NEW VENTURE CREATION

SECOND CANADIAN EDITION

STEPHEN SPINELLI, JR.
Philadelphia University

PRESCOTT C. ENSIGN
Wilfrid Laurier University

ROBERT J. ADAMS, JR.
The University of Texas at Austin

McGraw-Hill Education | McGraw-Hill Ryerson

NEW VENTURE CREATION: ENTREPRENEURSHIP FOR THE 21ST CENTURY
Second Canadian Edition

ISBN-13: 978-0-07-105146-0
ISBN-10: 0-07-1051465

2 3 4 5 6 7 8 9 0 WEB 1 9 8 7 6 5 4

Printed and bound in Canada.

Care has been taken to trace ownership of copyright material contained in this text; however, the publisher will welcome any information that enables it to rectify any reference or credit for subsequent editions.

Director of Product Management: Rhondda McNabb
Group Product Manager: Kim Brewster
Marketing Manager: Cathie Lefebvre
Group Product Development Manager: Kelly Dickson
Product Developer: Becky Ranger
Photo/Permissions Research: Robyn Craig
Senior Product Team Associate: Christine Lomas
Supervising Editor: Joanne Limebeer
Copy Editor: Cat Haggert
Plant Production Coordinator: Scott Morrison
Manufacturing Production Coordinator: Emily Hickey
Cover Design: Liz Harasymczuk
Cover Image: Philip and Karen Smith/Getty Images
Interior Design: Liz Harasymczuk
Page Layout: ArtPlus Limited/Valerie Van Volkenburg
Printer: Webcom, Ltd.

Library and Archives Canada Cataloguing in Publication

Spinelli, Stephen, author New venture creation : entrepreneurship for the 21st century / Stephen Spinelli, Jr., Philadelphia University, Prescott C. Ensign, Wilfred Laurier University, Robert J. Adams, Jr., The University of Texas at Austin.—2nd Canadian edition.

Based on: Timmons, Jeffry A. New venture creation.Includes bibliographical references and index.ISBN 978-0-07-105146-0 (pbk.)

1. New business enterprises—Handbooks, manuals, etc. 2. Entrepreneurship—Handbooks, manuals, etc. I. Ensign, Prescott C., author II. Adams, Robert J., Jr., author III. Title.

HD62.5.T53 2014   658.1'141   C2013-906044-8

DEDICATIONS

To our families—to our children, and grandchildren.
Thank you for propelling our dreams.

Jeff Timmons—Professor, Scholar, Mentor, Friend

Jeff Timmons is the original author of this textbook.
Although he passed away a few years ago, his presence remains
a powerful influence in this edition. Jeff's commitment to higher
education and to entrepreneurship was a statement of his belief
in humanity and his contributions to entrepreneurship in the
classroom and in practice changed the playing field.
Students and teachers across the globe have been affected
by his work and the world continues to be
a better place because of him.

ABOUT THE AUTHORS

JEFFRY A. TIMMONS
(December 7, 1941–April 8, 2008): In Memoriam

BA, Colgate University; MBA, DBA, Harvard University Graduate School of Business

Success magazine, in a feature article, called him "one of the two most powerful minds in entrepreneurship in the nation." Michie P. Slaughter, former president of the Kauffman Center for Entrepreneurial Leadership at the Ewing Marion Kauffman Foundation, calls him "the premier entrepreneurship educator in America." In 2007, *Forbes Small Business* called Dr. Timmons one of the country's best entrepreneurship educators.

In 1985, he designed and launched the Price-Babson College Symposium for Entrepreneurship Educators (SEE), aimed at improving teaching and research by teaming highly successful entrepreneurs with "an itch to teach" with experienced faculty. This unique initiative was in response to a need to create a mechanism enabling colleges and universities to attract and support entrepreneurship educators and entrepreneurs and help them create lasting collaborations that would enhance the classroom experience for their students. There is now a core group of over 2000 entrepreneurship educators and entrepreneurs from over 350 colleges and universities in the United States and 38 foreign countries who are alumni of the Price-Babson College Fellows Program. *INC.* magazine's "Who's Who" special edition on entrepreneurship called Jeff Timmons "the Johnny Appleseed of entrepreneurship education" and concluded that this program had "changed the terrain of entrepreneurship education."

In 2003 Dr. Timmons worked with Professor Steve Spinelli to conceive a sister program to the SEE program that would be available for engineering schools with an interest in entrepreneurship. They partnered with colleagues at the new Olin College of Engineering on the Babson campus, President Rick Miller, Provost David Kerns, Dean Michael Moody, and Professors John Bourne, Ben Linder, Heidi Neck, and Stephen Schiffman to win a three-year National Science Foundation grant to design, develop, and deliver such a program.

Dr. Timmons helped launch several new initiatives including the Babson-Kauffman Entrepreneurship Research Conference, the Kauffman Foundation/CEL Challenge Grant, the Price Challenge Grant, business plan competitions, and a president's seminar. He provided leadership in developing and teaching in initiatives that assist Native Americans seeking economic self-determination and community development, most notably through entrepreneurship education programs at the nation's several Tribal Colleges. In April 2001, Professor Timmons was recognized for these efforts in a citation voted by the legislature of the State of Oklahoma naming him Ambassador for Entrepreneurship.

A prolific researcher and writer, he wrote nine books, including this textbook first published in 1974. *New Venture Creation* has been rated by *INC.*, *Success,* and *The Wall Street Journal* as a "classic" in entrepreneurship, and has been translated into Japanese, Portuguese, and Chinese.

STEPHEN SPINELLI, JR.

President, Philadelphia University

BA, McDaniel College (formerly Western Maryland College); MBA, Babson Graduate School of Business; and PhD (Economics), Imperial College, University of London

The majority of Dr. Spinelli's professional experience has been in entrepreneurship. He was a founding shareholder, director, and manager of Jiffy Lube International. He was also founder, chairman, and CEO of American Oil Change Corporation. In 1991, he completed a sale of Jiffy Lube to Pennzoil Company. Formerly he was also the Babson College Vice Provost for Entrepreneurship and Global Management; Director, Arthur M. Blank Center for Entrepreneurship; and Chairman, Entrepreneurship Division, Paul T. Babson Chair in Entrepreneurship. Dr. Spinelli has led the Entrepreneurship Division at Babson and taught full-time. He has not abandoned his business roots. He continues to consult with regional, national, and international companies; serves as a director at several corporations; and participates as an angel investor with investments in more than a dozen start-ups.

Dr. Spinelli is the quintessential "pracademic"—a business practitioner turned academic. Having successfully harvested Jiffy Lube, Dr. Spinelli was invited to attend the Price-Babson College Fellows Program and his career in academia was launched. After several years of part-time teaching, he joined the ranks of full-time faculty after receiving his PhD in October 1995 from Imperial College, University of London. Dr. Spinelli's expertise is in start-up and growth management. His research has focused on an understanding of strategic entrepreneurial relationships. He is the author of more than two dozen journal articles, book chapters, academic papers, and teaching case studies. He is also the author of six books including *Franchising: Pathway to Entrepreneurship* (Prentice Hall, 2003). His latest book, *Never Bet the Farm,* is co-authored with Anthony Iaquinto. A superb educator, he served as a key member of the faculty of the Price-Babson College Fellows Program's Symposium for Entrepreneurship Educators (SEE) for 12 years, in addition to his teaching in the undergraduate, graduate, and executive education programs. Dr. Spinelli is a shining example of the many contributions that entrepreneurs can make to an academic institution. He has led the internationalization of SEE to Chile, Argentina, Costa Rica, China, and Europe. In 2003 Dr. Spinelli founded the Babson Historically Black Colleges and Universities case writing consortium. This group is dedicated to writing entrepreneurship teaching cases focused on African American entrepreneurs.

Dr. Spinelli has been a leading force in curriculum innovation at Babson and, with his colleagues in Entrepreneurship Division, continually defines and delivers new initiatives. In 1999, he led the design and implementation of an Entrepreneurship Intensity Track for MBAs seeking to launch new business ventures upon graduation. Building on this highly successful initiative, he led the design and development of ACE—an accelerated honors curriculum for aspiring entrepreneurs in Babson's undergraduate program. Dr. Spinelli's presentation to the United States Association for Small Business and Entrepreneurship (USASBE) resulted in the naming of the F.W. Olin Graduate School of Business as the 2002 National Model MBA program.

Dr. Spinelli has been a strong voice for entrepreneurship. He has been a keynote speaker for Advent International's CEO Conference, the MCAA National Convention and Allied Domecq International's Retailing Conference, the Entrepreneur's Organization at MIT and many others; he has been called to testify before the U.S. Senate Subcommittee on Small Business and Entrepreneurship. He is often quoted as an expert in the field in such leading publications as *The Wall Street Journal, Forbes, The Financial Times, Success* magazine, and *INC.* He also serves as a director for several local, regional, and national not-for-profits and community-based associations.

President Stephen Spinelli was touted as a new model of college president in a front-page story on May 17, 2008, in the *Philadelphia Inquirer.* He calls Philadelphia University a 126-year-old start-up, a university with the entrepreneurial zeal that drives an innovative curriculum and applied research.

PRESCOTT C. ENSIGN, PhD

Dobson Professor of Innovation & Entrepreneurship, School of Business and Economics, Wilfrid Laurier University

Dr. Ensign has served on the faculties of universities in Canada, state universities in California and Ohio, and has been a visiting professor in Ecuador. He is the recipient of a Fulbright Scholarship and has been honoured for both his teaching and research. With a background in industrial engineering and management, Dr. Ensign's research has focused on innovation and technology development. His research has also examined the strategy and structure of enterprises as they internationalize. Recently, Dr. Ensign has investigated entrepreneurship in remote locations as well as economic development and change in emerging markets. His research has been funded by the Carnegie Bosch Institute, Carnegie Mellon University; the Canadian International Development Agency; Export Development Canada; Aboriginal Affairs and Northern Development Canada; Canada Foundation for Innovation; Australian Research Council; and repeatedly by the Social Sciences and Humanities Research Council of Canada, for which he serves as a grant proposal reviewer.

He is the author of *Knowledge Sharing Among Scientists* (2009), which explores social interaction and innovative behaviour among R&D workers. Dr. Ensign co-edited *Demography at the Edge* (2010), which considers economic and social development in remote regions—such as the far North. He and colleagues are presently working on the follow-up *Settlements at the Edge* to be released in 2014. Dr. Ensign has authored or co-authored over 30 journal articles, 10 book chapters, 20 case studies, and has given more than 50 conference presentations. His case studies have been translated into French, Korean, and Spanish.

Dr. Ensign has supervised undergraduate, MSc, and PhD students. Much of this involves the study of market entry and expansion. Projects have included commercialization of green/clean technologies; integration of scientific know-how when company cultures merge; social networks of entrepreneurs; small firm-large firm cooperation vs. competition; and social entrepreneurship.

Dr. Ensign has presented workshops on new venture creation to Aboriginal, immigrant, and visible minorities, and is a supporter of several national and international organizations that foster entrepreneurial behaviour. He is also a frequent coach and judge for business plan competitions.

ROBERT J. ADAMS, JR.

Dr. Rob Adams is on the faculty of the MBA program at the University of Texas at Austin, where he teaches entrepreneurship and is the Director of Texas Venture Labs.

Dr. Adams is a former software executive, entrepreneur, and institutional fund manager. He has served on many corporate boards and has founded or financed more than 40 companies, which have launched more than 100 products and raised more than a billion dollars of capital. Dr. Adams is currently active with a number of technology and life sciences companies as a board member or advisor.

Prior to his appointment at the University of Texas he was in the venture capital industry, holding a partner position at TL Ventures and managing director and founder positions at AV Labs (Austin Ventures) and Tejas Venture Partners. Prior to the venture business he was a software operating executive for two decades. This career included positions in sales, marketing, and general management. He was with Lotus (NYSE: IBM), joining the company shortly after its public offering. Adams was their first corporate sales representative, and went on to be instrumental in the development and launch of both 1-2-3 for Macintosh and Lotus Notes. He then founded and was CEO of Business Matters, a venture-backed developer of financial modelling products that was acquired. He was an executive with Pervasive Software (NASDAQ: PVSW), a company he helped take public.

Dr. Adams holds a Bachelor's of Science degree in Industrial Engineering from Purdue University, where he is a Distinguished Alumnus; a Masters of Business Administration from Babson College's Olin School of Management; and a PhD in Management from Capella University. He has taught at the MBA programs of the Acton School of Business, Babson College, the University of Texas at Austin, and St. Edwards University.

Dr. Adams is a nationally recognized speaker on entrepreneurship and product and financing strategy. He recently keynoted the *INC. 500* business conference and consults for numerous Fortune 500 companies. He blogs for Inc.com, and is on the board of directors for Huffington Small Business. He has been covered in *Business Week, Forbes, Fortune, Money, The New York Times, The Wall Street Journal, Washington Post,* on Bloomberg Radio, public television, and public radio's nationally syndicated *Marketplace* program.

Dr. Adams is the author of *A Good Hard Kick in the Ass: Basic Training for Entrepreneurs* (Random House/Crown, 2002); and *If You Build It Will They Come? Three Steps to Test and Validate Any Market Opportunity* (Wiley, 2010). He provides expert testimony on technology-related business issues, and has consulted on economic development and early stage company investment and its impact on economies for various governments including Canada, Chile, Costa Rica, India, Malaysia, New Zealand, and Thailand.

Dr. Adams is a Fellow at the IC^2 Institute, a University of Texas–based foundation that runs the Austin Technology Incubator. He is a visiting Professor at Thammasat University in Thailand and the University of Manitoba. He is an avid downhill skier and runner. He was a collegiate rower and graduated from the Marine Corps' Officer Candidate School.

BRIEF CONTENTS

PART I
The Entrepreneurial Mind   1

CHAPTER 1
The Entrepreneurial Mind: Crafting a
Personal Entrepreneurial Strategy   3

PART II
The Opportunity   38

CHAPTER 2
The Entrepreneurial Process   40

CHAPTER 3
The Opportunity: Screening, Creating,
Shaping, Recognizing, Seizing   76

CHAPTER 4
The Business Plan   126

SAMPLE BUSINESS PLAN:
Edgar Bruce Eyewear   Online in Connect

PART III
The Founder and Team   160

CHAPTER 5
The Entrepreneurial Leader   162

CHAPTER 6
The New Venture Team   195

CHAPTER 7
Ethical Decision Making and
the Entrepreneur   223

PART IV
Financing Entrepreneurial Ventures   249

CHAPTER 8
Resource Requirements   250

CHAPTER 9
Financing the Venture   277

CHAPTER 10
The Deal: Valuation, Structure,
and Negotiation   317

CHAPTER 11
Obtaining Debt Capital   349

PART V
Start-up and Beyond   391

CHAPTER 12
Leading Rapid Growth:
Entrepreneurship Beyond Start-up   392

CHAPTER 13
Franchising   419

CHAPTER 14
The Family as Entrepreneur   439

CHAPTER 15
Leading through Trouble, the Harvest,
and Beyond   476

CASES   CA-1

ENDNOTES   EN-1

GLOSSARY   GL-1

WEBSITES   WE-1

INDEX   IN-1

TABLE OF CONTENTS

PREFACE xiv

ACKNOWLEDGMENTS xvii

PART I The Entrepreneurial Mind   1

CHAPTER 1 The Entrepreneurial Mind: Crafting a Personal Entrepreneurial Strategy   3

Achieving Entrepreneurial Greatness   4

Leadership and Human Behaviour   5

Research   7

Converging on the Entrepreneurial Mind   8

  Desirable and Acquirable Attitudes, Habits, and Behaviours   8

  Six Dominant Themes   8

Entrepreneurial Reasoning: The Entrepreneurial Mind in Action   17

The Concept of Apprenticeship   19

  Shaping and Managing an Apprenticeship   19

  Windows of Apprenticeship   19

  The Concept of Apprenticeship: Acquiring the 50 000 Chunks   22

  Role Models   22

Entrepreneur's Creed   22

Myths and Realities   23

What Can Be Learned?   26

A Word of Caution: What Grades, IQ Tests, GMATs, and Others Don't Measure   27

A Personal Strategy   29

Learning Objectives Summary   30

Study Questions   30

Mind Stretchers   30

Exercise: Crafting a Personal Entrepreneurial Strategy   31

Case: Torak Express   34

PART II The Opportunity   38

CHAPTER 2 The Entrepreneurial Process   40

Demystifying Entrepreneurship   41

Classic Entrepreneurship: The Start-up   41

Entrepreneurship in Post-Brontosaurus Capitalism: Beyond Start-ups   41

  "People Don't Want to Be Managed. They Want to Be Led!"   42

  Signs of Hope in a Corporate Ice Age   43

  Metaphors   43

  Entrepreneurship = Paradoxes   44

  The Higher Potential Venture: Think Big Enough   45

Smaller Can Mean Higher Failure Odds   47

  Getting the Odds in Your Favour   49

  Threshold Concept   49

Promise of Growth   49

  Venture Capital Backing   50

  Private Investors Join Venture Capitalists   51

  Find Financials Backers and Associates Who Add Value   52

  Option: The Lifestyle Venture   52

The Timmons Model: Where Theory and Practice Collide in the Real World   53

  Intellectual and Practical Collisions with the Real World   54

  Value Creation: The Driving Forces   54

  Change the Odds: Fix It, Shape It, Mould It, Make It   55

  Recent Research Supports the Model   64

Learning Objectives Summary   66

Study Questions   66

Mind Stretchers   66

Exercise: Visit with an Entrepreneur and Create a Lifelong Learning Log   67

Case: F&D Meats   69

CHAPTER 3 The Opportunity: Screening, Creating, Shaping, Recognizing, Seizing   76

Think Big Enough   77

Opportunity through a Zoom Lens   77

  Transforming Caterpillars into Butterflies   78

  New Venture Realities   78

  The Circle of Ecstasy and the Food Chain for Ventures   79

  When Is an Idea an Opportunity?   80

  The Real World   81

  Spawners and Drivers of Opportunities   82

  Search for Sea Changes   83

  Desirable Business/Revenue Model Metrics   86

The Role of Ideas   86

  Ideas as Tools   86

  The Great Mousetrap Fallacy   87

  Contributors to the Fallacy   87

Pattern Recognition   88

  The Experience Factor   88

  Enhancing Creative Thinking   89

  Approaches to Unleashing Creativity   89

  Team Creativity   91

  Big Opportunities with Little Capital   91

  Real Time   93

  Relation to the Framework of Analysis   94

Screening Opportunities   97

  Opportunity Focus   97

  Screening Criteria: The Characteristics of Higher Potential Ventures   98

  Industry and Market Issues   99

Economics 101
Harvest Issues 103
Competitive Advantages Issues 104
Venture Team Issues 105
Personal Criteria 106
Strategic Differentiation 107
Gathering Information 109
Finding Ideas 109
Industry and Trade Contacts 111
Shaping Your Opportunity 112
Published Sources 113
Guides and Company Information 113
Additional Sources of Intelligence 113
Internet Impact: Research and Learning 114
Screening Venture Opportunities 115
QuickScreen 115
Venture Opportunity Screening Exercise (VOSE) 115
Learning Objectives Summary 116
Study Questions 116
Mind Stretchers 117
Exercise: Idea Generation Guide 117
Case: Nanopix: European Gaming Opportunties 118

CHAPTER 4 The Business Plan 126
Developing the Business Plan 127
The Plan Is Obsolete at the Printer 128
Work in Progress—Bent Knees Required 128
The Plan Is Not the Business 128
Some Tips from the Trenches 130
How to Determine If Investors Can Add Value 131
The Dehydrated Business Plan 132
Who Develops the Business Plan? 132
Who Is the Business Plan For? 133
A Closer Look at the What 133
The Relationship between Goals and Actions 133
Segmenting and Integrating Information 134
Establishing Action Steps 134
Preparing a Business Plan 135
A Complete Business Plan 135
Business Model 136
Learning Objectives Summary 139
Study Questions 139
Mind Stretchers 139
Exercise: The Business Plan Guide 140
Case: SHAD 150

SAMPLE BUSINESS PLAN:
Edgar Bruce Eyewear   Online in Connect

PART III The Founder and Team 160

CHAPTER 5 The Entrepreneurial Leader 162

The Entrepreneurial Domain 163
Converging on the Entrepreneurial Leader 163

Principal Forces and Venture Modes 164
Stages of Growth 165
A Theoretical View 165
Managing for Rapid Growth 167
What Entrepreneurial Leaders Need to Know 171
Ethical Entrepreneurial Leadership 173
Competencies and Skills 174
Skills in Building Entrepreneurial Culture 174
Other Necessary Competencies 177
Learning Objectives Summary 181
Study Questions 181
Mind Stretchers 181
Exercise: Leadership Skills and Know-How
Assessment 182
Case: SPARK 189

CHAPTER 6 The New Venture Team 195
The Importance of the Team 196
The Connection to Success 196
Forming and Building Teams 197
Anchoring Vision in Team Philosophy and Attitudes 197
A Process of Evolution 200
Filling the Gaps 201
Additional Considerations 206
Common Pitfalls 207
Rewards and Incentives 208
Slicing the Founder's Pie 208
The Reward System 209
Critical Issues 210
Considerations of Timing 211
Considerations of Value 212
Internet Impact: Team 213
Attracting Talent 213
Learning Objectives Summary 214
Study Questions 214
Mind Stretchers 214
Exercise: Rewards 215
Case: Canica Design Inc. 219

CHAPTER 7 Ethical Decision Making and the
Entrepreneur 223
Overview of Ethics 224
Ethical Stereotypes 226
Should Ethics Be Taught? 227
Ethics Can and Should Be Taught 227
Integrity as Governing Ethic 228
Entrepreneurs' Perspectives 229
Thorny Issues for Entrepreneurs 231
Action under Pressure 231
Different Views 232
Problems of Law 235

Examples of the Ends-and-Means Issue   233
An Example of Integrity   235
Social Enterprises and Social Entrepreneurship   235
The Timmons Model Interpreted for Social Entrepreneurship   236
Ethics Redux   237
Learning Objectives Summary   238
Study Questions   238
Mind Stretchers   238
Exercise: Ethics   239
Case: Planet Bean: Growing Responsibly   242

PART IV   Financing Entrepreneurial Ventures   249
CHAPTER 8   Resource Requirements   250
The Entrepreneurial Approach to Resources   251
Bootstrapping Strategies: Marshalling and Minimizing
Resources   252
Using Other People's Resources   252
The Right Stuff—Does Canada Have What It Takes?   254
Outside People Resources   256
Build Your Brain Trust   256
Board of Directors   256
Alternatives to a Formal Board   260
Legal Counsel   260
Bankers and Other Lenders   263
Accountants   263
Consultants   265
Financial Resources   266
Analyzing Financial Requirements   266
Internet Impact: Resources   268
Extending Your Network   268
Fundraising for Nonprofits   268
Learning Objectives Summary   269
Study Questions   269
Mind Stretchers   269
Exercise: Build Your Brain Trust   270
Case: Exercise.app   271

CHAPTER 9   Financing the Venture   277
Venture Financing: The Entrepreneur's Achilles' Heel   278
Financial Management Myopia: It Can't Happen to Me   278
Critical Financing Issues   279
Entrepreneurial Finance: The Owner's Perspective   281
Determining Capital Requirements   284
Financial Strategy Framework   284
Free Cash Flow: Burn Rate, OOC, and TTC   286
Crafting Financial and Fundraising Strategies   287
Critical Variables   287
Financial Life Cycles   288
Investor Preferences   290
The Capital Markets Food Chain   290

Cover Your Equity   292
Timing   293
Angels and Informal Investors   293
Who They Are   293
Finding Informal Investors   294
Contacting Investors   295
Evaluation Process   295
The Decision   296
Venture Capital: Gold Mines and Tar Pits   297
What Is Venture Capital?   298
The Venture Capital Industry   299
The Venture Capital Process   299
Identifying Venture Capital Investors   301
Dealing with Venture Capitalists   303
Questions the Entrepreneur Can Ask   304
Due Diligence: A Two-Way Street   304
Other Equity Sources   305
Business Development Bank of Canada (BDC)   305
Scientific Research and Experimental Development Tax Credit
Program   306
Industrial Research Assistance Program (IRAP)   307
Corporate Venture Capital   307
Mezzanine Capital   307
Private Placements   308
Initial Public Share Offerings   309
Private Placement after Going Public   312
Employee Share Ownership Plans (ESOPs)   312
Keeping Current about Capital Markets   312
Learning Objectives Summary   314
Study Questions   314
Mind Stretchers   314
Case: Scavenger Energy: From the Ground Up   315

CHAPTER 10   The Deal: Valuation, Structure,
and Negotiation   317
The Art and Craft of Valuation   318
What Is a Company Worth?   318
Determinants of Value   318
Long-Term Value Creation versus Quarterly Earnings   318
Psychological Factors Determining Value   318
A Theoretical Perspective   319
Investor's Required Rate of Return   319
Investor's Required Share of Ownership   319
The Theory of Company Pricing   320
The Reality   322
The Down Round or Cram Down   322
Improved Valuations or Bouncing Back   325
Valuation Methods   325
The Venture Capital Method   325
The Fundamental Method   326
The First Chicago Method   326

Ownership Dilution   326
Discounted Cash Flow   328
Other Rule-of-Thumb Valuation Methods   329
Tar Pits Facing Entrepreneurs   329
Staged Capital Commitments   330
Structuring the Deal   331
What Is a Deal?   331
Understanding the Bets   334
Some of the Lessons Learned: The Dog in the Suitcase   335
Negotiations   336
What Is Negotiable?   336
The Specific Issues Entrepreneurs Typically Face   337
The Term Sheet   338
Black Box Technology, Inc., Term Sheet   338
Traps   339
Strategic Circumference   339
Legal Circumference   339
Attraction to Status and Size   340
Unknown Territory   340
Opportunity Cost   341
Underestimation of Other Costs   342
Greed   343
Being Too Anxious   343
Impatience   343
Take-the-Money-and-Run Myopia   344
Learning Objectives Summary   345
Study Questions   345
Mind Stretchers   345
Case: Terracycle Inc.   346

CHAPTER 11 Obtaining Debt Capital   349

A Cyclical Pattern: The Good Old Days Return but Fade
Again   350
A Word of Caution   350
The Lender's Perspective   350
Sources of Debt Capital   351
Trade Credit   353
Commercial Bank Financing   353
Line of Credit Loans   354
Time-Sales Finance   355
Term Loans   356
Personal Property Security Act   356
Purchase Money Security Interests and General Security
Agreements   357
Plant Improvement Loans   358
Commercial Finance Companies   358
Factoring   359
Leasing Companies   361
Before the Loan Decision   361
Approaching and Meeting the Banker   363
What the Banker Wants to Know   364
The Lending Decision   367
Lending Criteria   367

Loan Restrictions   368
Covenants to Look For   369
Personal Guarantees and the Loan   370
Building a Relationship   370
Handling a Banker or Other Lender   371
What to Do When the Bank Says "No"   371
Tar Pits: Entrepreneurs Beware   372
Beware of Leverage: The ROE Mirage   372
Neither a Lender Nor a Borrower Be, But If You Must...   373
Learning Objectives Summary   374
Study Questions   374
Mind Stretchers   374
Case: Minto Lake Resources Inc.: Finding the Value   375

PART V Start-up and Beyond   391

CHAPTER 12 Leading Rapid Growth:
Entrepreneurship Beyond Start-up   392

Inventing New Organizational Paradigms   393
Entrepreneurial Leaders Are Not Administrators or Managers   393
Leading Practices of High-Growth Companies   394
Growing Up Big   394
Stages of Growth Revisited   394
Core Leadership Mode   395
The Problem in Rate of Growth   396
Industry Turbulence   399
The Importance of Organizational Culture and Climate   400
Six Dimensions   400
Approaches to Entrepreneurial Leadership   403
Entrepreneurship for the 21st Century: Big
Breakthroughs   404
Austin Hill   404
Gabrielle Chevalier   405
Nina Gupta   406
Doug and Danny Elder   407
The Chain of Greatness   408
Learning Objectives Summary   409
Study Questions   409
Mind Stretchers   409
Case: Parlance Communications in Mexico   410

CHAPTER 13 Franchising   419

Introduction   420
Job Creation versus Wealth Creation   420
Franchising: A Story of Entrepreneurship   421
Franchising: Assembling the Opportunity   422
Primary Target Audience   422
Evaluating a Franchise   424
Franchisor as the High-Potential Venture   426
Key Components of a Franchise Offering   426
Service Delivery System   426
Training and Operational Support   428
Field Support   429

Marketing, Advertising, and Promotion   429
Supply   430
Franchising Frictions and Legal Considerations   431
Franchise Relationship Model   432
Learning Objectives Summary   436
Study Questions   436
Mind Stretchers   436
Case: Which Way to Grow?   437

CHAPTER 14 The Family as Entrepreneur   439
Families, Entrepreneurship, and the Timmons Model   440
Building Entrepreneurial Family Legacies   440
Large Company Family Legacies   440
Smaller and Mid-Size Family Legacies   442
The Family Contribution and Roles   444
Frame One: The Mindset and Method for Family
Enterprising   447
Enterprising Mindset and Methods   448
Creating the Dialogue for Congruence   451
Successful Next Generation Entrepreneurship   452
Frame Two: The Six Dimensions for Family
Enterprising   453
Leadership Dimension—Does Your Leadership Create a Sense
of Shared Urgency for Enterprising and Transgenerational
Wealth Creation?   454
Relationship Dimension—Does Your Family Have the Relationship
Capital to Sustain Their Transgenerational Commitments?   455
Vision Dimension—Does Your Family Have a Compelling
Multigenerational Vision That Energizes People at Every
Level?   455
Strategy Dimension—Does Your Family Have an Intentional
Strategy for Finding Their Competitive Advantage as a
Family?   456
Governance Dimension—Does Your Family Have Structures
and Policies That Stimulate Change and Growth in the
Family and Organization?   456
Performance Dimension—Does Your Performance Meet the
Requirements for Transgenerational Entrepreneurship and
Wealth Creation?   457
Frame Three: The Familiness Advantage for Family
Enterprising   458
Succession   461
Succession? Maybe.   463
Succession? No.   463
Succession Woes   463
Conclusion   464
Learning Objective Summary   464
Study Questions   465
Mind Stretchers   465
Exercise   466
Case: Sweet Success   470

CHAPTER 15 Leading through Trouble, the Harvest,
and Beyond   476
When the Bloom Is off the Rose   477

Getting into Trouble—The Causes   477
Strategic Issues   478
Leadership Issues   478
Poor Planning, Financial/Accounting Systems, Practices, and
Controls   479
Getting Out of Trouble   479
Predicting Trouble   480
Net-Liquid-Balance-to-Total-Assets Ratio   481
Non-quantitative Signals   481
The Gestation Period of Crisis   482
The Paradox of Optimism   482
The Bloom Is Off the Rose—Now What?   483
Decline in Organizational Morale   484
The Threat of Bankruptcy   484
Voluntary Bankruptcy   484
Bargaining Power   485
Intervention   485
Diagnosis   486
The Turnaround Plan   487
Longer-Term Remedial Actions   491
A Journey, Not a Destination   491
The Journey Can Be Addictive   492
First Build a Great Company   492
Create Harvest Options   493
A Harvest Goal   495
Crafting a Harvest Strategy: Timing Is Vital   495
Harvest Options   497
Capital Cow   497
Employee Share Ownership Plan   497
Management Buyout   497
Merger, Acquisition, and Strategic Alliance   498
Outright Sale   499
Public Offering   499
Beyond the Harvest   501
The Road Ahead: Devise a Personal Entrepreneurial
Strategy   502
Goals Matter—A Lot!   502
Values and Principles Matter—A Lot!   502
Seven Secrets of Success   503
Learning Objectives Summary   504
Study Questions   504
Mind Stretchers   504
Case: Cavendish Cove Cottages   505

CASES   CA-1

ENDNOTES   EN-1

GLOSSARY   GL-1

WEBSITES   WE-1

INDEX   IN-1

PREFACE

A BOOK FOR THE NEXT GENERATION OF ENTREPRENEURIAL LEADERS

The evolution of entrepreneurship over the years has had an extraordinary impact on the cultural and economic landscape in Canada and worldwide. While there will always be opportunities for improvement and innovation, the present entrepreneurial revolution has become a model for business people, educators, and policymakers around the globe.

People in every nation have enormous entrepreneurial qualities and aspirations, and that spirit is finding its way into nearly all world markets. Entrepreneurship is exploding in the for-profit and not-for-profit sectors. Entrepreneurs across Canada, from the rural and remote to the urban centres, are affecting positive social and economic change. Every day we see that social enterprises and social entrepreneurship are gaining in popularity and impact.

In our roles as student, teacher, researcher, observer, and participant in this revolution, we can honestly say that global adoption of the entrepreneurial mindset appears to be growing exponentially larger and faster. That mindset, while informed by new venture experiences, affects larger corporations and the not-for-profit world as well. In our assessment, we are at the dawn of a new age of entrepreneurial reasoning, equity creation, and philanthropy, whose impact in the coming years will dwarf what we experienced over the last century.

AN EDITION FOR AN ERA OF EXTRAORDINARY UNCERTAINTY AND OPPORTUNITY

Current business times are being defined as much by worldwide challenges and uncertainty as from the enormous opportunities afforded by technology, global communications, and the increasing drive to develop socially, economically, and environmentally sane and sensible new ventures. As with past generations, entrepreneurs in this arena face the ultimate and most demanding juggling act: how to simultaneously balance the insatiable requirements of marriage, family, new venture, service to community, and still have time for one's own pleasure and peace.

A BOOK ABOUT THE CANADIAN ENTREPRENEURIAL PROCESS

New Venture Creation is about the actual process of getting a new venture started, growing the venture, successfully harvesting it, and starting again.

There is a substantial body of knowledge, concepts, and tools that entrepreneurs need to know—before taking the start-up plunge—if they are to get the odds in their favour. Accompanying the explosion in entrepreneurship has been a significant increase in research and knowledge about the entrepreneurial process. Much of what was known previously has been reinforced and refined, while some has been challenged. Numerous new insights have emerged. *New Venture Creation* continues to be the product of experience and considerable research in this field, rooted in real-world application and refined in the classroom.

The design and flow of this book are aimed at creating knowledge, skills, and awareness. In a pragmatic way—through text, case studies, and hands-on exercises—students are engaged to discover critical aspects of entrepreneurship, and to find what levels of competency, know-how, experience, attitude, resources, and networks are required to pursue different entrepreneurial opportunities. No doubt about it: There is no substitute for the real thing—actually starting a company. But short of that, it is possible to expose students to many of the vital issues and immerse them in key learning experiences, such as critical self-assessment and the development of a business plan.

This book is divided into five parts, which detail the driving forces of entrepreneurship—the entrepreneurial mind, the opportunity, the founder and team, financing entrepreneurial ventures, and the start-up and beyond. Part I explores the entrepreneurial revolution and addresses the mindset required to tackle this tremendously challenging and rewarding pursuit. Part II lays out the process by which real opportunities—not just ideas—can be discovered and selected. This section examines the type of opportunity around which higher potential ventures can be built (with acceptable risks and trade-offs), and how such opportunities can profitably be shaped, recognized, and seized. Part III concerns entrepreneurial leadership, team creation, and personal ethics. Part IV addresses marshalling resources, entrepreneurial finance, and fundraising—including structuring and striking a deal. The book concludes in Part V with sections dealing with strategies for success, leading rapid growth, franchising as an entrepreneurial vehicle, family enterprise, and harvest issues.

Once the reader understands how winning entrepreneurs think, act, and perform, he or she can then establish goals to practise emulating those actions, attitudes, habits, and strategies. *New Venture Creation* challenges readers to think about the process of becoming an entrepreneur, and seeks to enable entrepreneurs to immerse themselves in the dynamics of launching and growing a company. The book addresses practical issues such as the following:

- What are my real talents, strengths, and weaknesses, and how can I exploit those talents and strengths, and minimize my weaknesses?

- How can I recognize when an opportunity is more than just another good idea, and whether it is one that fits with my personal mindset, capabilities, and life goals?

- Why do some firms grow quickly to several million dollars in sales, but then stumble, never growing beyond a single-product firm?

- What are the critical tasks and hurdles in seizing an opportunity and building the business?

- How much money do I need, and when, where, and how can I get it—on acceptable terms?

- What financing sources, strategies, and mechanisms can I bring to bear throughout the process—from prestart, through the early growth stage, to the harvest of my venture?

- What are the minimum resources I need to gain control over the opportunity, and how can I do this?

- Is a business plan needed? If so, what kind is required and how and when should I develop one?

- Who are the constituents for whom I must create or add value to achieve a positive cash flow, and to develop harvest options?

- What is my venture worth, and how do I negotiate what to give up?

- What are the critical transitions in entrepreneurial leadership as a firm grows from $1 million, to $5 million, to over $25 million in sales?

- What are some of the pitfalls, minefields, and hazards I need to anticipate, prepare for, and respond to?
- What are the contacts and networks I need to access and develop?
- Do I know what I do and do not know, and do I know what to do about it?
- How can I develop a personal "entrepreneurial game plan" to acquire the experience I need to succeed?
- How critical and sensitive is the timing in each of these areas?

The textbook also exposes the reader to the well-known paradoxes that characterize entrepreneurship and challenge entrepreneurial leaders, such as:

- ambiguity and uncertainty versus planning and rigour
- creativity versus disciplined analysis
- patience and perseverance versus urgency
- organization and management versus flexibility
- innovation and responsiveness versus systemization
- risk avoidance versus risk management
- current profits versus long-term equity

The *New Venture Creation* models are useful not only as a comprehensive textbook for a course in entrepreneurship, but may also serve as a roadmap for a curriculum in entrepreneurship. This textbook may also be successfully deployed for training and workshops offered by economic development offices. The real-world applications and exercises can be blended with theory to provide a solid basis for nascent entrepreneurs and would-be entrepreneurs.

WHAT TO EXPECT FROM THE CANADIAN EDITION

This edition is a significant update: Canadian cases, exercises, websites, and textual material have been added to capture the current financial, economic, technological, and globally competitive environment. A special effort has been made to include cases that capture the dynamic ups and downs new firms experience over an extended period of time. By grappling with decisions faced by entrepreneurs—from start-up to harvest—this textbook offers a broad and rich perspective on the often turbulent and unpredictable nature of the entrepreneurial process.

The Canadian edition features major changes and additions:

- *Tailored for Canadian institutions.* The structure and flow of the book is such that it begins with a focus on the reader as the aspiring entrepreneur. The table of contents is designed to reflect the subjects taught in Canadian higher learning institutions, and the 15-chapter format has been tailored to accommodate the length of the Canadian semester.

- *Written for a Canadian business context.* Based on extensive feedback and input from Canadian instructors, the new venture creation process has been grounded squarely in a Canadian context. The text teaches the universal applicability of many entrepreneurial and new venture creation tasks by focusing on the latest updates, and yet remains directly and deeply linked to the Canadian experience through examples of entrepreneurs in action coping with the aftermath of the global economic crisis and the new competitive realities.

- *Refinements to the Timmons Model of the entrepreneurial process.* We have included a dynamic financial planning model that can be a breakthrough tool for entrepreneurs evaluating or planning a venture. Plus, the textbook includes the addition of social, economic, and environmental sustainability factors.

- *The family as entrepreneur.* Chapter 14 outlines the significant economic and entrepreneurial contribution families make to communities and countries worldwide, and examines the different roles families play in the entrepreneurial process. The chapter describes the Six Dimensions for Family Enterprising, and provides a dynamic model to assess a family's relative mindset for enterprising, and to identify key issues for family dialogue. The running example in the chapter is Canadian (Backerhaus Veit of Toronto).

- *Canadian examples, data, and visuals.* Canadian examples are woven seamlessly throughout the chapters, and data, in the form of clear, easy-to-follow figures and tables, is derived from Canadian sources and Canadian industries whenever appropriate. Readers can expect to see the latest Canadian data and updates on the significant changes in the brave new world of capital markets, the economy, and the banking environment that are relevant to entrepreneurs.

- *In-chapter and online exercises.* In keeping with the practical focus of the text, both text chapters and the corresponding online material contain hands-on exercises to help reinforce the theory in the chapter or help the future entrepreneur assess his/her readiness for the next step in the new venture creation process. These exercises will challenge students to research, brainstorm, and identify what are likely to be the upcoming "sea changes" that will drive the next growth industries.

- *Canadian end-of-chapter and end-of-text cases.* Every chapter concludes with a short case featuring a Canadian company or individual that relates directly to the chapter content. The text also features eight end-of-text cases of varying lengths that relate more broadly to the concepts covered in the new venture creation process.

- *Business plan chapter and sample plan.* Chapter 4 presents a complete business plan guide along with tips, practical advice, and know-how from successful entrepreneurs and investors on the development and presentation of the plan. The guide has been updated to reflect current trends and includes material on social and environmental sustainability. The sample business plan, positioned as an appendix to chapter 4, features the plan from an actual Canadian start-up and is modelled on the guide found in the chapter.

ACKNOWLEDGMENTS

The Canadian edition of this book celebrates many years of intellectual capital acquired through research, case writing, course development, teaching, and practice. The latter has included a wide range of ventures, involving both former students and others. It has also been made possible by the support, encouragement, thinking, and achievements of many people: academic colleagues, former professors and mentors, entrepreneurs, former students, and our many friends who till this soil. A special thanks and debt of appreciation is due to all of our current and former students from whom we learn, and by whom we are inspired with each encounter. We marvel at your accomplishments!

Cases in this edition could not have been generated without the collaboration and support of sharing entrepreneurs. We wish to thank the case authors for their efforts in bringing these stories forward. The cases greatly enrich the educational experience of our students. Our contributors are:

Bill Barrett, *Planet Bean*
Carter Berezay, *Greaten Consulting Group*
Peggy Cunningham, *Dalhousie University*
Zeina Farhat, *University of Windsor*
Sean M. Hennessey, *University of Prince Edward Island*
Carson Kolberg, *Meal in a Jar*
Andrew Lunnie, *Canadian International Development Agency*
Barbara L. Marcolin, *University of British Columbia*
Ken Mark, *University of Western Ontario*
Eric Morse, *University of Western Ontario*
Charles E. Mossman, *University of Manitoba*
Elspeth J. Murray, *Queen's University*
Susan Myrden, *Memorial University of Newfoundland*
Lukas Neville, *University of Manitoba*
Roopa Reddy, *Wilfrid Laurier University*
Nicholas P. Robinson, *McGill University*
Corey Rochkin, *University of Western Ontario*
David Rose, *Wilfrid Laurier University*
Francine K. Schlosser, *University of Windsor*
Katrina Shaw, *Wilfrid Laurier University*
Peter Sianchuk, *Mount Allison University*
Donna M. Stapleton, *Memorial University of Newfoundland*
Ning Su, *University of Western Ontario*
Stewart Thornhill, *University of Western Ontario*
Erna van Duren, *University of Guelph*
Mary Weil, *University of Western Ontario*
Patrick Woodcock, *University of Ottawa*
Anthony A. Woods, *Incoho Inc.*
Sajjad Zahir, *University of Lethbridge*

We would like to extend a special thanks to those professors who reviewed and provided feedback for the first and second Canadian editions of *New Venture Creation*, as they have surely helped to shape the direction of the text.

Ronald Abraira, *Concordia University*
Angela Burlton, *McGill University*
Terri Champion, *Niagara College*
Jane Forbes, *Seneca College*
Anthony Goerzen, *Queen's University*
Vance Gough, *Mount Royal University*
Knud Jensen, *Ryerson University*
Ariff Kachra, *University of Western Ontario*
Rhonda Koster, *Lakehead University*
Sandra Malach, *University of Calgary*
Barbara Orser, *University of Ottawa*

Peter Pellatt, *University of Alberta*
Jason Perepelkin, *University of Saskatchewan*
Kojo Saffu, *Brock University*
Marnie Walker, *York University*

A number of individuals and organizations also deserve accolades for their contributions:

Stephen Daze, Agawa Entrepreneurship Development Corporation
John Dobson, The John Dobson Foundation
Cassandra Dorrington, Canadian Aboriginal and Minority Supplier Council
Steve Farlow, Schlegel Centre for Entrepreneurship, Wilfrid Laurier University
Nicholas P. Robinson, Merchant Law Group
Baffin Business Development Corporation
Business Development Bank of Canada
Canadian Association of Family Enterprise
Canadian Federation of Independent Business
Canadian Venture Capital & Private Equity Association
Capital for Aboriginal Prosperity and Entrepreneurship Fund
Industry Canada
Kitikmeot Economic Development Commission

A debt of gratitude is due to the John Dobson Foundation for providing a portion of the financing for this venture. They afforded me the most precious commodity—time. The Social Sciences and Humanities Research Council of Canada's support for case development was instrumental in producing this Canadian edition.

We are truly indebted to Jeffry Timmons and Stephen Spinelli who saw promise in this venture and gave us the "green light" to pursue it!

This Canadian edition came to fruition because of the tremendous effort of developmental editor Becky Ranger who took charge of shepherding this project from beginning to end. All of this was accomplished on schedule and with a most cheerful disposition. Extreme gratitude is due to publisher Kim Brewster for believing in this venture, who at the outset envisioned a Canadian edition of *New Venture Creation* and placed her confidence in this endeavour. Finally, we wish to express a special thank-you to a very capable array of individuals at McGraw-Hill Ryerson who showed great pride and professionalism in producing the finished product you see before you.

Prescott C. Ensign

CHAPTER WALKTHROUGH

IN-CHAPTER PEDAGOGY

The in-chapter pedagogy has been designed to facilitate learning and take the concepts from the Timmons Model and apply them to real-word situations. Whether a practical example of entrepreneurship in action, a trip to the Web, or highlighting relevant data through a figure or a table, these features reinforce chapter material and keep students focused on what is important in each chapter.

LEARNING OBJECTIVES. To help students identify key concepts, each chapter opens with a list of Learning Objectives related to the key topics in the chapter.

LEARNING OBJECTIVES

LO1 Articulate a definition of entrepreneurship and the entrepreneurial process—from lifestyle ventures to high potential enterprises.

LO2 Evaluate the practical issues and identify the requirements necessary to launch; include an appraisal of the array of stakeholders who play a role.

LO3 Show how entrepreneurs and their financial backers increase their odds for success by defying the pattern of disappointment and failure experienced by many.

LO4 Explain the Timmons Model of the entrepreneurial process, how it applies to your entrepreneurial career aspirations and ideas for businesses, and how recent research confirms its validity.

FIGURES AND TABLES. The most up-to-date charts and diagrams are included to illustrate relevant ideas and concepts. Canadian data are used where appropriate.

EXHIBIT 2.1   ENTREPRENEURSHIP IS A CONTACT SPORT

Remember, entrepreneurship is a full contact sport. The value comes in the "collision."

Spontaneity, Opportunism → $ ← Discipline, Processes

ENTREPRENEURS ACROSS CANADA. To tie the chapter concepts more directly to the Canadian experience, chapters include textboxes featuring the trials and tribulations of a Canadian enterprise or individual entrepreneurs.

ENTREPRENEURS ACROSS CANADA
Spin Master

A good example of the creativity generated by using more than one head is that of Spin Master. It was founded when three friends—who had just graduated from Western University, armed with $10 000—set out to build a business. Earth Buddy, a small, pantyhose-covered head filled with grass seeds that sprouted hair when watered was their first product. It was a huge hit—a Pet Rock-like phenomenon—providing the team a foundation to sprout their next idea. The venture boasts a willingness to take risks, creativity, playfulness, and constant scanning for great new innovative toys. Spin Master has also seen fit to give back. It sponsors the Spin Master Innovation Fund with the Canadian Youth Business Foundation. The Fund sponsors 10 awards of $50 000 for an innovative start-up.

Questions: Is it easier to behave entrepreneurially as an outsider? Spin Master has become an insider, part of the establishment. Now that it is a sizable enterprise with seasoned managers who have much to lose, can it retain its youthful exuberance and willingness to try new things?

EARTH BUDDY

PHOTOS New to this edition are photos, both illustrating key concepts and profiling Canadian companies and entrepreneurs.

A PORSCHE WRAPPED IN GOLD FOIL. CLEVER, BUT DOES IT CREATE VALUE?

END-OF-CHAPTER PEDAGOGY

Chapters conclude with a series of features that provide a tie-in to the chapter-opening features or reinforce chapter concepts through additional experiential material.

LEARNING OBJECTIVES SUMMARY

LO1 We began to demystify entrepreneurship by examining its classic start-up definition and a broader, holistic way of thinking, reasoning, and acting that is opportunity obsessed and leadership balanced.

LO2 No one works alone, make certain others are involved in the effort. Entrepreneurship has many metaphors and poses many paradoxes.

LO3 Getting the odds in your favour is the entrepreneur's perpetual challenge. Thinking big

enough can improve the odds significantly. Higher potential ventures are sought by successful entrepreneurs, venture capitalists, and private investors.

LO4 The Timmons Model is at the heart of spotting and building the higher potential venture and understanding its three driving forces: the team, opportunity, and resources. The concept of fit and balance is crucial. Research on entrepreneurs and their fast-growth ventures adds validity to the model.

LEARNING OBJECTIVES SUMMARY. This feature offers a point-by-point review of the Learning Objectives found at the beginning of each chapter.

STUDY QUESTIONS

1. Can you define what is meant by classic entrepreneurship and the high potential venture? Why and how are threshold concepts, cover your equity, bootstrapping of resources, fit, and balance important?
2. "People don't want to be managed, they want to be led." Explain what this means and its importance and implications for developing your own style and leadership philosophy.
3. What are the most important determinants of success and failure in new businesses? Who has the best and worst chances for success, and why?
4. What are the most important things you can do to get the odds in your favour?

5. What criteria and characteristics do high-growth entrepreneurs, venture capitalists, and private investors seek in evaluating business opportunities? How can these make a difference?
6. Define and explain the Timmons Model. Apply it and graphically depict, as in the Shopify example, the first five years or so of a new company with which you are familiar.
7. What are the most important skills, values, talents, abilities, and mindsets one needs to cultivate as an entrepreneur?

STUDY QUESTIONS. These questions provide a review of the material covered in the chapter and help students prepare for exams.

MIND STRETCHERS   Have you considered?

1. Who can be an entrepreneur? When?
2. More than 80 percent of entrepreneurs learn the critical skills they need after age 21. What does this mean for you?
3. In your lifetime, the odds are that leading firms today such as Sony, Research In Motion, Apple, Air Canada, and the Gap will be knocked off by McDonald's, and upstarts. How can this happen? Why does it present an opportunity, and for whom?

4. What do you need to be doing now, and in the next 12 months, to get the odds in your favour?
5. List 20 ideas and then pick out the best two that might be an opportunity. How can these become opportunities? Who can make them opportunities?
6. How many different ways can a new venture go off the tracks?

MIND STRETCHERS. Useful for more than just review purposes, these questions ask students to apply concepts in the chapter to their own lives and experiences.

CASES. The end-of-chapter cases feature a Canadian entrepreneur and tie directly into the major themes and topics covered in the chapter.

EXERCISES. The exercises help students apply and experience the concepts covered in the chapter and guide the future entrepreneur through the new venture creation process.

CASE   F&D MEATS

Preparation Questions

1. What are the two most valuable capabilities that F&D has, and do these capabilities lead to any negative consequences?
2. What are the different approaches to defining the market segments in this industry? Which do you think is more valuable from F&D's perspective and why?
3. What analysis would you suggest Dino do on the financial and operational figures provided? Complete any recommended analysis and provide any conclusions.

INTRODUCTION

It was 1:03 am on Saturday morning, and Franko D'Angelo, part owner and manager of F&D Meats, was making a final batch of custom, cognac bison sausage for a party tonight at a local embassy. Yet despite the late hour, Franko's mind had been occupied with important pending decisions. Key customers wanted new products requiring new expensive equipment, while others were demanding price breaks for volume purchases. Then recently a potential major customer made inquiries into supplying their Eastern Canadian store chain with a branded line sausages. Finally, his brother and partner in the business, Dino, had announced that he was going to enter MBA school in three months.

COMPANY BACKGROUND

A decade ago, Franko had pursued his love when he entered Le Cordon Bleu Culinary Arts School and subsequently apprenticed at one of Ottawa's most prestigious hotels as a sous-chef. Five years ago, Franko began producing handmade sausages in the basement apartment below his father's small Italian grocery store. For a summer job, Dino, a student, started selling sausages at Ottawa's Tulip Festival.[1] The sausages were a hit. A local radio personality described the sausages as the "most mouthwatering meat to ever grace his mouth." Based upon their success, Dino set up sausage kiosks at the other major summer festivals.

As the festival season ended, revenues slowed compelling the brothers to seek out new sales opportunities. Initially, Dino,

This case was written by Patrick Woodcock, Telfer School of Management, University of Ottawa.
[1] Ottawa has more than 50 summer festivals as well as some in the spring, fall, and winter.

the "sales manager," approached local Italian restaurants and grocery stores. Over the next year, five restaurants and two local grocery stores began purchasing regularly from them. However, more than 40 percent of their sales were walk-in order customers who would phone in their order and pickup it up from their downtown basement location. However, after two years the firm needed to find a larger production space furthermore, Dino's father had passed away requiring the operation to relocate. His passing also meant that his grocery store was sold and lost to condominium developers. Sales had initially been impacted, but Dino had managed to get more specialty food and deli retailers in the region as clients.

EXPANDING THE OPERATION

With the passing of their father and increased demand, Franko and Dino began searching for a larger production location. In the second year of operation, Franko found a vacated dairy and cheese operation, and thought it would make an excellent space as it had a large walk-in refrigerator, lots of space tiled space for production, two loading docks, and most of the sanitation, electrical, and water supply needed for food processing. It was located in an industrial park approximately 15 kilometers outside of Ottawa and the clincher was that rent was about half of anything they had considered previously. The only downside was that it was located some distance from most customers.

It took them almost six months to get the operation ready for production because of the complexity of getting permits and installing equipment. They moved in half way through the third year of operation.

THE MARKET & INDUSTRY

The greater Ottawa and Gatineau region encompasses about 1.2 million people and is growing at about 2% annually. The region's population is 60% English speaking and 30% French speaking, with the remaining 10% having another first language. The large French population and culture provide the region with a distinctly European flavour. Other cultures are also well represented as sections of the city are named little Italy and Chinatown because of their ethnic and commercial heritage.

EXERCISE   Visit with an Entrepreneur and Create a Lifelong Learning Log

Through interviews with entrepreneurs who have, within the past 5 to 10 years, started firms with significant growth and are profitable, you can gain insight into an entrepreneur's reasons, strategies, approaches, and motivations for starting and owning a business. Gathering information through interviewing is a valuable skill to practise. You can learn a great deal in a short time through interviewing if you prepare thoughtfully and thoroughly.

The Visit with an Entrepreneur Exercise has helped students interview successful entrepreneurs. While there is no right way to structure an interview, the format in this exercise has been tested successfully on many occasions. A breakfast, lunch, or dinner meeting is often an excellent vehicle.

Select two entrepreneurs and businesses about which you would like to learn. This could be someone you see as an example or role model to which you aspire, or which you know the least about but are eager to learn. Interview at least two entrepreneurs with differing experiences, such as a high potential (e.g., $5 million revenue plus) and a lifestyle business (usually much smaller, but not necessarily).

Create a Lifelong Learning Log

Create a computer file or acquire a notebook or binder in which you record your goals, triumphs and disappointments, and lessons learned. This can be done as key events happen or on some other frequent basis. You might make entries during times of crisis and at year's end to sum up what you accomplished and your new goals. The record of personal insights, observations, and lessons learned can provide valuable anchors during times of difficult decisions as well as interesting reading—for you at least.

A Visit with an Entrepreneur

Step 1   Contact the person you have selected and make an appointment.

Be sure to explain why you want the appointment and to give a realistic estimate of how much time you will need.

Step 2   Identify specific questions you would like to have answered and the general areas about which you would like information. (See Step 3, Conduct the interview.)

Using a combination of open-end questions, such as general questions about how the entrepreneur got started, what happened next, and so forth, and closed-end questions, such as specific questions about what his or her

goals were, if he or she had to find partners, and so forth, will help keep the interview focused and yet allow for unexpected comments and insights.

Step 3   Conduct the interview.

Recording the interview on audiotape can be helpful and is recommended unless you or the person being interviewed objects. Remember, too, that you will learn more if you are an interested listener.

The Interview
Questions for Gathering Information

- Would you tell me about yourself before you started your first venture?
  Who else did you know while you were growing up who had started or owned a business, and how did they influence you? Anyone later, after you were 21 years old?
  Were your parents, relatives, or close friends entrepreneurial? How so?
  Did you have role models?
  What was your education/military experience? In hindsight, was it helpful? In what specific ways?
  Did you have a business or self-employment during your youth?
  In particular, did you have any sales or marketing experience? How important was it, or a lack of it, to starting your company?
  When, under what circumstances, and from whom did you become interested in entrepreneurship and learn some of the critical lessons?

- Describe how you decided to create a job by starting your venture instead of taking a job with someone else.
  How did you spot the opportunity? How did it surface?
  What were your goals? What were your lifestyle needs or other personal requirements? How did you fit these together?
  How did you evaluate the opportunity in terms of the critical elements for success? The competition? The market? Did you have specific criteria you wanted to meet?
  Did you find or have partners? What kind of planning did you do? What kind of financing did you have?
  Did you have a start-up business plan of any kind? Please tell me about it.

INSTRUCTOR AND STUDENT RESOURCES

Great care was used in the creation of the supplemental materials to accompany *New Venture Creation*, Second Canadian Edition. Whether you are a seasoned faculty member or a newly minted instructor, you will find the support materials to be comprehensive and practical.

connect

McGraw-Hill Connect™ is a web-based assignment and assessment platform that gives students the means to better connect with their coursework, with their instructors, and with the important concepts that they will need to know for success now and in the future.

With Connect, instructors can deliver assignments, quizzes, and tests online. Instructors can edit existing questions and author entirely new problems. Track individual student performance—by question, assignment, or in relation to the class overall—with detailed grade reports. Integrate grade reports easily with learning management systems.

By choosing Connect, instructors are providing their students with a powerful tool for improving academic performance and truly mastering course material. Connect allows students to practice important skills at their own pace and on their own schedule. Importantly, students' assessment results and instructors' feedback are all saved online—so students can continually review their progress and plot their course to success.

Connect also provides 24/7 online access to an eBook—an online edition of the text—to aid students in successfully completing their work, wherever and whenever they choose.

KEY FEATURES

Simple Assignment Management

With Connect, creating assignments is easier than ever, so instructors can spend more time teaching and less time managing.

- Create and deliver assignments easily with selectable questions and test-bank material to assign online.
- Streamline lesson planning, student progress reporting, and assignment grading to make classroom management more efficient than ever.
- Go paperless with the eBook and online submission and grading of student assignments.

Smart Grading

When it comes to studying, time is precious. Connect helps students learn more efficiently by providing feedback and practice material when they need it, where they need it.

- Automatically score assignments, giving students immediate feedback on their work and side-by-side comparisons with correct answers.
- Access and review each response; manually change grades, or leave comments for students to review.
- Reinforce classroom concepts with practice tests and instant quizzes.

Instructor Library

The Connect Instructor Library is your course creation hub. It provides all the critical resources you'll need to build your course, just the way you want to teach it.

- Assign eBook readings and draw from a rich collection of textbook-specific assignments.
- Access instructor resources, including ready-made PowerPoint presentations and media to use in your lectures.
- View assignments and resources created for past sections.
- Post your own resources for students to use.

eBook

Connect reinvents the textbook learning experience for the modern student. Every Connect subject area is seamlessly integrated with Connect eBooks, which are designed to keep students focused on the concepts key to their success.

- Provide students with a Connect eBook, allowing for anytime, anywhere access to the textbook.
- Merge media, animation, and assessments with the text's narrative to engage students and improve learning and retention.
- Pinpoint and connect key concepts in a snap using the powerful eBook search engine.
- Manage notes, highlights, and bookmarks in one place for simple, comprehensive review.

INSTRUCTOR AND STUDENT SUPPLEMENTS

INSTRUCTOR'S MANUAL The Instructor's Manual, prepared by Canadian author Prescott Ensign, Wilfrid Laurier University, includes a wealth of information to assist instructors in presenting this text and their course to its best advantage.

COMPUTERIZED TEST BANK Created by Chris Galea, St. Francis Xavier University, this flexible and easy-to-use electronic testing program allows instructors to create tests from book-specific items. The Test bank contains a broad selection of multiple choice, true/false, and essay questions. Instructors may add their own questions, as well as edit existing questions. Each question identifies the learning objective, page reference, and difficulty level. Multiple versions of the test can be created and printed.

POWERPOINT PRESENTATIONS Prepared by Chris Galea, St. Francis Xavier University, the PowerPoint Presentation slides are based around course learning objectives and include many of the figures and tables from the ninth edition U.S. textbook as well as some additional slides that support and expand the text discussions. Slides can be modified by instructors.

ENTREPRENEURSHIP VIDEOS Entrepreneurship videos are available online with Connect and to Instructors on DVD with Closed Captioning. Please contact your Learning Solutions Consultant for more information.

SUPERIOR LEARNING SOLUTIONS AND SUPPORT

The McGraw-Hill Ryerson team is ready to help you assess and integrate any of our products, technology, and services into your course for optimal teaching and learning performance. Whether it's helping your students improve their grades, or putting your entire course online, the McGraw-Hill Ryerson team is here to help you do it. Contact your Learning Solutions Consultant today to learn how to maximize all of McGraw-Hill Ryerson's resources!

For more information on the latest technology and Learning Solutions offered by McGraw-Hill Ryerson and its partners, please visit us online: www.mcgrawhill.ca/he/solutions.

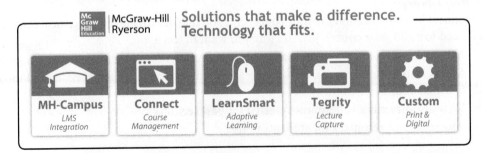

THE ENTREPRENEURIAL MIND

At the heart of the entrepreneurial process is the founder: the seeker, the creator, and initiator behind the start-up. The founder is leader, problem solver, and motivator; he or she is the strategizer and guardian of the mission, values, and culture of the venture. Without his or her energy, drive, and vitality, the greatest ideas—even when backed by an abundance of resources and staff—will fail, grossly underperform, or simply never get off the ground. In business, art, science, or sports, talent does not guarantee success. The difference lies in the intangibles: creativity, ingenuity, commitment, tenacity, and a passion to win. He or she must also possess leadership and team-building skills.

So, what is it that an aspiring entrepreneur needs to know? What habits, attitudes, and mindsets can be learned, practised, and developed to improve the odds of success? We begin with a focus on you—the aspiring entrepreneur. We examine the mindsets, attitudes, and habits that lead to entrepreneurial success—and failure. By examining patterns and practices of entrepreneurial thinking and reasoning, and the entrepreneurial mind in action, you can begin your own assessment and planning process to get you headed where you want to go. This personal entrepreneurial strategy will evolve into your personal business plan—a blueprint to help you learn, grow, attract mentors who can change your life and your venture's, and pursue the opportunities that best suit you.

Survival odds for a venture go up once you reach the benchmark of $1 million in sales and 20 employees. Launching or acquiring and then building a business that exceeds those levels is more fun and more challenging than operating a small one- or two-person operation. But perhaps most important, a business of this magnitude achieves the critical mass necessary to attract good people and significantly increases the likelihood of realizing a harvest. An entrepreneur is not simply creating a job; he or she can build a business that can lift a community.

A leader who thinks and acts with an "entrepreneurial mind" can make a critical difference as to whether a not-for-profit or for-profit enterprise is destined to be a traditional, very small lifestyle venture, a stagnant or declining large one, or a higher potential enterprise. Practising certain mental attitudes and actions can stimulate, motivate, and reinforce the kind of zest and entrepreneurial culture whose self-fulfilling prophecy is success.

It is impossible to give people a test to determine who will become an entrepreneur. Rather, it is useful for would-be entrepreneurs and others involved in entrepreneurship to study how successful entrepreneurs think, feel, and respond and how those factors that are significant can be developed and strengthened.

Entrepreneurs who create or recognize opportunities and then seize and shape them into higher potential ventures think and do things differently. They operate in an entrepreneurial domain, a place governed by certain modes of action and dominated by certain driving forces.

Take for example, Tim Horton, who began his career as a professional hockey player in 1950 and in 1964 opened his first Tim Horton Doughnut Shop with Jim Charade. But this was not Horton's first business. Prior to that, he and Charade had several hamburger restaurants that failed. And before that, Horton was a partner in an automobile dealership that bore his name; he worked in the off season in a sales capacity. It was early in his professional sports career that Horton realized hockey could not provide financial stability. In 1967, the third Tim Horton Doughnut shop opened, and by the time of his death in 1974, there were 35 franchises. In terms of passion and whether hockey was a job, Horton replied: "What I get paid for are the practices, I would play the games for nothing."

It makes a lot of sense for entrepreneurs to pay attention to picking partners, team members, and employees with an eye for complementing the entrepreneurs' own weaknesses and strengths and the needs of the venture. As will be seen, they seek people who fit. Not only can an entrepreneur's weakness be an Achilles' heel for a new venture, but also the whole is almost always greater than the sum of its parts.

Finally, ethics are terribly important in entrepreneurship. In highly unpredictable and fragile situations, ethical issues cannot be handled according to such simplistic notions as "always tell the truth." It is critical that an entrepreneur understands, develops, and implements an effective integrity strategy for the business.

CHAPTER 1

THE ENTREPRENEURIAL MIND: CRAFTING A PERSONAL ENTREPRENEURIAL STRATEGY[1]

" If you're going to lick the icing off somebody else's cake you won't be nourished and it won't do you any good. You will have to experiment and try things out for yourself. "

EMILY CARR

LEARNING OBJECTIVES

LO1 Evaluate whether being an entrepreneur gives sustaining energy or takes it away. Analyze what characteristics contribute to being an entrepreneur.

LO2 Describe the entrepreneurial mind—the strategies, habits, attitudes, and behaviours that work for entrepreneurs who build higher potential ventures.[2]

LO3 Defend the benefits of an apprenticeship and an entrepreneur's creed.

LO4 Describe the characteristics of various entrepreneurial groups.

LO5 Develop a personal entrepreneurial strategy, including a self-assessment and goal-setting process that can become a lifelong habit of entrepreneurial thinking and action.

ACHIEVING ENTREPRENEURIAL GREATNESS LO1

Jeffrey Skoll has left his mark in a number of business arenas and with a number of social endeavours. Most notably, Skoll was the first employee and first president of eBay. After university he backpacked around the world, then founded an IT consulting firm that operated from 1987 to 1994. He then co-founded a computer rental business in 1990 that flopped when the computers were never returned. But it was in 1996 when Skoll met eBay's **founder** Pierre Omidyar that things got really interesting. Skoll wrote the business plan that eBay followed from its emergence as a **start-up** to its smashing success, at which point Skoll realized a harvest by cashing in a portion of his equity.

founder: An individual (founder) or individuals (cofounders) who were present and contributed at the inception of the venture.

Skoll is credited with the establishment of the eBay Foundation and personally pushed off into the realm of philanthropic ventures. Skoll founded a media company to promote movies with a social message. He supports a global array of philanthropic ventures and social enterprises. Skoll has stated "I went from living in a house with five guys in Palo Alto and living off their leftovers, to all of a sudden having all kinds of resources. I wanted to figure out how I could take the blessing of these resources and share it with the world... 'Bet on good people doing good things' I was told, and that has really resonated with me." Skoll sees a growing 'opportunity gap'—that not all people have equal access to economic opportunities. At the heart of the entrepreneurial process is the opportunity, if a good portion of society is blocked from taking a stab at an opportunity, then resentment or even chaos may follow.

start-up: A newly established business.

Another extraordinary story of our time is that of **serial entrepreneur** Terry Matthews. His first start-up with fellow British Isles immigrant Michael Cowpland was Mitel, an abbreviation for Mike and Terry's Electric Lawnmowers. Those responsible for delivering the goods to the partners for later resale lost the shipping container. The lawnmowers arrived in winter. Matthews recalled, "That taught me a key lesson—the importance of timing...you can't cut grass when it's covered with snow."[3] Terry and Mike rebounded with a profitable and popular two-tone, multi-frequency receiver in the telephone voice communications market. The telephony device, which hastened the demise of rotary-dial phones, allowed them to sell a better product than their competitors' at

serial entrepreneur: An individual who has repeatedly gone through the venture-creation process.

TERRY MATTHEWS, SERIAL ENTREPRENEUR.

a fraction of the cost, garnering returns of 1000 percent. The pair purchased a silicon chip foundry and moved to newer technologies—microprocessors and semiconductor devices. Mitel went public and the company was later acquired by British Telecom. Cowpland went on to found the software company Corel and Matthews transitioned from voice to data networking with the launch of Newbridge Networks, which he subsequently turned over to Alcatel for $7.1 billion.

With some irony, Matthews bought back the Mitel name and PBX business from British Telecom. Mitel's manufacturing was spun off as Breconridge. Later, Matthews' March Networks became the first successful Canadian IPO in the tech industry after the bubble burst and high-tech crashed.

Matthews has founded 65 different ventures and remains active in about 20 of them. Successes include Celtic House Venture Partners, an early-stage technology **venture capital** firm with interests in telecom, storage, networking, and Internet infrastructure. Matthews is also founder and chairman of Wesley Clover, a **private equity** firm with assets in telecom, real estate, and leisure industries. Matthews offers many words of determination and drive: "Don't be boring, do something…make a mark, don't be part of the living dead."[4] "I don't think I'm stubborn, I just focus on the task at hand and do what it takes. Persistence is the single most important thing for success."[5] "I've always been a big believer in the early-mover advantage."[6] When the 65-year-old is pushed on the subject of retirement—why someone who does not need to work chooses to work and is not sitting on a beach or hot-air ballooning around the world— Matthews' reply is brief. "It's fun."[7]

On a smaller scale, Tom Heintzman and Greg Kiessling, with both conviction and depths of relevant experience, made the entrepreneurial leap and founded Bullfrog Power in 2004. Bullfrog delivered environmentally responsible electricity to the power grids in Ontario and Alberta and later to British Columbia, Nova Scotia, New Brunswick, and Prince Edward Island. Electricity consumers (residential, commercial, and governmental) can elect Bullfrog Power as their provider. Bullfrog and its partners then inject electricity derived from renewable sources into the system. For example, in August 2008, in Kingston, Ontario, 160 Queen's University students elected to have their housing complex get on the green grid. "While students won't be saving any money with Bullfrog Power, it is a conscious decision they made to assist the environment. On the contrary, it's going to cost them each $65 extra a year to reduce their carbon footprint by 56 tonnes."[8] In December of 2011, Bullfrog Power became one of Canada's first certified B Corporations. Certified B Corporations are legally required to consider the impact of their decisions on their employees, suppliers, community, consumers, and the environment. As of 2013, Bullfrog Power had over 8000 residential customers and more than 1300 commercial customers. Boyd Cohen of the University of Victoria observes that "young, entrepreneurial firms can contribute towards a more sustainable society through innovation."[9] Research conducted by Richard Hudson of Mount Allison University and Roger Wehrell of Saint Francis Xavier University shows that socially responsible investors have two goals: to obtain a market-based return and to make others act in a more socially responsible way.[10] Bullfrog's founders are hoping to do just that—to turn a profit and improve the planet.

The ultimate message is clear: Great companies can be built, but all the capital, technology, and latest information available cannot substitute for hard work and determination. An entrepreneur creates the culture in his or her own **new venture**. These ideals are at the very heart of the difference between good and great entrepreneurs and the enterprises they create.

venture capital: Cash invested in a new or expanding business or project in which there is significant risk.

private equity: Working capital provided to an enterprise that is not publicly traded; sources of private equity include a private equity firm, a venture capitalist, and an angel investor.

new venture: A recently created enterprise involving risk with expectation of gain.

LEADERSHIP AND HUMAN BEHAVIOUR

The entrepreneur of the twenty-first century is just as likely to be inside an established company like AbitibiBowater, BC Hydro, or Telus as an outsider or a start-up. Today entrepreneurship is indicative of a form of strategy rather than a size of company.

Effective entrepreneurs are intrinsically motivated, high-energy leaders who can tolerate ambiguity, mitigate risk, effectively commercialize, and innovate. These leaders identify and pursue opportunities by marshalling the diverse resources required to develop new markets and engage the inevitable competition.

A single psychological model of entrepreneurship has not been supported by research. However, social scientists, **venture capitalists**, investors, and entrepreneurs share the opinion that the eventual success of a new venture will depend a great deal upon the talent and behaviour of the lead entrepreneur and of his or her team.

Myths persist about entrepreneurs; among these is the belief that leaders are born, not made. The roots of this thinking reflect an earlier era, when rulers were royalty and leadership was part of the aristocracy. Fortunately, such notions have not withstood the tests of time or the scrutiny of scientific investigation of leadership and management. Research, as summarized in Exhibit 1.1, has shown that leadership is an extraordinarily complex phenomenon depending on the interconnections among the leader, the task, the situation, and those being led.

venture capitalists: Individuals who invest in a new or expanding business or project in which there is significant risk.

EXHIBIT 1.1	COMPARING MANAGEMENT AND LEADERSHIP	
	MANAGEMENT	**LEADERSHIP**
Creating an Agenda	Planning and budgeting—establishing detailed steps and timetables for achieving needed results, and then allocating the resources necessary to achieve these results	Establishing direction—developing a vision of the future, often the distant future, and strategies for producing the changes needed to achieve that vision
Developing a Human Network for Achieving the Agenda	Organizing and staffing—establishing some structure for accomplishing plan requirements, staffing that structure with individuals, delegating responsibility and authority for carrying out the plan, providing policies and procedures to help guide people, and creating methods or systems to monitor implementation	Aligning people—communicating the direction by words and deeds to all those whose co-operation may be needed to influence the creation of teams and coalitions that understand the vision and strategies
Execution	Controlling and problem solving—monitoring results versus plan in some detail, identifying deviations, and then planning and organizing to solve these problems	Motivating and inspiring—energizing people to overcome major political, bureaucratic, and resource barriers to change by satisfying very basic, often unfulfilled human needs
Outcomes	Producing a degree of predictability and order—having the potential of consistently producing key results expected by various stakeholders	Producing change—having the potential of producing extremely useful, and often dramatic, change

Source: John P. Kotter, *A Force for Change: How Leadership Differs from Management* (New York, NY: Free Press, 1990).

Numerous ways of analyzing human behaviour have implications in the study of entrepreneurship. The psychological motivation of entrepreneurial behaviour is a generally accepted part of the literature.[11] The theory states that people are motivated by three principal needs:

(1) the need for achievement, (2) the need for power, and (3) the need for affiliation. The *need for achievement* is the need to excel and for measurable personal accomplishment. A person competes against a self-imposed standard that does not involve competition with others. The individual sets realistic and challenging goals and likes to get feedback on how well he or she is doing to improve performance. The *need for power* is the need to influence others and to achieve an "influence goal." The *need for affiliation* is the need to attain an "affiliation goal"—the goal is to build a warm relationship with someone else and/or to enjoy mutual friendship. The prototypical entrepreneur has a high need for achievement and power and a low need for affiliation.

RESEARCH

Other research focuses on the common attitudes and behaviours of entrepreneurs. One study found that entrepreneurs are unique individuals and that particular motives do influence later performance of the venture.[12] Another study revealed that "those who like to plan are much more likely to be in the survival group than those who do not."[13] The get-rich-quick schemers are not the company builders, nor are they the planners of successful ventures. Rather, the entrepreneur is the visionary who participates in the day-to-day routine to achieve a long-term objective and who is generally passionate and not exclusively profit-oriented.

Academics have continued to characterize the special qualities of entrepreneurs. One finding was that entrepreneurs felt they had to concentrate on certain fundamentals: responsiveness, resiliency, and adaptiveness in seizing new opportunities.[14] Entrepreneurs often speak of other attitudes, including an ability "to activate vision" and a willingness to learn about and invest in new techniques, to be adaptable, to have a professional attitude, and to have patience. They talk about the importance of "enjoying and being interested in business," as well as the business of the entrepreneur as being "a way of life." Entrepreneurs believe that the ability to conceptualize their business and to engage in strategic planning are of growing importance, particularly when thinking five years ahead.

Entrepreneurs recognize and endorse the importance of human resource management; one entrepreneur said that one of the most challenging tasks was playing "a leadership role in attracting high-quality people, imparting your vision to them, and holding and motivating them." Entrepreneurs focus on building an organization and teamwork. The CEO of one firm stressed the ageless importance of sensitivity to and respect for employees: "It is essential that the separation between management and the average employee should be eliminated. Students should be taught to respect employees all the way down to the janitor and accept them as knowledgeable and able persons." One company that initially took this concept to heart was Ben & Jerry's Ice Cream. The company began operations with a covenant that "no boss got more than five times the compensation, including both pay and benefits, of the lowest-paid worker with at least one year at the company."[15] Since its inception, the covenant was modified to seven to one, while the company reported $63.2 million in revenue in the first half of 1992.[16] By 2000, the ratio had reached 17 to 1. In 2004 and after four consecutive years of workforce reductions, Ben & Jerry's stopped reporting this number.

A consulting report by McKinsey & Co. of medium-sized growth companies confirms that the CEOs of winning companies were notable for three common traits: perseverance, a builder's mentality, and a strong propensity for taking calculated risks.[17]

CONVERGING ON THE ENTREPRENEURIAL MIND LO2

 The entrepreneur is one of the most intriguing and at the same time most elusive characters.

WILLIAM BAUMOL

DESIRABLE AND ACQUIRABLE ATTITUDES, HABITS, AND BEHAVIOURS

Many successful entrepreneurs admit that attributes like initiative and a take-charge attitude, perseverance, resiliency, and adaptability are important—but it is what they *do* that matters most.[18]

Successful entrepreneurs share a common core of energy and raw intelligence, but possession of these characteristics does not necessarily an entrepreneur make. There is evidence that entrepreneurs—even if they *are* born—can be made better and that certain attitudes and behaviours can be acquired, developed, practised, and refined through a combination of experience and study.[19]

While not all attitudes, habits, and behaviours can be acquired by everyone at the same pace and with the same proficiency, entrepreneurs are able to significantly improve their odds of success by concentrating on those that work, by nurturing and practising them, and by eliminating, or at least mitigating, the rest. Painstaking effort may be required, and much will depend upon the motivation of an individual to grow, but it seems people have an astounding capacity to change and learn if they are motivated and committed to do so.

Evidence confirms attitudes and behaviours that successful entrepreneurs have in common. All mentioned the possession of three attributes as the principal reasons for their successes: (1) positive response to challenges and mistakes, (2) personal initiative, and (3) great perseverance.[20]

"Themes" have emerged from what successful entrepreneurs do and how they perform. Undoubtedly many attitudes and behaviours characterize the entrepreneurial mind, and there is no single set of attitudes and behaviours that every entrepreneur must have for every venture opportunity. Further, the *fit* concept argues that what is required in each situation depends on the mix and match of the key players and how promising and forgiving the opportunity is, given the founder's strengths and shortcomings. A team might collectively show many of the desired strengths, but even then there is no such thing as a perfect entrepreneur—as yet.

SIX DOMINANT THEMES

A consensus has emerged around six dominant themes, shown in Exhibits 1.2 and 1.3.

Commitment and Determination

Commitment and determination are seen as more important than any other factor. With commitment and determination, an entrepreneur can overcome incredible obstacles and compensate for other weaknesses.

Total commitment is required in nearly all entrepreneurial ventures. Almost without exception, entrepreneurs live under huge, constant pressures—first for their firms to survive start-up, then for them to stay alive, and, finally, for them to grow. A new venture demands top priority for the entrepreneur's time, emotions, and loyalty. Thus, commitment and determination usually require personal sacrifice. An entrepreneur's commitment can be measured in several ways— through a willingness to invest a substantial portion of his or her net worth in the venture,

EXHIBIT 1.2 SIX THEMES OF DESIRABLE AND ACQUIRABLE ATTITUDES AND BEHAVIOURS

THEME	ATTITUDE OR BEHAVIOUR
Commitment and Determination	Tenacious and decisive, able to recommit/commit quickly
	Intensely competitive in achieving goals
	Persistent in solving problems, disciplined
	Willing to undertake personal sacrifice
	Immersed
Leadership	Self-starter; high standards but not a perfectionist
	Team builder and hero maker; inspires others
	Treats others as he/she wants to be treated
	Shares the wealth with all the people who helped create it
	Honest and reliable; builds trust; practises fairness
	Not a lone wolf
	Superior learner and teacher; courage
	Patient and urgent
Opportunity Obsession	Has intimate knowledge of customers' needs and wants
	Market driven
	Obsessed with value creation and enhancement
Tolerance of Risk, Ambiguity, and Uncertainty	Calculated risk taker
	Risk minimizer
	Risk sharer
	Manages paradoxes and contradictions
	Tolerates uncertainty and lack of structure
	Tolerates stress and conflict
	Able to resolve problems and integrate solutions
Creativity, Self-Reliance, and Adaptability	Nonconventional, open-minded, lateral thinker
	Restless with status quo
	Able to adapt and change; creative problem solver
	Quick learner
	No fear of failure
	Able to conceptualize and "sweat details" (helicopter mind)
Motivation to Excel	Goal-and-results oriented; high but realistic goals
	Drive to achieve and grow
	Low need for status and power
	Interpersonally supporting (versus competitive)
	Aware of own weaknesses and strengths
	Has perspective and sense of humour

through a willingness to take a cut in pay because he or she will own a major piece of the venture, and through other major sacrifices in lifestyle and family circumstances.

The desire to win does not equal the will to never give up. This is a critically important distinction. Countless would-be entrepreneurs (and lots of other types of people for that matter) say that they really want to win. However, few have the dogged tenacity and unflinching perseverance to

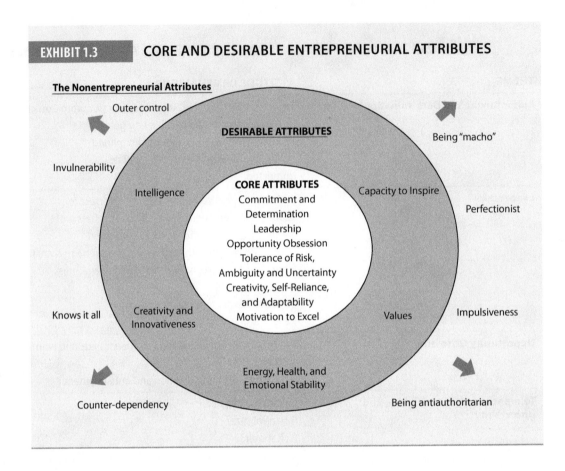

EXHIBIT 1.3 **CORE AND DESIRABLE ENTREPRENEURIAL ATTRIBUTES**

The Nonentrepreneurial Attributes

Outer control

Being "macho"

Invulnerability

DESIRABLE ATTRIBUTES

Intelligence

Capacity to Inspire

Perfectionist

CORE ATTRIBUTES
Commitment and
Determination
Leadership
Opportunity Obsession
Tolerance of Risk,
Ambiguity and Uncertainty
Creativity, Self-Reliance,
and Adaptability
Motivation to Excel

Knows it all

Creativity and
Innovativeness

Values

Impulsiveness

Energy, Health, and
Emotional Stability

Counter-dependency

Being antiauthoritarian

angel investor:
A high-net-worth
individual who
provides start-up
or growth capital
in exchange
for equity or
convertible debt.
They often play
an advisory role
to the venture
team.

make it happen. Take a young entrepreneur we shall call Stephen. One of the authors introduced him to a potentially invaluable lead—a brain trust prospect and mega-**angel investor**. Stephen placed several phone calls to the investor, but none were returned. He made a few more calls, each time leaving a message with the referral information. Still, no response.

Over the next week, the young entrepreneur made another series of over two dozen calls that once again received no response. At that point, what would you have done? Have you ever called anyone that many times and not gotten any sort of reply? Would you keep trying, or decide to move on and not waste any more time? Feeling that this individual was a potentially invaluable contact, Stephen refused to give up. He would make 12 more calls before finally getting a response. In the luncheon meeting that followed soon after, the mega-angel agreed to invest $1 million in Stephen's start-up, and serve as chairman of the board. The company became successful, and was sold four years later for $55 million.

Entrepreneurs are intensely competitive: they love to win and love to compete—at anything! The best of them direct all this competitive energy toward the goal and toward their external competitors. This is critical; founders who get caught up in competing with peers in the company invariably destroy team cohesion and spirit and, ultimately, the team.

Entrepreneurs who successfully build new enterprises seek to overcome hurdles, solve problems, and complete the job; they are disciplined and tenacious. They are able to commit and recommit quickly. They are not intimidated by difficult situations; in fact, they seem to think that the impossible just takes a little longer. However, they are neither aimless nor foolhardy in their relentless attack on a problem or obstacle that can impede their business. If a task is unsolvable, an entrepreneur will actually give up sooner than others. Most researchers share the opinion that while entrepreneurs are extremely persistent, they are also realistic in recognizing what they can and cannot do, and where they can get help to solve a very difficult but necessary task.

Leadership

Successful entrepreneurs are experienced, possess intimate knowledge of the technology and marketplace in which they will compete, demonstrate sound general management skills, and have a proven track record. They are self-starters and have an internal locus of control with high standards. They are patient leaders, capable of instilling tangible goals and managing for the longer haul. The entrepreneur is at once a learner and a teacher, a doer and a visionary. Building a substantial enterprise that will contribute something lasting and relevant to the world while realizing a capital gain requires the patience to stick to the task for 5 to 10 years or more.

Work by Alan J. Grant lends significant support to the fundamental "driving forces" theory of entrepreneurship that will be explored in chapter 3. Grant surveyed 25 senior venture capitalists to develop an entrepreneurial leadership paradigm. Three clear areas evolved from his study: the lead entrepreneur, the venture team, and the external environment, which are outlined in further detail in Exhibit 1.4. Furthermore, Grant suggested that to truly understand this paradigm, it should be "metaphorically associated with a *troika*, a Russian vehicle pulled by three horses of *equal* strength. Each horse represents a cluster of the success factors. The troika was driven toward success by the visions and *dreams* of the founding entrepreneurs."[21]

Successful entrepreneurs possess a well-developed capacity to exert influence without formal power. These people are adept at conflict resolution. They know when to use logic and when to persuade, when to make a concession, and when to exact one. To run a successful venture, an entrepreneur learns to get along with many different constituencies who often have conflicting aims: the customer, the supplier, the financial backer, the creditor, as well as the partners and others on the inside. Success comes when the entrepreneur is a mediator—a negotiator rather than a dictator.

Successful entrepreneurs are interpersonally supporting and nurturing—not interpersonally competitive. When a strong need to control, influence, and gain power over others characterizes the lead entrepreneur, or where he or she has an insatiable appetite for putting an associate down, the venture usually gets into trouble. Entrepreneurs should treat others as they want to be treated; they should share the wealth with those who contributed. A dictatorial, adversarial, and domineering management style makes it difficult to attract and keep people who thrive on a thirst for achievement, responsibility, and results. Under such a scenario, compliant partners and managers are often chosen. Destructive conflicts erupt over who has the final say, who is right, and whose prerogatives take precedence.

Entrepreneurs who create and build substantial enterprises are not lone wolves and super-independent. Neither do they need to collect all the credit for the effort. Instead, they actively build a team recognizing the reality that it is rarely possible to build a substantial business working alone. They have an uncanny ability to make heroes out of the people they attract to the venture by giving responsibility and sharing credit for accomplishments.

In the corporate setting, this "hero-making" ability is identified as an essential attribute of successful **intrapreneurs**.[22] These hero makers, of both the independent and corporate varieties, try to make the pie bigger and better, rather than jealously clutching and hoarding a tiny pie that is all theirs. They have a capacity for objective interpersonal relationships as well, which enables them to smooth out individual differences of opinion by keeping attention focused on the common goal.[23]

intrapreneurs: Managers within an organization who develop innovative solutions.

Opportunity Obsession

Successful entrepreneurs are obsessed first with opportunity—not with the money, the resources, the contacts and networking, and not with image or appearances. While some of these latter items have a place and time in the entrepreneurial process, they are not the source and driver for new ventures. Entrepreneurs, in their best creative mode, are constantly thinking of new ideas for businesses by watching trends, spotting patterns, and connecting the dots to shape and mould a unique enterprise. Dev Jennings of the University of Alberta and colleagues note that the formation of opportunity beliefs involves "overcoming ignorance and reducing doubt."[24]

EXHIBIT 1.4   THE ENTREPRENEURIAL LEADERSHIP PARADIGM

THE LEAD ENTREPRENEUR

Self-concept	Has a realist's attitude rather than one of invincibility
Intellectually honest	Trustworthy, his/her word is his/her contract Admits what and when he/she does not know
Pace maker	Displays a high energy level and a sense of urgency
Courage	Capable of making hard decisions: setting and beating high goals
Communication skills	Maintains an effective dialogue with the venture team, in the marketplace, and with other venture constituents
Team player	Competent in people management and team-building skills

THE VENTURE TEAM

Organizational style	The lead entrepreneur and the venture team blend their skills to operate in a participative environment
Ethical behaviour	Practises strong adherence to ethical business practices
Faithfulness	Stretched commitments are consistently met or bettered
Focus	Long-term venture strategies are kept in focus but tactics are varied to achieve them
Performance/reward	High standards of performance are created and superior performance is rewarded fairly and equitably
Adaptability	Responsive to rapid changes in product/technological cycles

EXTERNAL ENVIRONMENTAL INFLUENCES

Constituent needs	Organization needs are satisfied, in parallel with those of the public the enterprise serves
Prior experience	Extensive prior experiences are effectively applied
Mentoring	The competencies of others are sought and used
Problem resolution	New problems are immediately solved or prioritized
Value creation	High commitment is placed on long-term value creation for backers, customers, employees, and other stakeholders
Skill emphasis	Marketing skills are stressed over technical ones

Source: Adapted from Alan Grant, "The Development of an Entrepreneurial Leadership Paradigm for Enhancing Venture Capital Success," *Frontiers of Entrepreneurship Research* (Babson Park, MA: Babson College, 1992).

Take Tom Stemberg, for example. After business school—and after over 15 years in the supermarket business—he began to look for major new opportunities. He researched and rejected many decent ideas that were either not good "big" opportunities, or not the right fit for him. He then noted a recurring pattern with profound economic implications; every Main Street shop was selling ballpoint pens (wholesale cost: about 30 cents) for $2, $3, and more. He soon learned that these very large gross margins were common for a wide range of products used by small businesses and the self-employed: copy paper, writing and clerical supplies, calculators, and other electronics. Stemberg believed there was a new business model underlying this opportunity pattern—which, if well-developed and executed, could revolutionize the office supply business and become a major enterprise. He and Leo Kahn founded Staples, and they were certainly right.

Entrepreneurs realize good ideas are a dime a dozen, but good opportunities are few and far between. Fortunately, a great deal is now known about the criteria, the patterns, and the requirements that differentiate the good idea from the good opportunity. Dave Valliere of Ryerson University and Thomas Gegenhuber of Johannes Kepler University assert leaders must allocate their deliberate attention like any scarce and valuable resource; knowing when to cease one's awareness of and stop contemplation of a matter is vital.[25] Entrepreneurs rely heavily on their own previous experiences (or their frustrations as customers) to come up with their breakthrough opportunities.

In chapters 2 and 3, we will examine in detail how entrepreneurs and investors are "opportunity obsessed." We will see their ingenious, as well as straightforward, ways and patterns of creating, shaping, moulding, and recognizing opportunities that are not just another good idea, and then transforming these "caterpillars into butterflies." These practices, strategies, and habits are part of the entrepreneurial mindset, and are skills and know-how that are learnable and acquirable.

The entrepreneur's credo is to think opportunity first and cash last. Paul Kedrosky points out that Flickr took no venture capital. By not having all that money, "the Flickr folks were forced to compete smarter....They came up with many dandy ideas, and then cheerfully borrowed the best of everyone else's."[26] Time and again—even after harvesting a highly successful venture—lead entrepreneurs will start up another company. They possess all the money and material wealth anyone would ever hope for, yet it is not enough. Like the artist, scientist, athlete, or musician who, at great personal sacrifice, strives for yet another breakthrough discovery, new record, or masterpiece, the greatest entrepreneurs are similarly obsessed with what they believe is the next breakthrough opportunity.

An excellent example of this is Maynard Freeman Schurman, who in 1896 advertised in the Summerside, Prince Edward Island, newspaper that he was taking over a local company and would now be serving local residents. This family-controlled enterprise grew and became the prominent player in the Island's lumber and construction business. M. F. Schurman Co. Ltd. grew in the retail space and moved into steel fabrication, concrete, trusses, cartage, rentals, and property management. The legacy of the Schurman family was felt Island-wide and in 2004 the family sold their empire—10 separate companies—to J. D. Irving Ltd., the namesake of another legendary tycoon on the Atlantic coast.

Entrepreneurs like Stemberg, Schurman, and Irving think "big enough" about opportunities. They know that a mom-and-pop business can often be more exhausting and stressful, and much less rewarding, than a high potential business. Their opportunity mindset is how to create it, shape it, mould it, or fix it so that the customer/end-user will respond: Wow! Their thinking habits focus on what can go right here, what and how can we change the product or service to make it go right? What do we have to offer to become the superior, dominant product or service?

Tolerance of Risk, Ambiguity, and Uncertainty

Because high rates of change and high levels of risk, ambiguity, and uncertainty are almost a given, successful entrepreneurs tolerate risk, ambiguity, and uncertainty. They balance paradoxes and contradictions.

Entrepreneurs risk money, but they also risk reputation. Successful entrepreneurs are not gamblers; they take calculated risks. Like the parachutist, they are willing to take a risk; however, in deciding to do so, they calculate the risk carefully and thoroughly and do everything possible to get the odds in their favour. Entrepreneurs get others to share inherent financial and business risks with them. Partners put up money and put their reputations on the line, and investors do likewise. Creditors also join the party, as do customers who advance payments and suppliers who advance credit. For example, one researcher studied very successful entrepreneurs who initiated and orchestrated actions that had risk consequences.[27] It was found that while they shunned risk, these entrepreneurs sustained their courage by the clarity and optimism with which they saw the future. Entrepreneurs limited the risks they initiated by carefully defining and strategizing their ends and by controlling and monitoring their means—and by tailoring them both to what they saw the future to be. Further, they managed risk by transferring it to others.

One proposed concept of motivation–organizational fit contrasts a hierarchic (managerial) role with a task (entrepreneurial) role.[28] This study of motivational patterns showed that those who are task oriented (i.e., entrepreneurs) opt for the following roles because of the corresponding motivations:

ROLE	MOTIVATION
1. Individual achievement	A desire to achieve through one's own efforts and to attribute success to personal causation
2. Risk avoidance	A desire to avoid risk and leave little to chance
3. Seeking results of behaviour	A desire for feedback
4. Personal innovation	A desire to introduce innovative solutions
5. Planning and setting goals	A desire to think about the future and anticipate future possibilities

Entrepreneurs also tolerate ambiguity and uncertainty and are comfortable with conflict. Ask someone working in a large company how sure they are about receiving a paycheque this month, in two months, in six months, and next year. Invariably, they will say that it is virtually certain and will be amused at the question. Start-up entrepreneurs face just the opposite situation; there may be no revenue at the beginning, and if there is, a 90-day backlog in orders would be quite an exception. To make matters worse, lack of organization, structure, and order is a way of life. Constant changes introduce ambiguity and stress into every part of the enterprise. Jobs are undefined and changing continually, customers are new, co-workers are new, and setbacks and surprises are inevitable. There never seems to be enough time.

Successful entrepreneurs maximize the good "higher performance" effects of stress and minimize the negative reactions of exhaustion and frustration. Two surveys have suggested that very high levels of both satisfaction and stress characterize founders, to a greater degree than managers, regardless of the success of their ventures.[29]

Creativity, Self-Reliance, and Ability to Adapt

The high levels of uncertainty and rapid rates of change that characterize new ventures require fluid and highly adaptive forms of organization that can respond quickly and effectively.

Successful entrepreneurs believe in themselves. They believe that their accomplishments (and setbacks) lie within their own control and influence and that they can affect the outcome. Successful entrepreneurs have the ability to see and "sweat the details" and also to conceptualize (i.e., they have "helicopter minds" to hover above a situation). They are dissatisfied with the status quo and are restless initiators.

The entrepreneur has historically been viewed as an independent, highly self-reliant innovator, and champion (and occasional villain) of the free enterprise economy. More modern research and investigation have refined the agreement among researchers and practitioners alike that effective entrepreneurs actively seek and take initiative. They willingly put themselves in situations where they are personally responsible for the success or failure of the operation. They like to take the initiative to solve a problem or fill a vacuum where no leadership exists. They also like situations where personal impact on problems can be measured. Again, this is the action-oriented nature of the entrepreneur expressing him or herself.

Coralie Lalonde is such an example. Born in Calgary, she grew up in a middle-class family. After graduate school she started a product design and research company. Lalonde leveraged that success into an investment in Sybarus Technologies, which Lucent purchased for over $100 million. Able to retire at age 33, she then turned to helping start-ups and social causes: "If we want to have a strong community we have to get involved in that community, and that means not just putting money in, but putting in time and energy and skills."[30] Providing seed funding and expertise to both groups she expects strong returns on her efforts: "I love working with people, being engaged, having to make decisions, the anxiety. I just like to spend time with entrepreneurs."[31] Lalonde and her fellow angel investors placed bets on Softv.net, Quake Technologies, Galazar Networks, and several venture capital funds. Her philanthropic bets have paid hefty dividends as well. Coralie Lalonde's charitable endeavours include Junior Achievement (for which she serves as regional chairwoman), Community Foundation, Women in Technology mentoring program, Social Innovation Challenge, and Tech Venture Challenge.

Successful entrepreneurs are adaptive and resilient. They have an insatiable desire to know how well they are performing. They realize that to know how well they are doing and how to improve their performance they need to actively seek and use feedback. Seeking and using feedback is also central to the habit of learning from mistakes and setbacks, and of responding to the unexpected. For the same reasons, these entrepreneurs often are described as excellent listeners and quick learners.

Entrepreneurs are not afraid of failing; rather, they are more intent on succeeding, counting on the fact that "success covers a multitude of blunders," as George Bernard Shaw eloquently stated. People who fear failure will neutralize whatever achievement motivation they may possess. They

CORALIE LALONDE, SUCCESSFUL ENTREPRENEUR AND ANGEL INVESTOR

will tend to engage in a very easy task, where there is little chance of failure, or in a very difficult situation, where they cannot be held personally responsible if they do not succeed.

Further, successful entrepreneurs learn from failure experiences. They better understand not only their roles but also the roles of others in causing the failure, and thus are able to avoid similar problems in the future. There is an old saying to the effect that the cowboy who has never been thrown from a horse undoubtedly has not ridden too many! The iterative, trial-and-error nature of becoming a successful entrepreneur makes serious setbacks and disappointments an integral part of the learning process.

Motivation to Excel

Successful entrepreneurs are motivated to excel. Entrepreneurs are self-starters who appear driven internally by a strong desire to compete against their own self-imposed standards and to pursue and attain challenging goals. This need to achieve has been well established in the literature on entrepreneurs since the pioneering work of McClelland and Atkinson on motivation in the 1950s and 1960s. Seeking out the challenge inherent in a start-up and responding in a positive way is achievement motivation in action.

Conversely, these entrepreneurs have a low need for status and power, and they derive personal motivation from the challenge and excitement of creating and building enterprises. They are driven by a thirst for achievement, rather than by status and power. Ironically, their accomplishments, especially if they are very successful, give them power. But it is important to recognize that power and status are a result of their activities. Setting high but attainable goals enables entrepreneurs to focus their energies, be very selective in sorting out opportunities, and know what to say no to. Having goals and direction also helps define priorities and provides measures of how well they are performing. Possessing an objective way of keeping score, such as changes in profits, sales, or stock price, is also important. Thus, money is seen as a tool and a way of keeping score, rather than the object of the game by itself.

Successful entrepreneurs insist on the highest personal standards of integrity and reliability. They do what they say they are going to do, and they pull for the long haul. These high personal standards are the glue and fibre that bind successful personal and business relationships and make them endure. A study involving 130 participants in a small business training program at the Harvard Business School confirmed how important this issue is. It was the single most important factor in their long-term successes.[32]

The best entrepreneurs have a keen awareness of their own strengths and weaknesses and those of their partners and of the competitive environment surrounding and influencing them. They are coldly realistic about what they can and cannot do and do not delude themselves; that is, they have "veridical awareness" or "optimistic realism." It also is worth noting that successful entrepreneurs believe in themselves. They do not believe that fate, luck, or other powerful, external forces will govern the success or failure of their venture. They believe they personally can affect the outcome. This attribute is also consistent with achievement motivation, which is the desire to take personal responsibility, and self-confidence.

This veridical awareness is routinely accompanied by other valuable entrepreneurial traits—perspective and a sense of humour. The ability to retain a sense of perspective, and to "know thyself" in both strengths and weaknesses makes it possible for an entrepreneur to laugh, to ease tensions, and to get an unfavourable situation set in a more profitable direction.

ENTREPRENEURIAL REASONING: THE ENTREPRENEURIAL MIND[33] IN ACTION

How do successful entrepreners think, what actions do they initiate, and how do they start and build businesses? By understanding the attitudes, behaviours, management competencies, experience, and know-how that contribute to entrepreneurial success, one has some useful benchmarks for gauging what to do. Exhibit 1.5 examines the role of opportunity in entrepreneurship.

Successful entrepreneurs have a wide range of personality types. Most research about entrepreneurs has focused on the influences of genes, family, education, career experience, and so forth, but no psychological model has been supported. Studies have shown that an entrepreneur does not need specific inherent traits, but rather a set of acquired skills.[34] Individual learning leads to group learning which leads to enterprise-level learning.[35] Start-up intentions and venture-creation decisions depend upon cognitive processes, social context, cultural values, and characteristics of the entrepreneur. One study asserts that an entrepreneurial way of thinking is universal. Like culture, it is a common characteristic of entrepreneurs regardless of national origin.[36]

"There is no evidence of an ideal entrepreneurial personality. Great entrepreneurs can be either gregarious or low key, analytical or intuitive, charismatic or boring, good with details or terrible, delegators or control freaks. What you need is a capacity to execute in certain key ways."[37] Successful entrepreneurs share common attitudes and behaviours. They work hard and are driven by an intense commitment and determined perseverance; they see the cup half full, rather than half empty; they strive for integrity; they thrive on the competitive desire to excel and win; they are dissatisfied with the status quo and seek opportunities to improve almost any situation they encounter; they use failure as a tool for learning and eschew perfection in favour of effectiveness; and they believe they can personally make an enormous difference in the final outcome of their ventures and their lives.

EXHIBIT 1.5	OPPORTUNITY KNOCKS—OR DOES IT HIDE? AN EXAMINATION OF THE ROLE OF OPPORTUNITY RECOGNITION IN ENTREPRENEURSHIP

OPPORTUNITIES OF VARIOUS SOURCES AND TYPES

SOURCES OF OPPORTUNITIES	ENTREPRENEURS	NON-ENTREPRENEURS
Prior work	58%	48%
Network	22%	30%
Thinking by analogy	11%	22%
Partner	9%	—
TYPES OF OPPORTUNITIES	**ENTREPRENEURS**	**NON-ENTREPRENEURS**
Niche expansion/underserved niche	25%	29%
Customer need	30%	25%
Own firm's need	5%	4%
Better technology	40%	42%

Source: Charlene Zietsma, "Opportunity Knocks–Or Does It Hide? An Examination of the Role of Opportunity Recognition in Entrepreneurship," *Frontiers of Entrepreneurship Research* (Babson Park, MA: Babson College, 1999).

Note: Numbers equal total people in the sample allocated to each category.

Saunders Farm is a family-run enterprise. "Over the years we've worked hard, tried new ideas and never stopped innovating." It was in 1974 that Bill and Anne Saunders bought a run-down farm to "re-discover their family roots, and to satisfy their entrepreneurial spirits." It offered one of the region's original pick-your-own strawberry opportunities. In 1991 a new vision for the firm emerged: a fall season and a Halloween attraction. Initially it was just a four-scene hayride and a four-scene haunted house, but now it takes nearly 200 employees to take care of the thousands of visitors. One son, Mark, returned from university with his wife Anne to "help the farm navigate its new direction." With three generations on site, they now host corporate retreats in restored log buildings for groups to "play, learn, and grow." The mazes

were developed to create a summertime family attraction. Saunders Farm maintains a substantial footprint in the social media space with a Twitter feed and Facebook page. TripAdvisor also plays a role in directing customers their way, as does Yelp and two-for-one coupon websites. Saunders Farm boasts the world's largest collection of hedge mazes and has added a splash zone and farm shop with homemade food and products from the local community. Selling Christmas trees is a way to extend revenues later into the season. With apps for iPhone and Android, Saunders Farm is looking to stay modern and connected. With additions to the venue, such as jumping pillows, a puppet show, a fairy garden, and a pedal cart track the family is trying attract and retain customers. Mark Saunders, "director of fun," revealed that a 2000-square-foot commercial kitchen built in 2013 "will allow us to do more banquets and catering" and move boldly into weddings. Mark Saunders is conservative, however: "the company carefully nurses a cash balance, preferring to pay for capital improvements out of cash on hand rather than taking on debt."

QUESTION: This lifestyle business has transcended generations. The farm has had to evolve and innovate to remain competitive. Today, the farm competes with festivals and events that are nonprofits and receive government subsidies. What future developments and challenges to you foresee? Can the family ever expand beyond a single site? Does an exit necessitate selling to a third party or can a harvest be realized when passing the farm to the next generation?

Courtesy Mark Saunders, Saunder's Farm

ENTREPRENEURS ARE NOT CONTENT TO JUST BE PART OF THE PACK, THEY WANT TO LEAVE THEIR MARK ON SOCIETY.

Sources: http://www.saundersfarm.com/; http://www.tripadvisor.com/; http://www.yelp.com/; http://www.savourottawa.ca/; Elizabeth Howell, "Saunders Farm expansion targets weddings, corporate retreats" Ottawa Business Journal, 26 October 2012.

Those who have succeeded speak of these attitudes and behaviours time and again.[38] For example, David Large of the University of Ottawa, himself a founder or co-founder of several ventures and investor in others, knows the intense commitment and perseverance of entrepreneurs. He defines an entrepreneur as "someone who stands up and says I'm going to make that happen!" Other phrases that capture the spirit of the entrepreneur include: "seeing opportunities where others see problems," "never accepting no for an answer," "freedom to soar or sink," and "biting off more than you can chew."

Successful entrepreneurs possess not only a creative and innovative flair, but also solid management skills, business know-how, and sufficient contacts. Exhibit 1.6 demonstrates this relationship.

Inventors, noted for their creativity, often lack the necessary management skills and business know-how. Promoters usually lack serious general management and business skills and true creativity. Managers govern, police, and ensure the smooth operation of the status quo; their management skills, while high, are tuned to efficiency as well, and creativity is usually not required. Although the management skills of the manager and the entrepreneur overlap, the manager is more driven by conservation of resources and the entrepreneur is more opportunity-driven.[39]

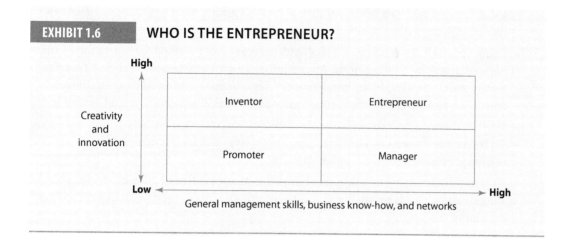

EXHIBIT 1.6 **WHO IS THE ENTREPRENEUR?**

THE CONCEPT OF APPRENTICESHIP LO3

It occurred to me how much knowledge I have gained in the short time I have worked as the 'apprentice.' Much of what I've learned can't be recorded….In my first week, I was off to the races with piles of reading material….The advantages of working with a small group of people are that I remain in 'the loop' and have a greater opportunity to explore various roles within the company. The challenges of growing quickly with such a small team are the increasing demands….This position requires a high level of confidentiality with a strong focus on business ethics. My experiences in the first few months have varied from attending a precious metals conference with fund managers and analysts to travelling to the Amazon for a mine opening….However, the most exciting and challenging event so far has been working on a hostile takeover!

MELANIE PILON

SHAPING AND MANAGING AN APPRENTICESHIP

When one looks at successful entrepreneurs, one sees profiles of careers rich in experience. Repeatedly there is a pattern among successful entrepreneurs. They have usually acquired 10 or more years of substantial experience, built contacts, garnered the know-how, and established a track record in the industry, market, and technology niche within which they eventually launch, acquire, or build a business. Frequently, they have acquired intimate knowledge of the customer, distribution channels, and market through direct sales and marketing experience. The more successful ones have made money for their employer before doing it for themselves. Consider the following examples:

- Apple Computer founders Steve Jobs and Steve Wozniak were computer enthusiasts as preteens and had accumulated a relatively lengthy amount of experience by the time they started the company in their mid-20s. In entirely new industries such as micro-computers, a few years can be a large amount of experience.

- Tim Morgan, a former WestJet Airlines executive and co-founder, is taking his experience to launch a new airline and tour company that promises "a refreshing new way to travel." He is also leveraging what he learned as founder and president of Morgan Air. In this social-network era, even before painting planes and getting them in the air, Morgan's new venture includes a discussion forum on the company website and a presence on Facebook.

- Frank Stronach apprenticed as a tool-and-die maker and worked for others for 10 years before starting his first business. After another 10-plus years, he landed his first automotive parts contract. From humble beginnings, he has gone on to create a colossal empire in auto parts manufacturing—including the ability to produce and assemble entire vehicles.
- Pixar Canada, located in Vancouver, is a subsidiary of Pixar Animation Studios and offers apprenticeships in a number of areas.
- Ashton Kutcher, angel investor, sees himself as an apprentice of the tech start-up ecosystem. His advice is to listen and learn—sit alongside smart people, ask questions, and do a lot of reading.

Thousands of similar examples exist. There are always exceptions to any such pattern, but if you want the odds in your favour, get the experience first. Successful entrepreneurs are likely to have at least 8 to 10 years of experience. They are likely to have accumulated enough net worth to contribute to funding the venture or to have a track record impressive enough to give investors and creditors the necessary confidence. Finally, they usually have nurtured a network and acquired relevant business contacts that ultimately contribute to the success of their ventures.

The first 10 or so years after leaving school can make or break an entrepreneur's career in terms of how well he or she is prepared for serious entrepreneuring. Evidence suggests that the most durable entrepreneurial careers, those found to last 25 years or more, were begun across a broad age spectrum, but the person had selected prior work and experiences to prepare him or her specifically for an entrepreneurial path.

Relevant experience, know-how, attitudes, behaviours, and skills appropriate for a particular venture opportunity can dramatically improve the odds for success. Alternatively, if an entrepreneur does not have these, then he or she will have to learn them while launching and growing the business. The tuition for such an approach is often greater than most entrepreneurs can afford.

Since entrepreneurs frequently evolve from an entrepreneurial heritage or are shaped and nurtured by their closeness to entrepreneurs and others, the concept of an apprenticeship can be a useful one. Much of what an entrepreneur needs to know about entrepreneuring comes from learning by doing. Knowing what to prepare for, where the windows for acquiring the relevant exposure lie, how to anticipate these, where to position oneself, and when to move on, can be quite useful.

As Howard Stevenson of the Harvard Business School reminds us:

> You have to approach the world as an equal. There is no such thing as being supplicant. You are trying to work and create a better solution by creating action among a series of people who are relatively equal. We destroy potential entrepreneurs by putting them in a velvet-lined rut, by giving them jobs that pay too much, and by telling them they are too good, before they get adequate intelligence, experience, and responsibility.

WINDOWS OF APPRENTICESHIP

Exhibit 1.7 summarizes the key elements of an apprenticeship and experience curve and relates these to age windows. Age windows are especially important because of the inevitable time it takes to create and build a successful activity, whether it is a new venture or within an existing organization.

There is a saying in the venture capital business that the "lemons," or losers, in a portfolio ripen in about two and one-half years and that the "plums," or winners, usually take seven or eight years to come to fruition. Therefore, seven years is a realistic time frame to expect to grow a higher potential business to a point where a capital gain can be realized.

EXHIBIT 1.7 **WINDOWS OF ENTREPRENEURIAL APPRENTICESHIP**

ELEMENTS OF THE APPRENTICESHIP AND EXPERIENCE CURVE	AGE			
	20s	**30s**	**40s**	**50s**
1. Relevant Business Experience	Low	Moderate to high	Higher	Highest
2. Management Skills and Know-How	Low to moderate	Moderate to high	High	High
3. Entrepreneurial Goals and Commitment	Varies widely	Focused high	High	High
4. Drive and Energy	Highest	High	Moderate	Lowest
5. Wisdom and Judgment	Lowest	High	Higher	Highest
6. Focus of Apprenticeship	Discussing what you enjoy; key is learning business, sales, marketing; profit and loss responsibility	General management, Division management, Founder	Growing and harvesting	Reinvesting
7. Dominant Life-Stage Issues*	Realizing your dream of adolescence and young adulthood	Personal growth and new directions and ventures	Renewal, regeneration, reinvesting in the system	

*Source: Daniel J. Levinson, *The Seasons of a Man's Life* (New York, NY: Random House, 1986).

The implications of this are quite provocative. First, time is precious. Assume an entrepreneur spends the first five years after college, university, or graduate school gaining relevant experience. He or she will be 25 to 30 years of age (or maybe as old as 35) when launching a new venture. By the age of 50, there will have been time for starting, at most, three successful new ventures. What is more, entrepreneurs commonly go through false starts or even a failure at first in the trial-and-error process of learning the entrepreneurial ropes. As a result, the first venture may not be launched until later (i.e., in the entrepreneur's mid- to late-30s). This would leave time to grow the current venture and maybe one more. But there are always exceptions. Aydin Mirzaee, for example, hit the ground running in his early 20s. And many others gained experience in their childhood through lemonade stands, babysitting, etc. Recently, it is common for aspiring entrepreneurs to launch multiple ventures even before the first succeeds or fails.

Exhibit 1.7 reveals other paradoxes and dilemmas. For one thing, just when an entrepreneur's drive, energy, and ambition are at a peak, the necessary relevant business experience and leadership skills are least developed, and those critical elements, wisdom and judgment, are in their infancy. Later, when an entrepreneur has gained the necessary experience in the "deep, dark canyons of uncertainty" and has thereby gained wisdom and judgment, age begins to take its toll. In addition, patience and perseverance to relentlessly pursue a long-term vision need to be balanced with the urgency and realism to make it happen. Flexibility to stick with the moving opportunity targets and to abandon some and shift to others is also required. However, flexibility and the ability to act with urgency disappear as the other commitments of life are assumed.

THE CONCEPT OF APPRENTICESHIP: ACQUIRING THE 50 000 CHUNKS

Recently, studies of entrepreneurs have confirmed what practitioners have known all along: that some attitudes, behaviours, and know-how can be acquired and that some of these attributes are more desirable than others.

Increasingly, research on the career paths of entrepreneurs and the self-employed suggest the role of experience and know-how is central to successful venture creation. Many successful entrepreneurs do not have prior industry experience. More critical to the entrepreneur is the ability to gain information and act on it.[40] Evidence also suggests that success is linked to preparation and planning.[41] This is what getting 50 000 chunks of experience is all about.

Although formal market research may provide useful information, it is also important to recognize the entrepreneur's collective, qualitative judgment must be weighted most heavily in evaluating opportunities. One study found that entrepreneurs view believing in the idea and experimenting with new venture ideas that result in both failures and successes as the most important components of opportunity recognition.[42]

Many successful entrepreneurs follow a pattern of apprenticeship, where they prepare for becoming entrepreneurs by gaining the relevant business experiences from parents who are self-employed or through job experiences. They do not leave acquisition of experience to accident or osmosis. As one entrepreneur said, "Know what you know and what you *don't* know."[43]

ROLE MODELS

Numerous studies show a strong connection between the presence of role models and the emergence of entrepreneurs. A number of entrepreneurs report the value of reading biographies; these might be from the business realm, but often are the telling of accomplishments of individuals from other realms. For instance, more than half of those starting new businesses had parents who owned businesses. Likewise, 70 percent of MIT graduates who started technology businesses had entrepreneurial parents.[44] The authors summarized it this way:

> Family firms spawn entrepreneurs. Older generations provide leadership and role modeling. This phenomenon cuts across industries, firm size, and gender.

ENTREPRENEUR'S CREED

So much time and space would not be spent on the entrepreneurial mind if it were just of academic interest. Entrepreneurs themselves believe that mindset is in large part responsible for success. When asked an open-ended question about what they believe are the most critical concepts, skills, and know-how for running a business—today and five years hence—their answers were very revealing. Most mentioned mental attitudes and philosophies based on entrepreneurial attributes, rather than specific skills or organizational concepts. These answers are gathered together in what might be called an entrepreneur's creed:

- Do what gives you energy—have fun.
- Figure out what can go right and make it happen.
- *Illegitimi non carborundum:* tenacity and creativity will triumph.
- If you don't know it can't be done, then you'll go ahead and do it.
- Be dissatisfied with the way things are—and look for improvement.

- Don't take a risk if you don't have to—but take a calculated risk if it's the right opportunity for *you*.
- Businesses fail; successful entrepreneurs learn—but keep the tuition low.
- It is easier to beg for forgiveness than to ask for permission in the first place.
- Make opportunity and results your obsession—not money.
- Money is a tool and a scorecard available to the right people with the right opportunity at the right time.
- Making money is even more fun than spending it.
- Make heroes out of others—a team builds a business; an individual makes a living.
- Take pride in your accomplishments—it is contagious!
- Sweat the details that are critical to success.
- Integrity and reliability equal long-run oil and glue.
- Accept the responsibility, less than half the credit, and more than half the blame.
- Make the pie bigger—don't waste time trying to cut smaller slices.
- Play for the long haul—it is rarely possible to get rich quickly.
- Don't pay too much—but don't let it get away!
- Only the lead dog gets a change of view.
- Success is getting what you want: Happiness is wanting what you get.

MYTHS AND REALITIES
LO4

Folklore and stereotypes about entrepreneurs and entrepreneurial success are remarkably durable, even in these informed and sophisticated times. More is known about the founders and the process of entrepreneurship than ever before. However, certain myths enjoy recurring attention and popularity, in part because while generalities may apply to certain types of entrepreneurs and particular situations, the great variety of founders tend to defy generalization. Exhibit 1.8 lists myths about entrepreneurs that have persisted and realities that are supported by research.

EXHIBIT 1.8   **MYTHS AND REALITIES ABOUT ENTREPRENEURS**

Myth 1— Entrepreneurs are born, not made.

Reality— While entrepreneurs are born with certain native intelligence, a flair for creating, and energy, these talents by themselves are not enough. The making of an entrepreneur occurs by accumulating the relevant skills, know-how, experiences, and contacts over a period of years and includes large doses of self-development. The creative capacity to envision and then pursue an opportunity is a direct descendant of at least 10 or more years of experience that leads to pattern recognition.

Myth 2— Anyone can start a business.

Reality— Entrepreneurs who recognize the difference between an idea and an opportunity, and who think big enough, start businesses that have a better chance of succeeding. Luck, to the extent it is involved, requires good preparation. And the easiest part is starting. What is hardest is surviving, sustaining, and building a venture so its founders can realize a harvest. Perhaps only 1 in 10 to 20 new businesses that survive five years or more results in a capital gain for the founders.

continued

Myth 3— Entrepreneurs are gamblers.

Reality— Successful entrepreneurs take very careful, calculated risks. They try to influence the odds, often by getting others to share risk with them and by avoiding or minimizing risks if they have the choice. Often they slice up the risk into smaller, quite digestible pieces; only then do they commit the time or resources to determine if that piece will work. They do not deliberately seek to take more risk or to take unnecessary risk, nor do they shy away from unavoidable risk.

Myth 4— Entrepreneurs want the whole show to themselves.

Reality— Owning and running the whole show effectively puts a ceiling on growth. It is extremely difficult to grow a higher potential venture by working single-handedly. Higher potential entrepreneurs build a team, an organization, and a company. Besides, 100 percent of nothing is nothing, so rather than taking a large piece of the pie, they work to make the pie bigger.

Myth 5— Entrepreneurs are their own bosses and completely independent.

Reality— Entrepreneurs are far from independent and have to serve many masters and constituencies, including partners, investors, customers, suppliers, creditors, employees, families, and those involved in social and community obligations. Entrepreneurs, however, can make free choices of whether, when, and what they care to respond to. Moreover, it is extremely difficult, and rare, to build a business beyond annual sales of $1 million single-handedly.

Myth 6— Entrepreneurs work longer and harder than managers do in big companies.

Reality— There is no evidence that all entrepreneurs work more than their corporate counterparts. Some do, some do not. Some actually report that they work less.

Myth 7— Entrepreneurs experience a great deal of stress and pay a high price.

Reality— Being an entrepreneur is stressful and demanding. However, there is no evidence that it is any more stressful than numerous other highly demanding professional roles, and entrepreneurs find their jobs very satisfying. They have a high sense of accomplishment, are healthier, and are much less likely to retire than those who work for others. Three times as many entrepreneurs as corporate managers say they plan to never retire.

Myth 8— Start a business and fail and you'll never raise money again.

Reality— Talented and experienced entrepreneurs—because they pursue attractive opportunities and are able to attract the right people and necessary financial and other resources to make the venture work—often head successful ventures. Further, businesses fail, but entrepreneurs do not. Failure is often the fire that tempers the steel of an entrepreneur's learning experience and street savvy.

Myth 9— Money is the most important start-up ingredient.

Reality— If the other pieces and talents are there, the money will follow, but it does not follow that an entrepreneur will succeed if he or she has enough money. Money is one of the least important ingredients in new venture success. Money is to the entrepreneur what the paint and brush are to the artist—an inert tool that in the right hands, can create marvels.

Myth 10— Entrepreneurs should be young and energetic.

Reality— While these qualities may help, age is no barrier. The average age of entrepreneurs starting high potential businesses is in the mid-30s, and there are numerous examples of entrepreneurs starting businesses in their 60s. What is critical is possessing the relevant know-how, experience, and contacts that greatly facilitate recognizing and pursuing an opportunity.

Myth 11— Entrepreneurs are motivated solely by the quest for the almighty dollar.

Reality— Entrepreneurs seeking high potential ventures are more driven by building enterprises and realizing long-term capital gains than by instant gratification through high salaries and perks. A sense of personal achievement and accomplishment, feeling in control of their own destinies, and realizing their vision and dreams are also powerful motivators. Money is viewed as a tool and a way of keeping score, rather than an end in itself. Entrepreneurs thrive on the thrill of the chase; and, time and again, even after an entrepreneur has made a few million dollars or more, he or she will work on a new vision to build another company.

Myth 12— Entrepreneurs seek power and control over others.

Reality— Successful entrepreneurs are driven by the quest for responsibility, achievement, and results, rather than for power for its own sake. They thrive on a sense of accomplishment and of outperforming the competition, rather than a personal need for power expressed by dominating and controlling others. By virtue of their accomplishments, they may be powerful and influential, but these are more the by-products of the entrepreneurial process than a driving force behind it.

Myth 13— If an entrepreneur is talented, success will happen in a year or two.

Reality— An old maxim among venture capitalists says it all: The lemons ripen in two and a half years, but the plums take seven or eight. Rarely is a new business established solidly in less than three or four years.

Myth 14— Any entrepreneur with a good idea can raise venture capital.

Reality— Of the ventures of entrepreneurs with good ideas who seek out venture capital, only 1 to 3 out of 100 are funded.

Myth 15— If an entrepreneur has enough start-up capital, he or she can't miss.

Reality— The opposite is often true; that is, too much money at the outset often creates euphoria and a spoiled-child syndrome. The accompanying lack of discipline and impulsive spending usually lead to serious problems and failure.

Myth 16— Entrepreneurs are lone wolves and cannot work with others.

Reality— The most successful entrepreneurs are leaders who build great teams and effective relationships working with peers, directors, investors, key customers, key suppliers, and the like.

Myth 17— Unless you attained 700-plus on your GMAT and have an "A" average, you'll never be a successful entrepreneur.

Reality— Entrepreneurial IQ is a unique combination of creativity, motivation, integrity, leadership, team building, analytical ability, and ability to deal with ambiguity and adversity.

Studies have indicated that 90 percent or more of founders start their companies in the same marketplace, technology, or industry they have been working in. Entrepreneurs are likely to have role models, have 8 to 10 years of experience, and be well educated. It also appears that successful entrepreneurs have a wide range of experiences in products/markets and across functional areas. Studies also show that most successful entrepreneurs start companies in their 30s. Exhibit 1.9 provides some average profile information of entrepreneurs by location.

EXHIBIT 1.9 **CHARACTERISTICS OF ENTREPRENEURS BY LOCATION**

	AVERAGE AGE (YEARS)	AVERAGE WORKDAY (HOURS)	SERIAL ENTREPRENEURS (% WHO HAVE HAD A PREVIOUS START-UP)
Silicon Valley	34.12	9.95	56
Boston	36.8	10.41	51
Toronto	35.63	8.69	44
Vancouver	36.7	9.5	50
Waterloo	33.43	9.8	32
Bangalore	37	10.86	24
Singapore	33.35	11	32

Entrepreneurs work both more and less than their counterparts in large organizations, they have high degrees of satisfaction with their jobs, and they are healthier.[45] One study showed that nearly 21 percent of the founders were over 40 when they embarked on their entrepreneurial career, the majority were in their 30s, and just over one-quarter did so by the time they were 25.

WHAT CAN BE LEARNED?

For over 40 years, the authors have been engaged as educators, cofounders, investors, advisors, and directors of new, higher potential ventures. Former students have launched many of these, and the cases in this book are about such founders. Do we believe that in 35 to 40 hours of class time, during a single semester, the average student can be converted into the next Richard Branson or Bill Gates? No, but perhaps we can get you geared up for your own entrepreneurial journey.

Henry Mintzberg of McGill University has been on a tirade over business school education for years. His assertion is that "MBA classrooms overemphasize the science of management while ignoring its art."[46] Practising managers should be learning from their own experiences—from each other. Ed McMullan and Vance Gough join in the assertion that entrepreneurs learn from seeing the successes and innovations of others. As early as 1993, the University of Calgary implemented an MBA in enterprise development that combined entrepreneurs and managers in the same classroom.[47]

New Venture Creation immerses you in the dynamics and realities of launching and growing lifestyle- to higher potential ventures. Throughout the text are cases and examples about real entrepreneurs, including students and recent graduates. You will face the same situations these aspiring entrepreneurs faced as they sought to turn dreams into reality. The cases and text, combined with other online resources, will enable you to grapple with the conceptual, practical, financial, and personal issues entrepreneurs encounter. This book will help you get the odds of success in your favour. It will focus your attention on developing answers for the most important of these questions, including:

- What is the difference between a good opportunity and just another idea?
- Is the opportunity I am considering the right opportunity for me now?
- Why do some firms grow quickly to several million dollars in sales but then stumble, never growing beyond a single-product firm?
- What are the critical tasks and hurdles in seizing an opportunity and building the business?
- How much money do I need and when, where, and how can I get it—on acceptable terms?
- What financing sources, strategies, and mechanisms can I use from pre-start through the early growth stage to the harvest of my venture?
- What are the minimum resources I need to gain control over the opportunity, and how can I do this?
- Is a business plan needed? If so, what kind is needed and how and when should I develop one?
- Who are the constituents for whom I must create or add value to achieve a positive cash flow and to develop harvest options?
- What is my venture worth and how do I negotiate what to give up?
- What are the critical transitions in entrepreneurial management as a firm grows from $1 million to $5 million to $25 million in sales?
- What is it that entrepreneurial leaders do differently that enables them to achieve such competitive breakthroughs and advantages, particularly over conventional practices, but also so-called best practices?

- What do I need to know and practise in entrepreneurial reasoning and thinking to have a competitive edge?
- What are some of the pitfalls, minefields, and hazards I need to anticipate, prepare for, and respond to?
- What are the contacts and networks I need to access and to develop?
- Do I know what I do and do not know, and do I know what to do about it?
- How can I develop a personal "entrepreneurial game plan" to acquire the experience I need to succeed?
- How critical and sensitive is the timing in each of these areas?
- Why do entrepreneurs who succeed in the long term seek to maintain reputations for integrity and ethical business practices?

We believe that we can significantly improve the quality of decisions students make about entrepreneurship and thereby further improve the fit between what they aspire to do and the requirements of the particular opportunity. In many cases, those choices lead to self-employment or meaningful careers in new and growing firms and, increasingly, in large firms that "get it." In other cases, students join larger firms whose customer base and/or suppliers are principally the entrepreneurial sector. Still others seek careers in the financial institutions and professional services firms that are at the vortex of the entrepreneurial economy: venture capital, private equity, investment banks, commercial banks, consulting, accounting, and the like.

Our view of entrepreneurship is that it need not be an end in itself. Rather, it is a pathway that leads to innumerable ideas and opportunities, and opens visions of what young people can become. You will learn skills, and how to use those skills appropriately. You will learn how to tap your own and others' creativity, and to apply your new energy. You will learn the difference between another good idea and a serious opportunity. You will learn the power and potential of the entrepreneurial team. You will learn how entrepreneurs finance and grow their companies, often with ingenious **bootstrapping** strategies that get big results with minimal resources. You will learn the joy of self-sufficiency and independence. You will learn how entrepreneurial leaders make this happen, and give back to society. You will discover anew what it is about entrepreneurship that sustains entrepreneurial reasoning and thinking and fuels your dreams.

bootstrapping:
A technique of starting with existing (minimal) resources and proceeding; to accumulate resources and grow organically. "Pull oneself up by the bootstraps" is a metaphor of independence without external assistance.

A WORD OF CAUTION: WHAT GRADES, IQ TESTS, GMATS, AND OTHERS DON'T MEASURE

Never, never, never give up.

If you are going through hell, keep going.

Success is going from failure to failure without losing enthusiasm.

Every day you may make progress. Every step may be fruitful. Yet there will stretch out before you an ever-lengthening, ever-ascending, ever-improving path. You know you will never get to the end of the journey. But this, so far from discouraging, only adds to the joy and the glory of the climb.

WINSTON CHURCHILL

The following data about Harvard Business School alumni whose careers were followed for nearly 25 years has surprised many. Regardless of the measure one applies, among the very top of the class were graduates who were both highly successful and not very successful. At the bottom of the class were alumni who became outrageously successful, and others who accomplished little.

ENTREPRENEURS ACROSS CANADA
StormFisher Biogas

StormFisher Biogas was founded by three MBA classmates. Ryan Little, who held a BA in arts from Queen's University and had earlier started CanadaHelps, Bas van Berkel, who had been working as a civil engineer in the Netherlands, and Chris Guillon, who held a BSc in agriculture and an MSc in biology from McGill University. The team wanted their start-up to do good for society and the environment. Renewable energy was the path they chose. The three saw an opportunity in transforming organic waste into biogas via anaerobic digestion. The waste would be material like household table scraps suitable for composting. The by-products of their process would be energy and organic fertilizer. In December 2007, they were working on a business plan to raise financing for their new venture to get off the ground. The business plan took shape and various partners were filled in. The team debated who to approach, the timing, and "the ask"—how much money and with what conditions attached. In 2008, they entered into a strategic partnership with Denham Capital Management to invest $350 million. In 2009, Loblaw Companies Ltd. agreed that 47 stores between Windsor and Waterloo, Ontario, would divert organic waste—such as from the produce department, the bakery, and deli counter—to StormFisher Biogas. In 2010 the company was sold to a joint venture of General Electric and AES. Ryan Little and Bas van Berkel then went on to start Rocksteady Investments, to focus on commercializing cleantech. Rocksteady sought to serve as an intermediary between investors and early-stage enterprises that had intellectual property and were seeking $1 million or less and were either pre-revenue or just beginning sales. Chris Guillon and another employee, Brandon Moffatt, remained on with their original start-up and subsequently led a management buyback of StormFisher Biogas. In 2011, Harvest Power purchased the StormFisher site. By this point, Bas van Berkel had returned to Europe to start Parmenion MFG, a synthetic wax producer. Chris Guillon and Brandon Moffatt went on to join Pushkar Kumar at GreenMantra Technologies, which breaks down recyclable plastics into valuable elements—wax, grease, and fuel.

QUESTION: Would you have joined this ride? For how long would you have held on?

Sources: "StormFisher Biogas and Loblaw Companies Limited to Create Electricity From Organic Trimmings," Market Wired, Press Release, October 19, 2009; "StormFisher Biogas and Denham Capital Management Announce $350 Million Partnership to Develop Biogas-Based Renewable Energy Projects," Market Wired, Press Release, February 14, 2008; Norman De Bono, "Loss of green leader leaves city blue, minus $20M plant," *London Free Press*, June 1, 2010; www.airwaterland.ca March 10, 2008. StormFisher Inks Deal To Develop Biogas Projects; Norman De Bono, "Biogas project revived," *London Free Press*, March 29, 2011.

The middle of the class achieved all points on the continuum of success. How could this be? "One of the little secrets of higher education is that conventional A students often end up working for creative and entrepreneurial C students."[48] One medical trade journal reports:

> "A" students often lack the personality skills essential when working with the public. There are delightful exceptions, but there is some truth to this cliché. The discipline and attention to detail necessary to do well on academic tests can be barriers to "connecting" with patients and building the rapport necessary for successful practice.[49]

In short, there are many different kinds of intelligence, a much greater bandwidth than most researchers and test architects ever imagined. The dynamic and subtle complexities of the entrepreneurial task require their own special intelligences. How else would one explain the enormous contradiction inherent in geniuses who fail in business and financially?

One only need consider the critical skills and capacities that are at the heart of entrepreneurial leadership and achievement, yet are not measured by the IQ tests, GMATs, and the like that rank and sort young applicants with such imprecision. Consider the skills and capacities not measured by these tests:

- ✔ leadership
- ✔ interpersonal skills
- ✔ team building and team playing
- ✔ creativity and ingenuity
- ✔ motivation
- ✔ learning skills (versus knowledge)

- ✔ persistence and determination
- ✔ values, ethics, honesty, and integrity
- ✔ goal-setting orientation
- ✔ self-discipline
- ✔ frugality
- ✔ resourcefulness
- ✔ resiliency and capacity to handle adversity
- ✔ ability to seek, listen, and use feedback
- ✔ reliability
- ✔ dependability
- ✔ sense of humour

Obviously, entrepreneurship is not for dummies. Quite the opposite is true. Intelligence is a very valuable and important asset for entrepreneurs, but by itself is a woefully inadequate measure of potential. Clearly, just being very smart will not help much if one does not possess numerous other qualities (see chapters 5, 6, and 7: "The Entrepreneurial Leader," "The New Venture Team," and "Ethical Decision Making and the Entrepreneur," respectively, for an elaboration on these other qualities). A fascinating article in Maclean's, "Do Grades Really Matter: Why A+ Students Often End Up Working for C+ Students," is well worth reading to get some powerful insights into why it is often not the class genius who becomes most successful.[50]

A PERSONAL STRATEGY LO5

An apprenticeship can be an integral part of the process of shaping an entrepreneurial career. A principal task is to determine what kind of entrepreneur you are likely to become, based on background, experience, and drive. Research published by Atul Gupta in 2013 shows that entrepreneurial traits and personality influence the strategy chosen by the entrepreneur and that this has bearing on job satisfaction.[51] Simon Parker of Western University and his colleagues observe that those strategies chosen have far-reaching and long-lasting consequences.[52] Through an apprenticeship, an entrepreneur can shape a strategy and prepare an action plan to make it happen. The "Crafting a Personal Entrepreneurship Strategy" exercise found in this chapter addresses this issue more fully. For a quick inventory of your entrepreneurial attributes, do the "QuickLook: The Personal Entrepreneurial Strategy" exercise available online in Connect.

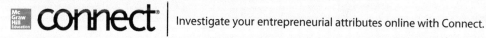

Investigate your entrepreneurial attributes online with Connect.

Despite all the work involved in becoming an entrepreneur, the bottom line is revealing. Evidence about careers and job satisfaction of entrepreneurs all points to the same conclusion: If they had to do it over again, not only would more of them become entrepreneurs again, but they would have done it sooner.[53] They report higher personal satisfaction with their lives and their careers than their managerial counterparts. Numerous other studies show that the satisfaction from independence and from living and working where and how they want to is a source of great joy.[54] Financially, successful entrepreneurs enjoy higher incomes and a higher net worth than career managers in large companies. In addition, the successful harvest of a company usually means a capital gain of several million dollars or more and, with it, a new array of very attractive options and opportunities to do whatever they choose to do with the rest of their lives.

LO1 Entrepreneurs are men and women of all ages, colours, cultures, religions, and backgrounds. There is no single profile or psychological template.

LO2 Successful entrepreneurs share six common themes that describe their ways of thinking and acting: commitment and dedication; leadership; opportunity obsession; tolerance of risk, ambiguity, and uncertainty; creativity, self-reliance, and adaptability; and motivation to excel. Rather than being innate, these six attitudes and behaviour can be nurtured, learned, and encouraged. Entrepreneurs love competition and actually avoid risks when they can, preferring carefully calculated risks.

LO3 Entrepreneurship can be learned; an apprenticeship is highly beneficial.

LO4 IQ tests, GMATs, and even grades do not measure some of the most important entrepreneurial abilities and aptitudes. Many entrepreneurial qualities, such as interpersonal skills, persistence, and reliability cannot be measured. The entrepreneurial mindset can benefit large, established companies today just as much as smaller firms.

LO5 Most successful entrepreneurs have had a personal strategy to help them achieve their dreams and goals, both implicitly and explicitly. A personal strategy provides many similar benefits as a business plan. Self-assessment is one of the hardest things for entrepreneurs to do, but if you don't do it, you will really get into trouble. If you don't do it, who will?

STUDY QUESTIONS

1. What is the difference between a manager and a leader?
2. Define the six major themes that characterize the mindsets, attitudes, and actions of a successful entrepreneur. Which are most important, and why? How can they be encouraged and developed?
3. Entrepreneurs are made, not born. Why is this so? Do you agree, and why or why not?
4. Explain what is meant by the apprenticeship concept, and why is it important to young entrepreneurs.
5. What is your personal entrepreneurial strategy? How should it change?
6. Can you evaluate your attraction to entrepreneurship?
7. Great athletic talent is not equal to a great athlete. Why? How does this apply to entrepreneurship?

MIND STRETCHERS *Have you considered?*

1. Who can be an entrepreneur, and who cannot? Why?
2. How do you personally stack up against the core and desirable entrepreneurial attributes (Exhibit 1.3)? What do you need to develop and improve?
3. What can a larger company do to attract and keep the best entrepreneurial talent?
4. Is Bill Gates, Oprah Winfrey, Ted Rogers, or David Thomson an entrepreneur, a leader, a manager? How can we know?
5. How will you personally define success in 5, 10, and 25 years? Why?
6. Assume that you have achieved a net worth between $25 million to $50 million. So what? Then what?

> *If you don't know where you're going, any path will take you there.*

Crafting a personal entrepreneurial strategy can be viewed as the personal equivalent of developing a business plan. As with planning in other situations, the process itself is more important than the plan.

The key is the process and discipline that puts an individual in charge of evaluating and shaping choices and initiating actions that makes sense, rather than letting things just happen. Having a longer-term sense of direction can be highly motivating. It also can be extremely helpful in determining when to say no (which is much harder than saying yes) and can temper impulsive hunches with a more thoughtful strategic purpose. This is important because today's choices, whether or not they are thought out, become tomorrow's record of accomplishment. They may end up shaping an entrepreneur in ways that he or she may not find so attractive 10 years hence and, worse, may result in failure to obtain just those experiences needed in order to have high-quality opportunities later on.

A personal strategy can be invaluable, but it need not be a prison sentence. It is a point of departure, rather than a contract of indenture, and it can and will change over time. The process of developing a personal strategy for an entrepreneurial career is a very individual one and one of self-selection.

Reasons for planning an entrepreneurial strategy are similar to those for developing a business plan (see chapter 4). Planning helps an entrepreneur to manage the risks and uncertainties of the future; helps him or her to work smarter, rather than simply harder; keeps him or her in a future-oriented frame of mind; helps him or her to develop and update a keener strategy by testing the sensibility of his or her ideas and approaches with others; helps motivate him or her; gives him or her a "results orientation"; helps him or her be effective in managing and coping with what is by nature a stressful role; and so forth.

Rationalizations and reasons given for not planning, like those that will be covered in chapter 4, are that plans are out of date as soon as they are finished and that no one knows what tomorrow will bring and, therefore, it is dangerous to commit to uncertainty. Further, the cautious, anxious person may find that setting personal goals creates a further source of tension and pressure and a heightened fear of failure. There is also the possibility that future or yet unknown options, which actually might be more attractive than the one chosen, may become lost or be excluded. Commitment to a career-oriented goal, particularly for an entrepreneur who is younger and lacks much real-world experience, can be premature. For the person who is inclined to be a compulsive and obsessive competitor and achiever, goal setting may add gasoline to the fire. And, invariably, some events and environmental factors beyond one's control may boost or sink the best-laid plans.

Personal plans fail for the same reasons as business plans, for reasons that include frustration when the plan appears not to work immediately and problems of changing behaviour from an activity-oriented routine to one that is goal-oriented. Other problems are developing plans that are based on admirable missions, such as improving performance, rather than goals, and developing plans that fail to anticipate obstacles, and those that lack progress milestones, reviews, and so forth.

A Conceptual Scheme for Self-Assessment

Exhibit 1.10 shows one conceptual scheme for thinking about the self-assessment process called the Johari Window. According to this scheme, there are two sources of information about the self: the individual and others.

EXHIBIT 1.10	PEELING THE ONION

	KNOWN TO ENTREPRENEUR AND TEAM	**NOT KNOWN TO ENTREPRENEUR AND TEAM**
Known to Prospective Investors and Stakeholders	Area 1 *Known area*: (what you see is what you get)	Area 2 *Blind area*: (we do not know what we do not know, but you do)
Not Known to Prospective Investors and Stakeholders	Area 3 *Hidden area*: (unshared—you do not know what we do, but the deal does not get done until you find out)	Area 4 *Unknown area*: (no venture is certain or risk free)

Source: James McIntyre, Irwin M. Rubin, David A. Kolb, *Organizational Psychology: Experiential Approach*, 2nd ed., © 1974. Adapted by permission of Pearson Education, Inc., Upper Saddle River, NJ.

According to the Johari Window, individuals can learn about themselves in three areas.

There are two potential obstacles to self-assessment efforts. First, it is hard to obtain feedback; second, it is hard to receive and benefit from it. Everyone possesses a personal frame of reference, values, and so forth, which influence first impressions. It is, therefore, almost impossible for an individual to obtain an unbiased view of himself or herself from someone else. Further, in most social situations, people usually present self-images that they want to preserve, protect, and defend, and behavioural norms usually exist that prohibit people from telling a person that he or she is presenting a face or impression that differs from what the person thinks is being presented. For example, most people will not point out to a stranger during a conversation that a piece of spinach is prominently dangling from between his or her front teeth.

The first step for an individual in self-assessment is to generate data through observation of his or her thoughts and actions and by getting feedback from others for the purposes of (1) becoming aware of blind spots and (2) reinforcing or changing existing perceptions of both strengths and weaknesses.

Once an individual has generated the necessary data, the next steps in the self-assessment process are to study the data generated, develop insights, and then establish apprenticeship goals to gain any learning, experience, and so forth.

Finally, choices can be made in terms of goals and opportunities to be created or seized.

Crafting an Entrepreneurial Strategy

Profiling the Past

One useful way to begin the process of self-assessment and planning is for an individual to think about his or her entrepreneurial roots (what he or she has done, his or her preferences in terms of lifestyle and work style, etc.) and couple this with a look into the future and what he or she would like most to be doing and how he or she would like to live.

In this regard, everyone has a personal history that has played and will continue to play a significant role in influencing his or her values, motivations, attitudes, and behaviours. Some of this history may provide useful insight into prior entrepreneurial inclinations, as well as into his or her future potential fit with an entrepreneurial role. Unless an entrepreneur is enjoying what he or she is doing for work most of the time, when in his or her 30s, 40s, or 50s, having a great deal of money without enjoying the journey will be a very hollow success.

Profiling the Present

It is useful to profile the present. Possession of certain personal entrepreneurial attitudes and behaviours (i.e., an "entrepreneurial mind") is linked to successful careers in entrepreneurship. These attitudes and behaviours deal with such factors as commitment, determination, and perseverance; the drive to achieve and grow; an orientation toward goals; the taking of initiative and personal responsibility; and so forth.

In addition, various role demands result from the pursuit of opportunities. These role demands are external in the sense that they are imposed upon every entrepreneur by the nature of entrepreneurship. As will be discussed in chapter 4, the external business environment is given, the demands of a higher potential business in terms of stress and commitment are given, and the ethical values and integrity of key actors are given. Required as a result of the demands, pressures, and realities of starting, owning, and operating a substantial business are such factors as accommodation to the venture, toleration of stress, and so forth. A realistic appraisal of entrepreneurial attitudes and behaviours in light of the requirements of the entrepreneurial role is useful as part of the self-assessment process.

Finally, part of any self-assessment is an assessment of management competencies and what "chunks" of experience, know-how, and contacts need to be developed.

Getting Constructive Feedback

A Scottish proverb says, "The greatest gift that God hath given us is to see ourselves as others see us." One common denominator among successful entrepreneurs is a desire to know how they are doing and where they stand. They have an uncanny knack for asking the right questions about their performance at the right time. This thirst to know is driven by a keen awareness that such feedback is vital to improving their performance and their odds for success.

Receiving feedback from others can be a most demanding experience. The following list of guidelines in receiving feedback can help:

- Feedback needs to be solicited, ideally, from those who know the individual well (e.g., someone he or she has worked with or for) and who can be trusted. The context in which the person is known needs to be considered. For example, a business colleague may be better able to comment upon an individual's leadership skills than a friend may. Or a personal friend may be able to comment on motivation or on the possible effects on the family situation. It is helpful to chat with the person before asking him or her to provide any specific written impressions and to indicate the specific areas he or she can best comment upon. One way to do this is to formulate questions first. For example, the person could be told, "I've been asking myself the following question…and I would really like your impressions in that regard."

- Specific comments in areas that are particularly important either personally or to the success of the venture need to be solicited and more detail probed if the person giving feedback is not clear. A good way to check if a statement is being understood correctly is to paraphrase the statement. The person needs to be encouraged to describe and give examples of specific situations or behaviours that have influenced the impressions he or she has developed.

- Feedback is most helpful if it is neither all positive nor all negative.

- Feedback needs to be obtained in writing so that the person can take some time to think about the issues, and so feedback from various sources can be pulled together.

- The person asking for feedback needs to be honest and straightforward with himself or herself and with others.

- Time is too precious and the road to new venture success too treacherous to clutter this activity with game playing or hidden agendas. The person receiving feedback needs to avoid becoming defensive and taking negative comments personally.

- It is important to listen carefully to what is being said and think about it. Answering, debating, or rationalizing should be avoided.

- An assessment of whether the person soliciting feedback has considered all important information and has been realistic in his or her inferences and conclusions needs to be made.

- Help needs to be requested in identifying common threads or patterns, possible implications of self-assessment data and certain weaknesses (including alternative inferences or conclusions), and other relevant information that is missing.

- Additional feedback from others needs to be sought to verify feedback and to supplement the data.

- Reaching final conclusions or decisions needs to be left until a later time.

Putting It All Together

Exhibit 1.11 shows the relative fit of an entrepreneur with a venture opportunity, given his or her relevant attitudes and behaviours and relevant general leadership skills, experience, know-how, and contacts, and given the role demands of the venture opportunity. A clean appraisal is almost impossible. Self-assessment is just not that simple. The process is cumulative, and what an entrepreneur does about weaknesses, for example, is far more important than what the particular weaknesses might be. After all, everyone has weaknesses.

EXHIBIT 1.11 FIT OF THE ENTREPRENEUR AND THE VENTURE OPPORTUNITY

Thinking Ahead

As it is in developing business plans, goal setting is important in personal planning. Few people are effective goal setters. Perhaps fewer than 5 percent have ever committed their goals to writing, and perhaps fewer than 25 percent of adults even set goals mentally.

Again, goal setting is a process, a way of dealing with the world. Effective goal setting demands time, self-discipline, commitment and dedication, and practice. Goals, once set, do not become static targets.

A number of distinct steps are involved in goal setting, steps that are repeated over and over as conditions change:

- Establishment of goals that are specific and concrete (rather than abstract and out of focus), measurable, related to time (i.e., specific about what will be accomplished over a certain time period), realistic, and attainable.

- Establishment of priorities, including the identification of conflicts and trade-offs and how these can be resolved.

- Identification of potential problems and obstacles that could prevent goals from being attained.

- Specification of action steps that are to be performed to accomplish the goal.

- Indication of how results will be measured.

- Establishment of metrics for reviewing progress and tying these to specific dates on a calendar.

- Identification of risks involved in meeting the goals.

- Identification of help and other resources that may be needed to obtain goals.

- Periodic review of progress and revision of goals.

Preparation Questions

1. What would Torak's costs per month be for operating mobile online payment services from each of the vendors (i.e., MS Systems and FP Systems)?

2. Calculate the amount that Torak would save per month by switching to a mobile online payment system because of time savings by drivers.

3. Should one consider only costs for vendor selection? What other factors would you consider?

Steve had just started reading the Sunday newspaper at the morning breakfast table at home. A news article on the third page, which mostly covered local business developments in Lethbridge, Alberta, drew his attention. He called to his father, Gerry, who was sitting on a sofa and watching TV, "Dad, Smart Courier is coming to Lethbridge. I heard about them before, and they are very technology intensive. We need to consider technology for our business while we're thinking of expanding it." Gerry got up, looked over Steve's shoulder, and had a quick reading of the article. "Steve, you mentioned the other day that some customers are not keeping enough cash at home to pay for their deliveries. Why don't you look into how we can improve the payment process using some new technologies? It will be something to start with," said Gerry. "Ok, I will explore it and discuss it in a week," Steve replied, looking at the calendar on the wall.

TORAK IS READY TO DELIVER YOUR STUFF

Torak Express was a family-owned and operated parcel delivery and courier service serving customers in Lethbridge, a city of nearly ninety thousand people located in Southern Alberta. Gerry Easthope, the CEO and President of the limited company, had started it in 1995 as a one-man business with one vehicle and two trusted and committed clients. Later it also provided employment for his son Steve, who was then out of high school and eager for something to do to earn income. Prior to starting his business Gerry worked for many years for a large transportation company in Calgary, about 200 kilometres north of Lethbridge. He came back to Lethbridge as a management student at the University of Lethbridge in 1986 and completed a bachelor degree in marketing in

1990. He appreciated the education he received at the university; however, the knowledge and experience he gained from his employment at the transportation company had been his special strength that he could depend on since the founding of Torak. One of his first two clients was a pharmacy store who hired Torak to deliver medicine and other health-related products to customers at their residences and to collect payments for the items. Torak's reliable, cost-effective, and high-quality service allowed the pharmacy to save $5000 in the first year, Gerry came to know later. The other initial client of Torak was a flower shop that asked Gerry to deliver flowers to individuals and offices on various occasions and again to collect payments for them. Torak quickly established a high reputation in a niche business. Gerry never looked for customers and he did not run any advertisements. Customers were referred to him by other clients who spread Torak's reputation by word of mouth. He never worried about competition; out of three other courier businesses operating in the city, two had already shut down.

NEED FOR EXPRESS SERVICES IN A SMALL CITY

As of 2012, Gerry still ran his business from home to keep costs down. Torak served a stable customer base consisting of 30 businesses primarily in four areas—pharmacies, law firms, flower shops, and grocery stores. Most of them were located in Lethbridge, but Torak also served a few in neighbouring small towns within a radius of 20 kilometres. Torak only delivered small packages and did not deal with large items such as furniture or appliances. About 75 percent of his delivery items were prescription medicines delivered from pharmacies to residences—homes or senior citizen's housing facilities. However, law firms were also very satisfied with Torak's efficient and reliable express delivery of documents.

OPERATIONS

Gerry ran the courier operation with his two sons, Steve and Allen, and three hourly employees, who essentially subcontracted the tasks from Torak on demand. Seven vehicles, all minivans, were used for business and Gerry kept the seventh one on reserve as a backup in case of breakdown. He opted

This case was written by Sajjad Zahir, University of Lethbridge. The author expressed thanks to Prof. Robert Ellis, Faculty of Management of the University of Lethbridge for carefully reading the manuscript and providing useful comments and suggestions for improving the case.

for minivans because they also could be used for occasionally delivering bags full of grocery items to customers. He understood that reliable vehicles were essential in any transportation business. These were the main equipment used in the operations and the items of major cost. To minimize breakdown time and maintenance costs, Gerry had decided to lease new vehicles from a local Dodge dealer every two years. Each minivan travelled about 100,000 kilometres by the end of a two-year term when Gerry contracted for a new set of minivans. This also helped him keep up with new technological upgrades in automobiles, especially for fuel efficiency and emission control. All resources allocated for Torak's business operations were sufficient to meet the steady demand from the 30 businesses it currently served to generate monthly revenue of about $50 000.

Torak was open for business 6 days a week, Monday to Saturday, from 8:00 a.m. to 8:00 p.m. Gerry actively participated in the delivery along with other drivers. He also prepared each day's schedule of pickups and deliveries the previous night. The delivery zone that included Lethbridge and some adjoining small towns was divided into six segments, one for each driver. Every couple of hours, the six drivers met together at a common place, usually a parking lot of a grocery store that also had a flower shop and a pharmacy of its own. The daily schedule was handed to each driver at the first meeting of the day. Communications were carried on using mobile phones, and Gerry did not plan to use the Internet. Therefore, tracking of drivers was also done by using phones. Drivers could synchronize their meeting times through voice communication subject to minimum unavoidable delays caused by traffic congestion or pick-up and delivery time uncertainties. At the meeting drivers brought items picked up from their segments, sorted them, and transferred them to other drivers for delivery in their segments. Following this simple logistic rule, drivers did not have to drive all the way from one end of the delivery zone to another and thus saved time and fuel. Fuel is a major cost of operation for any transportation business. Each driver kept a log sheet (i.e., a business form) that recorded delivery and pickup data and payment information. The drivers collected payment as cash or cheques from each delivery point as required.

Gerry collected payments for deliveries early the next day from all drivers and then turned these payments over to each business the next day. He billed each business at the end of month, for all services he provided to each business during that period, and businesses usually issued a cheque for the invoiced amount to Torak.

TECHNOLOGY FOR PAYMENT AND RECORD KEEPING: A PLAN TO IMPROVE

The world was gradually moving towards a cashless society. People were increasingly shopping with credit cards, debit cards, and online facilities such as PayPal. Many people would hardly carry much cash. Personal cheque use was also seeing a downturn. Banks stopped printing their own cheques; they outsourced such noncore tasks to others such as Davis and Henderson (http://dhltd.com/). Gerry lamented, "Besides, personal cheques would cost a lot more than what it used to be. A few years ago, one could order a hundred cheques for about $15.00; now they would cost about four times more. Banks were increasing fees for processing personal cheques, as well." Too often Gerry and other drivers had to return to delivery points later to pick up payments because the customers did not have enough cash or a cheque on hand.

Steve thought about handheld card-payment processing devices (mobile point-of-sale device) that each driver would carry with them and use to accept payments using debit cards and credit cards at the time of delivery. These devices used long-range wireless technology for Internet-based services provided by many vendors such as the major telephone companies. They would come with their own built-in printers that each driver would use to issue receipts right at the point of delivery. Most cards were already chip-enabled and could facilitate a contactless Paypass method. That would not only be very convenient for all parties concerned but also would save time for drivers. Funds would be transferred to Torak's merchant bank account immediately. Accepting credit cards or debit cards was almost essential in any online business today. Consumers enjoyed both the security and the convenience of buying with a credit card or debit card. However, as a merchant, accepting credit cards could be costly if one was not aware of the potentially numerous charges levied by card associations and merchant service providers.

Steve talked with Torak's bank about opening a merchant bank account to get an idea about the cost. Gerry would be able to transfer funds to each business he served online from Torak's merchant bank account in the evening of the same day from his home-office; there would be no need to wait until the next day to drive to each business to hand over cash and cheques. Steve searched for such services on the Internet and gathered information from two potential providers—MS Systems and FP Systems. He was ready to discuss the matter with Gerry during the upcoming meeting.

While researching information about online services, Steve also thought of sharing the daily schedule and keeping daily service logs using some kind of smartphone technology. He understood that there were many applications ("apps") available for smartphones that could help him. He was already aware of file sharing tools over the virtual environment called "the cloud." Gerry could post the schedules on a common area in the cloud using DropBox or Google Share and all drivers could access them on their smartphones. He needed more time to think about this.

MEETING WITH GERRY: BRAINSTORMING THE MOVE TO WIRELESS PAYMENT

Steve thought that at this meeting he would mainly provide pertinent cost and benefit information that he collected so far from MS Systems (MSS) and FP Systems (FPS) to Gerry and others. He might need to get information from other service providers as well on a later date. "We will accept payment by MasterCard, Visa, and bank debit cards from customers and try out this approach. But I know some folks will continue to use cash and cheques. So, can you let me know about these tools?" asked Gerry. Steve presented the following information about services provided by MSS and FPS.

1) MS Systems

MSS was one of North America's largest processors of debit and credit card transactions. For businesses needing to accept card payments from its customers, MSS offered a "single point of contact" for all major credit and debit cards and all point-of-sale solutions—from in-store to mobile wireless to e-commerce. It was created as a joint investment between two large Canadian financial groups in November 2001. By maintaining the tradition of security, stability, and strength of the parent banks, over the years MSS had become one of North America's leading processors of debit and credit card transactions for businesses of all sizes.

SUMMARY OF RATES FROM MSS

Sign Up Fee—Covers cost of setting up account	$300
Monthly Rental Fee—Amount to rent terminal	$65 + one time activation fee of $75/device
Monthly Wireless Network Access Fee	Included above

Monthly Account Service Package—Cost for keeping your merchant records up to date and on file, 24/7 customer service access, online statements	$5
Merchant Discount Rate (MDR) MasterCard—Cost of processing MasterCard transaction	1.71%
Merchant Discount Rate (MDR) Visa—Cost of processing Visa transaction	1.71%
Non-Qualified Fee—Additional cost of processing premium cards such as Visa Gold, Air Miles Credit Cards, and cards not swiped	0.50%
Debit Transaction Fee—Cost for processing debit transaction	$0.06
Card Brand Fee—Cost incurred for using Visa/MC cards used towards their branding initiatives	$0.10
Minimum MDR/month—Minimum amount of MDR a merchant must process—full amount or difference is charged if MDR is below this amount	$5
PCI Security Fee (Quarterly)	$45

2) FP Systems

FP Systems was one of Canada's leading providers of low-cost card processing and merchant account services for independent business owners. It offered wireless and virtual credit card processing for merchants "on-the-go." Untethered by traditional wired terminals, their cost-effective mobile solutions provided merchants with the freedom, flexibility, and convenience to accept credit cards quickly and securely whenever and wherever it was needed. It also offered a full range of advanced wireless credit card processing services and equipment for the "mobile" merchant. From plumbers and electricians, to car service operators and trade show exhibitors, their wireless solutions were claimed to be ideal for anyone receiving payments away from their office or business. Best of all, mobile units qualified to receive face-to-face rates, not the higher "card not present" rates.

SUMMARY OF RATES FROM FPS

Sign Up Fee—Covers cost of setting up account	None (promotion)
Monthly Rental Fee—Amount to rent terminal	$40
Monthly Wireless Network Access Fee	$25

Monthly Account Service Package—Cost for keeping your merchant records up to date and on file, 24/7 customer service access, online statements	Included
Merchant Discount Rate (MDR) MasterCard—Cost of processing MasterCard transaction	1.45%
Merchant Discount Rate (MDR) Visa— Cost of processing Visa transaction	1.45%
Non-Qualified Fee—Additional cost of processing premium cards such as Visa Gold, Air Miles Credit Cards, and cards not swiped	1.45%
Debit Transaction Fee—Cost for processing debit transaction	$0.10
Card Brand Fee—Cost incurred for using Visa/MC cards used towards their branding initiatives	$0.10
Minimum MDR/month—Minimum amount of MDR a merchant must process— full amount or difference is charged if MDR is below this amount	$1000
PCI Security Fee (Quarterly)	$30

Gerry provided some inputs about his delivery point customers for Steve to do some analysis. He would have to open a merchant bank account for credit card processing. He would find out how much that would cost. He expected that 25 percent of customers would still make payments using cash or cheques. Of the other 75 percent, 40 percent would use credit cards (he guessed equally divided between MasterCard and Visa) and 35 percent would use bank debit cards. The average amount of each debit transaction was estimated to be about $100.00. He also estimated that one-quarter of all credit card users were members of some loyalty program. Cards would be always swiped or inserted or tapped. There would be no card brand fee for Torak. Steve was confident that using the wireless point-of-purchase devices, the drivers and himself would save on the average one hour of work time per day. Gerry also asked Steve to use an hourly rate of $25.00 for the cost of each driver including himself. He wanted to convince himself that in addition to providing better services for delivery point customers, the new technology would also not be a financial burden for him in the long run. He wanted to have a comparative analysis of the potential providers and get an idea about the total investment and payback period. He looked at Steve and said, "Son, this is the time to make a decision about the payment process. By the way, you can tell me about the cloud based file sharing technology at the next meeting."

For more information on the resources available from McGraw-Hill Ryerson, go to www.mcgrawhill.ca/he/solutions.

PART II

THE OPPORTUNITY

One often hears, especially from younger, newer entrepreneurs, the exhortation: "Go for it! You have nothing to lose now. So what if it doesn't work out. You can do it again. Why wait?" While the spirit this reflects is commendable and there can be no substitute for doing, such itchiness can be a mistake unless it is focused on a solid opportunity.

Jumping at the wrong opportunity can preclude a later, better opportunity. Your attention, your team's attention, and resources (yours and investors) will already be occupied. Even if you wanted to disengage from the current opportunity, you probably cannot chase after that better opportunity as it passes by.

Most entrepreneurs launching businesses, particularly the first time, run out of cash quicker than they bring in customers and profitable sales. While there are many reasons for this, the first is that they have not focused on the *right* opportunities. Unsuccessful entrepreneurs usually equate an idea with an opportunity; successful entrepreneurs know the difference!

Successful entrepreneurs know that it is important to "think big enough." They understand that they are not simply creating a job for themselves and a few employees; they are building a business that can create value for themselves and their community.

While there are boundless opportunities for those with entrepreneurial zest, a single entrepreneur will likely be able to launch and build only a few good businesses—probably no more than three or four—during his or her energetic and productive years. (Fortunately, all you need to do is grow and harvest one quite profitable venture whose sales have exceeded several million dollars. The result will be a most satisfying professional life, as well as a financially rewarding one.)

How important is it, then, that you screen and choose an opportunity with great care? Very important! It is no accident that venture capitalists invest in no more than 1 or 2 percent of all the ventures that they review.

As important as it is to find a good opportunity, even good opportunities have risks and problems. The perfect deal has yet to be seen. Identifying risks and problems before the launch while steps can be taken to eliminate them or reduce any negative effect early is another dimension of opportunity screening.

A "blue ocean" approach calls for bravely heading off to a realm where there are no competitors, no customers, and no market in fact. But reasons may exist for why there are no enterprises treading in those waters. There are no lemonade stands set up on the surface of the moon—at least not yet. Perhaps, if Richard Branson is successful with Virgin Galactic there will be need as space tourists look to quench their thirsts on a lunar trip.

CHAPTER 2

THE ENTREPRENEURIAL PROCESS

"I don't make movies to make money. I make money to make movies."

WALT DISNEY

LEARNING OBJECTIVES

LO1 Articulate a definition of entrepreneurship and the entrepreneurial process—from life-style ventures to high potential enterprises.

LO2 Evaluate the practical issues and identify the requirements necessary to launch; include an appraisal of the array of stakeholders who play a role.

LO3 Show how entrepreneurs and their financial backers increase their odds for success by defying the pattern of disappointment and failure experienced by many.

LO4 Explain the Timmons Model of the entrepreneurial process, how it applies to your entrepreneurial career aspirations and ideas for businesses, and how recent research confirms its validity.

DEMYSTIFYING ENTREPRENEURSHIP

LO1

Entrepreneurship is a way of thinking, reasoning, and acting that is opportunity obsessed, holistic in approach, and leadership balanced for the purpose of value creation and capture. Entrepreneurship results in the creation, enhancement, realization, and renewal of value, not just for owners, but for all participants and stakeholders. At the heart of the process is the creation and/or recognition of opportunities,[1] followed by the will and initiative to seize these opportunities. It requires a willingness to take risks—both personal and financial—but in a very calculated fashion to constantly shift the odds of success, balancing the risk with the potential reward. Typically, entrepreneurs devise ingenious strategies to marshal their limited resources. Take for example Franko and Dino D'Angelo, who started F&D Meats, the subject of this chapter's case, a new venture formed to deliver fresh, made to order, specialty meat products.

Today, entrepreneurship has evolved beyond the classic start-up notion to include companies and organizations of all types, in all stages. Thus, *entrepreneurship can occur—and fail to occur—in firms that are old and new; small and large; fast- and slow growing; in the private, not-for-profit, and public sectors; in all geographic points; and in all stages of a nation's development, regardless of politics.*

Entrepreneurial leaders inject imagination, motivation, commitment, passion, tenacity, integrity, teamwork, and vision into their companies. They face dilemmas and must make decisions despite ambiguity and contradictions. Rarely is entrepreneurship a get-rich-quick proposition. On the contrary, it is one of continuous renewal, as entrepreneurs are never satisfied with the nature of their opportunity. The result of this value creation process is that the total economic pie grows larger and society benefits.

CLASSIC ENTREPRENEURSHIP: THE START-UP

The classic expression of entrepreneurship is the raw start-up company, an innovative idea that develops into a high-growth company. The best of these become entrepreneurial legends: Virgin Group, Microsoft, Amazon.com, Molson, Sony, Tim Hortons, Google, Canadian Tire, Samsung, and hundreds of others became household names. Though once famous, many have faded from glory: Netscape, Sun Microsystems, Kodak, Eaton's, and Sam the Record Man. Success, in addition to the strong leadership from the main entrepreneur, almost always involves building a team with complementary talents. The ability to work as a team and sense an opportunity where others see contradiction, chaos, and confusion are critical elements of success. Entrepreneurship also requires the skill and ingenuity to find and control resources, often owned by others, to pursue the opportunity. It means making sure the upstart venture does not run out of money when it needs it the most. Successful entrepreneurs hold together a team and acquire financial backing to chase an opportunity others may not recognize.

ENTREPRENEURSHIP IN POST-BRONTOSAURUS CAPITALISM: BEYOND START-UPS

The upstart companies of yesterday and today have had a profound impact on the competitive structure of Canadian and global industries. Giant firms, such as IBM (knocked off by Apple, then by Microsoft, and later divided when Lenovo acquired IBM's once-strong PC division), Zellers (another victim of competitive pressures), the music recording industry (hobbled by file-sharing Napster and then legally by Apple's iTunes), or Eaton's and Kmart (entirely disappearing from

Canada) once thought invincible, have been dismembered by the new wave of entrepreneurial force. The resulting downsizing during the 1980s returned in waves. Economic downturns, rising fuel prices, and shifting consumer preferences were responsible for restructuring in many industries. The future did not look bright for the dinosaurs. While large companies, like Nortel Networks, shrank their head count, new ventures added jobs. As autopsy after autopsy was performed on failing large companies, a fascinating pattern emerged, showing, at worst, a total disregard for the winning entrepreneurial approaches of their new rivals and, at best, a glacial pace in recognizing their impending demise and the changing course.

"PEOPLE DON'T WANT TO BE MANAGED. THEY WANT TO BE LED!"[2]

These behemoth firms can be characterized, during their high vulnerability periods, as hierarchical in structure with many layers of reviews, approvals, and vetoes. Their tired executive blood conceived of leadership as *managing and administering* from the top down, in stark contrast to powerful insights from Warren Bennis. In his book, *Managing People is Like Herding Cats*, he points out "Cats of course, won't be herded. And the most successful organizations in the 21st Century won't be managed—they'll be led." These stagnating giants tended to reward people who accumulated the largest assets, budgets, number of plants, products, and head count, rather than rewarding those who created or found new business opportunities, took calculated risks, and occasionally made mistakes, all with bootstrap resources. While very cognizant of the importance of corporate culture and strategy, the corporate giants' pace was tedious: Research on these dinosaurs concludes that it typically took six years for a large firm to change its strategy and 10 to 30 years to change its culture. Meanwhile, the median time it took start-ups to accumulate necessary capital was one month, but averaged six months.[3]

To make matters worse, these corporate dinosaurs had many bureaucratic tendencies, particularly arrogance. They shared a blind belief that if they followed the almost sacred best-management practices of the day, they could not help but prevail. Previously, these best-management practices did not include entrepreneurship, entrepreneurial leadership, and entrepreneurial reasoning. If anything, these were considered dirty words in the corporate world. Chief among these sacred cows was staying close to your customer. What may shock you is the following conclusion of a study of disruptive technologies:

> One of the most consistent patterns in business is the failure of leading companies to stay at the top of their industries when technologies or markets change....But a more fundamental reason lies at the heart of the paradox: Leading companies succumb to one of the most popular, valuable management dogmas. They stay close to their customers.[4]
>
> When they do attack, the [new] entrant companies find the established players to be easy and unprepared opponents because the opponents have been looking up markets themselves, discounting the threat from below.[5]

One gets further insight into just how vulnerable and fragile the larger, so-called well-managed companies can become, and why newcomers pose the greatest threats. This pattern also explains why there are tremendous opportunities for the entrepreneurial generation even in markets currently dominated by large players.

> The problem is that managers keep doing what has worked in the past: serving the rapidly growing needs of their current customers. The processes that successful, well-managed companies have developed to allocate resources among proposed investments are incapable of funnelling resources in programs that current customers explicitly don't want and whose profit margins seem unattractive.[6]

Coupled with the number of innovations and new firms and industries created in the past 30 years, it is no wonder that brontosaurus capitalism has found its ice age.

SIGNS OF HOPE IN A CORPORATE ICE AGE

Fortunately, for many giant firms, the entrepreneurial revolution may spare them from their own ice age. One of the more exciting developments of the decade is the response of some large, established corporations to the revolution in entrepreneurial leadership. After decades of experiencing the demise of giant after giant, corporate leadership, in unprecedented numbers, is launching experiments and strategies to recapture entrepreneurial spirit and to instill the culture and practices we would characterize as entrepreneurial reasoning. The present generation has too many attractive opportunities in truly entrepreneurial environments. They do not need to work for a brontosaurus that lacks spirit.

Increasingly we see examples of large companies adopting principles of entrepreneurship to survive and to renew. Research reveals how large firms are applying entrepreneurial thinking, in pioneering ways, to invent their futures, including companies such as Irving, Corning, Motorola, PotashCorp of Saskatchewan, Bombardier, and EnCana.[7] Most large brontosaurus firms could learn valuable lessons on how to apply entrepreneurial thinking from companies such as these.

METAPHORS

Improvisational, quick, clever, resourceful, and inventive all describe good entrepreneurs. Likewise, innumerable metaphors from other parts of life can describe the complex world of the entrepreneur and the entrepreneurial process. From music, it is jazz, with its uniquely impromptu flair. From sports, many metaphors exist: LeBron James's agility, the broken-field running of Pinball Clemons, the wizardry on ice of Sidney Crosby, or the competitiveness of Silken Laumann. Even more fascinating are the unprecedented comebacks of athletic greats such as Mario Lemieux, Picabo Street, and Greg LeMond.

A number of sports replicate the complex and dynamic nature of managing risk and reward, including all the intricate mental challenges faced in entrepreneuring. These include classic sports such as golf, gymnastics, soccer, and squash, or modern ones like wakeboarding, snowboarding, and kiteboarding! Sports can, at the same time, be physically demanding, complex, intricate, and delicate. They can simultaneously be so rewarding and punishing that one's will, patience, self-discipline, and self-control may all be tested. Teamwork and training pay off, but Team Canada's 14-year medal streak did come to an end in 2013 at the men's World Junior Hockey Championships. Entrepreneurs face these challenges and rewards—both financial and emotional.

An entrepreneur also faces challenges like a symphony conductor or a coach who must blend and balance a group of diverse people with different skills, talents, and personalities into a superb orchestra or team. On many occasions, it demands all the talents and agility of a juggler who, under great stress, must keep many balls in the air at once.

The complex decisions and numerous alternatives facing the entrepreneur also have many parallels with the game of chess. As in chess, the victory goes to the most creative player, who can imagine several alternate moves in advance and anticipate possible defences. This kind of mental agility is frequently demanded in entrepreneurial decision-making. Mike Chiasson and Chad Saunders, when both were at the University of Calgary, found that entrepreneurial actions were driven, as well as constrained, by mental processes. Recognizing and formulating entrepreneurial opportunity is a cyclical yin and yang where restrictions and possibilities must be reconciled.[8]

Regardless of the metaphor you choose for entrepreneurship, each is likely to describe a creative, even artistic, improvised act. Often, the outcomes are either rewarding successes or painfully visible misses. Always, urgency is on the doorstep.

ENTREPRENEURSHIP = PARADOXES

paradoxes:
Statements or relationships that are seemingly contradictory.

One of the most confounding aspects of the entrepreneurial process is its contradictions. Because of its dynamic, fluid, ambiguous, and chaotic character, the process's constant changes frequently pose **paradoxes**. Dirk De Clercq and Maxim Voronov, both of Brock University, suggest that entrepreneurs must conform and innovate—that is, "fit in" and "stand out."[9] Can you think of other paradoxes that you have observed or heard about? A sampling of entrepreneurial paradoxes follows.

✔ *An opportunity with no or very low potential can be an enormous opportunity.* A famous example of this paradox is Apple. Founders Steve Jobs and Steve Wozniak approached their employer, Hewlett-Packard, with the idea for a desktop, personal computer and were told this was not an opportunity for HP. Jobs and Wozniak then started their own company. Business plans rejected by some venture capitalists become legendary successes when backed by another investor. In addition to quite a few instances where some now famous and successful entrepreneurs had their ideas initially turned down, there are a growing number of cases where some entrepreneurs said "no" to investment money—despite indications from many that it is getting harder to find venture capital in Canada.[10] One such individual is Albert Lai. He turned down offers of funding and it turned out to be the right move—he later sold BubbleShare for $3 million…and did not have to share his winnings. In his blog Albert Lai writes:

> Lack of entrepreneurial support systems for students (and recent grads): students are not given the a) role models & motivation, b) knowledge & encouragement, c) support systems & funding, d) education/network, to enable them to succeed. Many of the most innovative start-ups/products on the net that you use everyday today were started in dorm rooms of university students—especially in the B2C space (i.e., Netscape, Napster, Yahoo, Google, Facebook, etc.). Virtually none of them are from Canadian university dorm rooms. The above points can be reduced to two things: lack of funding and lack of entrepreneurial culture/encouragement.
>
> How do we solve this? We need to provide Canadian students with more exposure to "what's possible" and a real support system.

✔ *To make money you have to first lose money.* It is commonly said in the venture capital business that the lemons, or losers, ripen in two-and-a-half years, while the plums take seven or eight years. A start-up, venture-backed company typically loses money, often $10 million or more, before sustaining profitability and going public, usually at least five to seven years later.

✔ *To create and build wealth one must relinquish wealth.* Among the most successful and growing companies the founders aggressively dilute their ownership to create ownership throughout the company. By rewarding and sharing the wealth with the people who contribute significantly to its creation, owners motivate stakeholders to make the pie bigger. A recurring theme on the popular CBC television show, *Dragons' Den*, is that the investors must relinquish some equity but the value of bringing a Dragon on board is worth the price.

✔ *To succeed, one first has to experience failure.* It is a common pattern that the first venture fails; yet the entrepreneur learns and goes on to create a high-performing company. Joseph Smallwood grew up in abject poverty in St. John's, Newfoundland. He finished day school but was unable to complete studies at Bishop Field College and, at age 15, became a printer's apprentice. He spent a number of years gaining experience as a reporter with various newspapers, including five years in New York City. He moved back to Newfoundland and his first venture in politics was a flop. He went on to serve as Newfoundland's premier for nearly 25 years and brought the island into Confederation.[11] A recent study finds those entrepreneurs who have previously failed increase their odds of success compared to those who are first time entrepreneurs. Of course, those with a track record of success do even better![12]

✔ *Entrepreneurship requires considerable thought, preparation, and planning, yet is basically an unplannable event.* The highly dynamic, changing character of technology, markets, and competition make it impossible to know all your competitors today, let alone five years from now. Yet great effort is invested in attempting to model and envision the future. The resulting **business plan** is inevitably obsolete when it comes off the printer. This is a creative process—like moulding clay.[13] You need to make a habit of planning and reacting as you constantly re-evaluate your options, blending the messages from your head and your gut, until this process becomes second nature.

✔ *For creativity and innovativeness to prosper, rigour and discipline must accompany the process.* For years, thousands of patents for new products and technologies lay fallow in government and university research labs because there was no commercial discipline.

✔ *Entrepreneurship requires a bias toward action and a sense of urgency, but also demands patience and perseverance.* While his competitors were acquiring and expanding rapidly, one entrepreneur's management team became outraged at his inaction. This entrepreneur reported he saved the company at least $50 million to $100 million during the prior year by just sitting tight. He learned this lesson from a case study in *New Venture Creation*.

✔ *The greater the organization, orderliness, discipline, and control, the less you will control your ultimate destiny.* Entrepreneurship requires great flexibility and nimbleness in strategy and tactics. One has to play with the knees bent. Overcontrol and an obsession with orderliness are impediments to the entrepreneurial approach. As the race-car driver Mario Andretti said, "If I am in total control, I know I am going too slow!"

✔ *Adhering to management best practice, especially staying close to the customer, created industry leaders, which became a seed of self-destruction and loss of leadership to upstart competitors.* We discussed earlier the study of "disruptive technologies."

✔ *To realize long-term equity value, you have to forgo the temptations of short-term profitability.* Building long-term equity requires large, continuous reinvestment in new people, products, services, and support systems, usually at the expense of immediate profits.

> **business plan:**
> A document that conveys the entrepreneur's vision for transforming an idea into a viable ongoing enterprise. It contains background on the venture team and how the goals will be realized.

The world of entrepreneurship is not neat, tidy, linear, consistent, and predictable, no matter how much we might like it to be that way.[14] In fact, it is from the collisions inherent in these paradoxes that value is created as illustrated in Exhibit 2.1. These paradoxes illustrate just how contradictory and chaotic this world can be. To thrive in this environment, one needs to be very adept at coping with ambiguity, chaos, and uncertainty, and at building management skills that create predictability.

THE HIGHER POTENTIAL VENTURE: THINK BIG ENOUGH

One of the biggest mistakes aspiring entrepreneurs make is strategic. They think too small. Sensible as it may be to think in terms of a very small, simple business as being more affordable, more manageable, less demanding, and less risky, the opposite is true. The chances of survival and success are lower in these small, job-substitute businesses, and even if they do survive, they are

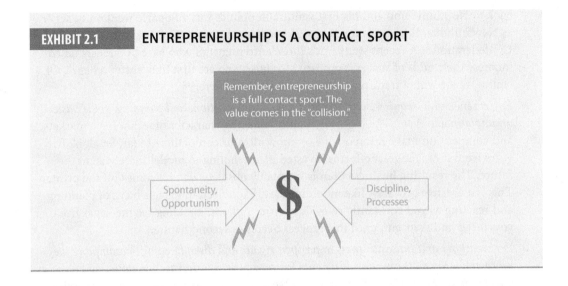

EXHIBIT 2.1   ENTREPRENEURSHIP IS A CONTACT SPORT

Remember, entrepreneurship is a full contact sport. The value comes in the "collision."

Spontaneity, Opportunism

$

Discipline, Processes

less financially rewarding. As one founder of numerous businesses put it: Unless this business can pay you at least five times your present salary, the risk and wear and tear won't be worth it.

One of the most highly regarded venture capital investors is Arthur Rock. His criterion for searching for opportunities is very simple: *look for business concepts that will change the way people live or work.* His home-run investments are legendary, including Intel, Apple, Teledyne, and dozens of others. Clearly, his philosophy is to think big. Today an extraordinary variety of people, opportunities, and strategies characterize the millions of proprietorships, partnerships, and corporations in the country. Remember, high potential ventures become high impact firms that often make the world a better place!

Nearly 10 percent of the Canadian population is actively working on a new venture.[15] More than 95 percent of start-ups have revenues of less than $1 million annually. Statistics Canada reports about 150 000 new businesses enter the playing field annually and nearly as many exit each year. Harry Bowen of Queen's University and Dirk De Clercq of Brock University find that entrepreneurial effort toward high-growth activities is related to financial conditions and educational factors that vary from place to place as well as over time.[16]

Not only can nearly anyone start a business, but also a great many can succeed. While it certainly might help, a person does not have to be a genius to create a successful business. As Nolan Bushnell, founder of Atari, one of the first desktop computer games in the early 1980s, and Pizza Time Theater, said, "If you are not a millionaire or bankrupt by the time you are 30, you are not really trying!"[17] It is an entrepreneur's preparedness for the entrepreneurial process that is important. Being an entrepreneur has moved from cult status in the 1980s to rock star infamy in the 1990s to become de rigueur at present. Amateur entrepreneurship is over. The professionals have arrived.

A stunning number of mega-entrepreneurs launched their ventures during their 20s. While the rigours of new ventures may favour the "young at start," age is *not* a barrier to entry. Studies show that about 25 percent of founders were over 40 when they embarked on their entrepreneurial careers, half were in their 30s, and just over one-quarter did so by the time they were 25. The Global Entrepreneurship Monitor finds that 25- to 34-year-olds are most active in entrepreneurship and that entrepreneurial activity declines after the age of 35.[18] However, numerous examples exist of founders who were over 60 at the time of launch, including the legendary Colonel Harland Sanders, who at 65 started franchising KFC with his first old-age pension cheque.

SMALLER CAN MEAN HIGHER FAILURE ODDS   LO3

Unfortunately, the record of survival is not good among all firms started. Most estimates place the failure rate for start-ups at 50 percent in the first few years. While government data, research, and business mortality statisticians may not agree on the precise failure and survival figures for new businesses, they do agree that failure is the rule, not the exception.

Complicating efforts to obtain precise figures is the fact that it is not easy to define and identify failures, and reliable statistics and databases are not available. One study reports after one year, 71 percent of new ventures are still in business, the number drops to 58 percent by year two and 49 percent by year three. At the five-year mark, 37 percent are still in business and going into the tenth year only 23 percent of those original start-ups remain in business (see Exhibit 2.2).

EXHIBIT 2.2	START-UP SURVIVAL RATES BY FIRM SIZE								

FIRM SIZE	NUMBER OF YEARS (PERCENT)								
	1	2	3	4	5	6	7	8	9
Small (1–4)	71	57	49	42	36	31	27	24	22
Medium (5–99)	74	61	53	47	42	38	34	31	29
Large (100+)	81	68	63	58	54	52	50	49	45
All	**71**	**58**	**49**	**42**	**37**	**32**	**28**	**25**	**23**

Source: *Longitudinal Employment Analysis Program (LEAP)*, Small Business Research and Policy, Industry Canada. Start-ups tracked from 2003 to 2008. Statistics based on firm size at start-up: 1 to 4 employees 130 021 observations; 5 to 99 employees 18 255 observations; 100+ employees 184 observations.

Exit rates vary widely across industries, but so too do entry rates. For instance, retail and services accounted for the majority of all failures. Restaurants come and go like clockwork, everybody thinks they have a better idea or menu. Chances of success also differ for other factors.

The likelihood that start-ups will survive their initial year differs across provinces. Firms in their initial year of life exhibit a much higher success rate in Ontario (75 percent) than in the Atlantic Provinces (59 percent). Business start-ups in British Columbia (75 percent), Quebec (74 percent), and Alberta (72 percent) are more likely to survive their first year than those in Saskatchewan or Manitoba (63 percent) (see Exhibit 2.3).

The following discussion provides a distillation of a number of failure-rate studies over many years. These studies illustrate that (1) failure rates are high, and (2) although the majority of the failures occur in the first two to five years, it may take considerably longer for some to fail.[19]

Finally, "failure" may not always be the most appropriate term. There are instances where an entrepreneur chooses to get out—either to close it or sell it off. Further, an idea may have run its course and no longer be viable, even after only one year—such as a product or service tied to an event like a music festival or a Winter Olympics. A better opportunity may come along and the entrepreneur may have to abandon the current venture for that more attractive one. Entrepreneurs that hop from one opportunity to another have been described as having a high churn rate. The serial entrepreneur is one who goes from venture to venture in succession, but there is also evidence of the portfolio entrepreneur, an individual who cannot concentrate his or her efforts on a single venture—perhaps even counting on some falling off along the way. Often data are unable to capture businesses that de-register or change name.

EXHIBIT 2.3

START-UP SURVIVAL RATES BY FIRM LOCATION

REGION	NUMBER OF YEARS (PERCENT)								
	1	2	3	4	5	6	7	8	9
Atlantic Canada	58.9	43.6	36.0	30.7	26.8	23.8	21.3	19.3	17.1
Quebec	74.2	56.0	46.8	40.7	36.3	32.6	29.6	27.1	24.8
Ontario	74.7	57.8	49.0	42.8	38.2	34.4	31.2	28.5	25.6
Prairies	63.2	49.4	41.6	35.9	31.7	28.5	25.7	22.9	20.2
Alberta	72.3	56.8	48.8	42.9	38.2	34.6	31.5	28.6	25.7
British Columbia	74.7	57.7	48.7	42.1	37.0	32.9	29.6	26.7	24.0
Canada	71.3	54.8	46.1	40.1	35.5	31.9	28.9	26.3	23.7

Source: Small Business Research and Policy, Industry Canada.

Failure rates across industries vary as well. The real estate industry, with a 37 percent rate of start-up failure, is the lowest. The technology sector has a high rate of failure at 54 percent. The software and services segment of the technology industry has an even higher failure rate; 55 percent of start-ups tracked closed their doors. Unfortunately, the record of survival is not good among all firms started.

To make matters worse, people think the failure rates are much higher. Since actions often are governed by perceptions rather than facts, this perception of failure, in addition to the dismal record, can be a serious obstacle to aspiring entrepreneurs.

creative destruction: The idea that innovation displaces old ideas and ways. Capitalism and market forces call for annihilation and reconfiguring of the status quo. Something newer or better is always out there, ready to topple established market offerings.

Still other studies have shown significant differences in survival rates among industry categories: retail trade, construction, and small service businesses accounted for 70 percent of all failures and bankruptcies. One study calculates a risk factor or index for start-ups by industry, which sends a clear warning signal to the would-be entrepreneur.[20] "The fishing is better in some streams versus others," is a favourite saying of the authors. Further, the vast majority of these failed companies had fewer than 100 employees. Through observation and practical experience, one would not be surprised by such reports. The implications for would-be entrepreneurs are important: Knowing the difference between a good idea and a real opportunity is vital. This will be addressed in detail in chapter 3. Monica Diochon of St. Francis Xavier University, Teresa Menzies of Brock University, and Yvon Gasse of the Université Laval point out that opportunity identification is not the same as opportunity pursuit. Factors that may help in identifying opportunities, such as education and experience, may even hamper pursuing opportunities.[21]

A certain level of failure is part of the "**creative destruction**" described by Joseph Schumpeter in his writings. It is part of the dynamics of innovation and economic renewal, a process that requires both births and deaths. More important, it is also part of the learning process inherent in an entrepreneurial apprenticeship.

Businesses fail, but entrepreneurs survive and learn.

The daunting evidence of failure poses two important questions for aspiring entrepreneurs. First, are there any exceptions to this general rule of failure, or are we faced with a punishing game of entrepreneurial roulette? Second, if there is an exception, how does one get the odds for success in one's favour?

GETTING THE ODDS IN YOUR FAVOUR

Fortunately, there is a decided pattern of exceptions to the overall rate of failure among the vast majority of small, marginal firms created each year. Most smaller enterprises that cease operation simply do not meet our notion of entrepreneurship. They do not create, enhance, or pursue opportunities that realize value. They tend to be job substitutes in many instances. Undercapitalized, undermanaged, and often poorly located, they soon fail.

THRESHOLD CONCEPT

Who are the survivors? The odds for survival and a higher level of success change dramatically if the venture reaches a critical mass of at least 10 to 20 people with $2 million to $3 million in revenues and is pursuing opportunities with growth potential. Survival rates for new firms increase steadily as the firm size increases. The survival rates at the three-year mark jump from approximately 49 percent for firms having up to five employees to approximately 63 percent for firms with over 100 employees.

Empirical evidence supports the *liability of newness* and *liability of smallness* arguments and suggests that being new and small make survival difficult. The authors of one study inferred, "Perceived satisfaction, cooperation, and trust between the customer and the organization [are] important for the continuation of the relationship. High levels of satisfaction, cooperation, and trust represent a stock of goodwill and positive beliefs which are critical assets that influence the commitment of the two parties to the relationship."[22] The authors of this study noted, "Smaller organizations are found to be more responsive, while larger organizations are found to provide greater depth of service....The entrepreneurial task is to find a way to either direct the arena of competition away from the areas where you are at a competitive disadvantage, or find some creative way to develop the required competency."[23]

Although any estimates based on sales per employee vary widely from industry to industry, this minimum translates roughly to a threshold of $50 000 to $100 000 of sales per employee annually. But great firms can generate much higher sales per employee.

PROMISE OF GROWTH

The definition of entrepreneurship implies the promise of expansion and the building of long-term value and durable cash-flow streams as well. It is perhaps not surprising that time frames and growth aspirations are idiosyncratic. Dev Dutta of the University of New Hampshire and Stewart Thornhill of Western University find that entrepreneurs vary in their cognitive styles. This outlook combined with their assessment of the competitive environment influences the growth intentions for their enterprise.[24]

However, as will be discussed later, it takes time for enterprises to become established and grow. Historically, two of every five small firms founded survive four years but few achieve growth during those first few years. Odds of survival increase substantially for those enterprises that grow, and the earlier in the life of the business that growth occurs, the higher the chance of survival.[25] The businesses listed on the 2012 INC. 500 exemplify this, with a median three-year growth rate of 1431 percent.[26] Profit's Hot 50 for 2012 achieved average two-year revenue growth of 1131 percent, but 20 percent of them were not yet profitable in the previous fiscal year.[27]

Of Canada's hottest 50 home-grown enterprises, 54 percent are headed by CEOs who have started ventures in the past.[28] The 2012 list of enterprises includes a wide range of products and services offered: storage tank manufacturer (West Fab Ltd), discount etailer (Beyond the Rack), software to convert PDFs to web pages (Uberflip), credit- and debt-card payment processing

©David Laurence

The odds of a restaurant continuing to attract patrons and remain in business are low. The industry has one of the highest failure rates for start-ups—on average. Common lore is that 9 out of 10 new restaurants close within three years. But the odds are not the same for everyone. One restaurateur might try many times, failing every time, while a celebrity chef might have a track record of many successful ventures. Max Rimaldi, proprietor of Libretto Restaurant Group, says the restaurant business is "not just about hype; at the end of the month revenues must exceed expenses." The Terroir 2013 hospitality symposium reported him as saying "providing great food and great service is not good enough and the elements of passion and love need to be added for a truly successful restaurant." It was in 2007 that he was declined by the banks and had to go it alone. His flagship restaurant, Pizzeria Libretto, won EnRoute's award for top ten new restaurants in Canada. In 2013, Chef Rocco Agostino won a Canadian pizza recipe challenge and came in third place at the International Pizza Expo. With the help of two partners, his second restaurant, Enoteca Sociale has also received much praise. In an interview with *The Globe and Mail* he pointed out the quality of the chef is as important as the quality of ingredients. Max Rimaldi has even received certification "Verace Pizza Napoletana" from Naples, Italy for the standards his pizza meets. "We're not going to do the type of chain where every location is exactly the same. We really want the integrity of each kitchen to stand out, by having unique chefs." His tips for success:

You should have a clearly defined business plan. The business plan has to be something that is easy to grasp so that anyone who looks at it will be able to immediately understand the concept. The business plan element helps to ask you questions in order to have really great answers for that day that you finally open.

The business plan is a road map. You're supposed to go back to it a year after operations and every year after that and to keep on updating it. When it's in your head you may forget things, but when it's on paper you can check things off.

QUESTION: *TorontoLife* **reported that Max Rimaldi might open as many as three new restaurants, taking him to a total of five; would you advise this bold move? Why or why not?**

Sources: Sandra Williams, "Three restaurateurs and their recipes for successful business," July 3, 2012, http://walletpop.ca/; Chris Nuttall-Smith, "Toronto's pizza wars heat up (to about 900°F)," *The Globe and Mail*, November 4, 2011; Gregory Furgala, "Pizzeria Libretto is rumoured to be opening three new locations," *Toronto Life*, October 26, 2012; http://www.thedailymeal.com/pizzeria-libretto/

(Zomaron Merchant Services), franchise driveway installation from recycled tires (Enviropaving Corp.), discount real estate broker (2 Percent Realty), and moving and storage (Firemen Movers). Some of the true excitement of entrepreneurship lies in conceiving, launching, and building firms such as these.

VENTURE CAPITAL BACKING

Another notable pattern of exception to the failure rule is found for businesses that attract start-up financing from successful private venture capital companies. However, as Exhibit 2.4 shows, venture-backed firms account for a very small fraction of the population each year.

Venture capital is not essential to a start-up, nor is it a guarantee of success. Of the companies making the 2001 INC. 500, only 18 percent raised venture capital and only 3 percent had venture funding at start-up.[29] Consider, for instance, that even in the dot-com heyday, in 2000 only 1300 Canadian enterprises received venture capital. However, companies with venture capital support

| | EXHIBIT 2.4 | CANADIAN VENTURE CAPITAL ACTIVITY |

YEAR	AMOUNT INVESTED	NUMBER OF DEALS	AVERAGE DEAL
1998	1.5 billion	850	$1.8 million
1999	2.75 billion	900	3.1 million
2000	5.9 billion	1300	4.5 million
2001	3.7 billion	925	4 million
2002	2.75 billion	790	3.5 million
2003	1.7 billion	680	2.5 million
2004	1.85 billion	600	3 million
2005	1.82 billion	630	2.9 million
2006	1.7 billion	408	4.2 million
2007	2.1 billion	412	5.1 million
2008	1.3 billion	371	3.5 million
2009	1.0 billion	331	3.0 million
2010	1.1 billion	354	3.2 million
2011	1.5 billion	393	3.8 million
2012	1.5 billion	395	3.7 million

Source: Courtesy of CVCA—Canada's Venture Capital and Private Equity Association and Thomson Reuters.

fare better overall. Perhaps as few as 1 percent of the venture-backed companies declare bankruptcy or become defunct.[30]

These compelling data have led some to conclude a threshold core of 10 to 15 percent of new companies will become the winners in terms of size, job creation, profitability, innovation, and potential for harvesting (and thereby realize a capital gain).

PRIVATE INVESTORS JOIN VENTURE CAPITALISTS

Tens of thousands of entrepreneurs who have cashed out, harvesting their enterprises, have become "angels" as private investors in the next generation of entrepreneurs. Many of the more successful entrepreneurs have created their own investment pools and compete directly with venture capitalists for deals, such as Skypoint Capital, Garage Technology Ventures, Golden Opportunities Fund, TriWest Capital, AVAC, or Wesley Clover. Their operating experiences and accomplishments provide a compelling case for adding value to an upstart company. Take, for example, Purple Angel, a Canadian group of former high-tech executives who came together in 2001 to give back—to support technology start-ups by investing resources: time, money, and effort. Some of their chosen projects have required business acumen (e.g., help with market identification or making an introduction to a key contact); others have needed technological expertise. While Purple Angel's mission explicitly mentions the goal of fun, generating wealth is a stated objective too.

Private investors and entrepreneurs have very similar selection criteria to the venture capitalists: They are in search of the high potential, higher growth ventures. Unlike the venture capitalists, however, private investors are not constrained by having to invest so much money in a relatively short period that they must invest it in minimum chunks of $3 million to $5 million or more (see chapter 9). Angel investors, therefore, are prime sources for less capital-intensive start-ups and early-stage businesses.

This overall search for higher potential ventures has become more evident in recent years. The next generation of entrepreneurs appears to be learning the lessons of these survivors, venture capitalists, private investors, and founders of higher potential firms. Thousands of students now have been exposed to these concepts over the years, and their strategies for identifying potential businesses are mindful of and disciplined about the ingredients for success. Unlike 20 or more years ago, it is now nearly impossible not to hear and read about these principles whether on television, in books, on the Internet, or in a multitude of seminars, courses, and programs for would-be entrepreneurs of all types.

FIND FINANCIAL BACKERS AND ASSOCIATES WHO ADD VALUE

One of the most distinguishing disciplines of these higher potential ventures is how the founders identify financial partners and key team members. They insist on backers and partners who do more than bring just money, friendship, commitment, and motivation to the venture. They surround themselves with backers who can add value to the venture through their experience, know-how, networks, and wisdom. Key associates are selected because they are smarter and better at what they do than the founder; and they raise the overall average of the entire company. This theme will be examined in detail in later chapters.

OPTION: THE LIFESTYLE VENTURE

For many aspiring entrepreneurs, issues of family roots and location take precedence. Accessibility to a preferred way of life, whether by access to skiing, hiking, music, surfing, canoeing, a rural setting, or the mountains, can be more important to the entrepreneur than how large a business

©alptraum/iStockphoto.com

FIND BACKERS ABLE TO ADD VALUE, NOT THOSE JUST WILLING TO TAKE A GAMBLE.

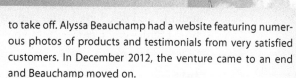

Alyssa Beauchamp, with schooling in graphic design and business—human resources in particular—was working as a recruitment coordinator when she started "My Cups Runneth Over" in January of 2010. This Calgary-based business offered "custom made bras, corsets, and bikinis for plus-sized women, as well as hand-made fabric bridal bouquets and hand-decorated footwear." Despite valiant efforts via social media (e.g., Pinterest) and devoted customers, the business had yet to take off. Alyssa Beauchamp had a website featuring numerous photos of products and testimonials from very satisfied customers. In December 2012, the venture came to an end and Beauchamp moved on.

QUESTION: What could Alyssa Beauchamp have done differently to improve the odds for success or was pulling the plug the right action?

Sources: Alyssa Beauchamp, LinkedIn, accessed October 2013; Profile for My Cups Runneth Over, Canadian Company Capabilities, Industry Canada; company website (no longer available).

one has or the size of one's net worth. Others vastly prefer to be with and work alongside their family or spouse. They want to live in a non-urban area that they consider very attractive or even pursue a noble cause. Maria Panínguakí Kjærulff is a full-time artist who, for now, calls Nuuk, Greenland, home. After graduating from Nova Scotia College of Art and Design with a Bachelor of Fine Arts, including a semester at Cooper Union School of Art in New York City, she chose to locate in her hometown. Though she has spent time in Minnesota and Denmark, she returned to comfortable surroundings, family, and friends. Despite the relative isolation of Greenland—a large island with low population, primarily within the Arctic Circle—Maria's art is exhibited in Denmark, Canada, Korea, Iceland, Finland, Sweden, and Norway.

Yet couples who give up successful careers in Toronto to buy a bed-and-breakfast in cottage country to avoid the rat race generally last only six to seven years. They discover the joys of self-employment, including seven-day, 70- to 90-hour workweeks, chefs and day help that do not show up, roofs that leak when least expected, and occasional guests from hell. The grass is always greener, so they say.

Methods of financing often separate ventures. Jean-Etienne de Bettignies of Queen's University finds that equity-type contracts are prevalent for high-growth ventures whereas debt-type contracts are typical of lifestyle ventures.[31]

THE TIMMONS MODEL: WHERE THEORY AND PRACTICE COLLIDE IN THE REAL WORLD LO4

How can aspiring entrepreneurs—and the investors and associates who join the venture—get the odds of success on their side? What do these talented and successful high potential entrepreneurs, their venture capitalists, and their private backers do differently? What accounts for their exceptional record? Are there general lessons and principles underlying their successes that can benefit aspiring entrepreneurs, investors, and those who would join a venture? If so, can these lessons be learned?

These are the central questions of our lifetime work. We have been immersed as students, researchers, teachers, and practitioners of the *entrepreneurial process*. As founding shareholders and investors of several high potential ventures (some of which are now public), advisors to ventures, and mentors to entrepreneurs—including many former students, we have each applied, tested, refined, and tempered academic theory as fire tempers iron into steel: in the fire of practice. Chances are that your instructor for this course has considerable background in entrepreneurship, perhaps advising government on policy matters or local/regional economic development agencies. Much of the wisdom we have gained, whether from activities such as judging and coaching business-plan and elevator-pitch competitions or a having a seat on a board of directors, comes from you—the student.

INTELLECTUAL AND PRACTICAL COLLISIONS WITH THE REAL WORLD

Throughout this period of evolution and revolution, *New Venture Creation* has adhered to one core principle: In every quest for greater knowledge of the entrepreneurial process and more effective learning, there must be intellectual and practical collisions between academic theory and the real world of practice. The standard academic notion of something being all right in practice but not in theory is unacceptable. This integrated, holistic balance is at the heart of what we know about the entrepreneurial process and getting the odds in your favour.

VALUE CREATION: THE DRIVING FORCES

A core, fundamental entrepreneurial process accounts for the substantially greater success pattern among higher potential ventures. Despite the variety of businesses, entrepreneurs, geographies, and technologies, central themes or driving forces dominate this highly dynamic entrepreneurial process:

- it is *opportunity* driven
- it is driven by a *lead entrepreneur* and an *entrepreneurial team*
- it is *resource parsimonious* and *creative*
- it depends on the *fit* and *balance* among these
- it is *integrated* and *holistic*
- it is *sustainable*

A PORSCHE WRAPPED IN GOLD FOIL. CLEVER, BUT DOES IT CREATE VALUE?

These are the controllable components of the entrepreneurial process that can be assessed, influenced, and altered. Founders and investors focus on these forces during their careful due-diligence process to analyze the risks and determine what changes can be made to improve a venture's chances of success.

First, we will elaborate on each of these forces to provide a blueprint and a definition of what each means. Then, using the early years of Shopify as an example, we will illustrate how the holistic, balance, and fit concepts pertain to a start-up.

CHANGE THE ODDS: FIX IT, SHAPE IT, MOULD IT, MAKE IT

The driving forces at the root of successful new venture creation are illustrated in Exhibit 2.5. The process starts with opportunity, not money, strategy, networks, team, or the business plan. Most genuine opportunities are much bigger than either the talent and capacity of the team or the initial resources available to the team. The role of the lead entrepreneur and the team is to juggle all these key elements in a changing environment. Think of a juggler bouncing up and down on a trampoline that is moving on a conveyor belt at unpredictable speeds and directions, while trying to keep objects of various shapes, weights, and sizes all in the air. That is the dynamic nature of an early-stage start-up. The business plan provides the language and code for communicating the quality of the three driving forces of the Timmons Model and of their fit and balance.

In the entrepreneurial process depicted in the Timmons Model, the shape, size, and depth of the opportunity establishes the required shape, size, and depth of both the resources and the team. We have found that many people are a bit uncomfortable viewing the opportunity and resources balanced precariously by the team. It is disconcerting to some because we show the three key elements of the entrepreneurial process as circles, and thus the balance appears tenuous. These reactions are justified, accurate, and realistic. The entrepreneurial process is dynamic. Those who recognize the risks better manage the process and garner higher returns.

EXHIBIT 2.5	THE TIMMONS MODEL OF THE ENTREPRENEURIAL PROCESS

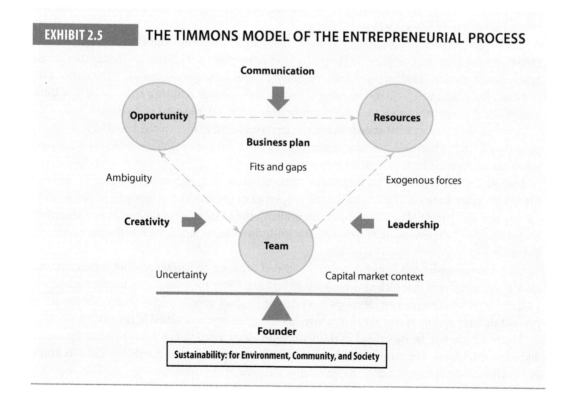

The lead entrepreneur's job is simple enough. He or she must carry the deal by *taking charge of the success equation*. In this dynamic context, ambiguity and risk are actually your friends. Central to the homework, creative problem solving and strategizing, and due diligence that lies ahead is analyzing the fits and gaps that exist in the venture. What is wrong with this opportunity? What is missing? What good news and favourable events can happen, as well as the adverse? What has to happen to make it attractive and a fit for me? What market, technological competitive, management, and financial risks can be reduced or eliminated? What can be changed to make this happen? Who can change it? What are the least resources necessary to grow the business the farthest? Is this the right team? By implication, if you can determine these answers and make the necessary changes by figuring out how to fill the gaps and improve the fit and attract key players who can add such value, then the odds for success rise significantly. In essence, the entrepreneur's role is to manage and redefine the risk–reward equation—all with an eye towards sustainability. Since part of the entrepreneur's legacy is to create positive impact without harming the environment, the community, or society, the concept of sustainability appears as the underlying foundation in the model.

The Opportunity

At the heart of the process is the opportunity. Successful entrepreneurs and investors know that a good idea is not necessarily a good opportunity. For every 100 ideas presented to investors in the form of a business plan or proposal, usually fewer than four get funded. More than 80 percent of those rejections occur in the first few hours; another 10 to 15 percent are rejected after investors have read the business plan carefully. Less than 10 percent attract enough interest to merit a more thorough review; that due diligence can take several weeks or months. These are very slim odds. Would-be entrepreneurs chasing ideas that are going nowhere have wasted countless hours and days. An important skill for an entrepreneur or an investor is to be able to quickly evaluate whether serious potential exists, and to decide how much time and effort to invest. Many give the aspiring entrepreneur the advice to visit a bank to ask for a loan even if you do not need the money. The rigour of the assessment is worthwhile and often the banker delivers medicine that others cannot see or friends will not share.

One senior partner at a prominent venture capital fund asserted, "There's never been a better time than now to start a company. In the past, entrepreneurs started businesses. Today they invent new business models. That's a big difference, and it creates huge opportunities."[32] Even after a big stock market crash, when financing often dries up, those words still ring true. In fact, of those enterprises that started during the toughest times and survived, most go on to thrive.

Another venture capitalist stated, "After the irrational exuberance of the late 90s, it is again a great time to start a business. Venture capital is plentiful, valuations make sense, and venture capitalists are anxious for high potential ventures."[33]

Exhibit 2.6 summarizes the important characteristics of good opportunities. Underlying market demand (because of the value-added properties of the product or service and the market's current size and potential for 20-plus percent growth), the economics of the business, particularly robust margins (40 percent or more), and free cash flow characteristics drive the value creation potential.

We build our understanding of opportunity by first focusing on market readiness: the consumer trends and behaviours that seek new products or services. Once these emerging patterns are identified, the aspiring entrepreneur develops a service or product concept, and, finally, the service or product delivery system is conceived. We then ask the questions articulated in the exhibit.

These criteria will be described in more detail in chapter 4 and can be applied to the search and evaluation of any opportunity. In short, the greater the growth, size, durability, and robustness of the gross and net margins and free cash flow, the greater the opportunity. The more *imperfect*

Market demand is a key ingredient to measuring an opportunity:
- Customer payback less than one year?
- Market share and growth potential of 20 percent annual growth that is durable? *
- Is the customer reachable?

Market structure and size help define an opportunity:
- Emerging and/or fragmented?
- $50 million or more, with a $1 billion potential?
- Proprietary barriers to entry?

Margin analysis helps differentiate an opportunity from an idea:
- Low cost provider (40 percent gross margin)?
- Low capital requirement versus the competition?
- Breakeven in 1–2 years?
- Value added increase of overall corporate P/E ratio?

*Durability of an opportunity is a widely misunderstood concept. In entrepreneurship, durability exists when the investor gets his or her money back plus a market or better return on investment.

the market, the greater the opportunity. The greater the rate of change, the **market failure**, and the chaos, the greater is the opportunity. The greater the inconsistencies in existing service and quality, in lead times and lag times, and the greater the vacuums and gaps in information and knowledge, the greater is the opportunity.

market failure: The existence of another means by which a market participant can be better off.

Resources: Creative and Parsimonious

A common misconception among untried entrepreneurs is that you first need to have all the resources in place, especially the money, to succeed with a venture. Thinking money first is a big mistake. Money follows high potential opportunities conceived of and led by a strong management team. Investors have bemoaned for years that there is too much money chasing too few deals. Some insist that there is a shortage of quality entrepreneurs and opportunities, not money. Successful entrepreneurs devise ingeniously creative and stingy strategies to marshal and gain control of resources (Exhibit 2.7). Surprising as it may sound, investors and successful entrepreneurs often say one of the worst things that can happen to an entrepreneur is to have *too much money too early*. This flies contrary to the most common advice from entrepreneurs: Get enough capital; then get some more.[34] These seemingly clashing perspectives will be reconciled in due course.

Howard Head is a wonderful example of succeeding with few resources. He developed the first laminate, metal-edged ski, which became the market leader, and then the oversize Prince tennis racket—developing two unrelated technologies is a rare feat. Head left his job at a large aircraft manufacturer during World War II and worked in his garage on a shoestring budget to create the modern ski. It took more than 40 iterations before he developed a ski that worked and could be

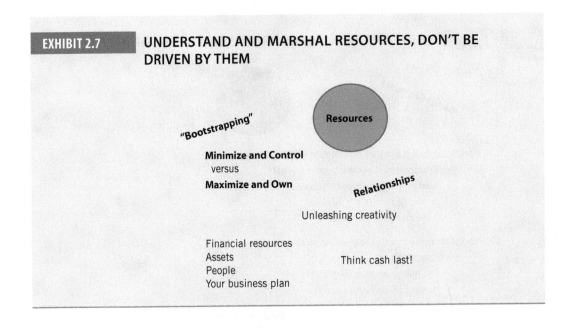

EXHIBIT 2.7 UNDERSTAND AND MARSHAL RESOURCES, DON'T BE DRIVEN BY THEM

"Bootstrapping"

Resources

Minimize and Control
versus
Maximize and Own

Relationships

Unleashing creativity

Financial resources
Assets
People
Your business plan

Think cash last!

marketed. He insisted that one of the biggest reasons he finally succeeded is that he had so little money. He argued that if he had complete financing he would have blown it all long before he evolved the ski into something that weighed half as much as solid wood skis and had better performance. Within a few years, the Head Ski company was making the majority of skis in use. The company went on to diversify into tennis and other racquet sports and manufactured an aluminium honeycomb tennis racquet. Howard Head sold his venture and retired. Head played more tennis in retirement with the aid of a tennis ball machine (built by Prince Manufacturing), and eventually Howard Head became the majority shareholder and chairman of the board of Prince. While he worked to improve the ball machine, his own game of tennis never got better. He went on to patent the oversize racquet and develop graphite composites—changing the game of tennis forever.[35]

Bootstrapping is a way of life in entrepreneurial companies and can create a significant competitive advantage. Doing more with less is a powerful competitive weapon. The necessary approach is to minimize and control the resources, not necessarily own them. Whether it is assets for the business, key people, the business plan, or start-up and growth capital, many successful entrepreneurs *think cash last*. Such strategies encourage a discipline of leanness, where everyone knows that every dollar counts, and the principle "conserve your equity" becomes a way of maximizing shareholder value.

The Entrepreneurial Team

There is little dispute today that the entrepreneurial team is a key ingredient in the higher potential venture. Investors are captivated "by the creative brilliance of a company's head entrepreneur...and bet on the superb track records of the management team working as a group."[36] French-born Georges Doriot's dictum was: I prefer a grade-A entrepreneur and team with a grade-B idea, over a grade-B team with a grade-A idea. "In the world today, there's plenty of technology, plenty of entrepreneurs, plenty of money, plenty of venture capital. What's in short supply is great teams. Your biggest challenge will be building a great team."[37] According to Toby Stuart of the Harvard Business School and Olav Sorenson of the University of Toronto, "social networks shape the emergence and development of nascent ventures."[38] Simon Parker of Western University explores the paradox that "Although venture teams whose founders are dissimilar tend to outperform teams whose founders are similar, most new venture teams are homogenous."[39] Founders need to be aware of cognitive biases in venture team formation.

"If you can find good people, they can always change the product. Nearly every mistake I've made has been I picked the wrong people, not the wrong idea."[40] Finally, as we noted earlier, ventures with more than 20 employees and $2 million to $3 million in sales are much more likely to survive and prosper than smaller ventures. In the vast majority of cases, it is very difficult to grow beyond this without a team of two or more key contributors.

Clearly, a new venture requires a lead entrepreneur who has personal characteristics described in Exhibit 2.8. But the high potential venture also requires interpersonal skills to foster communications and, therefore, team building.

Exhibit 2.8 summarizes the important aspects of the team. Invariably these teams are formed and led by a very capable entrepreneurial leader whose track record exhibits both accomplishments and several qualities that the team must possess. A pacesetter and culture creator, the lead entrepreneur is central to the team as both a player and a coach. Their ability and skill in attracting other key management members and then building the team is one of the most valued capabilities investors look for. The founder who becomes the leader does so by building heroes in the team. A leader adapts a philosophy that rewards success and supports honest failure, shares the wealth with those who help create it, and sets high standards for both performance and conduct. We will examine the entrepreneurial leader and the new **venture team** in detail in chapters 5 and 6.

venture team: The founder or cofounders and the core group responsible for the start-up's survival.

Importance of Fit and Balance

Rounding out the model of the three driving forces is the concept of fit and balance between and among these forces. Note that the team is positioned at the bottom of the triangle in the Timmons Model (Exhibit 2.5). Imagine the founder, the entrepreneurial leader of the venture, standing on a large ball, balancing the triangle over her head. This imagery is helpful in appreciating the constant balancing act since opportunity, team, and resources rarely match. When envisioning a company's future, the entrepreneur asks: What pitfalls will I encounter to get to the next boundary of success? Will my current team be large enough, or will we be over our heads if the company

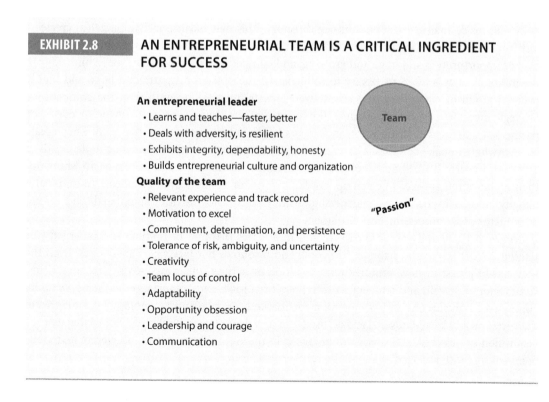

EXHIBIT 2.8   **AN ENTREPRENEURIAL TEAM IS A CRITICAL INGREDIENT FOR SUCCESS**

An entrepreneurial leader
- Learns and teaches—faster, better
- Deals with adversity, is resilient
- Exhibits integrity, dependability, honesty
- Builds entrepreneurial culture and organization

Quality of the team
- Relevant experience and track record
- Motivation to excel
- Commitment, determination, and persistence
- Tolerance of risk, ambiguity, and uncertainty
- Creativity
- Team locus of control
- Adaptability
- Opportunity obsession
- Leadership and courage
- Communication

Team

"Passion"

grows 30 percent over the next two years? Are my resources sufficient (or too abundant)? Vivid examples of the failure to maintain a balance are everywhere, such as when large companies throw too many resources at a weak, poorly defined opportunity. For example, Lucent Technologies' misplaced assumption and slowness to react to bandwidth demand resulted in an almost 90 percent reduction in market capitalization.

Exhibit 2.9 shows how this balancing act evolved for Shopify from inception through the pivot to become an ecommerce platform. While the drawings oversimplify these incredibly complex events, they help us to think conceptually—an important entrepreneurial talent—about the company building process, including the strategic and managerial implications of striving to achieve balance and the inevitable fragility of the process.

Tobias Lütke, a bricks-and-mortar retailer of snowboards, was stumped trying to sell online. With no easy and efficient means available, he took on the task himself and has since revolutionized the ecommerce platform. Lütke's genius was in recognizing that "he had created something new and potentially massive."[41] The opportunities were huge in this rapidly growing field and Shopify quickly expanded into apps. Though initially short on significant capital or other resources, the team had big ideas. Such a mismatch of ideas, resources, and talent could quickly topple out of the founder's control and fall into the hands of someone who could turn it into a real opportunity. Visually, the process can be appreciated as a constant balancing act, requiring continual assessment, revised strategies and tactics, an experimental approach. By addressing the types of questions necessary to shape the opportunity, the resources, and the team, the founder begins to mould the idea into an opportunity, and the opportunity into a business, just as you would mould clay from a shapeless form into a piece of artwork.

In 2005, Tobias Lütke and Scott Lake founded Jaded Pixel. In 2006, the two launched Shopify and business grew and employees were hired to keep up with demand—the opportunity was ballooning. At the outset, the venture team would have seen something like the first figure, Exhibit 2.9(a), with the huge opportunity far outweighing the team and resources. The gaps were major. Given the size and potential of the opportunity they were able to double in size every year for quite a few years. With great faith and many promises, they knew they could fill the resource gaps and build the team, both with inside management and outside directors. This new balance in Exhibit 2.9(b) creates a justifiable investment. Shopify received $7 million in a Series A round of investment.

The opportunity is still huge and growing, and competitors are inevitable (see Exhibit 2.9(c)). An influx of cash is often necessary to fully exploit the opportunity, attract a large and highly talented group of employees, and create even greater financial strength than the competitors. Strategic investors can greatly enhance the balance of the driving forces. Strategic investors, or partners, are defined as those who can fill gaps left by other members of the team. They create balance where imbalance exists. The role of the strategic investor differs according to the needs of a venture. In early 2010, Shopify bought MNDCreative, the developers of StoreSync, to "shore up" their mobile strategy—i.e., to catch up, not fall behind, or possibly even get ahead. In mid-2010, Shopify entered into a formal partnership with Webjistix to provide "automated, end-to-end ecommerce order processing and fulfillment."

In late 2011, Shopify secured $15 million in a Series B round of funding and emerged (see Exhibit 2.9(d)) larger and stronger in people and resources but faced new challenges. Even the best and brightest of new ventures tend to erode over time into slow-moving, reactive firms. Could Shopify sustain and reinvent its entrepreneurial roots and organization as the opportunity continued to mushroom and competition for markets, people, and technology became greater than ever? Would it be blindsided and eclipsed by a new disruptive technology? It hoped that its 2012 acquisition of Select Start Studios would take it in the right direction and "accelerate its mobile commerce growth strategy."

EXHIBIT 2.9(A) **SHOPIFY—JOURNEY THROUGH THE ENTREPRENEURIAL PROCESS: AT START-UP, A HUGE IMBALANCE**

EXHIBIT 2.9(B) **SHOPIFY—JOURNEY THROUGH THE ENTREPRENEURIAL PROCESS: TWO ROUNDS OF EQUITY INVESTMENT, TOWARD A NEW BALANCE**

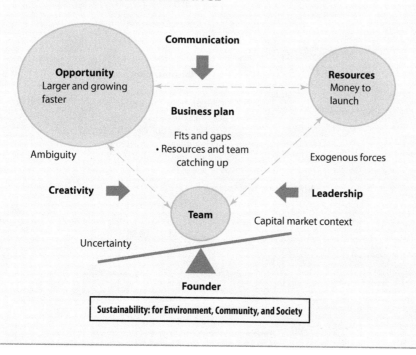

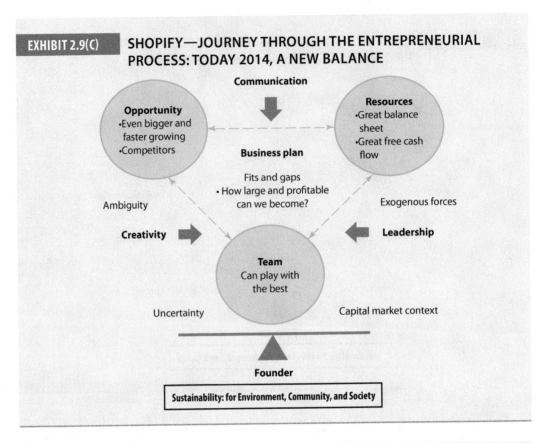

EXHIBIT 2.9(C) SHOPIFY—JOURNEY THROUGH THE ENTREPRENEURIAL PROCESS: TODAY 2014, A NEW BALANCE

Communication

Opportunity
•Even bigger and faster growing
•Competitors

Resources
•Great balance sheet
•Great free cash flow

Business plan

Fits and gaps
• How large and profitable can we become?

Ambiguity

Exogenous forces

Creativity

Leadership

Team
Can play with the best

Uncertainty

Capital market context

Founder

Sustainability: for Environment, Community, and Society

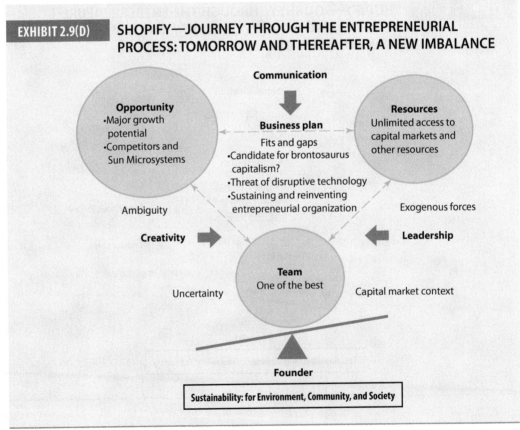

EXHIBIT 2.9(D) SHOPIFY—JOURNEY THROUGH THE ENTREPRENEURIAL PROCESS: TOMORROW AND THEREAFTER, A NEW IMBALANCE

Communication

Opportunity
•Major growth potential
•Competitors and Sun Microsystems

Resources
Unlimited access to capital markets and other resources

Business plan

Fits and gaps
•Candidate for brontosaurus capitalism?
•Threat of disruptive technology
•Sustaining and reinventing entrepreneurial organization

Ambiguity

Exogenous forces

Creativity

Leadership

Team
One of the best

Uncertainty

Capital market context

Founder

Sustainability: for Environment, Community, and Society

John H. Sleeman had been brewing beer in Canada since immigrating in 1834. His son, George Sleeman, kept things going strong and expanded to two breweries. The family then lost the business in 1902 due to debts incurred when George tried to develop a streetcar system in Guelph, Ontario. He recovered and bought back the brewery assets in 1906. The temperance movement put a damper on sales and George Sleeman's sons began delivering product to the United States during Prohibition—they got caught and the family business was forced to close in 1933.

John W. Sleeman, great-great grandson of John H. Sleeman, got married in England, returned home to Canada, and fought government regulations to become a major importer of British pub beers. He subsequently took a risk and imported inexpensive American beer just as a strike broke out among the Canadian brewers; John W. Sleeman recalled, "We were rewarded with so much cash we needed police escorts to make bank deposits." A few years passed and in 1988, John W. Sleeman, four generations removed from founder John H. Sleeman, brewed his first beer. The company went public in 1996 on the TSX and made its first acquisition—Okanagan Spring Brewery. Sleeman followed by acquiring Upper Canada Brewery in 1998, Maritime Brewing in 2000, and both Shaftsbury Brewing and Unibroue in 2004. In 2006, John W. Sleeman put the enterprise up for sale and Sapporo Breweries of Japan took ownership of his namesake for $400 million and promised to keep him on as CEO for at least a handful of years. As time passed, Sapporo found him indispensable and even talked about bringing in the next generation of Sleemans to help run the business.

QUESTION: John H. Sleeman was an entrepreneur in 1834, when he started the business. George Sleeman was certainly entrepreneurial—first taking a gamble on streetcars and then bootlegging alcohol into the United States. John W. Sleeman, in 1988, was entrepreneurial when he revived the family brewery. If John W. Sleeman no longer runs the business and is relegated to the position of figurehead or spokesperson, will he become restless? How likely is it that the next generation of Sleemans will chart their own entrepreneurial paths?

JOHN W. SLEEMAN

© The Canadian Press/Fred Lum/The Globe & Mail

Sources: Rob O'Flanagan, "Honorary Degree for Guelph's Beer Baron," *Guelph Mercury*, February 22, 2008. For an interesting discussion of financial and non-financial goals in family businesses, see "Nathan S. Greidanus and Stefan Märk, "An Exploration of Internal Corporate Venturing Goals in Family Firms," *Journal of Small Business and Entrepreneurship* 25, no. 2 (2012): 169–183. Further, the "trade-off between risky entrepreneurial income and riskless wage labor changes with age," see Moren Lévesque and Maria Minniti "Age Matters: How Demographics Influence Aggregate Entrepreneurship," *Strategic Entrepreneurship Journal* 5, no. 3 (2011): 269–284.

This iterative entrepreneurial process is based on both logic and trial and error. It is both intuitive and consciously planned. It is a process not unlike what the Wright brothers engaged in while creating the first self-propelled airplane. The aviators conducted more than 1000 glider flights before succeeding. These trial-and-error experiments led to the new knowledge, skills, and insights needed to fly. Entrepreneurs have similar learning curves.

The fit issue can be appreciated in terms of a question: This is a fabulous opportunity, but for whom? Some of the most successful enterprises were turned down by numerous investors before the founders received financial backing. If investors remain elusive, alternatives include licensing and franchising to fuel growth. Time and again, there can be a mismatch between the type of business and the investors, the chemistry between the founders and the backers, or a multitude of other factors that cause a rejection. Thus, how the unique combination of people, opportunity, and resources come together at a particular time may determine a venture's ultimate chance for success.

The potential for attracting outside funding for a proposed venture depends on this overall fit and how the investor believes he or she can add value to this fit and improve the fit, risk–reward ratio, and odds for success. Exhibit 1.11 in the previous chapter shows the possible outcome.

Importance of Timing

Equally important is the timing of the entrepreneurial process. Each of these unique combinations occurs in real time, where the hourglass drains continually and may be friend, foe, or both. Decisiveness in recognizing and seizing the opportunity can make all the difference. Do not wait for the perfect time to take advantage of an opportunity; there is no perfect time. Most new businesses run out of money before they can find enough customers and the right team for their great idea. Opportunity is a moving target.

RECENT RESEARCH SUPPORTS THE MODEL

The Timmons Model evolved from Jeffery Timmons' doctoral dissertation research at the Harvard Business School about new and growing ventures. Over four decades, the model has evolved and been enhanced by ongoing research, case development, teaching, and experience in high potential ventures and venture capital funds. The fundamental components of the model have not changed, but their richness and relationships of each to the whole have been steadily enhanced as they have become better understood. Numerous other researchers have examined a wide range of topics in entrepreneurship and new venture creation. The bottom line is that the model, in its simple elegance and dynamic richness, harnesses what you need to know about the entrepreneurial process to get the odds in your favour. As each of the chapters and accompanying cases, exercises, and issues expand on the process, addressing individual dimensions, a detailed framework with explicit criteria will emerge. If you engage this material fully, you cannot help but improve your chances of success.

A research effort focused on 906 high-growth companies provides important benchmarks of the practices in a diverse group of industries.[42] *Most significantly, the results of the research reconfirm the importance of the model and its principles: the team, the market opportunity, the resource strategies, most of the individual criteria, the concept of fit and balance, and the holistic approach to entrepreneurship.*

Exhibit 2.10 summarizes the 26 leading practices identified by the research in four key areas: marketing, finance, management, and planning.

EXHIBIT 2.10	**LEADING PRACTICES**

LEADING MARKETING PRACTICES OF FAST-GROWTH FIRMS

- Deliver products and services perceived as highest quality to expanding segments.

- Cultivate pacesetting new products and services that stand out in the market as best of the breed.

- Deliver product and service benefits that demand average or higher market pricing.

- Generate revenue flows from existing products and services that typically sustain approximately 90 percent of the present revenue base, while achieving flows from new products and services that typically expand revenue approximately 20 percent annually.

- Generate revenue flows from existing customers that typically sustain approximately 80 percent of the ongoing revenue base, while achieving flows from new customers that typically expand revenue flows by about 30 percent annually.

- Create high impact, new product and service improvements with development expenditures that typically account for no more than approximately 6 percent of revenues.

- Utilize a high-yield sales force that typically accounts for approximately 60 percent of marketing expenditures.

- Rapidly develop broad product and service platforms with complementary channels to help expand a firm's geographic marketing area.

LEADING FINANCIAL PRACTICES OF FAST-GROWTH FIRMS

- Anticipate multiple rounds of financing (on average every 2.5 years).

- Secure funding sources capable of significantly expanding their participation amounts.

- Utilize financing vehicles that retain the entrepreneur's voting control.

- Maintain control of the firm by selectively granting employee stock ownership.

- Link the entrepreneur's long-term objectives to a defined exit strategy in the business plan.

LEADING MANAGEMENT PRACTICES OF FAST-GROWTH FIRMS

- Use a collaborative decision-making style with the top management team.

- Accelerate organizational development by assembling a balanced top management team with or without prior experience of working together.

- Develop a top management team of three to six individuals with the capacity to become the entrepreneur's entrepreneurs. Align the number of management levels with the number of individuals in top management.

- Establish entrepreneurial competency first in the functional areas of finance, marketing, and operations. Assemble a balanced board of directors comprised of both internal and external directors.

- Repeatedly calibrate strategies with regular board of directors meetings.

- Involve the board of directors heavily at strategic inflection points.

LEADING PLANNING PRACTICES OF FAST-GROWTH FIRMS

- Prepare detailed written monthly plans for each of the next 12 to 24 months and annual plans for three or more years.

- Establish functional planning and control systems that tie planned achievements to actual performance and adjust management compensation accordingly.

- Periodically share with employees the planned versus actual performance data directly linked to the business plan.

- Link job performance standards that have been jointly set by management and employees to the business plan.

- Prospectively model the firm based on benchmarks that exceed industry norms, competitors, and the industry leader.

LO1 We began to demystify entrepreneurship by examining its classic start-up definition and a broader, holistic way of thinking, reasoning, and acting that is opportunity obsessed and leadership balanced.

LO2 No one works alone, make certain others are involved in the effort. Entrepreneurship has many metaphors and poses many paradoxes.

LO3 Getting the odds in your favour is the entrepreneur's perpetual challenge. Thinking big

enough can improve the odds significantly. Higher potential ventures are sought by successful entrepreneurs, venture capitalists, and private investors.

LO4 The Timmons Model is at the heart of spotting and building the higher potential venture and understanding its three driving forces: the team, opportunity, and resources. The concept of fit and balance is crucial. Research on entrepreneurs and their fast-growth ventures adds validity to the model.

STUDY QUESTIONS

1. Can you define what is meant by classic entrepreneurship and the high potential venture? Why and how are threshold concepts, cover your equity, bootstrapping of resources, fit, and balance important?
2. "People don't want to be managed, they want to be led." Explain what this means and its importance and implications for developing your own style and leadership philosophy.
3. What are the most important determinants of success and failure in new businesses? Who has the best and worst chances for success, and why?
4. What are the most important things you can do to get the odds in your favour?
5. What criteria and characteristics do high-growth entrepreneurs, venture capitalists, and private investors seek in evaluating business opportunities? How can these make a difference?
6. Define and explain the Timmons Model. Apply it and graphically depict, as in the Shopify example, the first five years or so of a new company with which you are familiar.
7. What are the most important skills, values, talents, abilities, and mindsets one needs to cultivate as an entrepreneur?

MIND STRETCHERS   *Have you considered?*

1. Who can be an entrepreneur? When?
2. More than 80 percent of entrepreneurs learn the critical skills they need after age 21. What does this mean for you?
3. In your lifetime, the odds are that leading firms today such as Sony, Research In Motion, Apple, Air Canada, McDonald's, and the Gap will be knocked off by upstarts. How can this happen? Why does it present an opportunity, and for whom?
4. What do you need to be doing now, and in the next 12 months, to get the odds in your favour?
5. List 20 ideas and then pick out the best two that might be an opportunity. How can these become opportunities? Who can make them opportunities?
6. How many different ways can a new venture go off the tracks?

Through interviews with entrepreneurs who have, within the past 5 to 10 years, started firms with significant growth and are profitable, you can gain insight into an entrepreneur's reasons, strategies, approaches, and motivations for starting and owning a business. Gathering information through interviewing is a valuable skill to practise. You can learn a great deal in a short time through interviewing if you prepare thoughtfully and thoroughly.

The Visit with an Entrepreneur Exercise has helped students interview successful entrepreneurs. While there is no right way to structure an interview, the format in this exercise has been tested successfully on many occasions. A breakfast, lunch, or dinner meeting is often an excellent vehicle.

Select two entrepreneurs and businesses about which you would like to learn. This could be someone you see as an example or role model to which you aspire, or which you know the least about but are eager to learn. Interview at least two entrepreneurs with differing experiences, such as a high potential (e.g., $5 million revenue plus) and a lifestyle business (usually much smaller, but not necessarily).

Create a Lifelong Learning Log

Create a computer file or acquire a notebook or binder in which you record your goals, triumphs and disappointments, and lessons learned. This can be done as key events happen or on some other frequent basis. You might make entries during times of crisis and at year's end to sum up what you accomplished and your new goals. The record of personal insights, observations, and lessons learned can provide valuable anchors during times of difficult decisions as well as interesting reading—for you at least.

A Visit with an Entrepreneur

Step 1   Contact the person you have selected and make an appointment.

Be sure to explain why you want the appointment and to give a realistic estimate of how much time you will need.

Step 2   Identify specific questions you would like to have answered and the general areas about which you would like information. (See Step 3, Conduct the interview.)

Using a combination of open-end questions, such as general questions about how the entrepreneur got started, what happened next, and so forth, and closed-end questions, such as specific questions about what his or her

goals were, if he or she had to find partners, and so forth, will help keep the interview focused and yet allow for unexpected comments and insights.

Step 3   Conduct the interview.

Recording the interview on audiotape can be helpful and is recommended unless you or the person being interviewed objects. Remember, too, that you will learn more if you are an interested listener.

The Interview
Questions for Gathering Information

- Would you tell me about yourself before you started your first venture?

  Who else did you know while you were growing up who had started or owned a business, and how did they influence you? Anyone later, after you were 21 years old?

  Were your parents, relatives, or close friends entrepreneurial? How so?

  Did you have role models?

  What was your education/military experience? In hindsight, was it helpful? In what specific ways?

  Did you have a business or self-employment during your youth?

  In particular, did you have any sales or marketing experience? How important was it, or a lack of it, to starting your company?

  When, under what circumstances, and from whom did you become interested in entrepreneurship and learn some of the critical lessons?

- Describe how you decided to create a job by starting your venture instead of taking a job with someone else.

  How did you spot the opportunity? How did it surface?

  What were your goals? What were your lifestyle needs or other personal requirements? How did you fit these together?

  How did you evaluate the opportunity in terms of the critical elements for success? The competition? The market? Did you have specific criteria you wanted to meet?

  Did you find or have partners? What kind of planning did you do? What kind of financing did you have?

  Did you have a start-up business plan of any kind? Please tell me about it.

How much time did it take from conception to the first day of business? How many hours a day did you spend working on it?

How much capital did it take? How long did it take to reach a positive cash flow and break-even sales volume? If you did not have enough money at the time, what were some ways in which you bootstrapped the venture (bartering, borrowing, and the like)? Tell me about the pressures and crises during that early survival period.

What outside help did you get? Did you have experienced advisors? lawyers? accountants? tax experts? patent experts? How did you develop these networks and how long did it take?

How did any outside advisors make a difference in your company?

What was your family situation at the time?

What did you perceive to be the strengths of your venture? Weaknesses?

What was your most triumphant moment? Your worst moment?

Did you want to have partners or do it solo? Why?

- Once you got going:

What were the most difficult gaps to fill and problems to solve as you began to grow rapidly?

When you looked for key people as partners, advisors, or managers, were there any personal attributes or attitudes you were particularly seeking because you knew they would fit with you and were important to success? How did you find them?

Are there any attributes among partners and advisors that you would definitely try to avoid?

Have things become more predictable? Or less?

Do you spend more time, the same amount of time, or less time with your business now than in the early years?

Do you feel more managerial and less entrepreneurial now?

In terms of the future, do you plan to harvest? To maintain? To expand?

In your ideal world, how many days a year would you want to work? Please explain.

Do you plan ever to retire? Would you explain?

Have your goals changed? Have you met them?

Has your family situation changed?

What do you learn from both success and failure?

What were/are the most demanding conflicts or trade-offs you face (e.g., the business versus personal hobbies or a relationship, children, etc.)?

Describe a time you ran out of cash, what pressures this created for you, the business, your family, and what you did about it. What lessons were learned?

Can you describe a venture that did not work out for you and how this prepared you for your next venture?

Questions for Concluding

- What do you consider your most valuable asset, the thing that enabled you to make it?
- If you had it to do over again, would you do it again, in the same way?
- As you look back, what do you believe are the most critical concepts, skills, attitudes, and know-how you needed to get your company started and grown to where it is today? What will be needed for the next five years? To what extent can any of these be learned?
- Some people say there is a lot of stress being an entrepreneur. What have you experienced? How would you say it compares with other "hot seat" jobs, such as the head of a big company, or a partner in a large law or accounting firm?
- What things do you find personally rewarding and satisfying as an entrepreneur? What have been the rewards, risks, and trade-offs?
- Who should try to be an entrepreneur? And who should not?
- What advice would you give an aspiring entrepreneur? Could you suggest the three most important lessons you have learned? How can I learn them while minimizing the tuition?
- Would you suggest any other entrepreneur I should talk to?
- Are there any other questions you wished I had asked, from which you think I could learn valuable lessons?

Step 4: Evaluate what you have learned.

Summarize the most important observations and insights you have gathered from these interviews. Contrast especially what patterns, differences, and similarities exist between lifestyle and high potential entrepreneurs. Who can be an entrepreneur? What surprised you the most? What was confirmed about entrepreneurship? What new insights emerged? What are the implications for you personally, your goals, career aspirations?

Step 5: Write a thank you note.

This is more than a courtesy; it will also help the entrepreneur remember you favourably should you want to follow up on the interview.

Preparation Questions

1. What are the two most valuable capabilities that F&D has, and do these capabilities lead to any negative consequences?

2. What are the different approaches to defining the market segments in this industry? Which do you think is more valuable from F&D's perspective and why?

3. What analysis would you suggest Dino do on the financial and operational figures provided? Complete any recommended analysis and provide any conclusions.

INTRODUCTION

It was 1:03 am on Saturday morning, and Franko D'Angelo, part owner and manager of F&D Meats, was making a final batch of custom, cognac bison sausage for a party tonight at a local embassy. Yet despite the late hour, Franko's mind had been occupied with important pending decisions. Key customers wanted new products requiring new expensive equipment, while others were demanding price breaks for volume purchases. Recently, a potential major customer made inquiries into supplying their Eastern Canadian store chain with a branded line sausages. Finally, his brother and partner in the business, Dino, had announced that he was going to enter MBA school in three months.

COMPANY BACKGROUND

A decade ago, Franko had pursued his love when he entered Le Cordon Bleu Culinary Arts School and subsequently apprenticed at one of Ottawa's most the prestigious hotels as a sous-chef. Five years ago, Franko began producing hand-made sausages in the basement apartment below his father's small Italian grocery store. For a summer job, Dino, a student, started selling sausages at Ottawa's Tulip Festival.[1] The sausages were a hit. A local radio personality described the sausages as the "most mouthwatering meat to ever grace his mouth." Based upon their success, Dino set up sausage kiosks at the other major summer festivals.

As the festival season ended, revenues slowed, compelling the brothers to seek out new sales opportunities. Initially, Dino, the "sales manager," approached local Italian restaurants and grocery stores. Over the next year, five restaurants and two local grocery stores began purchasing regularly from them. However, more than 40 percent of their sales were walk-in order customers who would phone in their order and pick it up from their downtown basement location. However, after two years the firm needed to find a larger production space. Furthermore, Dino's father had passed away, requiring the operation to relocate. His passing also meant that his grocery store was sold and lost to condominium developers. Sales had initially been impacted, but Dino had managed to get more specialty food and deli retailers in the region as clients.

EXPANDING THE OPERATION

With the passing of their father and increased demand, Franko and Dino began searching for a larger production location. In the second year of operation, Franko found a vacated dairy and cheese operation, and thought it would make an excellent space as it had a large walk-in refrigerator, lots of tiled space for production, two loading docks, and most of the sanitation, electrical, and water supply needed for food processing. It was located in an industrial park approximately 15 kilometres outside of Ottawa and the clincher was that rent was about half of anything they had considered previously. The only downside was that it was located some distance from most customers.

It took them almost six months to get the operation ready for production because of the complexity of getting permits and installing equipment. They moved in halfway through the third year of operation.

THE MARKET & INDUSTRY

The greater Ottawa and Gatineau region encompasses about 1.2 million people and is growing at about 2% annually. The region's population is 60% English speaking and 30% French speaking, with the remaining 10% having another first language. The large French population and culture provide the region with a distinctly European flavour. Other cultures are also well represented as sections of the city are named little Italy and Chinatown because of their ethnic and commercial heritage.

This case was written by Patrick Woodcock, Telfer School of Management, University of Ottawa.

[1] Ottawa has more than 50 summer festivals as well as some in the spring, fall, and winter.

Economically, the region relies mostly on government and tourism. Being a national capital, the government supports many festivals, cultural events, and museums (e.g., almost one hundred museums). There are many other tourist attractions including a major casino, numerous live production theaters, a symphony orchestra, a horse racing track, and several large arts and conference centres. Moreover, the city is home to five post secondary institutions and a number of major sports franchises. This makes Ottawa an attractive location for businesses that service tourism, including the sausage business.

TYPES OF SAUSAGES

Sausages can be classified in a number of ways. However, one of the most common is to classify sausages based upon the method of production.[2] Table 1 classifies sausages by production process. It also provides a brief market description of these segments.

The taste and desirability of a sausage is related to the quality and type of ingredients as well as the production process. "Quality" ingredients are fresher, include better cuts of meat, and do not include "fillers." Different production techniques can distinguish a producer's sausage in a number of ways including using longer natural smoking or drying processes; making smaller batches of unique products; and customizing products for clients.

THE SAUSAGE MARKET

Growth in the sausage market has been quite dramatic over the past several years, but most of the growth has occurred in the dinner "grilling sausage" segment. Table 2 illustrates some of these trends.

The growth in the dinner sausage market was attributed to several things including two income families requiring meals that demanded ease and speed of cooking, a trend toward low carbohydrate diets, and the increasing fashionability of specialty sausages. In the last five years, sausage demand had grown by over 9% annually. Analysts expected demand for sausages would continue to be strong, particularly for higher quality grilling sausage and low fat grilling sausage. The only potential negatives were concern for the "mad cow disease" (BSE) that had surfaced recently in Canada, and the high fat associated with some sausages.

TABLE 1	GENERAL CLASSIFICATION OF SAUSAGES (FROM LEAST TO MOST COMPLEX TO PROCESS)	
SAUSAGE TYPE	**PRODUCTION PROCESS DESCRIPTION**	**MARKET DESCRIPTION**
Fresh Sausage (must be cooked)	Raw ingredients produced into sausage. Easy to manufacture.	Represents 40% of market. Strong growth and includes all barbequing sausages. Prices range from $5 to $11 per kg.
Fresh Smoked Sausage (must be cooked)	Raw ingredients produced into a sausage and then smoked often using chemicals when in bulk.	Fastest growing market, but only represented 15% of the market. Prices range from $10 to $15 per kg for this more expensive sausage.
Cooked & Cooked Smoked Sausage	Sausages are produced and pre-cooked. They are eaten cold or re-heated.	Represents about 20% of market but low growth. Europeans have greater preference for these sausages. Average cost $10 per kg and $15 per kg for smoked.
Dried Sausage	Sausages are dried, or dry fermented which imparts a piquant taste. Top products are dried over weeks, but mass production techniques offer quick chemical alternatives. Sausages last weeks without refrigeration.	These sausages make up more than 15% of the market. Pepperonis type products make up a substantial of this market. Growth is average and the price ranges from $15 per kg for chemically dried to over $30 per kg for age-dried sausage.

Source: Food and Agriculture Organization of The United Nations, Rome. Small Scale Sausage Production, FAO Animal Production and Health Paper 52. 1985, by I.V. Savic (HYPERLINK "http://www.fao.org/docrep/003/x6556e/X6556E00.htm"\l "TOC") www.fao.org/docrep/003/x6556e/X6556E00.htm#TOC) Reproduced with permission.

[2] These different production methods give the sausages unique tastes and visual attributes.

TABLE 2 — CANADA'S CONSUMPTION OF SAUSAGES

SAUSAGE CATEGORY	AVERAGE RETAIL SALES	DOLLAR SALES % CHANGE VS. YEAR AGO	UNIT SALES (KG)	UNIT SALES % CHANGE VS. YEAR AGO
Fresh Dinner				
Total	$178 598 965	14.9	18 662 379	10.5
Private label	$13 581 229	0.4	1 519 063	-1.2
Frozen Dinner				
Total	$34 640 829	12.2	4 516 405	7.9
Private label	$2 782 176	4	347 338	-3.8
Breakfast				
Total	$94 937 406	2.3	12 743 276	-5
Private label	$7 425 599	8.5	1 085 896	-0.8
Dried*				
Total	$56 478 242	11	3 245 876	5.5

Source: National Hot Dog and Sausage Council Report, 2010

*Includes dried meat sausage snacks and imported specialty dried fermented sausages.

SAUSAGE MANUFACTURERS

The largest Canadian meat and sausage producer is Maple Leaf Foods, which owns two other large Canadian meat manufacturers: Schneider Foods and Mitchell's Gourmet Food's Inc. Maple Leaf Foods is a large, highly diversified food processing company that dominates the Canadian meat processing industry. It had sales of over $6 billion and just over $100 million in earnings last year, both of which had grown by about 10 percent annually during the past two years mostly through acquisitions.

Maple Leaf was divided into three main operating groups: the Agriproducts Group, the Bakery Products Group, and the Meat Products Group. In the past year, the company had derived 64.9% of their revenues from meat products group, but only 26.7% of their operating earnings from this group. Both the agribusiness and bakery product groups were more profitable from both return on sales and return on assets employed basis.

Mitchell's Gourmet Food's Inc., although part of Maple Leaf, operates independently out of a plant located in Saskatoon, Saskatchewan, and produces only processed meat products. Sausage production focuses on fresh and smoked products including bacon, sausages, wieners, dry smoked meat products, luncheon meats, and hams. This company was the first major producer of smoked meat and European sausage in the prairies. More recently, Mitchell had begun producing a line of haute cuisine sausages and dried pepperoni sausages. In 2002, Mitchell became a wholly owned subsidiary of Schneider Foods Inc. and subsequently of Maple Leaf.

Pillars Sausages & Delicatessens Limited is a privately owned meat processing company located in southwestern Ontario. It sells sausages, salami, ham, luncheon meats, cooked beef products, liver spreads, and cooked poultry meats all across Canada to retail outlets. In 1999, Pillars completed a 30 000 sq ft processing plant and nearby a brand new 90 000 sq ft distribution centre, both in Waterloo. Several years earlier, they had purchased Kretschmar Private Label Meat Specialists, a company that produced private–label meat products for various grocery chains throughout North America. This company is located in Toronto. In addition, Pillars had a joint venture with P&H Foods for processing poultry products and this company specialized in the production of classic European types of sausages.

Tour Effel is a subsidiary of McCain's Foods Inc., a multi-billion dollar international food business located in Atlantic Canada. Tour Effel has plants located in Quebec City and Montreal that make various types of processed and smoked meat products including pates, hams, and sausages. Their product focus is on new cuisine sausages. They also produce Loeb's private label brand called Merit Selection.

There are many other small regional and local sausage producers that produce specialized products and sell to local and regional markets. Examples are:

- Venetian Meat & Salami Co. Ltd. produces fresh, smoked and some dried sausages including pepperoni and salami. They are located in Hamilton and only ship their more expensive sausages outside of the local Toronto and Hamilton market.
- Grimm's Fine Foods Ltd. is a company located in British Columbia with sales of about $50 million. It focuses exclusively on fresh, dried, and cooked sausages. Recently, they were purchased by Helmuth of California.

Competition at the local level is intense. There are many local butchers and even grocery stores with meat departments that produce fresh sausages for their shelves. Making fresh sausages is relatively simple because one only needs a meat grinder, mixer, and sausage stuffer.

The Canadian market was also supplied by some international producers, although imports made up a very small amount of the market. Johnsonville Sausage, located in Wisconsin, had been particularly aggressive in Eastern Canada.

Johnsonville produced sausages, wieners, and other processed meat products such as burritos, although they had historically specialized in sausages. Johnsonville mass produces approximately 40 different types of sausages under the categories of brats, Italian, smoked, and breakfast sausages. Another US company that made several standard smoked sausages was Oscar Mayer Foods, which was a division of Kraft Foods. Both of these companies sold only to the large retail chains in Canada.

In addition, a number of European companies exported dried sausages into Canada. These specialty items were sold by agents specializing in European food merchandise. Possibly as much of half of all of Canada's very high quality dried sausages came from Europe. This represented less than 10 percent of the total dried sausage market segment.

F&D MEATS OPERATIONS

Franko and Dino manage the business in an incredibly frugal manner. The company has been profitable from its inception and both revenues and profits demonstrate growth (see Table 3).

TABLE 3	UN-AUDITED INCOME STATEMENT ON A CASH BASIS[1]		
ACCOUNTS	LAST YEAR	4TH YEAR OF OPERATION	3RD YEAR OF OPERATIONS[4]
Revenue	189 001	143 221	103 003
Meat	110 449	66 364	32 311
Other Ingredients	5 522	2 655	1 129
Labour[2]	17 340	14 336	12 935
Cost of Goods Sold	133 311	83 355	46 375
Operating Income	55 690	59 866	56 628
Rent	12 000	12 000	6 000
Building Maintenance and Repair	1 052	1 859	9 901
Utilities	5 647	5 463	5 154
Machinery Maintenance and Repair	854	2 648	6 975
Advertising and Promotion	1 075	4 424	4 623
Water and Sewage	3 298	2 976	2 894
Travel	357	1 058	1 412
Delivery Van Costs	8 446	5 925	3 763
Courier	356	245	266
Auto Repair	366	2 876	1 055
Miscellaneous Expenses[3]	3 515	2 975	2 254
Total Non-Operating Expenses	36 966	42 449	41 297
Net Income	18 724	17 417	12 331

Notes: 1. These statements were created by Dino, who was not an accountant. 2. This does not include salaries to Franko and Dino. 3. Includes all items such as cleaning, stationery, etc. 4. Some expenses are due to the cost of upgrading to the new facility and only had to pay 1/2 years' rent.

However, they still were not drawing a salary from the operation. Fortunately, an inheritance provided them with financial buffer for the near term.

Their concern over the next several years was to make the company into a strong operation that could financially support them both. Based upon the present financial statements they thought that revenues would have to grow five times before that goal was attainable.

PRODUCTION

Franko manages production for F&D, but his greatest skill is being a chef. He is superb at developing new, unique recipes and getting the best-quality ingredients for his products. He often said that his greatest joy is spending the night in the kitchen trying out new ingredients and recipes. "Watching peoples face when they dig into a superb sausage" he stated "was worth more than any salary."

Once the recipes are set, sausages are produced in a batch process. The grinding, mixing, stuffing equipment have a maximum capacity of 50 kilos of sausage per batch, and over an eight hour day, ten batches are easily attainable including the cleanup time between batches. The smoker room has the capacity to produce 50 kilos per day and this could be doubled if chemicals were added, which would half the smoking time. F&D did not have a drying room because this would require a considerable amount of capital and take up to a week per batch using traditional methods.

Franko is very particular about the ingredients, particularly the meat. Freshly slaughtered meat is delivered weekly and then aged for up to 28 days (depending on the type of meat). Although this is atypical in the industry, the aging process produces extraordinarily succulent and tender meat.[3] An abundance of refrigeration capacity allows Franko to inventory the meat for such a length of time. When ready, the meat is ground up, and blended with non-meat items. At this point, sausage sold to restaurants for ingredients is bulk packaged and shipped, while sausage destined to be made into actual sausages is sent to the stuffing machine. Sausages that required cooking and/or smoking were then hung in the smoker or cooked in large vats. Both operations required time but capacity was not a constraint except during some key times during the busy summer months when demand was often tripled. Finally, the sausages are packed and delivered.

Packaging at F&D is relatively rudimentary as the equipment just wraps the sausages in plastic wrap over a styrofoam plate. A labelling machine then attaches a paper label.

F&D had eight part-time employees to help with the production process.[4] The use of part-time employees eliminates many costs associated with full-time employees and it allows for flexibility when seasonal production requires change. However, the downside is that Franko spent a lot of time training and supervising workers.

Franko also spent a considerable amount of his time searching for new fresh ingredients or trying out new sausage recipes. Normally, he spent all of Sunday trying out new recipes and doing the odd batch of custom ordered specialized sausages, such as the smoke-cured rabbit and garlic knackwurst order that he had done last Sunday. During the busy summer season, Franko almost always had to work twelve and fourteen hour days, seven days a week to insure "things got done."

MARKETING AND SALES

Dino did not have experience in sales, but he uses a relatively straightforward approach to selling the product. He provides clients with a fresh product sample and a brochure explaining the company's philosophy, the products, and cooking instructions. The brochure also includes a personalized letter from Franko, the chef, to the client. However, the key to Dino's success is largely due to his gregarious Italian nature. While Franko's skill was cooking, Dino's skill was entertaining people with a funny tales or jokes. This combination slowly began to generate sales, and once they had a customer they seemed to keep them for good.

Table 4 illustrates the types of sausages F&D Meats produced.

Both Franko and Dino think quality and wide selection were important to F&D's growth and success. Customers often related tales of parties, events, etc. that had been a spectacular success because of the uniqueness of the sausages in the meal. They are a talking point at most occasions.

F&D Meats sells sausages to a variety of customers. Dino estimates that their primary customers are 21 independent local grocery stores or chains, 26 restaurants, the casino, the race track, and one caterer. They also sell at the festivals and supplied a few delis with specialized sausages. In addition,

---

[3] The top restaurants in the world age their beef in this manner, but it is rare for most restaurants or meat product producers to go to this extreme.
[4] All of these workers were untrained local high school students.

TABLE 4

TYPES OF SAUSAGES MADE BY F&D MEATS

Type of Sausage	Retail[1] Price	Volume (kg)		
		Year 6	Year 5	Year 4
Italian Medium	$10.50	3977	2932	2137
Italian Mild	$10.50	3088	2497	2137
Italian Hot	$10.50	599	545	350
Pork	$ 9.50	568	401	103
Smoked Italian Medium	$11.00	4810	3683	1720
Smoked Italian Hot	$11.00	377	420	402
Sicilian Spiced	$11.00	710	508	482
Bratwurst	$11.00	1381	1188	1012
Hungarian	$11.00	266	379	327
Knackwurst	$11.00	1500	1133	1223
Italian Chicken Medium	$12.50	1711	1432	560
Italian Chicken Hot	$12.75	1099	1019	850
Chicken Bratwurst	$12.00	1821	1552	79
Pork Apple	$11.00	308	485	43
Pork Honey Mustard	$12.76	497	288	161
Veal Sweet Garlic	$13.40	195	189	56
Breakfast Links	$ 9.00	245	386	137
Breakfast Patties	$ 9.00	241	189	35
Duck a la Orange	$18.90	52	58	n/a
Wild Boar & Blueberries	$27.40	36	22	n/a
Sea Food Cajun	$15.60	56	18	n/a
Italian Turkey	$11.00	816	608	n/a
Smoked Beef	$12.00	381	245	n/a
Cajun Turkey	$11.50	927	429	n/a
Cajun Chicken	$11.50	1326	679	n/a
Hot Smoked Cajun	$12.25	156	98	n/a
Maple Smoked Pork	$13.45	377	211	n/a
Maple Smoked Beef	$13.55	188	152	n/a
Smoked Pork & Apple	$13.00	221	159	n/a
Smoked Lamb Fennel	$15.65	320	147	n/a
Pork Apricot & Mustard	$13.95	326	162	n/a
Smoked Dried Tomatoes & Chicken	$14.55	221	n/a	n/a
Honeyed Pork & Pear	$13.60	326	n/a	n/a
Cajun Hot Pepper Beef	$13.00	180	n/a	n/a
Artichoke Almond Chicken	$15.67	162	n/a	n/a
Raisin Cajun Lamb	$15.00	56	n/a	n/a
Sun Dried Tomato and Basil Chicken	$16.50	176	n/a	n/a
Spicy Bleu Chicken Sausage	$15.50	162	n/a	n/a
Pistachio Pesto Chicken	$15.50	239	n/a	n/a
Sweet Sicilian	$11.00	108	n/a	n/a
Bison Sage	$17.55	51	n/a	n/a
Venison Cajun	$17.55	32	n/a	n/a
Trout Cajun	$18.90	26	n/a	n/a

Note: 1. This is recommended retail price.

they have many secondary customers who order sausage just during the summer or during special events. The only category of customers that had declined since the move to their new location was "walk-in" or "phone-in" clients. Dino surmised it was due to the inconvenience. During year five, the year after they moved, about 10 percent of the "phone-in" clients had failed to pick up their orders. Now he and Franko were reluctant to take orders over the phone for fear that they would not be picked up. Due to their JIT production schedule, "walk-in" customers have extremely limited product selection.[5]

Deliveries were handled either by Dino or an employee who would once a day or every other day (depending upon the need) deliver orders to the primary customers as well as any other important customer who had ordered.

THE KEEPING OF RECORDS!

The bookkeeping process is not a labour-of-love for either brother. Neither brother has the accounting training or inclination. Despite this, Dino was the bookkeeper and he diligently kept accounts on a cash basis. Dino thought that his accounts were accurate despite being unaudited, but what bothers him the most is that he doesn't know really what to do with the resulting numbers.

NEW POTENTIAL OPPORTUNITIES AND CONCERNS

A variety of opportunities were now confronting Franko and Dino. Quite a few delis were encouraging them to produce high quality dry/fermented sausage (e.g., very high quality salami, pepperoni, etc). These delis were finding that importing these products from Europe presents problems. Every now and then, ship delays or problems in shipment affected the reliability of delivery or quality of the product. These delis hope that F&D Meats will produce a high quality product at a good price, as they have done with their other products.

However, making dry fermented sausage will require substantial changes. More specifically, it requires a large, climate-controlled space because the temperature and humidity must be controlled and gradually changed to encourage the right molds to grow and aging to occur (i.e., fermentation for the piquant taste). The space required would have to be big enough to allow for considerable inventory because the process took an average of one week and could take several weeks depending upon the variety of sausage. Franko had the space to do this renovation in the present building, but a climate controlled room would have to be built. Initial estimates suggest this could cost at least $50 000.[6]

In addition, Dino had been approached by a national retailer to supply their stores in Eastern Canada.[7] They had just opened five more stores in Eastern Canada, and presently all their sausages were being imported. Their proposal is to have F&D Meats slowly begin supplying the Eastern Canadian stores with high quality sausages on a region by region basis. The objective is to make F&D the principal supplier of sausages for them in Canada. What has raised Franko's interest was that F&D could very quickly ramp up sales growth to the desired revenue levels in the next two or so years. If it worked, Dino thought this approach would surely provide the required volume to move F&D Meats to be a profitable company. In addition, this would allow Dino to attend MBA School full time rather than part-time as he was planning. It would certainly relieve Dino's sales and marketing role despite his commitment to Franko that he would continue as the sales manager of F&D.

Both Franko and Dino realize the next phase of development of F&D is crucial to the long-term success of their company. However, it was now almost 5 a.m. and Franko realized he needed to get a few hours of sleep before returning to work tomorrow morning.

---

[5] Dino estimated "phone-in" and "walk-in sales" declined to less than 5% of total sales.

[6] The cost depended upon the automation and energy efficiency. This was the lowest price quote and would be for a very basic room that would have to be operated manually.

[7] This retailer is actually an international retailer with a strong national presence across all of Canada.

For more information on the resources available from McGraw-Hill Ryerson, go to www.mcgrawhill.ca/he/solutions.

CHAPTER 3

THE OPPORTUNITY: SCREENING, CREATING, SHAPING, RECOGNIZING, SEIZING

You miss 100 percent of the shots you don't take.

WAYNE GRETZKY

LEARNING OBJECTIVES

LO1 Defend the importance of thinking big enough.

LO2 Illustrate how to assess opportunity using the criteria employed by successful entrepreneurs, angels, and venture capital investors in evaluating potential ventures.

LO3 Support the statements that most successful ventures track a "circle of ecstasy" and match investors' appetites in "the food chain."

LO4 Differentiate between an idea and an opportunity.

LO5 Explain the roles of ideas, pattern recognition, and the creative process in entrepreneurship.

LO6 Identify sources of information for finding and screening venture opportunities.

THINK BIG ENOUGH

Since first published in 1977, *New Venture Creation* has urged aspiring entrepreneurs to "think big enough." Time and again the authors have observed the classic small business owner who, almost like a dairy farmer, is enslaved by and wedded to the business. Extremely long work weeks of 70, 80, or even 100 hours and rare vacations are often the rule rather than the exception. Moreover, these hardworking owners rarely build equity, other than in the real estate they may own for the business. One of the big differences between the growth and equity minded entrepreneur and the traditional small business owner is that the entrepreneur thinks *bigger*. Patricia Cloherty puts it this way: "It is critical to think big enough. If you want to start and build a company, you are going to end up exhausted. So you might as well think about creating a BIG company. At least you will end up exhausted and *rich*, not just exhausted!"

Her theme of thinking bigger is embedded throughout this book. How can you engage in a "think big" process that takes you on a journey treading the fine line between high ambitions and being totally out of your mind? How do you know whether the idea you are chasing is a worthy endeavour or a waste of time and energy? You can never know which side of the line you are on—and can stay on—until you try and until you undertake the journey. This is not to say that being big is all that matters. A small business owner may judge their effort to be a success even if the business does not pass a certain size threshold. There are examples of firms that remained small by staying within their objectives and remaining true to their strengths, resources, and capabilities or were limited by the scope of the opportunity. Further, a lifestyle or hobby enterprise may satisfy the proprietor for many years despite low margins or revenues. But for those of you wanting more, the content in this book should provide a solid basis for reaching those goals!

OPPORTUNITY THROUGH A ZOOM LENS

Many, many proposals to launch new companies are turned down by venture capital investors each year. The opportunity recognition process is complex, subtle, and situational (at the time, in the market space, in relation to the investor's other alternatives, etc.). If the brightest, most knowledgeable, and most sophisticated investors in the world miss good opportunities and occasionally hop on board with the losers, we can conclude that the journey from idea to high-potential opportunity is illusive, contradictory, and perilous. Think of this journey as a race through varied terrain and weather conditions. At times, the journey takes place in full sun-shine on straight, smooth highways, as well as on twisting, turning, narrow one-lane passages that can lead to breathtaking views. Along the way you also will unexpectedly encounter fog, hail storms, white-out conditions, and freezing rain. All too often, you seem to run out of gas and find obstacles and hold-ups when you least expect them. This is the entrepreneur's journey. As Aydin Mirzaee put it, "You have to make every decision right every step of the way." One wrong move and you're done. If too much equity is doled out too quickly, later round investors won't hop on board.

If finding ideas is the starting point, then, why do we talk about it at the end of this chapter? We believe that knowing what to look for will aid you considerably in your search for a decent opportunity. In fact, a recent abundance of research supports this.[1] Having gone through the criteria laid out in this chapter and developed some of your own criteria—including work-life-balance, personal aspirations, and preferences—you will be able to best judge what constitutes a good idea and ultimately a promising opportunity for you.

TRANSFORMING CATERPILLARS INTO BUTTERFLIES

This chapter is dedicated to making that journey friendlier by focusing a zoom lens on the opportunity. It shares the road maps and benchmarks used by successful (and unsuccessful) entrepreneurs, venture capitalists, angels, and other private equity investors in their quest to transform the often amorphous, fuzzy idea into a spectacularly prosperous venture. These criteria comprise the core of their due diligence to ascertain the viability and profit potential of the proposed business, and therefore, the balance of risk and reward. It will examine the role of ideas and pattern recognition in the creative process of entrepreneurship.

business model:
A one-page flowchart or diagram describing the "engine of the enterprise" to demonstrate the value proposition of the venture, how it balances resources with the ecosystem in which it operates, and how it generates cash flow.

You will come to see the criteria used to identify higher potential ventures as jumping-off points at this rarefied end of the opportunity continuum, rather than mere endpoints. One to 10 out of 100 entrepreneurs create ventures that separate themselves from the pack. Scrutinized through our lens, these ventures reveal a highly dynamic, constantly changing work of art, rather than a product of a formula or the completion of certain items on a checklist. The highly organic and situational character of the entrepreneurial process underscores the criticality of determining *fit* and balancing *risk and reward*. As the authors have argued for decades: the business plan is obsolete as soon as it comes off the printer! It is in this shaping process that the best entrepreneurial leaders and investors add the greatest value to the enterprise and creatively transform an idea into a venture. In recent years, the mantra has become "show me your model." In addition to the business plan, we will consider the **business model** and the value it provides both to the team and to other constituents—including would-be investors.

NEW VENTURE REALITIES

It is useful to put the realities faced by countless entrepreneurs into perspective. Consider the following fundamental realities as normal as you seek to convert your amorphous idea into a successfully realized outcome:

New Ventures: Fundamental Realities

- ✔ Most new ventures are works in process and not works of art. What you start out to do is not what you end up doing.
- ✔ Most business plans are obsolete at the printer.
- ✔ Onset Venture Partners[2] found that 91 percent of portfolio companies that followed their business plans failed!
- ✔ Speed, adroitness of reflex, and adaptability are crucial. Keep those knees bent and be ready!
- ✔ The key to succeeding is failing quickly and recouping quickly, and keeping the tuition low.
- ✔ Success is highly situational, depending on time, space, context, and stakeholders.
- ✔ The best entrepreneurs specialize in only making "new mistakes."
- ✔ Starting a company is a lot harder than it looks, or you think it will be, but you can last a lot longer and do more than you think if you do not try to do it solo and you don't give up prematurely.

These realities are intended to convey the transient and at times chaotic nature of this beast, and the dynamic context within which most new ventures evolve. Such realities present so much room for the unexpected and the contradictory that it places a premium on thinking bold enough and doing everything you can to make sure your idea becomes an opportunity. Therefore, how can the aspiring entrepreneur think about this complex, even daunting challenge?

THE CIRCLE OF ECSTASY AND THE FOOD CHAIN FOR VENTURES

LO3

What most small businesses do not know about, but that is a way of life in the world of high-potential ventures, is what we will call the "circle of venture capital ecstasy" (Exhibit 3.1) and "the food chain for entrepreneurial ventures" (Exhibit 3.2). These concepts enable the entrepreneur to visualize how the company building-investing-harvesting cycle works. Understanding this cycle and the appetites of different suppliers in the capital markets food chain enables you to answer the questions for *what* reason does this venture exist and for *whom*? Knowing the answers to these questions has profound implications for fundraising, team building, and growing and harvesting the company—or coming up short in any of these critical entrepreneurial tasks.

Exhibit 3.1 shows that the key to creating a company with the highest value (e.g., market capitalization) begins with identifying an opportunity in the "best technology and market space," which creates the attraction for the "best venture team." Speed and agility to move quickly attracts the "best venture capitalists, board members, and other mentors and advisors" who can add value to the venture.

Exhibit 3.2 captures the food chain concept, which will be discussed in detail in chapter 9 "Financing the Venture." Different players in the food chain have very different capacities and preferences for the kind of venture in which they want to invest. The vast majority of start-up entrepreneurs spend inordinate amounts of time chasing the wrong sources with the wrong venture. One goal in this chapter, and again in chapter 9, is to provide a clear picture of what those criteria are and to grasp what "think big enough" means to the players in the food chain. This is a critical early step to avoid wasting time chasing venture capitalists, angels, and others when there is a misfit from the outset. As one CEO put it, "There are so many investors out there that you could spend the rest of your career meeting with them and still not get to all of them." In fact, the problem is compounded when seeking angel or informal investors since there are a hundred times more of them than there are venture capitalists.

| EXHIBIT 3.1 | CIRCLE OF VENTURE CAPITAL ECSTASY |

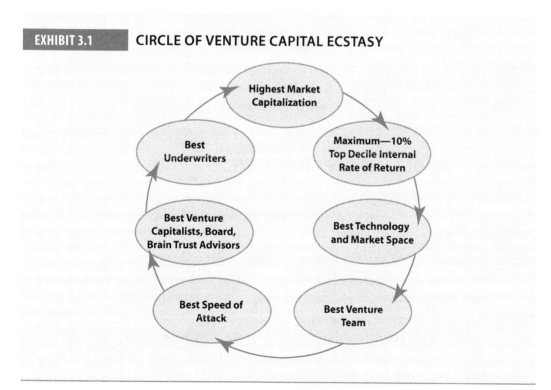

EXHIBIT 3.2 **THE CAPITAL MARKETS FOOD CHAIN FOR ENTREPRENEURIAL VENTURES**

STAGE OF VENTURE	R&D	SEED	LAUNCH	HIGH GROWTH
Enterprise Value	Less than $1 million	$1–$5 million	>$1–$50 million-plus	More than $100 million
Sources of Funding	Founders High net worth individuals FFF* SR&ED**	FFF* Angel funds Seed funds SR&ED**	Venture capital series A, B, C . . .† Strategic partners Very high net worth individuals Private equity	IPOs Strategic acquirers Private equity
Amount of Capital Invested	Up to $200 000	$10 000–$500 000	$500 000–$20 million	$10–$50 million-plus
% Company Owned at IPO	10%–25%	5%–15%	40%–60% by prior investors	15%–25% by public
Share Price and Number‡	$0.01–$0.50 1–5 million	$0.50–$1.00 1–3 million	$1.00–$8.00+/– 5–10 million	$12–$18+ 3–5 million

* Friends, Families, and Fools

** Scientific Research and Experimental Development tax incentive program.

† Venture Capital Series A, B, C . . . (Average Size of Round)

	A	@ $5.1 million—start-up
Round	B	@ $8.1 million—product development
	C+	@ $11.3 million—shipping product

Valuations vary markedly by industry (e.g., 2x)

Valuations vary by region and VC cycle

‡ At Post–IPO

Why waste time thinking too small and on ventures for which there is no appetite in the financial marketplace? Knowing how capital suppliers and entrepreneurs think about the opportunity creation and recognition process, their search and evaluation strategies, and what they look for is a key frame of reference.

WHEN IS AN IDEA AN OPPORTUNITY? LO4

The Essence: Four Anchors

If an idea is not an opportunity, what is an opportunity? Superior business opportunities have the following four fundamental anchors:

1. They create or add significant value to a customer or end-user.
2. They solve a significant problem, remove a serious pain-point, or meet a significant want or need—for which someone is willing to pay a premium.
3. They have robust market, margin, and moneymaking characteristics that will allow the entrepreneur to estimate and communicate sustainable value to potential stakeholders.
4. They are a good *fit* with the founder(s) and venture team at the time and marketplace—along with an attractive *risk-reward* balance.

If an opportunity has these qualities, the "window of opportunity" will be open and will remain open long enough. Further, entry into a market with the right characteristics will be feasible, and the venture team will be able to achieve it. The venture will have or will be able to gain a competitive advantage (i.e., to achieve leverage). Finally, the economics of the venture will be rewarding and forgiving enough to allow for significant profit and growth potential.

To summarize: *A superior opportunity has the qualities of being attractive, durable, and timely and is anchored in a product or service which creates or adds value for its buyer or end-user—usually by solving a painful, serious problem.*[3] The most successful entrepreneurs, venture capitalists, and private investors are opportunity-focused; that is, they start with what customers and the market-place want, and do not lose sight of this.

THE REAL WORLD

Opportunities are created, or built, using ideas and entrepreneurial creativity. Yet, while the image of a carpenter or mason at work is useful, in reality the process is more like the collision of particles in a nuclear reaction or like the spawning of hurricanes over the ocean. Ideas interact with real-world conditions and entrepreneurial ingenuity at a point in time. The product of this interaction is an opportunity around which a new venture can be formed.

The business environment in which an entrepreneur launches his or her venture cannot be altered significantly. For-profit businesses operate in a free enterprise system characterized by private ownership and profits. And, despite assumptions often made concerning social and non-profit organizations, they also are subject to market forces and economic constraints. Consider, for instance, what would happen to donations if it were perceived that a non-profit organization was not reinvesting its surplus returns, but instead was paying management excessive salaries. Or, what if a socially oriented organization concentrated all its efforts on the social mission, while neglecting revenues? Clearly, dealing with suppliers, production costs, labour, and distribution is critical to the health of these social corporations. Thus, social and non-profit organizations are just as concerned with positive cash flow and generating sufficient cash flows, even though they operate in a different type of market than for-profit organizations.

EVERY BOAT NEEDS A GOOD ANCHOR, AND A BIG SHIP REQUIRES A COUPLE OF THEM!

SPAWNERS AND DRIVERS OF OPPORTUNITIES

In a free enterprise system, changing circumstances, chaos, confusion, inconsistencies, lags or leads, knowledge and information gaps, and a variety of other vacuums in an industry or market spawn opportunities.

Changes in the business environment and the ability to anticipate these changes are so critical in entrepreneurship that constant vigilance for changes is a valuable habit. An entrepreneur with credibility, creativity, and decisiveness can seize an opportunity while others study it. Since the last edition of this text, the Kairos Society was formed. Its raison d'être is "to find and empower the young pioneers who will push the world forward through entrepreneurship and innovation—we do so with the support of the top universities, mentors, and corporations across the globe. At the Kairos Society, we view today's global problems as opportunities for entrepreneurs to focus on the meaningful businesses and innovations that will radically change the world for the better. Not only for our generation, but for the generations to come." Derin Kent and Tina Dacin, both of Queen's University, observe that modern microfinance was shaped by a cacophony of disparate forces emanating from commercial banking and poverty alleviation.[4] Further, open sourcing, open innovation, crowd sourcing, and crowd funding are sweeping mainstream business. Collective entrepreneurship is on the rise too.[5]

Opportunities are situational. Some conditions under which opportunities are spawned are idiosyncratic, while at other times they are generalizable and can be applied to other industries, products, or services. In this way, cross-association can trigger in the entrepreneurial mind the crude recognition of existing or impending opportunities. It is often assumed that a marketplace dominated by large, multi-billion-dollar players is impenetrable by smaller, entrepreneurial companies. You cannot possibly compete with entrenched, resource-rich, established companies. The opposite can be true for several seasons. It can take three to five years or more for a large company to change its strategy and even longer to implement the new strategy, since it can take 10 years or more to change the culture enough to operate differently. For a new or small company, 10 or more years can be forever.[6] It may even be easier for a large company to try something new by adopting a new name or spinning off a new division. General Motors created Saturn in 1985 to try something different and in 2010 distanced itself from Hummer when that experiment went awry.

Some of the most exciting opportunities have come from fields that conventional wisdom says are the domain of big business: technological innovation. Three engineering students came up with a "digital guidance" tool for hip replacement for a fourth-year project and went on to launch their enterprise, Avenir Medical. The performance of smaller firms in technological and design innovation is remarkable—95 percent of the radical innovations since World War II have come from new and small firms, not the giants. According to Tom Brzustowski, president of the Natural Sciences and Engineering Research Council from 1995 to 2005:

> As far as innovations are concerned, with the exception of Nortel, I believe that all radical innovations in Canada have come from companies with fewer than 10 000 employees. Take Magna, though a large company by Canadian standards, its radical innovation—pressure forming—emerged from one of their small constituent companies.
>
> Commercialization of radical innovations is not the same as being the source of the IP behind the innovation. The companies that produced the radical innovations may have acquired somebody else's intellectual property to do it.

In his book, *The Way Ahead*, Tom Brzustowski calls "for entrepreneurial managers in companies of all sizes in all sectors to be on the prowl for opportunities to add new value in what they do and make, and thus to produce innovations that will let them operate in a price-setting mode."[7]

There can be exciting opportunities in ordinary businesses that might never get the attention of venture capital investors. The revolution in computers, information systems, and networking has had a profound impact on businesses that had changed little in decades. The used-auto-parts business had been stagnant for generations. Yet, the team at Pintendre Auto Inc. saw a new opportunity in this field by applying the latest computer and information technology to a traditional business that relied on crude, manual methods to track inventory and find parts for customers.[8] In just three years, Pintendre Auto grew to $16 million in sales and eventually this Québec-based enterprise owned and operated over 100 facilities in the United States and Canada. Reaching sales of nearly $30 million drew the attention of LKQ Corporation, which in 2007 acquired Pintendre Auto for an undisclosed sum.

Technology and regulatory changes have profoundly altered and will continue to alter the way we conceive of opportunities. Cable television, with its hundreds of channels, came of age in the 1990s and brought with it new opportunities in the sale and distribution of goods from infomercials to shopping networks to pay-per-view. The Internet has created an even more diverse set of opportunities in sales and distribution, most notably Amazon.com, iTunes, Craigslist, Priceline, YouTube, and eBay.

Consider the example of Bulldog Interactive Fitness that illustrates the phenomenon of vacuums in which opportunities are spawned.

Exhibit 3.3 summarizes the major types of discontinuities, asymmetries, and changes that can result in high-potential opportunities. Creating such changes through technical and design innovation, influencing and creating the new rules of the game (airlines, telecommunications, financial services and banking, medical products), and anticipating the various impacts of such changes is central to recognizing opportunities.

SEARCH FOR SEA CHANGES

A simple criterion for the highest potential ventures comes from Vancouver's Ventures West, "We target companies that are addressing worldwide markets which are large enough to allow the portfolio company to grow to a significant size." Garage Technology Ventures states: "We're looking to invest in entrepreneurial teams with big ideas and a need for seed capital to turn their ideas into great companies. We are willing to invest in unproved teams attacking unproven markets with unproven solutions." The best place to start in seeking to identify such ideas in a macro sense is to identify a significant **sea change** that is occurring or will occur. Think of the profound impact that personal computing, biotechnology, and the Internet have had on the past generation. The great new ventures of the next generation will come about by the same process and will define these next great sea changes. Exhibit 3.4 summarizes some categories

sea change: A broad or substantial transformation.

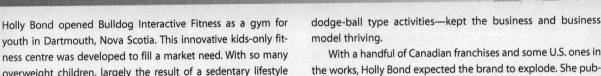

Holly Bond opened Bulldog Interactive Fitness as a gym for youth in Dartmouth, Nova Scotia. This innovative kids-only fitness centre was developed to fill a market need. With so many overweight children, largely the result of a sedentary lifestyle (TV, computer, videogames), she asked why not combine gaming with exercise? "She went looking for a high-tech solution, but found no specialized equipment on the market... Bond sensed a gap and decided to capitalize on the opportunity."

The gym, targeted at getting the "Xbox generation" off the couch, opened in 2005 after nearly a year of hard work and research. Holly became a certified personal trainer, and with her husband, drew up a business plan and secured financing, all in secrecy. "We didn't even tell our best friends what we were doing," said Bond. "We were so afraid that someone else was going to do it first." Niche fitness chains, like women-only Curves and Sisters Pace Fitness, proved that demographic-specific gyms could access a market that others missed.

About eighteen months into operations, Bond decided to franchise. "It was always our intention to franchise," says Bond, "but we thought we'd be doing that later, maybe in three or four years, once we had a few of our own open." With a steady stream of enquiries and $200 000 from angel investors in Halifax the franchising began. The interactive equipment was a hit: exercise bikes provided input to PlayStation games on big wall-mounted screens, rowing machines hooked up to display the user competing with others and escaping from sea monsters, Dance Dance Revolution, a rock climbing treadmill, Wii stations, and many others—including some old fashioned dodge-ball type activities—kept the business and business model thriving.

With a handful of Canadian franchises and some U.S. ones in the works, Holly Bond expected the brand to explode. She publicly shared her ambitious goal of 400 franchises worldwide by 2011 (as of 2013, there were four franchises in Canada and one in the United States failed to materialize). She picked up a 2007 Export Achievement Award and admitted, "We're all exhausted, but it's an exciting exhausted." With her sights set on launching a DVD, writing a book, developing a line of kid-size workout equipment, and creating a TV show, she caught the attention of DHX Media Ltd., an independent producer and distributor of TV programming and interactive content. David Regan, executive VP at DHX Media said, "We've been tracking these guys for awhile as they've been refining their model and think they've come a long way from where they started out." DHX Media acquired Bulldog Interactive Fitness Inc. for $625 000 and 99 333 shares in DHX (locked for one year). Bond stayed on at the helm and additional compensation was tied to meeting financial performance benchmarks. Holly indicated, "There is a huge amount of synergy between the two companies and this allows us to operate at an entirely new level." A Bulldog Interactive Fitness franchise started with a fee of $34 900, capital costs of between $250 000 and $400 000, and royalty fees of 7 percent gross sales and 2 percent for national advertising.

Question: Holly Bond bowed out of Bulldog Interactive Fitness in 2009. Did she give up the reins too early?

Sources: Graham Scott, "From Fat to Fit," *Canadian Business*, October 8, 2006; Allan Lynch, "From Baby Fat to Super-Fit," *Chatelaine*, August 2007; Bill Power, "Exercise Joins Entertainment: Children's TV Producer Buys Chain of Kids' Fitness Centres," *Chronicle Herald*, March 25, 2008.

for thinking about such changes. These include technology, market and societal shifts, and even opportunities spawned from the excesses produced by the Internet boom. Moore's Law (the computing power of a chip doubles every 18 months) has been a gigantic driver of much of our technological revolution over the past 40 years. Metcalfe's Law states that the value of belonging to a community grows as the number of members increases. See these and the other laws in Exhibits 3.3 and 3.4.

Breakthroughs in gene mapping and cloning, biotechnology, and nanotechnology and changes brought about by the Internet will continue to create huge opportunities for the next generation. Beyond the macro view of sea changes, how can one think about opportunities in a more practical, less abstract sense? What are some parameters of business/revenue models that increase the odds of thinking big enough and therefore appealing to the food chain? To go with this chapter is the Sea-Change Exercise on Connect, which will challenge you to think creatively and expansively about how new technology discoveries will drive the next new industries. This pattern continues to this day.

| EXHIBIT 3.3 | SUMMARY OF OPPORTUNITY SPAWNERS AND DRIVERS |

EXHIBIT 3.3   SUMMARY OF OPPORTUNITY SPAWNERS AND DRIVERS

ROOT OF CHANGE/CHAOS/ DISCONTINUITY	OPPORTUNITY CREATION
Regulatory changes	Airlines, insurance, telecommunications, medical, pension fund management, financial services, banking, tax laws and securities regulations
10-fold change in 10 years or less	Moore's Law—computer chips double in performance every 18 months; financial services, private equity, consulting, Internet, biotech, information age, publishing
Reconstruction of value chain and channels of distribution	Superstores—Loblaws, Walmart; publishing; automobiles; Internet sales and distribution of all services
Proprietary or contractual advantage	Technological innovation: patent, licence, contract, franchise, copyrights, distributorship
Existing management/investors burned out/undermanaged	Turnaround, new capital structure, new breakeven, new free cash flow, new team, new strategy; owners' desires for liquidity, exit; telecom, waste management service, retail businesses
Entrepreneurial leadership	New vision and strategy, new team equals secret weapon; organization thinks, acts like owners
Market leaders are customer obsessed or customer blind	New, small customers are low priority or ignored: hard disk drives, paper, chemicals, mainframe computers, centralized data processing, desktop computers, corporate venturing, office superstores, automobiles, software, most services

EXHIBIT 3.4   IDEAS VERSUS OPPORTUNITIES: SEARCH FOR SEA CHANGES

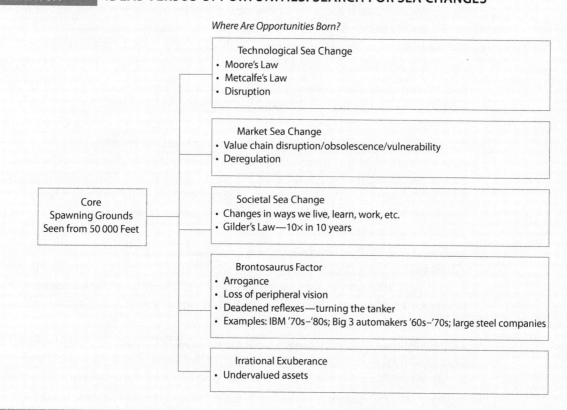

Where Are Opportunities Born?

Core Spawning Grounds Seen from 50 000 Feet

Technological Sea Change
- Moore's Law
- Metcalfe's Law
- Disruption

Market Sea Change
- Value chain disruption/obsolescence/vulnerability
- Deregulation

Societal Sea Change
- Changes in ways we live, learn, work, etc.
- Gilder's Law—10× in 10 years

Brontosaurus Factor
- Arrogance
- Loss of peripheral vision
- Deadened reflexes—turning the tanker
- Examples: IBM '70s–'80s; Big 3 automakers '60s–'70s; large steel companies

Irrational Exuberance
- Undervalued assets

DESIRABLE BUSINESS/REVENUE MODEL METRICS

We will emphasize time and again in *New Venture Creation* that *happiness is a positive cash flow!—but think cash last*. Further, you do not have an entry strategy until you have said no to lots of ideas, ideas that just come to you are not usually opportunities, and the number of ideas does not matter but the economics really do matter.

THE ROLE OF IDEAS

> *A bee puts to shame many an architect in the construction of her cells. But what distinguishes the worst architect form the best of bees is this, that the architect raises his structure in imagination before he erects it in reality.*

> KARL MARX, *CAPITAL*

IDEAS AS TOOLS

A good idea is nothing more than a tool in the hands of an entrepreneur. Finding a good idea is the first step in the process of converting an entrepreneur's creativity into an opportunity. The importance of the idea is often overrated at the expense of underemphasizing the need for products or services, or both, that can be sold in enough quantity to real customers.

Further, the new business that simply bursts from a flash of brilliance is rare. Usually a series of trial-and-error iterations is necessary before a crude and promising product or service fits with what the customer is willing to pay. Howard Head made 40 different metal skis before he finally arrived at the model that worked consistently. With surprising frequency, major businesses are built around very different products than those originally envisioned. Consider these examples:

- ✔ Swedish born Canadian Gideon Sundback patented a "separable fastener" in 1917. It took 20 years for this device—later dubbed "zipper"—to be adopted by the fashion industry.
- ✔ Polaroid Corporation was founded with a product based on the principle of polarized light. It was thought that polarized lamps would prevent head-on collisions between cars by preventing the "blinding" glare of oncoming headlights. The company pivoted and grew in stature and size based on another application of the same technology: instant photography. Polaroid excelled until a disruptive technology (digital imaging) pushed them into bankruptcy.
- ✔ Medical doctor Wilbur Franks led a team of Canadians that developed an anti-gravity suit in 1941 to prevent pilot blackout from acceleration (G-force). G-suits had been around since 1906 for clinical surgery. George Crile, a founder of the Cleveland Clinic, developed a rubber suit that could be inflated by bicycle pump to apply force and maintain blood pressure preventing loss of consciousness.
- ✔ William Steere, CEO of Pfizer, described the discovery of Viagra, the fastest-selling drug in history, as having "a certain serendipity" behind it. The drug was originally developed by Pfizer to treat angina—its real "potency" was discovered as a side effect.[9]
- ✔ In 1955 CBC-TV made use of the first instant replay on *Hockey Night in Canada*.

As one entrepreneur expressed it:

Perhaps the existence of business plans and the language of business give a misleading impression of business building as a rational process. But, as any entrepreneur can confirm, starting a business is very much a series of fits and starts, brainstorms and barriers. Creating a business is a round of chance encounters that leads to new opportunities and ideas, mistakes that turn into miracles.[10]

THE GREAT MOUSETRAP FALLACY

Perhaps no one did a greater disservice to generations of would-be entrepreneurs than Ralph Waldo Emerson in his oft-quoted line: "If a man can make a better mousetrap than his neighbour, though he builds his house in the woods the world will make a beaten path to his door."

What can be called the great mousetrap fallacy was thus spawned. It is often assumed that success is possible if an entrepreneur can just come up with a new idea. The truth is that ideas are inert and, for all practical purposes, worthless. Ideas are infinite but resources simply are not. Further, the flow of ideas is phenomenal. Venture capital investors, for instance, during the investing boom of the late 1990s, received as many as 100 to 200 proposals and business plans each month. Only 1 to 3 percent of these actually received financing, however. Further, VC investors and the enterprises they invest in both benefit by learning from each other, but the VCs may specialize and not diversify despite best intentions.[11]

The fallacy persists despite the lessons of practical experience noted long ago in the insightful reply to Emerson by Owen B. Winters: "The manufacturer who waits for the world to beat a path to his door is a great optimist. But the manufacturer who shows this 'mousetrap' to the world keeps the smoke coming out his chimney." Even today, with the advent of the Internet and social media, Becky Reuber of the University of Toronto and Eileen Fischer of York University find that young and small firms must overcome the liability of being an unknown and present their reputation to the world.[12] For example, rather than wait, Volkswagen has been proactive in seeking out design ideas by opening up a competition soliciting design ideas from the general public. TheFunTheory.com is a website that shows video clips of amazing ideas in action, with the premise that fun is the easiest way to change people's behaviour.

CONTRIBUTORS TO THE FALLACY

One cannot blame it all on Ralph Waldo Emerson. There are several reasons for the perpetuation of the fallacy. One is the portrayal in oversimplified accounts of the ease and genius with which such ventures as Xerox, Seagram's, and Polaroid made their founders wealthy. Unfortunately, these exceptions do not provide a useful rule to guide aspiring entrepreneurs.

Another is that inventors seem particularly prone to mousetrap myopia. Perhaps, like Emerson, they are substantially sheltered in viewpoint and experience from the tough, competitive realities of the business world. Consequently, they may underestimate, if not seriously discount, the importance of what it takes to make a business succeed. Frankly, inventing and brainstorming may be a lot more fun than the diligent observation, investigation, and nurturing of customers that are often required to sell a product or service. Canadian James Gosling created the Java programming language at Sun Microsystems. It quickly gained notoriety and became ubiquitous; it also quickly became open source free software.

Contributing also to the great mousetrap fallacy is the tremendous psychological ownership attached to an invention or to a new product. This attachment is different from attachment to a business. While an intense level of psychological ownership and involvement is certainly a prerequisite for creating a new business, the fatal flaw in attachment to an invention or product is the narrowness of its focus. The focal point needs to be the building of the business, rather than just one aspect of the idea.

Another source of mousetrap fallacy myopia lies in a technical and scientific orientation, that is, a desire to do it better. A good illustration of this is the experience of a Canadian entrepreneur who, with his brother, founded a company to manufacture truck seats. The entrepreneur's brother had developed a new seat for trucks that was a definite improvement over other seats. The entrepreneur knew he could profitably sell the seat his brother had designed, and they did so. When they needed more manufacturing capacity, one brother had several ideas on how to improve the seat. The first brother stated: "If I had listened to him, we probably would be a small custom shop today, or out of business. Instead, we concentrated on making seats that would sell at a profit, rather than just making a better and better seat. Our company has several million dollars of sales today and is profitable."

Related to "doing it better" is the idea of doing it first. Having the best idea first is by no means a guarantee of success. There can be a liability—a painful downside—to being first. Sometimes the first ones merely prove to the competition that a market exists to be snared. Therefore, unless having the best idea also includes the capacity to pre-empt other competitors by capturing a significant share of the market or by erecting insurmountable barriers to entry, first does not necessarily mean most viable. Sometimes, the quick follower sees things more clearly than the first-mover, capturing benefits of vicarious learning.

Spotting an opportunity within an existing market was a key aspect in the development of a mass-produced rotary electric toothbrush. The founding entrepreneur had noted a large pricing spread among retail products. At the low end were devices in the range of $5. There was then a jump to the $60 to $80 range, and then another jump to products that were selling for well over $100. His research showed that new battery technology, plus outsourcing and a new rotary design, could result in a disposable product that would fill the gaps, steal market share, and yield substantial profits. His $1.75-million business turned into $475 million when his company was sold to Procter & Gamble. This is an excellent example of a clear pricing pattern that can be applied elsewhere.

PATTERN RECOGNITION

THE EXPERIENCE FACTOR

One cannot build a successful business without ideas. In this regard, experience is vital in looking at new venture ideas. Time after time, experienced entrepreneurs exhibit an ability to quickly recognize a pattern—and an opportunity—while it is still taking shape. Nobel laureate Herbert Simon wrote extensively about pattern recognition. He described the recognition of patterns as a creative process that is not simply logical, linear, and additive but intuitive and inductive as well. It involves, he said, the creative linking, or cross-association, of two or more in-depth "chunks" of experience, know-how, and contacts.[13] Simon contended that it takes 10 years or more for people to accumulate what he called the "50 000 chunks" of experience that enable them to be highly creative and recognize patterns—familiar circumstances that can be translated from one place to another. Popularized by Malcolm Gladwell in his 2008 book *Outliers*, it was Anders Ericsson (a co-author of Herbert Simon's) who revealed that it takes 10 000 hours of practice to master an art, sport, or any number of activities.

Thus, the process of sorting through ideas and recognizing a pattern can also be compared to the process of fitting pieces into a three-dimensional jigsaw puzzle. It is impossible to assemble such a puzzle by looking at it as a whole unit. Rather, one needs to see the relationships between the pieces and be able to fit together some that are seemingly unrelated before the whole is visible. And sometimes, the perspective of others is necessary.

Recognizing ideas that can become entrepreneurial opportunities stems from a capacity to see what others do not—that one plus one equals three. Consider the following examples of the common thread of pattern recognition and new business creation by linking knowledge in one field or marketplace with quite different technical, business, or market know-how:

- ✔ Jim Treliving quit the RCMP to open a franchise restaurant—Boston Pizza. The leap was made after Jim ate at the original restaurant in Edmonton. Jim recounts, "It was love at first bite." Jim partnered with George Melville and over 10 years built up a chain of 16 franchised restaurants. They then turned the tables and took over the 44-restaurant chain for $3.8 million to become the franchisor. They divested 15 of the restaurants and kept one as a corporate training restaurant.

- ✔ During travel throughout Europe, the eventual founders of Crate & Barrel frequently saw stylish and innovative products for the kitchen and home that were not yet available in North America. When they returned home, the founders created Crate & Barrel to offer these products for which market research had, in a sense, already been done. In Crate & Barrel, the knowledge of consumer buying habits in one geographical region, Europe, was transferred successfully to another, the United States and Canada.

- ✔ Laurence Lewin worked in a variety of jobs before settling on the fashion industry in the mid-1970s. Lewin failed to complete medical school, joined the military where he lost his rifle, barely passed England's lowest level accounting qualification, and then worked in the computer industry. He went to work for Suzy Shier in 1987 and in 1990 co-founded La Senza. A few years later Suzy Shier was cast off for cash to fuel growth of La Senza. Lewin's empire of close to 800 stores—about half of which are in Canada and the remainder in 40 other countries—was purchased by Limited Brands in November of 2006 for $628 million in cash. Laurence Lewin passed away in November 2008.

ENHANCING CREATIVE THINKING

The creative thinking described above is of great value in recognizing opportunities, as well as other aspects of entrepreneurship. The notion that creativity can be learned or enhanced holds important implications for entrepreneurs who need to unlock imaginative solutions. Most people can certainly spot creative flair. Children seem to have it, and many seem to lose it. Several studies suggest that creativity actually peaks around the first grade because a person's life tends to become increasingly structured and defined by others and by institutions. Further, the development of intellectual discipline and rigour in thinking takes on greater importance in school than during the formative years, and most of our education beyond grade school stresses a logical, rational mode of orderly reasoning and thinking. Finally, social pressures may tend to be a taming influence on creativity.

Evidence suggests that one can enhance creative thinking in later years. The organization IDEO has been pushing the envelope for decades, and their blog, Design Thinking, at design-thinking.ideo.com gives insight into their creative processes.

APPROACHES TO UNLEASHING CREATIVITY

Since the 1950s, much has been learned about the workings of the human brain. Today, there is general agreement that the two sides of the brain process information in different ways. The left side performs rational, logical functions, while the right side operates the intuitive and non-rational modes of thought. A person uses both sides, actually shifting from one mode to the other (see Exhibit 3.5). Approaching ideas creatively and maximizing the control of these modes of thought can be of value to the entrepreneur.

More recently, attention has focused on the creativity process. For instance, evidence is mounting that administrative tasks crowd out more contemplative but non-urgent tasks:

> Entrepreneurs are creative people who follow passions and may toy with 101 ideas for a business before starting one. Then come the endless Things That Must Be Done: raising capital, closing sales, hiring staff, securing suppliers. Activities that don't have deadlines, such as inventing, designing, and concocting new products, can get pushed to the bottom of to-do lists. As more time-sensitive and urgent tasks accumulate at the top of those lists, the creative stuff simply falls off.[14]

Many have reported of the benefits of daydreaming. Daniel Kahneman, Nobel prize winner for his work in decision making, asserts in his 2011 book, *Thinking, Fast and Slow*, that there are two modes of processing in our brain: one is fast, instinctive, and emotional; the other is slower, deliberate, and logical. Psychology professor Mihaly Csikszentmihalyi labels full engagement in a work task as "flow" while thinking time away from work is "incubation"—and both are important. At least four hours of consecutive, uninterrupted time dedicated to a task is vital, but so too are distractions. Working on a complex problem is more likely to be solved when uninterrupted time is mixed with distractions than through dedicated conscious effort. This also allows one to break free of "associative barriers"—essentially, probable relationships we surmise based on our knowledge. And while stereotypes can be good, such as if that dog is giving cues that it might bite, stay back;

| EXHIBIT 3.5 | COMPARISON OF LEFT-MODE AND RIGHT-MODE BRAIN CHARACTERISTICS |

L-MODE	R-MODE
Verbal: Using words to name, describe, and define.	Nonverbal: Awareness of things, but minimal connection with words.
Analytic: Figuring things out step-by-step and part-by-part.	Synthetic: Putting things together to form wholes.
Symbolic: Using a symbol to stand for something. For example, the sign + stands for the process of addition.	Concrete: Relating to things as they are at the present moment.
Abstract: Taking out a small bit of information and using it to represent the whole thing.	Analogic: Seeing likenesses between things; understanding metaphoric relationships.
Temporal: Keeping track of time, sequencing one thing after another, doing first things first, second things second, etc.	Nontemporal: Without a sense of time.
Rational: Drawing conclusions based on reason and facts.	Nonrational: Not requiring a basis of reason or facts; willingness to suspend judgment.
Digital: Using numbers as in counting.	Spatial: Seeing where things are in relation to other things, and how parts go together to form a whole.
Logical: Drawing conclusions based on logic; one thing following another in logical order—for example, a mathematical theorem or a well-stated argument.	Intuitive: Making leaps of insight, often based on incomplete patterns, hunches, feelings, or visual images.
Linear: Thinking in terms of linked ideas, one thought directly following another, often leading to a convergent conclusion.	Holistic: Seeing whole things all at once; perceiving the overall patterns and structures, often leading to divergent conclusions.

associative barriers can keep us from forming new connections and new lines of thought. Steve Jobs defined creativity as "just connect things"—but seeing connections between seemingly unrelated elements is arduous for some whereas for other it is just plain elementary. Some people are just better at pulling together a set of observations and making new arrangements.

Nevertheless, fantasizing about positive outcomes or just spacing out might not be productive. If your goal-setting and goal imagining is unrealistic the chances of failure are greater. Rather, visualize the process not the outcome. Procrastination is still an enemy of the productive entrepreneur. Kalina Christoff, cognitive neuroscientist at the University of British Columbia, sates "Mind wandering is a much more active state than we ever imagined, much more active than during reasoning with a complex problem."[15]

To keep the creative visualization process alive, entrepreneurs need to carve out some time to think freely. A walk in the woods is often pointed to as a prime setting for the activity. Competition is another motivator.[16]

TEAM CREATIVITY

Teams of people can generate creativity that may not exist in a single individual. The creativity of a team of people is impressive, and comparable or better creative solutions to problems evolving from the collective interaction of a small group of people have been observed.

BIG OPPORTUNITIES WITH LITTLE CAPITAL

The bootstrap credo is self-capitalization: get by on a shoe-string budget, maintain control, and the windfall is yours. Within the dynamic free enterprise system, opportunities are apparent to a limited number of individuals—and not just to the individuals with financial means. Ironically, successful entrepreneurs such as Howard Head attribute a portion of their success to the discipline of limited capital resources. Many entrepreneurs have learned the key to success is in the art of bootstrapping, which "in a start-up is like zero inventory in a just-in-time system: it reveals hidden problems and forces the company to solve them."[17] Canadians take pride in their conservative nature—often avoiding risks associated with becoming highly leveraged (see chapter 11 "Obtaining Debt Capital")—growing through retained earnings. Consider the following:

- Approximately three-quarters of start-ups launch with $50 000 or less; half begin with $10 000 or less as seed capital. Further, the primary source of capital was, overwhelmingly, personal savings (77 percent), rather than outside investors with deep pockets.[18]

Prescott C. Ensign

DISNEY IS BUILT ON THE POWER OF TEAM CREATIVITY.

Spin Master Ltd.

EARTH BUDDY

A good example of the creativity generated by using more than one head is that of Spin Master. It was founded when three friends—who had just graduated from Western University, armed with $10 000—set out to build a business. Earth Buddy, a small, pantyhose-covered head filled with grass seeds that sprouted hair when watered was their first product. It was a huge hit—a Pet Rock-like phenomenon—providing the team a foundation to sprout their next idea. The venture boasts a willingness to take risks, creativity, playfulness, and constant scanning for great new innovative toys. Spin Master has also seen fit to give back: it sponsors the Spin Master Innovation Fund with the Canadian Youth Business Foundation. The Fund sponsors 10 awards of $50 000 for an innovative start-up.

Questions: Is it easier to behave entrepreneurially as an outsider? Spin Master has become an insider, part of the establishment. Now that it is a sizable enterprise with seasoned veterans who have much to lose, can it retain its youthful enthusiasm and willingness to try new things?

- In the 1930s, Josephine Esther Mentzer assisted her uncle by selling skin care balm and quickly created her own products with an initial investment of $100. After convincing the department stores rather than the drugstores to carry her products, Estee Lauder was on its way to becoming the corporation it is today with sales of US$8 billion.[19]

- Putting their talents (cartooning and finance) together, in 1923 Roy and Walt Disney moved to California and started their own film studio—with $290. By 2009, the Walt Disney Co. had a market capitalization exceeding $50 billion.

- While working in real estate, Montréal immigrant Assaad Abdelnour's vision for CLIC Foods began. He later bought and operated a supermarket and the full concept took shape. CLIC (Canadian Lebanese Investment Corporation) became a pioneer in ethnic foods and today is a leader in the production and distribution of international food products with annual sales of nearly $50 million. CLIC boasts 200 employees at six locations across Canada, derives 25 percent of revenues from exports, and in 2007 opened a facility in New Jersey.[20]

- With $100, Calgary-native Nicholas Graham, age 24, went to a local fabric store, picked out some fabrics, and made $100 worth of ties. Having sold the ties to specialty shops, Graham was approached by Macy's to place his patterns on men's underwear. Joe Boxer Corporation was born and "six months into Joe Boxer's second year, sales had already topped $1 million."[21] Graham, CUO (Chief Underpants Officer), successfully harvested the business a few years later when annual sales reached US$20 million.

REAL TIME

Opportunities exist or are created in real time and have what we call a window of opportunity. For an entrepreneur to seize an opportunity, the window must be open and remain open long enough to achieve market-required returns.

Exhibit 3.6 illustrates a window of opportunity for a generalized market. Markets grow at different rates over time and as a market quickly becomes larger, more and more opportunities are possible. As the market becomes established, conditions are not as favourable. Thus, at the point where a market starts to become sufficiently large and structured (e.g., at five years in Exhibit 3.6), the window opens; the window begins to close as the market matures (e.g., at 12 to 13 years in the exhibit).

The curve shown describes the rapid growth pattern typical of such new industries as microcomputers and software, cellphones, quick oil changes, and nanotechnology. For example, in the cellular phone industry, most major cities began service between 1984 and 1985. In 1996, U.S. and Canadian cellphone use was comparable, 13 in 100 U.S. residents and 9 in 100 Canadian residents had one, but by 2007, U.S. penetration reached 76 percent while Canada was at 60 percent. For 2012, U.S. penetration reached 103 percent while Canada was at 80 percent.[22] In other industries where growth is not so rapid, the slope of a curve would be less steep and the possibilities for opportunities fewer.

In considering the window of opportunity, the length of time the window will be open is important. It takes a considerable length of time to determine whether a new venture is a success or a failure. And, if it is to be a success, the benefits of that success need to be realized.

Evidence shows that for venture-capital-backed firms it takes about two and a half years to realize that the venture is a lemon, while the winners take seven or eight years to mature. An extreme example of the length of time it can take for a "plum" to be harvested is the experience of one Silicon Valley venture capital firm that invested in a new firm in 1966 and was finally able to realize a capital gain in early 1984. Another way to think of the process of creating and seizing an opportunity in real

---

EXHIBIT 3.6 **CHANGES IN THE PLACEMENT OF THE WINDOW OF OPPORTUNITY**

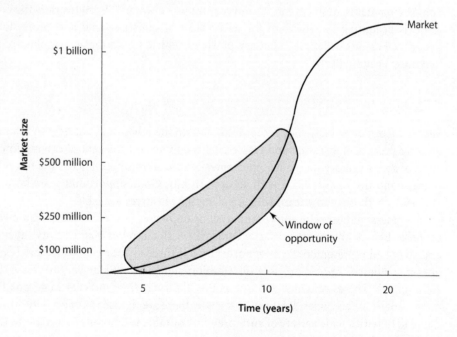

time is to think of it as a process of selecting objects (opportunities) from a conveyor belt moving through an open window, the window of opportunity. The speed of the conveyor belt changes, and the window through which it moves is constantly opening and closing. The continually opening and closing window and the constantly changing speed of the conveyor belt represent the volatile nature of the marketplace and the importance of timing. For an opportunity to be created and seized, it needs to be grabbed from the conveyor belt before the window closes.

The ability to recognize a potential opportunity when it appears and the sense of timing to seize that opportunity as the window is opening, rather than slamming shut, are critical. That opportunities are a function of real time is illustrated in a statement made in 1977 by Ken Olsen, then president and cofounder of Digital Equipment Corporation: "There is no reason for any individual to have a computer in their home." Though the statement is taken out of context, it illustrates how windows of opportunity open and close. Olsen was speaking of using computers to operate household functions such as opening doors and running faucets. That window of opportunity was closed in 1977, but appears to be opening now, as some people operate their house's lights, furnaces, and other appliances with their smartphones. Nevertheless, Ken Olsen was forced to resign in 1992 and within a decade the struggling company's assets were sold off.[23] It is not easy for even the world's leading experts to predict just which innovative concepts for new business will evolve into the major industries of tomorrow. This is vividly illustrated by several quotations from famous innovators. In 1901, two years before the famous flight, Wilbur Wright said, "Man will not fly for 50 years." In 1910, Thomas Edison said, "The nickel-iron battery will put the gasoline buggy...out of existence in no time." In 1932 Albert Einstein made it clear, "[There] is not the slightest indication that nuclear energy will ever be obtainable. It would mean that the atom would have to be shattered at will." In 1943 Thomas Watson, IBM Chairman predicted, "I think there is a world market for maybe five computers." And in 1981 Bill Gates, Microsoft Chairman stated, "640K ought to be enough for anybody."

Clearly predicting opportunity is tricky business. In 1899, Charles Duell, commissioner at the U.S. Office of Patents, stated, "Everything that can be invented has been invented." While today just about every appliance on the kitchen counter has a computer, some are foretelling that the desktop/home computer may fade as more "Net" devices and individuals tap into a CPU remotely. Sun Microsystems' business model and mantra was always: "The network is the computer." The cloud is becoming the standard for every facet of one's personal and professional existence. Presently, Edison's belief that a battery-powered vehicle would replace gasoline-powered ones is looking ever more likely.

RELATION TO THE FRAMEWORK OF ANALYSIS

Successful opportunities, once recognized, fit with the other forces of new venture creation. This iterative process of assessing and reassessing the fit among the central driving forces in the creation of a new venture was shown in chapter 2. Of utmost importance is the fit of the lead entrepreneur and the venture team with an opportunity. Good opportunities are both desirable and attainable by those on the team who are using the resources available.

To understand how the entrepreneurial vision relates to the analytical framework, it may be useful to look at an opportunity as a three-dimensional relief map with its valleys, mountains, and so on, all represented. Each opportunity has three or four critical factors (e.g., proprietary licence, patented innovation, sole distribution rights, an all-star venture team, breakthrough technology). These elements pop out at the observer; they indicate huge possibilities where others might see obstacles. It is easy to see why there are thousands of exceptional opportunities that will fit with a wide variety of entrepreneurs but that might not fit neatly into the framework outlined in Exhibit 3.7.

EXHIBIT 3.7 CRITERIA FOR EVALUATING VENTURE OPPORTUNITIES

	ATTRACTIVENESS	
CRITERIA	**HIGHEST POTENTIAL**	**LOWEST POTENTIAL**
Industry and Market	Changes way people live, work, learn, etc.	Incremental improvement only
Market:	Market driven; identified; recurring revenue niche	Unfocused; onetime revenue
Customers	Reachable; purchase orders Remove serious pain-point	Loyal to others or unreachable
User benefits	Less than one-year payback Solves an important problem/need	Three years plus payback
Value added	High; advance payments	Low; minimal impact on market
Product life	Durable	Perishable
Market structure	Imperfect, fragmented competition or emerging industry	Highly concentrated or mature or declining industry
Market size	$100 million to $1 billion sales potential	Unknown, less than $20 million or multibillion sales
Growth rate	Growth at 30%–50% or more	Contracting or less than 10%
Market capacity	At or near full capacity	Undercapacity
Market share attainable (Year 5)	20% or more; leader	Less than 5%
Cost structure	Low-cost provider; cost advantages	Declining cost
Economics		
Time to breakeven/positive cash flow	Under 1.5–2 years	More than 4 years
ROI potential	25% or more; high value	Less than 15%–20%; low value
Capital requirements	Low to moderate; fundable/bankable	Very high; unfundable or unbankable
Internal rate of return potential	25% or more per year	Less than 15% per year
Free cash flow characteristics:	Favourable; sustainable; 20%–30% or more of sales	Less than 10% of sales
Sales growth	Moderate to high (15%–20%)	Less than 10%
Asset intensity	Low/sales $	High
Spontaneous working capital	Low, incremental requirements	High requirements
R&D/capital expenditures	Low requirements	High requirements
Gross margins	Exceeding 40% and durable	Under 20%
After-tax profits	High; greater than 10%; durable	Low
Time to breakeven profit and loss	Less than two years; breakeven not creeping or leaping	Greater than four years; breakeven creeping or leaping up

(continued)

EXHIBIT 3.7   **CRITERIA FOR EVALUATING VENTURE OPPORTUNITIES** *(CONTINUED)*

	ATTRACTIVENESS	
CRITERIA	**HIGHEST POTENTIAL**	**LOWEST POTENTIAL**
Harvest Issues		
Value-added potential	High strategic value	Low strategic value
Valuation multiples and comparables	Price/earning = 20×; 8–10 × EBIT; 1.5–2× revenue: Free cash flow 8–10×	Price/earnings ≤ 5×, EBIT ≤ 3–4×; revenue ≤ 0.4
Exit mechanism and strategy	Present or envisioned options	Undefined; illiquid investment
Capital market context	Favourable valuations, timing, capital available; realizable liquidity	Unfavourable; credit crunch
Competitive Advantage Issues		
Fixed and variable costs	Lowest; high operating leverage	Highest
Control over costs, prices, and distribution	Moderate to strong	Weak
Barriers to entry:	Knowledge to overcome	
Proprietary protection	Have or can gain	None
Response/lead time	Competition slow; napping	Unable to gain edge
Legal, contractual advantage	Proprietary or exclusivity	None
Contracts and networks	Well-developed; accessible	Crude; limited
Key people	Top talent; an A team	B or C team
Venture Team		
Entrepreneurial team	All-star combination; free agents	Weak or solo entrepreneur; not free agents
Industry and technical experience	Top of the field; super track record	Underdeveloped
Integrity	Highest standards	Questionable
Intellectual honesty	Know what they do not know	Do not want to know what they do not know
Fatal-Flaw Issue Personal Criteria	Nonexistent	One or more
Goals and fit	Getting what you want; but wanting what you get	Surprises; only making money
Upside/downside issues	Attainable success/limited risks	Linear; on same continuum
Opportunity costs	Acceptable cuts in salary, etc.	Comfortable with status quo
Desirability	Fits with lifestyle	Simply pursuing big money
Risk/reward tolerance	Calculated risk; low risk/reward ratio	Risk averse or gambler
Stress tolerance	Thrives under pressure	Cracks under pressure

(continued)

EXHIBIT 3.7　　**CRITERIA FOR EVALUATING VENTURE OPPORTUNITIES** *(CONTINUED)*

CRITERIA	ATTRACTIVENESS	
	HIGHEST POTENTIAL	LOWEST POTENTIAL
Strategic Differentiation		
Degree of fit	High	Low
Team	Best in class; excellent free agents	B team; no free agents
Service management	Superior service concept	Perceived as unimportant
Timing	Rowing with the tide	Rowing against the tide
Technology	Groundbreaking; one of a kind	Many substitutes or competitors
Flexibility	Able to adapt; commit and decommit quickly	Slow; stubborn
Opportunity orientation	Always searching for opportunities	Operating in a vacuum; napping
Pricing	At or near leader	Undercut competitor; low prices
Distribution channels	Accessible; networks in place	Unknown; inaccessible
Room for error	Forgiving and resilient strategy	Unforgiving, rigid strategy

SCREENING OPPORTUNITIES

LO6

OPPORTUNITY FOCUS

Opportunity focus is the most fruitful point of departure for screening opportunities. The screening process should not begin with strategy (which derives from the nature of the opportunity), nor with financial and spreadsheet analysis, nor with estimations of how much the company is worth and who will own what shares.

These starting points, and others, usually place the cart before the horse. In addition, many entrepreneurs who start businesses—particularly those for whom the ventures are their first—run out of cash at a faster rate than they bring in customers and profitable sales. There are many reasons why this happens, but one thing is certain: These entrepreneurs have not focused on the right opportunity.

Over the years, those with experience in business and in specific market areas have developed rules to guide them in screening opportunities. For example, during the initial stages of the irrational exuberance about the dot-com phenomenon, number of "clicks" changed to attracting "eyeballs," which changed to pages viewed. Many investors got caught up in false metrics. Those who survived the stock market crash of 2000–2001 understood that dot-com survivors would be the ones who executed transactions. Number of customers, amount of the transaction, and repeat transactions became the recognized standards.[24] Moreover, in the aftermath of the 2009 financial downturn the winners and losers were revealed. A stout recession provided threats to established enterprises and opportunities for new ventures. During such transformation periods, the status quo is repeatedly proved to be no longer viable and business models are quickly evaluated and refined as consumers shift priorities dramatically. 2013 and 2014 ushered in a "new normal" with phrases like "negative growth" and "negative savings rate."

SCREENING CRITERIA: THE CHARACTERISTICS OF HIGHER POTENTIAL VENTURES

Venture capitalists, savvy entrepreneurs, and investors also use this concept of boundaries in screening ventures. Exhibit 3.7 summarizes criteria used by venture capitalists to evaluate opportunities, many of which tend to have a high-technology bias. As will be seen later, venture capital investors reject 60 to 70 percent of the new ventures presented to them very early in the review process, based on how the entrepreneurs satisfy these criteria.

However, these criteria are not the exclusive domain of venture capitalists. The criteria are based on good business sense used by successful entrepreneurs, angel investors, private investors, as well as venture capitalists. Consider the following examples of great small companies built without a dime of professional venture capital.

- Herb and Rhoda Singer established Discount Car & Truck Rentals in 1980. Discount has grown from the first location in Hamilton, Ontario, to 300 locations, most of which are franchises. It has a few locations in Australia and has expansion plans for the United States. Discount included hybrids in its fleet in 2004, and in 2008, during a looming Toronto Transit Authority strike, offered discounts to stranded public transportation riders. In 2011 the company announced a push toward sustainability, boasting of a fleet of fuel-efficient vehicles and other green initiatives.

- Wester's Garage, located in Tilley, Alberta (pop. 397), "in the heart of truck country, surrounded by oil fields and wide open space," provides custom performance tuning for trucks and cars. Owner Lyndon Wester offers reprogramming of the computer chip that controls the engine. It all started in late 1998 with some simple electronics work, but by 2000, they had developed custom performance profiles for the Pontiac Fiero and GM diesel trucks. Their first big break was an order in July 2002 to convert UPS vans across North America. In 2003, Lyndon Wester secured a U.S. military contract for 50 Chevy Suburbans and two local contracts for oil service company fleet vehicles to modify GM trucks to improve fuel economy, limit speed, and alter powertrain parameters. These contracts secured the future for Wester's Garage. While maintaining customers in Alberta's oil fields they thrived with performance tuning for car and truck enthusiasts— even the occasional boat engine. As one online bulletin board posting noted, "Seems amazing that someone living 13 miles from nowhere is getting computers shipped to him from all over North America." In late 2012, some of Lyndon's handiwork was attracting headlines at National Championship races in the United States.

- In 1986, Pleasant Rowland founded the Pleasant Company as a mail-order catalogue company selling the American Girls Collection of historical dolls. She had begun the company with the modest royalties she received from writing children's books and did not have enough capital to compete in stores with the likes of Mattel's Barbie.[25] By 1992, she had grown the company to US$65 million in sales.[26] Mattel acquired it in 1998 for US$770 million, and under Rowland's continued management the company had sales of US$350 million in 2001.

- Edgy musician Ashley MacIsaac offered half of his future revenues on eBay in the summer of 2008 with a minimum bid of $1.5 million. Seeking a patron of the arts, MacIsaac said, "I see this as no different than what they did in Mozart's day." David Bowie issued bonds in the late 1990s using future royalties as guarantee; Bowie collected tens of millions of dollars on the spot.[27] In 2007, Madonna came to a similar arrangement with concert promoter Live Nation Inc. for over $100 million. The point of departure here is opportunity and, implicitly, the customer, the marketplace, and the industry. Exhibit 3.7

shows how higher and lower potential opportunities can be placed along an attractiveness scale. The criteria provide some quantitative ways in which an entrepreneur can make judgments about industry and market issues, competitive advantage issues, economic and harvest issues, venture team issues, and fatal-flaw issues and whether these add up to a compelling opportunity. For example, *dominant* strength in any one of these criteria can readily translate into a winning entry, whereas a flaw in any one can be fatal.

Entrepreneurs contemplating opportunities that will yield attractive companies, not high-potential ventures, can also benefit from paying attention to these criteria. These entrepreneurs will then be in a better position to decide how these criteria can be compromised. As outlined in Exhibit 3.7, business opportunities with the greatest potential will possess many of the following, or they will dominate in one or a few for which the competition cannot come close.

INDUSTRY AND MARKET ISSUES

MARKET *Higher potential* businesses can identify a market niche for a product or service that meets an important customer need and provides high value-added or value-created benefits to customers. This invariably means the product or service eliminates or drastically reduces a major pain-point for a customer or end-user, or solves a major problem/bottleneck for which the customer is willing to pay a premium. Customers are reachable and receptive to the product or service, with no brand or other loyalties. The potential payback to the user or customer of a given product or service through cost savings or other value-added or value-created properties is one year or less and is identifiable, repeatable, and verifiable. Further, the life of the product or service exists beyond the time needed to recover the investment, plus a profit. And so much the better if the company is able to expand beyond a single product. If benefits to customers can be calculated in dollar terms, then the market potential is far less difficult and risky to ascertain.

Lower potential opportunities are unfocused regarding customer need, and customers are unreachable and/or have brand or other loyalties to others. A payback to the user of more than three years and low–value-added or value-created properties also makes an opportunity unattractive. Being unable to expand beyond a one-product company can make for a lower potential opportunity. The failure of one of the first portable computer companies, Osborne Computer, is a prime example of this. Adam Osborne's business plan called for sales of 10 000 of his Osborn 1 computer over the product's lifespan; sales peaked at 10 000 units per month. Despite market appeal, quality control fell during rushed production. Osborne's boasts of a second-generation model that was months away from release did not boost confidence. Customers poised to buy the current model held off and dealers cancelled orders for the Osborne 1. The young venture never recovered and his blunder came to be known as "Osborneing." Med-Eng CEO Richard L'Abbe recounts a similar—though non-fatal—scenario. It occurred several iterations into the product line. An update to their bomb disposal suit and helmet combo was introduced half-way through the usual cycle. The word got out and customers held off buying. Med-Eng quickly took note and went back to their normal update cycle.

MARKET STRUCTURE Market structure is significant in terms of the number of sellers, size distribution of sellers, whether products are differentiated, conditions of entry and exit, number of buyers, cost conditions, and sensitivity of demand to changes in price.

A fragmented, imperfect market or emerging industry often contains vacuums and asymmetries that create unfilled market niches—for example, markets where resource ownership, cost advantages, and the like can be achieved. In addition, those markets where information or knowledge gaps exist and where competition is profitable, but not so strong as to be overwhelming, are attractive. An example of a market with an information gap is that experienced by an entrepreneur who encountered a large out-of-town company that wanted to dispose of a small, old, downtown office building. This office building, because its book value was about $200 000, was viewed by the financially-oriented firm as a low-value asset, and the company wanted to dispose of it so the resulting cash could be put to work for a higher return. The buyer, who had done more homework than the out-of-town sellers, bought the building for $200 000 and resold it in less than six months for more than $8 million.

Industries that are highly concentrated, that are perfectly competitive, or that are mature or declining are typically unattractive. The capital requirements and costs to achieve distribution and marketing presence can be prohibitive, and price-cutting and other competitive strategies in highly concentrated markets can be a significant barrier to entry. (The most blatant example is organized crime and its life-threatening actions when territories are invaded.) Revenge by normal competitors who are well positioned through product strategy, legal tactics, and the like, also can be punishing to the newcomer.

The unattractiveness of perfectly competitive industries is captured by the comment of prominent venture capitalist William Egan, who put it this way: "I want to be in a non-auction market."

MARKET SIZE An attractive new venture sells to a market that is large and growing (i.e., one where capturing a small market share can represent significant and increasing sales volume). A minimum market size of more than $100 million in sales is attractive. In the medical and life sciences today, this target boundary is more like $500 million or $1 billion. Such a market size means it is possible to achieve significant sales by capturing roughly 5 percent or less and thus not threatening competitors. For example, to achieve a sales level of $1 million in a $100-million market requires only 1 percent of the market. Thus, a recreational equipment manufacturer entered a $60-million market that was expected to grow at 20 percent per year to over $100 million by the third year. The founders were able to create a substantial but smaller company without obtaining a major share of the market and possibly incurring the wrath of existing companies.

However, a market can be too large. A multi-billion-dollar market may be too mature and stable, and such a level of certainty can translate into competition from Fortune 500 firms and, if highly competitive, into lower margins and profitability. Further, an unknown market or one that is less than $10 million in sales also is unattractive. To understand the disadvantages of a large, more mature market consider the entry of a firm into the microcomputer industry today versus the entry of Apple into that market in 1975.

GROWTH RATE An attractive market is large and growing (i.e., one where capturing a good share of the increase is less threatening to competitors and where a small market share can represent significant and increasing sales volume). An annual growth rate of 30 to 50 percent creates niches for new entrants, and such a market is a thriving and expansive one, rather than a stable or contracting one, where competitors are scrambling for the same niches. Thus, for example, a $100-million market growing at 50 percent per year has the potential to become a $1-billion industry in a few years, and if a new venture can capture just 2 percent of sales in the first year, it can attain sales in the first year of $1 million. If it just maintains its market share over the next few years, sales will grow significantly.

MARKET CAPACITY Another signal of the existence of an opportunity in a market is a market at full capacity in a growth situation—in other words, a demand that the existing suppliers cannot meet. Timing is of vital concern in such a situation, which means the entrepreneur should be asking: Can a new entrant fill that demand before the other players can decide to and then actually increase capacity?

MARKET SHARE ATTAINABLE The potential to be a leader in the market and capture at least a 20-percent share can create a high value for a company that might otherwise be worth not much more than book value. For example, one such firm, with less than $15 million in sales, became dominant in its small market niche with a 70-percent market share. The company was acquired for $23 million in cash.

A firm that will be able to capture less than 5 percent of a market is unattractive in the eyes of most investors seeking a higher potential company.

COST STRUCTURE A firm that can become the low-cost provider is attractive, but a firm that continually faces declining cost conditions is less so. Attractive opportunities exist in industries where economies of scale are insignificant (or work to the advantage of the new venture). Attractive opportunities boast of low costs of learning by doing. Where costs per unit are high when small amounts of the product are sold, existing firms that have low promotion costs can face attractive market opportunities.

For instance, consider the operating leverage of Johnsonville Sausage. Its variable costs were 6 percent labour and 94 percent materials. What aggressive incentives could management put in place for the 6 percent to manage and to control the 94 percent? Imagine the disasters that would occur if the scenario were reversed!

A word of caution from Scott Kunkel and Charles Hofer, who observed:

Overall, industry structure...had a much smaller impact on new venture performance than has previously been suggested in the literature. This finding could be the result of one of several possibilities:

1. Industry structure impacts the performance of established firms, but does NOT have a significant impact on new venture performance.

2. The most important industry structural variables influencing new ventures are different from those which impact established firms and thus research has yet to identify the industry structural variables that are most important in the new venture environment.

3. Industry structure does NOT have a significant DIRECT impact on firm performance, as expected. Instead, the impact of industry structure is strongly mitigated by other factors, including the strategy selected for entry.[28]

ECONOMICS

PROFITS AFTER TAX High and durable gross margins usually translate into strong and durable after-tax profits. Attractive opportunities have potential for durable profits of at least 10 to 15 percent and often 20 percent or more. Those generating after-tax profits of less than 5 percent are quite fragile.

TIME TO BREAKEVEN AND POSITIVE CASH FLOW As mentioned above, breakeven and positive cash flow for attractive companies are possible within two years. Once the time to breakeven and positive cash flow is greater than three years, the attractiveness of the opportunity diminishes accordingly.

RETURN ON INVESTMENT POTENTIAL An important corollary to forgiving economics is reward. Very attractive opportunities have the potential to yield a return on investment of 25 percent or more per year. During the 1980s, many venture capital funds achieved only single-digit returns on investment. High and durable gross margins and high and durable after-tax profits usually yield high earnings per share and high return on shareholders' equity, thus generating a satisfactory "harvest" price for a company. This is most likely true whether the company is sold through an initial public offering or privately, or whether it is acquired. Given the risk typically involved, a return on investment potential of less than 15 to 20 percent per year is unattractive.

CAPITAL REQUIREMENTS Ventures that can be funded and have capital requirements that are low to moderate are attractive. Realistically, most higher potential businesses need significant amounts of cash—several hundred thousand dollars and up—to get started. Businesses that can be started with little or no capital are rare, but they do exist. In today's venture capital market, the first round of financing is typically $1 to $2 million or more for a start-up.[29] Some higher potential ventures, such as those in the service sector or "cash sales" businesses, have lower capital requirements than do technology-intensive firms with large research and development expenditures.

If the venture needs too much money or cannot be funded, it is unattractive. An extreme example is a venture that a team of students proposed to repair satellites. The students believed that the required start-up capital was in the $50 to $200 million range. Projects of this magnitude are in the domain of the government and large multinational corporation, rather than that of the entrepreneur and the venture capitalist. Think Richard Branson of Virgin Galactic launching commercial space flights!

INTERNAL RATE OF RETURN POTENTIAL Is the risk–reward relationship attractive enough? The response to this question can be quite personal, but the most attractive opportunities often have the promise of—and deliver on—a very substantial upside of 5 to 10 times the original investment in 5 to 10 years. Of course, the extraordinary successes can yield 50 to 100 times or more, but these are exceptions. A 25 percent or greater annual compound rate of return is considered very healthy. In economically stable times, those investments considered basically risk free have yields of 3 to 8 percent.

FREE CASH FLOW CHARACTERISTICS Free cash flow is a way of understanding a number of crucial financial dimensions of any business: the robustness of its economics; its capital requirements, both working and fixed assets; its capacity to service external debt and equity claims; and its capacity to sustain growth.[30] We define unleveraged free cash flow (FCF) as earnings before interest but after taxes (EBIAT) *plus* amortization (A) and depreciation (D) *less* spontaneous working capital requirements (WC) *less* capital expenditures (CAPex), or FCF = EBIAT + [A+D] − [+ or − WC] − CAPex. EBIAT is driven by sales, profitability, and asset intensity. Low-asset-intensive, high-margin businesses generate the highest profits and sustainable growth.[31] We will explore this in detail in chapter 9 "Financing the Venture."

GROSS MARGINS The potential for high and durable gross margins (i.e., the unit selling price less all direct and variable costs) is important. Gross margins exceeding 40 to 50 percent provide a tremendous built-in cushion that allows for more error and more flexibility to learn from mistakes than do gross margins of 20 percent or less. High and durable gross margins, in turn, mean that a venture can reach breakeven earlier, preferably within the first two years. Thus, for example, if gross margins are just 20 percent, for every $1 increase in fixed costs (e.g., insurance, salaries, rent, and utilities), sales need to increase $5 just to stay even. If gross margins are 75 percent, however, a $1 increase in fixed costs requires a sales increase of just $1.33. One entrepreneur, who built the international division of an emerging software company to $17 million in highly profitable sales in just five years (when he was 25 years old), offers an example of the cushion provided by high and durable gross margins. He stresses there is simply no substitute for outrageous gross margins by saying, "It allows you to make all kinds of mistakes that would kill a normal company. And we made them all. But our high gross margins covered all the learning tuition and still left a good profit."[32] Gross margins of less than 20 percent, particularly if they are fragile, are unattractive.

TIME TO BREAKEVEN—CASH FLOW AND PROFIT AND LOSS (P&L) New businesses that can quickly achieve a positive cash flow and become self-sustaining are highly desirable. It is often the second year before this is possible, but the sooner the better. Obviously, simply having a longer window does not mean the business will be lousy. Two great companies illustrate that a higher potential business can have a longer window. Pilkington Brothers, an English firm that developed plate glass technology, ran huge losses for over two and a half years before it was regarded as a great company. Similarly, Federal Express went through an early period of enormous negative cash flows of $1 million a month. More recently, auto giant General Motors managed $3.6 billion in negative cash flow for the second quarter of 2008 before turning around and posting a $4.9 billion profit in 2012.

HARVEST ISSUES

VALUE-ADDED POTENTIAL New ventures that are based on strategic value in an industry, such as valuable technology, are attractive, while those with low or no strategic value are less attractive. For example, most observers contend that technology services capacity of compelling strategic value to HP was acquired when it purchased EDS for $13.9 billion in 2008, whereas the merger with Compaq was of less strategic value. "In Compaq, HP grabbed more of what it already had;" with EDS, HP was getting something new.[33] Opportunities with extremely large capital commitments, whose value on exit can be severely eroded by unanticipated circumstances, are less attractive.

Thus, one characteristic of businesses that command a premium price is that they have high value-added strategic importance to their acquirer, such as distribution, customer base, geographic coverage, proprietary technology, contractual rights, and the like. Such companies might be valued at four, five, or even six times (or more) last year's sales, whereas perhaps 60 to 80 percent of companies might be purchased at 0.75 to 1.25 times sales.

VALUATION MULTIPLES AND COMPARABLES Consistent with the above point, there is a large spread in the value the capital markets place on private and public companies. Part of your analysis is to identify some historical boundaries for valuations placed on companies in the market/industry/technology area you intend to pursue. The rules outlined in Exhibit 3.7 are variable and should be thought of as a boundary and a point of departure.

EXIT MECHANISM AND STRATEGY Businesses that are eventually sold—privately or to the public—usually are started and grown with a harvest objective in mind. Whether put up for sale or approached by a buyer, attractive companies that realize capital gains from the sale of their businesses have, or envision, a harvest or exit mechanism. Unattractive opportunities do not have an exit mechanism in mind. Planning is critical because, as is often said, it is much harder to get out of a business than to get into it. Giving some serious thought to the options and likelihood that the company can eventually be harvested is an important initial and ongoing aspect of the entrepreneurial process.

CAPITAL MARKET CONTEXT The context in which the sale or acquisition of the company occurs is largely driven by the capital markets at that particular time. Timing can be a critical component of the exit mechanism because, as one study indicated, since World War II, the average bull market on Bay Street has lasted five and a half years, adding from 82 to 266 percent to the market's value and the average bull/bear cycle has been just over six years.[34] "Over the last half century, the average bear market has lasted 12 months. The shortest—four months between August and November 1987—included the Toronto market's biggest one-day crash. Bay Street shares lost 22 percent of their value on Monday, October 19. But that bear market ushered in the longest bull market in the exchange's history. The bulls ran for almost 10½ years, resulting in an overall return of 247 per cent." For a keener appreciation of the critical difference the capital markets can make, one only has to recall such stock market events or even a bank credit crunch. Initial public offerings are especially vulnerable to the vicissitudes of the capital markets; here the timing is vital. Some of the most successful companies seem to have been launched when debt and equity capital were most available and relatively cheap.

COMPETITIVE ADVANTAGES ISSUES

VARIABLE AND FIXED COSTS An attractive opportunity has the potential for being the lowest-cost producer and for having the lowest marketing and distribution costs. For example, Bowmar was unable to remain competitive in the market for electronic calculators after the producers of large-scale integrated circuits, such as Hewlett-Packard, entered the business. Being unable to achieve and sustain a position as a low-cost producer shortens the life expectancy of a new venture.

DEGREE OF CONTROL Attractive opportunities have potential for moderate-to-strong degree of control over prices, costs, and channels of distribution. Fragmented markets where there is no dominant competitor—no Rogers, Shaw, or Vidéotron—have this potential. These markets usually have a market leader with a 20-percent market share *or less*. For example, sole control of the source of supply of a critical component for a product or of channels of distribution can give a new venture market dominance even if other areas are weak.

Lack of control over such factors as product development and component prices can make an opportunity unattractive. For example, if a young enterprise's supplier is unable to produce inputs needed at low enough prices or high enough quantities that young enterprise is vulnerable. Maintaining control is a key factor in determining a venture's fate.

A market where a major competitor has a market share of 40 percent or more usually implies a market where power and influence over suppliers, customers, and pricing create a serious barrier and risk for a new firm. Such a firm will have few degrees of freedom. However, if a dominant competitor is at full capacity, is slow to innovate or to add capacity in a large and growing market, or routinely ignores or abuses the customer (Bell Canada is a frequent example), there may be an entry opportunity. However, entrepreneurs usually do not find such sleepy competition in dynamic, emerging industries dense with opportunity.

ENTRY BARRIERS Having a favourable window of opportunity is important. Having or being able to gain proprietary protection, regulatory advantage, or other legal or contractual advantage, such as exclusive rights to a market or with a distributor, is attractive. Having or being able to gain an advantage in response/lead times is important because these can create barriers to entry or expansion by others. For example, advantages in response/lead times in technology, product innovation, market innovation, people, location, resources, or capacity make an opportunity attractive. Possession of well-developed, high-quality, accessible contacts that are the product of years of building a top-notch reputation and that cannot be acquired quickly is also advantageous. Sometimes this competitive advantage may be so strong as to provide dominance in the marketplace, even though many of the other factors are weak or average. An example of how quickly the joys of start-up may fade if others cannot be kept out is the experience of firms in the hard disk industry that were unable to erect entry barriers into the market in the early to mid-1980s. During this period, nearly 100 hard disk drive companies were launched and severe price competition led to a major industry shakeout.

If a firm cannot keep others out or if it faces already existing entry barriers, it is unattractive. An easily overlooked issue is a firm's capacity to gain distribution of its product. As simple as it may sound, even venture-capital-backed companies fall victim to this market issue. Air Florida apparently assembled all the right ingredients, including substantial financing, yet was unable to secure sufficient gate space for its airplanes. Even though it sold passenger seats, it had no place to pick the passengers up or drop them off!

VENTURE TEAM ISSUES

ENTREPRENEURIAL TEAM Attractive opportunities have existing teams that are strong and contain industry superstars. The team has proven profit and loss experience in the same technology, market, and service area, and members have complementary and compatible skills. An unattractive opportunity does not have such a team in place or has no team.

INDUSTRY AND TECHNICAL EXPERIENCE A leadership record of significant accomplishment in the industry, with the technology, and in the market area, with a proven profit and lots of achievements where the venture will compete is highly desirable. A top-notch executive team can become the most important strategic competitive advantage in an industry. Imagine relocating the Chicago Bulls or the Phoenix Suns to Halifax, Nova Scotia. Do you think you would have a winning competitor in the National Basketball Association?

INTEGRITY Trust and integrity are the oil and glue that make economic interdependence possible. Having an unquestioned reputation in this regard is a major long-term advantage for entrepreneurs and should be sought in all personnel and backers. A shady past or record of questionable integrity is for B team players only.

INTELLECTUAL HONESTY There is a fundamental issue of whether the founders know what they do and do not know, as well as whether they know what to do about shortcomings or gaps in the team and the enterprise.

FATAL-FLAW ISSUES Attractive ventures have no fatal flaws; an opportunity is rendered unattractive if it suffers from one or more fatal flaws. Usually, these relate to one of the above criteria, and examples abound of markets that are too small, that have overpowering competition, where the cost of entry is too high, where an entrant is unable to produce at a competitive price, and so on. An example of a fatal-flaw entry barrier is experience. Linda Collier, former Canadian Woman Entrepreneur of the Year, president and CEO of Tri-ad International Freight Forwarding (i.e., air, sea, land) was doing "brisk business" and wanted to expand. She "hired a vice-president to assist with that task. Eight months later, he launched a rival company, taking five Tri-ad employees with him." Fortunately for Collier, the VP had a fatal flaw: inexperience. "This industry is easy to get into. To stay and grow in it is completely different." Within six months, his business was bankrupt. This incident with her VP was the second of four tries her employees have made to come after her business. "I must make it look easy," Collier jokes. She has since put multiple measures in place to protect databases, customer profiles, service rates, and noncompete agreements to stymie staff from becoming competitors.[35]

PERSONAL CRITERIA

GOALS AND FIT Is there a good match between the requirements of business and what the founders want out of it? The crux of this is contained in the adage: "Success is *getting* what you want. Happiness is wanting what you get."

UPSIDE/DOWNSIDE ISSUES An attractive opportunity does not have excessive downside risk. The upside and the downside of pursuing an opportunity are not linear, nor are they on the same continuum. The upside is easy, and it has been said that success has a thousand sires. The downside is another matter; it has also been said that failure is an orphan. An entrepreneur needs to be able to absorb the financial downside in such a way that he or she can rebound without becoming indentured to debt obligations. If an entrepreneur's financial exposure in launching the venture is greater than his or her net worth—the resources he or she can reasonably draw upon, and his or her alternative disposable earnings stream if it does not work out—the deal may be too big. While today's bankruptcy laws are generous, the psychological burdens of living through such an ordeal are infinitely more painful than the financial consequences. An existing business needs to consider if a failure will be too demeaning to the firm's reputation and future credibility, aside from the obvious financial consequences.[36]

OPPORTUNITY COST In pursuing any venture opportunity, there are also opportunity costs. An entrepreneur who is skilled enough to grow a successful, multi-million-dollar venture has talents that are highly valued by medium- to large-size firms as well. While assessing benefits that may accrue in pursuing an opportunity, an entrepreneur needs to heed other alternatives, including potential "golden handcuffs," and account honestly for any cut in salary that may be involved in pursuing a certain opportunity.

Further, pursuing an opportunity can shape an entrepreneur in ways that are hard to imagine. An entrepreneur will probably have time to execute between two and four multi-million-dollar ventures between the ages of 25 and 50. Each of these experiences will position him or her, *for better or for worse*, for the next opportunity. Since an entrepreneur in the early years needs to gain relevant experience and since building a venture (either one that works or one that does not) takes more time than is commonly believed, it is important to consider alternatives while assessing an opportunity.

DESIRABILITY A good opportunity is not only attractive but also desirable (i.e., good opportunity fits). An intensely personal criterion would be the desire for a certain lifestyle. This desire may preclude pursuing certain opportunities that may be excellent for someone else. The founders of new start-ups take time to consider the location of their work. Often that decision is based on a telephone area code, favourite mountain bike trail, or a host of other social, cultural, and demographic characteristics of a city or region. Richard Florida, of the University of Toronto, delivered a keynote address in Saint John, New Brunswick.[37] Florida, drawing on his book *Who's Your City?*, highlights that the creative economy is making the place where you live the most important decision of your life. Place is not only important, it is more important than ever. Place is becoming more relevant to our individual lives. Where to live is not an arbitrary choice.

The Canadian Institute for Rural Entrepreneurship asserts, "The new rural entrepreneur is bold, innovative, and connected." For the rural new venture, collaboration is a key element; communication of best practices and borrowing what works elsewhere contribute to competitiveness. Clusters, networks, and critical mass may be necessary for commercial longevity—reaching a minimum threshold increases the odds of survival. Time is a critical ingredient as well. It takes time to establish a rural enterprise and gain momentum. Putting a place or product on the map does not happen quickly. The process should be purposefully driven, with clear goals and objectives in mind. Listening to needs, motives, and expectations is important for any business, but in a rural or remote setting even more so.[38]

RISK/REWARD TOLERANCE Successful entrepreneurs take calculated risks or avoid risks they do not need to take. This is not to suggest that all entrepreneurs are gamblers or have the same risk tolerance; some are quite conservative while others actually seem to get a kick out of the inherent danger and thrill in higher risk and higher stake games. The issue is fit—recognizing that gamblers and overly risk-averse entrepreneurs are unlikely to sustain any long-term successes.

STRESS TOLERANCE Another important dimension of the fit concept is the stressful requirements of a fast-growth, high-stakes venture. But having to keep up may not be the sole reason for stress. One investigation of the 62 serial entrepreneurs in the 2007 Profit 100 found that the initial start-up stage was the most stressful time.[39] Brik Eksten of Markham, Ontario-based Digital Rapids Corp., which helps TV and film producers place content on the Internet, notes that things get easier the more ventures you have under your belt: Eksten went from "only the worried survive" to "there will always be setbacks. Eventually, you become accustomed to a certain level of bombardment." A 2008 study published in the *Journal of Business Venturing* revealed that thinking and planning for the future may reduce the stress an entrepreneur faces.[40]

STRATEGIC DIFFERENTIATION

DEGREE OF FIT To what extent is there a good fit among the driving forces (founders and team, opportunity, and resource requirements) and the timing given the external environment?

TEAM There is no substitute for an absolutely top-quality team. The execution of and the ability to adapt and to devise constantly new strategies are vital to survival and success. A team is nearly unstoppable if it can inculcate into the venture a philosophy and culture of superior learning, as well as teaching skills, an ethic of high standards, delivery of results, and constant improvement. Are those who are able to pursue the opportunity free agents—clear of employment, noncompete, proprietary rights, and trade secret agreements?

SERVICE MANAGEMENT Research was conducted with several hundred companies across a wide range of industries to determine why customers stopped buying these companies' products. The results were surprising: 15 percent of the customers defected because of quality and 70 percent stopped using a product or service because of bad customer service. Having a "turbo-service" concept that can be delivered consistently can be a major competitive weapon against small and large competitors alike. Home Depot, in the home supply business, and Lexus, in the auto industry, have set an entirely new standard of service for their respective industries. Studies have also shown that service recovery is an important ingredient. When things do go wrong, what transpires to "recover" can be crucial: We're sorry your meal is late, how can we make it up to you? We apologize for overbooking, how can we make this right? A loyal customer is worth a lot. Customer relations can be managed and the best individuals and organizations have learned how to keep customers loyal.

TIMING From business to historic military battles to political campaigns, timing is often the one element that can make a significant difference. Time can be an enemy or a friend; being too early or too late can be fatal. The key is to row with the tide, not against it. Strategically, ignoring this principle is perilous.

TECHNOLOGY A breakthrough, proprietary product is no guarantee of success, but it creates a formidable competitive advantage (see Exhibit 3.8).

FLEXIBILITY Maintaining the capacity to commit and uncommit quickly, to adapt, and to abandon if necessary is a major strategic weapon, particularly when competing with larger organizations. Larger firms can typically take six years or more to change basic strategy and 10 to 20 years or more to change the culture.

OPPORTUNITY ORIENTATION To what extent is there a constant alertness to the marketplace? A continual search for opportunities? As one insightful entrepreneur put it, "Any opportunity that just comes in the door to us, we do not consider an opportunity. And we do not have a strategy until we are saying no to lots of opportunities."

EXHIBIT 3.8	CANADIAN INVENTIONS IN THE 20TH CENTURY
Hydrofoil boat	Alexander Bell and Casey Baldwin (1908)
Jolly Jumper	Olivia Pool (1910)
Variable pitch propeller	Wallace Turnbull (1918)
Ski-Doo	Armand Bombardier (1922)
Snowblower	Arthur Sicard (1925)
Quartz clock	Warren Marrison (1927)
Pablum	Alan Brown, Theodore Drake, and Frederick Tisdall (1930)
Plexiglass	William Chalmers (1931)
Scanning electron microscope	James Hillier and Albert Prebus (1939)
Paint roller	Norman Breakey (1940)
Walkie-talkie	Donald L. Hings (1942)
Garbage bag	Harry Wasylyk and Larry Hansen (1950)
Electric wheelchair	George Klein (1952)
Alkaline battery	Lewis Urry (1959)
Wonderbra	Louise Poirier (1964)
IMAX	Grahame Ferguson, Roman Kroitor, and Robert Kerr (1968)
UV degradable plastics	James Guillet (1971)
Computerized braille	Roland Galarneau (1972)
Digital film colourization	Wilson Markle and Brian Hunt (1983)
Abdominizer	Dennis Colonello (1984)
Newt suit	Phil Nuytten (1987)
CPR mannequin	Diane Croteau and Richard Brault (1989)
Infant stretcher	Wendy Murphy (1990)
Closed-chest surgery	Douglas Boyd (1999)
Electric dicycle	Ben Gulak (2006)

ENTREPRENEURS ACROSS CANADA
Loughati.com

THE FOUNDERS AT SHOW YOUR LOVE TO ARABIC LANGUAGE, THE LAUNCH EVENT FOR LOUGHATI.COM.

Going live in 2013, "Loughati.com is a startup e-commerce company based in Canada, and provides shipment to the USA and worldwide." It claims to be the largest online Arabic bookstore for kids and offers books, DVDs, and educational toys for children from birth to age 16. A launch party was held in late January 2013 at BEIT Zatoun, a culture and art venue located in Toronto. Loughati.com seeks to serve as a point of dialogue and greater understanding between Arab and Israeli interests.

Questions: With or without competition, what will determine whether Loughati.com is successful? How can it best build and maintain interest in its product offerings?

PRICING One common mistake of new companies with high-value-added products or services in a growing market is to underprice. A price that is slightly below to as much as 20 percent below competitors is rationalized as necessary to gain market entry. In a 30-percent gross margin business, a 10-percent price increase results in a 20- to 36-percent increase in gross margin and will lower the breakeven sales level for a company with $900 000 in fixed costs to $2.5 million from $3 million. At the $3-million sales level, the company would realize an extra $180 000 in pre-tax profits.

DISTRIBUTION CHANNELS Having access to the distribution channels is sometimes overlooked or taken for granted. New channels of distribution can leapfrog and demolish traditional channels.[41] Some examples include direct mail, home shopping networks, infomercials, the World Wide Web, and the coming revolution in interactive television in your own home.

ROOM FOR ERROR How forgiving is the business and the financial strategy? How wrong can the team be in estimates of revenue costs, cash flow, timing, and capital requirements? How bad can things get, yet be able to survive? If some single-engine planes are more prone to accidents, by 10 or more times, in which plane do you want to fly? Higher leverage, lower gross margins, and lower operating margins are the signals in a small company of flights destined for fatality.

GATHERING INFORMATION

FINDING IDEAS

Finding a potential opportunity is most often a matter of being the right person, in the right place, at the right time. Certainly past experience and industry exposure can help, but one also has to be tuned in and astutely listening. Creativity again plays a role in sense-making and generating connections to make mental leaps. Ben Gulak's latest project is the DTV Shredder. The Oakville, Ontario, native was forced to pivot quickly when it became clear that regulatory hurdles would prevent success of his earlier idea—a vehicle that Dragon's Den angel investors committed $1.25 million to see to fruition.[42] How can you increase your chances of being the next young retiree or at least on the path to success like:

- April Glavine of Lean Machine Inc., which offers healthy vending machines with nutritious snacks and beverages.
- Monica Mei of Aime, WhatImWear.in, and The Shop Society, who developed a fashion label, a mobile app for trendsetters, and a mobile app that helps retailers form a personalized connection with their customers.
- Cassandra Rush of Sassy Cassy's Boots, who handles design and manufacturing of her boots that come in various calf sizes.
- Lauren Friese of TalentEgg, a web portal aiming to match college and university students and recent graduates with employers and career resources.
- Lisa Donaldson of Fiddleheads Kids Shop Inc., which provides confidence to new parents shopping for an assortment of baby products and toys.
- Lisa von Sturmer of Growing City, which provides composting for offices and businesses.

Numerous sources of information can help generate ideas.

Existing Businesses

Purchasing an ongoing business is an excellent way to find a new business idea. Such a route to a new venture can save time and money and can reduce risk as well. Investment bankers and business brokers are knowledgeable about businesses for sale, as are trust officers. However, brokers do not advertise the very best private businesses for sale, and the real gems are usually bought by the individuals or firms closest to them, such as management, directors, customers, suppliers, or financial backers. Bankruptcy judges have a continual flow of ventures in serious trouble. Excellent opportunities may be buried beneath all the financial debris of a bankrupt firm.

Franchises

Franchising is another way to enter an industry, by either starting a franchise operation or becoming a franchisee. This is a fertile area. The number of franchisors nationally stands at more than 500, according to the Canadian Franchise Association and franchisors account for well over $100 billion in sales annually and approximately one-fifth of all retail sales. See chapter 13 "Franchising" for a more complete discussion of franchises, including resource information.

Patents

Patent brokers specialize in marketing patents that are owned by individual inventors, corporations, universities, or other research organizations to those seeking new commercially viable products. Some brokers specialize in international product licensing, and occasionally a patent broker will purchase an invention and then resell it. Although a few unscrupulous brokers have tarnished the patent broker's image, over the years acquisitions effected by reputable brokers have resulted in significant new products. For example, Bausch & Lomb acquired, through the National Patent Development Corporation, the rights to hydron, a material used in contact lenses.

Product Licensing

A good way to obtain exposure to many product ideas available from universities, corporations, and independent investors is to check out Canada Business Network, www.canadabusiness.ca, which provides government services for entrepreneurs. Their web page on product licensing covers both licensing your intellectual property and licensing someone else's product. The Intellectual Property Institute of Canada, www.ipic.ca, is another source of useful information, as is the Canada/Manitoba Business Service Centre. INPEX (an invention and new product exposition) is an annual showcase of inventions, new products, and innovations that are available to license, market, or manufacture.

CORPORATIONS Corporations engaged in R&D often develop inventions or services that they do not exploit commercially. These inventions either do not fit existing product lines or marketing programs or do not represent sufficiently large markets to be interesting to major corporations. A good number of such corporations license these kinds of inventions, either through patent brokers, product-licensing information services, or their own patent-marketing efforts. Directly contacting a corporation with a licensing program may prove fruitful. Many large corporations have active internal patent-marketing efforts. *Fast Company* magazine annually lists their pick of the 50 most innovative companies, which is a helpful resource.

NOT-FOR-PROFIT RESEARCH INSTITUTES These non-profit organizations undertake R&D under contract to the government and private industry as well as some internally sponsored investigation of new products and processes that can be licensed to private corporations for further development, manufacturing, and marketing. One example of how this works is Battelle Memorial Institute's participation in the development of xerography and the subsequent license of the technology to the Haloid Corporation, now Xerox Corporation. Canada's National Research Council (NRC) is composed of over 20 institutes with active licensing programs.

UNIVERSITIES A number of universities are active in research in the physical sciences and seek to license inventions that result from this research either directly or through an associated research foundation that administers its patent program. Many universities publish periodic reports containing abstracts of inventions they own that are available for licensing. In addition, since a number of very good ideas developed in universities never reach formal licensing outlets, another way to find these ideas is to become familiar with the work of researchers in your area of interest. The website Futurity.org is a clearinghouse of the latest discoveries by scientists coming out of research universities in the United States, United Kingdom, Canada, and Australia.

INDUSTRY AND TRADE CONTACTS

TRADE SHOWS AND ASSOCIATION MEETINGS In some industries, trade shows and association meetings can be an excellent way to examine the products of many potential competitors, meet distributors and sales representatives, learn of product and market trends, and identify potential products. The Canadian Photonics Consortium is a good example of an association that holds such seminars and meetings.

CUSTOMERS Contacting potential customers of a certain type of product can identify a need and where existing products might be deficient or inadequate. For example, discussions with doctors who head medical services at hospitals might lead to product ideas in the biomedical equipment business.

DISTRIBUTORS AND WHOLESALERS Contacting people who distribute a certain type of product can yield extensive information about the strengths and weaknesses of existing products and the kinds of product improvements and new products that are needed by customers.

COMPETITORS Examining products offered by companies competing in an industry can show whether an existing design is protected by patent and whether it can be improved or imitated.

FORMER EMPLOYERS A number of businesses are started with products or services, or both, based on technology and ideas developed by entrepreneurs while others employed them. In some cases, research laboratories were not interested in commercial exploitation of technology, or the previous employer was not interested in the ideas for new products and the rights were given up or sold. In others, the ideas were developed under government contract and were in the public domain. In addition, some companies will help entrepreneurs set up companies in return for equity. Nortel Networks did this repeatedly.

PROFESSIONAL CONTACT Ideas can be found by contacting such professionals as patent agents, accountants, commercial bankers, and venture capitalists who encounter those seeking to license patents or to start a business using patented products or processes.

CONSULTING Another method for obtaining ideas that has been successful for technically trained entrepreneurs is to provide consulting and one-of-a-kind engineering designs for people in fields of interest. For example, an entrepreneur wanting to establish a medical equipment company can consult or can design experimental equipment for medical researchers. These kinds of activities often lead to prototypes that can be turned into products needed by a number of researchers. For example, this approach was used in establishing a company to produce psychological testing equipment that evolved from consulting done at a hospital. In another instance, the design and manufacture of oceanographic instruments came out of consulting done for an oceanographic institute.

NETWORKING Social networks can be a stimulant and source of new ideas, as well as a source of valuable contacts with people. Much of this requires personal initiative on an informal basis, but around the country, organized networks can facilitate and accelerate the process of making contacts and finding new business ideas. The Digital Moose Lounge is a network for Canadian expatriates living in Silicon Valley and greater San Francisco Bay area. TiE (The Indus Entrepreneurs) is another such organization; from its genesis in Silicon Valley, it has grown to over 50 chapters in a dozen countries. Outside of Canada, most Canadian embassies and consulates organize Terry Fox Runs—a great chance to meet up with fellow Canadians.

SHAPING YOUR OPPORTUNITY

You will need to invest in thorough research to shape your idea into an opportunity. *Data available about market characteristics, competitors, and so on, are frequently inversely related to the real potential of an opportunity*; that is, if market data are readily available and if the data clearly show significant potential, then a large number of competitors will enter the market and the opportunity will diminish. Industry Canada, www.ic.gc.ca, provides "small business profiles"—essentially, revenue, expense, and balance sheet data, as well as financial ratios for businesses with sales between $30 000 and $5 000 000. It is a great way to see the financial profiles of businesses by industry. Their SME Benchmarking Tool can be used to check out competition before entering a market and periodically as a comparison with competitors after market entry.

The good news: Most data will be incomplete, inaccurate, and contradictory, and their meaning will be ambiguous. For entrepreneurs, gathering the necessary information, seeing possibilities, and making linkages where others see only chaos is essential.

Jonathan Calof, director of the Canadian Institute of Competitive Intelligence, defines competitor intelligence as specific and timely information about a business adversary. Even in emerging industries, finding out about competitors' sales plans, key elements of their corporate strategies, the capacity of their plants and the technology used in them, who their principal suppliers and customers are, and what new products rivals have under development is difficult, but not impossible.[43]

Using published resources is one source of such information. Interviewing people and analyzing data are also critical. Leonard Fuld believes that because business transactions generate information, which flows into the public domain, one can locate intelligence sources by understanding the transaction and how intelligence behaves and flows.[44]

This can be done legally and ethically. There are, of course, less-than-ethical (not to mention illegal) tactics, which include conducting phony job interviews, getting customers to put out phony bid requests, and lying, cheating, and stealing. Entrepreneurs need to be careful to avoid such practices and are advised to consult legal counsel when in doubt.

The information sources provided below are just a small start. Creativity, work, and analysis will be involved to find intelligence and to extend the information obtained into useful form. For example, a competitor's income statement and balance sheet will rarely be handed out. Rather, this information must be derived from information in public filings or news articles or from credit reports, financial ratios, and interviews, many of which are available on the Internet.[45]

PUBLISHED SOURCES

The first step is a complete search of materials in libraries and on the Internet. You can find a huge amount of published information, databases, and other sources about industries, markets, competitors, and personnel. Some of this information will have been uncovered when you search for ideas. Listed below are additional sources that should help get you started.

GUIDES AND COMPANY INFORMATION

Valuable information is available in special issues and the websites of *Business 2.0*, *Canadian Business*, *INC.*, *Fast Company*, *Mercury News*, and *Fortune*.

ADDITIONAL SOURCES OF INTELLIGENCE

Not everything entrepreneurs need to know will be found in libraries because this information needs to be highly specific and current. This information is most likely available from people—industry experts, suppliers, and the like. Summarized below are some useful sources of intelligence.

TRADE ASSOCIATIONS Trade associations, especially the editors of their publications and information officers, are good sources of information. Trade shows and conferences are prime places to discover the latest activities of competitors.[46]

EMPLOYEES Employees who have left a competitor's company can often provide information about the competitor, especially if the employee departed on bad terms. In addition, a firm can hire people away from a competitor. While consideration of ethics in this situation is very important, the number of experienced people in any industry is limited, and competitors must prove that a company hired a person intentionally to get specific trade secrets to challenge any hiring legally. Students who have worked for competitors are another source of information.

CONSULTING FIRMS Consulting firms frequently conduct industry studies and then make this information available. Frequently, in such fields as computers or software, competitors use the same design consultants, and these consultants can be sources of information.

MARKET RESEARCH FIRMS Firms doing market studies, such as those listed under published sources above, can be sources of intelligence.

KEY CUSTOMERS, MANUFACTURERS, SUPPLIERS, DISTRIBUTORS, AND BUYERS These groups are often a prime source of information.

PUBLIC FILINGS Federal, provincial, and local filings, such as with the Canadian Securities Administrators, Canadian Intellectual Property Office, or Access to Information Act, can reveal a surprising amount of information. There are companies that process inquiries of this type.

REVERSE ENGINEERING Reverse engineering can be used to determine costs of production and sometimes even manufacturing methods. An example of this practice is the experience of Advanced Energy Technology, which learned firsthand about such tactics. No sooner had it announced a new product, which was patented, when it received 50 orders, half of which were from competitors asking for only one or two of the items.

NETWORKS The networks mentioned in chapter 2 as sources of new venture ideas also can be sources of competitor intelligence.

OTHER Classified ads, buyers guides, labour unions, real estate agents, courts, local reporters, and so on, can all provide clues.[47]

INTERNET IMPACT: RESEARCH AND LEARNING

The Internet has become an important resource for entrepreneurial research and opportunity exploration. The rapid growth of data sources, websites, sophisticated search engines, and consumer response forums allows for up-to-date investigations of business ideas, competitive environments, and value chain resources.

Google is currently the top search engine in the world, and yet it is not popular in the Czech Republic, China, Japan, Russia, and South Korea. One of the reasons for Google's success is its increasingly deep and wide platform of tools. Google offers the means to view, for example, the text of patents and scholarly publications, archives of news stories, and blogs on hundreds of subjects.

As virtual communities of people who share a common interest or passion, blogs can be a tremendously valuable resource of insights and perspectives on potential opportunities. Proactive, low- or no-cost research can also be conducted with emailed questionnaires or by directing potential subjects to a basic website set up to collect responses. In addition, the Internet provides entrepreneurs and other proactive searchers with the extraordinary capability to tap wisdom and advice from experts on virtually anything—anywhere in the world.

SCREENING VENTURE OPPORTUNITIES

Time is the ultimate ally and enemy of the entrepreneur. The harsh reality is that you will not have enough time in a quarter, a year, or a decade to pursue all the ideas for businesses you and your team can think of. Perhaps the cruelest part of the paradox is that you have to find and make the time for the good ones. To complicate the paradox, you do not have a strategy until you are saying no to lots of opportunities! This demand is part of the both punishing and rewarding Darwinian aspect of entrepreneurship: Many will try, many will fail, some will succeed, and a few will excel. While the number of new enterprises launched in Canada can vary widely from year to year, only a small percentage of those will ever prove to be opportunities that achieve sales of $1 million or more. Many live by the creed: "Go big or go home!" and feel being bold is critical to being noticed. Studies show that those who are outspoken are rewarded more.

QUICKSCREEN

If most sophisticated private equity investors and venture capitalists invest in only 2 to 3 out of 100 ideas, then one can see how important it is to focus on a few superior ideas. The ability to reject ideas quickly and efficiently is an important entrepreneurial mindset. To make the struggle more manageable, two methodologies are provided on Connect. The first, QuickScreen, should enable you to conduct a preliminary review and evaluation of an idea in an hour. Unless the idea has been, or you are confident it can be, moulded and shaped so that it has the four anchors, you will waste a lot of time on a lower-potential idea.

VENTURE OPPORTUNITY SCREENING EXERCISES (VOSE)

The second methodology, the Venture Opportunity Screening Exercises, is also located on Connect. These exercises are designed to segment the screening of ideas into manageable pieces. The QuickScreen provides a broad overview of an idea's potential. In a team effort, each member of the team should complete the exercise separately and then meet as a team to merge the results. After each VOSE, you should revisit the QuickScreen and reevaluate your scoring.

LEARNING OBJECTIVES SUMMARY

LO1 High-potential opportunities invariably solve an important problem, want, or need that someone is willing to pay for now. The effort to develop a big high-potential venture is often very little more than that expended by a small business owner, and the rewards are much greater.

LO2 The highest potential ventures are found in high growth markets with high gross margins and robust free cash flow characteristics because their underlying products or services add significantly greater value to the customer, compared with the next best alternatives. To find these ventures entrepreneurs must analyze the viability and profit potential of the proposed business to determine its balance of risk and reward.

LO3 The best opportunities often do not start out that way. They are crafted, shaped, moulded, and reinvented in real time and market space until they maximize all the factors that venture capitalists look for (the "circle of ecstasy"). A good fit between the venture, the capital markets with respect to resources, the timing, and the balance of risk and reward govern the ultimate potential.

LO4 Ideas are a dime a dozen. Perhaps 1 out of 100 becomes a truly great business, and 1 in 10 to 15 becomes a higher potential business. The complex transformation of an idea into a true opportunity is akin to a caterpillar becoming a butterfly.

LO5 There are decided patterns in superior opportunities, and recognizing these patterns is an entrepreneurial skill aspiring entrepreneurs need to develop.

LO6 Rapid changes and disruptions in technology, regulation, information flows, and the like result in opportunities. The journey from idea to high-potential opportunity requires navigating an undulating, constantly changing, three-dimensional relief map while inventing the vehicle and road map along the way. Experience, creativity, and conceptualizing are required to both find and screen venture opportunities.

STUDY QUESTIONS

1. What is the difference between an idea and a good opportunity?
2. Why is it said that ideas are a dime a dozen?
3. What role does experience play in the opportunity creation process, and where do most good opportunities come from? Why is trial-and-error learning not good enough?
4. List the sources of ideas that are most relevant to your personal interests, and conduct a search using the Internet.
5. What conditions and changes that may occur in society and the economy spawn and drive future opportunities? List as many as you can think of as you consider the next 10 years.
6. Evaluate your best idea against the summary criteria in Exhibit 3.7. What appears to be its potential? What has to happen to convert it into a higher potential business?

1. Steve Jobs and Steve Wozniak, co-founders of Apple, were kids when they built their first computers. Colonel Sanders was 65 years old when he started to expand Kentucky Fried Chicken. What is an opportunity for whom?

2. Most successful existing businesses are preoccupied with their most important, existing customers and therefore lack the peripheral vision to spot new products and services. Is this happening where you work? Is this an opportunity for you?

3. The most successful ventures have leadership and people as important competitive advantages. How does this change the way you think about opportunities?

4. Who can you work with during the next few years to learn a business and have the chance to spot new opportunities outside the weak peripheral vision of an established business?

5. Barriers to entry can create opportunities for those with the right knowledge and experience. Why is this so? Can you find some examples?

EXERCISE   Idea Generation Guide

Before beginning the process of generating ideas for new ventures, it is useful to reflect on an old German proverb that says, "Every beginning is hard." If you allow yourself to think creatively, you will be surprised at the number of interesting ideas you can generate once you begin.

The Idea Generation Guide is an exercise in generating ideas. The aim is for you to generate as many interesting ideas as possible. *While generating your ideas, do not evaluate them or worry about their implementation.* Discussion and exercises in the rest of the book will allow you to evaluate these ideas to see if they are opportunities and to consider your own personal entrepreneurial strategy.

Remember—in any creative endeavour, there are no right answers.

Name: _____

Date: _____

Step 1   Generate a list of as many new venture ideas as possible.

As a consumer or paid user, think of the biggest, most frustrating, and painful task or situation you continually must take, and one that would be worth a lot to eliminate or minimize. These are often the seeds of real opportunities. Thinking about any unmet or poorly filled customer needs you know of that have resulted from regulatory changes, technological changes, knowledge and information gaps, lags, asymmetries, inconsistencies, and so forth, will help you generate such a list. Also, think about various products and services (and their substitutes) and the providers of these products or services. If you know of any weaknesses or vulnerabilities, you may discover new venture ideas.

Step 2   Expand your list if possible.

Think about your personal interests, your desired lifestyle, your values, what you feel you are likely to do very well, and contributions you would like to make.

Step 3   Ask at least three people who know you well to look at your list, and revise your list to reflect any new ideas emerging from this exchange.

See the discussion about getting feedback in chapter 1.

Step 4   Jot down insights, observations, and conclusions that have emerged about your business ideas or your personal preferences.

Which ones solve the greatest pain-point/aggravation/frustration for which you (and others you have spoken with) would pay a significant premium to eliminate?

Preparation Questions

1. What were the key changes, both internal to the organization and external within the operating environment, that led to the re-evaluation of distribution options?

2. If you were Jean Louis Drapeau, which option would you choose, and why? Your explanation should consider both qualitative and financial considerations.

NANOPTIX: EUROPEAN GAMING OPPORTUNITIES

It was January 2010 and the senior management team at Nanoptix Inc. was considering how to establish a stronger sales presence in European gaming and lottery markets. VP Sales and Marketing, Jean Louis Drapeau had narrowed the options to establishing an in-house sales force to cover the European market or to enlist an experienced manufacturer's representative to cover the territory. For the latter option, he had shortlisted two possible companies: Demon Interactive based out of the United Kingdom or Germany-based distributor National Rejectors Inc. GmbH (NRI). He needed to make his recommendation to company president, Daniel Vienneau, as soon as possible to capitalize on emerging gaming opportunities in Europe.

COMPANY OVERVIEW

Nanoptix Inc. began operations in Dieppe, New Brunswick, in 1996. They were a one-product firm that developed specialized testing equipment to measure the thickness of manufactured materials such as plastic and glass. Business customers, government agencies, or non-profit organizations purchased the equipment for research and development work that involved measuring minutely thin levels of material. Since the term "nanometer" stood for one billionth of a meter, the corporate name included the term "nano." The technical term for the process was phototonics. The testing equipment was expensive and could cost as much as $500 000. The Nanoptix equipment had a competitive advantage with a selling price less than $100 000 but it still represented a significant capital outlay for most research-based organizations.

The phototonics market developed slowly for Nanoptix and in 2000, the company was approached by another New Brunswick–based business to develop a customized three-headed printer. Spielo Manufacturing Inc. was an emerging company in the global gaming industry providing video lottery terminals (VLT) and other related products and services. They needed a small, customized printer that could be incorporated into their VLT machines. The printer would provide receipts to wagering customers. They approached Nanoptix because of their familiarity with the strong engineering background of the employees.

The President of Nanoptix was Daniel Vienneau. He had performed consulting work for Spielo and was very knowledgeable of their products and engineering processes. Mr. Vienneau had a bachelor's degree in engineering from Laval University and over 15 years of experience in mechanical design. Other members of the Nanoptix management team included his brother, Michel, who had extensive experience as a firmware engineer; Pierre Doucet, an electronics engineer with over 12 years of experience in new product design; Paul Chiasson, an engineer with expertise in the design of lottery terminals and thermal printers; and Yves Page, an industrial engineer with an entrepreneurial background who joined Nanoptix as Plant Manager.

The company focus shifted completely into customized printers as they achieved early success in this market because of their world-class engineering and product design capabilities. Their relationship with Spielo provided them with a steadily increasing stream of revenue (See Exhibit 1 for a summary of the financial position in 2001 and 2002). They were also able to enter into a relationship with a company called Money Controls (a division of Coinco) using their engineering expertise to develop a printer that Money Controls manufactured and marketed. Nanoptix received product development and royalty fees. The printer was called Paycheck and became the core product in terms of sales for Nanoptix. In 2007, they bought back the license from Money Controls and began to manufacture the Paycheck printers themselves. However, this meant that they now had to exclusively develop business relationships with the major OEM companies in the casino gaming equipment industry such as IGT (International Game Technology), Novomatic, WMS Gaming, Bally, and Aristocrat Technologies.

This case was written by Peter Sianchuk, Mount Allison University.

EXHIBIT 1

NANOPTIX OPERATING STATEMENTS 2001 AND 2002 (CDN $)
YEAR END NOVEMBER 30

	2002	2001
Gross Revenue		
Sales	$3 204 661	$2 989 128
Interest Revenue	9 984	38 483
R&D Assistance	205 092	0
	$3 419 737	$3 027 611
Cost of Goods Sold	1 160 422	1 587 296
Gross Profit	2 259 315	1 440 315
Operating Expenses		
Salaries and Fringe Benefits	684 825	514 617
Advertising and Promotion	102 321	32 708
Foreign Exchange	38 946	19 592
Insurance	5 405	3 187
Interest and Bank Charges	23 566	3 040
Professional Fees	243 759	222 377
Light and Heat	1 678	0
Property Taxes	6 120	0
Rent	81 225	48 939
Repairs and Maintenance	12 214	27 966
Research and Development	0	5,479
Office Supplies	48 522	70 660
Telecommunications	38 552	23 137
Travel and Entertainment	219 341	102 843
Amortization	90 097	94 938
	1 596 571	1 169 483
Income Before Taxes	662 744	270 832
Income Taxes	295 751	29 666
Net Income	366 993	241 166

Source: Company Records

REFOCUSING IN 2003

By 2002, the relationship with Spielo and Money Controls had put Nanoptix in a somewhat precarious position. They were focused exclusively on only two customers with a single product line for each. The Nanoptix thermal printer product was considered by company officials to be as innovative as any customized printer on the market and well supported by the Nanoptix team of over 20 engineers and product designers, but Spielo sales were declining. As an engineering-based company, Nanoptix lacked the marketing orientation needed to ensure that they were effectively utilizing their world-class in-house expertise to develop products that responded to market needs in a timely manner. The engineers could create a vast array of highly technical products but there was an overriding need for products that (1) had clearly established markets, (2) were priced cost effectively in relation to market needs and the competition, and (3) had features demanded by the end users.

Mr. Drapeau was brought in as VP Sales and Marketing in 2002. He had over 20 years' experience in senior sales and executive marketing positions with international firms such as Clairol, Bristol-Myers Squibb, Johnson & Johnson, and AC Nielsen. When he arrived, the company faced a serious cash flow problem. Sales decreased by over 50 percent in 2003 and were insufficient to support the salary and R&D expenses that were increasing significantly (See Exhibit 2 for the 2003 income statement). The Nanoptix thermal printer brand was not well known in the gaming industry. They had a weak presence in the United States and no representation in Europe, which accounted for the two largest gaming and lottery markets in the world. Established manufacturer representatives or distributors were reluctant to represent firms such as Nanoptix because they were unknown players in the industry. Sales were driven to a large degree by personal relationships. Mr. Drapeau emphasized this when he said, "The number one marketing tool is getting your face in front of the client and establishing a personal relationship. As a small company we should be able to achieve an advantage in this respect over the big firms."

An analysis was performed of industries where Nanoptix could market their thermal printers. The management team had a strong background in the gaming and lottery industry through their association with Spielo so the decision was made to focus on that area as the primary market for improving sales performance. The automated teller machine (ATM) and kiosk markets were considered the best fits in terms of potential new market strategies so these became secondary markets. The latter two markets also exhibited strong growth potential and would allow the company to diversify printer product lines beyond gaming if they chose to pursue them. Using their existing relationships with Spielo they were able to strike up an alliance with a manufacturer's representative who helped to close a deal with the Swedish lottery. They used this strategy to take small but concrete steps in terms of refocusing the company in 2003 and creating sales that would increase their presence in the global gaming industry.

By the end of 2004, with sales increasing, Nanoptix had to decide if they would grow their business by developing an internal company sales force or by entering into further relationships with manufacturer representatives. The manufacturer rep option had only become viable because Drapeau had spent over 18 months travelling extensively developing personal relationships with lotteries and other gaming organizations throughout the world. He spent up to 40 weeks a year travelling internationally to develop business contacts. It was the strength of these relationships that would become the key part of the organization's sales and marketing strategies.

An internal sales force would have added significantly to the company salary and benefit expenses. In addition, there would be travel, entertainment, and other expenses that would need to be covered by Nanoptix. It was estimated that a sales force would have an immediate impact on company cost of goods sold and thus gross sales of between 3–5 percent. The extra expenses would be partially offset by the fact that the sales force would represent Nanoptix exclusively. They could be trained to company specifications and expectations of performance. As a salaried employee, they would report directly to the VP Sales and Marketing. Hiring a manufacturer's rep would cost a negotiated percentage of sales that could be 4–6 percent of sales but the costs were only borne by the company when a sale was made. Operating independently, the rep would set his or her own agenda and focus on the most profitable product lines. Both options had inherent risks.

Manufacturer reps typically wanted quick money and thus supported product lines with the fastest turns and best margins. They usually represented many companies. If they felt they could make more money from Nanoptix products then they would be motivated to further promote thermal printers. This in turn would make Nanoptix products a more important part of the reps' product portfolio, potentially resulting in better negotiating terms for Nanoptix.

The decision was made to hire a manufacturer rep. The management team felt that to address the cash flow problem it was the fastest way to get new sales in the global market. The strategy paid off as 2004 sales climbed back to pre-2003 levels.

EXHIBIT 2

NANOPTIX OPERATING STATEMENTS 2003 (CDN $)
YEAR ENDED NOVEMBER 30

	2003
Gross Revenue	
Sales	$1 497 086
Interest Revenue	10 000
R&D Assistance	350 000
	$1 857 086
Cost of Goods Sold	427 243
Gross Profit	1 429 843
Operating Expenses	
Salaries and Fringe Benefits	685 025
Advertising and Promotion	40 687
Foreign Exchange	48 233
Insurance	12 350
Interest and Bank Charges	42 558
Professional Fees	94 330
Light and Heat	24 221
Property Taxes	22 000
Rent	2 183
Repairs and Maintenance	15 181
Office Supplies	51 588
Telecommunications	28 292
Travel and Entertainment	255 778
Amortization	86 400
	1 408 826
Income Before Taxes	21 017
Income Taxes	0
Net Income	21 017

Source: Company Records

INDUSTRY OVERVIEW

The gaming and lottery industry was part of a global business that included both casino and non-casino gambling. Legal gambling in the US resulted in more than US$93 billion in annual client spending. Over US$5 billion in direct gaming taxes were contributed by casinos to state and local government taxes and these facilities employed more than 360 000 people. In Europe each country regulated its own gaming. The UK was one of the largest markets with over £5 billion in lottery sales while at the other end of the spectrum were small markets such as Latvia, with the state owned lottery Latvijas Loto, one of the smallest countries with 2.3 million inhabitants. There was a long history of gambling in Europe. For example, SAZKA the lottery commission in the Czech Republic (formerly Czechoslovakia) was formed in 1956.

A VLT was made from various subcomponents. The main housing unit was typically formed of plastic and various metals and was covered in the colourful graphics that personalized each gaming experience. There were also the touch points (buttons to press or arms to pull in the case of an older model slot machine), money acceptors, software and electronics that allowed the machine to interact with the operator's main computer system, and the printer. The various subcomponents were typically manufactured and supplied by different companies who could be from anywhere in the world. Nanoptix was only focused on the printer component.

Modern machines had gravitated toward a ticket-in ticket-out (TITO) printing system. Printed tickets came out of the machine instead of money. There were advantages to this system both for the operator and the player. It was more convenient for customers because they no longer had to carry around buckets of coins. The operator could utilize fewer attendants since coin hoppers no longer need to be serviced and there was less dependence on coin processing equipment. From a printing standpoint the thermal printer had many advantages over the dot matrix printer for TITO amusement with payout (AWP) applications. Thermal paper was heated to create a sharp clear printing image. These machines featured fast refills, fast printing times, and longer print runs, which meant less down time and were particularly well suited for high volume transaction environments of the type associated with kiosks, ATM, lottery, casino, and other amusement machines.

The thermal printing industry was dominated by large global companies. It was estimated that Seiko had a 90-percent share of the market and were one of the first companies to offer such products. Other industry leaders included Ithaca, JCM, and Epson. It was a broad-based industry with many market segments; Nanoptix products only focused on the gaming machine segment that required the printing functionality previously noted. They were highly technical products customized to the specifications quoted by each customer. As a small company Nanoptix could deliver smaller orders while responding to the needs of each customer. With an average per unit cost price of $300, the machines were competitively priced. Nanoptix' advantage in the market was that they could deliver high levels of customer service based upon their ability to establish personal relationships with clients, highly technical products designed by a world-class engineering team, and have the products delivered globally at an affordable price while earning gross margins of between 20 and 30 percent.

The gaming machine industry was dominated by large global corporations. The leader in the industry was IGT, a publicly traded company with revenues of US$2.5 billion in 2008 and a net income of US$342 million. Like its industry rivals, IGT had grown through acquisitions to offer a wide variety of slot and video games. Other major companies included Novomatic, WMS Gaming, Bally Technologies, Aristocrat Technologies, Aruze Gaming, Konami, VGT, and Lottomatica. Many of the industry leaders began with a single line of products (WMS Gaming origins were in 1943 as a manufacturer of pinball machines in Chicago, Illinois, moving into casino style gaming in the 1970s) expanding products and services over time. For example, the GTech Corporation of Rhode Island purchased Spielo Manufacturing in 2003 and was in turn purchased by the Italian gaming and lottery giant Lottomatica in August 2006. Lottomatica offered products in five key market segments, which were typical of the industry leaders: government lotteries, gaming solutions (VLT machines), sports betting, interactive entertainment, and commercial services.

There were many global companies that manufactured printers but only certain firms competed in the highly specialized and technical market for thermal printers that could be customized to the needs of the gaming industry. Privately held Future Logic of Glendale, California, and TransAct Technologies Inc. of Hamden, Connecticut, were the largest companies with annual per unit sales of approximately 130 000 and 90 000 respectively (see Table 1 for an overview of TransAct sales in 2008). Nanoptix was the third largest company with sales that were about 20 percent of the market leader followed by Custom Engineering SpA, located in Parma, Italy, and JCM American Corporation, Las Vegas, Nevada. Some companies such as JCM specialized in other technologies such as bill validators but also had a presence in the printing markets. As markets changed industry relationships adapted to emerging opportunities. For example, in 2006 JCM and TransAct entered into an agreement whereby the JCM sales force would carry Trans-Act's gaming thermal printers along with their own bill acceptors and currency handling products.

TABLE 1	TRANSACT SALES AT DECEMBER 31, 2008		
MARKET	**SALES**	**OVERALL % OF SALES**	**% CHANGE FROM 2007**
Banking & POS	US$11 866 000	19.1	7
Casino & Gaming	US$22 299 000	35.8	15
Lottery	US$15 731 000	25.3	167
Services Group	US$12 311 000	19.8	−1
Total	US$62 209 000		

Transact Inc. overall sales increased by 28% from the previous year.

Source: Form 10-K Annual Report Filed March 16, 2009.

DISTRIBUTION OPTION—IN-HOUSE SALES TEAM

Europe was a complex market. Each country had its own regulations and gaming characteristics that could vary between highly sophisticated and well-established markets such as the United Kingdom and France to emerging gaming markets like Romania and the Ukraine. The *Media & Entertainment Consulting Network* was a bi-monthly industry newsletter for the European gaming industry. They reported in December 2008 that the global gaming industry was now focused on the Balkan states of Turkey, Greece, Croatia, Bulgaria, Romania, Slovenia, Serbia, and Montenegro for growth and expansion. These markets accounted for €4.5 billion in gambling in 2007 and were seeing growth in all sectors which included lottery, casino, betting, gambling machines, and interactive (internet and mobile).

Nanoptix wanted a presence in these countries but was also targeting more developed markets in the United Kingdom, France, Germany, Austria, the Netherlands, the Czech Republic, Sweden, and Spain. Relationships would need to be established with the regulators in each country. Company officials estimated that the European market might represent 150 000 new gaming machines per year but only approxi-

mately 25 percent of these would have TITO printing requirements. Mr. Drapeau felt with a stronger presence in Europe, Nanoptix should be able to garner 25 percent of the TITO market in year one with similar results expected for 2011. Optimistically, this number could be as large as 50 percent but it could also be as low as 10 percent. A sales rep would require a salary of $80 000 and there would be additional expenses for benefits (15–22 percent of salary) and travel/entertainment (40–60 percent of salary). It was estimated that two reps would initially be needed for Europe to reach these sales forecasts. Future hiring would depend upon rates of market penetration. Nanoptix needed each reps' first year sales to be approximately 5–6 percent above current company sales levels to break even.

Creating their own European sales force would also provide Nanoptix with greater control over the training and activities of the people. They would be able to strongly influence the way the salesperson dressed and presented themselves to the client. They would be in a better position to monitor the activities of the salesperson and would have more flexibility in terms of making necessary changes. Due to the highly technical nature of the gaming industry, the products of exacting specifications, the highly regulated environment, and the relationships that were critical to success the sales representatives would ideally have experience in these markets. Otherwise, extra training would be needed and the sales revenue curve much flatter. Ideally the sales reps would be hired in Canada so that they would better understand the corporate culture of the company and its products and processes. It was not likely that sales reps could be hired with industry experience and extensive training and management would likely be required.

Since Nanoptix attended the major gaming shows around the world it was also possible that international-based sales reps could be found. Assimilating such people into the head office in Dieppe, New Brunswick, could prove to be a sales management challenge.

DISTRIBUTION OPTION— MANUFACTURER'S REPRESENTATIVE, DEMON INTERACTIVE

The second option available to the company was to hire a manufacturer's representative (also called a manufacturer's agent but depending on the country could go by a variety of names including commission agent, exclusive agent, or resident sales agent). The manufacturer's rep would act as the sales branch for Nanoptix while remaining independent.

These reps typically worked for several non-competing manufacturers representing complementary products. Their main role was transactional as it directly related to selling activities. They did not necessarily take physical possession of the products nor did they take title to the goods. The management team estimated that a manufacturer's rep would be paid a straight 5 percent commission based on gross sales. They would be responsible for paying their own expenses.

The first of the companies being considered was called Demon Interactive. Demon was located outside of London, England, and was headed up by John Temple. Mr. Temple had previously worked for the 3M Company in their touch screens division. Although touch screens had several applications they were also used extensively in the gaming and lottery industry. As a result, Temple had numerous contacts in the industry. He also had a technical background and thus was able to sell on benefits and not just price. Temple had extensive industry experience and seemed interested in entering into a relationship with Nanoptix. From his base near London, he was able to quickly access all European destinations.

Another advantage for Nanoptix was that Demon Interactive represented few other clients at the present time. For some OEMs, it was often difficult to get the manufacturer's representative to focus on its particular products. This was because the agent's company was an independent business with its own goals and strategies. Agents tended to promote the products in the portfolio that provided them with the highest commissions. Sometimes the OEM needed to provide extra financial incentives to the agent. There was less direct control over a manufacturer's representative compared to managing your own sales force.

DISTRIBUTION OPTION— MANUFACTURER'S REPRESENTATIVE, NATIONAL REJECTORS INC. GMBH

NRI was located in Buxtehude, Germany. It was a division of Crane Payment Solutions (St. Louis, Missouri). Crane was a large international company that offered products within five market segments: aerospace and electronics, engineered materials, fluid handling, controls, and merchandising systems. Within the merchandising systems segment was the payment solutions division with three brand names: NRI, Cash Code, and Telequip. Crane further segmented this division into vending, gaming/amusements, retail/kiosk, and parking/transportation. NRI produced and marketed coin validation machines throughout Europe and beyond. Its focus was on the amusement and kiosk markets; however, they also had a

lesser presence in the casino market, which was the primary target of Nanoptix.

Whereas Demon Interactive was a one-person operation, NRI had six sales representatives who called on European customers. Nanoptix customers consisted of both gaming machine OEMs and casinos. Approximately 80 percent of a reps time would be spent dealing with gaming machine OEMs. In North America the OEM market was dominated by four large players: IGT, WMS Gaming, Bally Technologies, and Aristocrat Technologies. However, in Europe the market was more fragmented. Besides the global giant Novomatic, the European market featured names such as Atronic, Impera, Apex, Orion, Franco, Bell Fruit Games, EGT, and at least 20 others. The high number of OEMs was an opportunity for Nanoptix and relationships would need to be developed with these companies along with the lottery and gaming commissions for each country. Novomatic focused on producing the cabinetry and gaming products themselves and did not manufacture many of the subcomponents of slot machines including printing functionality. The European market also differed in that a manufacturer such as Novomatic was allowed to vertically integrate within the channel of distribution by owning casinos. This was not the case in North America.

NRI had a size advantage in terms of sales representatives over Demon Interactive but company officials at Nanoptix were concerned about now much attention they would give to the Nanoptix line of printers. They questioned whether or not Nanoptix products would simply become an afterthought for the NRI reps who had several other products to represent. Financial remuneration would be similar to what would be offered to Demon.

THE EUROPEAN OPPORTUNITY

There was a light snow falling outside his office window as Jean Louis Drapeau sat at his desk reviewing notes pertaining to the European decision. The company had come a long way since facing cash flow problems in 2003. Sales were almost 200 percent higher than what they were in 2001. The company now had over 40 customers scattered across the planet. The majority of sales still came from a small percentage of these customers but the portfolio clearly demonstrated that Nanoptix was an emerging global player in a global market. Although many of Nanoptix sales were smaller orders in the 100–500 unit range, they were capable of delivering much larger quantities of product. A single large order of 10 000–15 000 units would have an enormous positive impact on the company.

Worldwide sales of thermal printers for gaming applications were expected to be upwards of 300 000 units. The volume of slot machine sales in Europe was estimated at 150 000 units but only about 25 percent would have printing applications and thus be the market Nanoptix was targeting. The UK market was almost 100 percent TITO while smaller emerging markets varied in terms of printing functionalities and often had limited printing applications. Forecasting 2010 sales was mitigated by the uncertainty of entering the European market with a more substantial focus than in the past however Drapeau was able to confidently estimate that the market potential for Nanoptix thermal TITO printers should be 10 percent, 25 percent or 50 percent respectively based upon sensitivity analysis that ranged from pessimistic to realistic and optimistic projections.

The decision to create an in-house sales force or to hire an experienced manufacturer's representative was based upon both financial and management issues. Some of the factors that needed to be assessed included cost effectiveness, unit volume potential, effect on profitability, customer relationship building, sales management and supervision issues, corporate culture and long-term viability. With these issues in mind, Drapeau sat down to formulate a recommendation to bring forward to the rest of the Nanoptix management team.

For more information on the resources available from McGraw-Hill Ryerson, go to www.mcgrawhill.ca/he/solutions.

CHAPTER 4

THE BUSINESS PLAN

A good plan today is better than a perfect plan tomorrow.

GEORGE S. PATTON

LEARNING OBJECTIVES

LO1 Develop a business plan based on a model proven and refined through years of use.

LO2 Identify some of the pitfalls in the business plan preparation process and how to avoid these.

LO3 Explain what needs to be included in the plan, why, and for whom. Remember, the business plan (which is not the business!) is written for an intended audience.

LO4 Identify what has to be done to develop and complete a business plan for your proposed venture.

LO5 Explain why a well-articulated business plan is an important part of the entrepreneurial process, not an end in itself.

LO6 Critically examine a business plan developed by three young entrepreneurs to raise capital for Edgar Bruce Eyewear—a new Internet-based venture with the mission to deliver fashionable glasses to customers for less and donate glasses to individuals in developing parts of the world.

DEVELOPING THE BUSINESS PLAN

The business plan itself is the culmination of a usually lengthy, arduous, creative, and iterative process that, as we explored in chapter 3 and the accompanying exercises, can transform a raw idea into a magnificent opportunity. The plan will carefully articulate the merits, requirements, risks, and potential rewards of the opportunity and how it will be seized. It will demonstrate how the *four anchors* noted below (and in the online exercises for chapter 3) reveal themselves to the founders and investors by converting all the research, careful thought, and creative problem solving from the online Venture Opportunity Screening Exercises into a thorough plan. The business plan for a high potential venture reveals the business's ability to:

- *Create* or add significant value to a customer or end-user.
- *Solve* a significant problem, or meet a significant want or need for which someone will pay a premium.
- *Have* robust market, margin, and moneymaking characteristics: large enough ($50-plus million), high growth (20-plus percent), high margins (40-plus percent), strong and early free cash flow (recurring revenue, low assets, and working capital), high profit potential (10 to 15 percent after tax), and attractive realizable returns for investors (25 to 30 percent IRR).
- *Fit* well with the founder(s) and venture team at the time, in the marketspace, and with the risk-reward balance.

The plan becomes the point of departure for prospective investors to begin their due diligence to ascertain potential and various risks of the venture: technology risks, market risks, management risks, competitive and strategic risks, and financial risks. Even if you do not intend to raise outside capital, this homework is vital. The collisions between founders and investors that occur during meetings, discussions, and investigations reveal a great deal to all parties and begin to set the code for their relationship and negotiations. Getting to know each other much more closely is

IN "ONE DESIGN" SAILING ALL MUST USE THE SAME EQUIPMENT UNDER THE SAME WIND CONDITIONS; NEVERTHELESS, THE SAILOR WITH THE BETTER SKILLS AND WHO HAS CHARTED A BETTER PATH WILL WIN.

a crucial part of the evaluation process. Everyone will be thinking: Are these intelligent people; can we work well with them during thick but especially thin times; are they creative; do they listen; can they add value to the venture; is this the right team; do I want them as business partners; are they honest; are we having fun yet? Recent research points to the important role that "storytelling" plays in securing funding.[1] Martin Martens of Concordia University, Jennifer Jennings, and Dev Jennings, both of the University of Alberta, discovered that effective narratives convey credible information to those that are in a position to invest.

The investors who can bring the most insight, know-how, and contacts to the venture, and thus add the greatest value, will reveal themselves as well. The most valuable investors will see weaknesses, even flaws, in how the market is viewed, the technology or service, the strategies, the proposed size and structure of the financing, and the team, and will propose strategies and people to correct these. If it is the right investor, it can make the difference between an average and a good or great venture.

THE PLAN IS OBSOLETE AT THE PRINTER

The authors have argued for decades that the plan is obsolete the instant it emerges from the printer. In today's fast-paced climate, it is obsolete before it goes into the printer! The pace of technological and information-age change, and the dynamism of the global marketplace shorten the already brief life expectancy of any business plan. It is nearly impossible to find a year-old venture today that is identical in strategy, market focus, products or services, and team as the original business plan described.

WORK IN PROGRESS—BENT KNEES REQUIRED

In such a rapidly changing environment, flexibility and responsiveness become critical survival skills. Developing an idea into a business and articulating how this will be done via a business plan requires an open mind and "bent knees," along with clear focus, commitment, and determination.

The business plan should be thought of as a work in progress. Though it must be completed if you are trying to raise outside capital, attract key advisors, directors, team members, or the like, it can never be considered finished. As Yuval Deutsch of York University and Thomas Ross of the University of British Columbia point out, having good reputable directors onboard allows a fledgling firm to send a positive signal of high quality.[2] Like a cross-country flight plan, many unexpected changes can occur along the way: a thunderstorm, smoke-impaired visibility, fog, or powerful winds can develop. One has to be prepared to continually adjust course to minimize risk and ensure successful completion of the journey. Such risk-reward management is inherent in the business planning process.

THE PLAN IS NOT THE BUSINESS   LO2

Developing the business plan and business model is one of the best ways to define the blueprint, strategy, resources, and people requirements for a new venture. It is this document that focuses and communicates the founder's vision. The vast majority of INC.'s 500 fastest growing companies had business plans at the outset. Without a business plan, it is exceedingly difficult to raise capital from informal or formal investors.

Too often first-time entrepreneurs jump to a simplistic conclusion: All that is needed is a fat, polished, and enticing business plan and the business will automatically be successful. They confuse the plan with building the business. Some of the most impressive business plans never become great businesses. And some of the weakest plans lead to extraordinary businesses. But on the whole, evidence suggests that good business plans lead to prosperous businesses. According to Kevin Hindle of the Australian Graduate School of Entrepreneurship and Brent Mainprize of Royal Roads University, "With a good plan in hand, an entrepreneur should not let a lack of resources inhibit his or her pursuit of opportunity."[3]

Tomas Karlsson and Benson Honig tracked six young established enterprises and found evidence that these businesses "rarely referred to their plans after writing them."[4] In a larger study—623 nascent entrepreneurs in Sweden—Honig and Samuelsson found that not all shared the same growth expectations or desires, but that growth aspirations were positively correlated with venture performance, but were unable to show that modifications to the business plan had any benefit on venture performance.[5]

The message here is two-sided. The odds can be shaped in your favour through the development of a business plan. But just because you have a plan does not mean the business will be an automatic success. Unless the fundamental opportunity is there, along with the requisite resources and team needed to pursue it, the best plan in the world will not make much difference. Some helpful tips in preparing a business plan are summarized in Exhibit 4.1.

EXHIBIT 4.1 **DO'S AND DON'TS FOR PREPARING A BUSINESS PLAN**

DO

Involve all of the venture team in the preparation of the business plan.

Make the plan logical, comprehensive, readable, and as short as possible.

Demonstrate commitment to the venture by investing a significant amount of time and some money in preparing the plan.

Articulate what the critical risks and assumptions are and how and why these are tolerable.

Disclose and discuss any current or potential problems in the venture.

Identify several alternative sources of financing.

Spell out the proposed deal—how much for what ownership share—and how investors will win.

Be creative in gaining the attention and interest of potential investors.

Remember that the plan is not the business and that an ounce of can-do implementation is worth two pounds of planning.

Accept orders and customers that will generate a positive cash flow, even if it means you have to postpone writing the plan.

Know your targeted investor group (e.g., venture capitalist, angel investor, bank, or leasing company) and what they really want and what they dislike, and tailor your plan accordingly.

Let realistic market and sales projections drive the assumptions underlying the financial spreadsheets, rather than the reverse.

DON'T

Have unnamed, mysterious people on the venture team (e.g., a "Mr. G" who is currently a financial vice president with another firm and who will join you later).

Make ambiguous, vague, or unsubstantiated statements, such as estimating sales on the basis of what the team would like to produce.

Describe technical products or manufacturing processes using jargon or in a way that only an expert can understand, because this limits the usefulness of the plan.

Spend money on developing fancy brochures, elaborate PowerPoint and Flash presentations, and other "sizzle," instead, show the "steak."

Waste time writing a plan when you could be closing sales and collecting cash.

Assume you have a done deal when you have a handshake or verbal commitment but no money in the bank. (The deal is done when the cheque clears!)

Julie Snache launched her venture in mid-2013. Her business's Facebook page claimed, "She'll customize and sell dream catchers with one-of-a-kind design elements." Snache, herself, stated her plan, "Once I establish a customer base and web presence, I'll expand the store to include the work of other Aboriginal artists." She also sees an opportunity: "There aren't a lot of companies that provide authentic Aboriginal products. I want to create a space that will allow artists to keep control of their intellectual property while celebrating the indigenous cultures alive and thriving in Canada."

With a background in arts, combined with business training, Julie Snache feels prepared for this entrepreneurial endeavour. Julie is motivated and sets goals for herself and her business. But beyond creativity and enthusiasm, a plan is necessary.

Question: What should Julie Snache's business model look like?

SOME OF JULIE SNACHE'S CREATIONS.

Sources: "Student Entrepreneur Launches OrigiNative Designs," *Georgian News*, April 15, 2013; Facebook; LinkedIn.

SOME TIPS FROM THE TRENCHES   LO3

The most valuable lessons about preparing a business plan and raising venture capital come from entrepreneurs who have succeeded in these endeavours. Thomas Huseby, founder and head of SeaPoint Ventures, is a remarkable entrepreneur who has raised more than $80 million of venture capital as CEO of two telecommunications start-up companies that subsequently became publicly traded. Consider the following wisdom gleaned from his own experience on both sides of the negotiating table: entrepreneur/CEO and venture capitalist.

RE: Venture Capitalists

- There are a lot of venture capitalists. Once you meet one you could end up meeting all 700-plus of them.
- Getting a "no" from venture capitalists is as hard as getting a "yes;" qualify your targets and force others to say "no."
- Be vague about what other venture capitalists you are talking to.
- Don't ever meet with an associate or junior member twice without also meeting with a partner in that venture capital firm.

RE: The Plan

- Stress your business concept in the executive summary.
- The numbers don't matter; but the economics (e.g., value proposition and business model) really matter.
- Make the business plan look and feel good.
- Prepare lots of copies of published articles, contracts, market studies, purchase orders, and the like.
- Prepare very detailed résumés and reference lists of key players in the venture.
- If you can't do the details, make sure you hire someone who can.

RE: The Deal

- Make sure your current investors are as desperate as you are.
- Create a market for your venture.
- Never say "no" to an offer price.
- Use a lawyer who is experienced at closing venture deals.
- Don't stop selling until the money is in the bank.
- Make it a challenge.
- Never lie.

RE: The Fundraising Process

- It is much harder than you ever thought it could be.
- You can last much longer than you ever thought you could.
- The venture capitalists have done this before and have to do this for the rest of their lives!

This is particularly valuable advice for any entrepreneur seeking outside capital and anticipating dealing with investors.[6]

What about the possible loss of critical members of your new venture team? The Edgar Bruce Eyewear sample business plan value proposition (found in the appendix online in Connect) is based heavily on the knowledge and skill found within key individuals. Shelley MacDougall of Acadia University and Deborah Hurst of Athabasca University point out that "knowledge-intensive businesses in the fast-moving high technology sector are dependent upon the creation and transfer of knowledge among skilled employees. Ironically, this critical feature of organizational success resides with employees who tend to be somewhat transient." MacDougall and Hurst identify how entrepreneurs can work to become adept at coping with these challenges by: (1) maintaining an environment that fosters creativity, thus encouraging employees to stay, and (2) managing the departure of those that leave.[7]

Reaching that receptive audience is key, particularly if the venture is pushing a product or service in a new realm. A certain amount of specific knowledge would be required to assess Edgar Bruce Eyewear's business model. Such businesses in general may not be readily appreciated. The "give-one-get-one" model is intuitive but its appeal may be lost on an older generation. Research by Gary Gorman of Memorial University of Newfoundland, Peter Rosa of the University of Edinburgh, and Alex Faseruk of Memorial University of Newfoundland examines how new knowledge-based ventures fare compared to ventures in traditional industries when it comes to external financing. The risk assessment practices of chartered banks and government agencies have modified traditional lending approaches to meet the needs of knowledge-based firms. Their findings show that specialized processes are only partially developed and still evolving to handle these new types of ventures. Those providing external financing learn very much during the course of the due diligence and the conclusion is that such lenders must be purposefully sought out![8]

HOW TO DETERMINE IF INVESTORS CAN ADD VALUE

One of the most frequently missed opportunities in the entire process of developing a business plan and trying to convince outside investors to part with their cash is a consequence of sell-sell-sell! myopia by the founders.

Selling ability is one of the most common denominators among successful entrepreneurs. Too often, however, entrepreneurs—typically out of cash, or nearly so—become so obsessed with selling to prospective investors that they fail to ask great questions and do little serious listening. As a result, these entrepreneurs learn very little from their prospects, even though they probably know a great deal about the technology, market, and competitors (after all, that is the investor's business).

Entrepreneurs who not only succeed at developing a great business concept but also attract the right investors (who can add a great deal of value to the venture through their experience, wisdom, and networks) are usually savvy listeners. They use the selling opportunity, beyond presenting their plan and promoting themselves, to carefully query prospective investors: You've seen our concept, our story, and our strategies, what have we missed? Where are we vulnerable? How would you knock us off? Who will knock us off? How would you modify our strategy? What would you do differently? Whom do we need with us to make this succeed? What do you believe has to happen to make this highly successful? Be as blunt as you wish.

Two powerful forces are unleashed in this process. First, as a founder, you will begin to discern just how smart, knowledgeable, and, most important, creative the investors are about the proposed business. Do they have creative ideas, insights, and alternative ways of thinking about the opportunity and strategy that you and your team may not have thought of? This enables you, the founder, to ascertain just what value the investors might add to the venture and whether their approach to telling you and your team that you are "all wet" on certain things is acceptable. Would the relationship be likely to wear you out over time and demoralize you? In the process, you will learn a great deal about your plan and the investors.

The second powerful force is the message implicitly sent to the investors when you make such genuine queries and listen, rather than become argumentative and defensive (which they may try to get you to do): We have given this our best shot. We are highly committed to our concept and believe we have the right strategy, but our minds are open. We listen; we learn; we have bent knees; we adapt and change when the evidence and ideas are compelling; we are not granite heads. Investors are much more likely to conclude that you are a founder and a team with which they can work.

THE DEHYDRATED BUSINESS PLAN

A dehydrated business plan usually runs from four to ten pages, but rarely more. It covers key points, such as those suggested for the executive summary in the business planning guide that follows. Essentially, such a plan analyzes information about the heart of the business opportunity, competitive advantages the company will enjoy, and creative insights that an entrepreneur often has.

Since it can usually be prepared in a few hours, it is preferred by entrepreneurs who cannot find slack time while operating a business to write a complete plan. In many instances, investors prefer a dehydrated plan in the initial screening phase. Andrew Fisher, Executive Vice President at Wesley Clover, on the subject of quickly capturing a VC's attention, revealed to students that often he only reviews the PowerPoint slides or executive summary on his BlackBerry. Enough interest has to be generated for him to send the complete business plan to the printer.

A dehydrated plan is not intended to be used exclusively in the process of raising or borrowing money; it can be a valuable compass to keep you on track. Consider it a map of the main battleground ahead, but remember that it will not provide the necessary details and tactics necessary to conduct the battle.

WHO DEVELOPS THE BUSINESS PLAN?

The venture team often considers hiring an outside professional to prepare the business plan, so they can use their time to obtain financing and start the business.

There are compelling reasons why it is not a good idea to hire outside professionals. In the process of planning and of writing the business plan, the consequences of different strategies and tactics and the human and financial requirements for launching and building the venture can be examined, before it is too late. For example, one entrepreneur discovered—while preparing his business plan—that the major market for his biomedical product was in nursing homes, rather than in hospital emergency rooms, as he and his physician partner had previously assumed. This realization changed the focus of the marketing effort. Had he left the preparation to an outsider, this might not have been discovered or, at the very least, it is unlikely he would have had the same sense of confidence and commitment to the new strategy.

WHO IS THE BUSINESS PLAN FOR?

Identifying and understanding the audience is important. Allan Riding, Deloitte Chair in the Management of Growth Enterprises at the University of Ottawa, notes, "I usually recommend multiple plans, varying according to the purpose. One business plan for VCs might stress the upside potential while a business plan for getting a loan might stress the value of the assets and the track record of the owner(s). Likewise, I would use an entirely different plan for managing day-to-day operations. So, my question back to the entrepreneur is always 'what is the purpose of this particular plan?' In my view the purpose should be stated right up front…along with a demonstration that the team and product have the vision and talent to make it all work!"

The sample business plan provided in the appendix, Edgar Bruce, is intended for a venture capital audience that might provide an A round of risk capital. This business plan from the real world is not perfect and some confidential information has been omitted. The goal for this business plan was to open doors and get a dialogue started. The plan contains greater justification for proof of concept; much market research detail is provided to project revenue generation but far less detail on the expense side. Is this enough to scare off readers? Does the reader need greater explanation for website development—the single largest expenditure? Do the increases in sales seem justifiable? What about salary and server costs?

A CLOSER LOOK AT THE WHAT   LO4

THE RELATIONSHIP BETWEEN GOALS AND ACTIONS

Consider a team that is enthusiastic about an idea for a new business and has done a considerable amount of thinking and initial work evaluating the opportunity (such as thoroughly working through the Venture Opportunity Screening Exercises, found online at Connect). Team members believe the business they are considering has excellent market prospects and fits well with the skills, experience, personal goals, values, and aspirations of its lead entrepreneur and the venture team. They now need to ask about the most significant risks and problems involved in launching the enterprise, the long-term profit prospects, and the future financing and cash flow requirements. To take action the team must determine the demands of operating lead times, seasonality, facility location, marketing and pricing strategy needs, and so forth.

These questions now need to be answered convincingly with the evidence for them shown *in writing*. The planning and the development of such a business plan is neither quick nor easy. In fact, effective planning is a difficult process that demands time, discipline, commitment, dedication, and practice. However, it also can be stimulating and fun as innovative solutions and strategies to solve nagging problems are found.

The skills to write a business plan are not necessarily the ones needed to make a venture successful (although some of these skills are certainly useful). The best single point of departure for, and an anchor during, the planning process is the motto "Can Do," and is an apt one for planning and for making sure that a plan serves the very practical purpose for which it is intended.

Further, if a venture intends to use the business plan to raise capital, it is important for the team to do the planning and write the plan itself. Investors attach great importance to the quality of the venture team *and* to their complete understanding of the business that they are preparing to enter. Thus, investors want to be sure that what they see is what they get—that is, the team's analysis and understanding of the venture opportunity and its commitment to it. Investors usually correlate a team's ability to communicate the vision with their ability to make it a reality. They are going to invest in a team and a leader, not in a consultant. Nothing less will do, and anything less is usually obvious.

SEGMENTING AND INTEGRATING INFORMATION

When planning and writing a business plan, it is necessary to organize information so that it can be managed and that is useful.

An effective way to organize information is to segment the information into sections, such as the target market, the industry, the competition, the financial plan, and so on, and then integrate the information into a business plan.

This process works best if sections are discrete and the information within them digestible. Then the order in which sections are developed can vary, and different sections can be developed simultaneously. For example, since the heart and soul of a plan lies in the analysis of the market opportunity, of the competition, and of a resultant competitive strategy that can win, it is a good idea to start with these sections and integrate information along the way. Because the financial and operations aspects of the venture will be driven by the rate of growth and the magnitude and the specific substance of the market revenue plans, these can be developed later.

The information is then further integrated into the business plan. The executive summary is prepared last.

ESTABLISHING ACTION STEPS

The following steps, centred on actions to be taken, outline the process by which a business plan is written. These action steps are presented in the exercise found at the end of the chapter, "The Business Plan Guide."

- *Segmenting information.* An overall plan for the project, by section, needs to be devised and needs to include priorities—who is responsible for each section, the due date of a first draft, and the due date of a final draft.
- *Creating an overall schedule.* Next, create a more specific list of tasks; identify priorities and who is responsible for them. Determine when they will be started, and when they will be completed. This list needs to be as specific and detailed as possible. Tasks need to be broken down into the smallest possible component (e.g., a series of phone calls may be necessary before a trip). The list then needs to be examined for conflicts and lack of reality in time estimates. Peers and business associates can be asked to review the list for realism, timing, and priorities.
- *Creating an action calendar.* Tasks on the do list then need to be placed on a calendar. When the calendar is complete, the calendar needs to be re-examined for conflicts or lack of realism.
- *Doing the work and writing the plan.* The necessary work needs to be done and the plan written. Adjustments need to be made to the do list and the calendar, as necessary. As part of this process, it is important to have a plan reviewed by a lawyer to make sure it

Bruce Poon Tip is the CEO of G Adventures, the company he founded in 1990 after returning from an inspiring backpacking trip in Asia. Armed with his "daring business plan [Poon Tip set out to] organize small-group adventure tours to off-the-beaten-path destinations. While he felt the idea was a sure winner, bank managers were less than enthused. Unfunded—save for those maxed-out credit cards—but unfazed, Bruce put the plan in motion, offering adventure-craving travellers an alternative to the resorts, cruises, and motor coach tours." For a view of Bruce Poon Tip's business model explained, see his Ted Talk at www .tedxtoronto.com/speakers/bruce-poon-tip.

Question: Travel giants have acquired many of G Adventures' rivals. If you were Bruce Poon Tip, how would you tackle the task of perpetuating the "spirit, creativity, and core values as the firm becomes a sprawling global entity run by professional managers rather than entrepreneurial instinct"?

BRUCE POON TIP

Sources: Nicholas Keung, "A 'far off' idea travels a long way," *The Toronto Star*. March 19, 2007. Dan Bigman, "Cracking the 'Founder's Code Dilemma'," *Forbes*. July 16, 2009. Candice So, "Hire people who stay relevant, or your business will become irrelevant," ITbusiness.ca June 19, 2013.

contains no misleading statements, unnecessary information, and caveats. The plan also needs to be reviewed by an objective outsider, such as an entrepreneurially minded executive who has significant profit and loss responsibility, or a venture capitalist who would not be a potential investor. No matter how good the lead entrepreneur and his or her team are in planning, there will be issues that they will overlook and certain aspects of the presentation that are inadequate or less than clear. A good reviewer also can act as a sounding board in the process of developing alternative solutions to problems and answers to questions investors are likely to ask.

 The best way to predict the future is to create it.

PETER DRUCKER

PREPARING A BUSINESS PLAN   LO5

A COMPLETE BUSINESS PLAN

It may seem to an entrepreneur who has completed the online exercises for chapter 3 and who has spent hours informally thinking and planning that jotting down a few things is all that needs to be done. *However, there is a great difference between screening an opportunity and developing a business plan.*

There are two important differences in the way these issues need to be addressed. First, a business plan can have two uses: (1) inducing someone to part with $250 000 to $2 million or more, and

(2) guiding the policies and actions of the firm over a number of years. Therefore, strategies and statements need to be well thought out, unambiguous, and capable of being supported.

Another difference is that more detail is needed. (The exception to this is the dehydrated business plan discussed earlier in this chapter.) This means the team needs to spend more time gathering detailed data, interpreting it, and presenting it clearly. "Exploitation should begin based primarily on when an entrepreneur's ignorance has been sufficiently reduced through knowledge accumulation."[9] For example, for the purpose of screening an opportunity, it may be all right to note (if one cannot do any better) that the target market for a product is in the $30 to $60 million range and the market is growing over 10 percent per year. For planning an actual launch, this level of detail is not sufficient. The size range would need to be narrowed considerably; if it were not narrowed, those reading or using the plan would have little confidence in this critical number. Moreover, saying the target market is growing at over 10 percent is too vague. Does that mean the market grew at the stated rate between last year and the year before, or does it mean that the market grew on average by this amount over the past three years? In addition, a statement phrased in terms of "over 10 percent" smacks of imprecision. The actual growth rate needs to be known and needs to be stated. Whether the rate will or will not remain the same, and why, also needs to be explained.

Preparing an effective business plan for a start-up can easily take 200 to 300 hours. Squeezing that amount of time into evenings and weekends can make the process stretch over 3 to 12 months.

A plan for a business expansion or for a situation such as a leveraged buyout typically takes half this effort because more is known about the business, including the market, its competition, financial and accounting information, and so on.

Exhibit 4.2 is a sample table of contents for a business plan. The information shown is included in most effective business plans and is a good framework to follow. Organizing the material into sections makes dealing with the information more manageable. While the amount of detail and the order of presentation may vary for a particular venture according to its circumstances, most effective business plans contain this information in some form. (The amount of detail and the order in which information is presented is important. These can vary for each particular situation and will depend upon the purpose of the plan and the age and stage of the venture, among other factors.)

BUSINESS MODEL

In addition to a business plan, many entrepreneurs and their venture teams will prepare a business model. The business model is a succinct presentation of much background work. Despite its brevity, a good model will be well thought out and defensible.

A business plan must put the pieces of the puzzle together, must demonstrate revenues and profit. The business model must show how the product or service is differentiated and how customers will be reached. It also shows what value proposition is presented and at what price point. This is a real challenge in a one-page diagram!

The model portrays the operations and resources in sufficient detail to convince the reader that the proposed relationships are sound and can be executed. Whether in words in boxes or diagrammatically with arrows, an opportunity must be expressed that can be captured by the venture team. Better business models include a synopsis of how the enterprise will organize and what role key individuals will play in commercializing the opportunity presented.

| | **EXHIBIT 4.2** | **BUSINESS PLAN TABLE OF CONTENTS** |

I. EXECUTIVE SUMMARY
   Description of the Business Concept and the Business Opportunity and Strategy
   Target Market and Projections
   Competitive Advantages
   Costs
   Sustainability
   The Team
   The Offering

II. THE INDUSTRY AND THE COMPANY AND ITS PRODUCT(S) OR SERVICE(S)
   The Industry
   The Company and the Concept
   The Product(s) or Service(s)

III. MARKET RESEARCH AND ANALYSIS
   Customers
   Market Size and Trends
   Competition and Competitive Edges
   Estimated Market Share and Sales
   Ongoing Market Evaluation

IV. THE ECONOMICS OF THE BUSINESS
   Gross and Operating Margins
   Profit Potential and Durability
   Fixed, Variable, and Semivariable Costs
   Months to Breakeven
   Months to Reach Positive Cash Flow

V. MARKETING PLAN
   Overall Marketing Strategy
   Pricing
   Sales Tactics
   Service and Warranty Policies
   Advertising and Promotion
   Distribution

VI. DESIGN AND DEVELOPMENT PLANS
   Development Status and Tasks
   Difficulties and Risks

Product Improvement and New Products
   Costs
   Proprietary Issues

VII. MANUFACTURING AND OPERATIONS PLAN
   Operating Cycle
   Geographical Location
   Facilities and Improvements
   Strategy and Plans
   Regulatory and Legal Issues

VIII. VENTURE TEAM
   Organization
   Key Personnel
   Compensation and Ownership
   Other Investors
   Employment and Other Agreements and Share Option and Bonus Plans
   Board of Directors
   Other Shareholders, Rights, and Restrictions
   Supporting Professional Advisors and Services

IX. OVERALL SCHEDULE

X. CRITICAL RISKS, PROBLEMS, AND ASSUMPTIONS

XI. THE FINANCIAL PLAN
   Actual Income Statements and Balance Sheets
   Pro Forma Income Statements
   Pro Forma Balance Sheets
   Pro Forma Cash Flow Analysis
   Breakeven Chart and Calculation
   Cost Control
   Highlights

XII. PROPOSED COMPANY OFFERING
   Desired Financing
   Offering
   Capitalization
   Use of Funds
   Investor's Return

XIII. APPENDICES

Business models have a place in designing new ventures from scratch as well as mobilizing resources for a new opportunity within an existing enterprise. Whether an offshoot or a new organization, the scheme should be clear. And just like with the business plan, the difference between success and not is the team holding the document and bringing it to life. For more on this point, see Bruce Firestone's blog entry "The Complete Business Model" at www.eqjournal.org

A FINAL CHECKLIST*

This list will help you allocate your time and maintain your focus!
These points will also be important as you prepare for an
oral presentation of your business plan or business model.

Make Your Point Quickly and Give Hierarchy to Your Data—
The Details Matter!

- ✔ Hook the readers, especially in the executive summary, by having a compelling opportunity where you can:
  - Identify a need or opportunity in a large and growing market.
  - Conceptualize a business that will fill that need, or take advantage of that opportunity.
  - Demonstrate that you have the know-how and the team to effectively build a profitable and sustainable business (or identify how you will create such a team).
- ✔ Prioritize the points you are making into three categories:
  - Essential—without this the plan makes no sense.
  - Good to know—directly supports and gives context to your essential points.
  - Interesting—provides a higher level of understanding of market dynamics, industry, etc., but may not relate directly to the nuts and bolts of your business plan. Interesting information should be relegated to the appendix so it doesn't get in the way of the reader.
- ✔ Articulate the size of your market: who are your customers, why they will purchase your product or service, how much they will buy at what price.
- ✔ Include evidence of customers—this will increase your credibility.
- ✔ Discuss the competition, and why the customer will buy your product or service versus the alternatives.
- ✔ Articulate your marketing strategy. How will customers become aware of your product and service, and how will you communicate the benefits?
- ✔ Be specific when discussing your team. Articulate what relevant experience each brings to the business. If you can't identify key managers, you should outline the type of experience you want and a plan for recruiting that person.
- ✔ Edit for the details—clarity and typos—a sloppy presentation says a lot!

* The authors are grateful to Greg White of Chicago Venture Partners who developed this list.

LEARNING OBJECTIVES SUMMARY

LO1 The business plan is more of a process and work in progress than an end in itself, but it should present the information that its audience needs and expects.

LO2 The numbers in a business plan don't matter, but the economics of the business model and value proposition matter enormously. Given today's pace of change in all areas affecting an enterprise, the plan is obsolete the moment it emerges from the printer.

LO3 Preparing and presenting the plan to prospective investors is one of the best ways for the team to have a trial marriage, to learn about the venture strategy, and to determine who can add the greatest value. The dehydrated business plan can be a valuable shortcut in the process of creating, shaping, and moulding an idea into a business.

LO4 The business plan is a blueprint and flight plan for a journey that converts ideas into opportunities, articulates and manages risks and rewards, and articulates the likely flight path and timing for a venture.

LO5 The plan is not the business; some of the most successful ventures were launched without a formal business plan or with one that would be considered weak or flawed.

LO6 Review the business plan for Edgar Bruce Eyewear in the appendix.

STUDY QUESTIONS

1. What is a business plan, for whom is it prepared, and why?
2. Why not hire someone else to write your business plan?
3. How is the plan used by potential investors, and what are the four anchors they are attempting to validate?
4. Please explain the expression: The numbers in the plan don't matter.
5. How can entrepreneurs use the business plan process to identify the best team members, directors, and value-added investors?

MIND STRETCHERS   *Have you considered?*

1. Under what conditions and circumstances is it not to your advantage to prepare a business plan?
2. Some of the most valuable critiques and inputs on your venture will come from outside your team. Who else should review your plan; who knows the industry/market/technology/competitors?
3. A good friend offers you a look at a business plan. You are a director of a company that is a potential competitor of the venture proposed in the plan. What would you do?

An Exercise and Framework

This Business Plan Guide follows the order of presentation outlined in Exhibit 4.2. Originally developed by Leonard Smollen and Brian Haslett, based on more than 30 years of observing and working with entrepreneurs and actually preparing and evaluating hundreds of plans, it is intended to make this challenging task easier.

There is no single best way to write a business plan; the task will evolve in a way that suits you and your situation. While there are many ways to approach the preparation for and writing of a business plan, it is recommended that you begin with the market research and analysis sections. In writing your plan, you should remember that although one of the important functions of a business plan is to influence investors, rather than preparing a fancy presentation, you and your team need to prove to yourselves and others that your opportunity is worth pursuing, and to construct the means by which you will do it. Gathering information, making hard decisions, and developing plans comes first.

The Business Plan Guide shows how to present information succinctly and in a format acceptable to investors. While it is useful to keep in mind who your audience is and that information not clearly presented will most likely not be used, it also is important not to be concerned just with format. The Business Plan Guide indicates specific issues and shows you what needs to be included in a business plan and why.

You may feel as though you have seen much of this before. You should. The guide is based on the analytical framework described in the book and builds upon the online Venture Opportunity Screening Exercises. If you have not completed these exercises, it is helpful to do so before proceeding. The Business Plan Guide will allow you to draw on data and analysis developed in the Venture Opportunity Screening Exercises as you prepare your business plan.

As you proceed through the Business Plan Guide, remember that statements need to be supported with data whenever possible. Note also that it is sometimes easier to present data in graphic, visual form. Include the source of all data, the methods and/or assumptions used, and the credentials of people doing research. If data on which a statement is based are available elsewhere in the plan, be sure to reference where.

Remember that the Business Plan Guide is just that—a guide. It is intended to be applicable to a wide range of product and service businesses. For any particular industry or market, certain critical issues are unique to that industry or market. Common sense should rule in applying the guide to your specific venture.

The Guide

Name: _____

Venture: _____

Date: _____

Step 1   Segment Information into Key Sections

Establish priorities for each section, including individual responsibilities. When you segment your information, it is vital to keep in mind that the plan needs to be logically integrated and that information should be consistent. Because the market opportunity section is the heart and soul of the plan, it may be the most difficult section to write; but it is best to assign it a high priority and to begin working there first.

SECTION OR TASK	PRIORITY	PERSON(S) RESPONSIBLE	DATE TO BEGIN	FIRST DRAFT DUE DATE	DATE COMPLETED OR FINAL VERSION DUE DATE

Step 2   List Tasks That Need to Be Completed

Devise an overall schedule for preparing the plan by assigning priority, persons responsible, and due dates to each task necessary to complete the plan. It is helpful to break larger items (fieldwork to gather customer and competitor intelligence, trade show visits, etc.) into small, more manageable components (such as phone calls or e-mails required before a trip can be taken) and to include the components as a task. *Be as specific as possible.*

TASK	PRIORITY	PERSON RESPONSIBLE	DATE TO BEGIN	DATE OF COMPLETION

Step 3   Combine the List of Segments and the List of Tasks to Create a Calendar

In combining your lists, consider if anything has been omitted and whether you have been realistic in what people can do, when they can do it, what needs to be done, and so forth. To create your calendar, place an X in the week when the task is to be started and an X in the week it is to be completed and then connect the Xs. When you have placed all tasks on the calendar, look carefully again for conflicts or lack of realism. In particular, evaluate if team members are overscheduled.

TASK	WEEK														
	1	2	3	4	5	6	7	8	9	10	11	12	13	14	15

Step 4 A Framework to Develop and Write a Business Plan

The framework follows the order of presentation of the table of contents shown in Exhibit 4.2. While preparing your own plan, you may consider sections in a different order from the one presented in this exhibit. (Also, when you integrate your sections into your final plan, you may choose to present material somewhat differently.)

Cover

The cover page includes the name of the company and its contact details (physical address, phone, and email), the date, and the securities offered. Usually, the name, contact information, and the date are centred at the top of the page and the securities offered are listed at the bottom. Also suggested on the cover page at the bottom is the following text:

> This business plan has been submitted on a confidential basis solely for the benefit of selected, highly qualified investors in connection with the private placement of the above securities and is not for use by any other persons. Neither may it be reproduced, stored, or copied in any form. By accepting delivery of this plan, the recipient agrees to return this copy to the corporation at the address listed above if the recipient does not undertake to subscribe to the offering. Do not copy, fax, reproduce, or distribute without permission.

Table of Contents

Included in the table of contents is a list of the sections, subsections, and any appendices, and the pages on which they can be found. (See Exhibit 4.2.)

I. Executive Summary The executive summary is short and concise (one or two pages). It articulates what the opportunity conditions are and why they exist, who will execute the opportunity and why they are capable of doing so, and how the firm will gain entry and market penetration—it answers the questions we asked in chapter 3: "For what reason does this venture exist and for whom?"

The summary for your venture needs to mirror the criteria shown in Exhibit 3.7 and the Venture Opportunity Screening Exercises available on Connect. This is your chance to clearly articulate how your business is durable and timely, and how it will create or add value to the buyer or end-user.

The summary is prepared after the hard work is done; it is the reward after the other sections of the business plan are completed. For the writers it is dessert, for the business plan reader it is the aperitif—taken before the meal to stimulate the appetite. As the other sections are drafted, it is helpful to note one or two key sentences, and some key facts and numbers from each. There might even be a competition among the team over what to include. The executive summary should be fun to write, keep the tone lively. Yes, there will be too much to fit in it and much editing will take place.

The summary is important for those ventures trying to raise or borrow money. Investors, bankers, managers, and other readers use the summary to quickly determine whether they find the venture of interest. Unless the summary is appealing and compelling, it may be the only section read, and you may never get the chance to make a presentation or discuss your business in person. It is a vehicle for the team to communicate its excitement about the venture.

Leave plenty of time to prepare the summary. The material in the executive summary should be presented with enthusiasm and flair—you need to keep the reader committed and win them over—you are searching for advocates who will lend support.

The executive summary usually contains a paragraph or two covering each of the following:

A. *Description of the business concept and the business.* Describe the business concept for the business you are or will be in. Be sure the description of your concept explains how your product or service will fundamentally change the way customers currently do certain things. For example, Arthur Rock, the lead investor in Apple and Intel, has stated that he focuses on concepts that will change the way people live and/or work. You need to identify when the company was formed, what it will do, what is special or proprietary about its product, service, or technology, and so forth. Include summary information about any proprietary technology, trade secrets, or unique capabilities that give you an edge in the marketplace. If the company has existed for a few years, a brief summary of its size and progress is in order. Try to make your description 25 words or less, and briefly describe the specific product or service.

B. *The opportunity and strategy.* Summarize what the opportunity is, why it is compelling, and the entry strategy planned to exploit it. Clearly, state the main point or benefit you are addressing. This information may be presented as an outline of the key facts, conditions, competitors' vulnerabilities ("sleepiness," sluggishness, poor service, etc.), industry trends (is it fragmented or emerging?), and other evidence and logic that define the opportunity. Note plans for growth and expansion beyond the entry products or services and into other market segments (such as international markets) as appropriate.

C. *The target market and projections*. Identify and briefly explain the industry and market, who the primary customer groups are, how the product(s) or service(s) will be positioned, and how you plan to reach and service these groups. Include information about the structure of the market, the size and growth rate for the market segments or niches you are seeking, your unit and dollar sales estimates, your anticipated market share, the payback period for your customers, and your pricing strategy (including price versus performance/value/benefits considerations).

D. *The competitive advantages*. Indicate the significant competitive edges you enjoy or can create as a result of your innovative product, service, and strategy; advantages in lead time or barriers to entry; competitors' weaknesses and vulnerabilities; and other industry conditions.

E. *Sustainability*. Discuss the social, economic, and environmental sustainability of your business model. Summarize the employment opportunities that your business is likely to create, and describe any plans for outsourcing or using offshore labour and how that might impact the community and your labour pool. Briefly, describe any environmental issues related to your business with regard to resources, waste generation, and legislative compliance.

F. *The team*. Summarize the relevant knowledge, experience, know-how, and skills of the lead entrepreneur and any team members, noting previous accomplishments, especially those involving profit and loss responsibility and general management and people management experience. Include significant information, such as the size of a division, project, or prior business with which the lead entrepreneur or a team member was the driving force.

G. *The offering*. Briefly indicate the dollar amount of equity and/or debt financing needed, how much of the company you are prepared to offer for that financing, what principal use will be made of the capital, and how the investor, lender, or strategic partner will achieve its desired rate of return. Remember, your targeted resource provider has a well-defined appetite and you must understand the "Circle of Venture Capital Ecstasy" (Exhibit 3.1).

II. The Industry and the Company and Its Product(s) or Service(s)   A major area of consideration is the company, its concept for its product(s) and service(s), and its interface with the industry in which it will be competing. The marketing information, for example, fits into this context. Information needs to include a description of the industry, a description of the concept, a description of your company, and a description of the product(s) or service(s) you will offer, the proprietary position of these product(s) or service(s), their potential advantages, and entry and growth strategy for the product(s) or service(s).

A. *The industry*.
- Present the current status and prospects for the industry in which the proposed business will operate. Be sure to consider industry structure.
- Discuss briefly market size, growth trends, and competitors.
- Discuss any new products or developments, new markets and customers, new requirements, new entrants and exits, and any other national or economic trends and factors that could affect the venture's business positively or negatively.
- Discuss the environmental profile of the industry. Consider energy requirements, supply chain factors, waste generation, and recycling capabilities. Outline any new green technologies or trends that may have an impact on this opportunity.

B. *The company and the concept*.
- Describe generally the concept of the business, what business your company is in or intends to enter, what product(s) or service(s) it will offer, and who are or will be its principal customers.
- By way of background, give the date your venture was incorporated and describe the identification and development of its products and the involvement of the company's principals in that development.
- If your company has been in business for several years and is seeking expansion financing, review its history and cite its prior sales and profit performance, and if your company has had setbacks or losses in prior years, discuss these and emphasize current and future efforts to prevent a recurrence of these difficulties and to improve your company's performance.

C. *The product(s) or service(s)*.
- Describe in some detail each product or service to be sold.
- Discuss the application of the product or service and describe the primary end use as well as any significant secondary applications. Articulate how you will

solve a problem, relieve pain, or provide a benefit or needed service.

- Describe the service or product delivery system.
- Emphasize any unique features of the product or service and how these will create or add significant value; also, highlight any differences between what is currently on the market and what you will offer that will account for your market penetration. Be sure to describe how value will be added and the payback period to the customer—that is, discuss how many months it will take the customer to cover the initial purchase price of the product or service as a result of its time, cost, or productivity improvements.
- Include a description of any possible drawbacks (including problems with obsolescence) of the product or service.
- Define the present state of development of the product or service and how much time and money will be required to fully develop, test, and introduce the product or service. Provide a summary of the functional specifications and photographs, if available, of the product.
- Discuss any head start you might have that would enable you to achieve a favoured or entrenched position in the industry.
- Describe any features of the product or service that give it an "unfair" advantage over the competition. Describe any patents, trade secrets, or other proprietary features of the product or service.
- Discuss any opportunities for the expansion of the product line or the development of related products or services. (Emphasize opportunities and explain how you will take advantage of them.)

D. *Entry and growth strategy.*
- Indicate key success variables in your marketing plan (e.g., an innovative product, timing advantage, or marketing approach) and your pricing, channel(s) of distribution, advertising, and promotion plans.
- Summarize how fast you intend to grow and to what size during the first five years and your plans for growth beyond your initial product or service.
- Show how the entry and growth strategy is derived from the opportunity and value-added or other competitive advantages, such as the weakness of competitors.
- Discuss the overall environmental and social sustainability of your growth plan.[10] Consider the effect on the community and examine the potential environmental impact of your business as it grows.

III. Market Research and Analysis This section needs to support the assertion that the venture can capture a substantial market in a growing industry and stand up to competition. Because of the importance of market analysis and the critical dependence of other parts of the plan on this information, you are advised to prepare this section of the business plan before any other. Take enough time to do this section very well and to check alternative sources of market data.

This section of the business plan is difficult to prepare; however, other sections of the business plan depend on the market research and analysis presented here. For example, the predicted sales levels directly influence such factors as the size of the manufacturing operation, the marketing plan, and the amount of debt and equity capital you will require. Most entrepreneurs seem to have great difficulty preparing and presenting market research and analyses that show that their ventures' sales estimates are sound and attainable.

A. *Customers.*
- Discuss who the customers for the product(s) or service(s) are or will be. Note that potential customers need to be classified by relatively homogeneous groups having common, identifiable characteristics (e.g., by major market segment). For example, an automotive part might be sold to manufacturers and to parts distributors supplying the replacement market, so the discussion needs to reflect two market segments.
- Show who and where the major purchasers for the product(s) or service(s) are in each market segment. Include national regions and foreign countries, as appropriate.
- Indicate whether customers are easily reached and receptive, how customers buy (wholesale, through manufacturers' representatives, etc.), where in their organizations buying decisions are made, and how long decisions take. Describe customers' purchasing processes, including the bases on which they make purchase decisions (e.g., price, quality, timing, delivery, training, service, personal contacts, or political pressures) and why they might change current purchasing decisions.
- List any orders, contracts, or letters of commitment that you have in hand. These are the most powerful data you can provide. List also any potential customers who have expressed an interest in the product(s) or service(s) and indicate why; also list any potential customers who have shown no interest in the proposed product or service and explain why they are not interested and explain what you will do to

overcome negative customer reaction. Indicate how fast you believe your product or service will be accepted in the market.

- If you have an existing business, list your principal current customers and discuss the trends in your sales to them.

B. *Market size and trends.*
- Show for five years the size of the current total market and the share you will have, by market segment, and/or region, and/or country, for the product or service you will offer, in units, dollars, and potential profitability.
- Describe also the potential annual growth for at least three years of the total market for your product(s) or service(s) for each major customer group, region, or country, as appropriate.
- Discuss the major factors affecting market growth (e.g., industry trends, socioeconomic trends, government policy, environmental impacts, and population shifts) and review previous trends in the market. Any differences between past and projected annual growth rates need to be explained.

C. *Competition and competitive edges.*
- Make a realistic assessment of the strengths and weaknesses of competitors. Assess the substitute and/or alternative products and services and list the companies that supply them, both domestic and foreign, as appropriate.
- Compare competing and substitute products or services based on market share, quality, price, performance, delivery, timing, service, warranties, and other pertinent features.
- Compare the fundamental value that is added or created by your product or service, in terms of economic benefits to the customer and to your competitors.
- Discuss the current advantages and disadvantages of these products and services and say why they are not meeting customer needs.
- Indicate any knowledge of competitors' actions that could lead you to new or improved products and an advantageous position. For example, discuss whether competitors are simply sluggish or nonresponsive or are asleep at the switch.
- Identify the strengths and weaknesses of the competing companies and determine and discuss each competitor's market share, sales, distribution methods, and production capabilities.
- Review the financial position, resources, costs, and profitability of the competition and their profit

trend. Note that you can utilize Risk Management Association data for comparison.
- Indicate who are the service, pricing, performance, cost, and quality leaders. Discuss why any companies have entered or dropped out of the market in recent years.
- Discuss the three or four key competitors and why customers buy from them, and determine and discuss why customers leave them. Relate this to the basis for the purchase decision examined in Part IIIA.
- From what you know about the competitors' operations, explain why you think they are vulnerable and you can capture a share of their business. Discuss what makes you think it will be easy or difficult to compete with them. Discuss, in particular, your competitive advantages gained through such "unfair" advantage as patents.

D. *Estimated market share and sales.*
- Summarize what it is about your product(s) or service(s) that will make it saleable in the face of current and potential competition. Especially, mention the fundamental value added or created by the product(s) or service(s).
- Identify any major customers (including international customers) who are willing to make, or who have already made, purchase commitments. Indicate the extent of those commitments, and why they were made. Discuss which customers could be major purchasers in future years and why.
- Based on your assessment of the advantages of your product or service, the market size and trends, customers, competition and their products, and the trends of sales in prior years, estimate the share of the market and the sales in units and dollars that you will acquire in each of the next three years. Remember to show assumptions used.
- Show how the growth of the company sales in units and its estimated market share are related to the growth of the industry, the customers, and the strengths and weaknesses of competitors. Remember, the assumptions used to estimate market share and sales need to be clearly stated.
- If yours is an existing business, also indicate the total market, your market share, and sales for two prior years.

E. *Ongoing market evaluation.*
- Explain how you will continue to evaluate your target markets; assess customer needs and service; guide product improvement, pricing, and new product programs; plan for expansions of your production facility, and guide product/service pricing.

IV. The Economics of the Business The economic and financial characteristics, including the apparent magnitude and durability of margins and profits generated, need to support the fundamental attractiveness of the opportunity. The underlying operating and cash conversion cycle of the business, the value chain, and so forth need to make sense in terms of the opportunity and strategies planned.

A. *Gross and operating margins.*

- Describe the magnitude of the gross margins (i.e., selling price less variable costs) and the operating margins for each of the product(s) and/or service(s) you are selling in the market niche(s) you plan to attack. Include results of your contribution analysis.

B. *Profit potential and durability.*

- Describe the magnitude and expected durability of the profit stream the business will generate—before and after taxes—and reference appropriate industry benchmarks, other competitive intelligence, or your own relevant experience.
- Address the issue of how perishable or durable the profit stream appears to be. Provide reasons why your profit stream is perishable or durable, such as barriers to entry you can create, your technological and market lead time, and environmental sustainability, which in some cases can be a driver for cost reduction.

C. *Fixed, variable, and semivariable costs.*

- Provide a detailed summary of fixed, variable, and semivariable costs, in dollars and as percentages of total cost as appropriate, for the product or service you offer and the volume of purchases and sales upon which these are based.
- Show relevant industry benchmarks.

D. *Months to breakeven.*

- Given your entry strategy, marketing plan, and proposed financing, show how long it will take to reach a unit breakeven sales level.
- Note any significant stepwise changes in your breakeven that will occur as you grow and add substantial capacity.

E. *Months to reach positive cash flow.*

- Given the above strategy and assumptions, show when the venture will attain a positive cash flow.
- Show if and when you will run out of cash. Note where the detailed assumptions can be found.
- Note any significant stepwise changes in cash flow that will occur as you grow and add capacity.

V. Marketing Plan The marketing plan describes how the sales projections will be attained. The marketing plan needs to detail the overall marketing strategy that will exploit the opportunity and your competitive advantages. Include a discussion of sales and service policies; pricing, distribution, promotion, and advertising strategies; and sales projections. The marketing plan needs to describe *what* is to be done, *how* it will be done, *when* it will be done, and *who* will do it.

A. *Overall marketing strategy.*

- Describe the specific marketing philosophy and strategy of the company, given the value chain and channels of distribution in the market niche(s) you are pursuing. Include, for example, a discussion of the kinds of customer groups that you already have orders from or that will be targeted for initial intensive selling effort and those targeted for later selling efforts; how specific potential customers in these groups will be identified and how they will be contacted; what features of the product or service, such as service, quality, price, delivery, warranty, or training, will be emphasized to generate sales; if any innovative or unusual marketing techniques will enhance customer acceptance, such as leasing where only sales were previously attempted; and so forth.
- Indicate whether the product(s) or service(s) will initially be introduced internationally, nationally, or regionally; explain why; and if appropriate, indicate any plans for extending sales at a later date.
- Discuss any seasonal trends that underlie the cash conversion cycle in the industry and what can be done to promote sales out of season.
- Describe any plans to obtain government contracts as a means of supporting product development costs and overhead.
- Describe any sustainability advantages you have or can develop, and how these aspects relate to building customer loyalty and community support for your product(s) or service(s).

B. *Pricing.*

- Discuss pricing strategy, including the prices to be charged for your product and service, and compare your pricing policy with those of your major competitors, including a brief discussion of payback (in months) to the customer.
- Discuss the gross profit margin between manufacturing and ultimate sales costs and indicate whether this margin is large enough to allow for distribution and sales, warranty, training, service, amortization of

development and equipment costs, price competition, and so forth, and still allow a profit.

- Explain how the price you set will enable you (1) to get the product or service accepted, (2) to maintain and increase your market share in the face of competition, and (3) to produce profits.
- Justify your pricing strategy and differences between your prices and those for competitive or substitute products or services in terms of economic payback to the customer and value added through newness, quality, warranty, timing, performance, service, cost savings, efficiency, and the like.
- If your product is to be priced lower than those of the competition, explain how you will do this and maintain profitability (e.g., through greater value added via effectiveness in manufacturing and distribution, lower labour costs, lower material costs, lower overhead, or other cost component).
- Discuss your pricing policy, including a discussion of the relationship of price, market share, and profits.

C. *Sales tactics.*
- Describe the methods (e.g., own sales force, sales representatives, ready-made manufacturers' sales organizations, direct mail, or distributors) that will be used to make sales and distribute the product or service and both the initial plans and longer-range plans for a sales force. Include a discussion of any special requirements (e.g., refrigeration).
- Discuss the value chain and the resulting margins to be given to retailers, distributors, wholesalers, and salespeople and any special policies regarding discounts, exclusive distribution rights, and so on, given to distributors or sales representatives and compare these to those given by your competition. (See the online Venture Opportunity Screening Exercises.)
- Describe how distributors or sales representatives, if they are used, will be selected, when they will start to represent you, the areas they will cover, the head count of dealers and representatives by month, and the expected sales to be made by each.
- If a direct sales force is to be used, indicate how it will be structured and at what rate (a head count) it will be built up; indicate if it is to replace a dealer or representative organization and, if so, when and how.
- If direct mail, magazine, newspaper, or other media, telemarketing, or catalogue sales are to be used, indicate the specific channels or vehicles, costs (per 1000), expected response rates, and so on. Discuss how these will be built up.

- Show the sales expected per salesperson per year and what commission, incentive, and/or salary they are slated to receive and compare these figures to the average for your industry.
- Present a selling schedule and a sales budget that includes all marketing promotion and service costs.

D. *Service and warranty policies.*
- If your company will offer a product that will require service, warranties, or training, indicate the importance of these to the customers' purchasing decisions and discuss your method of handling service problems.
- Describe the kind and term of any warranties to be offered, whether service will be handled by company employees, agencies, dealers and distributors, or returns to the factory.
- Indicate the proposed charge for service calls and whether service will be a profitable or breakeven operation.
- Compare your service, warranty, and customer training policies and practices to those of your principal competitors.

E. *Advertising and promotion.*
- Describe the approaches the company will use to bring its product or service to the attention of prospective purchasers.
- For original equipment manufacturers and for manufacturers of industrial products, indicate the plans for trade show participation, trade magazine advertisements, direct mailings, the preparation of product sheets and promotional literature, and use of advertising agencies.
- For consumer products, indicate what kind of advertising and promotional campaign will introduce the product, including sales aids to dealers, trade shows, and so forth.
- Present a schedule and approximate costs of promotion and advertising (direct mail, telemarketing, catalogues, etc.), and discuss how these costs will be incurred.

F. *Distribution.*
- Describe the methods and channels of distribution you will employ. Discuss the availability and capacity of these channels.
- Indicate the sensitivity of shipping cost as a percent of the selling price.
- Note any special issues or problems that need to be resolved or present potential vulnerabilities.

- If international sales are involved, note how these sales will be handled, including distribution, shipping, insurance, credit, and collections.

VI. Design and Development Plans The nature and extent of any design and development work and the time and money required before a product or service is marketable need to be considered in detail. (Note that design and development costs are often underestimated.) Design and development might be the engineering work necessary to convert a laboratory prototype to a finished product; the design of special tooling; the work of an industrial designer to make a product more attractive and saleable; or the identification and organization of employees, equipment, and special techniques, such as equipment, new computer software, and skills required for computerized credit checking.

A. *Development status and tasks.*
- Describe the current status of each product or service and explain what remains to be done to make it marketable.
- Describe briefly the competence or expertise that your company has or will require to complete this development.
- List any customers or end-users that are participating in the development, design, and/or testing of the product or service. Indicate results to date or when results are expected.

B. *Difficulties and risks.*
- Identify any major anticipated design and development problems and define approaches to their solution.
- Discuss the possible effect on the cost of design and development, on the time to market introduction, and so forth, of such problems.

C. *Product improvement and new products.*
- In addition to describing the development of the initial products, discuss any ongoing design and development work that is planned to keep the product(s) or service(s) that can be sold to the same group of customers. Discuss customers who have participated in these efforts and their reactions, and include any evidence that you may have.
- With regard to ongoing product development, outline any compliance issues relating to new, pending, or potential environmental legislation. Discuss any green technologies or production capabilities that could enhance sustainability.

D. *Costs.*
- Present and discuss the design and development budget, including costs of labour, materials, consulting fees, and so on.
- Discuss the impact on cash flow projections of underestimating this budget, including the impact of a 15 to 30 percent contingency.

E. *Proprietary issues.*
- Describe any patent, trademark, copyright, or intellectual property rights you own or are seeking.
- Describe any contractual rights or agreements that give you exclusivity or proprietary rights.
- Discuss the impact of any unresolved issues or existing or possible actions pending, such as disputed rights of ownership, relating to proprietary rights on timing and on any competitive edge you have assumed.

VII. Manufacturing and Operations Plan The manufacturing and operations plan needs to include such factors as plant location, the type of facilities needed, space requirements, capital equipment requirements, and labour force (both full- and part-time) requirements. For a manufacturing business, the manufacturing and operations plan needs to include policies on inventory control, purchasing, production control, and which parts of the product will be purchased and which operations will be performed by your workforce (called make-or-buy decisions). A service business may require particular attention to location (proximity to customers is generally a must), minimizing overhead, and obtaining competitive productivity from a labour force.

A. *Operating cycle.*
- Describe the lead/lag times that characterize the fundamental operating cycle in your business. (Include a graph similar to the one found in the online Venture Opportunity Screening Exercises.)
- Explain how any seasonal production loads will be handled without severe dislocation (e.g., by building to inventory or using part-time help in peak periods).

B. *Geographic location.*
- Describe the planned physical location of the business. Include any location analysis that you have done.
- Discuss any advantages or disadvantages of the site location in terms of labour (including labour availability, whether workers are unionized, wage rates, and outsourcing), closeness to customers and/or suppliers, access to transportation, provincial and

local taxes and laws (including zoning and environmental impact regulations), access to utilities (energy use and sustainability), and so forth.

C. *Facilities and improvements.*

- For an existing business, describe the facilities, including plant and office space, storage and land areas, special tooling, machinery, and other capital equipment currently used to conduct the company's business, and discuss whether these facilities are adequate and in compliance with health, safety, and environmental regulations. Discuss any economies of scale.

- For a start-up, describe how and when the necessary facilities to start production will be acquired.

- Discuss whether equipment and space will be leased or acquired (new or used) and indicate the costs and timing of such actions and how much of the proposed financing will be devoted to plant and equipment.

- Explain future equipment needs in the next three years.

- For start-ups expecting to outsource manufacturing, indicate the location and size of the firm, and discuss the advantages, risks, and monitoring regime.

- Discuss how and when, in the next three years, plant space and equipment will be expanded and capacities required by future sales projections and any plans to improve or add existing plant space. Discuss any environmental impacts related to those expansion requirements. If there are any plans to move the facility, outsource labour, or move production overseas, discuss the impact on the local community. Indicate the timing and cost of such acquisitions.

D. *Strategy and plans.*

- Describe the manufacturing processes involved in production of your product(s) and any decisions with respect to subcontracting of component parts, rather than complete in-house manufacture.

- Justify your proposed make-or-buy policy in terms of inventory financing, available labour skills, and other nontechnical questions, as well as production, cost, and capability issues.

- Discuss who potential subcontractors and/or suppliers are likely to be and any information about, or any surveys that have been made of, these subcontractors and suppliers.

- Present a production plan that shows cost/volume/inventory level information at various sales levels of operation with breakdowns of applicable material, labour, purchased components, and factory overhead.

- Describe your approach to quality control, production control, and inventory control; explain what quality control and inspection procedures the company will use to minimize service problems and associated customer dissatisfaction.

- Describe the environmental sustainability of your operations, including the activities of your subcontractors and suppliers.

E. *Regulatory and legal issues.*

- Discuss any relevant provincial, federal, or foreign regulatory requirements unique to your product, process, or service such as licences, zoning permits, health permits, and environmental approvals necessary to begin operation.

- Note any pending regulatory changes that can affect the nature of your opportunity and its timing.

- Discuss any legal or contractual obligations that are pertinent as well.

VIII. Venture Team This section of the business plan includes a description of the functions that will need to be filled, a description of the key personnel and their primary duties, an outline of the organizational structure for the venture, a description of the board of directors, a description of the ownership position of any other investors, and so forth. You need to present indications of commitment, such as the willingness of team members to initially accept modest salaries, and of the existence of the proper balance of technical, managerial, and business skills and experience in doing what is proposed.

A. *Organization.*

- Present the key management roles in the company and the individuals who will fill each position. (If the company is established and of sufficient size, an organization chart needs to be appended.)

- If it is not possible to fill each executive role with a full-time person without adding excessive overhead, indicate how these functions will be performed (e.g., using part-time specialists or consultants to perform some functions), who will perform them, and when they will be replaced by a full-time staff member.

- If any key individuals will not be on board at the start of the venture, indicate when they will join the company.

- Discuss any current or past situations where key people have worked together that could indicate how their skills complement each other and result in an effective venture team.

B. *Key personnel.*
- For each key person, describe in detail career highlights, particularly relevant know-how, skills, and track record of accomplishments that demonstrate his or her ability to perform the assigned role. Include in your description sales and profitability achievements (budget size, number of subordinates, new product introductions, etc.) and other prior entrepreneurial or general management results.
- Describe the exact duties and responsibilities of each of the key members of the venture team.
- Complete résumés for each key management member need to be included here or as an exhibit and need to stress relevant training, experience, and concrete accomplishments, such as profit and sales improvement, labour management success, manufacturing or technical achievements, and meeting budgets and schedules.

C. *Management compensation and ownership.*
- State the salary to be paid, the share ownership planned, and the amount of equity investment (if any) of each key member of the venture team.
- Compare the compensation of each key member to the salary he or she received at his or her last independent job.

D. *Other investors.*
- Describe here any other investors in your venture, the number and percentage of outstanding shares they own, when they were acquired, and at what price.

E. *Employment and other agreements and share option and bonus plans.*
- Describe any existing or contemplated employment or other agreements with key members.
- Indicate any restrictions on shares and investing that affect ownership and disposition of shares.
- Describe any performance-dependent share option or bonus plans.
- Summarize any incentive share option or other share ownership plans planned or in effect for key people and employees.

F. *Board of directors.*
- Discuss the company's philosophy about the size and composition of the board.
- Identify any proposed board members and include a one- or two-sentence statement of each member's background that shows what he or she can bring to the company.

G. *Other shareholders, rights, and restrictions.*
- Indicate any other shareholders in your company and any rights, restrictions, or obligations, such as notes or guarantees, associated with these. (If they have all been accounted for above, simply note that there are no others.)

H. *Supporting professional advisors and services.*
- Indicate the supporting services that will be required.
- Indicate the names and affiliations of the legal, accounting, advertising, consulting, and banking advisors selected for your venture and the services each will provide.

IX. Overall Schedule   A schedule that shows the timing and interrelationship of the major events necessary to launch the venture and realize its objectives is an essential part of a business plan. The underlying cash conversion and operating cycle of the business will provide key inputs for the schedule. In addition to being a planning aid, by showing deadlines critical to a venture's success, a well-presented schedule can be extremely valuable in convincing potential investors that the venture team is able to plan for growth in a way that recognizes obstacles and minimizes investor risk. Since the time to do things tends to be underestimated in most business plans, it is important to demonstrate that you have correctly estimated these amounts in determining the schedule. Create your schedule as follows:

1. Lay out (use a bar chart) the cash conversion cycle of the business for each product or service expected, the lead and elapsed times from an order to the purchase of raw materials, or inventory to shipping and collection.

2. Prepare a month-by-month schedule that shows the timing of product development, market planning, sales programs, production, and operations, and that includes sufficient detail to show the timing of the primary tasks required to accomplish an activity.

3. Show on the schedule the deadlines or milestones critical to the venture's success, such as:
- Incorporation of the venture.
- Completion of design and development.
- Completion of prototypes.
- Obtaining sales representatives.
- Obtaining product display at trade shows.
- Signing of distributors and dealers.
- Ordering of materials in production quantities.
- Starting of production or operation.

- Receipt of first orders.
- Delivery on first sale.
- Receiving the first payment on accounts receivable.

4. Show on the schedule the "ramp up" of the number of management personnel, the number of production and operations personnel, and plant or equipment and their relation to the development of the business.

5. Discuss in a general way the activities most likely to cause a schedule slippage, what steps will be taken to correct such slippages, and the impact of schedule slippages on the venture's operation, especially its potential viability and capital needs.

X. Critical Risks, Problems, and Assumptions   The development of a business has risks and problems, and the business plan invariably contains some implicit assumptions about them. You need to include a description of the risks and the consequences of adverse outcomes relating to your industry, your company and its personnel, your product's market appeal, and the timing and financing of your start-up. Be sure to discuss assumptions concerning sales projections, customer orders, and so forth. If the venture has anything that could be considered a fatal flaw, discuss why it is not. The discovery of any unstated negative factors by potential investors can undermine the credibility of the venture and endanger its financing. Be aware that most investors will read the section describing the executive team first and then this section.

Do not omit this section. If you do, the reader will most likely come to one or more of the following conclusions:

1. You think he or she is incredibly naive or stupid, or both.

2. You hope to pull the wool over his or her eyes.

3. You do not have enough objectivity to recognize and deal with assumptions and problems.

Identifying and discussing the risks in your venture demonstrates your skills as a leader and increases the credibility of you and your venture with a venture capital investor or a private investor. Taking the initiative on the identification and discussion of risks helps you to demonstrate to the investor that you have thought about them and can handle them. Risks then tend not to loom as large black clouds in the investor's thinking about your venture.

1. Discuss assumptions and risks implicit in your plan.

2. Identify and discuss any major problems and other risks, such as:
   - Running out of cash *before* orders are secured.
   - Potential price cutting by competitors.

- Any potentially unfavourable industry trends.
- Design or manufacturing costs in excess of estimates.
- Sales projections not achieved.
- An unmet product development schedule.
- Difficulties or long lead times encountered in the procurement of parts or raw materials.
- Difficulties encountered in obtaining needed bank credit.
- Larger-than-expected innovation and development costs.
- Running out of cash *after* orders pour in.

3. Indicate what assumptions or potential problems and risks are most critical to the success of the venture, and describe your plans for minimizing the impact of unfavourable developments in each case.

XI. The Financial Plan   The financial plan is basic to the evaluation of an investment opportunity and needs to represent your best estimates of financial requirements. Its purpose is to indicate the venture's potential and to present a timetable for financial viability. It also can serve as an operating plan for financial management using financial benchmarks. In preparing the financial plan, you need to look creatively at your venture and consider alternative ways of launching or financing it.

As part of the financial plan, financial exhibits need to be prepared. To estimate *cash flow needs*, use cash-based, rather than an accrual-based, accounting (i.e., use a real-time cash flow analysis of expected receipts and disbursements). This analysis needs to cover three years, including current- and prior-year income statements and balance sheets, if applicable; profit and loss forecasts for three years; pro forma income statements and balance sheets; and a breakeven chart. On the appropriate exhibits, or in an attachment, assumptions behind such items as sales levels and growth, collections and payables periods, inventory requirements, cash balances, and cost of goods need to be specified. Your analysis of the operating and cash conversion cycle in the business will enable you to identify these critical assumptions.

Pro forma income statements are the plan-for-profit part of financial management and can indicate the potential financial feasibility of a new venture. Because usually the level of profits, particularly during the start-up years of a venture, will not be sufficient to finance operating asset needs, and because actual cash inflows do not always match the actual cash outflows on a short-term basis, a cash flow forecast indicating these conditions and enabling management to plan cash needs is recommended. Further, pro forma balance sheets are used to detail the assets required to support the projected level of operations and, through liabilities, to show how these assets are to be financed. The projected balance sheets can indicate if debt-to-equity ratios, working capital, current ratios, inventory turnover, and the like are within the acceptable limits required to justify future financings that are projected for the venture. Finally, it is very useful to prepare a breakeven chart showing the level of sales and production that will cover all costs, including those costs that vary with production level and those that do not.

A. *Actual income statements and balance sheets.* For an existing business, prepare income statements and balance sheets for the current year and for the prior two years.

B. *Pro forma income statements.*
- Using sales forecasts and the accompanying production or operations costs, prepare pro forma income statements for at least the first three years.
- Fully discuss assumptions (e.g., the amount allowed for bad debts and discounts, or any assumptions made with respect to sales expenses or general and administrative costs being a fixed percentage of costs or sales) made in preparing the pro forma income statement and document them.
- Draw on Section X of the business plan and highlight any major risks, such as the effect of a 20 percent reduction in sales from those projected or the adverse impact of having to climb a learning curve on the level of productivity over time, which could prevent the venture's sales and profit goals from being attained, plus the sensitivity of profits to these risks.

C. *Pro forma balance sheets.* Prepare pro forma balance sheets semi-annually in the first year and at the end of each of the first three years of operation.

D. *Pro forma cash flow analysis.*
- Project cash flows monthly for the first year of operation and quarterly for at least the next two years. Detail the amount and timing of expected cash inflows and outflows. Determine the need for and timing of additional financing and indicate peak requirements for working capital. Indicate how necessary additional financing is to be obtained, such as through equity financing, bank loans, or short-term lines of credit from banks, on what terms, and how it is to be repaid. Remember they are based on cash, not accrual, accounting.

- Discuss assumptions, such as those made on the timing of collection of receivables, trade discounts given, terms of payments to vendors, planned salary and wage increases, anticipated increases in any operating expenses, seasonality characteristics of the business as they affect inventory requirements, inventory turnovers per year, capital equipment purchases, and so forth. Again, these are real time (i.e., cash), not accruals.
- Discuss cash flow sensitivity to a variety of assumptions about business factors (e.g., possible changes in such crucial assumptions as an increase in the receivable collection period or a sales level lower than that forecasted).

E. *Breakeven chart.*
- Calculate breakeven and prepare a chart that shows when breakeven will be reached and any stepwise changes in breakeven that may occur.
- Discuss the breakeven shown for your venture and whether it will be easy or difficult to attain, including a discussion of the size of breakeven sales volume relative to projected total sales, the size of gross margins and price sensitivity, and how the breakeven point might be lowered in case the venture falls short of sales projections.

F. *Cost control.* Describe how you will obtain information about costs and how often, who will be responsible for the control of various cost elements, and how you will take action on budget overruns.

G. *Highlights.* Highlight the important conclusions, including the maximum amount and timing of cash required, the amount of debt and equity needed, how fast any debts can be repaid, etc.

XII. Proposed Company Offering The purpose of this section of the plan is to indicate the amount of money that is being sought, the nature and amount of the securities offered to investors, a brief description of the uses that will be made of the capital raised, and a summary of how the investor is expected to achieve its targeted rate of return. It is recommended that you read the discussion about financing in Part IV of this book.

The terms for financing your company that you propose here are the first steps in the negotiation process with those interested in investing, and it is very possible that your financing will involve different kinds of securities than originally proposed.

A. *Desired financing.* Based on your real-time cash flow projections and your estimate of how much money is required over the next three years to carry out the development and/or expansion of your business as described, indicate how much of this capital requirement will be obtained by this offering and how much will be obtained via term loans and lines of credit.

B. *Offering.*

- Describe the type (e.g., common shares, convertible debentures, debt with warrants, debt plus shares), unit price, and total amount of securities to be sold in this offering. If securities are not just common shares, indicate by type, interest, maturity, and conversion conditions.

- Show the percentage of the company that the investors of this offering will hold after it is completed or after exercise of any share conversion or purchase rights in the case of convertible debentures or warrants.

- Securities sold through a private placement and that therefore are exempt from SEC registration should include the following statement in this part of the plan: *The shares being sold pursuant to this offering are restricted securities and may not be resold readily. The prospective investor should recognize that such securities might be restricted as to resale for an indefinite period. Each purchaser will be required to execute a Non-Distribution Agreement satisfactory in form to corporate counsel.*

C. *Capitalization.*

- Present in tabular form the current and proposed (post-offering) number of outstanding shares of common shares. Indicate any shares offered by key people and show the number of shares that they will hold after completion of the proposed financing.

- Indicate how many shares of your company's common shares will remain authorized but unissued after the offering and how many of these will be reserved for share options for future key employees.

D. *Use of funds.* Investors like to know how their money is going to be spent. Provide a brief description of how the capital raised will be used. Summarize as specifically as possible, what amount will be used for such things as product design and development, capital equipment, marketing, and general working capital needs.

E. *Investors' return.* Indicate how your valuation and proposed ownership shares will result in the desired rate of return for the investors you have targeted and what the likely harvest or exit mechanism (IPO, outright sale, merger, management buyout, etc.) will be.

XIII. Appendices Include pertinent information here that is too extensive for the body of the business plan but that is necessary (product specs or photos; lists of references, suppliers of critical components; special location factors, facilities, or technical analyses; reports from consultants or technical experts; and copies of any critical regulatory approval, licences, etc.).

Step 5   Integrate Sections

Integrate the discrete sections you have created into a coherent business plan that can be used for the purpose for which it was created.

Step 6   Get Feedback

Once written, it is recommended that you get the plan reviewed. No matter how good you and your team are, you will most likely overlook issues and treat aspects of your venture in a manner that is less than clear. A good reviewer can give you the benefit of an outside objective evaluation. Your lawyer can make sure that there are no misleading statements in your plan and that it contains all the caveats and the like.

Preparation Questions

1. What factors have been most responsible for Shad's current level of success?

2. Describe Shad's current business model. What options does Shad have now? What are the benefits and risks of each?

3. How would Shad's business model change depending on which option he chooses?

SHAD—WHAT'S NEXT FOR THIS JUNO AWARD-WINNING ARTIST?

"We need to figure out where to go next," thought G, manager of Canadian hip hop artist Shad, as he drove home from an intense day of meetings. Shad was recording his third and final album under contract with Black Box Recordings over the winter of 2013. The first two albums released under the Canadian label had achieved critical success, including a JUNO[1] win for the second album. The success of the third album would play a role in determining Shad's future, but G knew it was time to start considering "What next? Where do we take Shad's career from here?"

HOW IT ALL BEGAN—SHAD'S FIRST BIG BREAK

Shadrach Kabango was born in Kenya in 1982 to Rwandan parents, and was raised in London, Ontario. The youngest of two children growing up, he always had an interest in music, and began rapping as a hobby in high school. He pursued his undergraduate degree in business administration at Wilfrid Laurier University, where he also had his first taste of performing as part of a band called "Bread and Water."

In 2004, while at Laurier, a few of Shad's tracks were submitted to a "Rhythm of the Future" competition at a local Kitchener-Waterloo radio station. The competition awarded $17 500 to young talent to fund the recording of their first album.

Shad won the competition, which gave him his first big break; he recorded his first album, *When This Is Over*, independently at a studio in Ottawa later that year. The album was released in 2005, and Shad had his first show in Waterloo.

Album sales totalled 3000 units, most of which sold through independent stores on consignment or directly by Shad.

G was a classmate of Shad's at Laurier, and connected to Shad's music and message. He fell into the role of manager after helping to promote and organize a show at fabled downtown Toronto music venue, the El Mocambo, in 2006. Later that year, Shad opened for two prominent hip hop artists, Common and Lupe Fiasco, and began to draw the attention of local record labels, leading into the first big decision for the team.

BUILDING THE SHAD BRAND

Selecting a Record Label: Why Black Box Recordings?

As Shad and his team began exploring options for record labels in Canada, key considerations included the label's expertise with distribution and marketing for new artists, the attention they would be able to provide Shad as a client, and their willingness to partner with Shad's team at this early stage.

In the end, Black Box Recordings offered the most expertise in both marketing and distribution. As G explained:

> While some labels were interested in providing only distribution, leaving it to Shad and the team to decide how to allocate marketing dollars, Black Box was interested in a licensing deal, whereby they would license the master recordings of Shad's next three albums, set up distribution through Universal Music, and use their experience with other young artists to make decisions on how the marketing money should be spent. The alternative of dealing with a distributor on our own and having to decide on the marketing spend was less appealing and more risky at the time.

Although Black Box did not have other hip hop artists on their roster, they did have experience working with young bands and had strong knowledge of the Canadian music industry. Black Box was also willing to put in the time to attend to Shad as a client. This was especially important as, according to G:

> Shad isn't the kind of artist who has a big radio single which drives kids to the store to purchase albums. So we needed a team who would be able to stick around for the slow grind.

This case was written by Roopa Reddy and David Rose, Wilfrid Laurier University.

[1] Prestigious award presented to Canadian music artists, acknowledging achievements in various aspects of music (www.junoawards.ca).

At the time, Black Box fit the bill better than the other options being considered, so Shad signed a licensing deal with Black Box Recordings in April of 2007, a contract that would have him record three albums under the label.

Shad—Personality, Image, and Appeal

As an artist and an individual, Shad had a refreshing and unique personality. Having earned an Honour's Bachelor of Business Administration from Wilfrid Laurier University, and a Master of Arts in Liberal Studies from Simon Fraser University, Shad was an intelligent young man with passion and commitment towards his music. With growing recognition as an inspiring Canadian, Shad had garnered interesting achievements, including winning Canada Reads, the Canadian Broadcasting Corporation (CBC)'s annual "battle of the books" competition. ("What is Canada Reads?" 2013)[2]. Such opportunities had begun to make Shad more recognized in Canada beyond his young fan base.

Described as authentic and accessible, Shad was the same person on or off stage. As one journalist described, with Shad "there is no mask" (Featherstone, 2012). His persona as a genuine Canadian guy who was laid back and witty connected him to his fans, who often expressed they felt as if they already knew Shad through his music. This personal nature of the connection fans experienced was unique to Shad as an artist.

Shad maintained clean and honest lyrics, covering subjects ranging from still living at home as a young man in "The Old Prince Still Lives At Home," to the empowerment of women in "Keep Shining." Critics recognized him as an intelligent, "conscious" rapper, and "the thinking man's rapper" ("Meet Canada Reads," 2011). Furthermore, as G explained:

> Although finances are a means for him to create music, Shad has not changed his perspective or music in pursuit of profit. He makes music to tell his story and engage in dialogue without coming across as political as often happens with other "conscious" rappers. Shad is dedicated to his fan base and believes in organic growth.

The Core Fans

Shad's fans were primarily university-aged males and young adults (aged 17–24) who were drawn to his unique, relatable, and noncommercial indie rap feel. Although many of his fans were dedicated "hip hop heads," others were drawn to the accessibility of his music. As one radio announcer expressed

about Shad's music, "If I had to introduce a new listener to hip hop, I would say, listen to this. I think this will change your mind. He is that kind of an artist." (Featherstone, 2012)

At first fans were drawn in at universities through campus tours. As touring venues expanded and Shad began headlining shows, his fan base began to expand to other cities and countries (see Exhibit 2 for website hits by location). G explained it was difficult to pinpoint the exact number of fans Shad had, however his Facebook page had grown from 5711 fans in April 2009 to 44 065 by January 2013. Shad's fans were based primarily in Canada, while the United States, Iran, Germany, and the United Kingdom rounded out the top five markets for Shad fans, according to his Facebook fan page. (Facebook, 2013)

GROWING IMPORTANCE OF SOCIAL MEDIA

G managed Shad's Facebook page, as he was more comfortable maintaining an active social media presence. The channels to reach fans often shifted in the music industry and keeping up with the latest trends was a challenge. G explained:

> The means to reach fans changes every couple of years. Between 2006 and 2010, the emphasis shifted from MySpace to Facebook to Twitter. This is a real paradigm shift in the industry, from a time when the only important channel was the record label.

Other online channels such as soundcloud.com and bandcamp. com offered alternatives for artists to share and sell music to fans at "pay what you can" prices, and Shad had begun to have an online presence on these sites in 2012.

SHAD'S KEY PARTNERS AND SOURCES OF REVENUE

Besides his band, his DJ, and the record label, the parties involved in Shad's career included the distribution company, the booking agent, his creative partner/director, and his manager.

The distributor's role involved focusing the label's marketing efforts to reach fans, primarily by getting albums on store shelves. While Black Box Recordings was initially partnered with Universal Canada as their distributor, they changed to

---

[2] The following link includes a brief video of Shad presenting his arguments in support of his chosen book, "Something Fierce" by Carmen Aguirre: www.cbc.ca/books/canadareads/2011/12/meet-canada-reads-panelist-shad.html

Universal Canada's independent arm, Fontana North, in 2008. G felt this was a positive move for the team:

> Fontana was more connected to smaller players in the industry and they understood the underground world of hip hop. They also placed Shad's album at independent music stores across the country, where Shad's target audience would be reached.

Under the licensing deal with Black Box Recordings, album sales had not been a source of direct income for Shad, as proceeds of album sales went towards covering associated marketing costs. Thus far, income had been earned mainly from touring and merchandise (Exhibit 1).

Shad's booking agent was responsible for booking shows and tours. As shows were Shad's largest source of revenue, the booking agent played an important role in the business. Shad and the team established a relationship with his first agent in 2007 at a small Canadian agency, and stayed with him as he moved to a larger agency the following year. By 2009, Shad moved to Chicago-based Billions Corporation as his booking agent. Show revenues more than doubled between 2008 and 2009 and continued to have impressive growth thereafter (see Exhibit 1). G noted that their agent was excellent, as "He doesn't put Shad into cookie cutter tours. He finds and works with the right partners in the right cities for Shad's type of music."

Shad was fortunate to have Justin Broadbent onboard as a frequent creative partner. Justin and Shad had developed a strong working relationship and Justin had created most of Shad's album art and designed Shad's original website (http://shadk.com/whenthisisover.html). Justin also directed the majority of Shad's videos, including 'The Old Prince Still Lives at Home," which went viral, with 2 million views on YouTube within two days.

Finally G was Shad's manager. G explained his role:

> In the beginning, we didn't know what a manager did. I was just helping Shad in any way I could, because I believed in him and his music. After graduating, I worked at a corporate job for a couple of years before quitting to dedicate more time to Shad, along with my family's business. As manager, I deal with Shad's key partners on an ongoing basis. My role involves making sure each partner is doing their job and respecting Shad's brand, along with ensuring Shad is fulfilling his commitments to key partners. With Shad's strong understanding of the business side of the industry, and clear vision of his goals, my role is more "facilitator" than manager.

ALBUMS TO DATE: ACCOMPLISHMENTS AND CHALLENGES

First Album under Black Box: *The Old Prince* (2007)

Shad's first label-album *The Old Prince*, was released in 2007. During this time, G felt that the tension between the art and business sides of the industry became evident as both the label and the team had different views on how to grow Shad's career, and how fast. This was apparent, for example, in choosing lead singles. While the label suggested releasing the song most likely to gain success on radio first, Shad and G felt that releasing an underground track for his core fans was the right first step, building towards a broader audience with the release of subsequent singles, which is what they did.

Towards the end of 2008, Shad toured as opener for fellow Canadian rapper Classified, who had just hired Black Box to take over as his management, and Shad was well received across Canada. *The Old Prince* received critical acclaim in Canada, and sales reached 7000 units by the end of the record cycle, which was impressive for an indie hip hop record at the time.

In 2009, Shad was nominated for the prestigious Polaris Prize in Canadian music, which recognizes albums of the highest artistic integrity regardless of genre. ("About Polaris," 2013). Although he did not win, G explained that having the album shortlisted (one of only ten albums) placed Shad in front of a panel of approximately 180 judges, comprised of industry critics, writers, and bloggers, which increased Shad's exposure in the industry.

Second Album under Black Box: *TSOL* (2010)

Shad's second album, *TSOL*, was released in 2010. G felt the team experienced a similar tension with the label in terms of which singles to release in what order, however the album had a successful release overall.

The album was nominated and won the Juno Award for best rap recording of the year, beating out frontrunner Drake in what was called a "major upset" in the media. (Rayner, 2011) Despite the initial surprise to the team, the win demonstrated the strong critical acclaim Shad had garnered in a short time, and increased his exposure on the music scene. *TSOL* was also shortlisted for the Polaris Prize that year.

The album toured well in 2010, including Shad's first European tour, and shows with Canadian artists k-os and K'naan. The Juno win turned out to be timely the following year, as all shows on a scheduled Spring 2011 tour subsequently sold out, and some shows were moved to bigger venues. The track "Rose Garden" also received significant airplay on radio stations in the greater Toronto area and the video for the same track received a million hits on YouTube.

Shad partnered with US label Decon to release *TSOL* in the United States, United Kingdom, France, and Germany, with 12 000 albums sold across markets.

Third Album under Black Box: To Be Released in 2013

In early 2013, Shad was recording for the third and final album on the Black Box Recordings contract, to be released later that year.

WHERE TO FROM HERE?

There were tradeoffs to the options ahead for Shad and the team. Shad and G recognized the importance of maintaining Shad's core value proposition while working to expand his reach. G and Shad needed to decide their best move after the completion of the licensing deal with Black Box Recordings.

Moving to a major label such as Def Jam or BMG through a licensing deal was one option that Shad and G were considering. G recognized that with access to a much larger pool of resources Shad would have increased exposure and growth, and the chance to really become a star in Canada and beyond. In terms of their marketing, large labels tended to use a top-down "funnel" approach, (Godin, 2006) where they would market to a large number of potential fans using established channels and connections to major media outlets, and hope for their efforts to trickle down to the right people.

G felt that going with a major label would involve compromises as well, especially with respect to the loss of creative control. Recently, Somali-Canadian artist K'naan had publicly expressed his opinion in a *New York Times* piece entitled "Censoring Myself for Success," commenting on the impact of moving away from his roots in pursuit of success with a big label. "Some songs became far more Top 40 friendly, but infinitely cheaper," he wrote, comparing a more "Americanized" song on a recent album to "a body with no soul at all." (K'Naan, 2012)

Another option was to move to a larger indie label, such as XL Recordings, a UK-based label that had fueled the success of indie artists including Adele, MIA, and The xx. Adele had received critical and commercial success under XL Recordings, selling over 11 million albums globally and receiving two Grammy awards along the way. (Catucci, 2013) Larger indie labels managed to maintain a small feel despite increased resources. As one writer noted, they worked by "patiently searching out artists with a niche, and then marshaling the label's resources to help the artists find a wider audience. XL has, in a sense, recast artistic freedom as a business model." (Catucci, 2013) G still wondered whether the indie labels would have the networks to help Shad's growth into new markets.

The team could also continue with Black Box Recordings, which G described as a "If it ain't broke, don't fix it" mentality. Shad and G had established a strong working relationship with the label, and the label now understood Shad's purpose in making music. G did feel, however, that with Black Box Shad might have limited potential for further growth, as the label did not have an international following.

Finally, another option would be for Shad and his team to release the album on their own. As the team was now connected to fans through social media and networks, G felt they could either sell the albums exclusively online using a "pay what you can" model, or combine online sales with an indie distribution partner to also get the album in stores, and allocate marketing money as the team saw fit in a quickly shifting industry. It was trendy to go indie, as had been seen with bands such as Radiohead and Flying Lotus. With this option, Shad's team would take on the key activities that a label would normally help to manage.

As G pulled into his driveway, he reflected on his conversations with Shad, with the question clear in his mind: "What can we do to enable Shad's growth while staying true to Shad's values and his fans?"

EXHIBIT 1   REVENUES AND EXPENSES ($)*

REVENUES AND EXPENSES: 2008-2011

	2008	2009	2010	2011
Show Revenue	$23 000.00	$56 000.00	$63 000.00	$150 000.00
Merchandise Revenue	$1 250.00	$7 000.00	$11 000.00	$10 000.00
Grant Income + Other Income	$1 500.00	$66 000.00	$95 000.00	$80 000.00
TOTAL REVENUE	$25 750.00	$129 000.00	$169 000.00	$240 000.00
Advertising (Gifts/Webhosting)	$1 500.00	$2 000.00	$2 400.00	$3 000.00
Insurance		$1 100.00		
Interest, Bank Charges, Fees	$700.00	$800.00	$600.00	$1 000.00
Entertainment/Promo	$500.00	$750.00	$8 000.00	$13 000.00
Office Expenses	$100.00	$100.00		$300.00
Accounting and Legal Fees	$1 000.00	$1 250.00		$2 000.00
Rent (equipment)			$700.00	$2 000.00
Supplies (for Instruments etc.)	$300.00	$500.00		$1 000.00
Salaries, Wages, Band Labour	$6 200.00	$11 000.00	$26 000.00	$35 000.00
Travel	$2 300.00	$25 000.00	$27 000.00	$35 000.00
Other Expenses				
Merch + Other Expenses	$800.00	$5 000.00	$8 000.00	$10 000.00
Management Fees	$2 500.00	$16 000.00	$20 000.00	$25 000.00
Booking Agent Fees	$2 300.00	$5 500.00	$6 000.00	$15 000.00
Other Expenses	$1 400.00	$3 000.00	$4 000.00	$4 000.00
TOTAL EXPENSES	$15 900.00	$63 500.00	$102 700.00	$146 300.00
Net Income	$9 850.00	$65 500.00	$66 300.00	$93 700.00

*Please Note: Figures may have been disguised for confidentiality or educational purposes.

EXHIBIT 2	WEB HITS BY COUNTRY ON SHAD'S WEBSITE WWW.SHADK.COM)

COUNTRY/TERRITORY	VISITS
1. Canada	125 755
2. United States	49 256
3. United Kingdom	6 331
4. Germany	3 862
5. France	2 157
6. Australia	1 699
7. Netherlands	1 051
8. Brazil	1 038
9. Spain	940
10. Rwanda	745

Source: Google Analytics for Shadk.com

*Please Note: Figures may have been disguised for confidentiality or educational purposes.

REFERENCE LIST

Canadian Broadcasting Corporation. What is Canada reads?, retrieved January 22, 2013, from http://www.660news.com/entertainment/article/203395--shad-beats-drake-at-juno-awards- for-rap-recording-of-the-year

Canadian Broadcasting Corporation. Meet Canada Reads Panelist Shad, retrieved January 22, 2013, from http://www.cbc.ca/books/canadareads/2011/12/meet-canada-reads-panelist-shad.html

Catucci, N. XL Recordings, Where Small is the New Big, Creative Cultures, retrieved February 15, 2013 from http://www.fastcocreate.com/1679178/xl-recordings-where-small-is-the-new-big

Featherstone, J. (2012) Aux Presents: Shad [Documentary] Canada: AUX. (including quotes from CBC Radio Personality Richard Terfry, and Globe and Mail reporter Ben Kaplan).

Facebook Fan Page Statistics for Shad, accessed January 21, 2013.

Godin, S. (2006). Flipping the Funnel (E-book). Retrieved February 15, 2013 from: http://sethgodin.typepad.com/seths_blog/2006/01/flipping_the_fu.html

K'Naan, (2012, December 8). Censoring Myself for Success, New York Times, retrieved February 5, 2013 from http://www.nytimes.com/2012/12/09/opinion/sunday/knaan-on-censoring-himself-for-success.html?_r=0

Polaris Music Prize. About Polaris, retrieved December 10, 2012 from http://www.polarismusicprize.ca/about-polaris/

Rayner, B. (2011, March 27). Shad nips Drake for Rap Juno, Toronto Star, retrieved December 10, 2012, from http://www.thestar.com/entertainment/music/junos/article/962333--shad-nips-drake-for-rap-juno

BUSINESS PLAN

 View the business plan for Edgar Bruce Eyewear online in Connect.

connect

For more information on the resources available from McGraw-Hill Ryerson, go to www.mcgrawhill.ca/he/solutions.

PART III

THE FOUNDER AND TEAM

Entrepreneurial founders must take a personal role in attracting, motivating, inspiring, and retaining an effective team of both specialists and generalists. The quality of that team has never been more fundamental and important than it is now. The new millennium ushered in a wave of new opportunities requiring nimble and creative teams. Some pundits have characterized this time as the communication era, characterized by galloping innovation—fuelled by the ability of inventive engineers and creative entrepreneurs to instantly access and share information worldwide. Investors stung by the dot-com fallout and the recession that ensued regained confidence as another boom wave followed. This was interrupted more recently by a global slump that hit harder and deeper than expected; private and venture capital investors emerge with a renewed appreciation for the time-tested wisdom that prosperous new ventures are often all about the team. Chapter 5, "The Entrepreneurial Leader," looks at the leadership issues inherent in building a company from scratch—and the significant recruiting, sales, and management skills the founder(s) must bring to bear as the enterprise grows through various stages.

One of the most critical aspects of entrepreneuring is in being able to attract the *right* people: team players whose skills and know-how are critical to the success of the enterprise. Ambiguity, risk, and the need to collectively pivot in the face of shifting competitive landscapes require that entrepreneurial teams be greater than the sum of their parts. Forming and building that team can be a rather unscientific, occasionally unpredictable, and frequently surprising experience. In chapter 6, "The New Venture Team," we put a zoom lens on the "people" portion of the Timmons Model.

The solo entrepreneur may make a living, but it is the team builder who develops an organization and a company with sustainable value and attractive harvest options. The vision of what these founders are trying to accomplish provides the unwritten ground rules that become the fabric, character, and purpose behind the venture. Effective lead entrepreneurs are able to build a culture around the business mission and the brand by rewarding performance, supporting honest failure, sharing the wealth with those who helped to create it, and setting high ethical standards of conduct. Chapter 7, "Ethical Decision Making and the Entrepreneur," addresses the complex and thorny issues of ethics and integrity for the entrepreneur, and how those decisions and choices can have a significant impact on future success.

CHAPTER 5

THE ENTREPRENEURIAL LEADER

I have found that great people do have in common an immense belief in themselves and in their mission. They also have great determination as well as an ability to work hard. At the crucial moment of decision, they draw on their accumulated wisdom. Above all they have integrity.

YOUSUF KARSH
Canadian portrait photographer

LEARNING OBJECTIVES

LO1 Explain the difference between an entrepreneurial leader and a manager, and illustrate why the team is so important.

LO2 Identify stages of growth that entrepreneurial ventures go through, the venture modes characteristic of the entrepreneurial domain, and the principal forces acting in the domain.

LO3 Articulate the skills, competencies, and philosophies entrepreneurial-thinking founders apply as they form, build, and lead a new venture team, and discuss the critical issues and hurdles they face.

THE ENTREPRENEURIAL DOMAIN

CONVERGING ON THE ENTREPRENEURIAL LEADER

There are convergent pressures on being an entrepreneur and being a leader as a venture accelerates and grows beyond founder-driven and founder-dominated survival. Key to achieving sustained growth and an eventual harvest is an entrepreneur's ability to have or develop competencies as an entrepreneurial leader.

In the past we generally believed that the kind of person with the entrepreneurial spirit required to propel a new venture through start-up to a multi-million-dollar annual sales level was different from the kind of person with the capacity to lead a new firm as it grew from zero to $20 million or more in sales. Further, it has long been thought that the entrepreneur who clings to the lead role too long will limit or impede company growth. Further, many VCs will be set on replacing the entrepreneur with "professional talent" as the enterprise transitions through stages of growth. But "entrepreneurs should not automatically be forced from their firms early. Several factors decide when the founder should step aside."[1]

Canadian economist John Kenneth Galbraith explained in 1971, "The great entrepreneur must, in fact, be compared in life with the male honey bee. He accomplishes his act of conception at the price of his own extinction."[2] In short, conventional wisdom held that a good entrepreneur was usually not a good manager, since he or she lacked the necessary management skill and experience. Likewise, it was assumed that a manager was not an entrepreneur, since he or she lacked some intense personal qualities and the orientation required to launch a business from scratch.

Evidence suggests that entrepreneurs who are also effective leaders can head new ventures that flourish beyond start-up and grow to become substantial, successful enterprises. Researchers studied the tenure of 54 founders of corporations on the Fortune 1000 list. They assumed founders have three ways to adapt: (1) shift from creation to exploitation, (2) shift from passionate commitment to dispassionate objectivity, and (3) shift from direct personal control over organizational actions to indirect impersonal control. Taking into account the growth rate, the timing of the initial public offering, the founder's age, education, and other factors, this study found the following:

1. If the firm grows relatively slowly, and the founder is capable of some adaptation, then the firm can become quite large.

2. Founders with scientific or engineering backgrounds remain in control of the companies for shorter periods than do founders whose academic focus was business.

3. The founder's tenure will typically be longer in family-dominated firms.[3]

More recently, researchers "observed that many founders can and do manage growth successfully. The applicability of conventional wisdom regarding the 'leadership crisis' in rapid-growth entrepreneurial firms may no longer be valid, if, in fact, it ever was."[4] Terry Matthews returned to run the company he built—Mitel. Founder Bill Gates headed Microsoft until mid-2008. Ted Rogers, Jr. continued to lead his namesake—Rogers Communications—until his death in late 2008. Steve Jobs returned to the top spot at Apple after stepping aside, thinking that was best for the company he co-founded, and 40 years later Andy Grove is now the senior advisor to executive management at Intel. Numerous examples such as these clearly indicate founders can learn and grow as fast as their companies do.

These and other data defy the notion that entrepreneurs can start but cannot manage growing companies. While the truth is probably somewhere in between, one thing is apparent: Growing a higher potential venture requires leadership skills. According to Sal Sloan, Operating Partner at BrainRider, a business to business marketing agency based in Toronto, adaptability is key.

Clearly, a complex set of factors goes into making someone a successful entrepreneurial leader. Launching a new venture and then managing rapid growth involves skills not found in most mature or stable environments. Further, one of the greatest strengths of successful entrepreneurs is that they know what they do and do not know. They have disciplined intellectual honesty, which prevents their optimism from becoming myopic delusion and their dreams from becoming blind ambition. No individual has all these skills, nor does the presence or absence of any single skill guarantee success or failure. An entrepreneur who knows that he or she needs a certain skill and knows where to get it is as valuable as one who knows whether he or she already has it.

PRINCIPAL FORCES AND VENTURE MODES

Companies, whether new, growing, or mature, occupy a place in either a managerial or an entrepreneurial domain, an area influenced by certain principal forces and characterized by ways of acting, called venture modes. Exhibits 5.1 and 5.2 illustrate the entrepreneurial and managerial domains and the dynamic of the principal forces acting in the domains and the dominant venture modes that result.

In the exhibits, the four cells are defined by the stage of the venture (upper axis), the extent of change and uncertainty accompanying it (right axis), and the degree to which a venture is managerial (bottom axis) or entrepreneurial (left axis). The entrepreneurial domain is the two upper cells in both exhibits, and the domains are functions of both the change and uncertainty facing a venture and the stage of growth of the venture.

Each venture mode (i.e., way of acting) for firms in each cell is driven by certain principal forces. These forces are shown in Exhibit 5.2. Shown in Exhibit 5.1 are dominant venture modes characteristic of firms in each cell. Organizations at different stages are characterized by differing degrees of change and uncertainty and are therefore more or less entrepreneurial or more or less

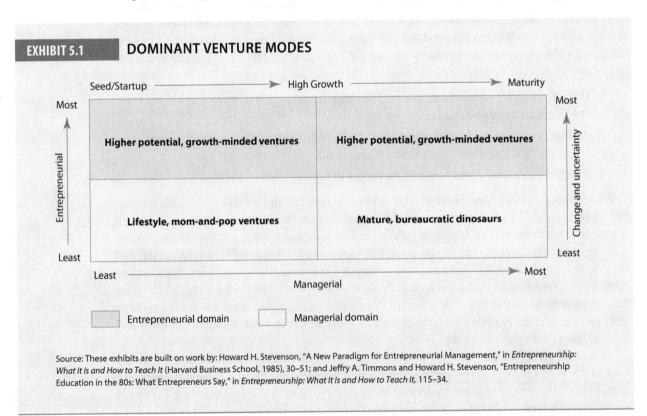

EXHIBIT 5.1   DOMINANT VENTURE MODES

Source: These exhibits are built on work by: Howard H. Stevenson, "A New Paradigm for Entrepreneurial Management," in *Entrepreneurship: What It Is and How to Teach It* (Harvard Business School, 1985), 30–51; and Jeffry A. Timmons and Howard H. Stevenson, "Entrepreneurship Education in the 80s: What Entrepreneurs Say," in *Entrepreneurship: What It Is and How to Teach It*, 115–34.

EXHIBIT 5.2   PRINCIPAL DRIVING FORCES

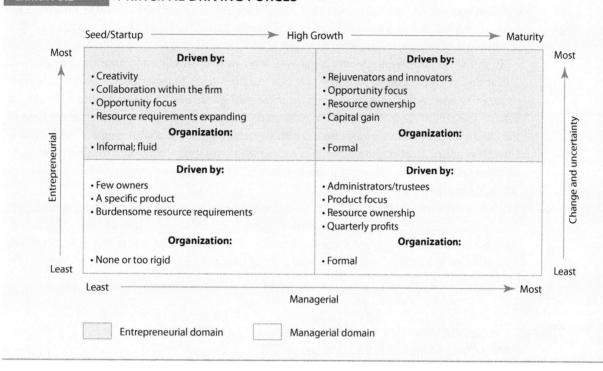

managerial. Thus, for example, a new venture in the seed/start-up stage, which is characterized by high change and uncertainty, is most entrepreneurial. These firms will be new, innovative, or backbone ventures; will be led by a team; will be driven by their founders' goals, values, commitment, and perceptions of the opportunities; and will minimize the use of resources. At the other extreme is a mature firm, one that is in the maturity stage and characterized by low change and uncertainty, is stable or contracting, is led by a manager, is driven by resource ownership and managerial efficiency, and is reactive. Other firms fall in between.

The managerial skills required of the firms in each cell are more evident upon examination of these principal forces and dominant venture modes. For example, creativity and comprehensive managerial skills are required to lead firms in both cells in the entrepreneurial domain. In the upper-left-hand cell, entrepreneurial leaders need to cope effectively with high levels of change and uncertainty. As the firm enters the high-growth stage, this changes.

STAGES OF GROWTH   LO2

A THEORETICAL VIEW

Entrepreneurship is not static. Exhibit 5.3 represents a *theoretical* view of the process of gestation and growth of new ventures and the transitions that occur at different boundaries in this process.[5] Ventures are sown, sprout, nurtured, and harvested.

The smooth, S-shaped curve in the exhibit is rarely replicated in the real world. If we tracked the progress of most emerging companies, the curve would be a jagged line; these companies would experience some periods of rapid progress followed by setbacks and accompanying crises.

In fact, many recommend seeking a respite after start-up to "catch your breath" before scaling up and being thrown into the perils of growth. A bit of stability early on allows one to calibrate, establish systems, and get things working before disequilibrium throws the new venture back on to the treadmill. But of course that lull may never be permitted by market forces. And a lull—self-induced or otherwise—may never go away!

In this illustration venture stages are shown in terms of time, sales, and number of employees. It is at the boundaries between stages that new ventures seem to experience transitions. Several researchers have noted that new ventures invariably go through transitions and face certain issues.[6] The exhibit shows the crucial transitions during growth and the key management tasks of the chief executive officer or founders. Most important and most challenging for the founding entrepreneur or a chief executive officer is coping with crucial transitions and the change in management tasks, going from leading to leading leaders, as a firm grows to roughly 30 employees, to 50, to 75, and then up.

The *research and development stage*, sometimes referred to as the nascent stage, is characterized by a single aspiring entrepreneur, or small team, doing the investigation and due diligence for their business idea. The nascent stage can be as short as a few months or can last years. Research indicates that if an idea is not turned into a going concern within 18 months, the chances of a

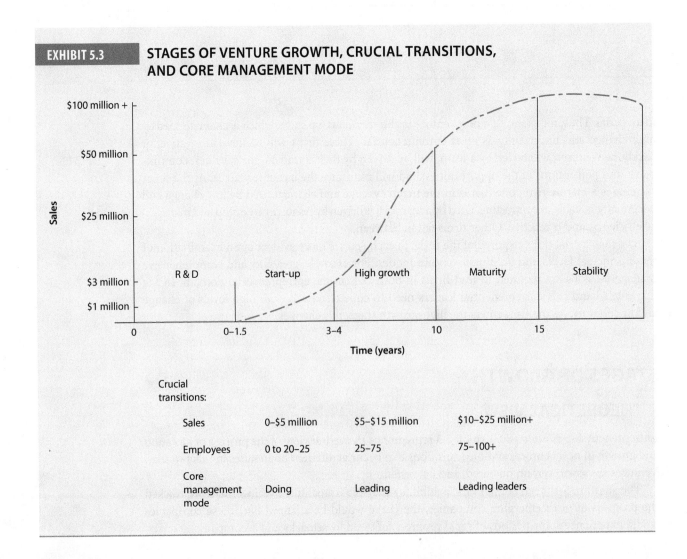

EXHIBIT 5.3   **STAGES OF VENTURE GROWTH, CRUCIAL TRANSITIONS, AND CORE MANAGEMENT MODE**

Crucial transitions:			
Sales	0–$5 million	$5–$15 million	$10–$25 million+
Employees	0 to 20–25	25–75	75–100+
Core management mode	Doing	Leading	Leading leaders

start-up fall dramatically. Nascent entrepreneurs have many fits and starts, and the business model can change often in the process.

The *start-up stage*, a stage that usually covers the first two or three years but perhaps as many as seven, is by far the most perilous stage and is characterized by the direct and exhaustive drive, energy, and entrepreneurial talent of a lead entrepreneur and a key team member or two. Here, the critical mass of people, market and financial results, and competitive resiliency are established, while investor, banker, and customer confidence is earned. The level of sales reached varies widely, but typically ranges from $2 to $20 million. A new company then begins its high-growth stage. The exact point at which this occurs can rarely be identified by a date on the calendar until well after the fact. It is in this stage that new ventures exhibit a failure rate exceeding 60 percent; that is, it is in this stage that the lemons ripen.

As with the other stages, the length of time it takes to go through the *high-growth stage*, as well as the magnitude of change occurring during the period, varies greatly. Probably the most difficult challenge for the founding entrepreneur occurs during the high-growth stage, when he or she finds it is necessary to let go of power and control (through veto) over key decisions that he or she has always had, and when key responsibilities need to be delegated without abdicating ultimate leadership and responsibility for results. But the challenges do not end there.

From the high-growth stage, a company then moves to what is called the *maturity stage*. In this stage, the key issue for the company is no longer survival; rather, it is one of steady, profitable growth. The *stability stage* usually follows.

MANAGING FOR RAPID GROWTH

Managing for rapid growth involves a leadership orientation not found in mature and stable environments. (This topic will be addressed again in chapter 12.) For one thing, the tenet that one's responsibility must equal one's authority is often counterproductive in a rapid-growth venture. Instead, results usually require close collaboration of a manager with other people than his or her subordinates, and managers invariably have responsibilities far exceeding their authority. Politics and personal power can be a way of life in many larger and stagnant institutions, as managers jockey for influence and a piece of a shrinking pie in a zero-sum game; but in rapid-growth firms, power and control are delegated. Everyone is committed to making the pie larger, and power and influence are derived not only from achieving one's own goals but also from contributing to the achievements of others as well. Influence also is derived from keeping the overall goals in mind, from resolving differences, and from developing a reputation as a person who gets results, who leads others, and who grows leadership talent.

Thus, among successful entrepreneurial leaders there is a well-developed capacity to exert influence *without* formal power. These people are adept at conflict resolution. They know when to use logic and when to persuade, when to make a concession and when to exact one. To run a successful venture, an entrepreneur learns to get along with many different constituencies, often with conflicting aims—the customer, the supplier, the financial backer, and the creditor, as well as the partners and others on the inside. Similarly, an entrepreneurial leader must operate in a world that is increasingly interdependent. Attempting to advise executives on how to exert "influence without authority," Allan Cohen and David Bradford assert, "You not only need to exercise influence skills with your peers and your own boss, but also to help the people who work for you learn to be effective influencers—even of you—since that will free you to spend more of your time seeking new opportunities and working the organization above and around you."[7]

Successful entrepreneurs are interpersonally supporting and nurturing—not interpersonally competitive—and successful entrepreneurial leaders understand their interdependencies and have learned to incorporate mutual respect, openness, trust, and mutual benefit into their leadership style. Fundamental to this progressive style is the awareness and practice of reciprocity for mutual gain.[8] When a strong need to control, influence, and gain power over others characterizes the lead entrepreneur, or when he or she has an insatiable appetite for putting an associate down, more often than not the venture gets into trouble. A dictatorial, adversarial, and dominating leader makes it difficult to attract and keep people who thirst for achievement, responsibility, and results. Compliant partners and managers are often chosen. Destructive conflicts often erupt over who has the final say, who is right, and whose prerogatives are what.

In the corporate setting, the "hero-making" ability is identified as an essential attribute of successful entrepreneurial leaders.[9] These hero makers try to make the pie bigger and better, rather than jealously clutching and hoarding a tiny pie that is all theirs. They have a capacity for objective interpersonal relationships as well, which enables them to smooth out individual differences of opinion by keeping attention focused on the common goal to be achieved.[10]

Exhibit 5.4 characterizes probable crises that growing ventures will face, including erosion of creativity by founders and team members; confusion or resentment, or both, over ambiguous roles, responsibilities, and goals; failure to clone founders; specialization and eroding of collaboration; desire for autonomy and control; need for operating mechanisms and controls; and conflict and divorce among founders and members of the team. The exhibit further delineates issues that confront entrepreneurial leaders.

Compounding of Time and Change

In the high-growth stage, change, ambiguity, and uncertainty seem to be the only things that remain constant. Change creates higher levels of uncertainty, ambiguity, and risk, which, in turn, compound to shrink time, an already precious commodity. One result of change is a series of

EXHIBIT 5.4	ENTREPRENEURIAL TRANSITIONS			
MODES/STAGES	**PLANNING**	**DOING**	**LEADING**	**LEADING LEADERS**
Sales	$0	$0–$5 million	$5–$15 million	$10 million or more
Employees	0–5	0–30	30–75	75 and up
Transitions	Characteristics:	Characteristics:	Probable crises:	Probable crises:
	Founder-driven	Founder-driven creativity	Erosion of creativity of founders	Failure to clone founders
	Wrenching changes			Specialization/eroding of collaboration versus practice of power, information, and influence
	Highly influential informal advisor	Constant change, ambiguity, and uncertainty	Confusion over ambiguous roles, responsibilities, and goals	
	Resource desperation	Time compression		Need for operating controls and mechanisms
	Very quick or very slow decision making	Informal communications	Desire for delegation versus autonomy and control	Conflict among founders
		Counterintuitive decision making and structure	Need for organization and operating policies	
		Relative inexperience		

shock waves rolling through a new and growing venture by way of new customers, new technologies, new competitors, new markets, and new people. In industries characterized by galloping technological change, with relatively minuscule lead and lag times in bringing new products to market and in weathering the storms of rapid obsolescence, the effects of change and time are extreme. For example, the president of a rapidly growing PC company said, "In our business it takes 6 to 12 months to develop a new computer, ready to bring to the market, and product technology obsolescence is running about 9 to 12 months." This time compression has been seen in such industries as electronics, telecommunications, fashion, and fast food.

Nonlinear and Nonparametric Events

Entrepreneurial leadership is characterized by nonlinear and nonparametric events. Just as the television did not come about by a succession of improvements in the radio, and the jet plane did not emerge from engineers and scientists attempting to develop a better and better piston engine plane, so too events do not follow straight lines, progress arithmetically, or even appear related within firms. Rather, they occur in bunches and in stepwise leaps. For example, a firm may double its sales force in 15 months, rather than over eight years, while another may triple its manufacturing capacity and adopt a new materials resource planning system immediately, rather than utilizing existing capacity by increasing overtime, then adding a third shift nine months later, and finally adding a new plant three years hence.

Relative Inexperience

In addition, the venture team may be relatively inexperienced. The explosive birth and growth of these firms are usually unique events that cannot be replicated, and most of the pieces in the puzzle—technology, applications, customers, people, the firm itself—are usually new. Stewart Butterfield from Victoria, B.C., and his wife Caterina Fake founded Ludicorp in Vancouver and began to work on an online multiplayer game. The tools for this project were re-deployed for Flickr—a far more promising opportunity. The move proved to be a shrewd one; Flickr launched in February 2004 and immediately captured users and industry attention. In March 2005, Yahoo! acquired this phenomenally growing enterprise.

Counterintuitive, Unconventional Decision Making

Yet another characteristic of rapidly growing ventures in the entrepreneurial domain is counterintuitive, unconventional patterns of decision making. For example, a computer firm needed to decide what approach to take in developing and introducing three new products in an uncertain, risky marketplace. Each proposed new product appeared to be aimed at the same end-user market, and the person heading each project was similarly enthusiastic, confident, and determined to succeed. A traditional approach to such a problem would have been to determine the size and growth rates of each market segment; evaluate the probable estimates of future revenue costs and capital requirements for their accuracy; compare the discounted, present-value cash flow that would emerge from each project; and select the project with the highest yield versus the required internal rate of return. Such an analysis sometimes overlooks the fact that most rapid-growth companies have many excellent alternatives and, more commonly, the newness of technology, the immaturity of the marketplace, and the rapid discovery of further applications make it virtually impossible to know which of any product proposals is best. The computer firm decided to support all three new products at once, and a significant new business was built around each one. New market niches were discovered simultaneously and the unconventional approach paid off.

Fluid Structures and Procedures

Most rapid-growth ventures also defy conventional organizational patterns and structures. It is common to find a firm that has grown $25 million, $50 million, or even $150 million per year in sales and that still has no formal organizational chart. If an organizational chart does exist, it usually has three distinguishing features: First, it is inevitably out of date. Second, it changes frequently. For example, one firm had eight major reorganizations in its first five years as it grew to $5 million. Third, the organizational structure is usually flat (i.e., it has few management layers), and there is easy accessibility to the top decision makers. However, the informality and fluidity of organization structures and procedures do not mean casualness or sloppiness when it comes to goals, standards, or clarity of direction and purpose. Rather, they translate into responsiveness and readiness to absorb and assimilate rapid changes while maintaining financial and operational cohesion.

Entrepreneurial Culture

Growing new ventures have a common value system, which is difficult to articulate, is even more elusive to measure, and is evident in behaviour and attitudes. There is a belief in and commitment to growth, achievement, improvement, and success and a sense among members of the team that they are "in this thing together." Goals and the market determine priorities, rather than whose territory or whose prerogatives are being challenged. Leaders worry less about status, power, and personal control. They are more concerned about making sure that tasks, goals, and roles are clear than whether the organizational chart is current or whether their office and rug reflect their current status. Likewise, they are more concerned about the evidence, competence, knowledge, and logic of arguments affecting a decision than the status given by a title or the formal position of the individual doing the arguing. Royston Greenwood and Roy Suddaby, both of the University of Alberta, explore institutional entrepreneurship, which is viewed as an oxymoron by some. How can those embedded within constraining structures, systems, and processes be motivated and able to promote change? Greenwood and Suddaby's research shows that such entrepreneurial actions are more likely at the periphery, among those less connected and who may be disadvantaged by

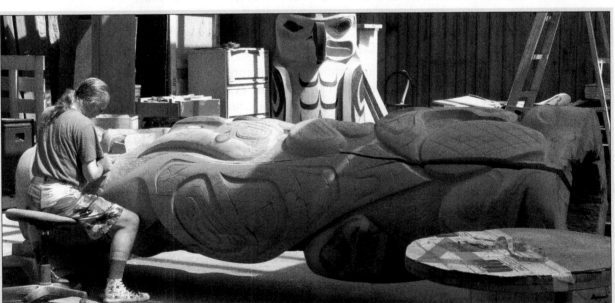

CULTURE MAY BE ETHNIC, NATIONAL, ORGANIZATIONAL, OR IT MAY EMANATE FROM ANY NUMBER OF IDENTITIES. CULTURE IS A SIGNIFICANT FACTOR IN AN INDIVIDUAL'S ATTITUDES AND ACTIONS.

Tal Dehtiar, founder of Oliberté Footwear, leads an empire of premium urban casual shoes sourced entirely from Africa. He speaks English, Russian, Hebrew, and Spanish and has a team mentality. Armed with an idea—vertical integration—and plans to source leather from Ethiopia and rubber in Liberia he was happy to fill in

the missing pieces. His answer for Africa is smart business and getting organized. In all his transactions he demands fair treatment and fair income for those involved. Tal Dehtiar "wanted to show that there is a better model," and he has led by example. He has already rejected at least two buy-out proposals. Patience and perseverance allow Dehtiar to continue to work in Africa to keep production rolling. Africa is a particularly trying environment for an entrepreneur. Market forces often have little bearing on decisions. Getting it right every time is important but not easy for a leader; selecting the wrong style or colour of leather means the shoes will flop in the western world. While inventory of unsellable shoes is dumped, retailers like Amazon.com and The Gap cannot get enough of the shoes they want.

Kinfe Sahlu Gulte

TAL DEHTIAR (RIGHT) WITH A FACTORY MANAGER IN ADDIS ABABA, ETHIOPIA.

Question: Although Tal Dehtiar draws inspiration from many sources, his work is consuming and often frustrating. As a leader do you show emotions such as aggravation or do you overcome and hide or disguise them?

Sources: Carlos Osorio, "Oakville Businessman Invests in Africa's Industrial Revolution," *The Toronto Star*, April 14, 2012; Tiana Reid, "Tal Dehtiar, President and CEO of Oliberte Premium Footwear," Trendhunter.com, April 3, 2011; "100 Most Creative People in Business 2012," *Fast Company*, June 2012.

prevailing arrangements and can benefit from change.[11] Japan and Korea are known to be discouraging environments for entrepreneurship whereas Taiwan encourages new business ventures and supports start-ups with the necessary resources to succeed.[12] Culture—be it national or corporate—clearly has a bearing on entrepreneurial activity.

This entrepreneurial climate, or culture, exists in larger firms also. Such a climate attracts and encourages the entrepreneurial achievers, and it helps perpetuate the intensity and pace so characteristic of high-growth firms. Rosabeth Moss Kanter, who has been studying "intrapreneurship" for many years, asserts that the global economy has experienced a postentrepreneurial revolution, which "takes entrepreneurship a step further, applying entrepreneurial principles to the traditional corporation, creating a marriage between entrepreneurial creativity and corporate discipline, co-operation, and teamwork."[13] This revolution has not made managing any easier; in fact, Kanter suggests, "This constitutes the ultimate corporate balancing act. Cut back and grow. Trim down and build. Accomplish more, and do it in new areas, with fewer resources."[14] Clearly, some corporations will embrace these challenges with more success than others; the following section will shed some light on how "giants learn to dance."[15]

WHAT ENTREPRENEURIAL LEADERS NEED TO KNOW

Traditionally business education has emphasized the managerial domain. There is nothing wrong with that, but to prepare students to start and lead vibrant, growing new ventures you cannot afford to emphasize managerial efficiency, maintenance tasks, resource ownership, and institutional formalization. Rather, the education needs to emphasize skills necessary for life in the entrepreneurial domain.

Effective entrepreneurial leaders need to be especially skilful at regulating conflict, resolving differences, balancing multiple viewpoints and demands, and building teamwork and consensus. These skills are particularly difficult when working with others outside one's immediate formal chain of command.

In talking of larger firms, Kanter identifies power and persuasion skills, skill in managing problems accompanying team and employee participation, and skill in understanding how change is designed and constructed in an organization as necessary.

> In short, individuals do not have to be doing "big things" in order to have their cumulative accomplishments eventually result in big performance for the company…They are only rarely the inventors of the "breakthrough" system. They are only rarely doing something that is totally unique or that no one, in any organization, ever thought of before. Instead, they are often applying ideas that have proved themselves elsewhere, or they are rearranging parts to create a better result, or they are noting a potential problem before it turns into a catastrophe and mobilizing the actions to anticipate and solve it.[16]

A study of mid-sized growth companies having sales or profit growth of more than 15 percent annually over five years confirms the importance of many of these same fundamentals of entrepreneurial management.[17] For one thing, these companies practised opportunity-driven management. According to the study, they achieved their first success with a unique product or distinctive way of doing business and often became leaders in market niches by delivering superior value to customers, rather than through low prices. They are highly committed to serving customers and pay close attention to them. For another thing, these firms emphasize financial control and managing every element of the business.

In a book that follows up on the implementation issues of how one gets middle managers to pursue and practise entrepreneurial excellence (first made famous in *In Search of Excellence* by Tom Peters and Bob Waterman), two authors note that some of the important fundamentals practised by team-builder entrepreneurs—who are more intent on getting results than just getting their own way—also are emulated by effective middle managers.[18] Or as John Sculley, of Apple, explained:

> The heroic style—the lone cowboy on horseback—is not the figure we worship anymore at Apple. In the new corporation, heroes won't personify any single set of achievements. Instead, they personify the process. They might be thought of as gatekeepers, information carriers, and teams. Originally heroes at Apple were the hackers and engineers who created the products. Now, more teams are heroes.[19]

The ability to shape and guide a cohesive team is particularly critical in high-tech firms where the competitive landscape can shift dramatically in the face of disruptive technologies. In his book *The Innovator's Dilemma*, Clayton Christensen finds that even aggressive, innovative, and customer-driven organizations can be rendered obsolete if they fail to take decisive, and at times radical, actions to stay competitive.[20] The point of greatest peril in the development of a high-tech market, writes Geoffrey Moore in his book *Crossing the Chasm*, lies in making the transition from an early market, dominated by a few visionary customers, to a mainstream market that is dominated by a large block of customers who are predominantly pragmatists in orientation.[21] In Exhibit 5.5, entrepreneur Edward Marram describes this as the "Blunder" stage of growth, perilously positioned between "Wonder" and Thunder." It has been suggested that a brief period of stability after the "Wonder" phase can allow the business to perform tests and get ready for "Thunder." And despite its name, "Blunder" need not be catastrophic. In fact, errors are to be expected: if you are not making mistakes, you are not trying hard enough.

Lead entrepreneurs whose companies successfully break into the mass market must find a way to manage the hyper-growth and gigantic revenues that can result from an international surge in demand.[22] Several entrepreneurial leaders who have skilfully negotiated these high-tech waters are as well known as the companies they founded: think Michael Dell, Robert

EXHIBIT 5.5 | STAGES OF GROWTH

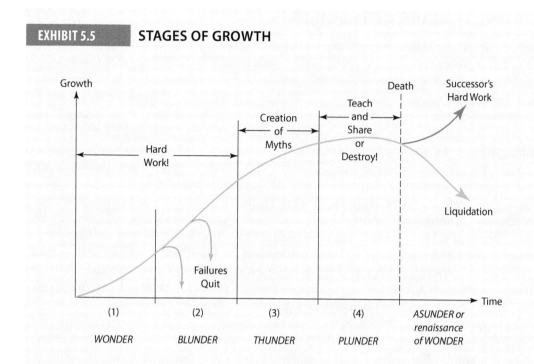

Herjavec, Michael Cowpland, and Suhayya Abu-Hakima. What sort of skills and personality are required to achieve such high levels of performance in a dynamic and uncertain marketplace? As portrayed in Stephen Covey's classic work, *The 7 Habits of Highly Effective People*, these individuals are curious, proactive team builders who have a passion for continuous improvement and renewal in their lives and in their ventures. Maybe most important in this context: these leaders have "the ability to envision, to see the potential, to create with their minds what they cannot at present see with their eyes . . . "[23]

ETHICAL ENTREPRENEURIAL LEADERSHIP

According to Donald Kuratko, an authority in the field, "No perspective of entrepreneurial leadership would be complete without the acknowledgement of the ethical side of enterprise....A leader has the unique opportunity to display honesty, integrity, and ethics in all key decisions." A leader's behaviour serves as a model for others to emulate.[24] Clearly the entrepreneurial leader's value system plays an important role, one that will be more fully explored in chapter 7, "Ethical Decision Making and the Entrepreneur."

"In entrepreneurial ventures, the ethical influence of the owner is more powerful than in larger corporations because his or her leadership is not diffused through layers of management."[25] A venture founder is readily recognized and under constant scrutiny by the whole team. Entrepreneurial owners have the potential to set high ethical standards in all business decisions.[26] It is worth noting that there is a "dark side" of entrepreneurial behaviour—a potentially destructive element resides within the energetic drive of successful entrepreneurs.[27] Leaders must monitor their entrepreneurial ego and know that an inflated self-view can have negative repercussions. Beyond the notion that "power corrupts," risk, control, trust, and optimism are all forces that entrepreneurs must embrace. Risk, for example, is something both sought after and avoided by entrepreneurs in a manner different from non-entrepreneurs.

COMPETENCIES AND SKILLS

Entrepreneurs who build substantial companies that grow to more than $10 million in sales and 75 to 100 employees are good entrepreneurs and good leaders. Typically, they will have developed a solid base and a wide breadth of leadership skills and know-how over a number of years working in different areas (e.g., sales, marketing, manufacturing, and finance). It would be unusual for any single entrepreneur to be outstanding in all areas. More likely, a single entrepreneur will have strengths in one area, such as strong people management, conceptual and creative problem-solving skills, and marketing know-how, as well as some significant weaknesses. While it is risky to generalize, often entrepreneurs whose background is technical are weak in marketing, finance, and general management. Entrepreneurs who do not have a technical background are, as you might expect, often weakest in the technical or engineering aspects. Honest self-assessment is therefore key. Knowing one's strengths and weaknesses is crucial to starting and growing a venture. Interestingly, Don Moore of Carnegie Mellon University, John Oesch of the University of Toronto, and Charlene Zietsma of Western University examined entrepreneurs and would-be entrepreneurs, conducting an experiment using undergraduate students at a Canadian university. Their results show that "entrepreneurs tend to overweight personal factors and underweight consideration of the competition when making venturing decisions."[28]

Throughout this book, the concept of fit has been stressed. Having a venture team whose skills are complementary is important, not the possession by an individual of a single, absolute set of skills or a profile. The art and craft of entrepreneuring involves recognizing the skills and know-how needed to succeed in a venture, knowing what each team member does or does not know, and then compensating for shortcomings, either by getting key people on board to fill voids or by accumulating the additional "chunks" of knowledge either before or after taking the plunge. After all, the venture and the people are works in progress.

SKILLS IN BUILDING ENTREPRENEURIAL CULTURE

Leaders of entrepreneurial firms need to recognize and cope with innovation, taking risks, and responding quickly, as well as with absorbing major setbacks. The most effective leaders seem to thrive on the hectic, and at times chaotic, pace and find it challenging and stimulating, rather than frustrating or overwhelming. They use a consensus approach to build a motivated and committed team, they balance conflicting demands and priorities, and they manage conflicts adroitly.

These leaders thus need interpersonal/teamwork skills that involve (1) the ability to create, through leadership, a climate and spirit conducive to high performance, including pressing for performance while rewarding work well done and encouraging innovation, initiative, and calculated risk-taking; (2) the ability to understand the relationships among tasks and between the leader and followers; and (3) the ability to lead in those situations where it is appropriate, including a willingness to lead actively, supervise and control activities of others through directions, suggestions, and the like.

Hao Ma of Peking University and Justin Tan of York University see the entrepreneur as a pioneer. Whether building a new venture or via intrapreneurship, pioneers are relentless champions of creativity and innovation.[29] Characteristics of pioneers include: passion, perseverance, and purposeful, persuasive, and relentless pursuit of goals. Bruno Dyck and Frederick Starke, both of the University of Manitoba, observed a number of instances where individuals either broke away from an existing business to start a new venture as a result of a polarizing event or were assuaged to stay. A leader can learn to handle such situations and recognize causes of conflict and instill harmony.[30]

These interpersonal skills can be called entrepreneurial influence skills, since they have a great deal to do with the way these leaders exact influence over others.

Leadership, Vision, Influence

Successful entrepreneurs are skilful in creating clarity out of confusion, ambiguity, and uncertainty. These entrepreneurial leaders are able to define and gain agreement on who has what responsibility and authority. Further, they do this in a way that builds motivation and commitment to cross-departmental and corporate goals, not just parochial interests. This is not perceived by other managers as an effort to jealously carve out and guard personal turf and prerogatives. Rather, it is seen as a genuine effort to clarify roles, tasks, and responsibilities, and to make sure there is accountability and appropriate approvals. This does not work unless the leader is seen as willing to relinquish his or her priorities and power in the interest of an overall goal. It also requires skill in making sure the appropriate people are included in setting cross-functional or cross-departmental goals and in making decisions. When things do not go as smoothly as was hoped, the most effective leaders work them through to an agreement. Those who are accustomed to traditional line/staff or functional chains of command are often baffled and frustrated in their new role. While some may be quite effective in dealing with their own subordinates, it is a new task to manage and work with peers, the subordinates of others, and even superiors outside one's chain of command.

Glenn Rowe of Memorial University of Newfoundland examines the paradox of leading and managing. He finds that strategic leadership is a necessary ingredient for wealth-creation in entrepreneurial and established organizations.[31] Rowe notes that visionary leaders are more future-oriented and embrace risk-taking more readily. He provides examples of enterprises that have benefitted by having both a visionary leader as well as a managerially minded leader. The managerially minded leader is concerned with financial controls and formal, traditional mechanisms and maintains rather than creates wealth.

Helping, Coaching, and Conflict Management

The most effective leaders are creative and skilful in handling conflicts, generating consensus decisions, and sharing their power and information. They are able to get people to open up, instead of clamming up; they get problems out on the table, instead of under the rug; and they do not become defensive when others disagree with their views. They seem to know that high-quality decisions require a rapid flow of information in all directions and that knowledge, competence, logic, and evidence need to prevail over official status or formal rank in the organization. The way they manage and resolve conflicts is intriguing. They can get potential adversaries to be creative and to collaborate by seeking a reconciliation of viewpoints. Rather than emphasizing differences and playing the role of hard-nose negotiator or devil's advocate to force their own solution, they blend ideas. They are more willing to risk personal vulnerability in this process—often by giving up their own power and resources—than are less-effective leaders. They insist on fairness and integrity in the short and long term, rather than short-term gain. The trade-offs are not easy: At the outset, such an approach involves more managers, takes more time, often appears to yield few immediate results, and seems like a more painful way to lead. Later, however, the gains from the motivation, commitment, and teamwork anchored in consensus are striking. For one thing, there is swiftness and decisiveness in actions and follow-through because the negotiating, compromising, and accepting of priorities is history. For another, new disagreements that emerge do not generally bring progress to a halt, since there is both high clarity and broad acceptance of the overall goals and underlying priorities. Without this consensus, each new problem or disagreement often necessitates a time-consuming and painful confrontation and renegotiation simply because it was not done initially. Apparently, the Japanese understand this quite well.

Teamwork and People Management

Another form of entrepreneurial influence has to do with encouraging creativity and innovation, and with taking calculated risks. Entrepreneurial leaders build confidence by encouraging

TERESA COADY AND BUNTING COADY ARCHITECTS

Teresa Coady's university thesis on "living breathing buildings" was rejected as not being architecture. Teresa overcame that obstacle and pushed for greener, cleaner building solutions. As CEO of the firm she founded with Tom Bunting, she led over 50 full-time employees on cutting-edge projects. The Vancouver-based firm has had a positive impact on resource use. Ahead of its time, the firm envisioned structures that would enhance, not harm, the natural environment—providing healthy and aesthetic surroundings for the buildings' inhabitants. On the subject of her clients, she said: "They love the way we work and they love our values."

The work climate at her firm was collaborative from start to finish when delivering a building. Teresa is credited with pioneering the integrated design process, which defies the traditional view of the architect as a sole creator, accepting no outside input. Both Teresa Coady and her firm contributed to causes of interest, including scholarships and hospital charities. Teresa sits on the boards of directors for both the U.S. and Canadian green building councils. In December of 2010, Bunting Coady Architects merged with B+H Architects.

VANCOUVER SKYLINE, ARCHITECTURAL CONFORMITY.

An employee described Teresa as an "inspirational leader" indicating that Teresa is very positive and asks others to never criticize. In an interview when she received a 2008 Canadian Woman Entrepreneur Award, Teresa said, "It's so important to find your passion in life. And once you do everything you learn will just go in effortlessly. And when you have a passion other people will recognize it in you and help you achieve your goals."

Sources: RBC Royal Bank Canadian Woman Entrepreneur Awards, December 8, 2008; www.buntingcoady.com; RBC Royal Bank Canadian Woman Entrepreneur Awards, December 8, 2008.

innovation and calculated risk-taking, rather than by punishing or criticizing whatever is less than perfect. They breed independent, entrepreneurial thinking by expecting and encouraging others to find and correct their own errors and to solve their own problems. This does not mean they follow a throw-them-to-the-wolves approach. Rather, their peers and others perceive them as accessible and willing to help when needed, and they provide the necessary resources to enable others to do the job. When it is appropriate, they go to bat for their peers and subordinates, even when they know they cannot always win. An ability to make heroes out of other team members and contributors and to make sure others are in the limelight, rather than accept these things oneself, is another critical skill.

The capacity to generate trust—the glue that binds an organization or relationship together—is critical. The most effective leaders are perceived as trustworthy; they behave in ways that create trust. They do this by being straightforward. They do what they say they are going to do. They are not the corporate rumour carriers. They are open and spontaneous, rather than guarded and cautious with each word. And they are perceived as being honest and direct. They treat their associates with respect, as they would want to be treated. They share the wealth with those who help create it by their high performance. Also, it is easy to envision the kind of track record and reputation these entrepreneurial leaders build for themselves. They have a reputation of getting results, because they understand that the task of managing in a rapid-growth company usually goes well beyond one's immediate chain of command. They become known as the creative problem solvers who have a knack for blending and balancing multiple views and demands. Their calculated risk-taking works out more often than it fails. And they have a reputation for developing human capital (i.e., they groom other effective and capable individuals to lead growth).

OTHER NECESSARY COMPETENCIES

Entrepreneurial leaders need a sound foundation in what are considered traditional management skills. Interestingly, in the study of practising entrepreneurs mentioned earlier, no one assigned much importance to capital asset-pricing models, beta coefficients, linear programming, and so forth, the prevailing and highly touted "new management techniques."[32] That is not to say that details are unimportant. The list of competencies below is divided into six areas.

Marketing

- *Market research and evaluation.* Ability to analyze and interpret market research study results, including knowing how to design and conduct studies and to find and interpret industry and competitor information. A familiarity with questionnaire design and sampling techniques. One successful entrepreneur stated that what is vital "is knowing where the competitive threats are and where the opportunities are and an ability to see the customers' needs."

- *Marketing planning.* Skill in planning overall sales, advertising, and promotion programs and in deciding on effective distributor or sales representative systems and setting them up.

- *Product pricing.* Ability to determine competitive pricing and margin structures and to position products in terms of price and ability to develop pricing policies that maximize profits.

- *Sales management.* Ability to organize, supervise, and motivate a direct sales force, and the ability to analyze territory and account sales potential and to manage a sales force to obtain maximum share of market.

- *Direct selling.* Skills in identifying, meeting, and developing new customers and in closing sales. Without orders for a product or service, a company does not really have a business.

- *Service management.* Ability to perceive service needs of particular products and to determine service and spare-part requirements, handle customer complaints, and create and manage an effective service organization.

- *Distribution management.* Ability to organize and manage the flow of product from manufacturing through distribution channels to ultimate customer, including familiarity with shipping costs, scheduling techniques, and so on.

- *Product management.* Ability to integrate market information, perceived needs, research and development, and advertising into a rational product plan, and the ability to understand market penetration and breakeven.

- *New product planning.* Skills in introducing new products, including market testing, prototype testing, and development of price/sales/merchandising and distribution plans for new products.

Operations/Production

- *Manufacturing management.* Knowledge of the production process, machines, personnel, and space required to produce a product and the skill in managing production to produce products within time, cost, and quality constraints.

- *Inventory control.* Familiarity with techniques of controlling in-process and finished goods inventories of materials.

- *Cost analysis and control.* Ability to calculate labour and materials costs, develop standard cost systems, conduct variance analyses, calculate overtime labour needs, and manage/control costs.

- *Quality control.* Ability to set up inspection systems and standards for effective control of quality of incoming, in-process, and finished materials. Benchmarking continuous improvement.
- *Production scheduling and flow.* Ability to analyze work flow and to plan and manage production processes, to manage work flow, and to calculate schedules and flows for rising sales levels.
- *Purchasing.* Ability to identify appropriate sources of supply, to negotiate supplier contracts, and to manage the incoming flow of material into inventory, and familiarity with order quantities and discount advantages.
- *Job evaluation.* Ability to analyze worker productivity and needs for additional help, and the ability to calculate cost-saving aspects of temporary versus permanent help.

Finance

- *Raising capital.* Ability to decide how best to acquire funds for start-up and growth; ability to forecast funds needs and to prepare budgets; and familiarity with sources and vehicles of short- and long-term financing, formal and informal.
- *Managing cash flow.* Ability to project cash requirements, set up cash controls, and manage the firm's cash position, and the ability to identify how much capital is needed, when and where you will run out of cash, and breakeven.
- *Credit and collection management.* Ability to develop credit policies and screening criteria, to age receivables and payables, and an understanding of the use of collection agencies and when to start legal action.
- *Short-term financing alternatives.* Understanding of payables management and the use of interim financing, such as bank loans, factoring of receivables, pledging and selling notes and contracts, bills of lading and bank acceptance; and familiarity with financial statements and budgeting/profit planning.
- *Public and private offerings.* Ability to develop a business plan and an offering memo that can be used to raise capital, a familiarity with the legal requirements of public and private share offerings, and the ability to manage shareholder relations and to negotiate with financial sources.
- *Bookkeeping, accounting, and control.* Ability to determine appropriate bookkeeping and accounting systems as the company starts and grows, including various ledgers and accounts and possible insurance needs.
- *Other specific skills.* Ability to read and prepare an income statement and balance sheet, and the ability to do cash flow analysis and planning, including breakeven analysis, contribution analysis, profit and loss analysis, and balance sheet management.

Entrepreneurial Leadership

- *Problem solving.* Ability to anticipate potential problems; ability to gather facts about problems, analyze them for real causes, and plan effective action to solve them; and ability to be very thorough in dealing with details of particular problems and to follow through.[33]
- *Stakeholder management.* Ability to accurately define the value of varying stakeholder groups and manage the company to deliver value.
- *Communications.* Ability to communicate effectively and clearly—orally and in writing—to media, public, customers, peers, and subordinates.
- *Planning.* Ability to set realistic and attainable goals, identify obstacles to achieving the goals, and develop detailed action plans to achieve those goals, and the ability to schedule personal time systematically.

Lane Merrifield, Lance Priebe, and Dave Krysko founded Club Penguin, a massively multiplayer online game that went live in late 2005. A little over two years later, Disney purchased Club Penguin for $350 million and another $350 million was promised once subsequent targets were met.

In 2009, Dave Krysko was the first to depart Disney. He started Davara Enterprises (Davara—a portmanteau of his and his wife's name, Donara). Davara Enterprises is the vehicle for "the family to build their version of a sustainable, healthy community with a vision to spur social change, attract new business, respect the environment, and bolster the arts." There is also the Krysko Family Foundation. Dave and his clan have a multi-family rental-housing unit; an organic farm; a café that streams live music; real estate development; and back the Keris Support Society, which provides 16 addiction recovery houses for women among other ventures.

Lance Priebe departed Disney in 2011 and went back to his roots, under the alias RocketSnail, a game studio located in Kelowna, British Columbia. RocketSnail launched MechMice in 2013 with Hyper Hippo Productions, with which Lance Priebe also was affiliated. Hyper Hippo was a mere three months old when MechMice was beta released, whereas RocketSnail had been around since 1999. Priebe did take a year off, but then got back into mentoring the next generation of game creators.

Lane Merrifield stayed on with Disney until the end of 2012, transitioning out fully in February 2013. At Disney he had a significant impact—Disney adopted many of Club Penguin's practices, including no in-game advertising. After his departure, Club Penguin had a record 1.8 million kid visitors in a single day. It was a perfect time to leave, "That, to me, was just further reinforcement that things were on a good path." With no plans to retire, he co-founded Fresh Grade, an online student assessment application. Lane Merrifield also considered plans to get his pilot's license, take a motorcycle trip to South America with friends, and take his family to Africa to visit some of the charities to which they have made contributions.

Hyper Hippo's new office space is above Krysko's new commercial development. "The three founders continue to be close." According to Merrifield, "The partnership we had was very special" and when it comes to future endeavours, none of them is ruling out working together again.

The Canadian Press/AP Photo/Rob Griffith

LANE MERRIFIELD, LAST FOUNDER TO LEAVE THE CLUB PENGUIN COLONY.

Question: How do you know when it's time to go? What are your plans after you have pocketed your $100 or $200 million?

Sources: Valerie McTavish "Club Penguin Leaves Behind Empty Nest," *BC Business*, March 4, 2013; Jennifer Smith, "Close-Up: Raising the Cultural Bar," *Kelowna Capital News*, November 22, 2011; Wendy Goldman Getzler, "Former Club Penguin Execs Into Hyper Hippo Games," iKids.com, June 25, 2013.

- *Decision making.* Ability to make decisions on the best analysis of incomplete data, when the decisions need to be made.
- *Project management.* Skills in organizing project teams, setting project goals, defining project tasks, and monitoring task completion in the face of problems and cost/quality constraints.
- *Negotiating.* Ability to work effectively in negotiations, and the ability to quickly balance value given and value received. Recognizing onetime versus ongoing relationships.
- *Managing outside professionals.* Ability to identify, manage, and guide appropriate legal, financial, banking, accounting, consulting, and other necessary outside advisors.
- *Human resources.* Ability to set up payroll, hiring, compensation, and training functions.

Law and Taxes

- *Corporate and securities law.* Familiarity with the commercial codes, including forms of organization and the rights and obligations of officers, shareholders, and directors; familiarity with securities regulations and other provincial and federal laws concerning the commercial activity of your firm, both registered and unregistered, and the advantages and disadvantages of different instruments.

- *Contract law.* Familiarity with contract procedures and requirements of government and commercial contracts, licences, leases, and other agreements, particularly employment agreements and agreements governing the vesting rights of shareholders and founders.

- *Law relating to patent and proprietary rights.* Skills in preparation and revision of patent applications and the ability to recognize a strong patent, trademark, copyright, and privileged information claims, including familiarity with claim requirements, such as intellectual property.

- *Tax law.* Familiarity with provincial and federal reporting requirements, including specific requirements of a particular form of organization, of profit and other pension plans, and the like.

- *Real estate law.* Familiarity with leases, purchase offers, purchase and sale agreements, and so on, necessary for the rental or purchase and sale of property.

- *Bankruptcy law.* Knowledge of bankruptcy law, options, and the forgivable and nonforgivable liabilities of founders, officers, and directors.

Information Technology

- Information and management systems tools from laptop to Internet: sales, supply chain, inventory, payroll, etc.

- Business to business, business to consumer, business to government via the Internet.

- Sales, marketing, manufacturing, and merchandising tools.

- Financial, accounting, and risk analysis and management tools (e.g., Cognos's business intelligence software).

- Telecommunications and wireless solutions for corporate information, data, and process management.

As has been said before, not all entrepreneurs will find they are greatly skilled in the areas listed above, and if they are not, they will most likely need to acquire these skills, either through apprenticeship, through partners, or through the use of advisors. However, while many outstanding advisors, such as lawyers and accountants, are of enormous benefit to entrepreneurs, these people are not always businesspeople and they often cannot make the best business judgments for those they are advising. For example, lawyers' judgments, in many cases, are so contaminated by a desire to provide perfect or fail-safe protection that they are totally risk averse.

LO1 The growing enterprise requires that the founder and team develop competencies as entrepreneurial leaders. Entrepreneurs create and invent new and unique approaches to organizing and leading teams. Ventures go through stages of growth from start-up, through rapid growth, to maturity, to decline and renewal. Leaders are also expected to evolve and go through transitions. As ventures grow, the core competencies need to be covered by the team.

LO2 Founders who succeed in growing their firms beyond $5 million in sales learn to adapt and grow quickly themselves as leaders, or they do not survive. The largest single factor that increases the complexity and difficulty of leading a young company is its rate of growth in orders and revenue. The faster the rate of growth, the more difficult and challenging are the issues, and the more flexible, adaptive, and quick learning must be the organization.

LO3 Founders of rapidly growing firms defy the conventional wisdom that entrepreneurs cannot manage growing beyond the start-up. The venture team must possess skills in marketing, operations/production, finance, entrepreneurial management, law and taxes, and information technology.

STUDY QUESTIONS

1. What is the difference between an entrepreneurial leader and a manager?
2. What must founders and teams do to grow their ventures? What leadership skills and abilities are necessary?
3. Define the stages that most companies experience as they grow, and explain the leadership issues and requirements anticipated at each stage.
4. What drives the extent of complexity and difficulty of management issues in a growing company?

MIND STRETCHERS   *Have you considered?*

1. It is often said, "You cannot hire an entrepreneur." What are the implications for large companies today?
2. How would you characterize the attitudes, behaviours, and mindsets of the most effective leaders and managers you have worked for? The worst? What accounts for the difference?
3. What would be your strategy for changing and creating an entrepreneurial culture in a large, nonentrepreneurial firm? Is it possible? Why, or why not?

Name: _____

Venture: _____

Date: _____

Part I—Competency Inventory

Part I of the exercise involves filling out the Competency Inventory and evaluating how critical certain competencies are either (1) for the venture or (2) personally over the next one to three years. How you rank the importance of competencies, therefore, will depend on the purpose of your assessment.

Step 1   Complete the Competency Inventory on the following pages.

For each competency, place a check in the column that best describes your knowledge and experience. Note that there is a section is at the end of the inventory for unique skills required by your venture; for example, if it is a service or franchise business, there will be some skills and know-how that are unique. Then rate the particular competencies in the inventory from 1 to 3 as follows:

1 = Critical

2 = Very Desirable

3 = Not Necessary

		COMPETENCY INVENTORY			
	RATING	THOROUGH KNOWLEDGE & EXPERIENCE (DONE WELL)	SOME KNOWLEDGE & EXPERIENCE (SO-SO)	NO KNOWLEDGE OR EXPERIENCE (NEW GROUND)	IMPORTANCE (1–3 YEARS)
MARKETING					
Market Research and Evaluation Finding and interpreting industry and competitor information; designing and conducting market research studies; analyzing and interpreting market research data; etc.					
Market Planning Planning overall sales, advertising, and promotion programs; planning and setting up effective distributor or sales representative systems; etc.					
Product Pricing Determining competitive pricing and margin structures and breakeven analysis; positioning products in terms of price; etc.					

		COMPETENCY INVENTORY			
	RATING	THOROUGH KNOWLEDGE & EXPERIENCE (DONE WELL)	SOME KNOWLEDGE & EXPERIENCE (SO-SO)	NO KNOWLEDGE OR EXPERIENCE (NEW GROUND)	IMPORTANCE (1–3 YEARS)
CUSTOMER RELATIONS MANAGEMENT					
Customer Service Determining customer service needs and spare-part requirements; managing a service organization and warranties; training; technical backup, telecom and Internet systems and tools; etc.					
Sales Management Organizing, recruiting, supervising, compensating, and motivating a direct sales force; analyzing territory and account sales potential; managing sales force; etc.					
Direct Selling Identifying, meeting, and developing new customers, suppliers, investors, brain trust and team; closing sales; etc.					
Direct Mail/Catalogue Selling Identifying and developing appropriate direct mail and catalogue sales and related distribution, etc.					
Electronic and Telemarketing Identifying, planning, implementing appropriate telemarketing programs, Internet-based programs, etc.					
SUPPLY CHAIN MANAGEMENT					
Distribution Management Organizing and managing the flow of product from manufacturing through distribution channels to customers; knowing the margins throughout the value chain; etc.					
Product Management Integrating market information, perceived needs, research and development, and advertising into a rational product plan, etc.					
New Product Planning Planning the introduction of new products, including market testing, prototype testing, and development of price, sales, merchandising, and distribution plans, etc.					

(continued)

COMPETENCY INVENTORY					
	RATING	THOROUGH KNOWLEDGE & EXPERIENCE (DONE WELL)	SOME KNOWLEDGE & EXPERIENCE (SO-SO)	NO KNOWLEDGE OR EXPERIENCE (NEW GROUND)	IMPORTANCE (1–3 YEARS)
OPERATIONS/PRODUCTION					
Manufacturing Management Managing production to produce products within time, cost, and quality constraints; knowledge of manufacturing resource planning; etc.					
Inventory Control Using techniques of controlling in-process and finished goods inventories, etc.					
Cost Analysis and Control Calculating labour and materials costs; developing standard cost systems; conducting variance analyses; calculating overtime labour needs; managing and controlling costs; etc.					
Quality Control Setting up inspection systems and standards for effective control of quality in incoming, in-process, and finished goods, etc.					
Production Scheduling and Flow Analyzing work flow; planning and managing production processes; managing work flow; calculating schedules and flows for rising sales levels; etc.					
Purchasing Identifying appropriate sources of supply; negotiating supplier contracts; managing the incoming flow of material into inventory; etc.					
Job Evaluation Analyzing worker productivity and needs for additional help; calculating cost-saving aspects of temporary versus permanent help; etc.					
FINANCE					
Accounting Determining appropriate bookkeeping and accounting systems; preparing and using income statements and balance sheets; analyzing cash flow, breakeven, contribution, and profit and loss; etc.					
Capital Budgeting Preparing budgets; deciding how best to acquire funds for start-up and growth; forecasting funds needs; etc.					

		COMPETENCY INVENTORY			
	RATING	THOROUGH KNOWLEDGE & EXPERIENCE (DONE WELL)	SOME KNOWLEDGE & EXPERIENCE (SO-SO)	NO KNOWLEDGE OR EXPERIENCE (NEW GROUND)	IMPORTANCE (1–3 YEARS)
Cash Flow Management Managing cash position, including projecting cash requirements, etc.					
Credit and Collection Management Developing credit policies and screening criteria, etc.					
Short-Term Financing Managing payables and receivables; using interim financing alternatives; managing bank and creditor relations; etc.					
Public and Private Offering Skills Developing a business plan and offering memo; managing shareholder relations; negotiating with financial sources deal structuring and valuation; etc.					
ENTREPRENEURIAL LEADERSHIP					
Problem Solving Anticipating problems and planning to avoid them; analyzing and solving problems; etc.					
Culture and Communications Communicating effectively and clearly, both orally and in writing, to customers, peers, subordinates, outsiders; treating others as you would be treated, sharing the wealth, giving back; etc.					
Planning Setting realistic and attainable goals; identifying obstacles to achieving the goals; and developing detailed action plans to achieve those goals; etc.					
Decision Making Making decisions based on the analysis of incomplete data, etc.					
Ethical Competency Defining and creating an organization's guiding values; fostering an environment that supports ethically sound behaviour; and instilling a sense of shared accountability among employees; etc.					
Project Management Organizing project teams; setting project goals; defining project tasks; monitoring task completion in the face of problems and cost/quality constraints; etc.					

(continued)

		COMPETENCY INVENTORY			
	RATING	THOROUGH KNOWLEDGE & EXPERIENCE (DONE WELL)	SOME KNOWLEDGE & EXPERIENCE (SO-SO)	NO KNOWLEDGE OR EXPERIENCE (NEW GROUND)	IMPORTANCE (1–3 YEARS)
Negotiating Working effectively in negotiations, etc.					
Personnel Management Setting up payroll, hiring, compensation, and training functions; identifying, managing, and guiding appropriate outside advisors; etc.					
Management Information Systems Knowing the relevant management information systems available and appropriate for growth plans, etc.					
Information Technology and the Internet Using spreadsheet, word processing, and other relevant software; using email, management tools, and other appropriate systems; etc.					
INTERPERSONAL TEAM					
Entrepreneurial Leadership/Vision/ Influence Actively leading, instilling vision and passion in others, and managing activities of others; creating a climate and spirit conducive to high performance; etc.					
Helping Determining when assistance is warranted and asking for or providing such assistance, etc.					
Feedback Providing effective feedback or receiving it, etc.					
Conflict Management Confronting differences openly and obtaining resolution; using evidence and logic; etc.					
Teamwork Working with others to achieve common goals; delegating responsibility and coaching subordinates; etc.					
Build a Brain Trust Connecting with experts and seeking advice and value, etc.					
LAW					
Corporations Understanding business law, forms of organization, and the rights and obligations of officers, shareholders, and directors, etc.					

COMPETENCY INVENTORY					
	RATING	THOROUGH KNOWLEDGE & EXPERIENCE (DONE WELL)	SOME KNOWLEDGE & EXPERIENCE (SO-SO)	NO KNOWLEDGE OR EXPERIENCE (NEW GROUND)	IMPORTANCE (1–3 YEARS)
Contracts Understanding the requirements of government and commercial contracts, licences, leases, and other agreements, etc.					
Taxes Understanding provincial and federal reporting requirements; understanding tax shelters, estate planning, fringe benefits; etc.					
Securities Understanding regulations of the provincial/territorial securities commission and agencies, etc.					
Patents and Proprietary Rights Understanding the preparation and revision of patent applications; recognizing strong patent, trademark, copyright, and privileged information claims; etc.					
Real Estate Understanding agreements necessary for the lease or purchase and sale of property, etc.					
Bankruptcy Understanding options and the forgivable and nonforgivable liabilities of founders, officers, directors, etc.					
Unique Skills List unique competencies required. 1. 2. 3.					

Part II—Competency Assessment

Part II involves assessing strengths and weaknesses, deciding which areas of competence are most critical, and developing a plan to overcome or compensate for any weaknesses and to capitalize on strengths.

Step 1   Assess leadership strengths and weaknesses:

- Which skills are particularly strong?

_____

_____

_____

- Which skills are particularly weak?

_____

_____

_____

- What gaps are evident? When?

_____

_____

_____

Step 2 **Circle the areas of competence most critical to the success of the venture, and cross out those that are irrelevant.**

Step 3 **Consider the implications for you and for developing the venture team.**

- What are the implications of this particular constellation of strengths and weaknesses?

  _____

  _____

  _____

- Who in your team can overcome or compensate for each critical weakness?

  _____

  _____

  _____

- How can you leverage your critical strengths?

  _____

  _____

  _____

- What are the time implications of the above actions? For you? For the team?

  _____

  _____

  _____

- How will you attract and fill the critical gaps in your strengths?

  _____

  _____

  _____

Step 4 **Obtain feedback.**

If you are evaluating your competencies as part of the development of a personal entrepreneurial strategy and planning your apprenticeship, refer back to exercise "Crafting a Personal Entrepreneurial Strategy" in chapter 1.

Preparation Questions

1. What is the core problem and issue(s) facing SPARK Marketing?

2. Based on your evaluation of the company and the external environment, what do you consider to be SPARK's main competitive advantage(s)?

3. Evaluate the alternatives proposed by Andrew to grow their business. Based on your analysis, what growth strategy would you recommend? How would you put this strategy into action?

SPARK MARKETING: RESPONDING TO MARKET OPPORTUNITIES AND AN INDUSTRY SHAKEUP

It was the middle of August 2010 and significant changes were occurring in the communications industry in Atlantic Canada. SPARK Marketing (SPARK) had been making its mark on the communications sector since its inception just one year before and had succeeded in making a name for itself. In fact, times had never been better for this full-service marketing and advertising agency. However, with the industry in flux, companies had to be in tune with changes that were occurring.

The past 10 years had seen the introduction of many small marketing and communications companies in the Atlantic Canadian market, plus the communications industry had experienced a technological revolution. Another change in the market was the recent announcement of a major player, Bristol Communications, shutting down operations. In an arrangement made before the announcement, it was determined that the majority of Bristol's employees would join m5 Communications, a large, full- service agency in the market. As a result of the acquisition of employees, many of Bristol's former clients moved to m5, at least in the short term.

Andrew Best, co-founder of SPARK, was responsible for strategic planning and business development and felt there were opportunities to take advantage of in the Atlantic Canadian market. As Andrew explained:

> The barriers to entry in this business are low. Competitors come and go. I am certain many of our competitors thought we did not stand a chance to survive as a newcomer when we entered this market just over a year ago, but we had a great year and our goal is to grow our revenue by 10% in our second year of business.

Andrew had identified several opportunities to grow the business. He wondered if he should expand the online capabilities of his company, focus on market segments that did not traditionally use agencies, or win clients from its closest competitors. Because of the competitive nature of the industry, timing was important, therefore he would need to make a final decision on the approach SPARK would take by the middle of September.

COMMUNICATIONS INDUSTRY

The communications industry was experiencing turbulent times, rife with hyper-competition and non-stop innovation. Large traditional agencies were struggling to redefine themselves, shift culture, add new services, and restructure. Times had been challenging for them as their way of doing things were ingrained and their traditional business models made it difficult for them to change and shift fast enough. The revolution in the industry was fuelled by a shift from analog to digital media, as there was a decline in traditional media audiences. Some agencies and companies failed to understand that simply shifting traditional content online was not an effective strategy.

The movement into the digital age has changed the face of the industry. According to the Society for Digital Agencies, in the past, industry leaders were known for their strengths in content development, packaging, and distribution. However, the new era was characterized by unprecedented levels of consumer choice, ubiquity, and interactivity. As a result, it was predicted that future industry growth would require agencies that had different competencies, substantially different from those that experienced success during the analog era. To accomplish this and become a market leader in this industry agencies needed to acquire and build new skills, develop deeper audience insights, and build closer relationships with clients and players within the value chain.

Technology was driving this movement since businesses had access to significantly more data about, and insight into, consumer interest and behaviours than ever before. Search traffic, social networking, and blogs, along with other elements of daily Internet activity, provided a continuous, real-time window into what audiences deemed important.

The industry saw a number of trends affecting agencies within the market. One high-growth area was the global emergence of mobile phones, which was due to the rapid

This case was written by Susan Myrden and Donna Stapleton, Memorial University of Newfoundland.

adoption of smartphone devices and growth of applications, changing the way audiences were reached. This trend is even more prominent for younger generations. In fact, four out of five teens carry a wireless device, up from 40% in 2004.[1]

The mobile content and advertising market was large and growing. Combined, it was estimated to be close to $1 billion, nearly 10 times the size of the desktop Internet market.[2] Mobile Internet usage had grown faster than desktop Internet adoption with 40 percent of iPod/iTouch users accessing the Internet more on their mobile devices than on their desktop. For lower-income segments, marketers were seeing many people abandoning computers and obtaining smartphones to stay connected at a lower cost.[3] This dominating trend further forced marketing agencies to provide increased innovation and high-quality content. Marketers had to build digital relationships with consumers, deliver winning experiences, and grab a position of greater influence within this rapidly evolving industry.

Another trend driving results in this highly competitive market was the increasing prevalence of social media outlets. They had become major distribution hubs for content, given consumers' propensity to share information, links, and networks. For marketing agencies, social media outlets represented potential opportunities to increase traffic to clients' digital sites; consequently, many marketers placed extra emphasis on "social media optimization" to increase audience size. The challenge associated with this was the difficulty of targeting specific user groups whose social networks were the most powerful, influential, and effective. The direct result was a demand for increased co-operation between marketing and information technology. The bottom line was if technology was not core to a marketing agency's operations they would not be able to compete.

Despite the growth opportunities that existed for agencies, there was also downward pressure on industry growth. The current worldwide recession saw many clients shift to smaller budgets and more digital, targeted approaches. Company spending was shifting to maximize success. Marketing was identified as the primary driver of this success and advertising, while still a critical part of the marketing mix, was seen to play a less significant role than it once had. Companies were not expected to invest large amounts of money into the thirty-second spot or flashy billboards; instead it was anticipated spending would be comprised of a number of differ-ent facets from many different parts of the marketing mix, with the majority of them being digital.

Coupled with the transition in spending, clients, who once used traditional agencies, were looking for more flexible and creative companies. Therefore, the larger agencies were experiencing layoffs or massive exits of talents who, like clients, were looking for something new and different. In fact, the entire industry was experiencing a shakeup.

Additional challenges that were occurring in the industry included increasing pressure to lower prices and rising customer expectations that went beyond service levels and the capabilities of most agencies. Consequently, keen players within the communications industry had to start searching for the right combinations of responses among unprecedented uncertainty regarding existing business models and prospects for future growth.

COMPANY BACKGROUND

SPARK began as a full-service advertising agency on May 1, 2009 (see Exhibit 1 for the company's launch advertisement), equally owned by Andrew Best and Christa Steeves. The company began in St. John's, Newfoundland and Labrador, but within a few months they had expanded into the Atlantic provinces. At the beginning, the majority of the company's business came from the Newfoundland market as the province had escaped the difficult economic times that had been felt globally. In fact, the economy in Newfoundland and Labrador was surprisingly strong and growing. However, Andrew quickly realized that there were opportunities to service clients across Atlantic Canada. As Andrew stated, "…while we began in St. John's, we never intended to focus on the provincial market. Bigger is better and we knew there were opportunities in Atlantic Canada." Servicing the Atlantic Canadian market was facilitated by opening a second office in Halifax, Nova Scotia.

SPARK's philosophy was to marry strategy with creativity and technology. As a full-service agency, SPARK offered a variety of strategic and creative services including strategic marketing planning, corporate identity and brand development, Internet marketing strategy, and marketing research. To carry out their clients' strategic initiatives, they combined online and offline tools to create consistent communication and conversation across mediums. The offline tools used included, but

---

[1] Lenhart, A. (2010). Teens and mobile phones. Pew Research Center. Retrieved from, http://pewinternet.org/Reports /2010 / Teens-and-Mobile-Phones.aspx

[2] Survival of the fittest in media evolution (2010). *The National*. Retrieved from, http://www.thenational.ae/business/media/ survival-of-the-fittest-in-media-evolution?pageCount=0#page2

[3] 2010 Digital Marketing Outlook. (2010). Society of Digital Agencies. Retrieved from, http://www.slideshare.net/gkrautzel/ 2010-digital-marketing-outlook-toolbox-com-analysis

EXHIBIT 1 **LAUNCH ADVERTISEMENT**

Source: Company files.

and Labrador. Many of the other agencies within the market differentiated themselves within their offline capabilities. However, very few focused on emerging trends within the online platform. SPARK planned to fill this gap. Based on how the industry was changing with technological developments coupled with recessionary times, SPARK was positioned as a cutting-edge agency with an extensive offering of online capabilities at a competitive price. Andrew felt that this was what clients were looking for in the local market. SPARK achieved this positioning strategy with low fixed overhead and by establishing a senior, seasoned team. Coupled with the capabilities of their in-house team with strong industry knowledge, they also had great industry contacts giving them access to research, production, and media services external to the company. This allowed the company to be creative, technologically-savvy, and cost-effective, providing mid-range priced service at high-priced service quality.

SPARK tried to foster a corporate culture that kept employees motivated and costs low. As Andrew explained, "We have a young team with no one close to retirement. We have fun and take a youthful approach to work. We are a small company and everyone has a role to play in how we build the business. We are collaborative, focused, and work to deadlines. We do not have financial perks to motivate our team. The incentive for employees to work hard is pride in their work, the company atmosphere and corporate culture, and being part of a start-up business." And as Andrew stated, "Our mantra for employees is—Grow with us and you will share in our success."

SPARK gained recognition almost immediately upon its launch. In fact, just four months after the company started, *Marketing Magazine* covered a story on the creation and launch of this new agency.[4] This helped in establishing the credibility of the agency in the Atlantic market.

THE TEAM

Having the right team, one that worked well together and with clients, was key to SPARK's success. The leadership team was comprised of Andrew and Christa, who brought a combined 18 years of industry experience, plus two key players in the creative department (See Exhibit 2 for the organizational chart). In total, 12 people worked at SPARK.

Andrew, CEO, had a business mind. He played multiple roles within the company including the management of the online and interactive marketing initiatives, staying on top of industry and technological changes, as well as running the

were not limited to, traditional mediums such as television, radio, out-of-home, and print as well approaches that have gained in popularity such as ambient and guerrilla marketing. The online mix of offerings included web design and development, website analytics, social network marketing, search engine optimization, email marketing, online advertising and buying, viral marketing, and mobile marketing. Despite the range of offerings provided by SPARK, they were committed to staying on top of emerging trends and technologies to evolve with the market. As Andrew explains, "...the tools we use will continue to change, so we look beyond what is working today. But the approach to strategy and need for creative, cost-effective, audience-focused marketing that drives the client's business forward will remain the same."

SPARK's business model was different than competitors in the St. John's market. SPARK's intention upon inception was to fill a gap that they perceived to exist in Newfoundland

---

[4] St. John's gets new agency Spark. *Marketing Magazine*. Retrieved from, http://www.marketingmag.ca/news/agency-news/st-johns-gets-new-agency-spark-10922

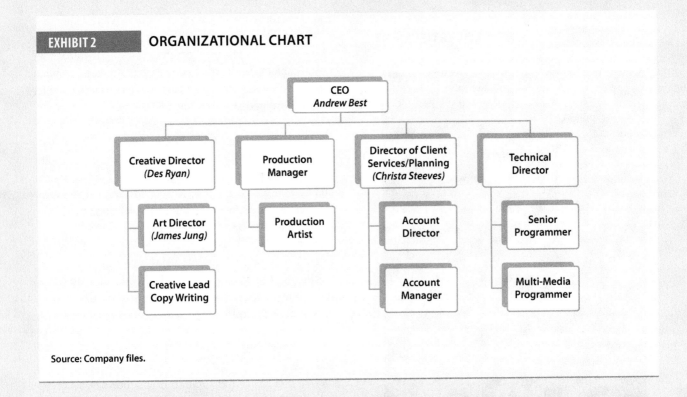

Source: Company files.

day-to-day operations. However, with his history of growing sales for start-up and established businesses, his primary role at SPARK was business development and driving the strategic direction of the company. Under his leadership and management, SPARK was able to drive sales and profitability for clients. Andrew's industry experience was diverse with a base in many industries including banking, communications, and online marketing.

Christa, Director of Client Services and Planning, had a knack for creativity. Her primary role in the agency was spearheading innovation and creative thinking for clients. She was a skilled and experienced marketing professional with competencies in strategic marketing planning and account management. She characterized herself as a big thinker and she believed in digging deep for consumer insights. She attributed this to her success during more than a decade as a marketing professional with some of Atlantic Canada's best agencies.

Des Ryan was the Creative Director. He had worked throughout Atlantic Canada and spent 15 years with Bristol Communications, a strong competitor of SPARK's until its recent closing. Andrew and Christa felt blessed to have acquired someone with Des's experience and talent, not to mention his knowledge of Bristol's clients and staff, when he joined the company in November 2009. According to Andrew, "When Des joined our team, Bristol took note. They

had already lost client work to us and now they lost a key employee."

James Jung was the veteran Art Director. He played the role of illustrator and designer at SPARK, bringing over 20 years of advertising industry experience. He had previously worked at award winning agencies in both Toronto and St. John's, combining solid business and strategic thinking with unparalleled insight and creativity. As Christa explains, "He just plain gets it. His work has made the cash registers ring, changed attitudes, and stirred the soul." James had won a number of awards from across the globe including Cannes, Advertising and Design Club of Canada, Marketing, among others.

COMPETITION

SPARK was operating in a market with many agency players. To date, 80 percent of its business was in Newfoundland and Labrador, with 20 percent generated from Nova Scotia. Therefore, SPARK needed to monitor its competition in both of these regions.

In Newfoundland and Labrador, SPARK was in direct competition with some of the major players in the St. John's market including Idea Factory and m5. These agencies were in the main consideration set for a client looking for a full-service agency. Although Target Marketing and Communications was a full-service agency in the St. John's market, they did not focus on local clients and therefore were not in direct competition with SPARK, but it was certainly an agency that Andrew needed to monitor closely as well.

Idea Factory, a relatively new player in the communications industry, was closest to SPARK in terms of its positioning and size and Andrew considered this company SPARK's closest competitor. In business for about a decade and focusing on the Newfoundland and Labrador market, they offered services in marketing and interactive communications, public relations, and marketing research. With less than 20 employees, Idea Factory was known for its strong ideas and interactive strategy.

m5, another of SPARK's close competitors, had been in business for 30 years, employing more than 200 people across Atlantic Canada and one office in New Hampshire, USA. The company was a fully integrated agency providing market research, public relations, creative development, web building, printing, audio/video production, and online, direct and small business marketing. They operated different profit centres within their business with m5Interactive, m5Public Relations and other core services. Since some of their clients had been with them for over 20 years, m5 had some of the highest retention rates among major agencies in Atlantic Canada. In the past, m5 was known as a retail shop, servicing a large number of retail clients, however, they had expanded their client base to include companies from a variety of industries.

Target, known for its creativity, had been in business for more than 30 years. They employed approximately 50 people, operating from one office in downtown St. John's, Newfoundland. They were rated in the top 10 creative agencies in Canada by *Strategy Magazine* for the past decade. The agency had won numerous client awards, including Gold at Cannes and the London Internationals. In addition, Target was the only agency east of Quebec to win Gold at the CASSIES (Canadian Advertising Success Stories), which rewards creative based on proven business effectiveness. Target focused on larger national clients, bidding on more expensive work than some of the local agencies.

The communications industry was shaken up when the Bristol Group, a major player in the Atlantic Canada market, entered voluntary receivership in July of 2010.[5] This created a major opportunity for those agencies left in the market. Bristol had been a leading marketing communications company for more than 30 years, with offices in St. John's, Newfoundland and Labrador; Halifax, Nova Scotia; Moncton, New Bruns-

wick; and Doha, Qatar. They offered many services including advertising, public relations, marketing research, event management, online marketing, and consulting services. Bristol was an experienced agency that serviced large, traditional clients. In an agreement made before their exit, nearly 80 of Bristol's employees, including senior executives, were offered jobs by m5 in a number of their offices.[6] With the move, m5 also acquired many of Bristol's clients, making the company the market leader on volume and number of employees in Atlantic Canada.

On a secondary level, SPARK competed with Applecore, DRAY Media, Colour, and Pilot; these agencies had carved out specific niches in the St. John's market but none had the full offering of the main competitive group. Finally, from a tertiary perspective there were a number of small shops, production houses, and independent freelancers, such as Waterwerks, Upstream, and Total, that were competing for clients' marketing dollars in this market.

In the Halifax market SPARK was competing with the same agencies as in the St. John's market. In addition, direct competitors also included the Extreme Group, Cossette, Revolve, and Trampoline. Secondary competitors included Chester & Co, Rapport, and Urban Orange. And there were over 50 tertiary competitors consisting of small boutique shops that specialized in specific areas or were seen as design shops. Like St. John's, Halifax also had a number of independent freelancers.

SELECTING A STRATEGY

To make the best use of the company's limited resources, Andrew knew SPARK needed a growth strategy that would help them move forward given the changes in the industry and the collapse of Bristol Communications. Because Andrew was pleased with the company's performance in the first year, he seriously considered maintaining the status quo. Since its inception, the company had been growing at a slow but steady pace and staying under the radar of most competitors. He wondered if that approach was preferred to minimize competitive retaliation or if he should take a more aggressive approach to growth. If he took a more aggressive approach, Andrew felt that there were three reasonable alternatives:

1. Expand online capabilities. Although SPARK had extensive online capabilities, the industry was moving towards social media as well as mobile and location based mar-

[5] Verrinder, J. (2010). Owners close Bristol group, but staff get new start with m5. *Research*. Retrieved from, http://www.research-live.com/news/m-and-a/owners-close-bristol-group-but-staff-get-new-start-with- m5/4003242.article

[6] Semansky, M. (2010). M5 scoops up clients and staff after Bristol folds. *Marketing Magazine*. Retrieved from, http://www.marketingmag.ca/news/agency-news/m5-scoops-up-clients-and-staff-after-bristol-folds-4130

keting. This option would involve hiring a person that had a strong background in these areas to serve existing clients and attract new ones.

2. Focus on a different segment. Many small businesses in the local market had in-house capabilities to conduct ad hoc marketing activities. However this option would involve SPARK targeting those clients who did not normally use agency firms and did not understand the benefits an agency could offer.

3. Target competitors' clients. With the exit of Bristol Communications from the market, many of its clients were in transition. This option would involve SPARK aggressively targeting clients that had moved to m5 but had yet to develop loyalties to the company.

Andrew pondered the decision. As he explained:

> If we are going to increase our sales in the Newfoundland and Nova Scotia markets we will have to steal business from the competition. I don't consider Target to be a competitor where we can take business as they do a different type of work, much bigger in size. They have bigger clients and strong client relationships. We will have to look to other competitors to take work, especially those that do not give full attention to both online and offline. There are many small players where we should be able to steal business. Plus, m5 is a major competitor and they have picked up Bristol's clients. The interesting thing about m5 is that they have a silo mentality with each of their operations separated (m5I, m5PR and Research). This may help us to attract some of their clients. It is my gut instinct that the Newfoundland market is worth about $25 million in agency work, and the Nova Scotia market is about three times that size. With so many large and small competitors in Atlantic Canada how can we differentiate our business from the competition to gain a reasonable share of this business? There are a number of strategic directions we can take to grow our business, but with limited human and financial resources, we need to prioritize our options to have a clear strategic approach to growth. Plus we need to attract clients from competitors without stirring up competitive retaliation.

Andrew knew this decision was important. He decided to weigh out the pros and cons of each alternative so that he would be prepared to operationalize the plan in the next few weeks.

CHAPTER 6

THE NEW VENTURE TEAM

In the world today, there's plenty of technology, plenty of entrepreneurs, plenty of venture capital. What's in short supply is great teams. Your biggest challenge will be building a great team.

JOHN DOERR,
Partner, Kleiner, Perkins, Caufield & Byers

LEARNING OBJECTIVES

LO1 Articulate the role and significance of teams in building successful new ventures.

LO2 Evaluate successful entrepreneurial philosophies and attitudes that can anchor vision in forming and developing effective new venture teams.

LO3 Identify the critical issues and hurdles, including common pitfalls, faced by entrepreneurs in forming and building new venture teams.

LO4 Analyze issues of reward that new teams face in slicing the equity pie.

LO5 Develop a reward system for your own venture.

THE IMPORTANCE OF THE TEAM

THE CONNECTION TO SUCCESS

team: A group who put effort into a common purpose. In sports, a team forms one side in a competitive game. Horses can even be harnessed together as a team pulling collectively. Team can be used as a noun or a verb.

Evidence suggests that the venture team can make all the difference in the enterprise's performance. There is a strong connection between the growth potential of a new venture (and its ability to attract capital beyond the founder's resources from private and venture capital backers) and the quality of its **team**.

The existence of a quality venture team is one of the major differences between a firm that simply provides its founder with a job substitute (and the ability to employ perhaps a few family members and others) and a higher potential venture. The lone-wolf entrepreneur may make a living, but the team builder creates an organization and a company—a company where substantial value and harvest options are created.

Ventures that do not have teams are not necessarily predestined for the new venture graveyard. Yet building a higher potential venture without a team is extremely difficult. Some entrepreneurs have acquired a distaste for partners, and some lead entrepreneurs can be happy only if they are in complete control; that is, they want employees, not partners, either internally or as outside investors. Take, for instance, an entrepreneur who founded a high-technology firm that grew steadily, but slowly, over 10 years to nearly $2 million in sales. As new patterns and technological advances in fibre optics drew much interest from venture capitalists, he had more than one offer of up to $5 million of funding, which he turned down because the investors wanted to own 51 percent or more of his venture. Plainly and simply, he said, "I do not want to give up control of what I have worked so long and hard to create." While clearly the exception to the rule, this entrepreneur has managed to grow his business to more than $20 million in sales.

Mahshad Koohgoli is the founder of Spacebridge Networks, Lantern Communications Canada, and Protecode. On the subject of his start-up Nimcat Networks, he revealed that when the money ran out he called his team together to deliver a difficult message. Koohgoli: "I have enough money to keep the heating on and the lights on; if you leave, I understand. But I'm not going to leave, and I suggest you don't either." Nobody left. Koohgoli explained: "There's no way I can get anything done unless these people succeed so my job is to take away any impediments that might be in their way to success. If they fail it's because I haven't taken care of them." Stephen Daze, executive director of the Entrepreneurship Centre added, "Koohgoli's faith in his team at Nimcat and their reciprocal faith in him turned out to be well placed. One month after that tough meeting, the first round of financing came through and within 18 months Nimcat was sold for $50 million, representing over eight times return on investment."[1]

For decades studies have pointed to the importance of a team approach to new venture creation. Solid teams are far more likely to attract venture capital, team-led start-ups have a greater chance of survival, and those enterprises often realize higher overall returns than ventures run by solo entrepreneurs.

Not only is the existence of a team important, but so too is the quality of that team. Because of this, venture capital investors are often very active in helping to shape—and reshape—venture teams. One study demonstrated the increasing importance of team formation, teamwork history, and cooperation between new venture teams and venture capitalists.[2] This is especially true today with highly technical ventures in areas such as biotechnology, nanotechnology, and photonics. Elicia Maine of Simon Fraser University and Elizabeth Garnsey of the University of Cambridge observe that "smaller and newer firms are playing an increasing role in the advanced materials sector."[3] Elicia Maine and other colleagues at Simon Fraser University also find that new technology-based firms also benefit from clustering near other start-ups, in that they share resources and bounce ideas off each other.[4] That such proximity provides opportunities for strengthening and growing young enterprises has been long observed.

There is, then, a valuable role that the right partner(s) can play in a venture. In addition, mounting evidence suggests that entrepreneurs face loneliness, stress, and other pressures. At the very least, finding the right partner can mitigate these pressures.[5] The key is identifying and working with the right partner or partners. Getting the right partners and working with them successfully usually involves anticipating and dealing with some critical issues and hurdles, when it is neither too early nor too late.

FORMING AND BUILDING TEAMS
LO2

ANCHORING VISION IN TEAM PHILOSOPHY AND ATTITUDES

The most successful entrepreneurs seem to anchor their vision of the future in certain entrepreneurial philosophies and attitudes (i.e., attitudes about what a team is, what its mission is, and how it will be rewarded). The soul of this vision concerns what the founder or founders are trying to accomplish and the unwritten ground rules that become the fabric, character, and purpose guiding how a team will work together, succeed and make mistakes together, and realize a harvest together. The rewards, compensation, and incentive structures rest on this philosophy and attitudes.

This fundamental mindset is often evident in later success. The anchoring of this vision goes beyond all the critical nuts-and-bolts issues covered in the chapters and cases on the opportunity, the business plan, financing, and so forth. Each of these issues is vital, but each by itself may not lead to success. A single factor rarely, if ever, does.

The capacity of the lead entrepreneur to craft a vision and then to lead, inspire, persuade, and cajole key people to sign up for and deliver the dream makes an enormous difference between success and failure, between loss and profit, and between substantial harvest and "turning over the keys" to get out from under large personal guarantees of debt. Henry Mintzberg of McGill University reminds us: "the vision can develop in an emergent fashion, within the new organization, as the founding leader learns from his or her experience."[6]

Marnie Walker grew Student Express, a special needs bussing company, to over $10 million in revenue, 300 employees, and a fleet of 250 vehicles before being offered more money for her start-up than she could say "no" to. Perhaps the words of others best capture Marnie Walker's ability to assemble and rally a cohesive group. There are many testimonials to her ability on her website. One member of her team, Sheila Gallagher, operations manager at Student Express, relates "I was given the opportunity to learn and grow under her leadership. Marnie allows everyone to develop their own style through excellent team leadership and project management skills." A colleague and leadership consultant, Elaine Todres, indicates "Marnie is straightforward, honest, incisive, focused, driven by the needs of the others, results-oriented, compassionate, and devoted to her people." And a customer from the York District School Board remarked: "She showed she really cared about our community, students, their parents and staff by helping out on committees and giving advice. She became part of our team."

Instilling a vision and the passion to win occurs very early, often during informal discussions, and seems to trigger a series of self-fulfilling prophecies that lead to success, rather than to "almosts" or to failure. In a study examining INC. 500 firms, it was found that the best lead entrepreneurs exhibit stronger entrepreneurial vision and greater self-efficacy or self-confidence to act on their vision and make it real.[7] In other words, lead entrepreneurs and team members who understand team building and teamwork have a secret weapon.

What are these team philosophies and attitudes that the best entrepreneurs have and are able to identify or instill in prospective partners and team members? These can be traced to the entrepreneurial mindset discussed in chapter 1—a mindset that can be seen actively at work around the team-building challenge. While there are innumerable blends and variations, most likely the teams of those firms that succeed in growing up big will share many of the following:

- *Cohesion*. Members of a team believe they are all in this together, and if the company wins, everyone wins. Members believe that no one can win unless everyone wins and, conversely, if anyone loses, everyone loses. Rewards, compensation, and incentive structures rest on building company value and return on capital invested, no matter how small or sizeable. Mahshad Koohgoli sums it up thus, "It's not about the path of least resistance. If it's easy, everybody else will be doing it…we are doing something that people said couldn't be done. Starting a company is not easy. But it's fun; I wouldn't change it for anything else."[8]

- *Teamwork*. A team that works as a team, rather than one where individual heroes are created, may be the single most distinguishing feature of the higher potential venture. Thus, on these teams, efforts are made to make others' jobs easier, to make heroes out of partners and key people, and to motivate people by celebrating their successes. As Harold Seigle, the highly successful, now retired, president and chief executive officer of the Sunmark Companies, likes to put it, "High performance breeds strong friendships!"

- *Integrity*. Hard choices and trade-offs are made regarding what is good for the customer, the company, and value creation, rather than being based on purely utilitarian or Machiavellian ethics or narrow personal or departmental needs and concerns. There is a belief in and commitment to the notion of getting the job done without sacrificing quality, health, or personal standards. Of Marnie Walker introduced earlier, Elaine Todres added: "She is ethical and hardworking. And most enduring of all, Marnie is modest and seeks to learn continuously." Marnie herself revealed that her aim is always to develop a culture of respect and accountability and to focus on long-term relationships.

share-vesting agreement: A schedule indicating what an individual's shares are worth and when. The arrangement takes into consideration when the person joined and when they leave. The agreement is structured so that at early departure the equity can be purchased back at a discount, which diminishes over time—typically three to five years—at which point the employee is fully vested and the shares can no longer be purchased back at a pro-rated amount. The agreement does not take into account how hard the person worked and whether or not they deserve the shares; share vesting is to encourage loyalty and dedication and to provide a reward.

- *Commitment to the long haul*. Like most organizations, new ventures thrive or wither according to the level of commitment of their teams. Members of a committed team believe they are playing for the long haul and that the venture is not a get-rich-quick drill. Rather, the venture is viewed as a delayed-gratification game in which it can take 5, 7, or even 10 or more years to realize a harvest. *No one gets a windfall profit by signing up now and then bailing out early or when the going gets tough.* **Share-vesting agreements** reflect this commitment. For example, shares (also known as stock) will usually be vested over five or seven years so that anyone who leaves early, for whatever reasons, can keep shares earned to date, but he or she is required to sell the remaining shares back to the company at the price originally paid. Of course, such a vesting agreement usually provides that if the company is unexpectedly sold or if a public offering is made long before the five-or-seven-year vesting period is up, then shares are 100 percent vested automatically with that event. Pat Quinn, former hockey player and coach sums up teamwork: "The big thing is commitment as a group. You have to develop trust amongst each other that revolves around that commitment, that onus on each other to be honest and have that common direction that the team all want to go to."

- *Harvest mindset*. A successful harvest is the name of the game. This means that eventual capital gain is viewed as the scorecard, rather than the size of a monthly paycheque, the location and size of an office, a certain car, or the like. Dan Martell founded Spheric Technologies in Moncton, New Brunswick, in 2004. Spheric Technologies created social network applications for corporations, essentially "Myspace for big business without the music." His venture grew to 28 full-time employees and revenues of more than $2.2 million in 2008. Mid-way through that year Dan Martell sold the venture and moved to other things—he co-founded Flowtown. He remained a senior advisor to Spheric Technologies, but in 2009 Spheric Technologies was forced to lay off another round of workers taking them down to 11 full-time employees.[9]

- *Commitment to value creation.* Team members are committed to value creation—making the pie bigger for everyone, including adding value for customers, enabling suppliers to win as the team succeeds, and making money for the team's constituencies and various stakeholders. Harry Chemko, Jason Billingsley, and Mark Williams graduated from university in 2000 and launched a consulting business for companies wanting an Internet presence. Soon they noticed a demand for online shopping software and jumped at it. They changed the venture's name and mission. Elastic Path's ecommerce platform is used by Aeroplan, Time Inc., Avis, Samsonite, and the Vancouver 2010 Olympic and Paralympic Winter Games. With approximately 200 customers worldwide, a staff of over 100, and $10 million in revenue they were identified by the *Financial Post* as a firm that would grow despite the economic slump of 2009–2010.[10] Vancouver-based Elastic Path remained privately held and grew organically without outside capital, but it has partnered extensively in order to expand internationally.

- *Equal inequality.* In successful emerging companies, democracy and blind equality generally do not work very well, and diligent efforts are made to determine who has what responsibility for the key tasks. The president is the one to set the ground rules and shape the climate and culture of the venture. Bill Foster, founder of Stratus Computer, was asked if he and his partners were all equal. He quipped, "Yes, we are, except I get paid the most and I own the most stock." Shares are usually not divided equally among the founders and key managers. In one company of four key people, shares were split as follows: 34 percent for the president, 23 percent each for the marketing and technical vice presidents, and 6 percent for the controller. The remainder went to outside directors and advisors. In another company, seven founders split the company as follows: 22 percent for the president, 15 percent for each of the four vice presidents, and 9 percent for each of the two other contributors. An example of how failure to differentiate in terms of ownership impacts a business is seen in a third firm, where four owners each had equal share. Yet, two of the owners contributed virtually everything, while the other two actually detracted from the business. Because of this unresolved problem, the company could not attract venture capital and was never able to grow significantly.

IN THE NORTHERN HEMISPHERE, HARVEST OCCURS IN THE FALL SEASON.

- *Fairness.* Rewards for key employees and share ownership are based on contribution, performance, and results over time. Since these can only be roughly estimated in advance, and since there will invariably be surprises and inequities, both positive and negative, as time goes on, adjustments are made. One good example is a company that achieved spectacular results in just two years in the cellular phone business. When the company was sold, it was evident that two of the six team members had contributed more than was reflected in their share ownership position. To remedy this, another team member gave one of the two team members shares worth several hundred thousand dollars. Since the team was involved in another venture, the president made adjustments in the various ownership positions in the new venture, with each member's agreement, to adjust for past inequities. In addition, it was decided to set aside 10 percent of the next venture to provide some discretion in making future adjustments for unanticipated contributions to ultimate success.

- *Sharing of the harvest.* This sense of fairness and justness seems to be extended by the more successful entrepreneurs to the harvest of a company, even when there is no legal or ethical obligation to do so. For example, as much as 10 to 20 percent of the "winnings" is frequently set aside to distribute to key employees. In one such recent harvest, employees were startled and awash with glee when informed they would each receive a year's salary after the company was sold. However, this is not always the case. In another firm, 90 percent of which was owned by an entrepreneur and his family, the president, who was the single person most responsible for the firm's success and spectacular valuation, needed to expend considerable effort to get the owners to agree to give bonuses to other key employees of around $3 million, an amount just over 1 percent of the $250-million sale price. (It is worth considering how this sense of fairness, or lack of it, affects future flows of quality people and opportunities from which these entrepreneurs can choose subsequent new ventures.)

So a real question remains: should incentives be individual or team based or a mix? Ideally the whole team is pulling together, but in reality tasks are divvied up. Some will be responsible for fundraising, some for developing the product or service, others for selling.

A PROCESS OF EVOLUTION

An entrepreneur considering issues of team formation will rarely discover black-and-white, bullet-proof answers that hold up over time. Nor is it being suggested that an entrepreneur needs answers to all questions concerning what the opportunity requires, and when, before moving ahead. Emphasis on the importance of new venture teams also does not mean every new venture must start with a full team that plunges into the business. It may take some time for the team to come together as a firm grows, and there will always be some doubt, a hope for more than a prospective partner can deliver, and a constant recalibration. Again, creative acts, such as running a marathon or entrepreneuring, will be full of unknowns, new ground, and surprises. Preparation is an insurance policy, and thinking through these team issues and team-building concepts in advance is very inexpensive insurance.

The combination of the right team of people and a right venture opportunity can be very powerful. The whole is, in such instances, greater than the sum of the parts. However, the odds for highly successful venture teams are rather thin. Even if a venture survives, the turnover among team members during the early years probably exceeds the national divorce rate. Jason Billingsley parted ways with his ElastiPath co-founders. Studies of new venture teams seeking venture capital show many never get off the ground. These usually exhaust their own resources and commitment before raising the venture capital necessary to launch their ventures.

Dan Martell, now located in the United States, and his co-founder and venture team had worked hard and Flowtown had received $750,000 in funding. But the team had to pivot rather quickly. Over privacy concerns, Facebook changed their terms of service and Flowtown could no longer do what they had promised investors they would do: match email addresses to social media marketing and ultimately convert targeted Facebookers into engaged customers. Flowtown's revenues of $100 000 per month stopped.

They went to the whiteboard, took an afternoon, and came up with three new ideas. Just over a year later, Demandforce acquired Flowtown for an undisclosed amount, but sufficient to cause the people involved to smile. Dan Martell now supports many start-ups and organizations that promote entrepreneurship. He is a vocal proponent of C100, which supports Canadian technology entrepreneurship and investing. Dan Martell launched Clarity.fm in New Brunswick in January 2012 and went public in May 2012. Clarity.fm provides a service as a matchmaker for start-ups seeking advice and entrepreneurs providing it.

Questions: What is Clarity.fm's business model? Does it make sense? What changes, if any, would you make?

Sources: Courtney Rubin, "Start-Up Flowtown Acquired by Demandforce," *Inc.*, October 17, 2011; Alexia Tsotsis, "Marketing Startup Flowtown Gets Swooped Up," *TechCrunch*, October 13, 2011; "Dan Martell" Wikipedia. Accessed 2013.

The formation and development of new venture teams seems to be idiosyncratic, and there seems to be a multitude of ways in which venture partners come together…and break apart. Some teams form by accidents of geography, common interest, or working together (see Angstrom's Team below). Perhaps the common interest is simply that the team members want to start a business, while in other instances the interest is an idea that members believe responds to a market need. Others form teams by virtue of past relationships. For example, roommates or close friendships in school frequently lead to business partnerships. Jiffy Lube was founded by college football coach Jim Hindman and some of his coaches and players—including Stephen Spinelli.

In the evolution of venture teams, two distinct patterns are identifiable. In the first, one person has an idea (or simply wants to start a business), and then three or four associates join the team over the next one to three years as the venture takes form. Alternatively, an entire team forms at the outset based on such factors as a shared idea, a friendship, an experience, and so forth.

FILLING THE GAPS

There is no simple solution—like a recipe from a cookbook—to team formation; rather, there are as many approaches to forming teams, as there are ventures with multiple founders.

Successful entrepreneurs search out people and form and build a team based on what the opportunity requires, and when.[11] Team members will contribute high value to a venture if they complement and balance the lead entrepreneur—and each other. Yet, ironically, while a substantial amount of thought usually accompanies the decision of people to go into business together, an overabundance of the thinking, particularly among the less experienced, can focus on less critical issues, such as titles or the corner office. Thus, teams are often ill-conceived from the outset and can easily plunge headlong into unanticipated and unplanned responses to crises, conflicts, and changes. Just as it is possible to recruit additions to the team from competitors or former employers, it should be noted that it is easy to lose team members that way too. Employees will leave to pursue their own best opportunities.[12]

A team starts with a lead entrepreneur (Ged McLean in the case of Angstrom Power Inc.). In a start-up situation, the lead entrepreneur usually wears many hats. Beyond that, comparison of the nature and demands of the venture and the capabilities, motivations, and interests of the

Angstrom Power Inc., located in North Vancouver, British Columbia, was a privately held enterprise "funded by venture partners with experience in advancing new energy technology." Angstrom's aim was to bring to market an integrated hydrogen fuel cell, with energy storage and micro-fluid components for hand-held portable electronics (e.g., smart phone). Take a look at the following individuals and their backgrounds. There are commonalities and differences in their areas of expertise and many have overlapped in working at various organizations.

- Paul Zimmerman, CEO, had built and run global businesses for the past 20 years. Paul brought to Angstrom contacts in the technology community (president of Oregon Scientific, senior executive at Cisco Systems, general manager at Samsung Electronics) as well as venture capital arena—including being a founding director of a $2-billion equity fund. His schooling included the University of Toronto (electrical engineering and computer science) and an executive MBA from the International Institute of Management Development in Switzerland.
- Dr. Ged McLean, founder, president, and CTO, was director of the Institute for Integrated Energy Systems at the University of Victoria, and held 40 patents and applications. He had past experience in start-up ventures.
- Godfrey Forssman, director of finance, was a chartered accountant with 12 years' experience in growing entrepreneurial ventures.
- Dr. Jeremy Schrooten, director of fuel cell systems, had BSc degrees in chemistry and ceramic engineering and a PhD in materials science. He previously worked at UTC Fuel Cells. He was credited with four patents before Angstrom and two while at Angstrom.
- Olen Vanderleeden, director of business development, had a BEng from the University of Victoria and an MBA from Simon Fraser University. He worked at Ballard Power for eight years. He held 11 patents and applications while at Ballard and 7 while with Angstrom.
- André van Vuuren, director of engineering, had a background in new product development from prototype through volume production.
- Bruce Townson, director of strategy and infrastructure, previously worked in partnership development in the hydrogen and fuel cell industries.
- Joerg Zimmermann, director of fueling R&D, worked in the R&D department of Ballard Power Systems for six years before joining Angstrom. He is a named inventor on 25 patents and patents pending.

The above lineup was listed on the venture's website in 2008, the individuals listed below were added in 2009 and Olen Vanderleeden and Bruce Townson were removed!

- John Lee, COO, 25 years of management experience at electrical and power technology companies—including alternative energy.
- Jim McBeth, director of manufacturing engineering, worked in a variety of industry positions including as a director general with the National Research Council of Canada.
- Steven Pratt, director of engineering, has 15 years of experience in maturing and commercializing emerging technologies and holds more than 40 patents.

Jim McBeth and Steven Pratt both left Angstrom in 2009 after six months of employment. In March of 2011, Joerg Zimmermann left Angstrom for General Fusion. In December of 2011, it was announced that BIC Group's Canadian subsidiary would acquire the assets of Angstrom Power for $18.7 million. In 2012, Paul Zimmerman left Angstrom after the sale to BIC, Ged McLean, Jeremy Schrooten stayed on with the new owners.

ANGSTROM'S BOARD OF DIRECTORS:

- Chairman: Ake Almgren, PhD, served on other boards, 26-year career at ABB, a worldwide power solutions company. President and CEO of Capstone Turbine 1998–2003.
- David Oxtoby, CFA, worked for Ontario Power Generation Ventures, Inc. from 2001–2005. He is currently CEO of CarbonFree Technology Inc.
- David Berkowitz has been with Ventures West since 1996 and leads the firm's cleantech practice.
- Wal van Lierop, PhD, is cofounder, president, and CEO of Chrysalix Energy Venture Capital.
- Mark Steinley was originally Angstrom's president and CEO while Ged McLean served as CTO and helped secure the venture's first round of financing ($2.85 million in 2002).
- Eric Schwitzer, managing partner at Enterprise Capital Management Inc.
- Daniel Muzyka, PhD, Dean, Sauder School of Business, University of British Columbia.

Question: Who will you surround yourself with?

Sources: Angstrom Power's Website, www.angstrom.com/; LinkedIn public listing for Angstrom Power; BusinessWeek Private Company listing for Angstrom Power Inc.

lead entrepreneur will signal gaps that exist and that need to be filled by other team members or by accessing other outside resources, such as a board of directors (see Angstrom's board of directors), consultants, lawyers, accountants, and so on.[13] Elicia Maine, Daniel Shapiro, and Aidan Vining, all of Simon Fraser University, examined the relationship between clusters and the growth performance of firms, finding that new ventures benefit by having access to a pool of valuable resources through proximity. Tod Rutherford of Syracuse University and John Holmes of Queen's University observe "entrepreneurs are active creators of institutional cluster development," but established firms erect barriers to protect their intellectual property in an attempt to reduce tacit knowledge flows within the cluster.[14]

Serial entrepreneur Mahshad Koohgoli, CEO of Protecode, has a product that examines a software developer's project and inspects the content to determine the underlying intellectual property and licensing attributes. With so much open source software it is important to trace the content for ownership. For example, lawsuits were filed against Cisco for including some code in its software that was in the public domain.[15]

If the strengths of the lead entrepreneur or a team member are technical in nature, other team members, or outside resources, need to fill voids in marketing, finance, and such (see Angstrom's team). Realistically, skills will overlap and responsibilities will be shared, but team members need to complement, not duplicate, the lead entrepreneur's capabilities and those of other team members.

A by-product of forming a team may be the alteration of an entry strategy if a critical gap cannot be filled. A firm may find that it simply cannot assault a certain market because it cannot hire the right design person. But it may find it could attract a top-notch person to exploit another niche with a modified product or service.

Most importantly, the process of evaluating and deciding who is needed, and when, is dynamic and not a one-time event. What know-how, skills, and expertise are required? What key tasks and action steps need to be taken? What are the requisites for success? What is the firm's distinctive competence? What external contacts are required? How extensive and how critical are the gaps? How much can the venture afford to pay? Will the venture gain access to the expertise it needs through additions to its board of directors (see Angstrom's board of directors) or outside consultants? Questions such as these determine when and how these needs could be filled. And answers to such questions will change over time.

The elements on the following pages, organized around the analytical framework introduced in chapter 2, can guide the formation of capable new venture teams.

The Founder

What kind of team is needed depends upon the nature of the opportunity and what the lead entrepreneur brings to the game.[16] One key step in forming a team is for the lead entrepreneur to assess his or her entrepreneurial strategy. (The personal entrepreneurial strategy exercise for chapter 1—found online in Connect—is a valuable input in approaching these issues.) Thus, the lead entrepreneur needs to first consider whether the team is desirable or necessary and whether he or she wants to grow a higher potential company. He or she then needs to assess what talents, know-how, skills, track record, contacts, and resources are being brought to the table; that is, what "chunks" have been acquired.[17] (See the leadership skills and know-how assessment exercise for chapter 5.) Once this is determined, the lead entrepreneur needs to consider what the venture has to have to succeed, who is needed to complement him or her, and when. The best entrepreneurs are optimistic realists and have a desire to improve their performance. They work at knowing what they do and do not know and are honest with themselves. The lead entrepreneur needs to consider issues such as:

- What relevant industry, market, and technological know-how and experience are needed to win, and do I bring these to the venture? Do I know the revenue and cost model better than anyone?
- Are my personal and business strengths in those specific areas critical to success in the proposed business?

Marnie Walker did not take long after the harvest of Student Express Ltd. to seek new opportunities. She got involved with other high-net-worth individuals to create Maple Leaf Angels to help start-up and growth companies. Maple Leaf Angels provides cash and other assistance, including coaching/mentoring, introductions, access to networks, and the support of belonging to a community. Receiving upwards of 400 applications for funding each year, Maple Leaf Angels selects six to eight to support. Get your business plan in order and submit it!

While still an active participant in Maple Leaf Angels, Walker founded 401 Bay Centre when her own search for a decent workspace turned up nothing suitable. 401 Bay Centre provides the services and financial benefits of a shared, managed office. Located in downtown Toronto, 45 furnished offices are available on a full or part-time basis—including daily rental, as highlighted by a testimonial from a Global film crew who were able to edit and upload breaking news from one of the day offices.

MARNIE WALKER, FOUNDER OF 401 BAY CENTRE.

Question: Draw 401 Bay Centre's business model. Are there limiting factors to revenue or growth?

Source: Susan Down, "Investment Angels," *The Toronto Star*, September 28, 2009; http://www.401bay.com/.

- Do I have the contacts and networks needed (and will the ones I have make a competitive difference), or do I look to partners in this area?
- Can I attract a team of all-star partners (first round picks) inside and externally, and can I lead these people and other team members effectively?
- Why did I decide to pursue this particular opportunity now, and what do I want out of the business (i.e., what are my goals and my income and harvest aspirations)?
- Do I know what the sacrifices and commitment will be, and am I prepared to make these?
- What are the risks and rewards involved, am I comfortable with them, and do I look for someone with a different risk-taking orientation?

Often a student going through this process will conclude that a more experienced person will be needed to lead the venture.

The Opportunity

The need for team members is something an entrepreneur constantly thinks about, especially in the idea stage before start-up. What is needed in the way of a team depends on the matchup between the lead entrepreneur and the opportunity, and how fast and aggressively he or she plans to proceed. (See the online Venture Opportunity Screening Exercises for chapter 3.) While most new ventures plan to bootstrap it and bring on additional team members only as the company can afford them, the Catch-22 is that if a venture is looking for venture capital or serious private investors, having an established team will yield higher valuation and a smaller ownership share that will have to be given up. Questions to consider are:

- Have I clearly defined the value added and the economics of the business? Have I considered how (and with whom) the business can make money? For instance, whether a company is selling razors or razor blades makes a difference in the need for different team members.

- What are the critical success variables in the business I want to start, and what (or who) is needed to influence these variables positively?

- Do I have, or have access to, the critical external relationships with investors, lawyers, bankers, customers, suppliers, regulatory agencies, and so forth, that are necessary to pursue my opportunity? Do I need help in this area?

- What competitive advantage and strategy should I focus on? What people are necessary to pursue this strategy or advantage?

Outside Resources

In reaction to corporate scandals (e.g., Bre-X, Hollinger, Nortel), governance issues have become more important in recent years, including for start-up enterprises.[18] Gaps can be filled by accessing outside resources, such as boards of directors, accountants, lawyers, consultants, and so forth.[19] Usually, tax and legal expertise can best be obtained initially on a part-time basis. Other expertise (e.g., to design an inventory control system) is specialized and needed only once. Generally, if the resource is a one-time or periodic effort, or if the need is peripheral to the key tasks, goals, and activities required by the business, then an alternative such as using consultants makes sense. However, if the expertise is a must for the venture at the outset and the lead entrepreneur cannot provide it or learn it quickly, then one or more people will have to be acquired. Some questions to consider are:

- Is the need for specialized, one-time, or part-time expertise peripheral or on the critical path?

- Will secrets be compromised if I obtain this expertise externally?

Rent frock Repeat is 100 percent Canadian owned and operated. RfR provides dresses for rent. This saves women the expense of purchase and customers indicate it also saves time and aggregation and fits into their schedules—a few clicks in the evening, including details about sizing, etc., and a dress and a back-up size conveniently arrive days later at their doorstep or wherever they wish. RfR's co-founders Lisa Delorme and Kristy Wieber appear to be pulling it off alone, but in reality an array of partners make it possible to source the latest fashions quickly without the costs of retail.

RENT FROCK REPEAT'S CO-FOUNDER, KRISTY WIEBER.

ChipCare boasts of a "strong team" and lists a varied array of partners. ChipCare offers a portable diagnostic device with potential to work in a number of applications—counting blood cells, measuring air pollution, and testing for food safety. But commercializing an invention is not easy!

ADDITIONAL CONSIDERATIONS

Forming and building a team is, like marriage, a rather unscientific, occasionally unpredictable, and frequently surprising exercise—no matter how hard one may try to make it otherwise! The analogy of marriage and family, with all the accompanying complexities and consequences, is a particularly useful one. Forming a team has many of the characteristics of the courtship and marriage ritual, involving decisions based in part on emotion. There may well be a certain infatuation among team members and an aura of admiration, respect, and often fierce loyalty. Similarly, the complex psychological joys, frustrations, and uncertainties that accompany the birth and raising of children (here, the product or service) are experienced in entrepreneurial teams as well. Thus, the following additional issues need to be considered:

- *Values, goals, and commitment.* It is critical that a team be well anchored in terms of values and goals. In any new venture, the participants establish psychological contracts and an entrepreneurially conducive environment. While these are most often set when the lead entrepreneur encourages standards of excellence and respect for team members' contributions, selection of team members whose goals and values are in agreement can greatly facilitate establishment of a psychological bond and an entrepreneurial climate. In successful enterprises, the personal goals and values of team members align well, and team members champion the goals of the enterprise too. While this alignment may be less exact in large publicly-owned corporations and greatest in small closely held firms, significant overlapping of a team member's goals with those of other team members and the overlap of enterprise goals and team members' goals is desirable. Practically speaking, these evaluations of team members are some of the most difficult to make.

- *Definition of roles.* A diligent effort needs to be made to determine who is comfortable with and who has what responsibility for the key tasks so duplication of capabilities or responsibilities is minimized. Roles cannot be pinned down precisely for all tasks, since some key tasks and problems simply cannot be anticipated and since contributions are not always made by people originally expected to make them. Maintaining a loose, flexible, flat structure with shared responsibility and information is desirable for utilizing individual strengths, flexibility, rapid learning, and responsive decision-making.

- *Peer groups.* The support and approval of family, friends, and co-workers can be helpful, especially when adversity strikes. Reference group approval can be a significant source of positive reinforcement for a person's career choice and, thus, his or her entire self-image and identity.[20] Ideally, peer group support for each team member should be there. (If it is not, the lead entrepreneur may have to accept the additional burden of encouragement and support in hard times, a burden that can be sizeable.) Therefore, questions of whether a prospective team member's spouse is solidly in favour of his or her decision to pursue an entrepreneurial career and the sweat equity required and of whether the team member's close friends will be a source of support and encouragement or of detraction or negativism need to be considered.

Dan Martell, profiled earlier, shares that choosing friends carefully is vital: "You are the average of the five people that you spend the most time with." To raise the average, if possible, you want to "hang" with folks better than yourself.

COMMON PITFALLS

There can be difficulties in the practical implementation of these philosophies and attitudes, irrespective of the venture opportunity and the people involved. The company may come unglued before it gets started, may experience infant mortality, or may live perpetually immersed in nasty divisive conflicts and power struggles that will cripple its potential, even if they do not kill the company.

Often, a team lacks skill and experience in dealing with such difficult start-up issues, does not take the time to go through an extended "mating dance" among potential partners during the **moonlighting** phase before actually launching the venture, or does not seek the advice of competent advisors. As a result, such a team may be unable to deal with such sensitive issues as who gets how much ownership, who will commit what time and money or other resources, how disagreements will be resolved, and how a team member can leave or be let go. Thus, crucial early discussions among team members sometimes lead to a premature disbanding of promising teams with sound business ideas. Or in the rush to get going, or because the funds to pay for help in these areas are lacking, a team may stay together but not work through, even in a rough way, many of these issues. Such teams do not take advantage of the moonlighting phase to test the commitment and contribution made by team members. For example, to build a substantial business, a partner needs to be totally committed to the venture. The success of the venture is the partner's most important goal, and other priorities, including his or her family, come second. Another advantage of using such a shakedown period effectively is that the risks inherent in such factors as premature commitment to permanent decisions regarding salary and shares are lower.

The common approach to forming a new venture team can also be a common pitfall for new venture teams. Here, two to four entrepreneurs, usually friends or work acquaintances, decide to demonstrate their equality with such democratic trimmings as equal share ownership, equal salaries, equal office space and cars, and other items symbolizing their peer status. Left unanswered are questions of who is in charge, who makes the final decisions, and how real differences of opinion are resolved. While some overlapping of roles and a sharing in and negotiating of decisions are desirable in new venture teams, too much looseness is debilitating. Even sophisticated buy-sell agreements among partners often fail to resolve the conflicts.

Another pitfall is a belief that there are no deficiencies in the lead entrepreneur or the venture team. Or the team is overly fascinated with or overcommitted to a product idea. For example, a lead entrepreneur who is unwilling or unable to identify his or her own deficiencies and weaknesses and to add appropriate team members to compensate for these, and who further lacks an understanding of what is really needed to make a new venture grow into a successful business, has fallen into this pitfall.[21]

Failing to recognize that creating and building a new venture is a dynamic process is a problem for some teams. Therefore, such teams fail to realize that initial agreements are likely not to reflect actual contributions of team members over time, regardless of how much time one devotes to team-building tasks and regardless of the agreements team members make before start-up. In addition, they fail to consider that teams are likely to change in composition over time. Richard Testa, a leading attorney whose firm has dealt with many start-ups and with numerous venture capital firms, startled those attending a seminar on raising venture capital by saying:

> The only thing that I can tell you with great certainty about this start-up business has to do with you and your partners. I can virtually guarantee you, based on our decade plus of experience, that five years from now at least one of the founders will have left every company represented here today.[22]

Woe is the team that fails to put in place mechanisms that will facilitate and help structure graceful divorces and provide for the internal adjustments required as the venture grows.

Destructive motivations in investors, prospective team members, or the lead entrepreneur spell trouble. Teams suffer if they are not alert to signs of misaligned motivations, such as an early concern for power and control by a team member. In this context, it has been argued that conflict

moonlighting: Having a second job beyond one's regular "daytime" employment. Many entrepreneurs do not give up their steady job to focus on the start-up: employee by day, entrepreneur by night.

management is a central task for members of teams. A study of self-empowered teams found that how team members resolve their conflicts could affect their self-efficacy, as well as overall team performance. Team members in this study were most effective when they recognized they wanted to resolve the conflict for mutual benefit and that the goal was to help each other get what each other really needs and values, and not to try to win or to outdo each other.[23]

Finally, new venture teams may take trust for granted. Integrity is important in long-term business success, and the world is full of high-quality, ethical people; yet predators, crooks, sharks, frauds, and impostors also inhabit the real world. Chapter 7 contains a detailed discussion on the importance of integrity in entrepreneurial pursuits. It is paradoxical that an entrepreneur cannot succeed without trust, but he or she probably cannot succeed with blind trust either. Trust is something that is earned, usually slowly, for it requires a lot of patience and a lot of testing in the real world. This is undoubtedly a major reason why investors prefer to see teams that have worked closely together. In the area of trust, a little cynicism goes a long way, and teams that do not pay attention to detail, such as performing due diligence with respect to a person or firm, fall into this pit.

REWARDS AND INCENTIVES   LO4

SLICING THE FOUNDER'S PIE

One of the most frequently asked questions from start-up entrepreneurs is: How much share ownership should go to whom? (Chapter 9 "Financing the Venture" examines the various methods used by venture capitalists and investors to determine what share of the company is required by the investor at different rounds of investment.) Consider discussions with Jed, a former student, who secured early-stage funding from John Doerr of Kleiner Perkins Caufield & Byers. The advice for Jed and all others is the same.

First, start with a philosophy and set of values that boil down to this great principle: Share the wealth with those who help to create the value and thus the wealth. Once over that hurdle, you are less likely to get hung up on the percentage of ownership issue. After all, 51 percent of nothing is nothing. The key is making the pie as large as possible. Second, the ultimate goal of any venture-capital-backed company is to realize a harvest at a price 5 to 10 times the original investment or more. Thus, the company will either be sold via an initial public offering (IPO) or to a larger company. It is useful to work backward from the capital structure at the time of the IPO to envision and define what will happen and who will get what. Most venture-capital-backed, smaller company IPOs during the robust capital markets would have 12 to 15 million shares outstanding after the IPO. In most situations 2.5 to 4 million shares are sold to the public (mostly to institutional investors) at $12 to $15 per share, depending on the perceived quality of the company and the robustness of the appetite for IPOs at the time. In less than 10 years, Motricity went from zero to filing an IPO for $250 million offering shares for $10. Seven years after inception, renewable products company Amyris had its initial public offering pricing shares at $16 looking to raise $85 million. The number could be halved or doubled. Typically, the founder/CEO will own 1 to 3 million shares after the IPO, worth somewhere between $12 and $45 million. Put in this perspective, it is much easier to see why finding a great opportunity, building a great team, and sharing the wealth with widespread ownership in the team is far more important than what percentage of the company is owned.

Finally, especially for young entrepreneurs in their 20s or 30s, this will not be their last venture. The single most important thing is that it succeeds. Make this happen, and the future opportunities will be boundless. All this can be ruined if the founder/CEO simply gets greedy and overcontrolling, keeping most of the company to himself or herself, rather than creating a sizeable, shared pie.

THE REWARD SYSTEM[24]

The reward system of a new venture includes both the financial rewards—such as shares, salary, and fringe benefits—and the chance to realize personal growth and goals, exercise autonomy, and develop skills in particular venture roles. Also, what is perceived as a reward by any single team member will vary. This perception will depend very much upon personal values, goals, and aspirations. Some may seek long-range capital gains, while others desire more short-term security and income.

The reward system established for a new venture team should facilitate the interface of the venture opportunity and the executive team. It needs to flow from team formation and enhance the entrepreneurial climate of the venture and the building of an effective team. Being able to draw in and hold onto high-quality team members depends, to a great extent, on financial and psychological incentives. The skills, experience, commitment, risk, and concern of these team members are secured through these payoffs.

The rewards available to an entrepreneurial team vary over the life of a venture. While intangible benefits, such as opportunity for self-development and realization, may be available continuously, some of the financial rewards are more or less appropriate at different stages of the venture's development.

Because these rewards are so important and because, in its early stages, a venture is limited in the rewards it can offer, the total reward system over the life of the venture needs to be thought through carefully and efforts made to ensure that the venture's capacity to reward is not limited as levels of contribution change or as new personnel are added.

External issues also have an impact on the reward system created for a new venture. The division of equity between the venture and external investors will affect how much equity is available to team members. Further, the way a venture deals with these questions will influence its credibility with investors and others, because these people will look to the reward system for signs of commitment by the venture team.

CRITICAL ISSUES

Dividing ownership among the founding team, based on the philosophy and vision discussed earlier, is an early critical task for the lead entrepreneur. Investors may provide advice but will, more often than not, dump the issue squarely back in the lap of the lead entrepreneur, since whether and how these delicate ownership decisions are resolved often is seen by investors as an important litmus test. Also, the process by which a reward system is decided and the commitment of each team member to deal with problems in a way that will ensure rewards continue to reflect performance are of utmost importance. Each key team member needs to be committed to working out solutions that reflect the commitments, risks, and anticipated relative contributions of team members as fairly as possible.[25]

A good reward system reflects the goals of the particular venture and is in tune with valuations. If a venture is not seeking outside capital, outside owners need not be considered; but the same issues need to be resolved. For example, if a goal is to realize a substantial capital gain from the venture in the next 5 to 10 years, then the reward system needs to be aimed at reinforcing this goal and encouraging the long-term commitment required for its attainment.

No time-tested formulas or simple answers exist to cover all questions of how distributions should be made. However, the following issues should be considered:

- *Differentiation*. The democracy approach can work, but it involves higher risk and more pitfalls than a system that differentiates based on the value of contributions by team members. As a rule, different team members rarely contribute the same amount to the venture, and the reward system needs to recognize these differences.

LEVEL OF COMMITMENT MATTERS. WHAT'S THE STORY ABOUT BACON AND EGGS FOR BREAKFAST? THE CHICKEN CONTRIBUTED, BUT THE PIG WAS COMMITTED.

- *Performance.* Reward needs to be a function of performance (as opposed to effort) during the early life of the venture and not during only one part of this period. Many ventures have been torn apart when the relative contributions of the team members changed dramatically several years after start-up without a significant change in rewards. (Vesting goes a long way toward dealing with this issue.)
- *Flexibility.* Regardless of the contribution of any team member at any given time, the probability is high that this will change. The performance of a team member may be substantially more or less than anticipated. Further, a team member may have to be replaced and someone may have to be recruited and added to the existing team. Flexibility in the reward system, including such mechanisms as vesting and setting aside a portion of shares for future adjustments, can help to provide a sense of justice.

CONSIDERATIONS OF TIMING

Division of rewards, such as the split of shares between the members of the entrepreneurial team, will most likely be made early in the life of the venture. Rewards may be a way of attracting significant early contribution; however, it is performance over the life of the venture that needs to be rewarded.

For example, regarding equity, once the allocation of shares is decided, changes in the relative share positions of team members will be infrequent. New team members or external investors may dilute each member's position, but the relative positions will probably remain unchanged.

However, events may occur during the initial stages of a venture. First, a team member who has a substantial portion of shares may not perform and need to be replaced early on. A key team member may find a better opportunity and quit. In each of these instances, the team will then be faced with the question of what will happen to the shares held by the team member. In each case, shares were intended as a reward for performance by the team member during the first several years of the venture, but the team member will not perform over this time period.

Several mechanisms are available to a venture when the initial share split is so made to avoid the loss or freezing of equity. A venture can retain an option of returning shares to its treasury at the price at which it was purchased in certain cases, such as when a team member needs to be replaced. A **buyback agreement** also achieves this purpose.

To guard against the event that some portion of the shares have been earned and some portion will remain unearned, as when a team member quits or dies, the venture can place shares purchased by team members in **escrow** to be released over a two- or three-year period. Such a mechanism is called a share-vesting agreement, and such an agreement can foster longer-term commitment to the success of the venture, while also providing a method for a civilized no-fault corporate divorce if things do not work out. Such a share-vesting agreement is attached as a restriction on the share certificate. Typically, the vesting agreement establishes a period of years, often four or more. During this period, the founding shareholders can "earn out" their shares. If a founder decides to leave the company before completion of the vesting period, he or she may be required to sell the shares back to the company for the price originally paid for them, usually nothing. The departing shareholder, in this instance, would not own any shares after the departure. Nor would the departing founder realize any capital gain windfall. In other cases, founders may vest a certain portion each year, so they have some shares even if they leave. Such vesting can be weighted toward the last year or two of the vesting period. Other restrictions can give the executive team and the board control over the disposition of shares, whether the shareholder stays or leaves the company. In essence, a mechanism such as a share-vesting agreement confronts team members with the reality that "this is not a get-rich-quick exercise."

Other rewards, such as salary, share options, bonuses, and fringe benefits, can be manipulated more readily to reflect changes in performance. But the ability to manipulate these is also somewhat dependent upon the stage of development of the venture. In the case of cash rewards, there is a trade-off between giving cash and the growth of the venture. Thus, in the early months of a venture, salaries will necessarily be low or nonexistent, and bonuses and other fringe benefits usually will be out of the question. Salaries, bonuses, and fringe benefits all drain cash, and until profitability is achieved, cash can always be put to use for operations. Salaries can become competitive once the venture has passed breakeven, but bonuses and fringe benefits should probably be kept at a minimum until several years of profitability have been demonstrated and growth objectives realized.

Mahshad Koohgoli advocates strict adherence to checkpoints. On the subject of timing with regard to his young venture Protecode, he revealed "We are keeping our focus. I've got 18 people in here right now. Eighteen payrolls; 18 families. I have no right to mislead them. I have no right to mislead myself. I hate to waste my time in life. Doing things quickly is very good. Something I've heard is 'you want to fail fast if you have to fail'—you don't want to drag it on for years." Koohgoli sees a statute of limitations, "If two years have gone by and nothing's happened, there's something wrong."[26] Finally, Eugene Kleiner, pioneer of venture capitalism asserts, "There is a time when panic is the appropriate response."

CONSIDERATIONS OF VALUE

The contributions of team members will vary in nature, extent, and timing. In developing the reward system, particularly the distribution of shares, contributions in certain areas are of particular value to a venture, as follows:

- *Idea.* In this area, the originator of the idea, particularly if trade secrets or special technology for a prototype was developed or if product or market research was done, needs to be considered.

- *Business plan preparation.* Preparing an acceptable business plan, in terms of dollars and hours expended, needs to be considered.

buyback agreement: Sale of a security with the provision that the seller can repurchase the security at a later date.

escrow: Money held in trust by a third party on behalf of the transacting parties until stipulated conditions are met.

- *Commitment and risk.* A team member may invest a large percentage of his or her net worth in the company, be at risk if the company fails, have to make personal sacrifices, put in long hours and major effort, risk his or her reputation, accept reduced salary, or already have spent a large amount of time on behalf of the venture. This commitment and risk needs to be considered.

- *Skills, experience, track record, or contacts.* A team member may bring to the venture skills, experience, track record, or contacts in such areas as marketing, finance, and technology. If these are of critical importance to the new venture and are not readily available, these need to be considered.

- *Responsibility.* The importance of a team member's role to the success of the venture needs to be considered.

Being the originator of the idea or expending a great amount of time or money in preparing the business plan is frequently overvalued. If these factors are evaluated in terms of the real success of the venture down the road, it is difficult to justify much more than 15 to 20 percent of equity for them. Commitment and risk, skills, experience, and responsibility contribute more by far to the success of a venture.

Anthony Woods and a classmate from Queen's University started TravelHangar, hoping to become an Internet-based travel agency for students. They immediately made an acquaintance a partner in the venture with 30 percent of the equity in return for information and a contact that could have been secured with a telephone call of their own. This blunder cost them both headaches and a good portion of their first year's revenue.

The list above is valuable when attempting to weigh the relative contributions of each team member. Contributions in each of these areas have some value; it is up to a team to agree on how to assign value to contributions and, further, to leave enough flexibility to allow for changes.

INTERNET IMPACT: TEAM

ATTRACTING TALENT

The Internet has changed the economics and capabilities of the job market. The ease and low cost of posting detailed employment openings, the extremely large databases of job seekers, and the speed of candidate response have many hiring managers and entrepreneurs devoting more time than ever before to recruiting online.

Since employers can delimit résumé searches to specified skill sets, years of experience, and salary requirements with a few keystrokes, a single Internet site such as Monster.com can serve as a targeted recruiting engine that is equal to a dozen or more recruiters. Jeff Taylor, Monster.com's founder and CEO, commented, "Post an opening for somebody fluent in Japanese and English, and you're as apt to hear from applicants in Tokyo and Dublin as from those in Los Angeles. We get 11 million visitors a month, and in many cases, small businesses get as many as 400 responses from one posting."

Websites representing professional associations such as Women in Technology International also have large databases of qualified individuals. These sites will often post job openings for a nominal fee.

LEARNING OBJECTIVES SUMMARY

LO1 A strong team is usually the difference between a success and a marginal or failed venture, and between a so-so and a great company.

LO2 Core philosophies, values, and attitudes, particularly sharing the wealth and ownership with those who create it, are key to team building.

LO3 The fit concept is central to anticipating gaps and building the team.[27] Numerous pitfalls await the entrepreneur in team building and need to be avoided. The lead entrepreneur and the entire team need to remain vigilant in their honest assessment of immediate and potential pitfalls.

LO4 Compensating and rewarding team members requires both a philosophy and technical know-how, and can have enormous impact on the odds of success.

LO5 Complete the Exercise "Rewards" found below.

STUDY QUESTIONS

1. Why is the team so important in the entrepreneurial process? How far can you get alone?
2. Describe what is meant by "team" philosophy and attitudes. Why are these important? How is this different from the quip "teamwork is everyone doing what I say."
3. What are the most critical questions an entrepreneur needs to consider in thinking through the team issues? What are some common pitfalls in team building? Can they be avoided or prepared for?
4. What are the critical rewards, compensation, and incentive issues in putting a team together? Why are these so crucial and difficult to manage?
5. How does the lead entrepreneur allocate share ownership and options in the new venture? Who should get what ownership and why?

MIND STRETCHERS   *Have you considered?*

1. Think about a team in which you have been a member or a captain. What leadership and coaching principles characterized the most and least successful teams?
2. What is a team? What is its antithesis? Who is part of the team? Are suppliers and buyers included? What about competitors?
3. Even sole proprietors do not work alone. How do you see the fit between you and the team concept?
4. One expert insists that the only guarantee he can make to a start-up team is that in five years, at least one or two members will leave or be terminated. What causes this? Why will your team be different?
5. Ask five people who have worked with you in a team to give you feedback about your team-building skills.

The following exercise can help an entrepreneur devise a reward system for a new venture. In proceeding with the exercise, it is helpful to look at these issues from an investor's point of view and to imagine that the venture is in the process of seeking capital from an investor group to which a presentation was made several weeks ago and which is favourably impressed by the team and its plan for the new venture. Imagine then that this investor group would like a brief presentation (of 10 to 15 minutes) about how the team plans to reward its members and other key contributors.

Name: _____

Venture: _____

Date: _____

Part I

Part I is to be completed by each individual team member—*alone.*

Step 1   Indicate who will do what during the first year or two of your venture, what contributions each has made or will make to creating a business plan, the commitment and risk involved for each, and what unique critical skills, experience, contacts, and so forth, each brings to the venture. Try to be as specific as possible, and be sure to include yourself.

TEAM MEMBER	RESPONSIBILITY	TITLE	CONTRIBUTION TO BUSINESS PLAN	COMMITMENT AND RISK	UNIQUE/CRITICAL SKILLS, ETC.

Step 2   Indicate below the approximate salary and number of shares (and as a percent) each member should have upon closing the financing of your new venture.

TEAM MEMBER	SALARY	NUMBER OF SHARES (AND %)

Step 3   Indicate below what fringe benefits you believe the company should provide during the first year or two.

TEAM MEMBER	VACATION	HOLIDAYS	HEALTH/LIFE INSURANCE	RETIREMENT PLAN	OTHER

Step 4   List other key contributors, such as members of the board of directors, and indicate how they will be rewarded.

NAME	EXPERTISE/ CONTRIBUTION	SALARY	NUMBER OF SHARES (AND %)	OTHER

Part II

Part II involves meeting as a team to reach consensus on the responsibilities of each team member and how each will be rewarded. In addition to devising a reward system for the team and other key contributors, the team will examine how consensus was reached.

Step 1   Meet as a team and reach consensus on the following team issues and indicate the consensus solution below.

RESPONSIBILITIES/CONTRIBUTIONS				
TEAM MEMBER	**RESPONSIBILITY**	**CONTRIBUTION TO BUSINESS PLAN**	**COMMITMENT AND RISK**	**UNIQUE/CRITICAL SKILLS, ETC.**

REWARDS		
TEAM MEMBER	**SALARY**	**NUMBER OF SHARES (AND %)**

		REWARDS (CONTINUED)				
TEAM MEMBER	TITLE	VACATION	HOLIDAYS	HEALTH/LIFE INSURANCE	RETIREMENT PLAN	OTHER

Step 2   Meet as a team and reach consensus on issues involving other key contributors and indicate the consensus solution below.

NAME	EXPERTISE/ CONTRIBUTION	SALARY	NUMBER OF SHARES (AND %)	OTHER

Step 3   Discuss as a team the following issues and indicate any important lessons and implications:

- What patterns emerged in the approaches taken by each team? What are the differences and similarities?

- How difficult or easy was it to reach agreement among team members? Did any issues bog down?

- If salaries or shares were equal for all team members, why was this so? What risks or problems might such an approach create?

- What criteria, either implicit or explicit, were used to arrive at a decision concerning salaries and shares? Why?

Preparation Questions:

1. How can Canica shore up or improve market position? Should Canica respond by trumping its own product? Will this build or dilute brand recognition?

2. Canica's corporate objective is to license the intellectual property (IP) upon reaching $10 million in annual scalpel sales. Is there evidence to suggest this corporate objective is in jeopardy?

3. Suppose your recommendation is approved and executed, but within 18 months revised forecasts for scalpel sales indicate BD is regaining lost ground at Canica's expense. Combined annual scalpel sales have now reached $4 million. Acting as Executive Vice President, outline your response / recommendation to the board.

CANICA DESIGN INC.

The Good and the Bad News

While reviewing the minutes from yesterday's board of directors meeting, Alden Rattew, Executive Vice President of Canica Design Inc., assessed the realities of the fledgling company's situation.

Scanning quickly through the record of items discussed at yesterday's meeting, it was clear that the board was excited when the president announced another milestone in the company's brief history. Canica's flagship product, an improved surgical scalpel and the first notable advancement since the original 1915 patent, had just reached revenues of US$1 million dollars for the fiscal year.

The first-generation scalpel, the Canica Standard, had been a solid performer since hitting the market in 2000 (see Figure 1). Alden recalled remarking to the board that when the second-generation scalpel, the Canica Safety Scalpel, was released in 2005, "the company really opened up internationally; Canica Design established a strong distribution network—particularly in the U.S." Now selling in seven markets including Canada, the United States, Japan, and select countries in the European Union, it was understandable that the mere mention of the product generated excitement among the board's investors.

However, that mood quickly turned sour when the president followed up with the downside of the agenda. The largest market player had recently introduced a product positioned to directly compete with Canica's flagship product. The recent release of the competition's "Protected Blade System" was a serious challenge to Canica's operations, its bottom line, and perhaps even its future.

Canica had fought hard to get this far and sensing the seriousness of the threat the board "requested" an assessment and strategic recommendations to be presented at the next meeting—four weeks away.

CANICA'S ROOTS

Canica Design's inception was in 1998, born out of Lee Valley Tools in Ottawa, Ontario. Leonard Lee was at the helm of Lee Valley Tools, a successful company producing high-quality cabinet hardware and supplies for woodworking and gardening. As founder and owner Mr. Lee thought he had seen it all.

Product Description

The Canica Standard Scalpel liberates the full level of surgical skill in an ergonomic ejectable blade scalpel handle.

Product Benefits

- New level of surgical control and operating room safety.
- Push-button blade ejection for minimal disposal risk.
- Ergonomically-shaped for enhanced surgical dexterity.
- Comes to hand like a fine writing instrument.

At the same time, Dr. Michael Bell, a highly regarded Canadian plastic reconstructive surgeon, was operating his own Ottawa-based clinic where he used a number of Lee Valley products. That year Dr. Bell contacted Lee Valley Tools to suggest corrosion prevention modifications to a wood carving knife he had been using. Unknown to Mr. Lee, the doctor had been using that wood carving knife in surgery and the corrosion was the result of repeated autoclaving.[1]

Sensing a new challenge, Mr. Lee assembled a small team from his tool design program to meet Dr. Bell and further discuss his ideas. Dr. Bell insisted the improvised Lee Valley instruments were better than existing industry products. After a frank discussion Dr. Bell made a strong case for the team to design a new surgical scalpel, "there just weren't any good ones on the market."

Later on that year, Lee Valley's industrial designer, Tim Maxwell, completed the scalpel design (the Canica Stan-

This case was written by Andrew Lunnie, Canadian International Development Agency, Gatineau, Québec and Prescott C. Ensign.

[1] A device to expose items to steam at a high pressure in order to decontaminate them and render them sterile.

dard) and shortly thereafter a new company, Canica Design Inc., was born. Canica became a designer and developer of medical/surgical tools and supplies for the healthcare industry, but was foremost a company of innovation. The company's website (http://www.canica.com/index.asp) described more succinctly:

> Canica Design is a medical/surgical instrument company based in Almonte, Ontario, Canada. The company has developed an exceptional proficiency in designing high-quality medical devices for clinicians. Canica's approach to medical device development is to work directly with doctors, translating their needs directly to new products through a vigorous research and development program.

Alden commented, "A notable corporate character trait is the loyalty Canica management has to our core business model." Anchored in product design and development, management was particularly cautious of the risks and costs of adopting new competencies—especially manufacturing. Alden remarked, "This strategy is not without its own risks. Taking a good idea through the iterative process to sale in the marketplace can be a long, intensive ordeal—often as many as 100 iterations of a single product before its release," while gesturing upstairs to the workstations where Tim Maxwell and the others toiled away in front of computer monitors manipulating three dimensional drawings.

Alden continued, "Eventually, the market tests the capability of the product. If the product is a success and can cultivate stable sales of US$10 million per year, then the intellectual property would qualify to be licensed to the industry blue chips." There may be some variability in the value, but one "blue chip"—Johnson & Johnson—had made these terms clear. Alden pointed, "This old rejection letter from J&J hangs in the company kitchen as a reminder that any Canica product has to grow and thrive in order to get noticed, but once a market had been developed the big players are interested—they'll coming knocking once we make a splash."

CANICA'S VALUE PROPOSITION

From concept to design, from design to prototype, and then to final product; as research and development costs mounted so too did the pressures to seek higher profit margins and greater cost savings, but Alden wondered what were the true costs?

The burden of adopting new roles and applying production techniques were perceived as a risk to the credo of the organization—to innovate. There had been the pressure to develop larger scale production in house—beyond mere prototypes. The reason for expanding operations were often debated and had validity in the traditional sense of the market, but bigger was not always better. Among the pressures that sparked debate were the need for product design feedback from manufacturing, need for oversight to ensure production quality, economies of scale opportunities, shorter return on investment timelines, and most important of all, protecting intellectual property.

With only 15 employees, Canica pushed against these pressures by relying on the existing teams to share the challenges and burden of prototype/demo and small quantity production—large-scale production was outsourced. As well, the design team and management had developed an acute expertise in manufacturing and final packaging. From source materials specifications (metals, composites, etc.), inspection scheduling/statistical sampling, and record keeping, quality control was actively monitored by Canica design staff despite the location of their production facility of choice.

For the scalpel, this transition to outsourced manufacturing was eased with the need for sterile products. National and international regulatory bodies in Canada, the United States, and the European Union required scalpels to be manufactured in a sterile environment. Canica management decided it was not cost effective to make such a large-scale investment to develop a sterile, in-house production environment; and thus remained true to their original business model.

"OPPORTUNITY MEETS THE PREPARED"

Work on improving scalpel design began in 1998 with the first-generation product (the Standard Scalpel), before Canica's incorporation; but the real boost in market potential for the product was realized in 2001 with a new law in the United States, the Needlestick Safety and Prevention Act. With the push of a button on the top of the scalpel (similar to a ball point pen that retracted) the blade could be ejected safely (without being touched) into the trash for proper disposal later. Previously removing a scalpel bade would have required additional handling—carefully holding the scalpel blade between thumb and index finger.

This new law authorized the Occupational Safety and Health Administration (OSHA) of the US Labor Department to revise the 1991 Bloodborne Pathogens Standard to require the use of safety-engineered sharp devices. OSHA published the revised standard on January 18, 2001, and it took effect on April 18, 2001.[2] The OSHA revision to the Bloodborne Pathogens Standard prompted Canica to evaluate and introduce safety-engineered sharp devices and needleless systems in order to reduce employees' occupational exposure to HIV, Hepatitis C, and other blood borne diseases.

While the new law did not recommend specific products to be procured for compliance, it did require workplaces to conduct their own evaluations of available safety devices on the market. Healthcare facilities evaluated and chose appropriate safety devices and often with the input of the workers, or in the case of the scalpel, consultation with medical professionals.

With development of the second-generation scalpel already in progress, Canica was well positioned to capitalize on the revision to the law and welcomed it. Canica moved quickly to establish sales distribution in the United States, the world's largest market. More than 1200 hospitals and surgical centres in the United States were stocking up on Canica's successful invention and Canica was quickly becoming one of the significant suppliers of scalpels in the United States.

THE PRODUCT: CANICA SAFETY SCALPEL™

Developed by Canica's industrial designer, Tim Maxwell, the Canica Standard Scalpel began with input from Dr. Michael Bell, a Canadian plastic surgeon. According to Dr. Bell, "while many complicated new devices have been created for medicine by modern technology, simpler instruments such as sutures, scalpels, and clamps haven't changed much in the last 100 years."

According to Leonard Lee, the Canica Standard Scalpel "is the first major change in the scalpel since 1915."[3] Despite the deceptively simple design, the scalpel was the result of dozens of iterations and heavy R&D investment. Detailed considerations were given to product design including source materials for the metal composite, functionality for the user, safety during handling from user to assistant, autoclaving/cleaning procedures, and compatibility with surgical blades, etc.

With the Canica Safety Scalpel, "The beauty of the blade is that it comes out easily and it retracts," said Dr. Bell, "you can hand someone something that is not dangerous."

The Canica Safety Scalpel was similar in the length, weight, and feel of a traditional scalpel handle to provide surgeons the familiarity and comfort they experienced when using familiar handles. It was ambidextrous in design for use by both right- and left-handed surgeons, was available in various length/weight combinations, came with a two-year warranty, and it even had a ruler etched along the length of it.

The Canica Safety Scalpel handle met OSHA[4] requirements and had integrated features that allowed both the touchless retraction and ejection of scalpel blades to reduce the risk of surgical blade injury and for safe passing. The reusable handle could also be disassembled for simplified cleaning and sterilizing. In addition, the handle accepted most conventional carbon and stainless steel blades. Finally, the two-piece reusable safety handle was suitable for sterilization using standard hospital protocols (see Figure 2).

Product Features

- Safe exchange between surgical team members during procedures. Allows retraction of the scalpel blade inside the handle before passing to reduce the risk of "sharps" injuries.
- Retractable scalpel handle specifically designed to significantly reduce the risk of "sharps" injuries occurring during blade removal.
- Slider activation allows touchless disposal of used blades.
- Is the only reusable handle that accepts most conventional carbon and stainless steel blades for easy conversion and maximum savings.
- Ambidextrous design for both right and left-handed surgeons.
- High-quality stainless steel and anodized aluminum construction feels like a traditional scalpel handle
- Easily sterilized using standard protocols; can be autoclaved.
- Laser-etched scale on back for quick measurements.
- Latex safe.
- Two-year warranty.

Product acceptance in the marketplace was a long process and profits were not quickly realized no matter how good the product was. This was a tough lesson to learn for Canica management, its design team, and its investors. Time to market was known to be a drawn out and arduous battle. The success that the Safety Scalpel afforded Canica was exceptional in the medical industry.

[2] http://www.osha.gov/SLTC/bloodbornepathogens/index.html

[3] Sean McKibbon, "Firm eyes EU operation: Regulators OK hi-tech medical gear." *Ottawa Sun.* July 5, 2002.

[4] The second-generation Canica product was launched in 2005, in response to BD's launch of a safe passing scalpel system which had raised the bar on what could be considered a "safety scalpel." Alden noted, "It was also developed in response to requests from our distributor to develop a product that would comply with OSHA's definition of a safety scalpel, since our Standard Scalpel did not."

THE COMPETITION

The challenge was significant. Headquartered in the United States and with offices in nearly 50 countries worldwide, Becton, Dickinson and Company (www.bd.com) was a medical technology company serving healthcare institutions, clinical laboratories, industry, and the general public. BD manufactured and sold a broad range of medical supplies, devices, laboratory equipment, and diagnostic products.

BD was the self-proclaimed world's largest manufacturer/supplier of metal blades of any kind and the holder of the original 1915 scalpel patent. Perhaps sensing pressure externally from OSHA, or responding to fluctuations in their scalpel sales, or possibly even taking a proactive stance on innovation, BD created a proprietary scalpel handle and custom fitting blades to match. Their scalpel design was also compliant with OSHA's revised Bloodborne Pathogens Standard and was positioned to compete directly with Canica's Safety Scalpel.

Upon the scrutiny of Canica's design team, BD's "Protected Blade System" was not as simple in design or as pragmatic as the Canica Safety Scalpel, and had fewer unique selling features:

- A clear, protective shield that locked before and after use.
- One handed activation.
- An audible button click and tactile sensation that confirmed the lock was in place.
- Allowed clinicians to retract the protective shield, easily and safely with one hand.

Alden remarked, "Although in Canica's estimation the BD offering has far less functionality and benefits to the user, a well-established and resourced industry giant backed the product. Meeting OSHA standards was the minimum criteria to compete; BD's name goes a long way in the eyes of customers worldwide—its client base is simply massive."

BD had been around since the beginning. For the past 100 years this industry patriarch had developed a mature global

FIGURE 4   CANICA DESIGN INC.'S ORGANIZATIONAL CHART

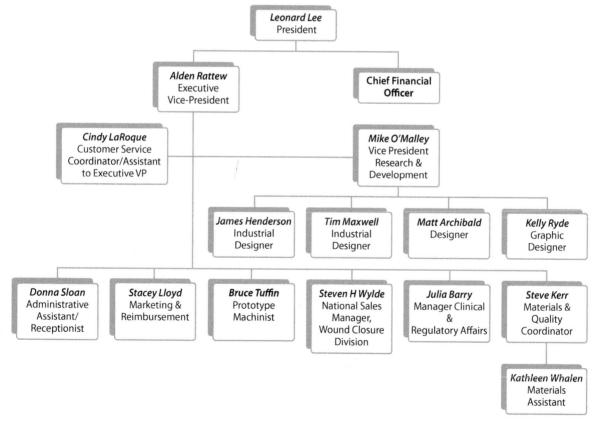

sales distribution network and impressive corporate financial resources to back their research and development programs. In addition, BD was widely considered a brand of quality and innovation, which would serve the product well in securing immediate sales.

The BD website contained some compelling, even alarming, evidence compiled by the International Health Care Worker Safety Center at the University of Virginia. With regard to operating rooms, the 2003 Exposure Prevention Information Network Data Reports "show that surgery attendants sustained the largest proportion of blade injuries (36 percent), followed by nurses (26 percent) and physicians (18 percent). In 76 percent of the cases, the injured worker was not the original user of the blade. The largest proportion of scalpel injuries (41 percent) occurred between steps of a multi-step procedure."

NEXT STEPS...

The Canica Safety Scalpel was the only offering in the company's product lineup that had extended beyond the break-even point. It was now generating a positive per unit return on investment and in the most recent fiscal year represented almost 60 percent of Canica Design's revenue; most of this revenue streamed from US sales. As a result, Canica was projecting to have its first profitable year since incorporation and revenues were expected to reach $5 million in the next three years. In June and July, several patents applied for almost three years earlier were finally issued.

Revenue growth and an improved cash flow allowed the spin-off to expand to 15 full-time staff (see Figure 4), maintain the interest of dozens of private investors, and stabilize Canica's research and development program permitting forays into other new and innovative products.

With forty-something products from three distinct product lines already on the market, and another cache of products at various stages of iteration, Canica was maturing and now beginning to reap the rewards for its heavy investment into R&D. Alden knew that Canica would soon be free of the "one trick pony" persona imposed by the success of the Safety Scalpel, but it must first address this market threat.

Now faced with the possibility of losing hard-fought ground to a vastly better resourced competitor, the Canica team needed to respond to this level of challenge with a corporate strategy to mitigate the immediate risk. Besides simply standing firm, the strategy should also be true to the corporate model; remaining nimble seemed an essential advantage.

Sitting behind an antique desk in Canica Design's office—a converted 130-year-old hardware storefront on the main street in Almonte, a community of about 4,500 residents 20 minutes west of Ottawa—Alden reflected on the nuances of the challenge his team faced. Alden surmised that managing the operations in an international, highly technical business environment should be like a ballet, but at this point it seemed more like a hockey game.

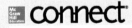

For more information on the resources available from McGraw-Hill Ryerson, go to www.mcgrawhill.ca/he/solutions.

ETHICAL DECISION MAKING AND THE ENTREPRENEUR

" *A creative man is motivated by the desire to achieve, not by the desire to beat others.* "

AYN RAND

LEARNING OBJECTIVES

LO1   Analyze the nature of business ethics and develop a context for thinking about ethical behaviour.

LO2   Defend the importance of high ethical standards in an entrepreneurial career.

LO3   Evaluate the role of social entrepreneurship in today's world and consider the value proposition of social enterprises.

LO4   Discuss with others the ethical implications of the decisions you make and identify how they might affect you, your partners, your customers, and your competitors.

OVERVIEW OF ETHICS

Most successful entrepreneurs believe that high ethical standards and integrity are exceptionally important to long-term success. For example, a study of 128 presidents/founders attending the Harvard Business School's Owner/President Management program were asked to name the most critical concepts, skills, and know-how for success at their companies at the time and what they would be in five years. Seventy-two percent stated that high ethical standards were the single most important factor in long-term success. A study of 1700 MBA students from the United States, Canada, and the United Kingdom by the Aspen Institute found that MBA students are concerned that their schools are not doing enough to prepare them for ethical dilemmas they may face in the business world.[1] Their concern and awareness is not surprising given the recent spate of corporate scandals. Ethical lapses like those of executives at Ravelston Corporation and Hollinger International, for example, erode the confidence in business activity at all levels. It should also be noted that business students have a marked propensity to cheat. In a study of 5331 students in the United States and Canada, 56 percent of MBA students indicated that they had cheated in the past year.[2] It has been reported that 73 percent of university students admitted to "serious cheating incidents" on written work while in high school.[3] "A recent University of Guelph study has discovered that more than half the student body in Canada is cheating its way through school."[4] And research has shown that those who "engage in dishonest behaviour in their college classes were more likely to engage in dishonest behaviour on the job."[5] The Internet has made both plagiarism and catching offenders easier. Technology has aided those aspiring to break the rules; text messaging during exams and camera phones copying an exam are common tactics. Ryerson University had to deal with a situation where students were working on solutions via Facebook.[6] Some contend that blame should be placed on the instructors and academic administrators who enable or do not properly handle dishonesty.

An article appearing in the *Journal of Business Ethics* finds that with regard to moral principles in business, "the argument is about values: are they universal or emergent? In entrepreneurship, it is about opportunities—are they discovered or constructed?" The authors of the article conclude that ethics and entrepreneurship are quite similar; both require a decision maker who has prepared for the unexpected.[7] Entrepreneurship carries ethical challenges beyond those that may confront a manager in an established organization. While entrepreneurs may be praised as innovators who contribute to society by developing new products, generating employment opportunities, and opening further possibilities, entrepreneurs are often only bound by the dynamic value creation process. In contrast, the manager in an established corporation has guidance from colleagues, rules/regulations, and company culture to direct him or her through ethical obstacles.[8] The assertion follows that the tenacity to succeed may push the entrepreneur to bend his or her own personal values.[9]

In the search for profits, quite often moral dilemmas enter the mix. Unethical behaviour is found among a range of stakeholders in the business world.[10] Financial pressures, short-term tactics, and heightened competition push entrepreneurs to do the "wrong things," just as they do others—including health care providers and educators. Richard Hudson of Mount Allison University and Roger Wehrell of Saint Francis Xavier University found that those pursuing a socially responsible cause often experience inferior profit margins; those putting profits first may be forced to push other considerations aside.[11] However, it becomes easier to have a "voice" where a fledgling enterprise is concerned; how much harm can you do by protesting Air Canada's corporate activity by boycotting their services or selling your few shares?

A provocative article in the *Harvard Business Review* asserted that the ethics of business were not those of society but rather those of the poker game.[12] The author of the article argued, "Most businessmen are not indifferent to ethics in their private lives, everyone will agree. My point is that in their office lives they cease to be private citizens; they become game players who must be guided by a somewhat different set of ethical standards." The author further argued that personal ethics and business ethics are often not in harmony, and by negotiation or compromise, a resolution must be reached. The article provoked a storm of response. The question remains, how are businesspeople supposed to operate in this capitalist system?

One individual has shown that hard work, determination, and high ethical standards are the proper response. Prem Watsa grew up in Hyderabad, India, and after earning a chemical engineering degree at the Indian Institute of Technology moved to Canada to study, working at night to support himself. Watsa founded Fairfax Financial Holdings, which posted over US$1.5 billion in profits for 2008. Some have labelled Prem Watsa the "Canadian Warren Buffet" and the *Globe and Mail* awarded him 2008's CEO of the Year, noting his company's success in the face of economic downturn. In challenging times, Watsa points out "a good university education is more important than ever." He has recently become Chancellor of the University of Waterloo and aims to "foster a new generation of entrepreneurs." His words of wisdom: "Stay positive and look at adversity as opportunity. Integrity, a solid work ethic, and the right attitude are essential tools for tomorrow's business leaders."[13]

In addition, the law, which one might expect to be black and white, is full of thorny issues. Laws not only have authority but also limitations. Laws are made with forethought and with the deliberate purpose of ensuring justice. They are, therefore, ethical in intent and deserve respect. However, laws are made in legislatures, not in heaven. They do not anticipate new conditions; they do not always have the effect they were intended to have; they sometimes conflict with one another; and they are, as they stand, incapable of making judgments where multiple ethical considerations hang in the balance or seem actually to war with one another. Thus, from the beginnings of recorded history, a code of laws was always accompanied by a human interpreter of laws, a judge, to decide when breaking the letter of the law did not violate the spirit or situation that the law was intended to cover.

©Prescott C. Ensign

DONALD TRUMP AND OTHERS HAVE PUT THEIR NAMES ATOP TALL BUILDINGS—EGO OR ADVERTISING?

ETHICAL STEREOTYPES

Canada, now as in the past, is seen as providing an inviting and nurturing climate for those wishing to start their own enterprises and reap the rewards. In part, this is because the federal and provincial governments have encouraged an atmosphere under which market forces, private initiative, and individual responsibility and freedom can flourish. But as has been pointed out, an entrepreneur need not be a decent and law-abiding individual; a criminal can be regarded as enterprising.[14] Just as surely as there is illegal business activity, there is immoral entrepreneurship. A study published by the Canadian Council for Small Business and Entrepreneurship in 2009 compared the legitimate entrepreneur with the illegitimate entrepreneur. Whether an entrepreneur adds value to society or extracts value from society, he or she will utilize similar enterprising skills and managerial capabilities.[15]

Laws, enacted in response to society's changing perceptions of what constitutes ethical business practices, have had the desirable effect of encouraging those in many industries to develop codes of ethics—in large part because they wished to set their own rules, rather than to have rules imposed on them.

As the ethical climate of business has changed, so has the image of the entrepreneur. Most "rags to riches" stories personify the good stereotype. Entrepreneurs doing business in the unfettered economic climate of the nineteenth century—the era of the robber barons, where acts of industrial sabotage were common—represent the ruthless stereotype. The exploitation of immigrant labour to build the railroads leaves an unsavoury aftertaste for today's more ethically conscious entrepreneurs.

Yet, thoughtful historians of entrepreneurship will also recall that regardless of standards by which they are judged or of the motivations attributed to them, "great" entrepreneurs gave back to society with libraries, concert halls, and charitable foundations. Guraj Deshpande, Jaishree Deshpande, and Gerry Pond pooled their resources to build the Pond-Desphande Centre for Innovation and Entrepreneurship at the University of New Brunswick. Their $5-million gift is intended to promote economic and social venture creation. Seymour Schulich has provided funds and his name to six universities across Canada.

A touch of suspicion still tinges entrepreneurial activity, and the word *entrepreneur* may still connote to some a person who belongs to a ruthless, scheming group. In 1975, *Time* suggested that a businessman might make the best-qualified candidate for U.S. president but noted the "deep-rooted American suspicion of businessmen's motives."[16] "Anyone with previous business experience becomes immediately suspect. Certain segments think he can't make a decision in the public interest."[17] Critics are much more inclined to examine and dissect the ethical behaviour of the commercial sector, rather than that of the clergy or of academia. However, in many comparisons, the behaviour of business moguls would look quite pure.

In 1988 the prophecy of *Time* magazine was fulfilled when George Bush, an oil entrepreneur, was elected president of the United States, and later reinforced in 2000 when his son, George W. Bush, a Harvard MBA, became president. Canada has largely avoided having business leaders go into politics—a recent exception being Paul Martin. Many politicians have legal backgrounds. In Europe it is common for leaders from industry to go into politics or vice-versa, but Canada remains critical of conflicts of interest and mixed motives (witness investigations of Brian Mulroney and Jean Chrétien).

Jeremy Hall of the University of Calgary and Philip Rosson of Dalhousie University explored entrepreneurial opportunities and ethical dilemmas. Their study divides entrepreneurship into three types: productive, unproductive, and destructive (criminal).[18] They observe that technological turbulence in particular, which creates opportunities for the newcomer and challenges incumbents as well as established regulations, may generate ethical dilemmas. From photocopying to file sharing, technology can push the boundaries of the rules of the game. A key challenge is to be prepared for the inevitable confrontations an entrepreneur will encounter.

SHOULD ETHICS BE TAUGHT?

Just as recent years have ushered in a new era of worldwide entrepreneurship, the landscape of business ethics has redefined itself. According to Andrew Stark of the University of Toronto:

> Advocates of the new business ethics can be identified by their acceptance of two fundamental principles. While they agree with their colleagues that ethics and interest can conflict, they take that observation as the starting point, not the ending point, of an ethicist's analytical task....Second, the new perspective reflects an awareness and acceptance of the messy work of mixed motives.[19]

The challenge facing this new group of business ethicists is to bridge the gap between the moral philosophers and the managers. The business ethicists talk of "moderation, pragmatism, minimalism"[20] in their attempt to "converse with real managers in a language relevant to the world they inhabit and the problems they face."[21] With this focus on the practical side of decision making, courses on ethics can be useful to entrepreneurs and all managers.

ETHICS CAN AND SHOULD BE TAUGHT

Derek Bok, former president of Harvard University, argues that ethics can and should be taught by educational institutions and that this teaching is both necessary and of value:

> Precisely because its community is so diverse, set in a society so divided and confused over its values, a university that pays little attention to moral development may find that many of its students grow bewildered, convinced that ethical dilemmas are simply matters of personal opinion beyond external judgment or careful analysis.[22]

Brenda Zimmerman of York University points out that 20 years ago, doing charitable work was an extra, something on the side, but today's MBAs "want to see much greater integration between their causes and the way they make money."[23] Many are choosing a career path where the returns are not measured entirely by salary. Tal Dehtiar and Michael Brown founded MBAs Without Borders while at McMaster University with the idea that there has to be another use for all their great business knowledge.[24] The University of Toronto has NeXus—"a non-profit management consulting service established to help non-profit organizations and social enterprises build capacity, explore new revenue streams, and broaden their networks for financial and community support."[25] Ann Armstrong of the University of Toronto explains that with social entrepreneurship, "if you had to choose between the social and economic outcome, you'd pick the social."[26] It brings to altruistic ventures "the ruthless efficiency of traditional business—something typically missing from charities, nonprofits, and government aid agencies. "The ratio of social benefit to invested dollar is often not very good with those organizations," according to Dirk Matten of York University. Canadian Jeff Skoll, the first president of eBay, is a big supporter of social enterprises. His Skoll Foundation, which started with about US$1 billion, has backed numerous social enterprises. Skoll championed the creation of the eBay Foundation, which is a philanthropic program supporting children, education, volunteerism, economic and community revitalization, as well as the natural environment.

John Shad, a former chairman of the New York Stock Exchange, gave more than $20 million to the Harvard Business School to include ethics in the MBA curriculum. J. Gregory Dees, an ethics professor at Duke University, stresses that the "primary objective of such courses is to get people thinking about issues that are easy to avoid....What we want people to leave with is a commitment to raising these issues in other settings, other courses, and on the job, with [an acceptable] comfort level in doing so."[27]

In addition, we have recently seen the emergence of numerous courses on socially responsible behaviour, social innovation, and on the role of environmentally sustainable business practices. A study published in 2009 in *Business Ethics* showed that personal values of entrepreneurs translated positively into economic performance of their ventures. Socially responsible business practices toward employees, customers, and society benefited the bottom line.[28]

INTEGRITY AS GOVERNING ETHIC

Lynn Paine, a specialist in management ethics, distinguishes among avoiding legal sanctions, compliance, and the more robust standard of integrity.

> From the perspective of integrity, the task of ethics management is to define and give life to an organization's guiding values, to create an environment that supports ethically sound behavior, and to instill a sense of shared accountability among employees.[29]

Paine goes on to characterize the hallmarks of an effective integrity strategy and the strategies for ethics management (see Exhibit 7.1). Clearly, the call for ethical strategies and practices is being heard. That is good news for our society, our economy, and you!

Paine points out formal codes of conduct "often have little to do with a company's response to ethical questions."[30] More important are the company's leadership, culture, structure/design, and institutional context.

David Allwright's research shows that companies may have morals and ethics tied to one location and may even project those halfway around the world, but ultimately the local environment

---

EXHIBIT 7.1 **STRATEGIES FOR ETHICS MANAGEMENT**

CHARACTERISTICS OF COMPLIANCE STRATEGY		CHARACTERISTICS OF INTEGRITY STRATEGY	
Ethos	Conformity with externally imposed standards	Ethos	Self-governance according to chosen standards
Objective	Prevent criminal misconduct	Objective	Stable responsible conduct
Leadership	Lawyer driven	Leadership	Management driven with aid of lawyers, HR, others
Methods	Education, reduced discretion, auditing and controls, penalties	Methods	Education, leadership, accountability, organizational systems and decision processes, auditing and controls, penalties
Behavioural Assumptions	Autonomous beings guided by material self-interest	Behavioural Assumptions	Social beings guided by material self-interest, values, ideals, peers

IMPLEMENTATION OF COMPLIANCE STRATEGY		IMPLEMENTATION OF INTEGRITY STRATEGY	
Standards	Criminal and regulatory law	Standards	Company values and aspirations, social obligations, including law
Staffing	Lawyers	Staffing	Executives and managers with lawyers, others
Activities	Develop compliance standards, train, and communicate	Activities	Lead development of company values and standards; train and communicate; integrate into company systems; provide guidance and consultation; assess values performance; identify and resolve problems; oversee compliance activities
Education	Compliance standards and system	Education	Decision making and values; compliance standards and system

Source: Lynn Sharp Paine, "Managing for Organizational Integrity," *Harvard Business Review* 72, no. 2 (1994): 113. Copyright © by the Harvard Business School Publishing Corporation; all rights reserved.

will have bearing on attitudes and actions.[31] Allwright observed, "Executives become outraged that they may be accused of behaving unethically." David Allwright of Mount Allison University and Harrie Vredenburg of the University of Calgary assert that partnering may seem to be a suitable risk reduction strategy, but beware—a partner with different (lower) standards will inevitably lead to conflicts and resource threatening crises.[32]

ENTREPRENEURS' PERSPECTIVES

Most entrepreneurs also believe ethics should be taught. In the research project previously mentioned, entrepreneurs and chief executive officers attending a management program at the Harvard Business School were asked the question: Is there a role for ethics in business education for entrepreneurs? Of those responding, 72 percent said ethics can and should be taught as part of the curriculum. (Only 20 percent said it should not, and two respondents were not sure.)

The most prominently cited reason for including ethics was that ethical behaviour is at the core of long-term business success, because it provides the glue that binds enduring successful business and personal relationships together. In addition, the responses reflected a serious and thoughtful awareness of the fragile but vital role of ethics in entrepreneurial attainment and of the long-term consequences of ethical behaviour for a business. Typical comments were:

- If the free enterprise system is to survive, the business schools better start paying attention to teaching ethics. They should know that business is built on trust, which depends upon honesty and sincerity.

- If our society is going to move forward, it won't be based on how much money is accumulated in any one person or group. Our society will move forward when all people are treated fairly—that's my simple definition of ethics. I know of several managers, presidents, etc., who you would not want to get between them and their wallets or ambitions.

- In my experience the business world is by and large the most ethical and law-abiding part of our society.

- Ethics should be addressed, considered, and thoroughly examined; it should be an inherent part of each class and course....Instead of crusading with ethics, it is much more effective to make high ethics an inherent part of business—and it is.

However, these views were not universally held. One entrepreneur who helped to found a large company with international operations warned: "For God's sake, don't forget that 90 percent of the businessman's efforts consist of just plain hard work." Another argument holds that certain conditions make it is easier to be ethical, perhaps even a luxury. "If you've got a job and a pension, it's a lot easier to buy organic foods." Whereas, for the poor and unemployed—survival may be the primary driver; taking the higher ground and worrying about the planet may not be a primary concern.[33]

There is also some cynicism. The 40-year-old head of a real estate and construction firm with 300 employees and $75 million in annual sales said: "There is so much hypocrisy in today's world that even totally ethical behaviour is questioned since many people think it is some new negotiating technique."

It would be unfortunate if the entrepreneur did not realize his or her potential for combining action with ethical purpose because of the suspicion that the two are unrelated or inimical. "Business ethics" need not be an oxymoron; there is no reason they need be considered generically opposed. Nevertheless, in analyzing ethics, the individual can expect no substitute for his or her own effort and intelligence.

In 2012, Clayton Christensen and colleagues wrote the book *How Will You Measure Your Life?* to turn models and management theories toward ourselves and attain happiness. Christensen notes that "the marginal cost of doing something wrong 'just this once' always seems alluringly

ENTREPRENEURS ACROSS CANADA
Awake

Matt Schnarr, Dan Tzotsis, and Adam Deremo launched Awake—a caffeinated chocolate bar. The trio collectively gathered their 50 000 chunks of experience in consumer packaged goods by chiefly working at PepsiCo, ConAgra, Kraft Foods, etc.

SPOKES OWL NEVIL AND QUEENS UNIVERSITY COMMERCE STUDENTS DURING FROSH WEEK.

AWAKE Chocolate

While the concept seems original to most of us, there have been similar products. Snickers Charged was offered in 2008 and Butterfinger Buzz in 2009. Bang!! Ice Cream, Cracker Jack'D, NRG Potato Chips, Perky Jerky, Turbo Truffle, and Wrigley's Alert Energy Gum are some other offerings of caffeinated products.

It was reported that the Snickers and Butterfinger products both had a 90-minute aftertaste and the Wrigley's gum had a bitter, medicinal flavour. Mastering the taste of the added caffeine to chocolate is tricky and according to Matt Schnarr, developing brand character is too. Hopefully these are not too easily replicated. Matt reported in late 2013, "business was definitely progressing" and Awake had growth objectives for the U.S. market in 2014.

Question: Whether Awake is new or not, it is different. According to "the Dragons," it tastes pretty good too. Partnerships have played a key role in Awake's success thus far. Partnerships involve give and take. In trying to balance what is gained and what is lost, what ethical considerations might this—or any venture—face?

Sources: www.awakechocolate.com; Candyblog.net January 25, 2008; Hollie Shaw, "Caffeine fuels Awake Chocolate's success," *National Post* January 28, 2013; Mary Teresa Bitti, "Dragons eat up Awake chocolate's pitch," *National Post* February 11, 2013.

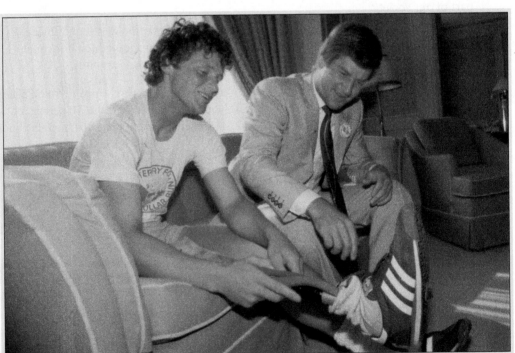

©David Cooper/Getstock.com

TERRY FOX AND BOBBY ORR, THE EPITOME OF INTEGRITY, COURAGE, AND HIGH STANDARDS. FEW CANADIANS ARE AS HERALDED AS THESE INDIVIDUALS.

low. You don't see the end result to which that path leads. The key is to define what you stand for and draw the line in a safe place." Christensen also points out that of the 32 Rhodes scholarship recipients (of which he is one), two went to jail.

THORNY ISSUES FOR ENTREPRENEURS   LO2

Although the majority of entrepreneurs take ethics seriously, researchers in this area are still responding to David McClelland's call for inquiry: "We do not know at the present time what makes an entrepreneur more or less ethical in his dealings, but obviously there are few problems of greater importance for future research."[34] Exhibit 7.2 outlines topics for consideration. Clearly, opportunities for further research exist.

ACTION UNDER PRESSURE

An entrepreneur will have to act on issues under pressure of time and when struggling for survival. In addition, the entrepreneur will most likely decide ethical questions that involve obligations on many sides—to customers, employees, shareholders, family, partners, himself, or a combination of these. Walking the tightrope and balancing common sense with an ethical framework is precarious.

To cope with the inevitable conflicts, an entrepreneur should develop an awareness of his or her own explicit and implicit ethical beliefs, those of his or her team and investors, and those of the milieu within which the company competes for survival. As noted above, in the long run,

EXHIBIT 7.2	SELECTED ETHICAL DILEMMAS OF ENTREPRENEURIAL MANAGEMENT
DILEMMA: ELEMENTS	**ISSUES THAT MAY ARISE**
Promoter: Entrepreneurial euphoria Impression management Pragmatic versus moral considerations	What does honesty mean when promoting an innovation? Does it require complete disclosure of the risks and uncertainties? Does it require a dispassionate analysis of the situation, with equal time given to the downside as well as the upside? What sorts of influence tactics cross the line from encouragement and inducement to manipulation and coercion?
Relationship: Conflicts of interest and roles Transactional ethics Guerrilla tactics	Tension between perceived obligations and moral expectations. Changes in roles and relationships: pre- versus post-venture status. Decisions based on affiliative concerns rather than on task-based concerns. Transition from a trust-based work environment to one that is more controlled.
Innovator: "Frankenstein's problem" New types of ethical problems Ethic of change	Side effects and negative externalities force a social reconsideration of norms and values. Heightened concern about the future impact of unknown harms. Who is responsible for the assessment of risk? Inventor? Government? Market? Breaking down traditions and creating new models.
Other dilemmas: Finders-keepers ethic Conflict between personal values and business goals Unsavoury business practices	Is there a fair way to divide profits when they are the result of co-operative efforts? Should the entrepreneur take all the gains that are not explicitly contracted away? Managing an intimate connection between personal choices and professional decisions. Coping with ethical pressures with creative solutions and integrity. Seeking industry recognition while not giving in to peer pressure to conform.

Source: J. Gregory Dees and Jennifer A. Starr, "Entrepreneurship Through an Ethical Lens," in *The State of the Art of Entrepreneurship*, Donald L. Sexton and John D. Kasarda, eds. (Boston, MA: PWS-Kent Publishing Company, 1992).

STUMBLES, TUMBLES, AND FALLS FROM GRACE

The following examples illustrate some of the ethical challenges experienced by Canadian companies in recent years.

NORTEL: QUICK SHAKE-UPS AT THE TOP

Jean Monty was CEO from 1993 to 1997; John Roth from 1997 to 2001, during which time he lobbied the authorities for lower taxes and threatened to move Nortel to the United States. In addition, market capitalization plummeted from $398 billion to $5 billion, 60 000 employees were laid off, and Roth cashed in $135 million in share options. Frank Dunn was CEO from 2001 to 2004, when he was fired with other financial executives; Dunn came under investigation by the U.S. Securities and Exchange Commission as well as the Ontario Securities Commission, and was arrested by the RCMP in mid-2008. U.S. Admiral William Owens took the helm from 2004 to 2005 to right the sinking ship, and then Mike Zafirovski took over and steered Nortel into bankruptcy in 2009 amid calls for a new captain! The shares were delisted from the TSX at 18.5 cents per share and Zafirovski resigned. At the end of 2009, Roth filed for a $1 billion indemnification from Nortel. Auctions for Nortel assets and legal filings occurred in 2011, some settlements were reached in 2013, and Ernst & Young was criticized for the way it handled Nortel's bankruptcy. Frank Dunn was "found not guilty of falsifying financial reports." A Canada–US cross-border trial was not ruled out by the Ontario Courts, so with further legal action on the horizon, the end was not in sight.

BRE-X: SMOKE AND MIRRORS, NO SUBSTANCE

Bre-X was a Canadian mining company that had a short, stratospheric economic rise on prospects of discovering gold. Its shares soared from just about nothing to $285 per share and it had a market capitalization of $6 billion. The discovery of gold was found to be a hoax and key players went into hiding. After a fleeting, tumultuous ride, investors were left holding worthless paper.

LIVENT: LIGHTS, CURTAIN, LEGAL ACTION

Garth Drabinsky and Myron Gottlieb wrestled their favourite division away from Cineplex Odeon, taking a business unit that included the Pantages Theatre in Toronto and *The Phantom of the Opera*. The company went public on the TSX and within a few years and under heavy financial losses, Drabinsky and Gottlieb were escorted by security guards out the door. Live Entertainment Corporation of Canada, Inc. (Livent) subsequently filed a $225-million lawsuit against the pair. Livent went bankrupt as the RCMP launched a criminal investigation and U.S. and Canadian securities regulators began investigating the company's books. Drabinsky and Gottlieb were indicted in a New York courtroom at which they failed to appear and therefore had fugitive arrest warrants entered against them. More recently, Canadian police charged four Livent senior executives with fraud totalling nearly half a billion dollars. In 2009 the Supreme Court of Canada denied Drabinsky and Gottlieb's appeal for their civil case. In their criminal case both were convicted on two counts of fraud and one count of uttering forged documents. Gottlieb was granted day parole after serving 11 months of his four-year sentence and Drabinsky granted day parole after serving about 14 months of his five-year sentence. In 2013, Drabinsky was fighting to not have his Order of Canada revoked.

Sources: "The Good, the Bad & the Ugly," *Canadian Business*, March 30, 2009; Barry Critchley, "Ernst & Young's multiple Nortel roles shrouded in mystery," *Financial Post*, March 13, 2013; Linda Nguyen, "Nortel case to go ahead with Canada-U.S. trial, Ontario court rules," *The Globe and Mail*, June 21, 2013; Wikipedia entry for "Bre-X," www.en.wikipedia.org/wiki/Bre-X; "Theatre Impresario Awaiting Sentencing on Fraud, Forgery," CBC News, May 14, 2009; Shannon Kari, "Months, Years before Livent Duo Face Any Prison Time," *Financial Post*, March 25, 2009; Barbara Shecter, "Livent Dazzled Audiences, Investors While Taking on Hollywood," *Financial Post*, May 3, 2009; "Myron Gottlieb of former Livent gets full parole," *The Toronto Star*, March 28, 2013.

succumbing to the temptations of situational ethics will, in all likelihood, result in a tumble into the quicksand, not a safety net—just ask executives or co-founders who are in prison or who have lost family, fortune, and reputation.

An appreciation of this state of affairs is succinctly stated by Fred Allen, chairman and president of Pitney-Bowes:

> We must learn to weigh short-term interests against long-term possibilities. We must learn to sacrifice what is immediate, what is expedient, if the moral price is too high. What we stand to gain is precious little compared to what we can ultimately lose.[35]

DIFFERENT VIEWS

Different reactions to what is ethical may explain why some aspects of venture creation go wrong for no apparent reason, both during start-up and in the heat of the battle. Innumerable examples can be cited to illustrate that broken partnerships often can be traced to apparent differences in the personal ethics among the members of a venture team. So, too, with investors. While the experienced venture capital investor seeks entrepreneurs with a reputation for integrity, honesty, and ethical behaviour, the definition is necessarily subjective and depends in part on the beliefs of the investor himself and in part on the prevailing ethical climate in the industry sector in which the venture is involved. In fact, the term *vulture capitalist* describes those who use an investment deal to seize ownership outright or control over valuable assets.

Business ethics has evolved and continues to change over time. Acceptable behaviour changes, sometimes quite quickly. In the present era of transparency, Mark Wexler of Simon Fraser University observes that as a firm grows in size, "you need a lot more internal vigilance and self-auditing," while a smaller enterprise can be run as an extension of the leader's personality.[36]

PROBLEMS OF LAW

For entrepreneurs, situations where one law directly conflicts with another are increasingly frequent. For example, a small-business investment company got in serious financial trouble. The federal authorities stated the company should begin to liquidate its investments, because it would otherwise be in defiance of its agreement with them. However, the securities regulatory authorities stated that this liquidation would constitute unfair treatment of shareholders, due to the resulting imbalance in their portfolios. After a year and a half of agonizing negotiation the company was able to satisfy all the parties, but compromises had to be made on all sides.

Legal demands involve labour practices that mandate particular treatment of Aboriginal peoples, members of visible minorities, women, and persons with disabilities. In addition, the Canadian government frequently campaigns to promote the hiring of immigrants. And, not all laws apply to all businesses; for example, the Employment Equity Act and Employment Equity Regulations cover 400 private sector employers and Crown corporations. These laws are based on valid ethical intent, but the administration and interpretation of them is no simple matter. Recently a number of individuals have been accused of fraudulently obtaining Aboriginal status solely to receive government contracts.

Further, there is no international code of business ethics. When doing business abroad, entrepreneurs may find that those with whom they wish to do business have little in common with them—no common language, no common historical context for conducting business, and no common set of ethical beliefs about right and wrong and everything in between. For example, in Canada, bribing a high official to obtain a favour is considered both ethically and legally unacceptable; in many parts of the world, it is the only way to get things done. What we see as a bribe, those in other parts of the world see as acceptable, even necessary.

"Do what the locals do" is one approach to this problem. Consulting a lawyer with expertise in international business before doing anything is another. Assuming that the object of an entrepreneur's international business venture is to make money, he or she needs to figure out some way that is legally tolerable under the laws that do apply and that is ethically tolerable personally.

EXAMPLES OF THE ENDS-AND-MEANS ISSUE

A central question in any ethical discussion concerns the extent to which a noble end may justify ignoble means—or whether using unethical means for assumed ethical ends may subvert the aim in some way. As an example of a noble end, consider the case of a university agricultural extension service in the United States whose goal was to aid small farmers to increase their crop productivity. The end was economically constructive and profit oriented only in the sense that the farmers might prosper from better crop yields. However, to continue to receive funding, the extension service was required to provide predictions of the annual increase in crop yield it could achieve, estimates it

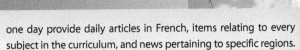
could not provide at the required level of specificity. Further, unless it could show substantial increases in crop yields, its funding could be heavily reduced. In this case, the extension service decided, if need be, to fudge the figures. It felt that even though the presentation of overly optimistic predictions was unethical, the objectives of those running the organization were highly ethical and even the unethical aspects could be condoned within the context of the inability of the various groups involved to speak each other's language clearly. The funding source finally backed down in its demand, ameliorating the immediate problem. But if it had not, the danger existed that the individuals in this organization, altruistic though their intentions were, would begin to think that falsification was the norm and would forget that actions that run contrary to one's ethical feelings gradually would build a debilitating cynicism.

A legendary Harvard Business School case recounts the story of how for many years executives at Heinz exaggerated numbers to meet unrealistic targets that ratcheted up every year. Sports have been plagued with scandals—players using performance enhancing drugs, fixed results, and games thrown by players, referees, fans, etc. Ryder Hesjedal won the Giro d'Italia in 2012 and many hoped that the sport of cycling would be cleaner. But cycling has not been clean for generations; cases of questionable activity date back to at least the 1880s. Since its inception the Tour de France has had rampant drug use; the rulebook distributed to riders in the 1930s reminded participants that drugs would not be provided by race organizers.

In another example, a merger of a small rental-service business with a mid-sized conglomerate forced the business's principals to realize that a law's intent was in direct opposition to what would occur if the law were enforced literally. In this instance, a partner in the rental firm became involved in a severe automobile accident and suffered multiple injuries shortly before the merger and was seemingly unable to return to work. The partner also knew that the outlook for his health in the immediate future was unpredictable. For the sake of his family, he was eager to seek some of the shares acquired in the merger and make a large portion of his assets liquid. However, federal law does not allow quick profit-taking from mergers and therefore did not allow such a sale. The partner consulted the president and officers of the larger company, and they acquiesced in his plans to sell portions of his shares and stated their conviction that no adverse effect on the shares would result. Still unsure, the man then checked with his lawyer and found that the federal law in question had almost never been prosecuted. Having ascertained the risk and having probed the rationale of the law as it applied to his case, the man then sold some of the shares acquired in the merger to provide security for his family in the possible event of his incapacitation or death. Although he subsequently recovered completely, this could not have been foreseen.

In this instance, the partner decided that a consideration of the intrinsic purpose of the law allowed him to act as he did. In addition, he made as thorough a check as possible of the risks involved in his action. He was not satisfied with the decision he made, but he believed it was the best he could do at the time. One can see in this example the enormous ethical tugs-of-war that go with the territory of entrepreneurship. In a similar example, was Apple's vague disclosure of Steve Jobs' health a violation of securities laws?

AN EXAMPLE OF INTEGRITY

The complicated nature of entrepreneurial decisions also is illustrated in the following example. At age 27, an entrepreneur joined a new computer software firm with sales of $1.5 million as vice president of international marketing of a new division. His principal goal was to establish profitable distribution for the company's products in the major industrialized nations. Share incentives and a highly leveraged bonus plan placed clear emphasis on profitability, rather than on volume. In one European country, the choice of distributors was narrowed to 1 from a field of more than 20. The potential distributor was a top firm, with an excellent track record and management, and the chemistry was right. In fact, the distributor was so eager to do business with the entrepreneur's company that it was willing to accept a 10-percent commission, rather than the normal 15-percent royalty. The other terms of the deal were acceptable to both parties. In this actual case, the young vice president decided to give the distributor the full 15-percent commission, even though it would have settled for less. This approach was apparently quite successful because, in five years, this international division grew from zero to $18 million in very profitable sales, and a large firm acquired the venture for $80 million. In describing his reasoning, the entrepreneur said his main goal was to create a sense of long-term integrity. He said further:

> I knew what it would take for them to succeed in gaining the kind of market penetration we were after. I also knew that the economics of their business definitely needed the larger margins from the 15 percent, rather than the smaller royalty. So I figured that if I offered them the full royalty, they would realize I was on their side, and that would create such goodwill that when we did have some serious problems down the road—and you always have them—then we would be able to work together to solve them. And that's exactly what happened. If I had exploited their eagerness to be our distributor, then it only would have come back to haunt me later on.

SOCIAL ENTERPRISES AND SOCIAL ENTERPRENEURSHIP

LO3

Social entrepreneurship has turned into a worldwide phenomenon effecting positive social change. Some view social entrepreneurship as applicable only for the nonprofit sector. Social entrepreneurship, in theory and in practice, does not have a unifying, agreed-upon definition. Jeff Stamp offered a thought-provoking perspective: "All ventures require investment; all ventures require return. The social question is who pays and what is the return horizon."

The *entrepreneurial process* (chapter 2) is all the "creation, enhancement, realization, and renewal of value." The result of social entrepreneurship is no different, but it helps clarify the concept of value. Specifically, social value is derived from entrepreneurial activities that seek to address problems related to people and the planet—regardless of profit orientation. In other words, social entrepreneurship seeks creative and valuable solutions to such issues as education, poverty, health care, global warming, water shortages, and energy.

A single unified definition of social entrepreneurship is not critical; what is most important is understanding the key differentiating factors between social and traditional entrepreneurship. Social purpose ventures are founded to solve a social problem through an economically viable entity.

We might argue that any nonprofit start-up is entrepreneurial. However, consistent with the focus of this book and research in entrepreneurship, the scaling and sustainability of new ventures are incredibly important to the economy (as with for-profit ventures) and to systemic change (as with nonprofit organizations). It is not enough, from both an economic and social perspective, to simply start a venture; it must be scalable and sustainable. With longevity, innovation, and an eye toward growth, significant impact can be made.

There are two types of enterprising nonprofits. The first type utilizes earned-income activities, a form of venturing, to generate all or a portion of total revenue. In many ways enterprising nonprofits apply the principles of entrepreneurship to generate revenue and sustain their mission-driven organizations. The second type has a focus on growth and economic sustainability. Such an enterprising nonprofit may incorporate outside investment, in the form of philanthropy, to scale the organization for increased social impact.

THE TIMMONS MODEL INTERPRETED FOR SOCIAL ENTREPRENEURSHIP

Chapter 3 introduced the Timmons Model of the entrepreneurial process. The three major components of the Timmons Model—opportunity, resources, and teamwork—certainly apply to social entrepreneurship; but the model requires a few contextual changes. Social opportunities are driven not only by markets but also by mission and social need. The brain trust aspect of the team—the external stakeholders—is especially important because collaboration across boundaries is paramount in social entrepreneurship. As with traditional start-ups, the art of bootstrapping is a necessary method of resource acquisition. Encouragingly, capital markets exist for social entrepreneurs, and available funds are increasing in both the for-profit and not-for-profit sectors. The concepts of fit and balance remain because sustainability and growth are the essence of *any* entrepreneurial endeavour.

Not like the traditional entrepreneurial ventures discussed throughout this text, resource acquisition is critical to the success of social ventures, enterprising nonprofits, and even hybrid forms. Most social entrepreneurs will admit that access to capital is a burgeoning challenge as more social ventures emerge, especially with high growth aspirations and visions of international scalability. Bootstrapping is prevalent among passionate social entrepreneurs, who are often quiet in their approach as they struggle to build sustainable business models.

Venture philanthropy provides value-added funding for nonprofit organizations to increase their potential for social impact. Though the origin of venture philanthropy has been attributed to John D. Rockefeller III in 1969 when he spoke before the U.S. Congress in support of tax reform, the modern version looks more like venture capital but with a social return on investment.

The brain trust in social entrepreneurship can include the community, investors, the government, customers, suppliers, and manufacturers. The list is endless in many respects and depends on the venture. Social ventures, while working toward a positive mission, must still deliver value for key stakeholders. What the value is and to whom will vary, but it is important that the social entrepreneur understand the interactions among brain trust stakeholders as well as the potential value derived from being associated with the venture.

The spirit of giving among entrepreneurs should be recognized and applauded; but is such giving sufficient? The story of a successful entrepreneur building a company, creating personal wealth, and *then* making significant charitable contributions is common. Social entrepreneurs, however, do not wait to give, but build businesses where economic value and societal contribution are two sides of the same coin. Social entrepreneurs use fundamental principles of entrepreneurship to promote positive change and permanent impact to help create and sustain our future.

ETHICS REDUX

The following statements are often made, even by practising entrepreneurs:

- How can we think about ethics when we haven't enough time even to think about running our venture?
- Entrepreneurs are doers, not thinkers—and ethics is too abstract a concept to have any bearing on business realities.
- When you're struggling to survive, you're not worried about the means you use—you're fighting for one thing: survival.

However, the contemplation of ethical behaviour is not unlike poetry—emotion recollected in tranquillity. This chapter is intended to provide one such tranquil opportunity.

By contemplating decisions made or not made an individual becomes more aware of his or her own value system and how making ethical decisions can be affected by the climate in which these decisions are made. However, in the online exercise for this chapter, participants are asked only to answer questions. They are not asked to carry out an action. Between intent and action lies a large gap, which can be filled only by confronting and working through a number of ambiguous situations. Visit Connect to try the exercise and test your ethical mettle.

LEARNING OBJECTIVES SUMMARY

LO1 The majority of CEOs, investors, and entrepreneurs believe that a high ethical standard is the most important factor in long-term success. Ethical dilemmas challenge entrepreneurs at the most crucial moments of survival.

LO2 Historically, ethical stereotypes of businesspeople ranged widely, and today the old perceptions have given way to a more aware and accepting notion of the messy work of ethical decisions. Entrepreneurs can rarely, if ever, finish a day without facing at least one or two ethical issues, and have found that behaving ethically is wiser in the long run.

LO3 Most business schools today have incorporated ethical issues into their curricula. Social ventures and nonprofit entrepreneurship are a growing phenomenon and have a marked impact on society.

LO4 Complete the Exercise "Ethics" found below.

STUDY QUESTIONS

1. Many professional exams (e.g., CA, CMA, CFA) test ethics. Can ethics be tested on paper? Actual behaviour is not being tested, so wouldn't an unethical person be able to get ethics questions correct just as likely as a truly ethical person?
2. What are the most thorny ethical dilemmas that entrepreneurs face, and why?
3. Describe an actual example of how and why taking a high ethical ground results in a good decision for business.
4. What are the differences among socially responsible ventures, social ventures, and enterprising nonprofits?
5. Why are corporate social responsibility (CSR) activities not considered to be part of the domain of social entrepreneurship?

MIND STRETCHERS   *Have you considered?*

1. How would you define your own ethics?
2. What was the toughest ethical decision you have faced? How did you handle it, and why? What did you learn?
3. How do you personally determine whether someone is ethical or not?
4. How would you describe the ethics of the prime minister of Canada? Would these ethics be acceptable to you from an investor, a partner, a spouse? Are the ethics of elected leaders different from those in the private sector, such as the CEO of a chartered bank or the CEO of a multinational oil company?

First Part

Make decisions in the following situations.

You will not have all the background information on each situation; instead, you should make whatever assumptions you feel you would make if you were actually confronted with the choices described. Select the choice that most closely represents the decision you would make personally. You should select choices even though you can envision other creative solutions that were not included in the exercise.

Situation 1

You are taking a very difficult statistics course, which you must pass to maintain your scholarship and to avoid damaging your application for graduate school. Statistics is not your strong suit, and because of a just-below-failing average in the course, you must receive a grade of 90 or better on the final exam, which is two days away. A janitor who is aware of your plight informs you that he found the statistics final in a blue box and saved it. He will make it available to you for a price, which is high but which you could afford. What would you do?

_____ (a) I would tell the janitor thanks, but no thanks.

_____ (b) I would report the janitor to the proper officials.

_____ (c) I would buy the exam and keep it to myself.

_____ (d) I would not buy the exam myself, but I would let some of my friends, who are also flunking the course, know that it is available.

Situation 2

You have been working on some complex analytical data for two days now. It seems that each time you think you have them completed, your boss shows up with a new assumption or another what-if question. If you only had a copy of a new software program for your personal computer, you could plug in the new assumptions and revise the estimates with ease. Then a colleague offers to let you make a copy of some software that is copyrighted. What would you do?

_____ (a) I would readily accept my friend's generous offer and make a copy of the software.

_____ (b) I would decline to copy it and plug away manually on the numbers.

_____ (c) I would decide to go buy a copy of the software myself for $300 and hope I would be reimbursed by the company in a month or two.

_____ (d) I would request another extension on an already overdue project date.

Situation 3

Your small company is in serious financial difficulty. A large order of your products is ready to be delivered to a key customer, when you discover that the product is simply not right. It will not meet all performance specifications, will cause problems for your customer, and will require rework in the field; but this, you know, will not become evident until after the customer has received and paid for the order. If you do not ship the order and receive the payment as expected, your business may be forced into bankruptcy. And if you delay the shipment or inform the customer of these problems, you may lose the order and also go bankrupt. What would you do?

_____ (a) I would not ship the order and place my firm in voluntary bankruptcy.

_____ (b) I would inform the customer and declare voluntary bankruptcy.

_____ (c) I would ship the order and inform the customer, after I received payment.

_____ (d) I would ship the order and not inform the customer.

Situation 4

You are the cofounder and president of a new venture, manufacturing products for the recreational market. Five months after launching the business, one of your suppliers informs you it can no longer supply you with a critical raw material since you are not a large-quantity user. Without the raw material the business cannot continue. What would you do?

_____ (a) I would grossly overstate my requirements to another supplier to make the supplier think I am a much larger potential customer to secure the raw material from that supplier, even though this would mean the supplier will no longer be able to supply another, non-competing small manufacturer who may thus be forced out of business.

_____ (b) I would steal raw material from another firm (non-competing) where I am aware of a sizeable stockpile.

_____ (c) I would pay off the supplier, since I have reason to believe that the supplier could be persuaded to meet my needs with a sizeable under-the-table payoff that my company could afford.

_____ (d) I would declare voluntary bankruptcy.

Situation 5

You are on a marketing trip for your new venture for the purpose of calling on the purchasing agent of a major prospective client. Your company offers a service that you hope the purchasing agent will buy. During the course of your conversation, you notice on the cluttered desk of the purchasing agent several copies of a cost proposal for a system from one of your direct competitors. This purchasing agent has previously reported mislaying several of your own company's proposals and has asked for additional copies. The purchasing agent leaves the room momentarily to get you a cup of coffee, leaving you alone with your competitor's proposals less than an arm's length away. What would you do?

_____ (a) I would do nothing but await the man's return.

_____ (b) I would sneak a quick peek at the proposal, looking for bottom-line numbers.

_____ (c) I would put the copy of the proposal in my briefcase.

_____ (d) I would wait until the man returns and ask his permission to see the copy.

Second Part

Step 1

Based on the criteria you used, place your answers to each of the above situations along the continuum of behaviour shown below. Duty: doing the right thing, regardless of outcome (telling the truth even if it hurts someone). Contractual: a person's obligations are based on a contract or agreement. Utilitarian: seeking the greatest good for the greatest number of people. Situational: action to be taken based on context; no absolutes, only relative to the situation.

	DUTY	CONTRACTUAL	UTILITARIAN	SITUATIONAL
Situation 1				
Situation 2				
Situation 3				
Situation 4				
Situation 5				

Step 2

After separating into groups of five to six people, record the answers made by each individual member of your group on the form below. Record the answers of each group member in each box and the group's solution in the column on the far right.

MEMBER NAME						GROUP ANSWER
Situation 1						
Situation 2						
Situation 3						
Situation 4						
Situation 5						

Step 3

Reach a consensus in each situation (if possible) and record the decision that your group has reached above. Allow 20 to 30 minutes.

Step 4

Report to the class your group's conclusions and explain how the consensus, if any, was reached. The discussion should focus on the following questions:

- Was a consensus reached by the group?
- Was this consensus difficult or easy to achieve and why?
- What kinds of ethical issues emerged?
- How were conflicts, if any, resolved, or were they left unresolved?
- What creative solutions did you find in order to solve the difficult problem without compromising your integrity?

Step 5

Discuss with the class the following issues:

- What role do ethical issues play and how important are they in the formation of a new venture team?
- What role do ethical issues play and how important are they in obtaining venture capital? That is, how do investors feel about ethics and how important are they to them?

- What feelings bother participants most about the discussion and consensus reached? For example, if a participant believes that his or her own conduct was considered ethically less than perfect, does he or she feel a loss of self-respect or a sense of inferiority? Does he or she fear others' judgment, and so on?

Step 6

Define each group member's general ethical position and note whether his or her ethical position is similar to or different from yours:

MEMBER NAME	POSITION	DIFFERENT/SIMILAR

Step 7

Decide whom you would and would not want as a business partner based on their ethical positions:

WOULD WANT	WOULD NOT WANT

Preparation Questions

1. What are Planet Bean's components of strategy, and how do they relate to corporate social responsibility?

2. Discus the key strengths, weaknesses, opportunities, and threats facing Planet Bean.

3. What are some strategic options that Planet Bean could consider? Evaluate their advantages and disadvantages, using the components of strategy from your answer to question 1.

It is late spring in Guelph, Ontario, and the sun is streaming into Planet Bean's east-end coffee bar. Byron Cunningham takes a long drink of "Freedom Fighter" and muses, "Opening up another coffee bar is just one of many decisions we need to make to continue growing responsibly. As well as obtaining socially responsible capital, sourcing fair-trade coffee, pricing competitively, and just keeping up with the day-to-day decisions, we do need to grow. We need to grow responsibly, that is the type of business we are at Planet Bean."

Planet Bean was established in 1997 as a roastery specializing in fair-trade and organic gourmet coffee. A member of the Specialty Coffee Association roasts the beans in a Probat batch coffee roaster to create single-origin or blended coffees with names such as Freedom Fighter, Café Femenino, and Dark Sidamo. From 2005 to 2010, Planet Bean's sales tripled to over C$1.5 million and retail sales now exceed wholesale revenues.

Planet Bean's market positioning and passion is excellent coffee, but their vision is being an innovative business that is fair, sustainable, and passionate. Their mission is creating the best tasting coffee and linking producers and consumers in a meaningful way. It is committed to developing the moral economy, to ethical business, and to fair trade for producers, workers, stakeholders, and customers. They believe success is measurable, not just financially, but also through their ability to reduce their ecological footprint, improve the health of the planet, and advance organic production and the capability to manage a democratic workplace based on co-operation that can be a model for a people-centred economy. According to Byron, Planet Bean is known for "commitment to great coffee and commitment to business change based on a social structure that puts people first."

In the spirit and practice of the triple bottom line, Planet Bean embraces its stakeholders in its business model. Social, environmental, and economic stakeholders' interests are described by Planet Bean's concern for "people, planet, and profit." As part of a co-operative that focused on fair trade, it aspires to provide a living wage for its employees and pays producer-farmers a fair price. People at Planet Bean know that "our social commitment is part of our whole vision and mission statement—it's what we are and how we live it, which provides our workers and customers a model for change that they can see and believe in." Planet Bean's credentials include membership in Fairtrade Canada, FLO, Ecocert Canada, as well as the Ethiopian Fine Coffee Network and more.

Clearly, the people at Planet Bean run a business and know that without customers, the "upstreaming" of value generated is not economically sustainable. A triple bottom line business must generate profits without subsidies, exploitation, and negative impact on the environment and communities.

COFFEE

According to urban legend, coffee is the world's second largest traded commodity after oil, and for those who just cannot function without it, this may seem just right. However, after adjusting for the value of roasting and distribution, coffee is closer to a $20 billion per year business than the $90 billion used in the urban legend (Pendergrast, 2009). The estimated global value of coffee was US$12.7 billion in 2007, when Robusta beans accounted for $3.32 billion and Arabica US$9.38 billion (Pay, 2009).

Over 70 countries produce coffee. Robusta beans, which are easier to produce, grow at lower altitudes, have higher yields, are more disease resistant and have a higher caffeine content. They account for about 30 percent of production, while the finer-flavoured and more aromatic Arabica beans account for the rest. Approximately three-quarters of all coffee is consumed in developed countries. Among major producing countries, only Brazilians and Ethiopians are significant coffee drinkers.

Coffee is cultivated in tropical climates, and traditionally grown on shrubs planted in the shade. Efforts to increase production during the 1970s resulted in farmers switching to sun-cultivation. Now coffee can be grown in rows and treated with fertilizers and pesticides, which allows for faster maturation. Traditional, shade-grown coffee matures mores slowly and many coffee aficionados feel the quality is better. It also provides a habitat for many indigenous species, requires less water and preserves soil quality.

This case was written by Professor Erna van Duren, University of Guelph, and Bill Barrett for purposes of class discussion.

Coffee is the seed of berries that grow on bushes. After harvesting, washing, and milling, coffee is sold as green beans in 60-lb. bags. Generally, the green bean equivalent (GBE) is used to measure volumes and prices of coffee. Coffee roasters and distributors capture a large share of the final value of coffee in a highly concentrated market dominated by Kraft, Nestle, Proctor and Gamble, Sara Lee, and Douwe Egberts. Roast and ground coffee accounts for about 80 percent of the value added at the roasting level of the value chain. Instant coffee accounts for most of the remainder. The European Union accounts for about half of all coffee sales. Large-scale roasters are protected from competition by their economies of scale and scope, along with phytosanitary barriers, patents on processing technology, and marketing and distribution arrangements.

Specialty Coffee

Specialty coffees have flavours based on soil, climate, and other growing conditions and generally are Arabica varieties. In the United States the share of the coffee market accounted for by specialty coffees increased from 1 percent in the 1980s to approximately 20 percent in 2007 to a US$13.5 billion market. Innovation continues in this segment of the industry through differentiating coffees by place of origin, gourmet or production attributes, relationship-based value chains as well as the creation of new beverages and positioning of specialty coffee bars as desirable social destinations.

Fair-Trade Coffee

Fair-trade coffee is among an increasing number of products being traded using a market-based approach that aims to help producers improve their economic and social condition and promote sustainability. Coffee was the first fair-trade product introduced in 1988 under the Max Havelaar brand in the Netherlands. Although coffee is the certified fair-trade product with the greatest economic value, its share of the international coffee market is estimated to be just one percent (Pay, 2009). This excludes other coffees that are marketed as fair trade such as Nestlé's AAA coffee, Starbucks' C.A.F.E. label, and others. There is no recognized legal definition of fair trade internationally or in Canada, and a number of organizations or networks are involved in the development of principles, guidelines, certification processes, labelling initiatives, and self-regulation initiatives. The Fairtrade Certification Mark is the independent certification mark of Fairtrade International (FLO) and is used in over 50 countries.

FLO-certified coffee must meet a minimum price, an organic premium when relevant, a fair-trade price premium, and adhere to other social and environmental practices. Farmers must also organize democratically; this is usually done through co-operatives. In 2006, more than 450 tonnes of coffee sold in Canada under various fair-trade labels was not officially certified (CBC, 2007). During 2011, Transfair U.S.A. dropped out of the international network after it proposed allowing estate farmers membership under a "Fair Trade for All" designation. Now a new version of FLO is being developed. From 1962 to 1989 the International Coffee Agreement brought some stability to prices. It abandoned price regulation during the 1990s in response to what many participants in the fair-trade movement refer to as "neo-liberal trade philosophies."

Organic and Eco-Friendly Coffee

Organic coffee refers to coffee grown using organic techniques without herbicides, pesticides, or synthetic fertilizers. Beginning in the 1970s private associations certified organic producers. By the 1990s, organic certification was available in many countries and internationally through initiatives such as the International Federation of Organic Agriculture. To be labelled organic in Canada, imports have to meet Canada's standards. According to the Canadian Food Inspection Agency, Canada's organic logo may only be used on products that have organic content that is greater than 95 percent. However, as with fair-trade designations, some organic regulations and standards have been co-opted by corporate interests. The Organic Consumers Association feels this is the case with the USDA organic label, which was significantly weakened in 2005 (Jaffee, 2010). Generally, consumers perceive organic coffee to be grown naturally, but there appears to great variation in what this means. Some consumers know that "Certified Organic" goes beyond farming practices, but many find it confusing. Eco-friendly or environmentally friendly products are generally considered to cause less or minimal harm to the environment. Various labelling standards exist nationally and internationally for eco-friendly products and increasing volumes of coffee are being marketed as such.

COFFEE VALUE CHAINS

Traditionally coffee was grown on estates, which have been associated with poor treatment of indigenous labour. Such issues at the producer end of the value chain remained hidden from consumers in developed countries until the 1990s when fair trade concerns and awareness began to increase among more affluent and younger consumers. Until then the typical value chain for coffee comprised large growing estates, coffee buyers or intermediaries, exporters, importers, roasters and retailers, and finally consumers. Large growers were sometimes able to deal with importers or roasters directly, while coffee buyers were often able to extract lower prices from smaller coffee growers and retain the difference as profit. Large buyer-importers have been able to buy large volumes, hold large inventories, and sell them over a longer period at higher prices. The asymmetry in market power, the long lead-time involved in increasing production, and other industry characteristics resulted in significant price volatility for coffee.

Fair-trade value chains have focused on removing links in the value chain and increasing the proportion of the consumer price of coffee captured by the producer. Fair-trade value chains generally seek to bypass organizations in the middle and deal with grower co-operatives. By working directly with co-operatives, Planet Bean has been able to develop one-on-one relationships with growers. As Byron indicates, "this allows us to pay them the full compensation for their hard work. It provides proper pay recognition, as well as allowing participation in community building through their co-operative."

Large companies increasingly take the same approach, and position coffee sourced through a simplified value chain as "fair trade." This threat is becoming more serious as aspects of the fair-trade movement are co-opted, and more businesses use their non-fair-trade products to subsidize their fair-trade products. Planet Bean became the first Canadian company to sign a licensing agreement with the government of Ethiopia, allowing it to use the regional designations for Ethiopian coffees such as the Sidamo, Yirgacheffe, and Harar beans that it buys directly from the Oromia Coffee Farmers Union. As well, Planet Bean's coffee is certified through Ecocert. Maintaining this certification costs between $1500 and $2000 and at least eight hours of paperwork annually.

PLANET BEAN

Planet Bean's primary product is certified fair-trade organic coffee, which provides over 95 percent of the contribution margin in the wholesale division and over 90 percent in retail. Whole bean coffee sales account for 40–45 percent of sales, while beverage and other retail sales account for the remainder. In late 2009, Planet Bean's coffee bar became the first in the region to serve single-brew coffees, thereby allowing customers to choose from 18 types of coffee along with a variety of coffee, tea, or chocolate drinks and locally baked goods made with organic flour.

Planet Bean's marketing emphasizes the flavour, freshness, and pedigree of its coffees using three themes: earth, fire, and water. Earth is for organic coffee grown under fair trade and sustainable conditions. Fire is for the roasting that develops full flavours. Water is for the coffee brewing processes. These marketing themes are also used in operations. Earth refers to working with growers to source and develop high-quality coffee, fire refers to the batch roasting processes, and water to working with the baristas to ensure that customers have excellent coffee! The themes are also used in the décor of the coffee bars, packaging, community events, other branding initiatives, and the website.

Currently, Planet Bean has a coffee shop in downtown Guelph, a roastery and retail location in the east end, and a new south-Guelph location on a main street that merges onto Highway 401. The south-end store is the new model for future locations. The main competition there is Starbucks, which is closer to the highway and has a drive-through in a new mall. According to Bill Barrett, "people might come to us originally because they've heard we're fair trade and organic, but they come back because the coffee tastes good." The recent expansion came a result of the growth strategy Planet Bean realized was necessary about five years ago. As Barrett indicates, we realized "that for us to succeed we have to increase our retail operations in the city" and although "the retail coffee market is very expensive…when we get down to selling it in our own coffee shops, we can compete."

A diverse management and coffee bar team manage Planet Bean's current operations. Byron Cunningham focuses on overall strategy, wholesale sales, and developing relationships in fair-trade value chain. John Brouwer, a former urban planner, manages finances in tune with the larger geopolitical situation and its implications for the fair-trade movement. Bill Barrett is responsible for marketing and continues to position Planet Bean as a specialty coffee supplier, with the added dimensions of fair trade and organics. His work on emphasizing quality has enabled Planet Bean to develop a unique niche, and his recent trips to work with grower cooperatives have resulted in several compelling photographs of the people who grow Planet Bean's coffee being added to the coffee bars' distinctive décor. Bill feels that it is important to show the real faces of people who grow coffee, not caricatures such as Juan Valdez. Dave Barrett, the master roaster, and Elijah Lederman, brew master and production manager, ensure that coffee beans are roasted to consistent qualities and flavours for each particular coffee. Steve Cutts ensures that orders, production, and shipping run smoothly, while the training of the baristas is managed by Emma Howart-Withers. Planet Bean's logo is designed locally by LINDdesign, and is used on its cups, T-shirts, mugs, retail items, and retail and bulk packaging.

Planet Bean is a division of the SUMAC Community Worker Co-operative. SUMAC employs over 40 people and 9 of those are worker-owners who work at Planet Bean. Currently individuals can make RRSP-eligible investment in Planet Bean through SUMAC. Exhibit 1 provides an overview of Planet Bean's finances.

Planet Bean buys fair-trade coffee from Guatemala, Mexico, Ethiopia, Peru, and Sumatra. These coffees offer Planet Bean customers a connection with the source of their coffee, and as Bill Barrett's poster-sized photographs portray, "the human face of our coffees." Fair-trade businesses such as Planet Bean still need to make a profit, and they choose to do so responsibly. The cost of the green coffee and consumer product prices form the bookends of their participation in the capitalist economy. Planet Bean's green coffee costs reflect the amount of coffee purchased, the contracted price with growers, transportation, trade and shipping related fees, and exchange rate costs. Since Planet Bean purchases its green coffee beans in US$, the level and volatility of the C$–US$ exchange rate can have a substantial impact on margins. Accordingly, Planet Bean has developed an arrangement with a local credit union to purchase forward contracts for US$ to lock in the cost of coffee bean purchases. John Brouwer, who manages this participation in the capitalist economy, sees many ethical dilemmas in using futures markets and bank financing. His most recent concern is related to the value of the Canadian dollar. He is troubled that the "recent blood being spilled in the Middle East has raised the value of the Canadian dollar and oil pricing which our country has benefited from, while other have lost their lives in that relationship."

Market research also poses somewhat of an ethical dilemma for Planet Bean. Everyone agrees word of mouth, reputation-based marketing is best and most consistent with their aim to build "'deeper' customer relationships." If Planet Bean does not grow responsibly and "generate" a certain level of surplus, it cannot sustain being a fair-trade business. "We do need to have surplus to invest in our operations, pay sustainable wages, attract talent, and provide a nest egg for poor years and deal with emergency situations," and as Byron sums up, "without a viable business, we cannot support our social objectives."

Local Environment

Wholesale and retail pricing focuses on being competitive with other specialty coffee offerings in Guelph and surrounding communities. Pricing surveys are undertaken periodically to ensure that retail and wholesale prices are competitive. Planet Bean shares these results with their wholesale customers so that they are able to price accordingly.

Guelph's high growth rate, agriculture, environmental, food, and arts foci, combined with the influence of the University of Guelph and a manufacturing sector that accounts for roughly 1/5th of economic activity make for a socio-economically and culturally diverse city. Guelph has a considerable range of restaurants and coffee shops ranging from Coffee Time and Tim Hortons to Starbucks, Second Cup, and Planet Bean. A "good cup of coffee" can also be enjoyed at several small independent restaurants and cafés such as the Red Brick, With the Grain, and many similar cafés as well as at chains such as Williams and even McDonalds, which serves 100-percent Arabica coffee.

In 2010, Planet Bean updated its preprinted consumer bag to refresh its retail shelf look and to deal with the competitive pressures of the recession and the increased numbers of varieties of "fair-trade" coffees now competing for shelf space. The website was redesigned with the earth, fire, and water theme. Given that its web-based and mail-order business was miniscule and caused more problems than profits, Planet Bean does not do or plan to do "ecommerce."

Guelph's growth has mainly been to the south, although subdivisions are growing in the east and west areas of Guelph. Starbucks is opening more locations, and has a drive-through, which Planet Bean would never do. Planet Bean aims to continue being the premier supplier of a wide range of high quality, freshly roasted fair-trade and organic coffee beans in southern Ontario. Given that that its retail coffee bars proved to be more recession proof that its wholesale business, Byron and his team have just opened a third coffee bar in south Guelph. When asked about the new location, Bill Barrett said "We're like coffee missionaries....We feel like south Guelph is devoid of excellent coffee, so we have to bring flavour to the people of south Guelph."

About 18 months were needed from the time they decided to open their third location to the "official opening date." The process involved securing socially responsible financing and planning for the operational aspects of opening, managing, and running the third coffee bar. The Bank of Montreal provided the debt financing since a local manager was interested in figuring out how BMO could work with socially responsible businesses. According to Byron, movement during these 18 months was "painstakingly slow, mainly because a bank hadn't seen our seen our model before. Banks are not comfortable with something new…so although our bank representative was very helpful, we had to a do a considerable amount of education." Because of this experience, future expansions should be faster.

Planet Bean's longer-run objective is to open three additional coffee bars in the south-central Ontario market.

Good location options appear to be downtown Hamilton or close to the University of Waterloo, both of which are within an hour's drive of downtown Guelph. Other communities within 45 minutes to an hour's drive of Guelph may also be good candidates. Byron and his team will be looking for a 1000- to 1200-square-foot location, with good parking and visibility on high traffic streets as well as quick ingress and egress. Exhibit 2 summarizes demographic and selected other data for the original Guelph, newest Guelph, and three other possible locations for another Planet Bean coffee bar.

GROWING RESPONSIBLY

Social entrepreneurism's time may have come. Two of three Canadians believe that government pays too little attention to the environment and that nearly three in four think GDP is an insufficient measure of progress, which should be augmented with health, social, and environmental data (AngusReid, 2011). Making larger strategic decisions and smaller day-to-day decisions in an economically, socially, and environmentally responsible manner takes vision and commitment. Byron, Bill, and the management team at Planet Bean are committed to responsible growth. They need to develop and evaluate options for growing responsibly. What advice would serve them best?

EXHIBIT 1	PLANET BEAN—FINANCES

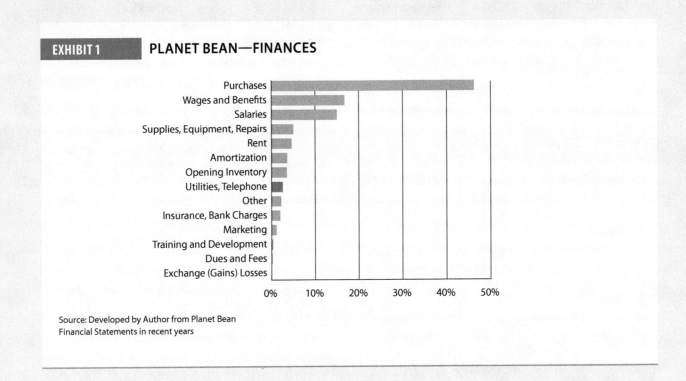

Source: Developed by Author from Planet Bean Financial Statements in recent years

EXHIBIT 2   LOCATION ASSESSMENT

| | | GUELPH | | KITCHENER-WATERLOO | | HAMILTON |
		DOWNTOWN	SOUTH	BEECHWOOD	KINGSWAY	LOCKE ST.
Population		10 812	6386	7922	8620	22 347
Households		5293	2475	3015	3813	12 925
Age of Household Head	Under 25	7.4%	2.1%	5.5%	7.7%	9.7%
	25–34	22.7%	9.9%	11.4%	19.7%	23.6%
	35–44	19.1%	13.5%	13.4%	21.4%	15.9%
	45–54	20.3%	24.7%	28.2%	16.3%	16.3%
	55–64	12.7%	20.5%	24.4%	15.9%	14.3%
	65–74	7.0%	13.6%	11.3%	10.4%	9.3%
	75 & over	10.7%	15.7%	5.8%	8.6%	10.9%
Household Size	1 person	37.7%	16.0%	18.8%	29.0%	54.8%
	2 people	34.6%	39.6%	33.9%	37.1%	29.8%
	3 people	13.4%	15.0%	16.0%	16.3%	8.4%
	4 people or more	14.4%	29.4%	31.2%	17.6%	7.0%
Household Type	Couple, with children	38.9%	48.6%	50.5%	39.4%	30.3%
	Couple, no children	44.4%	44.9%	35.7%	40.7%	52.7%
	Lone-Parent	16.7%	6.5%	13.8%	19.9%	17.1%
	One family	55.2%	79.4%	74.5%	62.5%	38.7%
	Non-Family	44.0%	19.2%	23.8%	37.0%	60.8%
	Never married	43.0%	27.9%	34.7%	37.9%	44.8%
	Married	36.8%	61.9%	54.9%	41.1%	31.7%
Age of Children at home	Under 10	37.9%	23.9%	26.8%	39.9%	43.1%
	10–14	20.8%	20.5%	18.7%	18.5%	17.8%
	15–17	12.8%	16.2%	13.9%	11.6%	11.2%
	18 & over	28.5%	39.5%	40.6%	30.1%	27.9%
Housing	Owned	51.1%	95.9%	78.4%	36.8%	27.5%
	Single detached	36.2%	77.0%	64.0%	19.7%	15.3%
	Low Rise Apartment	30.7%	1.7%	7.3%	18.5%	18.7%
	High Rise Apartment	13.4%	0.0%	1.8%	42.4%	57.8%
	Row, Duplex	19.8%	21.4%	26.9%	19.5%	8.2%
Housing Age	After 2006	2.3%	11.6%	6.0%	10.2%	0.2%
	1991–2006	8.4%	41.9%	16.8%	16.8%	2.5%
	1971–1990	13.5%	38.5%	66.8%	41.4%	25.2%
	1946–1971	28.9%	15.7%	10.1%	30.3%	37.4%
	Before 1946	46.9%	1.4%	0.3%	1.3%	33.2%

(continued)

EXHIBIT 2

LOCATION ASSESSMENT

		GUELPH		KITCHENER-WATERLOO		HAMILTON
		DOWNTOWN	SOUTH	BEECHWOOD	KINGSWAY	LOCKE ST.
Employment, in Labour Force		74.6%	66.1%	67.6%	66.7%	64.4%
Education	No certificate or degree	19.9%	14.0%	12.2%	24.6%	18.2%
	High School or equivalent	27.4%	22.0%	24.3%	32.6%	24.0%
	Apprenticeship or Trades	7.3%	6.4%	3.5%	7.3%	6.4%
	College, Some University	13.0%	16.5%	11.0%	16.9%	18.6%
	University degree	28.8%	36.2%	43.9%	13.6%	29.0%
Average Household Income		$66 010	$119 260	$137 215	$60 808	$51 243
Commuting	Vehicle	73.85%	87.9%	85.5%	78.0%	59.5%
	Public Transit	9.04%	3.7%	4.2%	11.3%	19.8%
	Walked or Cycled	15.27%	7.80%	9.11%	10.30%	19.9%
Language, Immigration	Immigrant	17.8%	23.5%	26.9%	34.5%	25.9%
	Visible Minority	10.4%	16.9%	21.9%	25.9%	20.1%
	Non-official Language	12.0%	18.6%	26.4%	34.4%	24.8%

Developed from Census Tract Data (StatisticsCanada, 2011)
Source: Developed by the author.

REFERENCE LIST

AngusReid. 2011. *Canadians and Americans call for more Action on the Environment*. New York: Angus Reid.

CBC. 2007. Fair Trade: An Alternative Economic Model. *CBC News*, April 23, 2007.

Jaffee, D, P.H. Howard. 2010. Corporate Cooptation of Organic and Fair Trade Standards. *Agricultural Human Values*, 27: 387-399.

Pay, E. 2009. *The Market for Organic and Fair Trade Coffee*. Rome: Food and Agricultural Organization of the United Nations.

Pendergrast, M. 2009. Coffee second only to oil? Is coffee really the second largest commodity? T*ea and Coffee Trade Journal*, April, 38-41.

connect

For more information on the resources available from McGraw-Hill Ryerson, go to www.mcgrawhill.ca/he/solutions.

PART IV

FINANCING ENTREPRENEURIAL VENTURES

A financing strategy is driven by corporate and personal goals, by resulting financial requirements, and ultimately by the available alternatives. In the final analysis, these alternatives are governed by the entrepreneur's relative bargaining power and skill in orchestrating the fundraising opportunities. In turn, that bargaining power is governed to a large extent by the cruelty of real time. It is governed by when the venture will run out of cash given its current cash burn rate.

More numerous alternatives for financing a company exist now than ever before. Even in the wake of economic turmoil, many contend that money remains plentiful for well-managed emerging firms with the promise of profitable growth. Savvy entrepreneurs should remain vigilant for the warnings noted here to avoid the myopic temptation to "take the money and run." The cost of money can vary considerably.

While some of these alternatives look distinct and separate, a financing strategy probably will encompass a combination of both debt and equity capital. In considering which financial alternatives are best for a venture at any particular stage of growth it is important to draw on the experience of other entrepreneurs, investors, lenders, accountants, and other professionals.

In the search for either debt or equity capital, it is important that entrepreneurs take a professional approach to selecting and presenting their ventures to both investors and lenders.

CHAPTER
8

RESOURCE REQUIREMENTS

It's almost like you see too much, because when it happens for real, everything flies at you so fast, you never get a sense of the ice and where everyone is at that one moment.

STEVE YZERMAN

LEARNING OBJECTIVES

LO1 Describe the successful entrepreneur's unique attitudes about and approaches to resources—people, capital, and other assets.

LO2 Evaluate the ways in which entrepreneurs turn less into more (e.g., bootstrapping, lease not buy, control rather than own).

LO3 Identify the important issues in selecting and effectively utilizing outside professionals, such as advisors, board of directors, lawyers, accountants, and consultants.

LO4 Articulate decisions about financial resources.

THE ENTREPRENEURIAL APPROACH TO RESOURCES LO1

Resources include (1) people, such as the venture team, the board of directors, lawyers, accountants, and consultants; (2) financial resources; (3) assets, such as plant and equipment; and (4) a business plan and other intellectual property. Nick Bontis of McMaster University sees knowledge and know-how in people and processes as the key ingredient for a new venture to survive and ultimately thrive. Successful entrepreneurs view the need for and the ownership and control of these resources in the pursuit of opportunities differently from the way managers in many large organizations view them. This different way of looking at resources is reflected in a definition of entrepreneurship given in chapter 1—the process of creating or seizing an opportunity *and pursuing it regardless of the resources currently controlled.*[1]

Successful entrepreneurs have a unique approach to resources.[2] The decisions on what resources are needed, when they are needed, and how to acquire them are strategic decisions that fit with the other driving forces of entrepreneurship. Entrepreneurs seek to use the minimum possible amount of all types of resources at each stage in their ventures' growth. Rather than own the resources they need, they seek to control them.

Entrepreneurs with this approach reduce some of the risk in pursuing opportunities, including:

- *Less capital.* The amount of capital required is simply smaller due to the quest for prudence. The financial exposure is therefore reduced as is the dilution of the founder's equity. As Michael Dunleavy with the business law firm LaBarge Weinstein in Kanata, Ontario, admonishes: don't give away too much equity too early—otherwise there is damage to be undone in order to capture the interest of later investors.

- *Staged capital commitments.* The capital infusions are staged to match critical objectives that will signal whether it is prudent to keep going, and thus infuse the second stage of capital, or abort the venture. Both the founder's and investor's financial exposure, and dilution of equity ownership, are thereby reduced.

- *More flexibility.* Entrepreneurs who do not own a resource are in a better position to commit and decommit quickly.[3] One price of ownership of resources is an inherent inflexibility. With the rapidly fluctuating conditions and uncertainty with which most entrepreneurial ventures have to contend, inflexibility can be a curse. Response times to evaluate quick changes and take action need to be short if a firm is to be competitive. Decision windows are most often small and elusive. And it is extremely difficult to accurately predict the resources that will be necessary to execute the opportunity. The entrepreneurial approach to resources permits iterations or strategic experiments in the venture process—that is, ideas can be tried and tested without committing to the ownership of all assets and resources in the business, to markets and technology that change rapidly, and so forth. For example, Howard Head says that if he had raised all the money he needed at the outset, he would have failed by spending it all too early on the wrong version of his metal ski. Consider also, for example, the inflexibility of a company that commits to a certain technology, software, or management system.

- *Low sunk cost.* In addition, sunk costs are lower if the firm exercises the option to abort the venture at any point. Consider, instead, the enormous upfront capital commitment of a nuclear power plant and the cost of abandoning such a project.

- *Lower costs.* Fixed costs are lowered, thus favourably affecting breakeven. Of course, the other side of the coin is that variable costs may rise. If the entrepreneur has found an opportunity with forgiving and rewarding economics, then there still will most likely be ample gross margins in the venture to absorb cost increases.

- *Reduced risk.* In addition to reducing total exposure, other risks, such as the risk of obsolescence of the resource, are also lower. For example, venture leasing has been used by biotechnology companies as a way to supplement sources of equity financing.

While some might scoff at those who do not own all their assets, assuming erroneously that the firm cannot afford to buy a resource, in fact not owning a resource can provide advantages and options. These decisions are often extremely complex, involving consideration of such details as the tax implications of leasing versus buying, and so forth.

BOOTSTRAPPING STRATEGIES: MARSHALLING AND MINIMIZING RESOURCES LO2

Minimizing resources is referred to in colloquial terms as bootstrapping. More formally it is referred to as a lack of resource intensity, defined as a multistage commitment of resources with a minimum commitment at each stage or decision point.[4] When discussing his philosophy on bootstrapping, Greg Gianforte (who retired at the age of 33 after he and his partners sold their software business, Brightwork Development, to McAfee Associates for more than $10 million) stated, "A lot of entrepreneurs think they need money...when actually they haven't figured out the business equation."[5] According to Gianforte, lack of money, employees, equipment—even lack of product—is actually a huge advantage because it forces the bootstrapper to concentrate on selling to bring cash into the business. Thus, to persevere, entrepreneurs ask at every step how they can accomplish a little more with a little less and pursue the opportunity (see for yourself by trying the online exercise "How Entrepreneurs Turn Less into More" on Connect.

As was outlined in Exhibit 1.3, the opposite attitude is often evident in large institutions that are usually characterized by a trustee or custodial viewpoint. Managers in larger institutions seek to have not only enough committed resources for the task at hand but also a cushion against the tough times.

USING OTHER PEOPLE'S RESOURCES

Obtaining the use of other people's resources, particularly in the start-up and early-growth stages of a venture, is an important approach for entrepreneurs. In contrast, large firms assume that virtually all resources have to be owned to control their use, and decisions centre around how these resources will be acquired and financed—not so with entrepreneurs.

Having the use of the resource and being able to control or influence the deployment of the resource are key. The quote at the beginning of the chapter illustrates being able to see everything unfolding quickly and sensing how it all comes together and fits into place. Scott Nichol founded 6N Silicon in September 2006, bringing his own expertise in metallurgy to tackle the purification of silicon for solar power. He located 6N Silicon "in the heart of Canada's metal processing industry, surrounded by Canada's extensive metal processing knowledge. 6N has benefited from access to considerable industry experience in processing other metals and applying collective skills to refine the 6N solution."[6]

Other people's resources can include, for example, money invested or lent by friends, relatives, business associates, or other investors. Or resources can include people, space, equipment, or other material loaned, provided inexpensively or for free by customers or suppliers, or secured by bartering future services, opportunities, and the like. In fact, using other people's resources can be as simple as benefiting from free booklets and pamphlets, such as those published by many of the Big Four accounting firms, or using low-cost educational programs or government-funded

ENTREPRENEURS ACROSS CANADA
Mustering Resources at Genuwine Cellars Inc.

Genuwine Cellars

COFOUNDERS ROBB DENOMME AND LANCE KINGMA

Robb Denomme co-founded Genuwine Cellars with wood craftsman Lance Kingma. They have been building custom-made wine cellars for high-end hotels, business moguls, and celebrities worldwide. From their base in Winnipeg, Manitoba, they do their own manufacturing—something that sets them apart from competitors. Having necessary resources in-house

settles well with clients and importing additional components from Asia cuts costs. Genuwine Cellars has set up a design office in Latin America for reasons of efficiency and to access skilled professionals. BDC awarded Denomme a Young Entrepreneur of the Year Award and noted that in addition to lean manufacturing and an organizational structure that incorporates sales, design, and manufacturing functions, "Hiring an outside business consultant, who has become Denomme's mentor, also helped." Denomme gives much credit to a great team of talented people. He notes that the greatest challenge he has faced as proprietor came a few years ago, when he had to lay off a handful of his 50-person team because they were not dedicated. Denomme stated, "We always felt we needed every warm body, but after that, we were able to do more with less people. I was shocked to learn that." Denomme also acknowledges the value of learning vicariously through the experience of others.

Question: Is this a cyclical business that follows economic trends? When business is good designers and carpenters are needed. Would you hire part-timers or full-time employees to meet demand? If orders are down, do you devote more time and money on advertising and sales?

Sources: BDC "2008 YEA Winners" BDC etc., January 2009; Daryl-Lynn Carlson, "Outlook 2009: Gen Y Takes Recession in Stride," National Post, December 29, 2008 ; Canadian Newswire, "Genuwine Cellars Captivates Discriminating Tastes— Robb Denomme Wins BDC's Young Entrepreneur Award for Manitoba," www.newswire.ca (accessed October 21, 2008).

management assistance programs. Extending accounts payable is one of the primary sources of working capital for many start-ups and growing firms.

How can you as an entrepreneur begin to tap into these resources? Howard Stevenson and William Sahlman suggest that you have to do "two seemingly contradictory things: seek out the best advisors—specialists if you have to—and involve them more thoroughly, and at an earlier stage, than you have in the past. At the same time, be more skeptical of their credentials and their advice."[7] A recent study found that social capital, including having an established business network and encouragement from friends and family, is strongly associated with entrepreneurial activity.[8] In addition to networking with family, friends, classmates, and advisors, the human touch enhances the relationship between the entrepreneur and the venture's advisors. Accuracy in social perception, skill at impression management, skill at persuasion and influence, and a high level of social adaptability may be relevant to the activities necessary for successful new ventures.[9] Paola Dubini of the University of Bocconi, Italy, and Howard Aldrich of the University of North Carolina have contributed to the growing body of knowledge about how these "social assets" may benefit the bottom line of a new venture; see Exhibit 8.1 for the strategic principles they have identified. However, a handful of studies have failed to demonstrate the effectiveness of networking activities on the performance of ventures.[10]

HYPOTHESES CONCERNING NETWORKS AND ENTREPRENEURIAL EFFECTIVENESS

Effective entrepreneurs are more likely than others to systematically plan and monitor network activities.

- Effective entrepreneurs are able to chart their present network and to discriminate between productive and symbolic ties.
- Effective entrepreneurs are able to view effective networks as a crucial aspect for ensuring the success of their company.
- Effective entrepreneurs are able to stabilize and maintain networks to increase their effectiveness and their efficiency.

Effective entrepreneurs are more likely than others to undertake actions toward increasing their network density and diversity.

- Effective entrepreneurs set aside time for purely random activities—things done with no specific problem in mind.
- Effective entrepreneurs are able to check network density, so as to avoid too many overlaps (because they affect network efficiency) while still attaining solidarity and cohesiveness.
- Effective entrepreneurs multiply, through extending the reachability of their networks, the stimuli for better and faster adaptation to change.

Source: Adapted from Paola Dubini and Howard Aldrich, "Personal and Extended Networks Are Central to the Entrepreneurial Process," *Journal of Business Venturing* 6, no. 5 (1991): 305–313.

There are many examples of controlling people resources, rather than owning them. In real estate, even the largest firms do not employ top architects full-time but, rather, secure them on a project-by-project basis. Most smaller firms do not employ lawyers but obtain legal assistance as needed. Technical consultants, design engineers, and programmers are other examples. An illustration of this approach is a company that grew to $20 million in sales in about 10 years with $7500 cash, a liberal use of credit cards, reduced income for the founders, and hard work and long hours. This company has not had to raise any additional equity capital.

An example of the opposite point of view is a proposed new venture in the iPhone applications software industry. The business plan called for about $300 000, an amount that would pay for only the development of the first products. The first priority in the deployment of the company's financial resources outlined in the business plan was to buy outright office equipment and sign a one-year lease on space costing approximately $150 000. The founders refused to consider other options, such as renting the equipment or working from home with what they had. The company was unable to attract venture capital, even though, otherwise, it had excellent prospects. The $150 000 raised from informal private investors was not enough money to execute the opportunity, and the founders decided to give it back and abandon the venture. A more entrepreneurial team would have figured out a way to keep going under these circumstances.

THE RIGHT STUFF—DOES CANADA HAVE WHAT IT TAKES?

Some contend that Canada is too conservative, resistant to innovation and risk, and stuck on its history of natural resources for competitive advantage. Michael Treacy, serial entrepreneur

BITHEADS—RESOURCES FOR HIRE

18 years ago, three software developers left a large company to form a small company that ultimately didn't go anywhere. But from that small company, lessons were learned and they formed bitHeads, inc. to deliver cool technology and products to its customers. Over the years, the company and their team of talented strategists, developers, designers, and software architects have solved challenging technical problems and delivered more than 500 sophisticated mobile apps, games, and enterprise-level software tools.

bitHeads has partnered with well-known brands, delivering solutions that entertained people, improved services and efficiency, strengthened customer relationships, and helped their customers increase revenue or open up new revenue streams. Since 1995, the organization has been a leader in the National Capital Region, and has grown from a team of three founders to more than 100 staff members who specialize in mobile, cloud and backend infrastructures, big data, and M2M solutions. In 2007, the company created a gaming division, Playbrains, and acquired a gaming studio in Toronto to add to their team of experts to expand the organization's service offerings and expertise in the media and entertainment spaces.

Remaining true to the company's original ideals, it's not uncommon to find the three founders working on a client's project, catching up with employees at the 40-foot bar or functional movie theater housed in the office, helping to raise funds for the employee-driven charity of the month, or giving back to the local technology community by sitting on public and private boards and mentoring start-ups and young entrepreneurs.

Source: www.bitheads.com; twitter.com/bitHeads

---

and strategy expert, knows that trade-offs have to be made to catch up and pursue things in a knowledge-based economy. "The only way to keep attracting work without suppressing wages," Treacy reasons, "is to improve productivity, and that means investing in innovation. Knowledge talent will be the only basis of real, sustainable competitive advantage over time."[11] According to Treacy, Canada is not prepared for a world where knowledge rules. This he finds in notable contrast to the United States, where innovation thrives. "That massive, consumer-driven culture opens up a world of opportunity for new ventures, because the market recognizes and warmly receives the value of a new product or service. And the people who can provide early-stage financing are willing to back it."[12]

Some have questioned whether or not entrepreneurship is the same everywhere. In France, entrepreneurs are more often part of the "corporate" establishment, whereas in Japan "network" entrepreneurs rely on the organization of industry. The "informal" entrepreneur characterizes the entrepreneur in Africa and parts of Asia. The western notion of the entrepreneur is that of an individualist with competitive instincts not part of a collective, as opposed to other regions where trust may be more prominent.[13]

Most contend that entrepreneurial attributes are more universal than idiosyncratic; it is the institutional environment that drives economic activity and latent behaviours. For example, recent research has shown that Labour Sponsored Venture Capital Corporations "crowd out" other types of venture capital funds, clearly frustrating one of the key governmental goals of this program.[14] These vehicles for new venture creation were supposed to foster additional financing (expand the aggregate pool of risk capital) not displace it! It is most probable that it is the incentive structures that arise from institutional arrangements that produce entrepreneurs. Finally, it should be noted that differences in entrepreneurial activity are often greater within a country (e.g., Québec vs. Saskatchewan) than between countries (e.g., Texas vs. Alberta).

Treacy concludes with that critical question about the future supply of Canadian entrepreneurs: "What are we doing to nurture them, and what are we doing to keep them here?"

BUILD YOUR BRAIN TRUST

Building a brain trust—a group of close advisors selected for their various expertises—for your venture is a huge part of improving the "fit" vis-à-vis the Timmons Model, and managing risk and reward. The adage "it's not just what you know, it's who you know that matters" conveys the message. While networking for its own sake is ill-advised, making connections pays dividends—some of these payoffs may be delayed, options to be exercised in the future.

After assessing the venture and entrepreneur's background through a basic gap analysis and applying the Timmons Model to the venture, it becomes clear what is missing and where value can be added during the creation, launch, and building of the enterprise. Aydin Mirzaee, founder of bOK Systems, was able to add Michael Cowpland of Corel and a Toronto VC to his brain trust. Aydin gained access to their knowledge, their relevant and extensive experience, and their contacts with other talent pools and capital. It was then up to Aydin, through his entrepreneurial energy, promise, and salesmanship, to capture their interest, gain their confidence, and tap into their talent. When this all comes together, drawing on the considerable strength of others, a better venture opportunity can be realized. The key is getting investors and directors to recognize high potential and see how they could personally make a large impact on the odds of success *because* they know what to do and how to do it to add value to this specific opportunity. The "Build Your Brain Trust," exercise at the end of this chapter will walk you through the key issues and tasks necessary to assemble a brain trust that can add maximum value to your venture.

The right advisors and brain-trust members are very important parts of your extended team and provide critical value to your venture. The most successful entrepreneurs think this through *before* they launch. They know what they need to fill in the gaps that exist on the team, and they ask themselves what they do not know. They focus on identifying individuals with the know-how, experience, and networks who have access to critical talent, experience, and resources that can make the difference between success and failure. Spend enough time—but not too much—planning and looking before you leap. James Chrisman of Mississippi State University, and Ed McMullan and Jeremy Hall both of the University of Calgary studied new ventures that had outside advisors; their research showed that start-up counselling assistance was positively related to a ventures growth up to a point where more help adds less and less value (marginal returns to outside assistance), eventually adding no value and ultimately reaching a point where guided preparation was actually detrimental.[15] Jean Lorrain of the Université du Québec á Trois-Rivières and Sylvie Laferté of Télé-université du Québec find that the support needs of young entrepreneurs are unique: "young entrepreneurs experience serious personal problems...feel at a particular loss with respect to self-management issues, including stress and time management."[16]

BOARD OF DIRECTORS

Initial work in evaluating the need for people resources is done when forming a new venture team (see chapter 6). Once resource needs have been determined and a team has been selected, it will usually be necessary to obtain additional resources from outside the venture in the start-up stage and during other stages of growth as well.

The decision of whether to have a board of directors and, if the answer is yes, the process of choosing and finding the people who will sit on the board are troublesome for new ventures.[17]

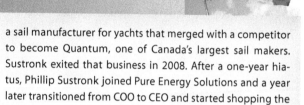

ENTREPRENEURS ACROSS CANADA
Phillip Sustronk

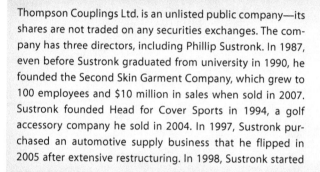

Thompson Couplings Ltd. is an unlisted public company—its shares are not traded on any securities exchanges. The company has three directors, including Phillip Sustronk. In 1987, even before Sustronk graduated from university in 1990, he founded the Second Skin Garment Company, which grew to 100 employees and $10 million in sales when sold in 2007. Sustronk founded Head for Cover Sports in 1994, a golf accessory company he sold in 2004. In 1997, Sustronk purchased an automotive supply business that he flipped in 2005 after extensive restructuring. In 1998, Sustronk started

a sail manufacturer for yachts that merged with a competitor to become Quantum, one of Canada's largest sail makers. Sustronk exited that business in 2008. After a one-year hiatus, Phillip Sustronk joined Pure Energy Solutions and a year later transitioned from COO to CEO and started shopping the company for a buyer.

Question: Phillip Sustronk is a remarkable resource; would you have any concerns working with/for him or hiring him to lead/ join your start-up?

Sources: thompsoncouplings.com; investing.businessweek.com; linkedin.com; Nicak Waddell, "Interviews Phil Sustronk, CEO of PureEnergy Solutions," Cantech Letter, February 26, 2011.

The Decision

The decision of whether to have a board of directors is influenced first by the form of organization chosen for the firm. If the new venture is organized as a corporation, it must have a board of directors, which must be elected by the shareholders. There is flexibility regarding a board with other forms of organization.

In addition, certain investors will require a board of directors. Venture capitalists almost always require that the firms they invest in have a board of directors, and also that they be represented on the board.

Beyond that, deciding whether to involve outsiders is worth careful thought. This decision making starts with identifying missing relevant experience, know-how, and networks, and determining if the venture has current needs that can be provided by outside directors. Their probable contributions can then be balanced against the resultant greater disclosure to outsiders of plans for operating and financing the business. Also, since one responsibility of a board of directors is to appoint officers for the firm, the decision whether to have a board also is tied to financing decisions and ownership of the voting shares in the company.

Boards are dominated by company executives and venture capitalists.[18] At least half of a board's members should be outside directors in order to provide independent, outside viewpoints. When Art Spinner of Hambro International was interviewed by *INC.*, he explained:

> Entrepreneurs worry about the wrong thing...that the boards are going to steal their companies or take them over. Though entrepreneurs have many reasons to worry, that's not one of them. It almost never happens. In truth, boards don't even have much power. They are less well equipped to police entrepreneurs than to advise them.[19]

The expertise that members of a board can bring to a venture, at a price it can afford, can far outweigh any of the negative factors. A board can play a crucial role, so it is important to intentionally choose a board by focusing on "holes" that need to be filled. According to noted business writer, David Gumpert, "The board continually challenged us—in terms of tactics, strategy and overall business philosophy." These challenges benefited the venture by (1) preventing dumb mistakes, (2) keeping them focused on what really mattered, and (3) stopping them from getting gloomy.[20]

A GOOD GUIDE CAN KEEP YOU ON TRACK. BE CERTAIN YOUR VENTURE HAS MENTORS THAT CAN PROVIDE DIRECTION. SO MUCH THE BETTER IF THEY HAVE FOLLOWED THE START-UP PATH THEMSELVES A FEW TIMES!

Selection Criteria: Add Value with Know-How and Contacts

Once the decision to have a board of directors has been made—and remember that it may not be optional, it may be a legal requirement—finding the appropriate people for the board is a challenge. It is important to be objective and to select trustworthy people. Most ventures typically look to personal acquaintances of the lead entrepreneur or the team or to their lawyers, bankers, accountants, or consultants for their first outside directors. While such a choice might be the right one for a venture, the process also involves finding the right people to fill the gaps discovered in the process of forming the venture team.

This issue of filling in the gaps relates to one criteria of a successful venture team, intellectual honesty; that is, knowing what you know and what you need to know. In a study of boards and specifically venture capitalists' contribution to them, entrepreneurs seemed to value operating experience over financial expertise.[21]

Defining expectations and minimum requirements for board members might be a good way to get the most out of a board of directors. A "wish list" of attributes and areas of knowledge may be constructed or alternatively if a list of candidates is identified, pros and cons for each individual may be tallied. Again, one must be mindful that the whole, the sum of the individuals, is the goal. These individuals must work together.

A top-notch outside director usually spends *at least* 9 to 10 days per year on his or her responsibilities. Four days per year are spent for quarterly meetings, a day of preparation for each meeting, a day for another meeting to cope with an unanticipated issue, plus up to a day or more for various phone calls. Yearly fees are usually paid for such a commitment.

Quality directors most often become involved for the learning and professional development opportunities, rather than for the money. Compensation to board members varies widely. Fees can range from as little as $500 to $1000 for a half- or full-day meeting to $10 000 to $30 000 per year for four to six full-day to day-and-a-half meetings, plus accessibility on a continuous basis. Directors are also usually reimbursed for their expenses incurred in preparing for and attending meetings. Shares in a start-up company, often 2 to 5 percent, or options, for 5000 to 50 000 shares, are common incentives to attract and reward directors.

As a director of 11 companies and an advisor to two other companies, Art Spinner suggested the following as a simple set of rules to guide you toward a productive relationship with your board:

- ✔ treat your directors as individual resources
- ✔ always be honest with your directors
- ✔ set up a compensation committee
- ✔ set up an audit committee
- ✔ never set up an executive committee[22]

New ventures are finding that, for a variety of reasons, people who could be potential board members are increasingly cautious about getting involved.

Liability

Motivated by an apparent wave of corporate fraud scandals that many felt could lead to a crisis of confidence in the capital marketplace, in 2002 the U.S. government passed the Sarbanes-Oxley Act (SOX). SOX requires companies to file paperwork with the Securities and Exchange Commission faster, create a more transparent means of collecting and posting financial data, maintain volumes of data, and test their procedures for posting accurate, timely information. The potential consequences of running afoul of this law are ominous, including prison time and huge fines for the company's chief officers. According to Tara Gray of the Economics Division of the Parliamentary Research Information and Research Service, Canada's response to SOX has been to emulate it, particularly given that many Canadian firms are listed on U.S. exchanges and must comply with SOX even when it conflicts with Canadian regulations. "Canadian firms make up the single largest group of foreign firms listed on U.S. stock exchanges."[23] But there are some stark differences between Canada and the United States:

- ✔ securities regulation is not under federal control in Canada
- ✔ a greater proportion of Canadian firms have a controlling shareholder
- ✔ many Canadian public corporations have relatively low market capitalizations

While start-ups are usually not subject to the technical requirements of the act, the spirit of the law and emerging case law create higher disclosure standards for even small and growing firms. Audit committees sitting on start-up boards, for example, could have real SOX-like exposure.

As well, directors of a company can be held personally liable for its actions and those of its officers. A climate of litigation exists in many areas. For example, some specific grounds for liability of a director have included voting a dividend that renders the corporation insolvent, voting to authorize a loan out of corporate assets to a director or an officer who ultimately defaults, and signing a false corporate document or report. Courts have held that if a director acts in good faith, he or she can be excused from liability. However, it can be difficult for a director to *prove* that he or she has acted in good faith, especially in a start-up situation. This proof could be complicated by several factors, including an inexperienced venture team, the financial weaknesses and cash crises that occur and demand solution, and the lack of good and complete information and records, which are necessary as the basis for action.

One solution to liability concerns is for the firm to purchase indemnity insurance for its directors. But this insurance is expensive. Despite the liability problems noted above, few enterprises report difficulty in recruiting board members. In dealing with this issue, new ventures will want to examine a possible director's attitude toward risk in general and evaluate whether this is the type of attitude the team needs to have represented.

Harassment

Outside shareholders, who may have acquired shares through a private placement or through the over-the-counter market, can have unrealistic expectations about the risk involved in a new venture, the speed at which a return can be realized, as well as the size of the return. Such shareholders are a source of continual annoyance for boards and for their companies.

Time and Risk

Experienced directors know that often it takes more time and intense involvement to work with an early-stage venture with sales of $5 million or less than with one having sales of $25 million or more, and the former is riskier. But the rewards—which may never be measured financially—are often substantial. The thrill of seeing others succeed or even simply navigate away from catastrophe can be satisfying. And we know that the initial break-in period for a start-up is crucial. Monica Diochon of St. Francis Xavier University, Teresa Menzies of Brock University, and Yvon Gasse of the Université Laval report that "sustainable operating ventures can be distinguished from others according to the activities undertaken during start-up."[24]

"Outsider assistance during the early stages of a venture's development can influence its subsequent development,"[25] observe James Chrisman and Ed McMullan both of the University of Calgary. The researchers found that ventures receiving such help "had higher than expected rates of survival, growth, and innovation." The online exercise "How Entrepreneurs Turn Less into More," on Connect is a great place to start.

ALTERNATIVES TO A FORMAL BOARD

The use of advisors and quasi-boards can be a useful alternative to having a formal board of directors—assuming a board is not legally required.[26] A board of advisors—which may complement a board of directors—is designed to dispense advice, rather than make decisions, and therefore advisors are not exposed to personal liability. A firm can solicit objective observations and feedback from these advisors. Such informal boards can bring needed expertise without the legal entanglements and formalities of a regular board. Also, the possible embarrassment of having to remove someone who is not serving a useful role can be avoided. Informal advisors are usually much less expensive, with honorariums of $500 to $1000 per meeting common. Remember, however, the level of involvement of these advisors probably will be less than that of members of a formal board. The firm also does not enjoy the protection of law, which defines the obligations and responsibilities of members of a formal board.

An informal group of advisors can also be a good mechanism through which a new venture can observe a number of people in action and select one or two as regular directors. The entrepreneur gains the advantages of counsel and advice from outsiders without being legally bound by their decisions.

LEGAL COUNSEL

The Decision

Nearly all companies need and use the services of lawyers, and newly created ventures perhaps more than most. Since it is critical that entrepreneurs fully understand the legal aspects of any decisions and agreements they make, they should never completely outsource that responsibility to their lawyer. Leslie Charm, a partner in the firm Youngman & Charm, put it this way, "You must understand the meaning of any document you're considering as well as your attorneys do. That's because at the end of the day, when you close that deal, you are the one who has to live with it, not your lawyers." In addition, Charm noted that lawyers should be viewed as teachers and advisors; use them to explain legalese and to articulate risk and ramifications, and in negotiations, use them to push to close the deal.

Various authors describe the importance of choosing and managing legal counsel. By following some legal basics and acquiring appropriate legal services, companies can achieve better legal health, including fewer problems and lower costs over the long term.[27] Some of the legal work can be done by entrepreneurs who do not have law degrees by using self-help legal guides and pre-printed forms. However, one should not rely exclusively on these materials. Factors to consider in choosing a lawyer include availability, comfort level with the lawyer, experience level and appropriateness to the task, cost, and whether or not the lawyer knows the industry and has connections to investors and venture capital.

Just how lawyers are used by entrepreneurial ventures depends on the needs of the venture at its particular stage. Size is also a factor. As company size increases, so does the need for advice in such areas as liability, mergers, and benefit plans. Contracts and agreements were almost uniformly the predominant use by entrepreneurs, regardless of the venture's size.

Entrepreneurs will most likely need to get assistance with the following areas of the law:

- *Incorporation.* Issues such as the forgivable and non-forgivable liabilities of founders, officers, and directors or the form of organization chosen for a new venture are important. As tax laws and other circumstances change, they are important for more established firms as well. How important this area can be is illustrated by the case of a founder who nearly lost control of his company as a result of the legal manoeuvring of the clerk and another shareholder. The clerk and the shareholder controlled votes on the board of directors, while the founder had controlling interest in the shares of the company. The shareholder tried to call a directors' meeting and not re-elect the founder president. The founder found out about the plot and adroitly called a shareholders' meeting to remove the directors first.

- *Franchising and licensing.* Innumerable issues concerning future rights, obligations, and what happens in the event of non-performance by either a franchisee or lessee or a franchisor or lessor require specialized legal advice.

- *Contracts and agreements.* Firms need assistance with contracts, licences, leases, and other such agreements such as non-compete employment agreements and those governing the vesting rights of shareholders.

- *Formal litigation, liability protection, and so on.* In today's litigious climate, sooner or later most entrepreneurs will find themselves as defendants in lawsuits and require counsel.

- *Real estate, insurance, and other matters.* It is hard to imagine an entrepreneur who, at one time or another, will not be involved in various kinds of real estate transactions, from rentals to the purchase and sale of property, which require the services of a lawyer.

- *Copyrights, trademarks, patents, and intellectual property protection.* Products are hard to protect. But pushing ahead with product development before ample protection from the law is provided can be expedient in the short term but disastrous in the long term. For example, an entrepreneur—facing the loss of a $2.5-million sale of his business and uncollected fees of over $200 000 if his software was not protected—obtained an expert on the sale, leasing, and licensing of software products. The lawyer devised subtle but powerful protections, such as internal clocks in the software that shut down the software if they were not changed.

- *Employee plans.* Benefit and share ownership plans have become complicated to use effectively and to administer. They require the special know-how of lawyers to avoid common pitfalls.

- *Tax planning and review.* Too frequently the tail of the accountant's tax avoidance advice wags the dog of good business sense. Entrepreneurs who worry more about finding good opportunities to make money than about finding tax shelters are infinitely better off.

- *Federal, provincial, and other regulations and reports.* Understanding the impact of and complying with regulations often is not easy. Violations of federal, provincial, and other regulations often can have serious consequences.

- *Mergers and acquisitions.* Specialized legal knowledge is required when buying or selling a company. Unless an entrepreneur is highly experienced and has highly qualified legal advisors in these transactions, he or she can either lose the deal or end up having to live with legal obligations that can be costly.

- *Bankruptcy law.* Many people have heard tales of entrepreneurs who did not make deposits to pay various federal and provincial taxes in order to use that cash in their business. These entrepreneurs perhaps falsely assumed that if their companies went bankrupt, the government was out of luck, just like the banks and other creditors. They were wrong. The owners, officers, and often the directors are held personally liable for those obligations.

- *Other matters.* These matters can range from assistance with collecting delinquent accounts to labour relations.

- *Personal needs.* As entrepreneurs accumulate net worth (i.e., property and other assets), legal advice in estate, tax, and financial planning is important.

Selection Criteria: Add Value with Know-How and Contacts

In a survey of the factors that enter into the selection of a law firm or a lawyer, 54 percent of the respondents said personal contact with a member of the firm was the main factor.[28] Reputation was a factor for 40 percent, and a prior relationship with the firm for 26 percent. Equally revealing was the fact that fees were mentioned by only 3 percent.

Many areas of the country have lawyers who specialize in new ventures and in firms with higher growth potential. The best place to start in selecting a lawyer is with acquaintances of the lead entrepreneur, of members of the venture team, or of directors. Recommendations from accountants, bankers, and associates also are useful. Other sources are partners in venture capital firms, partners of a leading accounting firm (those who specialize in privately owned and emerging companies), or a provincial bar association. To be effective, a lawyer needs to have the experience and expertise to deal with specific issues facing a new venture. Hooking up with the vast resources of a large law firm or national accounting firm may be beneficial, but we do not necessarily advise that strategy. You can usually get reasonable tax or estate-planning advice from a big law firm merely by picking up a telephone. The trade-off is that, if you are a small company and they have a dozen General Electrics as clients, you may get short shrift. One- or two-person firms can have an excellent network of specialists to refer to for problems outside their bailiwick. Use the specialist when you have to.[29]

As with members of the venture team, directors, and investors, the chemistry also is important. Finally, it is sound advice to expect to get what you pay for and to be highly selective. It is also important to realize that lawyers are not leaders of entrepreneurial enterprises and that they do not usually make business judgments. Rather, they seek to provide perfect or fail-safe legal protection.

Most lawyers are paid on an hourly basis. Retainers and flat fees are sometimes paid, usually by larger ventures. The amount an enterprise pays for legal services expectedly rises as the firm grows. Many law firms will agree to defer charges or initially to provide services at a lower than normal rate to obtain a firm's business. According to Michael Dunleavy of LaBarge Weinstein, it is a good sign if your lawyer will defer payment until the venture is thriving. If your lawyer wants fees paid up front or charges market rates, it is a sign that he or she is not very confident in your start-up's viability.

BANKERS AND OTHER LENDERS

The Decision

Deciding whether to have a banker or another lender usually involves decisions about how to finance certain needs. Most companies will need the services of a banker or other lender at some time. The decision also can involve how a banker or other lender can serve as an advisor.

As with other advisors, the banker or other lender needs to be a partner, not a difficult minority shareholder. First and foremost, therefore, an entrepreneur should carefully pick the right banker or lender rather than just pick a bank or a financial institution, although picking the bank or institution is also important. Different bankers and lenders have reputations ranging from "excellent" to "just OK" to "not OK" in how they work with start-ups and growing enterprises. Their institutions also have reputations for how well they work with entrepreneurial companies. Ideally, an entrepreneur needs an excellent banker or lender with an excellent financial institution, although an excellent banker or lender with a just OK institution is preferable to a just OK banker or lender with an excellent institution.

For an entrepreneur to know clearly what he or she needs from a lender is an important starting point. Some will have needs that are asset-based, such as money for equipment, facilities, or inventory. Others may need working capital to fund short-term operations.

Having a business plan is invaluable preparation for selecting and working with a lender. Also, because a banker or other lender is a "partner," it is important to invite him or her to see the company in operation, to avoid late financial statements (as well as late payments and overdrafts), and to be honest and straightforward in sharing information—even if it is bad news.

Selection Criteria: Add Value with Know-How and Contacts

Bankers and other lenders are known to other entrepreneurs, lawyers, accountants, and venture capitalists. Starting with their recommendations is ideal. From among four to seven or so possibilities, an entrepreneur will find the right lender and the right institution.

Today's banking and financial services marketplace is much more competitive than in the past. There are more choices, and it is worth the time and effort to shop around.

ACCOUNTANTS

The Decision

The accounting profession has come a long way from the "green eyeshades" stereotype one hears reference to occasionally. Today, virtually all the larger accounting firms have discovered the enormous client potential of new and entrepreneurial ventures, and a significant part of their business strategy is to cater specifically to these firms.

Accountants often are maligned, especially after the fallout of ethical scandals. The activities that accountants engage in have grown and no longer consist of solely counting numbers.[30] Accountants who are experienced as advisors to emerging companies can provide valuable services in addition to audits and taxation advice. An experienced general business advisor can be invaluable when helping to evaluate strategy, raising debt and equity capital, facilitating mergers and acquisitions, locating directors, and even balancing business decisions with important personal needs and goals. In fact, when Prescott Ensign's wife was launching a venture her accountant advised her on much more than the simple tax questions she initially inquired about. She was given advice on partnership arrangements (and why they often do not work), incorporation, cross-border shipping, and monitoring expenses and cash flow. Accountants and others may not have "lived it"—but their second-hand experience relayed by a multitude of clients may cut across industries and stages of the venture's lifecycle.

Selection Criteria: Add Value with Know-How and Contacts

In selecting accountants, the first step is for the venture to decide whether to go with a smaller local firm, a regional firm, or one of the major accounting firms. Although each company should make its own decision, many entrepreneurs prefer working with smaller regional accounting firms, because of lower costs and better personal attention.[31] In deciding on an accountant, you will need to address several factors:[32]

- *Service*. The levels of service offered and the attention likely to be provided need to be evaluated. Chances are, for most start-ups, both will be higher in a small firm than a large one. But if an entrepreneur of a higher potential firm seeking venture capital or a strategic partner has aspirations to go public, a national firm is a good place to start.

- *Needs*. Needs, both current and future, have to be weighed against the capabilities of the firm. Larger firms are more equipped to handle highly complex or technical problems, while smaller firms may be preferable for general advice and assistance because the principals are more likely to be involved in handling the account. In most instances, those companies in the early stages of planning or that do not plan to go public do not require a top-tier accounting firm. However, one exception to this might be those start-ups that are able to attract formal venture capital funds from day one.[33]

- *Cost*. Most major firms will offer cost-competitive services to start-ups with significant growth and profit potential. If a venture needs the attention of a partner in a larger firm, services of the larger firm are more expensive. However, if the firm requires extensive technical knowledge, a larger firm may have more experience and therefore be cheaper. Many early-growth phase companies are not able to afford to hire a leading national accounting firm and therefore a smaller local firm is best. However, these firms should tell you when you are ready to move on to a larger firm that provides more extensive services.[34]

- *Chemistry*. Rapport and personal interaction are always important considerations.

The recent trend in the accounting market has led to increased competition, spiralling capital costs, declining profit margins, and an increase in lawsuits.[35] Entrepreneurs should shop around in such a buyer's market for competent accountants who provide the most suitable and appropriate services. Sources of reference for good lawyers are also sources of reference for accountants; trade groups may also provide recommendations.

Once a firm has reached any significant size it will have many choices. The founders of one firm, which had grown to about $5 million in sales and had a strong potential to reach $20 million in sales in the next five years and eventually go public, put together a brief summary of the firm, including its background and track record, and a statement of needs for both banking and accounting services. The founders were startled by the aggressive response they received from several banks and major accounting firms.

The accounting profession is straightforward enough. Whether the accounting firm is small or large, it sells time, usually by the hour.

CONSULTANTS

The Decision[36]

Consultants are hired to solve particular problems and to fill gaps not filled by the venture team. There are many skilled consultants who can be of invaluable assistance and are a great source of "other people's resources." Advice needed can be quite technical and specific or general and far-ranging. Problems and needs also vary widely, depending upon whether the venture is just starting or is an existing business.

Start-ups usually require help with critical onetime tasks and decisions that will have lasting impact on the business. Consultants are employed by start-ups for the following reasons:

✔ to compensate for a lower level of professional experience

✔ to target a wide market segment (possibly to do market research)

✔ to undertake projects that require a large start-up investment in equipment[37]

These tasks and decisions might include assessing business sites, evaluating lease and rental agreements, setting up record and bookkeeping systems, finding business partners, obtaining start-up capital, and formulating initial marketing plans.

Existing businesses face ongoing issues resulting from growth. Many of these issues are so specialized that rarely is the expertise available within the venture team. Issues of obtaining market research, evaluating when and how to go about computerizing business tasks, deciding whether to lease or buy major pieces of equipment, and determining whether to change inventory valuation methods can be involved.

While it is not always possible to pinpoint the exact nature of a problem, sometimes a fresh, outside view helps when a new venture tries to determine the broad nature of its concern, such as whether it involves a personnel problem, manufacturing problem, or marketing problem.

Karl Bayer, of Germany's Institute for Systems and Innovation Research, reported that the use of consultants had a negative effect on sales three to five years later. Additionally, his research found that "the work delivered by the consultants...[was] inadequate for the task."[38] He suggests that the entrepreneur can most likely find and adequately prepare a consultant so that gaps are filled and the firm benefits in the long run, but it takes diligence.

Selection Criteria: Add Value with Know-How and Contacts

Unfortunately, nowhere are the options so numerous, the quality so variable, and the costs so unpredictable as in the area of consulting. The number of people calling themselves consultants is large and growing steadily. More than half the consultants were found to work on their own, while the remainder work for firms. In addition, government agencies employ consultants to work with businesses; various private and non-profit organizations provide assistance to entrepreneurs; and others, such as professors, engineers, and so forth, provide consulting services part time. Such assistance also may be provided by other professionals, such as accountants and bankers. A new and vital arena concerns Web presence. For example, Couple of Chicks e-marketing provides Internet marketing, distribution, and revenue measurement. The "chicks," Alicia Whalen of St. Catharines, Ontario, and Patricia Brusha of Mississauga, Ontario, use their expertise in search engine strategies and online metrics to boost website performance.

The right rapport is critical in selecting consultants. One company president who was asked what he had learned from talking to clients of the consultant he finally hired said, "They couldn't really pinpoint one thing, but they all said they would not consider starting and growing a company without him!"

As unwieldy and risky as the consulting situation might appear, there are ways of limiting the choices. Consultants tend to have specialties; while some consultants claim wide expertise, most will indicate the kinds of situations they feel most comfortable with and skilful in handling. In seeking a consultant, consider the following:[39]

- ✔ Good consultants are not geographically bound; they will travel and can work via electronic means.
- ✔ The best referral system is word of mouth. This point cannot be stressed enough.
- ✔ Always check references carefully. It is important to look at the past solutions consultants have utilized.
- ✔ People skills are essential and therefore should be assessed when interviewing a consultant.
- ✔ Ask about professional affiliations and call them to verify the person is in good standing.

Three or more potential consultants can be interviewed about their expertise and approach and their references checked. Candidates who pass this initial screening then can be asked to prepare specific proposals.

A written agreement, specifying the consultant's responsibilities and objectives of the assignment, the length of time the project will take, and the type and amount of compensation, is highly recommended. Some consultants work on an hourly basis, some on a fixed-fee basis, and some on a retainer-fee basis. Huge variations in consulting costs for the same services exist. At one end of the spectrum are government agencies, which provide consultants to small businesses without charge. At the other end of the spectrum are well-known consulting firms that may charge large amounts for minimal marketing studies or technical feasibility analysis.

While the quality of many products roughly correlates with their price, this is not so with consulting services. It is difficult to judge consultants solely on the basis of the fees they charge.

FINANCIAL RESOURCES   LO4

ANALYZING FINANCIAL REQUIREMENTS

Once the opportunity has been assessed, once a new venture team has been formed, and once all resource needs have been identified, then is the time for a new venture to evaluate what financial resources are required and when. 6N Silicon Inc., which "makes silicon that can be combined with scrap from the chip manufacturing industry to make crystalline silicon,"[42] was able to obtain federal funding from Sustainable Development Technology Canada and get money from Ontario's Innovation Demonstration Fund. Founded in 2006, 6N raised $6 million in its first round of venture funding in July 2007, $20 million in second-round funding in April 2008, and in early 2009 another $5 million was found for equipment lease financing. In 2010 6N Silicon was acquired by Calisolar, itself founded in 2006. The company's name was changed to Silicor Materials in 2012, and the company expanded that year as well as in 2013.

As has been noted before, there is a temptation to place the cart before the horse. Entrepreneurs are tempted to begin their evaluation of business opportunities—and particularly their thinking about formal business plans—by analyzing spreadsheets, rather than focusing first on defining the opportunity, deciding how to seize it, and then preparing the financial estimates of what is required.

However, when the time comes to analyze financial requirements, it is important to realize that cash is the lifeblood of a venture. As James Stancill of the University of Southern California, has said: "Any company, no matter how big or small, moves on cash, not profits. You can't pay bills with profits, only cash. You can't pay employees with profits, only cash."[41] Financial resources are almost always limited, and important and significant trade-offs need to be made in evaluating a company's needs and the timing of those needs.

Spreadsheets

Computers and spreadsheet programs are tools that save time and increase productivity and creativity enormously. Spreadsheets are nothing more than pieces of accounting paper adapted for use with a computer.

The origins of the first spreadsheet program, VisiCalc, reveal its relevance for entrepreneurs. It was devised by business school student Dan Bricklin. Faced with analyzing pro forma income statements and balance sheets, cash flows, and breakevens for his cases, he was asked the question: "What if you assumed such and such?"

The major advantage of using spreadsheets to analyze capital requirements is having the ability to quickly examine different scenarios. This takes on particular relevance also when one considers, as James Stancill points out, "Usual measures of cash flow—net income plus depreciation (NIPD) or earnings before interest and taxes (EBIT)—give a realistic indication of a company's cash position only during a period of steady sales."[42]

Take cash flow projections, for example. An entrepreneur could answer a question such as, What if sales grow at just 5 percent, instead of 15 percent, and what if only 50 percent, instead of 65 percent, of amounts billed are paid in 30 days? The impact on cash flow of changes in these projections can be seen.

The same what-if process also can be applied to pro forma income statements and balance sheets, budgeting, and breakeven calculations. To illustrate, by altering assumptions about revenues and costs such that cash reaches zero, breakeven can be analyzed. Thus, for example, return merchandise authorization (RMA) assumptions could be used as comparative boundaries for testing assumptions about a venture.

An example of how computer-based analysis can be of enormous value is the experience of a colleague who was seriously considering starting a new publishing venture. His analysis of the opportunity was encouraging, and important factors such as relevant experience and commitment by the lead entrepreneur were there. Assumptions about fixed and variable costs, market estimates, and probable start-up resource requirements had also been assembled. What needed to be done next was to generate detailed monthly cash flows to determine more precisely the economic character of the venture, including the impact of the quite seasonal nature of the business, and to determine the amount of money needed to launch the business and the amount and timing of potential rewards. In less than three hours, the assumptions about revenues and expenditures associated with the start-up were entered into a computer model. Within another two hours, he was able to see what the venture would look like financially over the first 18 months and then to see the impact of several different what-if scenarios. The net result was that the new venture idea was abandoned because the amount of money required appeared to outweigh the potential.

The strength of computer-based analysis is also a source of problems for entrepreneurs who place the "druther" before the fact. As the quote from Yzerman at the start of the chapter makes clear, with so many moving parts, analysis that is not grounded in sound perceptions about an opportunity is most likely to be confused.

INTERNET IMPACT: RESOURCES

EXTENDING YOUR NETWORK

An entrepreneur can greatly increase his or her reach for resources via the Internet. The Web offers a platform for which many tools are available (e.g., LinkedIn, Xing, Yahoo! Kickstart, Plaxo, Jigsaw, and Spoke). Nick Bontis was the Chief Knowledge Officer of Knexa, founded as an online auction for knowledge. Knexa evolved to provide knowledge exchange tools. Online groups and bulletin boards might also be a source for answers to challenges new ventures and their leaders face. And if you are short of ideas, check out Springwise.com, which "scans the globe for the most promising business ventures, ideas, and concepts."[43] Springwise is the brainchild of Reiner Evers, the creator of Trendwatching.com, a site devoted to spotting and tracking "the most promising consumer trends, insights, and related hands-on business ideas."[44]

In addition to intellectual resources the Web provides access to physical and financial assets (e.g., VenCorps, Alibaba, and Tradekey). Whether sourcing capital or equipment, just about anything can be found with some patience and a systematic search. Whether opening a restaurant or a carwash, used appliances and tools can readily be found. It is now even possible to pitch your idea and broadcast it on the Internet (e.g., Under the Radar).

FUNDRAISING FOR NONPROFITS

A dynamic online service model has emerged that is changing the way nonprofits conduct their fundraising auctions. Charity auctions, which account for millions of dollars in charitable giving in Canada, often attract high-income individuals and freely donated, high-quality items. But coordinating and staffing those venues has always been a challenge, particularly since volunteer turnover requires the retraining of a majority of the workforce each time an auction is held. In addition, physical auctions are typically catered affairs that are attended by only a small percentage of an organization's support base. Tom Williams of Victoria, British Columbia, has started GiveMeaning.com, a site that hosts fundraising pages and serves as a system for charities seeking support and those wishing to make online donations. CanadaHelps.org is a donation portal for 83 000 charities that can be browsed under a number of categories. It was created in 2000 by Queen's University students Matthew Choi, Ryan Little, and Aaron Pereira to help charities reduce overhead costs. Since its inception it has facilitated $60 million in donations.

LEARNING OBJECTIVES SUMMARY

LO1 Successful entrepreneurs use ingenious approaches to marshal and minimize resources.

LO2 Control of resources rather than ownership of resources is the key to a "less is more" resource strategy. Entrepreneurs are also creative in identifying other people's money and resources, thereby spreading and sharing the risks.

LO3 Building a brain trust of the right mentors, advisors, and coaches is one of the entrepreneur's most valuable "secret weapons." Selecting outside advisors, directors, and other professionals boils down to one key criterion: Do they add value through their know-how and networks?

LO4 Today, access to financial and non-financial resources is greater than ever before and is increasing because of the Internet.

STUDY QUESTIONS

1. Entrepreneurs think and act ingeniously when it comes to resources. What does this mean and why is it so important?
2. Describe at least two creative bootstrapping examples you know of.

3. In selecting outside advisors, a board, consultants, and others, what are the most important criteria, and why?

MIND STRETCHERS *Have you considered?*

1. Many successful entrepreneurs and private investors say it is just as bad to start out with too much money as it is too little. Why is this so? Can you find some examples?
2. It is said that money is the least important part of the resource equation and of the entrepreneurial process. Why is this so?

3. Within the first six months of start-up, which strategies will enable the entrepreneur to conserve cash and stretch resources?

Building a cadre of mentors, advisors, coaches, and directors can be the difference between success and failure in a venture. Building this brain trust will require your professionalism, thoroughness, salesmanship, and tenacity. You gain the trust and confidence of these mentors through your performance and integrity.

This exercise is intended to provide a framework and key steps in thinking through your requirements and developing a brain trust for your ventures.

Part I: Gap and Fit Analysis vis-à-vis the Timmons Model

1. At each phase of development of a venture, different know-how and access to experience, expertise, and judgment external to the founding team are often required. A key risk-reward management tool is the gap and fit analysis using the model.
   - Who has access to key know-how and resources that we do not?
   - What is missing that we have to have to obtain a very good chance?
   - Who can add the most value, insights, and solid experience to the venture now and in the next two years and how?
   - Who are the smartest, most insightful people given what we are trying to do?
   - Who has the most valuable perspective and networks that could help the venture or in an area that you know least about?

2. Break down the Timmons Model to focus on each dimension.
   - Core opportunity: If they are not on your team now, who are the people who know more than anyone else on the planet about: the revenue and cost model, and underlying drivers and assumptions; how to price, get sales, marketing, customer service, and distribution; IT and e-business; the competition; the free cash flow characteristics and economics of the business?
   - Resources: Who can help you get the necessary knowledge of and access to people, networks, money, and key talent?
   - Team: Who has 10 to 20 years more experience and scar tissue than you do in building a venture from ground zero?

   - Context: Who understands the context, changes, and timing of the venture in terms of the capital markets, any key regulatory requirements, and the internal drivers of the industry/technology/market?

3. Conclusions: What and who can make the biggest difference in the venture? Usually just one to three key people or resources can make a huge difference.

Part II: Identify and Build the Brain Trust

1. Once you've figured out what and who can make the greatest difference, you need to arrange for an introduction. Faculty, family, friends, roommates, and the like are good places to start.

2. If you can't get the introductions, then you have to go with your wits and creativity to get a personal meeting.
   - Be highly prepared and articulate.
   - Send an executive summary and advance agenda.
   - Know the reasons and benefits that will be most appealing to this person.
   - Follow up and follow through: send a handwritten note, not just another email.

3. Ask for blunt and direct feedback to such questions as:
   - What have we missed here? What flaws do you see in our team, our marketing plan, our financial requirements, our strategy, etc.?
   - Are there competitors we don't know about?
   - How would you compete with me?
   - Who would reject and accept us for an investment? Why?
   - Who have we missed?
   - Who else should we talk with?

You will gain significant insight into yourself and your venture, as well as how knowledgeable and insightful the potential brain trust member is about your business, from the questions he or she asks, and from your own. You will soon know whether the person is interested and can add value.

4. Grow the brain trust to grow the venture. Think two years ahead and add to the brain trust people who have already navigated the difficult waters you expect to travel.

IVEY | Publishing

Preparation Questions

1. What business model does ExerciseApp compete on in the marketplace? What decision criteria does Bowen face to find customers, markets and revenues, while constraining company costs?

2. What features should they design? Create a list.

3. What does Bowen need to do to set up the company ExerciseApp, including regulations? What management team does he need?

4. How much money does he need for the first year? When will his funding run out? Where does he get more funding?

Randy Bowen, chief executive officer (CEO) and founder of ExerciseApp,[1] decided to take the plunge and spec out the features for his new iPhone mobile application and supporting website. Bowen planned for ExerciseApp to download exercise workouts from professional (pro) athletes to followers who wanted to "Train. Play. Be. Like the Pros" and get an edge on their workouts. As Bowen envisioned the application, he realized he would need a lot of help to tackle the technology and the setup of this entrepreneurial venture in order to successfully bring it to market. With just enough funding to last the next eight months, Bowen had to prepare himself for the coming launch of ExerciseApp, hoping to attract additional funding in the process.

RANDY BOWEN AND THE CREATION OF EXERCISEAPP

Bowen always knew he wanted to start a venture and had invested much time over the past few years networking with other entrepreneurs and investors, while brainstorming potential business ideas. His past experience in launching businesses, including a mobile and online trading platform, had equipped him with some understanding of what a venture needed to succeed.

As an amateur athlete and competitive swimmer, Bowen attended sports camps when he was younger and had been mentored by professional athletes. Bowen realized the value of having his favourite athletes motivating him. Out of all the existing fitness applications, none catered to the needs of amateur athletes who were looking to supplement current coaching and workout plans. Bowen believed many amateurs wanted to be like their favourite professional athletes—to be like them, they had to train like them.

ExerciseApp was not Bowen's only idea, but he knew he had limited resources. He began with only his credit cards and a Cdn$20 000[2] line of credit. Bowen was able to convince his friend Tim Smith,[3] an all-star defenseman in the National Lacrosse League and a Mann Cup Champion, to be his first athlete. Smith then helped attract other athletes. Armed with letters of intent and sample videos from these athletes who were willing to develop content and beta test the platform, Bowen approached some of the investors he had met while networking and brought on an additional $25 000 in seed money. Only with these actual tangible results was Bowen able to work on closing larger amounts of funding and pursue government funding such as the Business Development Bank[4] and NRC-IRAP.[5]

THE BUSINESS MODEL

Bowen found a niche by focusing on amateur athletes' desire to be like their favourite professional athletes. He also knew that a tool for professional athletes to interact with their fan-bases would be very valuable to the pros. This application would enable these pro athletes to grow and monetize their fan-bases, while extending their careers past their active professional em-

[1] This general experience case is disguised.

[2] All funds are in Canadian dollars unless specified otherwise.

[3] Fictitious name

[4] The Business Development Bank of Canada (BDC) is a financial institution owned by the government of Canada with the mandate to finance qualified growing small and medium sized businesses in Canada. The BDC offers a range of financing options, but generally require at least twelve months of sales to qualify. http://www.bdc.ca

[5] National Research Council of Canada's (NRC) Industrial Research Assistance Program (IRAP) provides funding and other services to small and medium-sized businesses in Canada to be invested into technology innovation. Factors evaluated include the company's and management's ability to achieve the result proposed and their plan with the developed technology. http://www.nrc-cnrc.gc.ca/eng/irap/services/financial_assistance.html

ployment. They could maintain the relevance of their brands and maximize the value they extracted from fans while playing. The use of elite professional athletes who connected directly with their followers in a unique way would be very hard for competitors to easily copy. ExerciseApp gained first mover advantage and benefited from an innovative spirit that would be important in maintaining this leading position. Bowen could also leverage the brand of the athletes to attract users, turning the pros into the application's marketing engines.

Bowen designed the application to attract the athletes' fans and engage them through free workout samples. The fans had to pay $3 for a complete 40-minute session that they would then own and could access as many times as they liked. This price was a premium relative to alternatives, but Bowen believed using professional athletes to guide users through workouts justified the inflated price. Of the $3, only approximately 30 per cent to 35 per cent was returned to ExerciseApp. A 30 per cent royalty had to go to the operating system developer. Bowen then provided a 5 per cent to 10 per cent royalty to agents and financial advisors who helped him bring pro-athletes on board. The remaining 30 per cent went to the athletes, creating almost an equal partnership between the athletes and ExerciseApp. The fans also had access to supporting materials, including blogs, links and advice from the athletes and were encouraged to rate the workout sessions through Twitter and Facebook.

If ExerciseApp was to be a success, co-creating exercise video content and website features with athletes would be critical. Bowen realized he did not know how many professional athletes he needed, in what order they would be needed, how much time each athlete would need to commit, or what tools he would need to provide for these athletes. These were questions Bowen had to answer. He understood the interdependence between the athletes' and fans' use of the application and the value both parties could derive from it, but that the time each athlete would need to commit would have to be minimized in order for the athletes to be willing to participate. Athlete time was very valuable and would be a high priority for feature creation.

Business Services Value Chain

Bowen learned about the concept of open services innovation and decided to include these ideas as a part of his ExerciseApp business model. Business services value chain included systems thinking that featured input-processing-output as central ideas in technology business models.

Bowen knew these concepts had to be part of his business decisions, including how he would structure the organization and what internal systems he would put into place.

Primary concepts of applying Open Services[6] thinking included positioning ExerciseApp to its customer as a "service-oriented" technology business, rather than a more traditional "product-oriented" technology business. In their delivery to customers, the services would wrap around the products and technologies. Other significant concepts included defining parts of a product and services ecosystem that saw partners, content experts, and collaborators working together in developing iterations of the technology. This ecosystem of co-creation had appealing resources and skills ExerciseApp could employ in a pilot or at full launch.

Bowen would need to define both customer and supplier co-creation processes to ensure successful retention and growth. He realized these co-creation processes were quite similar (see Exhibit 1). The customer co-creation ideas follow Chesbrough's co-creation techniques and the service usage experiences need to describe the user's workout experience points. The main suppliers to Bowen's business were athletes providing workout videos and social media content delivered to their followers. Asynchronous and live synchronized workouts would offer great flexibility to athletes and improved excitement for customers. Bowen also had to consider that other suppliers, including gyms, filming companies, testers and testing sites, and other potential customer groups, would impact his services value chain ecosystem.

TECHNOLOGY STRUCTURING

As Bowen pictured the usage scenarios in his mind (see Exhibit 2), he defined many of his wants and needs, but also understood he did not have all the necessary technological knowledge. The usage scenarios would need to be translated into use cases, a potential task for his IT team. He would certainly need to be available for questions as Bowen had to ensure ExerciseApp provided a good experience for both the athletes and fans. In order to bring these elements together, Bowen had to form an agile team to develop quickly and create a testable user experience with the limited time and funds available.

As CEO, Bowen managed all support and business development functions, including finance, human resources and sales. He brought together a small, yet highly entrepreneurial team with diverse skillsets, relying primarily on equity for remuneration. Bowen knew he had

[6] Henry Chesbrough, *Open Services Innovation: Rethinking Your Business to Grow and Compete in a New Era*, Jossey-Bass, A Wiley Imprint, San Francisco, 2011, Chapter 2, Figure 2.2 Open Services Value Chain, p. 35.

FAST FEATURES: CO-CREATING SYSTEMS IN FAST-PACED WORK PLACES

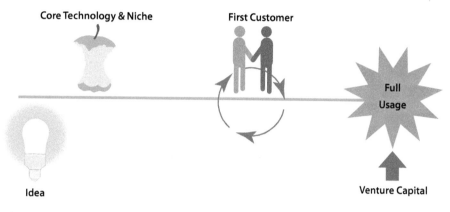

Core Technology & Niche

First Customer

Full Usage

Idea

Venture Capital

© 2012 Barbara L Marcolin

Source: Barbara L. Marcolin, 2012.

USE SCENARIOS

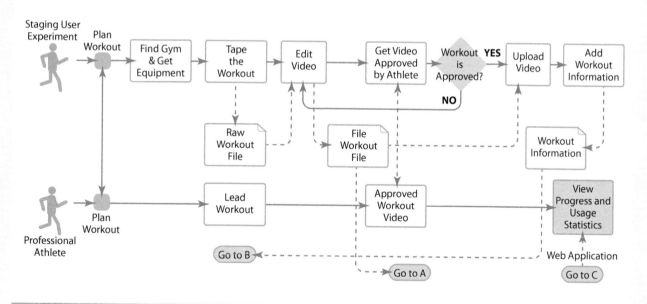

to be cautious to ensure the equity was effectively managed to maintain enough for future investors, while maintaining his controlling interest. He brought on two of the top 100 iPhone developers in the world, but still needed a CTO, a research director, a manager for professional athletes and a network operator to prepare for growth. Bowen had already had to release a few contract-based employees who did not have the necessary skillsets.

Bowen had to decide how he would merge the agile development process used by the developers with the customer and supplier co-creation processes. He also had to set up the development group roles and responsibilities, and create the supporting agile development toolkits to ensure code was produced quickly in sprints and modules.

With only two developers at his side, Bowen tentatively began with the iPhone architecture for the mobile platform

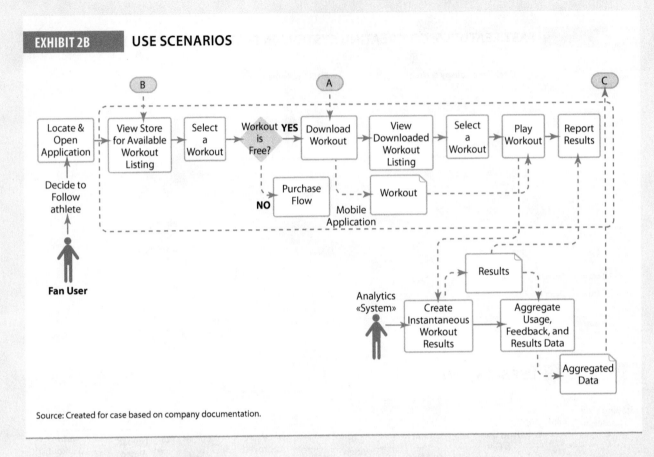

Source: Created for case based on company documentation.

to complement the web-based platform. Based on the success of the iPhone application, Bowen and his team would choose if and when to launch on Google's Android and RIM's BlackBerry platforms. Bowen remained unsure about how many IT platforms they could create at once. If they could not create all, he would have to decide on the order.

The Mobile Architecture

While many of iPhone's and Android's specifications were similar, Apple's iOS was developed in Objective-C and XCode, while the Android application would need to be developed in Java (see Exhibit 3). While the supporting architectures could be shared, a different front-end would have to be developed for each platform. The first platform developed would take six months and $100 000, but then the second would only take four months and $60 000.

Supporting Website Architecture

The developers had already begun developing the supporting website architecture (see Exhibit 4) with MySQL databases, a leading open-source database recently purchased by Oracle, on Kumulos's servers, with a Gravity Labs Multimedia Server to store the videos. The website played a crucial

role as it would include the primary athlete content editing dashboard.

User Feature Selection

Bowen needed to quickly decide which features to build for the iPhone application. An entrepreneurship faculty member suggested the developers create all the technology, but Bowen was not certain about this strategy. His system development classes suggested methods for Bowen to identify these features and build business-focused roadmaps. With the help of a systems faculty member, Bowen began a process of defining these features. He realized there was no way the developers knew of all the features he had conceived of so far. To create all the specifications and systems needed, developers would have to define the architectures with operating systems, devices, basic standards and development toolkits. Bowen would need to create the advanced features and usage situation features he envisioned. The ideas of open services innovation drove him to outline the usage scenarios and service blueprints that mapped out the processes within the business's ecosystem.

Tension arose between the two developers and Bowen as the push for both an agile development method and systems

EXHIBIT 3	MOBILE ARCHITECTURE

	Apple IOS Devices	Google Android Devices
Application Framework	iOS v5.1	Android v4.0.1
	Objective-C	Java
Hardware	Communication: Wi-Fi and Cellular	Gyroscope & Accelerometer
Data Sources	MySQL Database Servers (Kumulos)	Multimedia Servers (Gravity Labs)

Source: Created for case based on company documentation

thinking began to take its toll. Bowen pushed for use of the fast features process, a process in which technology and feature options are continually matched and re-matched to the evolving needs of the customer and company's resources. The initial list of features was primarily determined by the developers because the majority of the initial work had to be focused on setting up the IT platform. Bowen now had to implement a process in which suppliers (i.e., professional athletes), management and development teams could all decide on the feature priorities and delivery schedule. He also had to decide when to bring real customers into this process.

Bowen knew it was not only critical to bring the application quickly to market but that the application also had to be exceptional. Early poor reviews and ratings would sink the business shortly after the launch and risk destroying the reputations of the professional athletes involved. Bowen believed fans would likely first download and use the application at home; only if the first experience was compelling enough would they then pay for workouts and actually use the application at the gym.

Performance Criteria

Bowen not only needed strict performance criteria to ensure an optimum user experience, but also had to collect and analyse data on usage measures for determining success metrics and where future improvements would be required (see Exhibit 5). With all this sensitive data being collected, Bowen had to consider its protection and security according to the laws and ethics councils. He had to define exactly what data he wanted to collect, how to analyse it and how to protect it.

Research Pilot

Once a testable application was developed, Bowen wanted to run a research pilot with delivery experts to test the integrated usage experience points in its entirety with sample polished video content, sample social media feeds, polished icons and graphics, workable and scalable telecommunications infrastructure, fun exercise events over a few weeks for about 30 people, website support material and the athlete video creation dashboard. In order to build a compelling

EXHIBIT 4	WEBSITE ARCHITECTURE

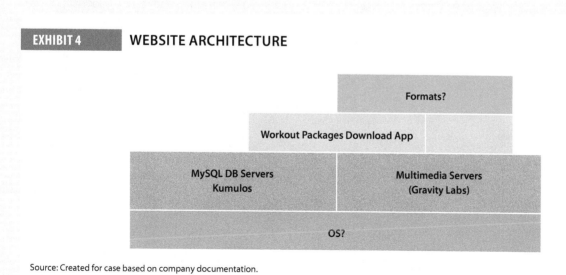

Source: Created for case based on company documentation.

opportunity to better understand the athletes and fans so he could uncover what truly motivated them to use ExerciseApp. Bowen's research questions surrounded business, usage, technical, co-creating processes and evidence-based outcomes (e.g., improved exercise, avoided harmful exercises, increased quality of exercise technique).

Bowen planned for the application to go through multiple levels of testing, from individual units and features, through to the multiple stages of the application as a whole. Bowen had to decide which features to include in the various stages of testing and who should be a part of these stages. Single testers could include Bowen himself, athletes, the research director, non-hostile potential customers, friends and family. Bowen realized, at later stages, he would need a larger and more objective sample.

ISSUES REALIZED ALONG THE WAY

Bowen faced a few issues with his original business plan that he had to resolve before launching. He discovered the iPhone handhelds posed problems when exercising—the user's hands were busy and it was not clear how they would modify the technology for that usage situation. Holders and wristbands were an acceptable stop-gap measure, but Bowen wanted to reach non-invasive technology as a part of the long-term platform roadmap. Bowen also realized he had underestimated how important the user experience for the athletes would be. He had to ensure they could easily upload and customize their workouts without having to commit too much of their valuable time.

As he sat in his office, Bowen began to lay out his remaining decisions. These included defining the structure of his team, outlining user features and roadmap for both the fans and the athletes, defining the plans for testing and proving the technology, orienting his developers and management team to the direction he wanted to take, finalizing his business, and locating more professional athletes, all while working in a cash-strapped environment while trying to raise more funding.

technology value proposition, Bowen would require this research data as evidence to devise the value statements, which then could be used to gain the confidence of users, athletes, customers and investors.

In designing the data collection during testing, Bowen had to decide what data to collect and what he wanted to learn from the data. This would include evaluating the functionality and processes of the software and effectiveness in improving users' exercise habits. He also needed to use this

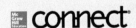

CHAPTER
9

FINANCING
THE VENTURE

Happiness to an entrepreneur is a positive cash flow.

FRED ADLER
Venture Capitalist

LEARNING OBJECTIVES

LO1 Describe critical issues in financing new ventures.

LO2 Differentiate entrepreneurial finance from conventional managerial or corporate finance.

LO3 Explain the process of crafting financial and fundraising strategies and identify the critical variables involved, including the financial life cycles of new ventures, a financial strategy framework, and investor preferences.

LO4 Describe the capital markets food chain and analyze its implications.

LO5 Identify informal investment sources of equity capital.

LO6 Evaluate the importance of vigilance in finding, contacting, and dealing with equity investors.

LO7 Explain how venture capital investors make decisions.

VENTURE FINANCING: THE ENTREPRENEUR'S ACHILLES' HEEL

There are three core principles of entrepreneurial finance: (1) more cash is preferred to less cash, (2) cash sooner is preferred to cash later, and (3) less-risky cash is preferred to more-risky cash. While these principles seem simple enough, entrepreneurs, chief executive officers, and division managers often seem to ignore them.[1] To these individuals, financial analysis seems intimidating, regardless of the size of the company. Even management teams, comfortable with the financial issues, may not be adept at linking strategic and financial decisions to their companies' challenges and choices. Dave Valliere of Ryerson University has shown that signalling plays an important role in valuation; the network of investors and entrepreneurs are constantly evaluating and being evaluated.[2]

FINANCIAL MANAGEMENT MYOPIA: IT CAN'T HAPPEN TO ME

Financial management myopia is a combination of self-delusion and just plain not understanding the complex dynamics and interplay between financial management and business strategy. Why is this so?

Getting Beyond "Collect Early, Pay Late"

During our many years as educators, authors, directors, founders, and investors in entrepreneurial companies, we have met a few thousand entrepreneurs and managers, company founders, presidents, and the chief executive officers of middle-market companies. By their own admission, they felt uniformly uncomfortable, if not downright intimidated and terrified, by their lack of expertise in financial analysis and its relationship to management and strategy. The vast majority of entrepreneurs and non-financial managers are disadvantaged. Beyond "collect early, pay late," there is precious little sophistication and an enormous level of discomfort when it comes to these complex and dynamic financial interrelationships. Even good managers who are revelling in major sales increases and profit increases often fail to realize until it is too late the impact increased sales have on the cash flow required to finance the increased receivables and inventory.

The Spreadsheet Mirage

It is hard to imagine any entrepreneur who would not want ready answers to many financial vigilance questions, such as those in Exhibit 9.1. Until now, however, getting the answers to these questions was a rarity. If the capacity and information are there to do the necessary analysis (and all too often they are not), it can take up to several weeks to get a response. In this era of spreadsheet mania, more often than not, the answers will come in the form of a lengthy report with innumerable scenarios, pages of numbers, backup exhibits, and possibly a presentation by a staff financial analyst, controller, or chief financial officer.

Too often the barrage of spreadsheet exhibits is really a mirage. What is missing? Traditional spreadsheets can only report and manipulate the data. The numbers may be there, the trends may be identified, but the connections and interdependencies between financial structure and business decisions inherent in key financial questions may be missed. As a result, gaining true insights and getting to creative alternatives and new solutions may be painfully slow, if not interminable. By themselves, spreadsheets cannot model the more complex financial and strategic interrelationships that entrepreneurs need to grasp. And for the board of directors, failure to get this information would be fatal and any delay would mean too little and too late. Such a weakness in financial know-how becomes life threatening for entrepreneurs when it comes to anticipating the financial and risk-reward consequences of their business decisions. During a financial crisis, such a weakness can make an already dismal situation worse.

To avoid financial management myopia, entrepreneurs need answers to questions that link strategic business decisions to financial plans and choices. The crux of it is anticipation: *What is most likely to happen? When? What can go right along the way? What can go wrong? What has to happen to achieve our business objectives and to increase or to preserve our options?* Financially savvy entrepreneurs know that such questions trigger a process that can lead to creative solutions to their financial challenges and problems. At a practical level, financially astute entrepreneurs and managers maintain vigilance over numerous key strategic and financial questions:

- What are the financial consequences and implications of crucial business decisions such as pricing, volume, and policy changes affecting the balance sheet, income statement, and cash flow? How will these change over time?
- How can we measure and monitor changes in our financial strategy and structure from a managerial, not just a GAAP, perspective?
- What does it mean to grow too fast in our industry? How fast can we grow without requiring outside debt or equity? How much capital is required if we increase or decrease our growth by X percent?
- What will happen to our cash flow, profitability, return on assets, and shareholder equity if we grow faster or slower by X percent?
- How much capital will this require? How much can be financed internally and how much will have to come from external sources? What is a reasonable mix of debt and equity?
- What if we are 20 percent less profitable than our plan calls for? Or 20 percent more profitable?
- What should be our focus and priorities? What are the cash flow and net income breakeven points for each of our product lines? For our company? For our business unit?
- What about our pricing, our volume, and our costs? How sensitive are our cash flow and net income to increases or decreases in price, variable costs, or volume? What price/volume mix will enable us to achieve the same cash flow and net income?
- How will these changes in pricing, costs, and volume affect our key financial ratios and how will we stack up against others in our industry? How will our lenders view this?
- At each stage—start-up, rapidly growing, stagnating, or mature company—how should we be thinking about these questions and issues?

Time and again, the financially fluent and skilful entrepreneurs push what would otherwise be an average company toward and even beyond the brink of greatness. Clearly, financially knowledgeable CEOs enjoy a secret competitive weapon that can yield a decisive edge over less financially astute entrepreneurs.

CRITICAL FINANCING ISSUES

Exhibit 9.2 illustrates the central issues in entrepreneurial finance. These include creating value, slicing and dividing the value pie among those who have a stake or have participated in the venture, and handling the risks inherent in the venture. Developing financing and fundraising strategies, knowing what alternatives are available, and obtaining funding are tasks vital to the survival and success of higher potential ventures.

Entrepreneurs face certain critical issues and problems that influence the financing of entrepreneurial ventures, such as:

- *Creating value.* For whom must value be created or added to achieve a positive cash flow and to develop harvest options?

- *Slicing the value pie.* How are deals, both for start-ups and for the purchases of existing ventures, structured and valued, and what are the critical tax consequences of different venture structures? What is the legal process and what are the key issues involved in raising outside risk capital?

- *Selling the idea.* How do entrepreneurs make effective presentations of their business plans to financing and other sources? What are some of the nastier pitfalls, minefields, and hazards that need to be anticipated, prepared for, and responded to? How critical and sensitive is timing in each of these areas?

- *Covering risk.* How much money is needed to start, acquire, or expand the business, and when, where, and how can it be obtained on acceptable terms? What sources of risk and venture capital financing—equity, debt, and other innovative types—are available, and how is appropriate financing negotiated and obtained?

- Who are the financial contacts and networks that need to be accessed and developed?

- How do successful entrepreneurs marshal the necessary financial resources and other financial equivalents to seize and execute opportunities, and what pitfalls do they manage to avoid, and how?

- Can a staged approach to resource acquisition mitigate risk and increase return?

A clear understanding of the financing requirements is especially vital for new and emerging companies because new ventures go through financial "hell" compared to existing firms, both

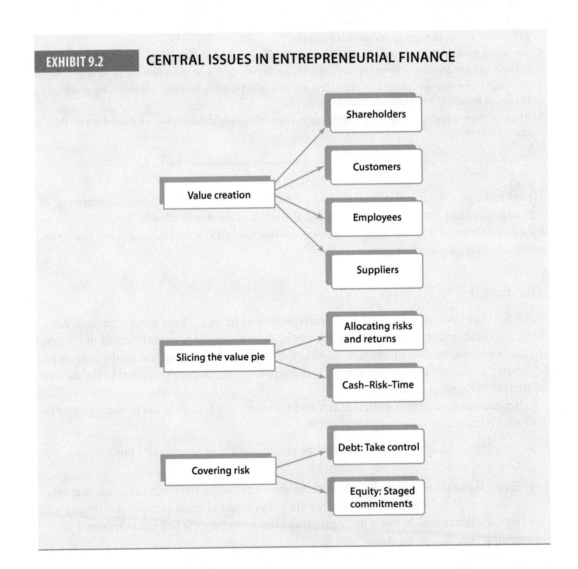

EXHIBIT 9.2   **CENTRAL ISSUES IN ENTREPRENEURIAL FINANCE**

smaller and larger, that have a customer base and revenue stream. In the early going, new firms are gluttons for capital, yet are usually not very debt-worthy. To make matters worse, the faster they grow, the more gluttonous is their appetite for cash.

This phenomenon is best illustrated in Exhibit 9.3 where loss as a percentage of initial equity is plotted against time.[3] The shaded area represents the cumulative cash flow of 157 companies from their inception. For these firms, it took 30 months to achieve operating breakeven and 75 months (or going into the seventh year) to recover the initial equity. As can be seen from the illustration, *cash goes out for a long time before it starts to come in*. This phenomenon is at the heart of the financing challenges facing new and emerging companies.

ENTREPRENEURIAL FINANCE: THE OWNER'S PERSPECTIVE   LO2

If an entrepreneur who has had responsibility for financing in a large established company and in a private emerging firm is asked whether there are differences between the two, the person asking will get an earful. While there is some common ground, there are both stark and subtle differences, both in theory and in practice, between entrepreneurial finance as practised in higher potential ventures and corporate or administrative finance, which usually occurs in larger, publicly traded companies. Further, there are important limits to some financial theories as applied to new ventures.

Students and practitioners of entrepreneurial finance have always been dubious about the reliability and relevance of much of so-called modern finance theory, including the capital asset pricing model (CAPM), beta, and so on.[4] Apparently, this skepticism is gaining support from a

| EXHIBIT 9.3 | INITIAL LOSSES BY SMALL NEW VENTURES |

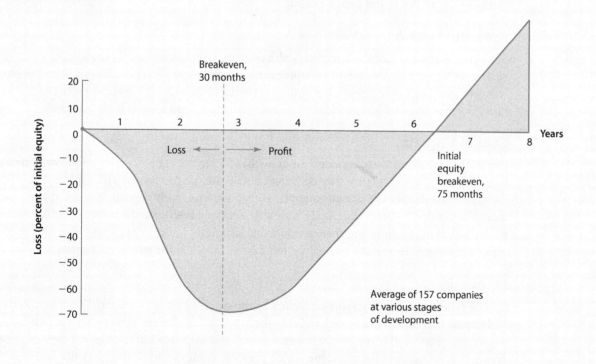

most surprising source, corporate finance theorists. As reported in a *Harvard Business Review* article by Nancy Nichols:

> One of the strongest attacks is coming from a man who helped launch modern finance, University of Chicago Professor Eugene Fama. His research has cast doubt on the validity of a widely used measure of stock volatility: beta. One group, however, eschews the scientific approach altogether, arguing that investors aren't always rational and that managers' constant focus on the markets is ruining corporate America. In their view, the highly fragmented U.S. financial markets do a poor job of allocating capital and keeping tabs on management.[5]

Continuing to challenge the basic assumptions of corporate finance, the author continued: "These three concepts, the efficient market hypothesis, portfolio theory, and CAPM, have had a profound impact on how the financial markets relate to the companies they seek to value....They have derailed and blessed countless investment projects."[6] Nichols concluded that "despite tidy theories, there may be no single answer in a global economy."[7]

It is especially noteworthy that even the most prestigious of modern finance theorists, prominent Nobel laureate Robert Merton of Harvard University, may have a lot to learn. His works and theories of finance were the basis for Long Term Capital Management, Inc. The total collapse of that firm in the late 1990s threatened to topple the entire financial system worldwide.

Acquiring knowledge of the limits of financial theories, of differences in the domain of entrepreneurial finance, and of understanding the implications is a core task for entrepreneurs. To begin to appreciate the character and flavour of these limits and differences, consider the following sampling.

Cash Flow and Cash

Cash flow and cash are the king and queen of entrepreneurial finance. Accrual-based accounting, earnings per share, or creative and aggressive use of the tax legislation and testing rules of the securities regulatory bodies are not. Just ask Enron or Nortel! Or consider the plight of Bernie Madoff, Conrad Black, and Jeffrey Skilling.

Time and Timing

Financing alternatives for the financial health of an enterprise are often more sensitive to, or vulnerable to, the time dimension. In entrepreneurial finance, time for critical financing moves often is shorter and more compressed, the optimum timing of these moves changes more rapidly, and financing moves are subject to wider, more volatile swings from lows to highs and back.

Capital Markets

Capital markets are relatively imperfect for more than 95 percent of the financing of private entrepreneurial ventures, in that they are frequently inaccessible, unorganized, and often invisible. Virtually all the underlying characteristics and assumptions that dominate such popular financial theories and models as the capital asset pricing model simply do not apply, even up to the point of a public offering for a small company. In reality, there are so many significant information, knowledge, and market gaps and asymmetries that the rational, perfect market models suffer enormous limitations.

Emphasis

Capital is one of the least important factors in the success of higher potential ventures. Rather, higher potential entrepreneurs seek not only the best deal but also the backer who will provide the most value in terms of know-how, wisdom, counsel, and help. In addition, higher potential entrepreneurs invariably opt for the value added (beyond money), rather than just the best deal or share price.

Strategies for Raising Capital

Strategies that optimize or maximize the amount of money raised can actually increase risk in new and emerging companies, rather than lower it. Thus, the concept of "staged capital commitments," whereby money is committed for a 3- to 18-month phase and is followed by subsequent commitments based on results and promise, is a prevalent practice among venture capitalists and other investors in higher potential ventures. Similarly, wise entrepreneurs may refuse excess capital when the valuation is less attractive and when they believe that valuation will rise substantially.

Downside Consequences

Consequences of financial strategies and decisions are eminently more personal and emotional for the owners of new and emerging ventures than for the managers of large companies. The downside consequences for such entrepreneurs of running out of cash or failing are monumental and relatively catastrophic, since personal guarantees of bank or other loans are common. Contrast these situations with that of the 100 highest paid executives in Canada. The average one of these 100 CEOs has earned as much by January 2 at 9:46 a.m. (assuming he or she works 9 to 5) as the average Canadian earns in a full year. By the end of the workday on January 2, the average of the 100 top-paid CEOs in Canada will have earned $70 000. The highest paid Canadian executive will have earned more than $570 000 in those two days of work. "The average of the top 100 CEOs is paid as much in a year as 238 average Canadians....The highest paid CEO makes as much as a small town—1969 people—working at the average of wages and salaries, or 4696 people working full-year at the minimum wage."[8] With much of these compensation packages independent of performance, the downside for these executives is obviously quite low.

Risk-Reward Relationships

While the high-risk/high-reward and low-risk/low-reward relationship (a so-called law of economics and finance) works fairly well in efficient, mature, and relatively perfect capital markets (e.g., those with money market accounts, deposits in credit unions, widely held and traded shares and bonds, and certificates of deposit), the opposite occurs too often in entrepreneurial finance to permit much comfort with this law. Some of the most profitable, highest return venture investments have been quite low-risk propositions from the outset. Many leveraged buyouts using extreme leverage are probably much more risky than many start-ups. Yet, the way the capital markets price these deals is just the reverse. The reasons are anchored in the second and third points noted above—timing and the asymmetries and imperfections of the capital markets for deals. Entrepreneurs or investors who create or recognize lower risk/high-yield business propositions, before others jump on the Brink's truck, will defy the laws of economics and finance.

Valuation Methods

Established company valuation methods, such as those based on discounted cash flow models used in Wall Street and Bay Street mega deals, seem to favour the seller, rather than the buyer, of private emerging entrepreneurial companies. A seller loves to see an investment banker show up with a notebook computer and then proceed to develop "the 10-year discounted cash flow stream." The assumptions normally made and the mindset behind them are irrelevant or grossly misleading for valuation of smaller private firms because of dynamic and erratic historical and prospective growth curves.

Conventional Financial Ratios

Current financial ratios are misleading when applied to most private entrepreneurial companies. For one thing, entrepreneurs often own more than one company at once and move cash and assets from one to another. For example, an entrepreneur may own real estate and equipment in one entity and lease it to another company. Use of different fiscal years compounds the difficulty of interpreting what the balance sheet really means and the possibilities for aggressive tax avoidance. Further, many of the most important value and equity builders in the business are off the balance sheet or are hidden assets: the excellent venture team; the best scientist, technician, or designer; know-how and business relationships that cannot be bought or sold, let alone valued for the balance sheet.

Goals

Creating value over the long term, rather than maximizing quarterly earnings, is a prevalent mindset and strategy among highly successful entrepreneurs. Since profit is more than just the bottom line, financial strategies are geared to build value, often at the expense of short-term earnings. The growth required to build value is often heavily self-financed, thereby eroding possible accounting earnings.

DETERMINING CAPITAL REQUIREMENTS

How much money does my venture need? When is it needed? How long will it last? Where and from whom can it be raised? How should this process be orchestrated? These are vital questions to any entrepreneur at any stage in the development of a company. These questions are answered in the next two sections.

FINANCIAL STRATEGY FRAMEWORK

The financial strategy framework shown in Exhibit 9.4 is a way to begin crafting financial and fundraising strategies. The exhibit provides a flow and logic with which an otherwise confusing task can be met. *The opportunity leads and drives the business strategy, which in turn drives the*

EXHIBIT 9.4	FINANCIAL STRATEGY FRAMEWORK

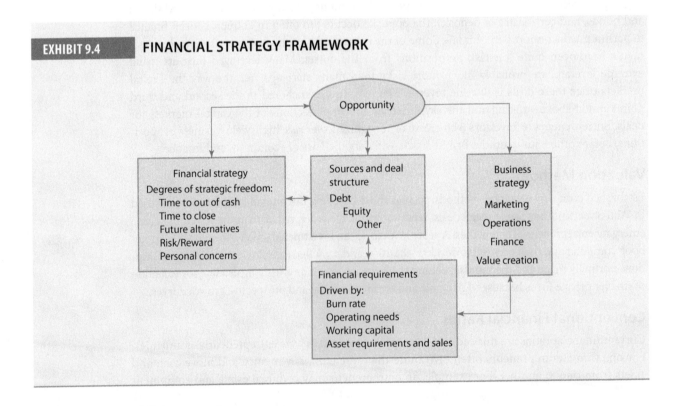

ENTREPRENEURS ACROSS CANADA
Kik Interactive

A NEW VENTURE TEAM OUTSIDE THEIR HEADQUARTERS

Kik Interactive began in 2009, the product of students attending the University of Waterloo, led by Ted Livingston. It was not Livingston's first iteration of the product; in fact, he even had a few other ventures before Kik that flopped. Shortly after launch Kik Messenger reached a million users, then 2 million users less than six months later. After an initial close working relationship, Research In Motion dropped them from their BlackBerry App World and filed a lawsuit against them. RRE, an early-stage venture capital firm, hopped in with an offer for $5 million of a $10 million **term sheet**.

Two other VC firms, Spark and USV, wanted to put in $2.5 million each, but at a lower valuation than RRE because of the dispute with RIM. To avoid dilution, Kik downgraded the funding round to $8 million, "meaning RRE had to take back $2 million, which they didn't want to do but agreed to."

Livingston mentions later, "I sold $1 million to RRE to keep them whole, as they really supported us in tough times." But Livingston was uncomfortable holding his first $1 million. "I didn't know what to do with it," he said. Not wanting to have the money drive a spike between himself and his team, he gave the entire sum to the University of Waterloo to create a venture fund for start-ups.

After the A round of funding in 2011, Kik reached 10 million users in April 2012 and 50 million users in April 2013. Series B financing of $19 million was announced later that month. Along with the earlier investors, Kik now had Foundation Capital helping them move toward goals and monetization options. Foundation Capital "was chosen precisely based on strengths in those areas." Anamitra Benerji, a partner at Foundation Capital, was a particularly valuable ally—he was Twitter's first product manager and was responsible for core revenue generation.

Question: If you were Ted Livingston, would you have donated the $1 million, kept it, or distributed it to the team?

Sources: Andrew James, "Ted Livingston: The shape of Canadian tech to come," Pandodaily.com, July 11, 2012; Darrell Etherington, "Kik raises $19.5M series B, bets on its cards platform play to take on WhatsApp and others," techcrunch.com , April 22, 2013.

financial requirements, the sources and deal structures, and the financial strategy. (Again, until this part of the exercise is well-defined, developing spreadsheets and "playing with the numbers" is just that—playing.)

Once an entrepreneur has defined the core of the market opportunity and the strategy for seizing it (of course, these may change, even dramatically), he or she can begin to examine the financial requirements in terms of (1) asset needs (for start-up or for expansion facilities, equipment, research and development, and other apparently onetime expenditures) and (2) operating needs (i.e., working capital for operations). This framework leaves ample room for crafting a financial strategy, for creatively identifying sources, for devising a fundraising plan, and for structuring deals.

Each fundraising strategy, along with its accompanying deal structure, commits the company to actions that incur actual and real-time costs and may enhance or inhibit future financing options. Similarly, each source has particular requirements and costs—both apparent and hidden—that carry implications for both financial strategy and financial requirements. The premise is that successful entrepreneurs are aware of potentially punishing situations, and that they are careful to "sweat the details" and proceed with a certain degree of wariness as they evaluate, select, negotiate, and craft business relationships with potential funding sources. In doing so, they are more likely to find the right sources, at the right time, and on the right terms and conditions. They are also more likely to avoid potential mismatches, costly sidetracking for the wrong sources, and the disastrous marriage to these sources that might follow.

term sheet:
A short, non-binding document outlining the conditions for financing a start-up company that summarizes the acceptable terms of the agreement.

Certain changes in the economic climate, such as the aftershocks felt following October 1987, March 2000, and fall 2008, cause repercussions across financial markets and institutions serving smaller companies. These take the form of greater caution by both lenders and investors as they seek to increase their protection against risk. When the financial climate becomes harsher, an entrepreneur's capacity to devise financing strategies and to effectively deal with financing sources can be stretched to the limit and beyond. Also, certain lures of cash that come in unsuspecting ways turn out to be a punch in the wallet. Later in this chapter we cover some of these potentially fatal lures and some of the issues and considerations needed to recognize and avoid these traps while devising a fundraising strategy and evaluating and negotiating with different sources.

FREE CASH FLOW: BURN RATE, OOC, AND TTC

The core concept in determining the external financing requirements of the venture is free cash flow. Three vital corollaries are the burn rate (projected or actual), time to OOC (when will the company be Out Of Cash), and TTC (or the Time To Close the financing and have the cheque clear). These have a major impact on the entrepreneur's choices and relative bargaining power with various sources of equity and debt capital, which is represented in Exhibit 9.5. Chapter 10 addresses the details of deal structuring, terms, conditions, and covenants.

The message is clear: If you are out of cash in 90 days or less, you are at a major disadvantage. OOC even in six months is perilously soon. But if you have a year or more, the options, terms, price, and covenants that you will be able to negotiate will improve dramatically. The implication is clear: raise money when you do not need it.

The cash flow generated by a company or project is defined as follows:

	Earnings before interest and taxes (EBIT)
Less	Tax exposure (tax rate times EBIT)
Plus	Depreciation, amortization, and other non-cash charges
Less	Increase in operating working capital
Less	Capital expenditures

EXHIBIT 9.5	ENTREPRENEUR'S BARGAINING POWER BASED ON TIME TO OUT OF CASH

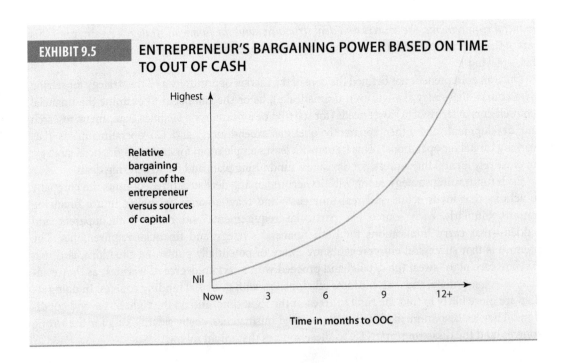

Economists call this result free cash flow. The definition takes into account the benefits of investing, the income generated, and the cost of investing, the amount of investment in working capital and plant and equipment required to generate a given level of sales and net income.

The definition can fruitfully be refined further. Operating working capital is defined as:

	Transactions cash balances
Plus	Accounts receivable
Plus	Inventory
Plus	Other operating current assets (e.g., prepaid expenses)
Less	Accounts payable
Less	Taxes payable
Less	Other operating current liabilities (e.g., accrued expenses)

Finally, this expanded definition can be collapsed into a simpler one:[9]

	Earnings before interest but after taxes (EBIAT)
Less	Increase in net total operating capital (FA + WC)

where the increase in net total operating capital is defined as:

	Increase in operating working capital
Plus	Increase in net fixed assets

CRAFTING FINANCIAL AND FUNDRAISING STRATEGIES

LO3

CRITICAL VARIABLES

When financing is needed, a number of factors affect the availability of the various types of financing and their suitability and cost:

- accomplishments and performance to date
- investor's perceived risk
- industry and technology
- venture upside potential and anticipated exit timing
- venture anticipated growth rate
- venture age and stage of development
- investor's required rate of return or internal rate of return
- amount of capital required and prior valuations of the venture
- founders' goals regarding growth, control, liquidity, and harvesting
- relative bargaining positions
- investor's required terms and covenants

Numerous other factors, especially an investor's or lender's view of the quality of a business opportunity and the venture team, will also play a part in a decision to invest in or lend to a firm.

Generally, a company's operations can be financed through debt and some form of equity financing.[10] Moreover, it is generally believed that a new or existing business needs to obtain both equity and debt financing if it is to have a sound financial foundation for growth without excessive dilution of the entrepreneur's equity.

Short-term debt (i.e., debt incurred for one year or less) usually is used by a business for working capital and is repaid out of the proceeds of its sales. Longer-term borrowings (i.e., term loans of one to five years or long-term loans maturing in more than five years) are used for working capital and/or to finance the purchase of property or equipment that serve as collateral for the loan. Equity financing is used to fill the non-bankable gaps, preserve ownership, and lower the risk of loan defaults.

However, a new venture just starting operations will have difficulty obtaining either short-term or longer-term bank debt without a substantial cushion of equity financing or long-term debt that is subordinated or junior to all bank debt.[11] As far as a lender is concerned, a start-up has little proven capability to generate sales, profits, and cash to pay off short-term debt and even less ability to sustain profitable operations over a number of years and retire long-term debt. Even the underlying protection provided by a venture's assets used as loan collateral may be insufficient to obtain bank loans. Asset values can erode with time; in the absence of adequate equity capital and good management, they may provide little real loan security to a bank.

A bank may lend money to a start-up to some maximum debt-to-equity ratio. As a rough rule, a start-up may be able to obtain debt for working capital purposes that is equal to its equity and subordinated debt. A start-up can also obtain loans through such avenues as Business Development Bank of Canada, manufacturers and suppliers, or leasing.

An existing business seeking expansion capital or funds for a temporary use has a much easier job obtaining both debt and equity. Sources such as banks, professional investors, and leasing and finance companies often will seek out such companies and regard them as important customers for secured and unsecured short-term loans or as good investment prospects. Furthermore, an existing and expanding business will find it easier to raise equity capital from private or institutional sources and to raise it on better terms than the start-up.

Awareness of criteria used by various sources of financing—whether for debt, equity, or some combination of the two—that are available for a particular situation is central to devise a time-effective and cost-effective search for capital.

FINANCIAL LIFE CYCLES

One useful way to begin identifying equity financing alternatives, and when and if certain alternatives are available, is to consider what can be called the financial life cycle of firms. Exhibit 9.6 shows the types of capital available over time for different types of firms at different stages of development (i.e., as indicated by different sales levels).[12] It also summarizes, at different stages of development (research and development, start-up, early growth, rapid growth, and exit), the principal sources of risk capital and costs of risk capital.

As can be seen in the exhibit, sources have different preferences and practices, including how much money they will provide, when in a company's life cycle they will invest, and the cost of the capital or expected annual rate of return they are seeking. The available sources of capital change dramatically for companies at different stages and rates of growth, and there will be variations in different parts of the country.

Many of the sources of equity are not available until a company progresses beyond the earlier stages of its growth. Some sources available to early-stage companies, especially personal sources,

EXHIBIT 9.6   **FINANCING LIFE CYCLES**

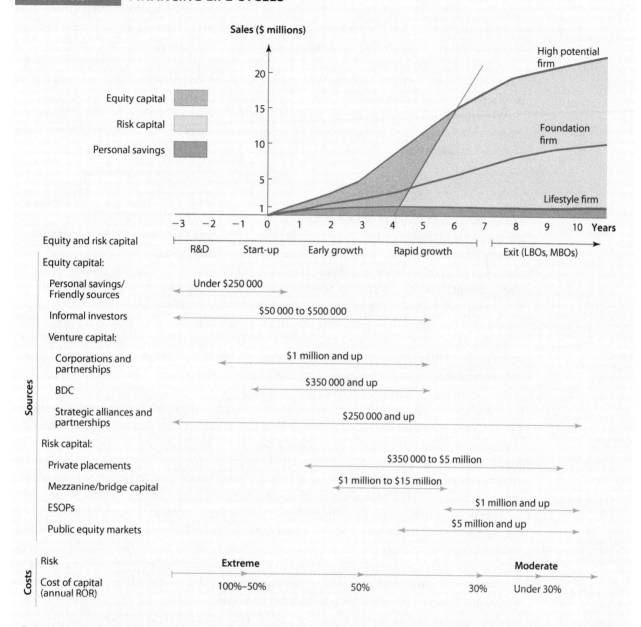

Source: Adapted and updated from W. H. Wetzel, Jr., "The Cost and Availability of Credit and Risk Capital in New England," in A Region's Struggling Savior: Small Business in New England, J. A. Timmons and D. E. Gumpert, eds. (Waltham, MA: Small Business Foundation of America, 1979).

friends, and other informal investors or angels, will be insufficient to meet the financing requirements generated in later stages if the company continues to grow successfully.

Another key factor affecting the availability of financing is the upside potential of a company. Of the new businesses of all kinds expected to launch in Canada in the coming year, probably 5 percent or fewer will achieve the growth and sales levels of high-potential firms. Foundation firms will total about 8 to 12 percent of all new firms, which will grow more slowly but exceed $1 million in sales and may grow to $5 to $15 million. Remaining are the traditional, stable lifestyle firms. High-potential firms (those that grow rapidly and are likely to exceed $20 to $25 million or more in sales) are strong prospects for a public offering and have the widest array of financing alternatives, including combinations of debt and equity and other alternatives (which are noted later), while foundation firms have fewer, and lifestyle firms are limited to the personal resources of their founders and whatever net worth or collateral they can accumulate.

In general, investors believe the younger the company, the more risky the investment. This is a variation of the old saying in the venture capital business: The lemons ripen in two-and-a-half years, but the plums take seven or eight.

While the timeline and dollar limits shown are only guidelines, they do reflect how these money sources view the riskiness, and thus the required rate of return, of companies at various stages of development.

INVESTOR PREFERENCES

Precise practices of investors or lenders may vary between individual investors or lenders in a given category, may change with the current market conditions, and may vary in different areas of the country from time to time. Identifying realistic sources and developing a fundraising strategy to tap them depend upon knowing what kinds of investments investors or lenders are seeking. While the stage, amount, and return guidelines noted in Exhibit 9.6 can help, doing the appropriate homework in advance on specific investor or lender preferences can save months of wild-goose chases and personal cash, while significantly increasing the odds of successfully raising funds on acceptable terms.

In the wake of the global recession, Canadian VC financing mostly vanished. Financing from south of the border also retreated. Though not as quickly as it retreated, money on both sides of the border did re-emerge, a bit more wary and a bit more demanding. Joshua Geist of Geminare notes, "We would not have a problem getting a deal done in Canada, but the deal would be so poor, and there would be so little value out of it for the company that I already know this isn't for us." "VCs are having a hard time exiting earlier deals to extract cash and with the cash on hand that is being doled out carefully to existing picks. The historically biggest players, big pension funds, have switched to adding private equity buyouts to their portfolios and not backing new ventures seeking risk capital. And those still in the game 'think long and hard' before putting a deal together," says Mike Middleton of Q1 Capital Partners.[13] For Canada, tougher times lead to tougher deals. inventureLab, an early-stage venture creation and finance business, proclaimed in big bold letters on its website that "Venture capital is broken." Arguing that "The priorities of venture capital do not help innovators build value. Their need for deal flow and rapid exits is not aligned with the process of transforming innovations into businesses, nor with the interests of the creators of the intellectual property." Providing business and sector expertise, inventureLab's approach was to focus on the needs of inventors and investors and create new paths to market for an innovation. inventureLab hoped to play a role in commercializing IP, but failed to gain traction and was shuttered. While start-ups come and go, the same holds true for VCs.

THE CAPITAL MARKETS FOOD CHAIN   LO4

Consider the capital markets for equity as a "food chain," whose participants have increasing appetites in terms of the deal size they want to acquire (Exhibit 9.7). This framework can help entrepreneurs identify and appreciate the various sources of equity capital at various stages of the venture's development, the amount of capital they typically provide, and the portion of the company and share price one might expect should the company eventually have an initial public offering (IPO) or trade sale.

STAGE OF VENTURE	R&D	SEED	LAUNCH	HIGH GROWTH
Enterprise Value at Stage	Less than $1 million	$1–$5 million	$1–$5 million	More than $100 million
Sources	Founders High Net Worth Individuals FFF* SR&ED	FFF* Angel Funds Seed Funds SR&ED	Venture Capital Series A, B, C . . . Strategic Partners Very High Net Worth Individuals Private Equity	IPOs Strategic Acquirers Private Equity
Amount of Capital Invested	Less than $50 000–$200 000	$10 000–$500 000	$500 000–$20 million	$10–$50 million-plus
% Company Owned at IPO	10%–25%	5%–15%	40%–60% by prior investors	15%–25% by public
Share Price	$0.01–$0.50	$0.50–$1.00	$1.00–$8.00	$12–$18
Number of Shares†	1–5 million	1–3 million	3–5 million	5–10 million

*Friends, families, and fools.

†At post–IPO.

The bottom row in Exhibit 9.7 shows this ultimate progression from R&D stage to IPO, where the capital markets are typically willing to pay $12 to $18 per share for new issues of small companies. Obviously, these prices are lower when the so-called IPO window is tight or closed, such as after the dot-com bubble. Prices for the few offerings that did exist (1 to 3 per week versus more than 50 per week in June 1996) were $5 to $9 per share. In hot IPO periods, 1999 for instance, offering prices reached as high as $20 per share and more. The modest revival that began in late 2003 continued into 2005. Again the IPO markets suffered a severe decline and were basically shut down after the market trouble and economic turmoil beginning in late 2008, continuing through 2009 and well into 2010. In the third quarter of 2008 no private companies went public in Canada—no IPOs at all. In the first half of 2008 there were 53 public equity issues sold to Canadian investment markets with a value of $680 million—a fraction of what occurred in the boom years between 1996 and 1999. It was not until 2012/2013 that things looked promising again.

One of the toughest decisions for the founders is whether to give up equity, and implicitly control, to have a run at creating very significant value. The row, "% Company Owned at IPO," shows that by the time a company goes public, the founders may have sold 70 to 80 percent or more of their equity. As long as the market capitalization of the company is at least $100 million or more, the founders have created significant value for investors and themselves. During the peak of the dot-com mania, companies went public with market capitalizations of $1 to $2 billion and more. Founders' shares on paper were at least initially worth $200 to $400 million and more. These were truly staggering, unprecedented valuations, which were not sustainable.

In the remainder of the chapter, we will discuss these various equity sources and how to identify and deal with them. Exhibit 9.8 summarizes the venture capital food chain. In the first three rounds, series A, B, C, one can see that on average, the amount of capital invested was quite substantial: $1–$4 million, $6–$10 million, and $10–$15 million.

EXHIBIT 9.8

EXHIBIT 9.8   THE VENTURE CAPITAL FOOD CHAIN FOR ENTREPRENEURIAL VENTURES

Venture Capital Series A, B, C, ... (Average size of round): Example of three staged rounds

Round*
{
"A" @ $1–4 million—Start-up
"B" @ $6–10 million—Product development
"C"** @ $10–15 million—Shipping product
}

*Valuations vary markedly by industry.

**Valuations vary by region and venture capital cycle.

COVER YOUR EQUITY

One of the toughest trade-offs for any young company is to balance the need for start-up and growth capital with preservation of equity. Holding on to as much as you can for as long as you can is generally good advice for entrepreneurs. As was evident in Exhibit 9.6, the earlier the capital enters, regardless of the source, the more costly it is. Creative bootstrapping strategies can be great preservers of equity, as long as such parsimony does not slow the venture's progress so much that the opportunity weakens or disappears.

Three central issues should be considered when beginning to think about obtaining risk capital: (1) Does the venture need outside equity capital? (2) Do the founders want outside equity capital? and finally, (3) Who should invest? While these three issues are at the centre of the venture team's thinking, it is also important to remember that a smaller percentage of a larger pie is preferred to a larger percentage of a smaller pie. Or as one entrepreneur stated, "I would rather have a piece of a watermelon than a whole raisin."[14]

After reviewing the online Venture Opportunity Screening Exercises, the business plan for chapter 4, and the free cash flow equations (including OOC, TTC, and breakeven) from earlier in this chapter, it may be easier to assess the need for additional capital. Deciding whether the capital infusion will be debt or equity is situation specific, and it may be helpful to be aware of the trade-offs involved; see chapter 11 for an introduction to debt capital. In the majority of the high-technology start-ups and early-stage companies, some equity investment is normally needed to fund research and development, prototype development and product marketing, launch, and early losses.

Once the need for additional capital has been identified and quantified, the venture team must consider the desirability of an equity investment. As was mentioned in chapter 8, boot-strapping continues to be an attractive source of financing. Many entrepreneurs suggest getting customers to pay quickly.[15] Entrepreneurs in certain industries can tap vendors by getting them to extend credit.[16] Such credit is termed "spontaneous" financing and arises in the normal course of business activity.

While it may appear a blessing at the time, tables can turn. As an example, in 2009 Air Canada came "perilously close to violating debt covenants. When its cash holdings fall below $900 million, for example, its credit card processing company can withhold a portion of ticket sales."[17] The threshold set by the credit card processing company was expected to rise to $1.3 billion—while Air Canada's reserves hovered around $1 billion. Standard and Poor's downgraded the airline's debt, adding greater pressure. Air Canada raised $1.20 billion in additional liquidity through a series of financing and other transactions with lenders and stakeholders (GE Capital, Export Development Canada, Aeroplan Canada, ACE Aviation Holdings). In 2012, Moody's Investor Service cut the airline's credit rating, believing there was an increased possibility the airline would default on its debt obligations. This was only 10 years after Air Canada had been in bankruptcy protection. With its pension solvency deficit in excess of $4 billion, by mid-2013, Air Canada posted lower revenue and admitted increasing competitive pressures.

An equity investment requires that the executive team firmly believes that investors can and will add value to the venture. With this belief, the team can begin to identify those investors who bring expertise to the venture. Cash flow versus high rate of return required is an important aspect of the "equity versus other" financing decision.

Deciding *who* should invest is a process more than a decision. The venture team has a number of sources to consider. There are both informal and formal investors, private and public markets. The single most important criterion for selecting investors is what they can contribute to the value of the venture—beyond just funding. Angels or wealthy individuals are often sought because the amount needed may be less than the minimum investment required by formal investors (i.e., venture capitalists and private placements). Whether a venture capitalist would be interested in investing can be determined by the amount needed and the rate of return expected.

TIMING

 There are two times for a young company to raise money; when there is lots of hope, or lots of results, but never in between.

GEORGES DORIOT
Venture Capitalist

Timing is critical. A venture should not wait to look for capital until it has a serious cash shortage. For a start-up, especially one with no experience or success in raising money, it is unwise to delay seeking capital because it is likely to take six months or more to raise money. In addition to the problems with cash flow, the lack of planning implicit in waiting until there is a cash shortage can undermine the credibility of a venture's executive team and negatively impact its ability to negotiate with investors.

On the other hand, if a venture tries to obtain equity capital too early, the equity position of the founders may be unnecessarily diluted and the discipline instilled by financial leanness may be eroded inadvertently.

ANGELS AND INFORMAL INVESTORS   LO5

WHO THEY ARE

Wealthy individuals are an important source of capital for start-up and emerging businesses today. They have made it on their own, have substantial business and financial experience, and are likely to be in their 40s or 50s. They are also well educated; 95 percent hold university degrees, and 51 percent have graduate degrees. Of the graduate degrees, 44 percent are in a technical field and 35 percent are in business or economics.

Since the typical informal investor will invest from $10 000 to $250 000 in any one deal, informal investors are particularly appropriate for the following:[18]

- Ventures with capital requirements of between $50 000 and $500 000.
- Ventures with sales potential of between $2 and $20 million within 5 to 10 years.

- Small, established, privately held ventures with sales and profit growth of 10 to 20 percent per year, a rate that is not rapid enough to be attractive to a professional investor, such as a venture capital firm.
- Special situations, such as very early financing of high-technology inventors who have not developed a prototype.
- Companies that project high levels of free cash flow within three to five years.

These investors may invest alone or in syndication with other wealthy individuals, may demand considerable equity for their interests, or may try to dominate ventures. They also can get impatient when sales and profits do not grow as they expected.

Usually, these informal investors will be knowledgeable and experienced in the market and technology areas in which they invest. If the right angel is found, he or she will add a lot more to a business than just money. As an advisor or director, his or her savvy, know-how, and contacts that come from having "made it" can be far more valuable than the $10 000 to $250 000 invested. The New Brunswick Small Business Investor Tax Credit gives a 30-percent tax break on investment amounts up to $80 000. The Yukon Small Business Investment Tax Credit grants a 24-percent break on investments of $100 000 or less. Generally, the evaluations of potential investments by such wealthy investors tend to be less thorough than those undertaken by organized venture capital groups, and such non-economic factors as the desire to be involved with entrepreneurship may be important to their investment decisions. There is a clear geographic bias of working within a one-hour driving radius of the investor's base. For example, a successful entrepreneur may want to help other entrepreneurs get started, or a wealthy individual may want to help build new businesses in his or her community.

Michael Robinson and Thomas Cottrell, both of the University of Calgary, investigated the three main categories of informal investors in private equity markets: relationship investors, opportunity-based investors, and angel investors. They found evidence "that the first two investor types are a major total source of capital and they prefer to invest in smaller amounts close to home and in the context of existing relationship. With respect to angel investors…their investments evolve through a life cycle of investing."[19]

FINDING INFORMAL INVESTORS

Finding these backers is not easy. One expert noted: "Informal investors, essentially individuals of means and successful entrepreneurs, are a diverse and dispersed group with a preference for anonymity. Creative techniques are required to identify and reach them."[20] The Internet has provided entrepreneurs with an effective method of locating such investors. Formal sources such as Garage Technology Ventures and Brightspark Capital provide invaluable advice, assistance, and information regarding potential investors and help forge the link between investors and entrepreneurs seeking capital.

Invariably, financial backers are also found by tapping an entrepreneur's own network of business associates and other contacts. Other successful entrepreneurs know them, as do many tax attorneys, accountants, bankers, and other professionals. Apart from serendipity, the best way to find informal investors is to seek referrals from lawyers, accountants, business associates, university faculty, and entrepreneurs who deal with new ventures and are likely to know such people. Because such investors learn of investment opportunities from their business associates, fellow entrepreneurs, and friends, and because many informal investors invest together in a number of new venture situations, one informal investor contact can lead the entrepreneur to contacts with others.

In most larger cities, there are law firms and private placement firms that syndicate investment packages as offerings to networks of private investors. They may raise from several hundred thousand dollars to several million. The National Angel Capital Organization (NACO) is the national clearinghouse and lists 25 angel networks, but many angels fly under the radar. New Brunswick has only one readily identifiable angel network, which is not even included in the national registry. That New Brunswick angel network counts 25 individual angels, which completed two deals in 2007 for $1.1 million.[21] Manitoba, Newfoundland and Labrador, Quebec, and Saskatchewan each have only one network identified in the NACO directory.

CONTACTING INVESTORS

If an entrepreneur has obtained a referral, he or she needs to get permission to use the name of the person making a referral when the investor is contacted. A meeting with the potential investor can then be arranged. At this meeting, the entrepreneur needs to make a concise presentation of the key features of the proposed venture by answering the following questions:

- What is the market opportunity?
- Why is it compelling?
- How will/does the business make money?
- How soon can the business reach positive cash flow?
- Why is this the right team at the right time?
- How does an investor exit the investment?

After the dot-com crash investors throughout the capital markets food chain returned to these fundamental basics for evaluating potential deals. The drought following the financial meltdown in late 2008 was expected to subside as investors cautiously tested the waters once again in 2010. But generating confidence and momentum has come slowly. News headlines in 2013 spoke of a global pressure cooker, the European economic crisis, and growing concerns that China's economic growth stretch would come to a close.

Entrepreneurs need to avoid meeting with more than one informal investor at the same time. Meeting with more than one investor often results in any negative viewpoints raised by one investor being reinforced by another. It is also easier to deal with negative reactions and questions from only one investor at a time. Like a wolf on the hunt, if an entrepreneur isolates one target "prey" and then concentrates on closure, he or she will increase the odds of success.

Whether or not the outcome of such a meeting is continued investment interest, the entrepreneur needs to try to obtain the names of other potential investors from this meeting. If this can be done, the entrepreneur will develop a growing list of potential investors and will find his or her way into one or more networks of informal investors. If the outcome is positive, often the participation of one investor who is knowledgeable about the product and its market will trigger the participation of other investors.

EVALUATION PROCESS

An informal investor will want to review a business plan, meet the full executive team, see any product prototype or design that may exist, and so forth. The investor will conduct background checks on the venture team and its product potential, usually through someone he or she knows who knows the entrepreneur and the product. The process is not dissimilar to the due diligence of the professional investors (see below) but may be less formal and structured. The new venture entrepreneur, if given a choice, would be wise to select an informal investor who can add knowledge, wisdom, and networks as an advisor and whose objectives are consistent with those of the entrepreneur.

THE DECISION

If the investor decides to invest, he or she will have an investment agreement drafted by a lawyer. This agreement may be somewhat simpler than those used by professional investors, such as venture capital firms. All the cautions and advice about investors and investment agreements that are discussed later in the chapter apply here as well.

Most likely, the investment agreement with an informal investor will include some form of a "put," whereby the investor has the right to require the venture to repurchase his or her shares after a specified number of years at a specified price. If the venture is not harvested, this put will provide an investor with a cash return.

WILL IT FLOAT?

Late-night television host David Letterman had a segment testing various items to see if they would float. To much fanfare, the item would be presented, analyzed, and a verdict would be reached before being dropped in a large tank of water for the real test. The verdict is still out on whether or not these entrepreneurs and their ideas will receive funding.

A BETTER MOUSETRAP

Frank Naumman of Waterloo, Ontario, has added a light emitting diode to his mousetrap as an indicator of whether or not it has been triggered. Although the modern mousetrap has been around since at least the 1880s, the last patent filing for an improved mousetrap was in 1993.

ENERGY GENERATOR

Thane Heins of Almonte, Ontario, has developed "Perepeteia," what some say may be a perpetual motion machine. While these claims may be grandiose, the efficiency of his generator has caught the attention of scientists, the YouTube community, and at least one investor.

DRYWALL FASTENER

Sean Ledoux of North Bay, Ontario, has come up with the idea of a single broad-headed screw to attach two drywall sheets to a wall instead of two screws, one on each side of the seam. He also has modified the screw threads but will not reveal details. Sean is already in talks to license the invention to Robertson Inc.—the founder of which lays claim to the creation of the square-notched screw.

MASCARA REMOVER

Robyn Mumford of Cobourg, Ontario, has designed a device that removes mascara just from the eyelashes without having to rub the sensitive skin around the eyes. Though the potential is huge, Anthony Gussin of Nytric, an innovation consulting company—points out that it will take "considerable financial resources to develop."

TRAILER HITCH ALIGNER

Ortwin Groh of Chilliwak, British Columbia, has developed a trailer-hitch alignment system to aid in backing up a vehicle to make proper contact to attach a trailer before towing. One piece attaches to the vehicle's bumper and another piece attaches to the trailer and then the driver lines them up in the mirrors while backing up the vehicle.

TRAILER HITCH ALIGNER

Dave Underwood of London, Ontario, has the "Hitch Docker" to quickly, easily, efficiently line up and hook up a trailer with no damage to your bumper—guaranteed. He has already had success across Ontario and his product is available through several specialty Internet firms based in the United States, but Dave is still seeking backing to make it big (e.g., Canadian Tire and Walmart).

TRAILER HITCH ALIGNER

Jack Julicher of Bowmanville, Ontario, has patented the "Easy-Hitch" to "allow you to safely, and without hassle, hitch up any type of trailer system to your vehicle." One telescopic rod with flashing light attaches to the hitch-ball on the vehicle while another telescopic rod with flashing light attaches to the trailer. This permits visibility to insure alignment while backing up the vehicle. Jack and his wife were featured on *Dragons' Den* on CBC Television.

Sources: Joe Castaldo, "The Next Great Canadian Idea: A Better Mousetrap," *Canadian Business*, July 11, 2008; Sharda Prashad, "The Next Great Canadian Idea: Peripiteia Generator," *Canadian Business*, July 11, 2008; Andrew Wahl, "Semifinalist 3: Drywall Fastener," *Canadian Business*, June 4, 2007; Zena Olijnyk, "Semifinalist 2: Mascara Remover," *Canadian Business*, June 4, 2007; Joe Castaldo, "Semifinalist 1: Trailer Hitch Aligner," *Canadian Business*, June 4, 2007; www. hitchdocker.com; www.easyhitch.net.

eral years ago—primarily digital piracy and a loss of revenue." Most students already had devices that could utilize a digital copy of a book, but what sort of user experience would students expect? Hardcopy was familiar and practical, but multimedia content offered possibilities. Students were accustomed to reading, turning the page, and marking up a personal copy of a textbook. But students today have grown up online.

PWC suggested that for 2015 and beyond "printed books will still account for the majority of sales. Technology may change rapidly, but people's habits do not." Chapters of this textbook are available (in print or electronically) on a chapter-by-chapter basis, just as individual songs from an album may be purchased through iTunes.

Educational publishers have evolved to publish and distribute both print and digital educational products. Industry leaders had adapted and had had great success, but times are changing yet again. Campus bookstores across Canada report that even required textbooks are not being purchased with the same regularity they once were. Textbooks are expensive, but so too is campus parking!

PricewaterhouseCoopers, in their report *Turning the page: The future of eBooks*, asked "Will the industry face the same issues that music publishers did during its digital transformation sev-

Question: What will the transition to digital books look like and what will be the appropriate business model? Would publishers go direct to students or still include the bookstore? A transition period whereby print and digital would coexist was predicted. For how long would both formats be supported? Would textbooks continue to be revised every four years or continuously in real time? Would the role of authors change? Consider that Stephen King and others distribute their books directly through their own websites. Is that model likely for textbooks? How might pricing, distribution, and revenue generation change?

Source: *Turning the page: The future of ebooks*, http://www.pwc.com/gx/en/entertainment-media/publications/future-of-ebooks.jhtml.

VENTURE CAPITAL: GOLD MINES AND TAR PITS   LO6

There are only two classes of investors in new and young private companies: value-added investors and all the rest. If all you receive from an investor, especially a venture capitalist or a substantial private investor, is money, then you may not be getting a bargain. One of the keys to raising risk capital is to seek investors who will truly add value to the venture well beyond the money. Research and practice show that investors may add or detract value in a young company. Therefore, carefully screening potential investors to determine how they might fill some gaps in the founders' know-how and networks can yield significant results. Adding key team members, new customers or suppliers, or referring additional investment are basic ways to add value.

A young founder of an international telecommunications venture landed a private investor who also served as an advisor. The following are examples of how this private investor provided critical assistance: introduced the founder to other private investors, to foreign executives (who became investors and helped in a strategic alliance), to the appropriate legal and accounting firms; served as a sounding board in crafting and negotiating early rounds of investments; and identified potential directors and other advisors familiar with the technology and relationships with foreign investors and cross-cultural strategic alliances.

Numerous other examples exist of venture capitalists' being instrumental in opening doors to key accounts and vendors that otherwise might not take a new company seriously. Venture capitalists may also provide valuable help in such tasks as negotiating original equipment manufacturer (OEM) agreements or licensing or royalty agreements, making key contacts with banks and leasing companies, finding key people to build the team, and helping to revise or to craft a strategy.

It is always tempting for an entrepreneur desperately in need of cash to go after the money that is available, rather than wait for the value-added investor. These quick solutions to the cash problem usually come back to haunt the venture.

WHAT IS VENTURE CAPITAL?[22]

The word *venture* suggests that this type of capital involves a degree of risk and even something of a gamble. Specifically, "The venture capital industry supplies capital and other resources to entrepreneurs in business with high growth potential in hopes of achieving a high rate of return on invested funds."[23] The whole investing process involves many stages, which are represented in Exhibit 9.9.

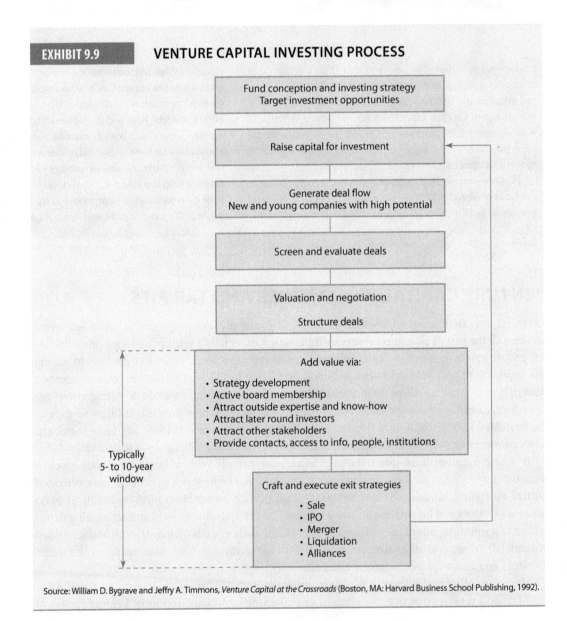

EXHIBIT 9.9 **VENTURE CAPITAL INVESTING PROCESS**

Source: William D. Bygrave and Jeffry A. Timmons, *Venture Capital at the Crossroads* (Boston, MA: Harvard Business School Publishing, 1992).

Throughout the investing process, venture capital firms seek to add value in several ways: identifying and evaluating business opportunities and entry or growth strategies; negotiating and closing the investment; tracking and coaching the company; providing technical and managerial assistance; and attracting additional capital, directors, team members, suppliers, and other key stakeholders and resources.

The process begins with the conception of a target investment opportunity or class of opportunities, which leads to a written proposal or prospectus to raise a venture capital fund. Once the money is raised, the value creation process moves from generating deals to crafting and executing harvest strategies and back to raising another fund. The process usually takes up to 10 years to unfold, but exceptions in both directions often occur.

THE VENTURE CAPITAL INDUSTRY

Although the roots of venture capital can be traced from investments made by wealthy families in the 1920s and 1930s, the venture capital industry did not experience a growth spurt until the 1980s, when the industry took off. Before 1980, venture capital investing activities could be called dormant; but in the 1980s the industry roared up. The sleepy cottage industry of the 1970s was transformed into a vibrant, at times frenetic, occasionally myopic, and dynamic market for private risk and equity capital. And it was deals galore through the 1990s with year after year reaching ever-higher levels. A sobering wake-up came in 2001 and the brakes came on hard in the ensuing years. Due diligence increased to six or eight months, closer to historical norms, rather than the 45 days or less during the dot-com feeding frenzy. Things gained momentum and in subsequent years the money started to flow once again—until everything came apart with the economic turmoil that began in late 2008 and continues today. The money still flows—some say like molasses—and deals are struck, but caution reigns in the search for plums.

The stark reality of all this is that the venture capital cycle—much like real estate—seems to repeat itself. Scarcity of capital leads to high returns, which attracts an overabundance of new capital, which drives returns down. The meltdown side of the venture capital and private equity markets can be expected with the certainty—though fortunately not frequency—as the change of seasons.

THE VENTURE CAPITAL PROCESS   LO7

Exhibit 9.10 represents the core activities of the venture capital process. At the heart of this dynamic flow is the collision of entrepreneurs, opportunities, investors, and capital.[24] In addition to money, the venture capitalist brings experience, networks, and industry contacts. A professional venture capitalist can therefore be very attractive to a new venture. Moreover, a venture capital firm has deep pockets and contacts with other groups that can facilitate raising more money as the venture develops.

The venture capital process occurs in the context of mostly private, quite imperfect capital markets for new, emerging, and middle-market companies (i.e., those companies with $5 to $200 million in sales). The availability and cost of this capital depend on a number of factors:

- perceived risk, in view of the quality of the venture team and the opportunity
- industry, market, attractiveness of the technology, and fit
- upside potential and downside exposure
- anticipated growth rate

EXHIBIT 9.10   **FLOWS OF VENTURE CAPITAL**

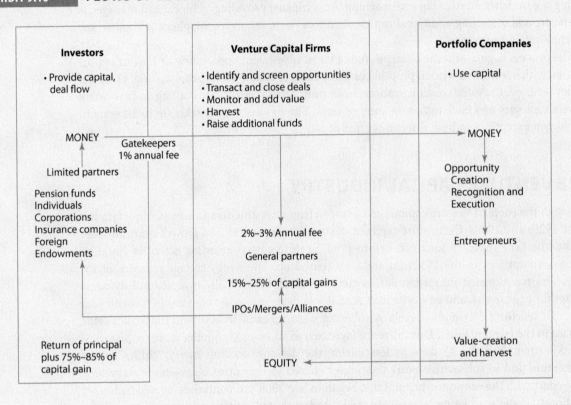

- age and stage of development
- amount of capital required
- founders' goals for growth, control, liquidity, and harvest
- fit with investors' goals and strategy
- relative bargaining positions of investors and founders given the capital markets at the time

However, no more than 2 to 4 percent of those contacting venture capital firms receive financing from them. Despite the increase in funds in the recent boom years, observers comment that the repeat fundraisers "stay away from seed and early-stage investments largely because those deals tend to require relatively small amounts of capital, and the megafunds, with $500 million-plus to invest, like to make larger commitments."[25] Further, an entrepreneur may give up 15 to 75 percent of his or her equity for seed/start-up financing. Thus, after several rounds of venture financing have been completed, an entrepreneur may own no more than 10 to 20 percent of the venture.

The venture capitalists' stringent criteria for their investments limit the number of companies receiving venture capital money. Venture capital investors look for ventures with high growth potential where they can quintuple their investment in five years; they place a high premium on the quality of leadership in a venture; and they like to see a venture executive team with complementary business skills headed by someone who has previous entrepreneurial or profit-and-loss (P&L) managerial experience. In fact, these investors are searching for the "superdeal." Superdeals meet the investment criteria outlined in Exhibit 9.11.

CHARACTERISTICS OF THE CLASSIC SUPERDEAL FROM THE INVESTOR'S PERSPECTIVE

MISSION

- Build a highly profitable and industry-dominant market leading company
- Go public or merge within four to seven years at a high price-earnings (P/E) multiple

COMPLETE VENTURE EXECUTIVE TEAM

- Led by industry "superstar"
- Possess proven entrepreneurial, general managerial, and P&L experience in the business
- Have leading innovator or technologies/marketing head
- Possess complementary and compatible skills
- Have unusual tenacity, imagination, and commitment
- Possess reputation for high integrity

PROPRIETARY PRODUCT OR SERVICE

- Has significant competitive lead and "unfair" and sustainable or defensible advantages
- Has product or service with high value-added properties resulting in early payback to user
- Has or can gain exclusive contractual or legal rights

LARGE, ROBUST, AND SUSTAINABLE MARKET

- Will accommodate a $100-million entrant in five years
- Has sales currently at $200 million, or more, and growing at 25 percent or more per year
- Has no dominant competitor now
- Has clearly identified customers and distribution channels
- Possesses forgiving and rewarding economics, such as:
  - Gross margins of 40 to 50 percent, or more
  - 10 percent or more profit after tax
  - Early positive cash flow and breakeven sales

DEAL VALUATION AND RATE OF RETURN (ROR)

- Has "digestible" first-round capital requirements (i.e., greater than $1 million and less than $10 million)
- Able to return 10 times original investment in five years at P/E of 15 times or more
- Has possibility of additional rounds of financing at substantial mark-up
- Has anti-dilution and IPO subscription rights and other identifiable harvest/liquidity options

Source: William D. Bygrave and Jeffry A. Timmons, *Venture Capital at the Crossroads* (Boston, MA: Harvard Business School Publishing, 1992).

IDENTIFYING VENTURE CAPITAL INVESTORS

Venture capital corporations or partners have an established capital base and professional management. Their investment policies cover a range of preferences in investment size and the maturity, location, and industry of a venture. Capital for these investments can be provided by one or more wealthy families, one or more financial institutions (e.g., insurance companies or pension funds), and wealthy individuals. Most are organized as limited partnerships, in which the fund managers are the general partners and the investors are the limited partners. Today, most of these funds prefer to invest from $2 to $5 million or more. Although some of the smaller funds will invest less, most of their investments are in the range of $500 000 to $1.5 million. Some of the so-called megafunds with more than $500 million to invest do not consider investments of less than $5 to $10 million. The investigation and evaluation of potential investments by venture capital corporations and partnerships are thorough and professional. Most of their investments are in high-technology businesses, but many will consider investments in other areas.

Sources and Guides

If an entrepreneur is searching for a venture capital investor, a good place to start is with Canada's Venture Capital and Private Equity Association (CVCA), which has a membership directory of venture capital firms. CVCA boasts over 1900 members with over $88 billion in capital under management in three domains: buyout, mezzanine, and venture capital. Entrepreneurs also can seek referrals from accountants, lawyers, investment and commercial bankers, and businesspeople who are knowledgeable about professional investors. Especially good sources of information are other entrepreneurs who have recently tried, successfully or unsuccessfully, to raise money.

Sometimes professional investors find entrepreneurs. Rather than wait for a deal to come to them, a venture capital investor may decide on a product or technology it wishes to commercialize and then put its own deal together. Michael Dunleavy and his fellow partners at Labarge Weinstein are always on the lookout for great companies to launch. They attend new technology showcases and other venues to discover the next great entrepreneurs who have not yet been called up to the big league.

What to Look For

Entrepreneurs are well advised to screen prospective investors to determine the appetites of such investors for the stage, industry, technology, and capital requirements proposed. It is also useful to determine which investors have money to invest, which are actively seeking deals, and which have the time and people to investigate new deals. Depending on its size and investment strategy, a fund that is a year or two old will generally be in an active investing mode.

Early-stage entrepreneurs need to seek investors who (1) are considering new financing proposals and can provide the required level of capital; (2) are interested in companies at the particular stage of growth; (3) understand and have a preference for investments in the particular industry (i.e., market, product, technology, or service focus); (4) can provide good business advice, moral support, and contacts in the business and financial community; (5) are reputable, fair, and ethical and with whom the entrepreneur gets along; and (6) have successful track records of 10 years or more advising and building smaller companies.[26]

Entrepreneurs can expect a number of value-added services from an investor. Ideally, the investor should define his or her role as a coach, thoroughly involved, but not a player. In terms of support, investors should have both patience and bravery. The entrepreneur should be able to go to the investor when he or she needs a sounding board, counselling, or an objective, detached perspective. Investors should be helpful with future negotiations, financing, private and public offerings, as well as in relationship building with key contacts.

What to Look Out For

There are also some things to be wary of in finding investors. These warning signs are worth avoiding unless an entrepreneur is so desperate that he or she has no real alternatives:

- *Attitude.* Entrepreneurs need to be wary if they cannot get through to a general partner in an investment firm and keep getting handed off to a junior associate, or if the investor thinks he or she can run the business better than the lead entrepreneur or the new venture team.

- *Overcommitment.* Entrepreneurs need to be wary of lead investors who indicate they will be active directors but who also sit on the boards of six to eight other start-up and early-stage companies or are in the midst of raising money for a new fund.
- *Inexperience.* Entrepreneurs need to be wary of dealing with venture capitalists who have an MBA; are under 30 years of age; have worked only on Bay Street or as a consultant; have no operating, hands-on experience in new and growing companies; and have a predominantly financial focus.
- *Unfavourable reputation.* Entrepreneurs need to be wary of funds that have a reputation for early and frequent replacement of the founders or those where more than one-fourth of the portfolio companies are in trouble or failing to meet projections in their business plans.
- *Predatory pricing.* During adverse capital markets, investors who unduly exploit these conditions by forcing large share price decreases in the new firms and punishing terms on prior investors do not make the best long-term financial partners.

How to Find Out

How does the entrepreneur learn about the reputation of the venture capital firm? The best source is the CEO/founders of prior investments. Besides the successful deals, ask for the names and phone numbers of CEOs the firm invested in whose results were only moderate to poor, and where the portfolio company had to cope with significant adversity. Talking with these CEOs will reveal the underlying fairness, character, values, ethics, and potential of the venture capital firm as a financial partner, as well as how it practises its investing philosophies. It is always interesting to probe regarding the behaviour at pricing meetings.

DEALING WITH VENTURE CAPITALISTS[27]

Do not forget that venture capitalists see lots of business plans and proposals, sometimes 100 or more a month. Typically, they invest in only one to three of these. The following suggestions may be helpful in working with them.

If possible, obtain a personal introduction from someone that is well-known to the investors (a director or founder of one of their portfolio companies, a limited partner in their fund, a lawyer or accountant who has worked with them on deals) and who knows you well. After identifying the best targets, you should create a market for your company by marketing it. Have several prospects. Be vague about who else you are talking with. You can end up with a rejection from everyone if the other firms know who was the first firm that turned you down. Beware, it is often just as hard to get a "no" as it is to get a "yes." You can waste an enormous amount of time before getting there.

When pushed by the investors to indicate what other firms/angels you are talking to, simply put it this way: "All our advisors believe that information is highly confidential to the company, and our team agrees. We are talking to other high quality investors like yourselves. The ones with the right chemistry who can make the biggest difference in our company and are prepared to invest first will be our partner. Once we have a term sheet and deal on the table, if you also want co-investors we are more than happy to share these other investors' names." Failing to take such a tack usually puts you in an adverse negotiating position.

Most investors who have serious interest will have some clear ideas about how to improve your strategy, product line, positioning, and a variety of other areas. This is one of the ways they can add value—if they are right. Consequently, you need to be prepared for them to take apart your business plan and to put it back together. They are likely to have their own format and their own financial models. Working with them on this is a good way to get to know them.

Never lie. As one entrepreneur put it, "You have to market the truth, but do not lie." Do not stop selling until the money is in the bank. Let the facts speak for themselves. Be able to deliver on the claims, statements, and promises you make or imply in your business plan and presentations. Tom Huseby of SeaPoint Ventures adds some final wisdom: "It's much harder than you ever thought it could be. You can last much longer than you ever thought you could. They have to do this for the rest of their lives!" Finally, never say no to an offer price. There is an old saying that your first offer may be your best offer.

QUESTIONS THE ENTREPRENEUR CAN ASK

The presentation to investors when seeking venture capital is demanding and pressing, which is appropriate for this high-stakes game. Venture capitalists have an enormous legal and fiduciary responsibility to their limited partners, not to mention their powerful self-interest. Therefore, they are thorough in their due diligence and questioning to assess the intelligence, integrity, nimbleness, and creativity of the entrepreneurial mind in action (see chapter 1).

Once the presentation and question-answer session is complete, the founders can learn a great deal about the investors and enhance their own credibility by asking a few simple questions:

- Tell us what you think of our strategy, how we size up the competition, and our game plan. What have we missed? Who have we missed?
- Are there competitors we have overlooked? How are we vulnerable and how do we compete?
- How would you change the way we are thinking about the business and planning to seize the opportunity?
- Is our team as strong as you would like? How would you improve this and when?
- Give us a sense of what you feel would be a fair range of value for our company if you invested $_____?

Their answers will reveal how much work they have done and how knowledgeable they are about your industry, technology, competitors, and the like. This will provide robust insight as to whether and how they can truly add value to the venture. At the same time, you will get a better sense of their forthrightness and integrity: Are they direct, straightforward, but not oblivious to the impact of their answers? Finally, these questions can send a favourable message to investors: Here are entrepreneurs who are intelligent, open-minded, receptive, and self-confident enough to solicit our feedback and opinions even though we may have opposing views.

DUE DILIGENCE: A TWO-WAY STREET

It can take several weeks or even months to complete the due diligence on a start-up, although if the investors know the entrepreneurs, it can go much more quickly. The verification of facts, backgrounds, and reputations of key people, market estimates, technical capabilities of the product, proprietary rights, and so on is a painstaking investigation for investors. They will want to talk with your directors, advisors, former bosses, and previous partners. Make it as easy as possible for them by having detailed résumés and lists of 10 to 20 references (with phone numbers and addresses) such as former customers, bankers, vendors, and others who can attest to your accomplishments. Prepare extra copies of published articles, reports, studies, market research, contracts or purchase orders, technical specifications, and other documentation that can support your claims.

One recent research project examined how 86 venture capital firms nationwide conducted their intensive due diligence. To evaluate the opportunity, the executive team, the risks, the competition, and to weigh the upside against the downside, firms spent from 40 to 400 hours, with the typical

BEWARE OF ONCOMING TRAFFIC

firm spending 120 hours. That is nearly three weeks of full-time effort. At the extreme, some firms engaged in twice as much due diligence.[28] Central to this investigation were careful checks of the venture team's references and verification of track record and capabilities.

While all this is going on, do your own due diligence on the venture fund. Ask for the names and phone numbers of some of their successful deals, some that did not work out, and the names of any presidents they ended up replacing. Who are their legal and accounting advisors? What footprints have they left in the sand regarding their quality, reputation, and record in truly adding value to the companies in which they invest? Finally, the chemistry between the venture team and the general partner who will have responsibility for the investment and, in all likelihood, a board seat, is crucial. If you do not have a financial partner you respect and can work closely with, then you are likely to regret ever having accepted the money.

OTHER EQUITY SOURCES

BUSINESS DEVELOPMENT BANK OF CANADA (BDC)

Promoting small and medium-sized enterprises by guaranteeing long-term loans, venture capital, and subordinate financing, Business Development Bank of Canada has been supporting start-up and high-potential ventures since 1944 (see Exhibit 9.12). According to their 2012 annual report, BDC had 28 000 clients:

- **BDC *Financing*** clients accepted $3.6 billion new loans in 2012. Income from BDC Financing was $504.7 million.

 See BDC's Financing by Stage of Development online in Connect.

- **BDC *Subordinate Financing*** clients accepted $163.8 million. Income from BDC Subordinate Financing was $36.2 million.

- BDC *Venture Capital* authorized direct investments for a total of $126.8 million in 2012. BDC Venture Capital recorded a $42.7 million loss for 2012.

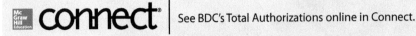

See BDC's Total Authorizations online in Connect.

- BDC *Consulting* offers entrepreneurs tailored, affordable, high-quality services to help them become more competitive. In 2012, 2236 mandates were started and a net loss of $11 million was reported.

BDC pays special attention to start-ups, innovators, fast growth companies, manufacturers, and exporters who face lower financing approval rates. BDC also pays special attention to entrepreneurs who are working to commercialize the fruits of research and development—university or lab discoveries—to create innovative products and globally successful companies in sectors such as life sciences and information technology.

Market data shows that approximately 5 percent of Canadian businesses are start-ups. BDC finds that after five years, 67 percent of the start-up businesses it supported survive, compared to the Statistics Canada industry benchmark of 36 percent.

BDC states its single mandate is to support Canadian entrepreneurs. It promotes an entrepreneurial culture across the country and targets. According to BDC:

- *Aboriginal* We help promote economic development through the Aboriginal Business Development Fund. Our strategy includes management training, ongoing mentorship, and loans. To raise entrepreneurship awareness among Aboriginal youth, we also organize E-Spirit, an Aboriginal youth business-plan competition.

EXHIBIT 9.12   **BUSINESS DEVELOPMENT BANK OF CANADA**

- BDC Venture Capital is a Canadian leader in the critically important early-stage (including seed) investment phase. In fiscal 2012, BDC made 87 percent of the dollar value of its direct investments in early-stage firms, including 16 percent devoted to seed investments.
- BDC offers subordinate financing, a hybrid financing that combines debt and equity features, to entrepreneurs who need working capital to grow their businesses but do not have the tangible security that conventional lenders require, or who do not want to dilute their ownership of the firm.
- Female entrepreneurs lead businesses of all sizes in all sectors. They also enter the small business marketplace at twice the rate men do. Over the past two decades, their number has more than doubled.
- Young entrepreneurs lead about 9 percent of Canadian small businesses. Many of them find it hard to secure financing because they have limited net worth, little or no managerial experience, and have no proven track record. Through its Entrepreneurship Centres across Canada, BDC granted 260 loans for a total of $6 million to young entrepreneurs across the country.
- BDC maintains formal partnerships with more than 200 Community Futures Development Corporations. These partnerships enable BDC to reach entrepreneurs who live near these centres. Using this network, BDC supported more than 1000 entrepreneurs in 2012.
- BDC helps promote economic development in Aboriginal communities through a grassroots approach. This strategy delivers management training, ongoing mentorship, and loans of $2000 to $20 000, with terms that vary depending on the cash flow expectations for the project.

Source: Business Development Bank of Canada, Annual Report 2012.

- *Rural* We have partnerships with more than 220 Community Futures Development Corporations, a cross-country network of contact points located mostly in rural areas.
- *Young Canadians* Many young entrepreneurs find it hard to secure financing because they have little or no management experience, financial resources, or track record. We celebrate the creativity and success of young entrepreneurs with our annual Young Entrepreneur Awards. Over the past eight years, we have authorized over $1.2 billion in financing to them.[29]

 | See BDC's Venture Capital Direct Investments Authorized by Stage of Development online in Connect.

SCIENTIFIC RESEARCH AND EXPERIMENTAL DEVELOPMENT TAX CREDIT PROGRAM

The risk and expense of conducting serious research and development are often beyond the means of start-ups and small businesses. For a number of decades, the SR&ED federal tax incentive program has encouraged companies to invest in and pursue innovation by offering tax credits of up to 35 percent on the first $2 million of qualified expenditures and 20 percent on amounts over that cap. In addition, provincial incentives vary from 10 to 20 to 37.5 percent. The Canada Revenue Agency administers the program and receives claims from over 18 000 enterprises, three-quarters of whom are small with claims varying from $20 000 to $2 million; in 2010 CRA doled out over $4 billion in investment tax credits.

However, many point out that although the concept is seemingly clear and appears easy, in reality there are difficulties. The process is time consuming, documentation required is extensive, quality of financial information to be provided in support is demanding, and there is a long time lag until payment is received.

INDUSTRIAL RESEARCH ASSISTANCE PROGRAM (IRAP)

The National Research Council-Industrial Research Assistance Program provides assistance for small and medium-sized enterprises. Financial assistance is geared toward technology innovation projects, digital technology adoption, HIV technology development, and a youth employment program designed to help both the enterprise and recent post-secondary graduates. Funds are provided to cover a portion of the salary costs of a post-secondary graduate who will work on technical opportunities or technology-related projects, such as R&D, engineering, development of new products/processes, market analysis for a new technology-based product, improvement of customer service, etc.

CORPORATE VENTURE CAPITAL

While corporate venture capitalists are similar to traditional VCs in that they look for promising young companies on the verge of a spike in sales, corporations tend to be more risk-averse and specialized. Business investing is highly cyclical in nature and follows a pattern of ebb and flow. Since investing in a relevant technology can reduce the costs of their own research and development, fit is usually an important aspect of the funding decision. When working with corporate funding sources, make sure you consider the corporation's philosophy and culture as well as their investment track record with small businesses before agreeing to any deal.

MEZZANINE CAPITAL

At the point where the company has overcome many of the early-stage risks, it may be ready for mezzanine capital.[30] The term **mezzanine financing** refers to capital that is between **senior debt** financing and common shares.

In some cases it takes the form of redeemable preferred shares, but in most cases it is subordinated debt that carries an equity "**kicker**" consisting of warrants or a conversion feature into common shares. This subordinated-debt capital has many characteristics of debt but also can serve as equity to underpin senior debt. It is generally unsecured, with a fixed coupon and maturity of 5 to 10 years. A number of variables are involved in structuring such a loan: the interest rate, the amount and form of the equity, exercise/conversion price, maturity, call features, sinking fund, covenants, and put/call options. These variables provide for a wide range of possible structures to suit the needs of both the issuer and the investor.

Offsetting these advantages are a few disadvantages to mezzanine capital compared to equity capital. As debt, the interest is payable on a regular basis, and the principal must be repaid, if not converted into equity. This is a large claim against cash and can be burdensome if the expected growth and/or profitability does not materialize and cash becomes tight. In addition, the subordinated debt often contains covenants relating to net worth, debt, and dividends.

Mezzanine investors generally look for companies that have a demonstrated performance record, with revenues approaching $10 million or more. Because the financing will involve paying interest, the investor will carefully examine existing and future cash flow and projections.

Mezzanine financing is utilized in a wide variety of industries, ranging from basic manufacturing to high technology. As the name implies, however, it focuses more on the broad middle spectrum of business, rather than on high-tech, high-growth companies. Specialty retailing, broadcasting, communications, environmental services, distributors, and consumer or business service industries are more attractive to mezzanine investors.

PRIVATE PLACEMENTS

Private placements are an attractive source of equity capital for a private company that for whatever reason has ruled out the possibility of going public. If the goal of the company is to raise a specific amount of capital in a short time, this equity source may be the answer. In this transaction, the company offers shares to a few private investors, rather than to the public as in a public offering. A private placement requires little paperwork compared to a public offering.

If the venture team knows of enough investors, then the private placement could be distributed among a small group of friends, family, relatives, or acquaintances. Or the company may decide to have a broker circulate the proposal among a few investors who have expressed an interest in small companies. The following four groups of investors might be interested in a private placement:[31]

1. Let us say you manufacture a product and sell to dealers, franchisors, or wholesalers. These are the people who know and respect your company. Moreover, they depend on you to supply the product they sell. They might consider it to be in their interest to buy your shares if they believe it will help assure continuation of product supply, and perhaps give them favoured treatment if you bring out a new product or product improvement. One problem is when one dealer invests and another does not; can you treat both fairly in the future? Another problem is that a customer who invests might ask for exclusive rights to market your product in a particular geographical area, and you might find it hard to refuse.

2. A second group of prospective buyers for your shares are those professional investors who are always on the lookout to buy a good, small company in its formative years, and

---

mezzanine financing: Financing utilized to finance expansion of existing enterprises. It is a debt/equity hybrid: the lender has the right to convert debt capital to an equity position. It usually provides the borrower a quick hit of cash; with little due diligence or collateral the financing is priced aggressively and the lender expects a 20–30 percent return. In architecture, a mezzanine is a middle level between two other floors.

senior debt: Money borrowed that must be repaid first if the enterprise fails; debt that takes priority over other unsecured or "junior" or subordinate debt owed.

kicker: An exercisable warrant, right, or other feature added to a debt instrument to satisfy investors; the debt holder thus has the option to purchase shares. Often the kicker has a breakpoint that must be obtained (e.g., share price reaching a particular level) before having real value. Kickers are included to lure investors and seal the deal or reach the entire issue.

ride it to success. Often, these sophisticated investors choose an industry and a particular product or service in that industry they believe will become hot and then focus 99 percent of their attention on the calibre of the venture. If your executive team, or one key individual, has earned a high reputation as a star in leadership, technology, or marketing, these risk-minded investors tend to flock to that person. (The high-tech industry is an obvious example.) Whether your operation meets their tests for stardom as a hot field may determine whether they find your private placement a risk to their liking.

3. Other investors are searching for opportunities to buy shares of smaller growth companies in the expectation that the company will soon go public and they will benefit as new investors bid the price up, as often happens. For such investors, news of a private placement is a tip-off that a company is on the move and worth investigating, always with an eye on the possibility of its going public.

4. Private placements also often attract venture capitalists who hope to benefit when the company goes public or when the company is sold. To help ensure that happy development, these investors get seriously active at the level of the board of directors, where their skill and experience can help the company reach its potential.

INITIAL PUBLIC SHARE OFFERINGS

Commonly referred to as an IPO, an initial public offering raises capital through provincially registered and underwritten sales of the company's shares. Numerous federal and provincial securities laws and regulations govern these offerings; thus, it is important that the venture's executives consult with lawyers and accountants who are familiar with the current regulations.

In the past, such as during strong bull markets for new issues, it was possible to raise money for an early-growth venture or even for a start-up. These boom markets are easy to identify because the number of new issues jump astoundingly. The flip side is that sharp decreases follow just as quickly as investor enthusiasm grinds to a halt. In these more difficult financial environments, such as following the 2008 recession and subsequent global economic slowdown, the new-issues market became very quiet for entrepreneurial companies. As a result, exit opportunities are limited. In addition, it becomes very difficult to raise money for early-growth or even more mature companies from the public market.

The more mature a company is when it makes a public offering, the better the terms of the offering. A higher valuation can be placed on the company, and less equity will be given up by the founders for the required capital.

There are a number of reasons an entrepreneurial company would want to go public. The following are some of the advantages:

- To raise more capital with less dilution than occurs with private placements or venture capital.
- To improve the balance sheet and/or to reduce or to eliminate debt, thereby enhancing the company's net worth. To obtain cash for pursuing opportunities that would otherwise be unaffordable.
- To access other suppliers of capital and to increase bargaining power, as the company pursues additional capital when it needs it least.
- To improve credibility with customers, vendors, key people, and prospects. To give the impression: "You're in the big leagues now."
- To achieve liquidity for owners and investors.

A PRIVATE PLACEMENT TIMELINE: JOURDAN RESOURCES OF VAL-D'OR, QUEBEC.

A mining company with exploration and development projects across northern Quebec, Jourdan Resources experienced success in finding phosphate, tantalum, lithium, beryllium, molybdenum, gold, uranium, and investor capital.

- 17 September 2007—closing of a $315 000 private placement; 2 070 000 common shares at a price of $0.15 per share and 2 070 000 common share purchase warrants. Each warrant entitles the holder to purchase one common share for a period of 24 months at an exercise price of $0.20 per share within six months of closing; thereafter at an exercise price of $0.30 per share during the second six months; thereafter at an exercise price of $0.40 per share during the third six months; and finally at a price of $0.50 per share at the remaining six months. In connection with the offering, Jourdan Resources paid finder's fees totalling $24 450. The proceeds of the offering to be used for working capital.

- 17 December 2007—closing of a $400 000 private placement; 2 858 000 units at a price of $0.14 per unit, with each unit consisting of one flow-through common share and one common share purchase warrant. The proceeds of the offering to be used for working capital.

- 20 December 2007—closing of a $235 000 private placement. 2 350 000 common shares at a price of $0.10 per share, including purchase warrants.

- 20 December 2007—closing of a $150 000 private placement. 1 071 428 units at $0.14 per unit. The securities issued pursuant to the offering are subject to a four month hold period.

- 21 December 2007—closing of a $225 000 private placement. 1 607 142 units at $0.14 per unit. Finder's fee representing 80 357 units (5 percent of the gross proceeds) and a 24-month 10 percent broker options exercisable.

- 22 October 2009—closing of a $682 775 private placement. 9 952 857 non–flow-through common shares were issued at a price of $0.035 per share and 4 976 429 common share purchase warrants. Also issued 7 431 667 flow-through common shares at $0.045 per share and 4 976 429 common share purchase warrants. Finder's feeds totalled $43 217.50 and 666 666 common share purchase warrants.

- 4 January 2010—closing of a $250 380 private placement.

- 28 June 2010—restructuring proposed: one new common share for each tranche of four outstanding common shares.

- 1 October 2010—restructuring approved: 72 131 833 shares becomes approximately 18 032 958.

- 3 December 2010—offering of a $1.7 million private placement; units at $0.15 and flow-through shares at $0.20.

- 23 December 2010—closing of $1 486 250 private placement. Agent paid a cash commission of $106 292.05 and issued 380 200 non-transferable broker warrants. Closing of a concurrent placement for $235 750 paying finder's fees in cash of $3600.

- 30 December 2010—closing of a $538 888 private placement.

- 8 June 2011—plans to spin out of uranium asset to maximize shareholder value by allowing the market to independently value separate property portfolios. Two strategically positioned companies is the result sought; one focused on uranium, the other focused on rare metals or high-technology metals. Jourdan Resources would transfer its uranium property to a new company in return for $300 000 in shares of the new company to be distributed to Jourdan shareholders.

- 5 October 2011—Émilien Séguin steps down as President and CEO, but continues as a director; Michael Dehn becomes President, CEO, and a director of the company.

- 19 October 2011—Donald R. M. Quick becomes a director of the company. Quick has expertise in mining mergers and acquisitions, having been involved with at least six deals, including the largest deals in Canada.

- 24 October 2011—enters into an acquisition and transfers its uranium assets with a book value of $600 000 to Gimus Resources and completes a private placement for $370 000.

- 12 December 2011—announces a private placement for a maximum of $2 500 000.

- 17 January 2012—Jourdan Resources closes the IPO of its subsidiary Gimus Resources.

- 20 January 2012—Second and final tranche of private placement announced in 12 December 2011 closes. 1 250 000 (half of what was announced) was raised. CEO announces "We are very pleased to have raised the current private placement in difficult market conditions."

- 22 February 2012—announces acquisition of Dissimieux Lake phosphate property.

- 29 February 2012—appoints new CFO. Departing CFO will manage the spinoff Gimus Resources.

- 11 September 2012—announces a private placement for a maximum of $1 700 000.

- 22 October 2012—first tranche of private placement closes for $152 750.

(continued)

- 24 December 2012—closing of a $200 000 private placement.
- 27 December 2012—closing of a flow-through private placement for $200 000.
- 22 February 2013—Jourdan Resources issues 2 300 000 incentive share options exercisable at $0.10 with an expiry of 22 February 2013.

- 9 May 2013—Jourdan Resources announces first tranche closing of private placement for $200 000.
- 31 July 2013—Jourdan Resources announces closing of second and final tranche for $102 500.

| EXHIBIT 9.13 | JOURDAN RESOURCES SHARE PRICE ON THE TSX VENTURE |

- To create options to acquire other companies with a tax-free exchange of shares, rather than having to use cash.
- To create equity incentives for new and existing employees.

Notwithstanding the above, IPOs can be disadvantageous for a number of reasons:

- The legal, accounting, and administrative costs of raising money via a public offering are more disadvantageous than other ways of raising money.
- A large amount of administrative effort, time, and expense are required to comply with securities regulations and reporting requirements and to maintain the status of a public company. This diversion of time and energy from the tasks of running the company can hurt its performance and growth.
- The executive team can become more interested in maintaining the price of the company's shares and computing capital gains than in running the company. Short-term activities to maintain or increase a current year's earnings can take precedence over longer-term programs to build the company and increase its earnings.
- The liquidity of a company's shares achieved through a public offering may be more apparent than real. Without a sufficient number of shares outstanding and a strong "market maker," there may be no real market for the shares and, thus, no liquidity.
- The investment banking firms willing to take a new or unseasoned company public may not be the ones with whom the company would like to do business and establish a long-term relationship.

PRIVATE PLACEMENT AFTER GOING PUBLIC[32]

Sometimes a company goes public and then, for any number of reasons that add up to bad luck, the high expectations that attracted lots of investors early on turn sour. Your financial picture worsens; there is a cash crisis; down goes the price of your shares in the public marketplace. You find that you need new funds to work your way out of difficulties, but public investors are disillusioned and not likely to cooperate if you bring out a new issue.

Still, other investors are sophisticated enough to see beyond today's problems; they know the company's fundamentals are sound. While the public has turned its back on you, these investors may be receptive if you offer a private placement to tide you over. In such circumstances, you may use a wide variety of securities—common shares, convertible preferred shares, convertible debentures. There are several types of exempt offerings, usually described by reference to the securities regulation that applies to them.

EMPLOYEE SHARE OWNERSHIP PLANS (ESOPS)

ESOPs are another potential source of funding used by existing companies that have high confidence in the stability of their future earnings and cash flow. An ESOP is a program in which the employees become investors in the company, thereby creating an internal source of funding. "The combination of being able to invest in employer shares and to benefit from its many tax advantages make the ESOP an attractive tool."[33] The ESOP Association of Canada claims that enterprises with ESOPs have higher profit growth, higher profit margins, increased productivity, and better returns on both total equity as well as capital.

Another way to encourage employee commitment and purchase of shares in the company is through a self-administered RRSP program set up to enable purchase of the company shares (with percentage ownership limits). This would also qualify for federal tax credit as well as a provincial tax incentive.

KEEPING CURRENT ABOUT CAPITAL MARKETS

One picture is clear from all this: capital markets, especially for closely held, private companies right through the initial public offering, are dynamic, volatile, asymmetrical, and imperfect. Research published in 2012 by Cécile Carpentier of Laval University, Jean-François L'Her of Caisse de dépôt et placement du Québec, and Jean-Marc Suret of Laval University shows that "individual investors do not price the stocks correctly around the issue and incur significant negative returns...entrepreneurial outside equity attracts lemons and individual investors cannot invest wisely in emerging ventures." Keeping abreast of what is happening in the capital markets

PRESS RELEASE: RIFCO INC. ISSUES COMMON SHARES UNDER EMPLOYEE SHARE OWNERSHIP

The Red Deer, Alberta, company operates through its wholly owned subsidiary Rifco National Auto Finance Corporation to provide automobile loans through its dealership network across Canada.

Shareholders approved the reservation of a maximum of 200 000 common shares for issuance under the ESOP within the year. Employees may contribute a maximum of 10 percent of their gross salaries, which will be matched 50 percent by Rifco with the issue price based on the weighted average trading price of the last five days of each month.

- On 1 March 2013, 3075 common shares were issued to employees, including 1590 common shares to officers at an issue price of $4.69. Shares issued to officers are subject to a four month hold period expiring 1 July 2013.

- On 1 April 2013, 3711 common shares were issued to employees, including 1455 common shares to officers at an issue price of $3.93. Shares issued to officers are subject to a four month hold period expiring 1 August 2013.

- On 1 May 2013, 6623 common shares were issued to employees, including 2904 common shares to officers at an issue price of $4.05. Shares issued to officers are subject to a four month hold period expiring 1 September 2013.

- On 2 July 2013, 6953 common shares were issued to employees, including 4425 common shares to officers at an issue prices of $4.61.

- On 1 August 2013, 4657 common shares were issued to employees, including 1307 common shares to officers at an issue price of $4.60. Shares issued to officers are subject to a four month hold period expiring 1 December 2013.

in the 6 to 12 months before a major capital infusion can save invaluable time and hundreds of thousands and occasionally millions of dollars. Below are listed the best sources currently available to keep you informed:

- ✔ Canada's Venture Capital & Private Equity Association
- ✔ *Venture Capital Journal*
- ✔ *Red Herring*, a Silicon Valley magazine
- ✔ Internet searches for "raising capital in Canada" and "U.S. capital markets" should produce a number of leads; the Conservative government's 2013 budget isolates money for incubator and accelerator organizations across Canada

LO1 Cash flow is king and cash is queen. Happiness is a positive cash flow. More cash is preferred to less cash. Cash sooner is preferred to cash later. Less-risky cash is preferred to more-risky cash.

LO2 Financial know-how, issues, and analysis are often the entrepreneurs' Achilles' heels. Entrepreneurial finance is the art and science of quantifying value creation, slicing the value pie, and managing and covering financial risk.

LO3 Determining capital requirements, crafting financial and fundraising strategies, and managing and orchestrating the financial process are critical to new venture success.

LO4 Characterizing the capital markets as a food chain, where enterprise size matches the inves-

tors looking for companies to invest in, is key to understanding motivations and requirements.

LO5 Entrepreneurs have to determine the need for outside investors, whether they want outside investors, and if so, whom. Canada's unique capital markets include a wide array of private investors, from "angels" to venture capitalists.

LO6 The search for capital can be very time consuming and requires creativity and hard work. Often your source of money is more important than how much.

LO7 It is said that the only thing that is harder to get from a venture capitalist than a "yes" is a "no." Entrepreneurs who know what and whom to look for—and look out for—increase their odds for success.

1. Define the following and explain why they are important: burn rate, free cash flow, OOC, TTC, financial management myopia, spreadsheet mirage.
2. Why is entrepreneurial finance simultaneously both the least and most important part of the entrepreneurial process? Explain this paradox.
3. What factors affect the availability, suitability, and cost of various types of financing? Why are these factors critical?
4. Why do financially savvy entrepreneurs ask the financial and strategic questions in Exhibit 9.1? Can you answer these questions for your venture?
5. What does one look for in an investor, and why?
6. How can the founders prepare for the due diligence and evaluation process?
7. Describe the venture capital investing process and its implications for fundraising.
8. What other sources of capital are available and how are these accessed?
9. Explain the capital markets food chain and its implications for entrepreneurs and investors.

1. With regard to your new venture, to what extent might you be suffering from financial myopia and spreadsheet mirage?
2. People who believe that you first have to have money, in large amounts, to make money are naive and ignorant. Why is this so? Do you agree?
3. Who do you need to get to know well to strengthen the entrepreneurial finance know-how on your team?
4. Some entrepreneurs say you shouldn't raise venture capital unless you have no other alternative. Do you agree or disagree, and why?
5. Identify a founder/CEO who has raised outside capital, and was later fired by the board of directors. What are the lessons here?
6. How do venture capitalists make money? What are the economics of venture capital as a business?

Preparation Questions

1. With no significant assets and no track record as a CEO, can Raza Hasanie make it?

2. What financing structure will satisfy investors?

3. How much will Raza Hasanie have to give up?

On the kitchen counter of Raza Hasanie's Calgary home, there were a dozen neatly bound copies of a business plan, ready for distribution to prospective investors. Hasanie, a geologist, had developed the business concept while studying for his MBA.

The plan outlined an oil-and-gas opportunity that could exploit suspended wells to yield a 5 to 15 times return on investment, and called for roughly $1 million in seed-capital funding. The business model was a common one for hundreds of small-scale companies and independent operators: Scavenger would bid on mineral rights for sites with intact wells, equipment, and infrastructure left over from previous drilling activities, and extract smaller deposits left behind by large-scale exploration and extraction operations. These bypassed opportunities weren't individually big enough to meet the investment hurdle rates set by large energy firms, but could offer excellent returns for a company ready to pursue many bypassed wells in parallel—precisely Scavenger's business model.

But there was a hitch: The company existed only in the pages of Hasanie's business plan. Scavenger Energy had no employees, no operations, and no customers. Its CEO, freshly graduated from business school, had no resources of his own to invest in the firm. In fact, Hasanie was still working a day job at IBM's geological software group. And while he was a skilled earth scientist, he had no experience leading a start-up company.

Hasanie needed to work his personal networks to get in front of investors. But even if he could find angels to pitch to, it would be a tough sell: The young entrepreneur would be asking investors to take a million-dollar gamble on an unproven founder with little to offer but some technical know-how and an idea.

FIRST PITCH

Hasanie's first calls were to a handful of well-connected supporters. While completing his MBA in Ontario, he pitched the Scavenger concept in a pair of business-plan competitions, netting him some $15 000 in prize money and providing an introduction to two seasoned angel investors and an Ottawa venture capitalist. The VC provided Hasanie with introductions into a small circle of Ottawa investors, to whom Hasanie made his first pitch.

That pitch took place in the national capital during the summer of 2004. Not one potential investor could boast of any experience in the energy industry, but everyone's ears perked up when a particular phrase rose above the technical lingo: "5× to 15× returns."

The story they were being told was about overlooked opportunities. There were millions of barrels of oil left behind in the Alberta oilfields, Hasanie explained to his audience, ignored and all but forgotten by Canadian energy companies. Hasanie himself had exploited one of these wells while with a small Calgary firm, and turned the company's $30 000 investment into $300 000 in natural gas production.

It wasn't just dumb luck: With the right software and technical expertise, public-domain information could be used to zero in on only those wells with a high chance for hydrocarbon recovery. Hasanie did enjoy some good fortune too, however—because the oil and gas industry is built on high risks and stratospheric rewards, few energy-industry titans were eager to pick through the modest remains of shut-in wells when they had larger, more attractive opportunities to pursue.

The only people interested in these overlooked opportunities were independent operators and very small-scale companies, which would pursue wells individually and within certain geographical boundaries—the oilpatch version of a lifestyle business. Each individual well would ultimately yield under half a million dollars—enough to keep slow-growth individual operators comfortable, but far less than needed to attract the interest of the energy giants. By pursuing large numbers of these small opportunities, Hasanie hoped to develop a low-risk, high-margin business—profitable after the first operation, and reaching after-tax net annual income exceeding $3.5 million by the third year.

The Ottawa investors followed up Hasanie's pitch with several rounds of meetings and due diligence. Their interest had been piqued, and by the end of the summer, they had informally committed $500 000 in financing to launch Scavenger.

FEEDBACK

That half-million wouldn't be enough. The same summer, in parallel with his Ottawa meetings, Hasanie met with a number of Calgary oil-and-gas investors and consultants, hoping

This case was written by Lukas Neville, PhD student, Queen's School of Business, and Professor Elspeth J. Murray, CIBC Teaching Fellow in Entrepreneurship, Queen's School of Business, Queen's University. This case was developed with the support of the CIBC Curriculum Development Fund at the Queen's Centre for Business Venturing, for purposes of classroom discussion.

they'd validate his concept and maybe lead him to some industry "greyhair" who would join his advisory board. Following a meeting with one energy-sector private equity lender, Hasanie dashed off an email to a former professor, a trusted advisor. "He's concerned that I'm only looking for $500K," he typed. "He was thinking upwards of $5 million would be needed. I'm not sure we need that much, but he did make some good points about the cost of delays or problems in the field. The first shut-in well I did with my previous company went flawlessly, so I hoped Scavenger would have similar luck. That might be a bit naive."

Scavenger's approach was incredibly economical, avoiding the immense costs of drilling, testing, and surface-rights negotiation usually borne by traditional exploration companies. "We're not even going after low-hanging fruit," Hasanie joked in his presentation. "This is picking up the berries off the ground." But Hasanie quickly discovered that everyone felt he needed more—whether it was oilpatch veterans saying $5 million or his conservative advisors in Toronto, who suggested a minimum of $2 million. Scavenger's expenses would come from its analysis process, land purchases, facility-use negotiations, and the cost of extraction. Using publicly available data, Scavenger would identify sites with the right mineral rights and infrastructure available, and then select those with a reasonably high recoverable amount of natural gas. With sites identified, they would bid on the land in an auction, negotiate usage rights for the facilities, and hire independent contractors to reopen the well. Commodity price increases could lead to volatility in labour markets and in auction prices for mineral rights. Moreover, it was entirely possible that problems with decades-old well equipment could push up costs. "I do need to take into consideration that field problems will ultimately occur," Hasanie wrote to his advisor, "and I should be prepared to 'spend' my way out of trouble when needed." Hasanie worked in consultation with his advisors and experts to arrive at a more realistic target for his fundraising. After three rounds of revised financials, it was clear he would need to expand his financing round beyond his early supporters in Ottawa—and would need to be seeking some $2 million in financing, with at least $750 000 in the immediate term.

Hasanie returned, hat in hand, to his alma mater. He met with prominent alumni over drinks at the storied National Club in Toronto and was reunited with one of the judges from his business-plan competition. That judge, a serial entrepreneur and angel investor himself, wanted to help: "What I wanted to do is to give the business a chance to succeed," he explains. "So I helped him get the right supporters with the right resources." With Hasanie ready to seek a larger and more complicated financing deal, he'd need top-notch legals. The B-plan judge introduced Hasanie to a senior partner and the chair of Stikeman Elliott, a white-shoe Toronto law firm. The partner agreed to help Hasanie with complimentary legal work.

Hasanie's new evangelist also helped introduce him to potential investors. Meeting at his alma mater's satellite office in downtown Toronto, Hasanie pitched to a host of high-profile business leaders, venture capitalists, and angel investors. They, too, were attracted by Scavenger's risk-and-reward profile. But they also had a range of serious concerns.

First, Hasanie had no "skin in the game"—he had sunk a few thousand dollars of B-plan prize money into registering his business and doing preliminary research, but the investors wanted to see more on the line for the young CEO. Hasanie noted to the investors that his family and close friends were all willing to invest, but the angels were not necessarily keen on that idea: It would secure founder commitment, but it would also add complexity and risk to the capitalization structure. The investors were concerned that a cluttered list of investors would make governance and the structure of an eventual exit more difficult.

Secondly, the investors were nervous about the lack of operational experience—Hasanie had never run a company, they noted. Lacking oil-and-gas experience themselves, they wanted a director from the energy industry, something Hasanie hadn't been able to secure.

Finally, there was a considerable challenge in terms of ownership and founder incentives. While there was interest on all sides to keep the founder happy and focused on growing the business, the angels couldn't justify giving the founder a fifth of the business simply for having the idea. They needed Hasanie to invest upfront—or find a way for him to earn his equity stake.

Hasanie, grappling with the feedback from investors, wrote again to his former professor to convey his concerns. "It looks like my ownership of the company is going to be significantly reduced from what I had expected," he confessed. "Once the investors and lawyers get their hands into the agreement, my stake is going to be pretty diluted."

connect®

For more information on the resources available from McGraw-Hill Ryerson, go to www.mcgrawhill.ca/he/solutions.

CHAPTER 10

THE DEAL: VALUATION, STRUCTURE, AND NEGOTIATION

> *When one door closes another door opens; but we so often look so long and so regretfully upon the closed door that we do not see the ones which open for us.*
>
> ALEXANDER GRAHAM BELL

LEARNING OBJECTIVES

LO1 Discuss how and why equity proportions are allocated to investors.

LO2 Classify methods used by venture capitalists and professional investors to estimate the value of a company.

LO3 Evaluate how deals are structured, including critical terms, conditions, and covenants.

LO4 Explain key aspects of negotiating and closing deals.

LO5 Characterize good versus bad deals and identify some of the traps entrepreneurs face in venture financing.

THE ART AND CRAFT OF VALUATION

The entrepreneur's and private investor's world of finance is very different from the corporate finance arena where public companies jostle and compete in well-established capital markets. The private company and private capital world of entrepreneurial finance is more volatile, more imperfect, and less accessible than corporate capital markets. The sources of capital are very different. The companies are much younger, more dynamic, and the environment more rapidly changing and uncertain. The consequences, for entrepreneurs and investors alike, of this markedly different context are profound. Cash flow is king, and beta coefficients and elegant corporate financial theories are irrelevant. Also, liquidity and timing are everything, and there are innumerable, unavoidable conflicts between users and suppliers of capital. Finally, the determination of a company's value is elusive and more art than science.

WHAT IS A COMPANY WORTH?

The answer: It all depends! Unlike the market for public companies, where millions of shares are traded daily and the firm's market capitalization (total shares outstanding times the price per share) is readily determined, the market for private companies is very imperfect. A new venture may be sitting on intellectual property that cannot be readily judged. How does a team reveal its value and what it expects from investors? Investors too must provide evidence that they can be part of a win-win solution.

DETERMINANTS OF VALUE

The criteria and methods applied in corporate finance to value companies traded publicly in the capital markets, when cavalierly applied to entrepreneurial companies, have severe limitations. The ingredients to the entrepreneurial valuation are cash, time, and risk. In chapter 9 you determined the burn rate, OOC, and the TTC for your venture, so it is not hard to infer that the amount of cash available and the cash generated will play an important role in valuation. Similarly, Exhibit 9.5 showed that time also plays an influential role. Finally, risk or perception of risk contributes to the determination of value. The old adage, "The greater the risk, the greater the reward" has considerable bearing on how investors size up the venture.

LONG-TERM VALUE CREATION VERSUS QUARTERLY EARNINGS

The core mission of the entrepreneur is to build the best company possible and, if possible, to create a great company. This is the single surest way of generating long-term value for all the stakeholders and society. Such a mission has quite different strategic imperatives than one aimed solely at maximizing quarterly earnings to attain the highest share price possible given price/earnings ratios at the time. More will be said about this in chapter 15.

PSYCHOLOGICAL FACTORS DETERMINING VALUE

Time after time companies are valued at preposterous multiples of any sane price/earnings or sales ratios. In the best years, with the bull market charging ahead, equities trading on the Toronto Stock Exchange were trading at nearly 20 times earnings. The shares of many of these companies were being traded at 50 or more times earnings and several were at 95 to 100 times earnings and six to seven times sales! Even more extreme valuations were seen during the peak of the dot-com bubble from 1998 to early 2000. Some companies were valued at 100 times revenue and more during this classic frenzy. High multiples did come back down but then pressed into 2005 and beyond until the rude awakening of late 2008 and early 2009. In mid-2005 the TSX composite index was at nearly 20 times earnings but by the fall of 2008 the P/E ratio for the Toronto Stock Exchange index was at half its former glory. The TSX composite index did bounce back and by 2011 was strong again, but not a the heights of years prior. In 2012 it dropped significantly and had ups and downs into 2013.

Often a psychological wave is behind extraordinarily high valuations; a combination of euphoric enthusiasm for a fine company, exacerbated by greed and fear of missing the run-up. The same psychology can also drive prices to undreamed of heights in private companies. The Bre-X fiasco is one such story that did not end well.

A THEORETICAL PERSPECTIVE

Establishing Boundaries and Ranges, Rather than Calculating a Number

Valuation is much more than science, as can be seen from the examples just noted. As will be seen shortly, there are at least a dozen different ways of determining the value of a private company. A lot of assumptions and a lot of judgment calls are made in every valuation exercise. In one instance, for example, an entrepreneur consulted 13 experts to determine how much he should bid for the other half of a $10 million in sales company. The answer ranged from $1 to $6 million. He subsequently acquired the other half for $3.5 million.

shotgun clause: A buy–sell agreement delivered as an ultimatum generally when a partnership is strained or an impasse is reached and a buyout cannot amicably be reached. Cash on hand and accessible as well as ability to run the firm play a role in evaluation and offer.

It can be a serious mistake to approach the valuation task in hopes of arriving at a single number or even a narrow range. All you can realistically expect is a range of values with boundaries driven by different methods and underlying assumptions for each. Within that range, the buyer and the seller need to determine the comfort zone of each. At what point are you basically indifferent to buying and selling? Determining your point of indifference can be an invaluable aid in preparing you for negotiations to buy or sell.

For example, Tom Culligan and Frank O'Dea started Second Cup in 1975 in a shopping mall in the outskirts of Toronto. The venture grew and eventually Frank O'Dea delivered a **shotgun clause** to his partner (an offer to buy out the partner at a specified price; the partner must either sell or buy out the other partner at that offer price) and Tom Culligan decided to buy rather than sell.

INVESTOR'S REQUIRED RATE OF RETURN

Various investors will require a different rate of return (ROR) for investments in different stages of development and will expect holding periods of various lengths. For example, Exhibit 10.1 summarizes, as ranges, the annual rates of return that venture capital investors seek on investments by stage of development and how long they expect to hold these investments. Several factors underlie the required ROR on a venture capital investment, including premiums for systemic risk, illiquidity, and value added. Of course, these can be expected to vary regionally and from time to time as market conditions change because the investments are in what are decidedly imperfect capital market niches to begin with.

INVESTOR'S REQUIRED SHARE OF OWNERSHIP   LO1

The rate of return required by the investor determines the investor's required share of the ownership, as Exhibit 10.2 illustrates. The future value of a $1-million investment at 50 percent

EXHIBIT 10.1

RATE OF RETURN SOUGHT BY VENTURE CAPITAL INVESTORS

STAGE	ANNUAL RATE OF RETURN (%)	TYPICAL EXPECTED HOLDING PERIOD (YEARS)
Seed and start-up	50–100 or more	More than 10
First stage	40–60	5–10
Second stage	30–40	4–7
Expansion	20–30	3–5
Bridge and mezzanine	20–30	1–3
LBOs	30–50	3–5
Turnarounds	50	3–5

compounded is $1 million $\times (1.5)^5$ = $1 million $\times 7.59$ = $7.59 million. The future value of the company in year 5 is profit after tax $\times$ price/earnings ratio = $1 million $\times 15$ = $15 million. Thus, the share of ownership required in year 5 is:

$$\frac{\text{Future value of the investment} = \$7.59 \text{ million}}{\text{Future value of the company} = \$15.00 \text{ million}} = 51\%$$

One can readily see that by changing any of the key variables, the results will change accordingly.

If the venture capitalists require the RORs mentioned earlier, the ownership they also require is determined as follows: In the start-up stage, 25 to 75 percent for investing all of the required

EXHIBIT 10.2

INVESTOR'S REQUIRED SHARE OF OWNERSHIP UNDER VARIOUS ROR OBJECTIVES

Assumptions:
    Amount of initial start-up investment = $1 million   Year 5 After-tax profit = $1 million
    Holding period = 5 years   Year 5 Price/earnings ratio = 15
    Required rate of return = 50%
Calculating the required share of ownership:

	INVESTOR'S RETURN OBJECTIVE (PERCENT/YEAR COMPOUNDED)			
Price/Earning Ratio	30%	40%	50%	60%
10×	37%	54%	76%	106%
15×	25	36	51	70
20×	19	27	38	52
25×	15	22	30	42

funds; beyond the start-up stage, 10 to 40 percent, depending on the amount invested, maturity, and track record of the venture; in a seasoned venture in the later rounds of investment, 10 to 30 percent to supply the additional funds needed to sustain its growth.

THE THEORY OF COMPANY PRICING

In chapter 9, we introduced the concept of the food chain, which we have included here as Exhibit 10.3. This chart depicts the evolution of a company from its idea stage through an initial public offering (IPO). The appetite of the various sources of capital—from family, friends, and angels, to venture capitalists, strategic partners, and the public markets—varies by company size, stage, and amount of money invested. We argue that entrepreneurs who understand these appetites and the food chain are better prepared to focus their fundraising strategies on more realistic sources, amounts, and valuations. Economic conditions also play a role. Gregory Smith, then president of Canada's Venture Capital and Private Equity Association (CVCA) stated, "It is not surprising that the buyout industry's investment and fundraising levels have subsided in the first quarter. The worldwide economic crisis that began in Q4 2008 continued in Q1 2009 and our

EXHIBIT 10.3   **THE CAPITAL MARKETS FOOD CHAIN FOR ENTREPRENEURIAL VENTURES**

	STAGE OF VENTURE			
	R&D	**SEED**	**LAUNCH**	**HIGH GROWTH**
Enterprise Value at Stage	Less than $1 million	$1–$5 million	$1–$50 million-plus	More than $100 million
Sources	Founders High net worth individuals FFF* SR&ED	FFF* Angel funds Seed funds SR&ED	Venture capital Series A, B, C...† Strategic partners Very high net worth individuals Private equity	IPOs Strategic acquirers Private equity
Amount of Capital Invested	Less than $50 000–$200 000	$10 000–$500 000	$500 000–$20 million	$10–$50 million-plus
% Company Owned at IPO	10%–25%	5%–15%	40%–60% by prior investors	15%–25% by public
Share Price and Number‡	$0.01–$0.50 1–5 million	$0.50–$1.00 1–3 million	$1.00–$8.00 3–5 million	$12–$18-plus 5–10 million

*Friends, families, and fools

†Venture capital series A, B, C, ...(average size of round)

Round $\left\{\begin{array}{l}\end{array}\right.$ "A" @ $3–5 million—start-up
"B" @ $5–10 million—product development
"C"** @ $10 million—shipping product

Valuations vary markedly by industry

Valuations vary by region and VC cycle

‡ At post–IPO

industry, in common with most economic sectors, has not been immune from its effects."[1] But Smith was optimistic, Canadian financial institutions are strong, with most still having "considerable capital available for deployment." They are just choosing to cautiously remain on the sidelines. However, the harsh reality was not encouraging; half as many deals in Q1 2009 compared to Q1 2008 and the average buyout was for less than one-quarter of the value of the average deal a year prior. In 2009 VC investment was at a 13-year low of $1.0 billion. In 2012 VC investments hit $1.5 billion, the highest level since 2002. In February 2013, Peter van der Velden, president of the CVCA, pointed out that six of the Canadian deals: Desire2Learn, Engineered Power, Thrasos Innovation, D-Wave Systems, Lightspeed Retail, and Securekey Technologies, were among the largest in North America.[2]

The theory of company pricing is depicted simplistically in Exhibit 10.4. In the ideal scenario a venture capital investor envisions two to three funding rounds, starting at a $1.00 per share equivalent, then a four to five times mark-up to Series B, followed by a double mark-up to Series C, and then doubling that $8.00 round at an IPO. This generic pattern would characterize the majority of deals that succeeded to an IPO, but there are many variations to this central tendency. In truth, many factors can affect this theory.

THE REALITY

The past 25 years have seen the venture capital industry explode from investing only $5 to $10 million per year to nearly $6 billion in 2000 before things slowed precipitously. Exhibit 10.5 shows the many realities of the capital marketplace at work, and how current market conditions, deal flow, and relative bargaining power influence the actual deal struck. The dot-com explosion and the plummeting of the capital markets led to much lower values for private companies. The S&P/TSX

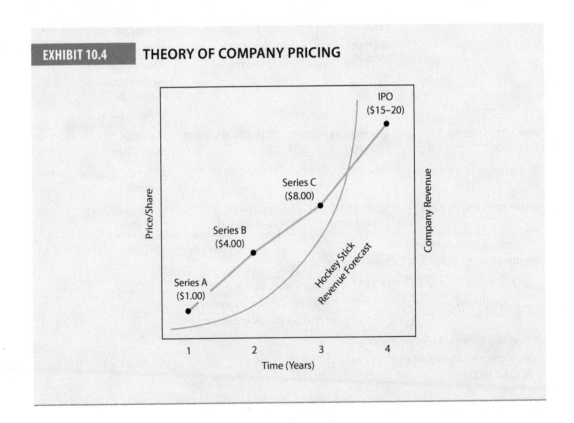

| EXHIBIT 10.4 | THEORY OF COMPANY PRICING |

TRICOLOUR VENTURE FUND

The TriColour Venture Fund at Queen's School of Business is Canada's first student-run venture capital fund. Students learn to evaluate business plans while seeking a return on the money provided by alumni of the school. Annually, the students screen proposals and then select companies for deeper analysis. After the due diligence is over, the students invest up to $150 000 in those companies chosen (in one year, no companies were chosen). Investment terms are then negotiated. Criteria include having existing investors, early stage ventures trying to fund growth, and an investment round of up to $1 million. Check out the TricClour Venture Fund's portfolio at http://business.queensu.ca/centres/qcbv/tricolour_venture_fund.php.

Queen's University School of Business

EXHIBIT 10.5   **THE REALITY**

Deal Deal Flow Today & Best Alternatives	1996: $1 billion 1998: $1.5 billion 2000: $6 billion 2002: $2.6 billion 2004: $1.8 billion 2006: $1.7 billion 2008: $1.3 billion 2010: $1.1 billion 2012: $1.5 billion
Competition for the Deal	
Relative Bargaining Power The Company vs. The VC	Company > VC Company = VC Company < VC
Today's Market Valuations	$1–5 million Pre-Money at 40–50% Ownership
The Final Deal	Negotiated Price & Terms

Composite Index fell from nearly 11 500 in September 2000 to half that by October 2002. The market rebounded and record levels were seen again, breaking 13 000 in 2006, breaking 14 000 in 2007, and 15 155 in June 2008 before landing at 7647 in November 2008—nearly a 50-percent drop!

THE DOWN ROUND OR CRAM DOWN

In the environment that existed after the October 1987 stock market crash after the dot-com bubble burst and after the economic meltdown in late 2008, entrepreneurs face rude shocks in the second or third round of financing. Instead of a substantial four or even five times increase in the valuation from Series A to B, or B to C, they are jolted with what is called a "cram-down" round or "down" round. The price is typically one-fourth to two-thirds of the last round, as shown in Exhibit 10.6. This severely dilutes the founders' ownership, where investors are normally protected against dilution. Founder dilution as a result of failing to perform is one thing, but dilution because the TSX and IPO markets collapse seems rudely unfair. Nevertheless, that is part of the reality of valuation.

Take, for example, two excellent young companies, one launched in 2002 and one in 2003. By mid-2004 the first had secured two rounds of venture financing, was on target to exceed $20 million in revenue, and was seeking a $25-million round of private equity. The previous round was at $4.50 per share. The Series C round was priced at $2.88 per share, a 36-percent discount from the prior round. The second company met or exceeded all its business plan targets and was expected to achieve $25 million of EBITDA in 2004. Its prior Series B round was priced at $8.50 per share. The new Series C was set at $6.50 per share, or nearly a 24-percent discount.

Lately onerous additional conditions have been imposed on financing, such as a three to five times return to the Series C investors *before* Series A or B investors receive a dime! Both the founders and early-round investors are severely punished by such cram-down financings. The principle of the last money in governing the deal terms still prevails.

One can sense just how vulnerable and volatile the valuation of a company can be in these imperfect markets when external events, such as a stock market collapse, trigger a downward spiral. One also gains a new perspective on how critically important timing is. Even the two strongly performing companies in the preceding example were crammed down. Imagine those companies that did not meet their plans: They were pummelled, if financed at all. What a startling reversal from the dot-com boom in 1998–1999 when companies at *concept stage* (with no product,

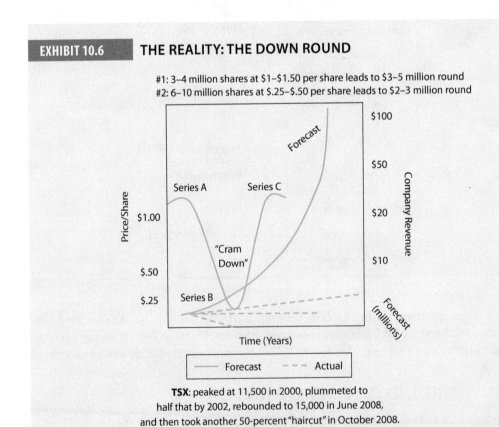

EXHIBIT 10.6   **THE REALITY: THE DOWN ROUND**

#1: 3–4 million shares at $1–$1.50 per share leads to $3–5 million round
#2: 6–10 million shares at $.25–$.50 per share leads to $2–3 million round

TSX: peaked at 11,500 in 2000, plummeted to half that by 2002, rebounded to 15,000 in June 2008, and then took another 50-percent "haircut" in October 2008.

no identifiable or defensible model of how they would make money or even breakeven, and a venture team without proven experience) raised $20, $50, $70 million, and more *and* had an IPO with multibillion-dollar valuations. History asks: What is wrong with this picture! History also offers the answer: Happiness is still a positive cash flow!

IMPROVED VALUATIONS OR BOUNCING BACK

As we saw in the last chapter, both the number of deals and average investment per deal slowly increase following a downturn. Valuations generally rise, and punishing cram-down rounds with severe preferential returns tend to be the exception rather than the norm. In 2009 there was a general sense that the capital climate was improving. One of the laws of physics is that for every action there is an equal and opposite reaction, and we hope that the same holds true in the financial world and that rebounds, such as the one to follow the global economic turmoil that began in late 2008, prove to be strong and sustained. In 2009 the CVCA gave a rallying cry:

> We are at a crisis point in Canada's venture industry. At several levels, the data conclusively demonstrate that there is a venture capital financing "gap" in Canada, and this means Canada's ability to drive innovation will weaken and we will see the overall economy suffer. Time is critical and we must act now. After all, the impact of venture-backed companies on the Canadian economy is significant, they generate jobs, contribute to the GDP and...they grow 5 times faster than the overall economy.[3]

The CVCA and Thompson Reuters reported that "New commitments of capital going to domestic venture capital funds totalled a mere $149 million, which is 74.4 percent lower than the $418 million committed during the same period in 2008. These numbers are in stark contrast to the situation in the U.S. where a total of US$4.3 billion was raised in Q1 2009, 39 percent below the US$7.1 billion raised in Q1 2008."[4] Gregory Smith stated, "This fundraising gap with the U.S. must be addressed if Canada is to compete in the knowledge-based economy of the future. Venture capital is the lifeblood of Canada's industries of tomorrow and the shortage of venture capital will have a profound impact on our ability to take a leadership role in those industries ranging from information technologies to cleantech upon which a prosperous future depends."[5] By 2013, the CVCA and Thompson Reuters were reporting a 73 percent gain in 2012 over 2011 numbers. It remained unclear whether this would be a blip, partly fuelled by pent-up demand, or if this level would be sustainable or even increase.

VALUATION METHODS   LO2

THE VENTURE CAPITAL METHOD[6]

This method is appropriate for investments in a company with negative cash flows at the time of the investment, but which in a number of years is projected to generate significant earnings. As discussed in chapter 9, venture capitalists are the most likely professional investors to partake in this type of an investment, thus the reference to the venture capital method. The steps involved in this method are as follows:

1. Estimate the company's *net income* in a number of years, at which time the investor plans on harvesting. This estimate will be based on sales and margin projections presented by the entrepreneur in his or her business plan.

2. Determine the appropriate *price-to-earnings ratio*, or P/E ratio. The appropriate P/E ratio can be determined by studying current multiples for companies with similar economic characteristics.

3. Calculate the projected *terminal value* by multiplying net income and the P/E ratio.

4. The terminal value can then be discounted to find the *present value* of the investment. Venture capitalists use discount rates ranging from 35 to 80 percent because of the risk involved in these types of investments.

5. To determine the investor's *required percentage of ownership*, based on their initial investment, the initial investment is divided by the estimated present value.

   To summarize the above steps, the following formula can be used:

$$\text{Final ownership required} = \frac{\text{Required future value (investment)}}{\text{Total terminal value}}$$

$$= \frac{(1 + \text{IRR})^{\text{years}} \text{ (investment)}}{\text{P/E ratio (terminal net income)}}$$

6. Finally, the number of shares and the share price must be calculated by using the following formula:

$$\text{New shares} = \frac{\text{Percentage of ownership required by the investor}}{1 - \text{Percentage of ownership required by the investor} \times \text{old shares}}$$

By definition, the share price equals the price paid divided by the number of shares. This method is commonly used by venture capitalists because they make equity investments in industries often requiring a large initial investment with significant projected revenues; in addition, the percentage of ownership is a key issue in the negotiations.

THE FUNDAMENTAL METHOD

This method is simply the present value of the future earnings stream (see Exhibit 10.7).

THE FIRST CHICAGO METHOD[7]

Another alternative valuation method, developed at First Chicago Corporation's venture capital group, employs a lower discount rate, but applies it to an expected cash flow. That expected cash flow is the average of three possible scenarios, with each scenario weighted according to its perceived probability. The equation to determine the investor's required final ownership is:

$$\text{Required final ownership} = \frac{\text{Future value of investment} - \text{Future value of non-IPO cash flow}}{\text{Probability (of success) (Forecast terminal value)}}$$

This formula[8] differs from the original basic venture capital formula in two ways: (1) the basic formula assumes there are no cash flows between the investment and the harvest in year 5; the future value of the immediate cash flows is subtracted from the future value of the investment because the difference between them is what must be made up for out of the terminal value; and (2) the basic formula does not distinguish between the forecast terminal value and the expected terminal value. The traditional method uses the forecast terminal value, which is adjusted through the use of a high discount rate. The formula employs the expected value of the terminal value. Exhibit 10.8 is an example of using this method.

OWNERSHIP DILUTION[9]

The previous example is unrealistic because in most cases, several rounds of investments are necessary to finance a high-potential venture. Take, for instance, the pricing worksheet presented in Exhibit 10.9 in which three financing rounds are expected. In addition to estimating the

EXHIBIT 10.7

EXAMPLE OF THE FUNDAMENTAL METHOD

HITECH, INC.

YEAR	REVENUE GROWTH (%)	REVENUE (MILLIONS)	AFTER-TAX MARGIN (%)	AFTER-TAX PROFIT (MILLIONS)	PRESENT VALUE FACTOR	PRESENT VALUE OF EACH YEAR'S EARNINGS (MILLIONS)
1	50%	$3.00	-0-	-0-	1.400	-0-
2	50	4.50	4.0%	$0.18	1.960	$0.09
3	50	6.75	7.0	0.47	2.744	0.17
4	50	10.13	9.0	0.91	3.842	0.24
5	50	15.19	11.0	1.67	5.378	0.31
6	40	21.26	11.5	2.45	7.530	0.33
7	30	27.64	12.0	3.32	10.541	0.32
8	20	33.17	12.0	3.98	14.758	0.27
9	15	38.15	12.0	4.58	20.661	0.22
10	10	41.96	12.0	5.03	28.926	0.17
Total present value of earnings in the super-growth period						2.12
Residual future value of earnings stream				$63.00	28.926	2.18
Total present value of company						4.30

EXHIBIT 10.8

EXAMPLE OF THE FIRST CHICAGO METHOD

	SUCCESS	SIDEWAYS SURVIVAL	FAILURE
1. Revenue growth rate (from base of $2 million)	60%	15%	0%
2. Revenue level after 3 years	$8.19 million	$3.04 million (liquidation)	$2 million
3. Revenue level after 5 years	$20.97 million (IPO)	$4.02 million	
4. Revenue level after 7 years		$ 5.32 million (acquisition)	
5. After-tax profit margin and earnings at liquidity	15%; $3.15 million	7%; $ 0.37 million	
6. Price-earnings ratio at liquidity	17	7	
7. Value of company liquidity	$53.55 million	$2.61 million	$0.69 million
8. Present value of company using discount rate of 40%	$9.96 million	$0.25 million	$0.25 million
9. Probability of each scenario	0.4	0.4	0.2
10. Expected present value of the company under each scenario	$3.98 million	$0.10 million	$0.05 million
11. Expected present value of the company		$4.13 million	
12. Percentage ownership required to invest $2.5 million		60.5%	

appropriate discount rate for the current round, the first-round venture capitalist must now estimate the discount rates that are most likely to be applied in the following rounds, which are projected for years 2 and 4. Although a 50-percent rate is still appropriate for year 0, it is estimated that investors in Hitech, Inc., will demand a 40-percent return in year 2 and a 25-percent return in year 4. The final ownership that each investor must be left with, given a terminal price/earnings ratio of 15, can be calculated using the basic valuation formula:

Round 1

$$\frac{\text{Future value (Investment)}}{\text{Terminal value (Company)}} = \frac{1.50^5 \times \$1.5 \text{ million}}{15 \times \$2.5 \text{ million}} = 30.4\% \text{ ownership}$$

Round 2

$$(1.40^3 \times \$1 \text{ million}) / (15 \times \$ 2.5 \text{ million}) = 7.3\%$$

Round 3

$$(1.25^1 \times \$1 \text{ million}) / (15 \times \$1.5 \text{ million}) = 3.3\%$$

DISCOUNTED CASH FLOW

In a simple discounted cash flow method, three time periods are defined: (1) years 1–5; (2) years 6–10; and (3) year 11 to infinity.[10] The necessary operating assumptions for each period are initial sales, growth rates, EBIAT/sales, and (net fixed assets + operating working capital)/sales. While using this method, one should also note relationships and trade-offs. With these assumptions, the discount rate can be applied to the weighted average cost of capital (WACC).[11] Then the value for free cash flow (years 1–10) is added to the terminal value. This terminal value is the growth perpetuity.

EXHIBIT 10.9	**EXAMPLE OF A THREE-STAGE FINANCING**					
HITECH, INC. (NUMBERS IN THOUSANDS)						
	YEAR 0	**YEAR 1**	**YEAR 2**	**YEAR 3**	**YEAR 4**	**YEAR 5**
Revenues	500	1250	2500	5000	8100	12 800
New income	(250)	(62)	250	750	1360	2500
Working capital at 20%	100	250	500	1000	1600	2560
Fixed assets at 40%	200	500	1000	2000	3200	5120
Free cash flow	(550)	(512)	(500)	(750)	(440)	(380)
Cumulative external financial need	500	1653	1543	2313	2753	3133
Equity issues	1500	0	1000	0	1000	0
Equity outstanding	1500	1500	2500	2500	3500	3500
Cash balance	950	436	938	188	748	368
Assume: long-term IRR required each round by investors	50%	45%	40%	30%	25%	20%

Source: William A. Sahlman, "A Method for Valuing High-Risk, Long-Term Investments," Harvard Business School Note 9-288-006.

OTHER RULE-OF-THUMB VALUATION METHODS

Several other valuation methods are also employed to estimate the value of a company. Many of these are based on similar, most recent transactions of similar firms, established by a sale of the company, or a prior investment. Such comparables may look at several different multiples, such as earnings, free cash flow, revenue, EBIT, and book value. Knowledgeable investment bankers and venture capitalists make it their business to know the activity in the current marketplace for private capital and how deals are being priced. These methods are used most often to value an existing company, rather than a start-up, since there are so many more knowns about the company and its financial performance.

TAR PITS FACING ENTREPRENEURS

There are several inherent conflicts between entrepreneurs, or the users of capital, and investors, or the suppliers of capital.[12] While the entrepreneur wants to have as much time as possible for the financing, the investors want to supply capital just in time or to invest only when the company needs the money. Entrepreneurs should be thinking of raising money when they do not need it, while preserving the option to find another source of capital.

Similarly, users of capital want to raise as much money as possible, while the investors want to supply just enough capital in staged capital commitments. The investors, such as venture capitalists, use staged capital commitments to manage their risk exposure over 6- to 12-month increments of investing.

In the negotiations of a deal, the entrepreneur sometimes becomes attracted to a high valuation with the sentiment "My price, your terms." The investors will generally attempt to change this opinion because it is their capital. The investors will thus focus on a low valuation, with the sentiment, "My price *and* my terms."

This tension applies not only to financial transactions but also to the styles of the users versus the styles of the suppliers of capital. The users value their independence and treasure the flexibility their own venture has brought them. However, the investors are hoping to preserve their options as well. These options usually include both reinvesting and abandoning the venture.

These points of view also clash in the composition of the board of directors, where the entrepreneur seeks control and independence, and the investors want the right to control the board if the company does not perform as well as was expected. This sense of control is an emotional issue for most entrepreneurs, who want to be in charge of their own destiny. Prizing their autonomy and self-determination, many of these users of capital would agree with the passion Walt Disney conveyed in this statement: "I don't make movies to make money. I make *money* to make movies." The investors may believe in the passions of these users of capital, but they still want to protect themselves with first refusals, initial public offering rights, and various other exit options.

The long-term goals of the users and suppliers of capital may also be contradictory. The entrepreneurs may be content with the progress of their venture and happy with a single or double. It is their venture, their baby; if it is moderately successful, many entrepreneurs believe they have accomplished a lot. The investors will not be quite as content with moderate success, but instead want their capital to produce extraordinary returns—they want a home run from the entrepreneur. Thus, the pressures put on the entrepreneur may seem unwarranted to the entrepreneur, yet necessary for the investor.

These strategies contradict each other when they are manifested in the management styles of the users and providers of capital. While the entrepreneur is willing to take a calculated risk, or is working to minimize or avoid unnecessary risks, the investor has bet on the art of the exceptional and thus is willing to bet the farm every day.

Aydin Mirzaee

SERIAL ENTREPRENEUR AYDIN MIRZAEE

A Canadian start-up, bOKnow had successfully been able to launch its VoIP product in the market but was looking to "take it to the next level" and increase the adoption of its service among the masses. The team was facing challenges such as a lack of time and money; it would be ideal if the founder and his venture team could devote their entire energy and attention to the company.

The team had bootstrapped until now, although things hadn't been as easy as they had all assumed they would be.

The fact that so many competitors had successfully raised money did not bode well for their venture. Investors were afraid to act since there were so many competitors popping up in the field already. This is a common problem for new ventures; having the competition raise money first can be both a positive and negative phenomenon. It can be a good sign since it points out that other people also believe in the existence of the market that the founders are going after. It can be a bad sign since it is less clear that the company will be the leader in the market.

Aydin Mirzaee quit his day job when he came to a crossroads with the start-up, devoting his full effort to the venture. Far from pondering whether to hand over the reigns to a new, "seasoned," professional CEO, the few angel investors whose ear he could reach insisted that he remain at the helm. Part of their draw was him, personally, despite his deficiencies in leadership experience. However, being out-funded ultimately proved to be an insurmountable hurdle to the company.

bOKnow remained viable and profitable up until the point when it was shuttered. It was ultimately closed down because a new opportunity presented itself to the team!

Question: Were there any avenues the team should have pursued? Did they pull the plug too earlier? Or not soon enough?

Entrepreneurs possess the ability to see opportunities and, more importantly, to seize those opportunities. They possess an instinctual desire to change, to adapt, or to de-commit in order to seize new opportunities. Yet, the investors are looking for clear steady progress, as projected in the business plan, which leaves little room for surprises.

Finally, the ultimate goals may differ. The entrepreneur who continues to build his or her company may find operating a company enjoyable. At this point, the definition of success both personally and for the company may involve long-term company building, such that a sustainable institution is created. But the investors will want to cash out in two to five years, so that they can reinvest their capital in another venture.

STAGED CAPITAL COMMITMENTS[13]

Venture capitalists rarely, if ever, invest all the external capital that a company will require to accomplish its business plan; instead they invest in companies at distinct stages in their development. As a result, each company begins life knowing that it has only enough capital to reach the next stage. By staging capital, the venture capitalists preserve the right to abandon a project whose prospects look dim. The right to abandon is essential because an entrepreneur will almost never stop investing in a failing project as long as others are providing capital.

Staging the capital also provides incentives to the entrepreneurial team. Capital is a scarce and expensive resource for individual ventures. Misuse of capital is very costly to venture capitalists but not necessarily to the venture team. To encourage the team to conserve capital, venture capital firms apply strong sanctions if it is misused. These sanctions ordinarily take two basic forms. First, increased capital requirements invariably dilute the venture team's equity share at an increasingly punitive rate. Second, the staged investment process enables venture capital firms to shut down operations. The credible threat to abandon a venture, even when the firm might be economically viable, is the key to the relationship between the entrepreneur and the venture capitalists. By denying capital, the venture capitalist also signals other capital suppliers that the company in question is a bad investment risk.

Short of denying the company capital, venture capitalists can discipline wayward venture team executives by firing or demoting them. Other elements of the share purchase agreement then come into play. For example, the company typically has the right to repurchase shares from departing venture team members, often at prices below market value, and vesting schedules limit the number of shares employees are entitled to if they leave prematurely. Finally, non-compete clauses can impose strong penalties on those who leave, particularly if their human capital is closely linked to the industry in which the venture is active.

Entrepreneurs accept the staged capital process because they usually have great confidence in their own abilities to meet targets. They understand that if they meet those goals, they will end up owning a significantly larger share of the company than if they had insisted on receiving all of the capital up front.

STRUCTURING THE DEAL   LO3

WHAT IS A DEAL?[14]

Deals are defined as economic agreements between at least two parties. In the context of entrepreneurial finance, most deals involve the allocation of cash flow streams (with respect to both amount and timing), the allocation of risk, and hence the allocation of value between different groups. For example, deals can be made between suppliers and users of capital, or between management and employees of a venture.

A Way of Thinking about Deals over Time

To assess and to design long-lived deals, William Sahlman of the Harvard Business School suggests the following series of questions as a guide for deal makers when structuring a deal and for understanding how deals evolve:[15]

- Who are the players?
- What are their goals and objectives?
- What risks do they perceive and how have these risks been managed?
- What problems do they perceive?
- How much do they have invested, both in absolute terms and relative terms, at cost and at market value?
- What is the context surrounding the current decision?
- What is the form of their current investment or claim on the company?
- What power do they have to act? To precipitate change?
- What real options do they have? How long does it take them to act?
- What credible threats do they have?

ENTREPRENEURS ACROSS CANADA
Learn the VC's Buttons and Push Them

Avrio Ventures Ltd. looks for growth stage industrial bio-products, nutraceutical ingredients, and food technology enterprises to invest in. In 2009 Avrio closed a Series A round investment into Manitoba Harvest to support Manitoba Harvest's rapid growth in channels of distribution, research, and new product development. Manitoba Harvest needed the capital to realize market opportunities and broaden their line of hemp-based nutraceuticals and natural foods. In 2013 Avrio provide $3 million in equity financing to Quebec-based Hortau Inc. Founded by Jean Caron and Jocelyn Boudreau in 2002, the company specialized in the design and manufacture of irrigation management technologies. In addition to Avrio, Hortau's current investors included Telesystem, Desjardins, Capital financière agricole, SDÉ Lévis, and SOLIDE.

Avrio looks for particular attributes in ventures it is considering and lists its investment criteria as:

- an experienced growth-oriented management team
- a sustainable competitive advantage either through proven science, proprietary intellectual property, or a strong brand franchise
- a large addressable market opportunity or a high-growth niche market segment
- a sound business model
- an entrepreneurial desire to build an enduring, world class organization

Avrio "focuses on commercialization and growth stage investments. Typically, the use of proceeds is to commercialize products, initiate product rollouts, expand distribution and market presence, or fund growth (organically or through acquisitions). Avrio will invest up to $10 million over the life of any single portfolio company. The Avrio team is patient, recognizing that successful companies require support over at least five years to realize their potential value. If your company meets these criteria, please submit a business plan."

Questions: NatureBox—a subscription, ecommerce venture that provides monthly parcels of healthy snacks—closed $9.25 million in funding in the second half of 2013. The cofounders were college friends. NGEN Partners led the round, with Avrio Capital and Silas Capital co-investing. The money will be used to accelerate growth (expand capacity), add to the management team, build the brand, and fund working capital. How would you find the right VC or VCs? How will you determine what they want to see and hear? Will you go after additional VC money simultaneously or will you wait—or how long?

Source: www.avrioventures.com/criteria

- How and from whom do they get information?
- How credible is the source of information?
- What will be the value of their claim under different scenarios?
- How can they get value for their claims?
- To what degree can they appropriate value from another party?
- How much uncertainty characterizes the situation?
- What are the rules of the game (e.g., tax, legislative)?[16]
- What is the context (e.g., state of economy, capital markets, industry specifics) at the current time? How is the context expected to change?

The Characteristics of Successful Deals[17]

While deal making is ultimately a combination of art and science, it is possible to describe some of the characteristics of deals that have proven successful over time:

- They are simple.
- They are robust (they do not fall apart when there are minor deviations from projections).

- They are organic (they are not immutable).
- They take into account the incentives of each party to the deal under a variety of circumstances.
- They provide mechanisms for communications and interpretation.
- They are based primarily on trust rather than on legalese.
- They are not patently unfair.
- They do not make it too difficult to raise additional capital.
- They match the needs of the user of capital with the needs of the supplier.
- They reveal information about each party (e.g., their faith in their ability to deliver on the promises).
- They allow for the arrival of new information before financing is required.
- They do not preserve discontinuities (e.g., boundary conditions that will evoke dysfunctional behaviour on the part of the agents of principals).
- They consider the fact that it takes time to raise money.
- They improve the chances of success for the venture.

The Generic Elements of Deals

A number of terms govern value distribution, as well as basic definitions, assumptions, performance incentives, rights, and obligations. The deal should also cover the basic mechanisms for transmitting timely, credible information. Representations and warranties, plus negative and positive covenants, will also be part of the deal structure. Additionally, default clauses and remedial action clauses are appropriate in most deals.

Tools for Managing Risk/Reward

In a deal, the claims on cash and equity are prioritized by the players. Some of the tools available to the players are common shares, partnerships, preferred shares (dividend and liquidation preference), debt (secured, unsecured, personally guaranteed, or convertible), performance conditional pricing (ratchets or positive incentives), puts and calls, warrants, and cash. Some of the critical aspects of a deal go beyond just the money:[18]

- number, type, and mix of shares (and perhaps of shares and debt) and various features that may go with them (such as puts) that affect the investor's rate of return
- the amounts and timing of takedowns, conversions, and the like
- interest rates on debt or preferred shares
- the number of seats, and who actually will represent investors, on the board of directors
- possible changes in the venture's executive team and in the composition of the board
- registration rights for investor's shares (in the case of a registered public offering)
- right of first refusal granted to the investor on subsequent private placements or an IPO
- employment, non-compete, and proprietary rights agreements
- the payment of legal, accounting, consulting, or other fees connected with putting the deal together
- specific performance targets for revenues, expenses, market penetration, and the like, by certain target dates

UNDERSTANDING THE BETS

Deals, because they are based on cash, risk, and time, are subject to interpretation. The players' perceptions of each of these factors contribute to the overall valuation of the venture and the subsequent proposed deal. As was described earlier, there are a number of different ways to value a venture, and these various valuation methods contribute to the complexity of deals. Consider, for instance, the following term sheets:[19]

- A venture capital firm proposes to raise $150- to $200 million to acquire and build an enterprise. The venture capital firm will commit between $15- and $30 million in equity and will lead in raising senior and subordinated debt to buy licences. Licensees will have to claim about 30 percent of the future equity value in the new company, the venture capital firm will claim 60 percent (subordinated debt claim is estimated at 10 percent), and the venture team will get 5 to 10 percent of the future equity but only after all prior return targets have been achieved. The venture capital firm's worst-case scenario will result in 33 percent ROR to the firm, 9 percent ROR to licensees, and 0 percent for the venture team. The non-compete agreements extend for 12 years, in addition to the vesting.

- An entrepreneur must decide between two deals:

  Deal A: A venture capital firm will lead a $3-million investment and requires the venture team to invest $1 million. Future gains are to be split 50–50 after the venture capital firm has achieved a 25 percent ROR on the investment. Other common investment provisions also apply (vesting, employment agreements, etc.). The venture capital firm has the right of first refusal on all future rounds and other deals the venture team may find.

FIND BACKERS ABLE TO ADD VALUE, NOT THOSE JUST WILLING TO TAKE A GAMBLE.

Deal B: Another venture capital firm will lead a $4-million investment. The venture team will invest nothing. The future gains are to be split 75 percent for the venture capital firm and 25 percent for the venture team on a side-by-side basis. Until the venture achieves positive cash flow, this venture capital firm has the right of first refusal on future financing and deals the venture team may find.

- A group of talented money managers is given $40 million in capital to manage. The contract calls for the venture team to receive 20 percent of the excess return on the portfolio over the government bond return. The contract runs for five years. The venture team cannot take out any of their share of the gains until the last day of the contracts (except to pay taxes).

While reading and considering these deals, try to identify the underlying assumptions, motivations, and beliefs of the individuals proposing the deals. Following are some questions that may help in identifying the players' bets.

- What is the bet?

- Who is it for?

- Who is taking the risk? Who receives the rewards?

- Who should be making these bets?

- What will happen if the entrepreneurs exceed the venture capitalists' expectations? What if they fall short?

- What are the incentives for the money managers? What are the consequences of their success or failure to perform?

- How will the money managers behave? What will be their investing strategy?

SOME OF THE LESSONS LEARNED: THE DOG IN THE SUITCASE

A few years ago a friend, living in an Edmonton, Alberta high-rise, called in great distress. Her beloved barkless dog had died in the middle of the night. She wanted a decent burial for the dog, but since it was the dead of winter, she did not know what to do. It was suggested that she contact a pet cemetery in nearby St. Albert and take the dog there. It would be frozen until spring, at which time it would be properly buried.

She gathered her courage, placed the dog in a suitcase, and headed down the elevator to the outdoors. As she struggled toward the nearest intersection to catch a cab, a young man noticed her struggle and offered to help. Puffing by now, she sized up the young man quickly and accepted his offer to carry the bag. In no time, she turned to find the young man sprinting down the street with her suitcase. Imagine the look on the faces of the young man and his buddies when they opened the suitcase and discovered the loot!

The moral of this story is that raising capital can have all the surprises of a dog in the suitcase for the entrepreneur. The following tips may help to minimize many of these surprises:

- Raise money when you do not need it.

- Learn as much about the process and how to manage it as you can.

- Know your relative bargaining position.

- If all you get is money, you are not getting much.

- Assume the deal will never close.

- Always have a backup source of capital.

- The legal and other experts can blow it—sweat the details yourself!
- Users of capital are invariably at a disadvantage in dealing with the suppliers of capital.
- If you are out of cash when you seek to raise capital, suppliers of capital will eat you for lunch.
- Start-up entrepreneurs are raising capital for the first time; suppliers of capital have done it many times, every day, for a living.

NEGOTIATIONS

LO4

Negotiations have been defined by many experts in a variety of ways, as the following examples demonstrate. Herb Cohen, the author of *You Can Negotiate Anything*, defines negotiations as "a field of knowledge and endeavor that focuses on gaining the favor of people from whom we want things"[20] or similarly, as "the use of information and power to affect behavior within a 'web of tension.'"[21] Other experts in the field of negotiations, Roger Fisher and William Ury, assert that negotiations are a "back-and-forth communication designed to reach an agreement when you and the other side have some interests that are shared and others that are opposed."[22]

WHAT IS NEGOTIABLE?

boilerplate:
Originally referred to the steel label on a steam boiler. The boilerplate was cast iron and unalterable. Later the term referred to printing plates which were also stamped iron. Today the term refers to a standard that can be changed little, if any. It may apply to legal contracts or even computer code.

Far more is negotiable than entrepreneurs think.[23] For instance, a normal ploy of the lawyer representing the investors is to insist, matter of factly, that "this is our **boilerplate**" and that the entrepreneur should take it or leave it. It is possible for an entrepreneur to negotiate and craft an agreement that represents his or her needs.

During the negotiation, the investors will be evaluating the negotiating skills, intelligence, and maturity of the entrepreneur. The entrepreneur has precisely the same opportunity to size up the investor. If the investors see anything that shakes their confidence or trust, they probably will withdraw from the deal. Similarly, if an investor turns out to be arrogant, hot-tempered, unwilling to see the other side's needs and to compromise, and seems bent on getting every last ounce out of the deal by locking an entrepreneur into as many of the "burdensome clauses" as is possible, the entrepreneur might want to withdraw.

Throughout the negotiations, entrepreneurs need to bear in mind that a successful negotiation is one in which both sides believe they have made a fair deal. The best deals are those in which neither party wins and neither loses, and such deals are possible to negotiate. This approach is further articulated in the works of Fisher and Ury, who have focused neither on soft nor hard negotiation tactics, but rather on principled negotiation, a methodical approach. This method asserts that the purpose of negotiations is "to decide issues on their merits rather than through a haggling process focused on what each side says it will and won't do. It suggests that you look for mutual gains wherever possible, and that where your interests conflict, you should insist that the result be based on some fair standards independent of the will of either side."[24] They continue to describe principled negotiations in the following four points:

- ✔ *People*: Separate the people from the problem
- ✔ *Interests*: Focus on interests, not positions
- ✔ *Options*: Generate a variety of possibilities before deciding what to do
- ✔ *Criteria*: Insist that the result be based on some objective standard

Others have spoken of this method of principled negotiation. Generally the adage holds to treat others as you would like to be treated. For example, Mario Lemieux states, "One thing I hate is people screaming at me. If you want me to do something, talk to me. When someone screams at me to hurry up, I slow down."

THE SPECIFIC ISSUES ENTREPRENEURS TYPICALLY FACE[25]

Whatever method you choose in your negotiations, the primary focus is likely to be on how much the entrepreneur's equity is worth and how much is to be purchased by the investor's investment. Even so, numerous other issues involving legal and financial control of the company and the rights and obligations of various investors and the entrepreneur in various situations may be as important as valuation and ownership share. Not the least of which is the value behind the money that a particular investor can bring to the venture, such as contacts and helpful expertise, additional financing when and if required, and patience and interest in the long-term development of the company. The following are some of the most critical aspects of a deal that go beyond "just the money":

- number, type, and mix of shares (and perhaps of shares and debt) and various features that may go with them (such as puts) that affect the investor's rate of return

- the amounts and timing of takedowns, conversions, and the like

- interest rate on debt or preferred shares

- the number of seats, and who actually will represent investors, on the board of directors

- possible changes in the venture team and in the composition of the board of directors

- registration rights for investor's shares (in case of a registered public offering)

- right of first refusal granted to the investor on subsequent private or initial public share offerings

- share vesting schedule and agreements

- the payment of legal, accounting, consulting, or other fees connected with putting the deal together

Entrepreneurs may find some subtle but highly significant issues negotiated. If they, or their lawyers, are not familiar with these, they may be missed as just boilerplate when, in fact, they have crucial future implications for the ownership, control, and financing of the business. Some issues that can be burdensome for entrepreneurs are:

- *Co-sale provision*. This is a provision by which investors can tender their shares of their shares before an initial public offering. It protects the first-round investors but can cause conflicts with investors in later rounds and can inhibit an entrepreneur's ability to cash out.

- *Ratchet anti-dilution protection*. This enables the lead investors to get for free additional common shares if subsequent shares are ever sold at a price lower than originally paid. This protection allows first-round investors to prevent the company from raising additional necessary funds during a period of adversity for the company. While nice from the investor's perspective, it ignores the reality that, in distress situations, the last money calls the shots on price and deal structure.

- *Washout financing.* This is a strategy of last resort, which wipes out all previously issued shares when existing preferred shareholders will not commit additional funds, thus diluting everyone.
- *Forced buyout.* Under this provision, if the venture team does not find a buyer or cannot take the company public by a certain date, then the investors can proceed to find a buyer at terms they agree upon.
- *Demand registration rights.* Here, investors can demand at least one IPO in three to five years. In reality, such clauses are hard to invoke because the market for new public share issues, rather than the terms of an agreement, ultimately governs the timing of such events.
- *Piggyback registration rights.* These grant to the investors (and to the entrepreneur, if he or she insists) rights to sell shares at the IPO. Since the underwriters usually make this decision, the clause normally is not enforceable.
- *Key-person insurance.* This requires the company to obtain life insurance on key people. The named beneficiary of the insurance can be either the company or the preferred shareholders.

THE TERM SHEET

Regardless of whether you secure capital from angels or venture capitalists, you will want to be informed and knowledgeable about the terms and conditions that govern the deal you sign. Many experienced entrepreneurs will argue that the terms and who your investor is are more important than the valuation. Today, the technical sophistication in deal structures creates an imperative for entrepreneurs and their legal counsel: if you do not know the details you will get what you deserve—not what you want.

To illustrate this point, consider the choice among four common instruments: (1) fully participating preferred shares, (2) partially participating preferred shares (4× return), (3) common preference ($1.00/share to common), and (4) non-participating preferred shares. Then, consider a $200-million harvest realized either through an IPO or an acquisition by another company. Why does any of this matter? Aren't these details better left to the legal experts?

Consider the economic consequences of each of these deal instruments under the two harvest scenarios in Exhibit 10.10. The graph shows there can be up to a $24-million difference in the payout received, even though, in the example, there are equal numbers of common shares, typically owned by the founders, and preferred shares, owned by investors. The acquisition exit is more favourable to investors, especially since periodically the IPO market is closed to new companies.

BLACK BOX TECHNOLOGY, INC., TERM SHEET

The best single presentation and discussion we have seen of the deal structure, term sheet contents, and their implications for negotiating the deal is presented in Black Box Technology, Inc.—Term Sheet (found online with Connect). This was developed by the former Boston law firm of Testa, Hurwitz & Thibeault, LLP. We highly recommend its careful reading before any negotiations with private investors and selecting very experienced counsel. "Getting a term sheet from an investor is like getting an invitation to the Prom in January—you've got a long way to go before you dance" according to start-up lawyer Ryan Roberts.[26] "VCs love to be the first to be second. They don't want to be the first to issue a term sheet, but will issue one quickly once someone else has," observes Mark Davis of DFJ Gotham Ventures.[27]

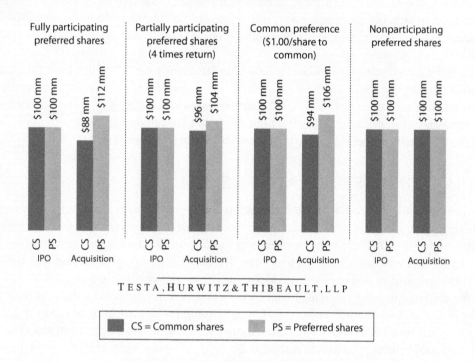

EXHIBIT 10.10 **CONSIDERING THE ECONOMICS:
$200 MILLION IPO OR ACQUISITION?**

Source: Testa, Hurwitz & Thibeault, LLP, presentation by Heather M. Stone and Brian D. Goldstein at Babson College, October 3, 2001.

TRAPS LO5

STRATEGIC CIRCUMFERENCE

Each fundraising strategy sets in motion some actions and commitments by the venture team that will eventually scribe a strategic circumference around the company in terms of its current and future financing choices. These future choices permit varying degrees of freedom as a result of the previous actions. Those who fail to think through the consequences of a fundraising strategy and the effect on their degrees of freedom fall into this trap.

While it is impossible to avoid strategic circumference completely, and while in some cases scribing a strategic circumference is clearly intentional, others may be unintended and, unfortunately, unexpected. For example, a company that plans to remain private or plans to maintain a 1.5 to 1.0 debt-to-equity ratio has intentionally created a strategic circumference.

LEGAL CIRCUMFERENCE

Many people have an aversion to becoming involved in legal or accounting minutiae. Many believe that since they pay sizeable professional fees, their advisors should and will pay attention to the details.

Legal documentation spells out the terms, conditions, responsibilities, and rights of the parties to a transaction. Because different sources have different ways of structuring deals, and because these legal and contractual details come at the *end* of the fundraising process, an entrepreneur may arrive at a point of no return, facing some onerous conditions and covenants that are not only difficult to live with, but also create potentially disastrous limitations and constraints—legal circumference—on future choices. Entrepreneurs cannot rely on lawyers and advisors to protect them in this vital matter.

To avoid this trap, entrepreneurs need to have a fundamental precept: "The devil is in the details." It is risky for an entrepreneur *not* to carefully read final documents and risky to use a lawyer who is *not* experienced and competent. Whether it is seen as wiggle room, Plan B, or a way out, not being boxed in legally or strategically is vital. It is helpful to keep a few options alive and to conserve cash. This also can keep the other side of the table more conciliatory and flexible.

ATTRACTION TO STATUS AND SIZE

It seems there is a cultural attraction to higher status and larger size, even when it comes to raising capital. Simply targeting the largest or the best-known or most-prestigious firms is a trap into which entrepreneurs often fall. These firms are often most visible because of their size and investing activity and because they have been around a long time. Yet, as the venture capital industry has become more heterogeneous, as well as for other reasons, such firms may or may not be a good fit.

Take, for example, an entrepreneur who had a patented, innovative device that was ready for use by manufacturers of semiconductors. He was running out of cash from an earlier round of venture capital investment and needed more money for his device to be placed in test sites and then, presumably, into production. Although lab tests had been successful, his prior backers would not invest further because he was nearly two years behind schedule in his business plan. For a year, he concentrated his efforts on many of the largest and most well-known firms and celebrities in the venture capital business, but to no avail. With the help of outside advice, he then decided to pursue an alternative fundraising strategy. First, he listed firms that were most likely prospects as customers for the device. Next, he sought to identify investors who already had investments in this potential customer base, because it was thought that these would be the most likely potential backers since they would be the most informed about his technology, its potential value-added properties, and any potential competitive advantages the company could achieve. Less than a dozen venture capital firms were identified (from among a pool of over 700, at the time), yet none had been contacted previously by this entrepreneur. In fact, many were virtually unknown to him, even though they were active investors in this particular industry. In less than three months, offers were on the table from three of these and the financing was closed.

It is best to avoid this trap by focusing your efforts toward financial backers, whether debt or equity, who have intimate knowledge and first-hand experience with the technology, marketplace, and networks of expertise in the competitive arena. Focus on those firms with relevant know-how that would be characterized as a good match.

UNKNOWN TERRITORY

Venturing into unknown territory is another problem. Entrepreneurs need to know the terrain in sufficient detail, particularly the requirements and alternatives of various equity sources. If they do not, they may make critical strategic blunders and waste time.

Douglas Cumming observed that in Canada "there is no single unique optimal form of venture finance." This is in contrast to the United States where tax laws lead to convergence on only one security. Canada's mix of financing instruments match up with the entrepreneurial firm depending upon its unique attributes and needs. Cumming found that in Canada, "seed stage firms are more likely to be financed with either common equity or straight preferred equity, and less likely to be financed with straight debt, convertible debt, or mixes of debt and common equity....Seed stage firms were also less likely to be financed with straight debt, convertible debt, or mixes of debt and common equity"—nascent firms without cash flows are simply less suited for debt finance. On the other hand, high-tech firms are likely to be financed through convertible preferred equity.[28]

For example, a venture that is not a "mainstream" venture capital deal may be overvalued and directed to investors who are not a realistic match, rather than being realistically valued and directed to small and more specialized funds, private investors, or potential strategic partners. The preceding example is a real one. The founders went through nearly $100 000 of their own funds, strained their relationship to the limit, and nearly had to abandon the project.

Another illustration of a fundraising strategy that was ill conceived and, effectively, a lottery— rather than a well-thought-out and focused search—is a venture in the fibre optics industry we'll call Opti-Com.[29] Opti-Com was a spin-off as a start-up from a well-known public company in the industry. The venture team was entirely credible, but members were not considered superstars. The business plan suggested the company could achieve the magical $50 million in sales in five years, which the entrepreneurs were told by an outside advisor was the minimum size that venture capital investors would consider. The plan proposed to raise $750 000 for about 10 percent of the common shares of the company. Realistically, since the firm was a custom supplier for special applications, rather than a provider of a new technology with a significant proprietary advantage, a sales estimate of $10 to $15 million in five years would have been more plausible. The same advisor urged that their business plan be submitted to 12 mainstream venture capital firms in the immediate vicinity. Four months later, they had received 12 rejections. The entrepreneurs then were told to "go see the same quality of venture capital firms in New York." A year later, the founders were nearly out of money and had been unsuccessful in their search for capital. When redirected away from mainstream venture capitalists to a more suitable source, a small fund specifically created in the area to provide risk capital for emerging firms that might not be robust enough to attract conventional venture capital but would be a welcome addition to the economic renewal of the province, the fit was right. Opti-Com raised the necessary capital, but at a valuation much more in line with the market for start-up deals.

OPPORTUNITY COST

The lure of money often leads to a common trap—the opportunity cost trap. An entrepreneur's optimism leads him or her to the conclusion that with good people and products (or services), there has to be a lot of money out there with "our name on it!" In the process, entrepreneurs tend to grossly underestimate the real costs of getting the cash in the bank. Further, entrepreneurs also underestimate the real time, effort, and creative energy required. Indeed, the degree of effort fundraising requires is perhaps the least appreciated aspect in obtaining capital. In both these cases, there are opportunity costs in expending these resources in a particular direction when both the clock and the calendar are moving targets.[30]

For a start-up company, for instance, founders can devote nearly all their available time for months to seeking out investors and telling their story. It may take six months or more to get a "yes" and up to a year for a "no." In the meantime, a considerable amount of cash and human capital has been flowing out, rather than in, and this cash and capital might have been better spent elsewhere.

One such start-up began its search for venture capital and within 12 months the founders had exhausted $100 000 of their own seed money and had quit their jobs to devote themselves full time to the effort. Yet they were unsuccessful after approaching more than 35 sources of capital. The opportunity costs are clearly high.

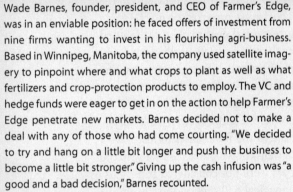

Wade Barnes, founder, president, and CEO of Farmer's Edge, was in an enviable position: he faced offers of investment from nine firms wanting to invest in his flourishing agri-business. Based in Winnipeg, Manitoba, the company used satellite imagery to pinpoint where and what crops to plant as well as what fertilizers and crop-protection products to employ. The VC and hedge funds were eager to get in on the action to help Farmer's Edge penetrate new markets. Barnes decided not to make a deal with any of those who had come courting. "We decided to try and hang on a little bit longer and push the business to become a little bit stronger." Giving up the cash infusion was "a good and a bad decision," Barnes recounted.

In the subsequent season, too much rain in Canada and Russia reduced revenues by about 20 percent because crops couldn't be planted. In a drought, however, crops are still planted and Farmer's Edge gets paid.

Barnes then entered into an arrangement with partner Viterra—Canada's largest grain handler. Eight days later Viterra went up for sale and Barnes waited anxiously. The result was favourable; Farmer's Edge was now allied with the acquirer—a Swiss commodities trading giant able to open additional doors.

Despite the good news, Farmer's Edge was feeling a financial pinch: "Our biggest issue was we'd been growing so rapidly that we were going to have to make a decision whether to slow down on growth to heal a bit from the bad year, or try to keep growing the company and going into these different markets."

Barnes was approached by Avrio Capital and struck a deal on Halloween, 2012. Simultaneously, Barnes gave the company's 60 employees an opportunity to invest and about 20 did. Avrio and the employees took a 15 percent stake in Farmer's Edge in return for approximately $4 million in new capital.

Question: Wade Barnes appears to have played the situation right. Is there anything you would have done differently? What do you expect the future will hold for Farmer's Edge?

There are opportunity costs, too, in existing emerging companies. In terms of human capital, it is common for top management to devote as much as half of its time trying to raise a major amount of outside capital. Again, this requires a tremendous amount of emotional and physical energy as well, of which there is a finite amount to devote to the daily operating demands of the enterprise. The effect on near-term performance is invariably negative. In addition, if expectations of a successful fundraising effort are followed by a failure to raise the money, morale can deteriorate and key people can be lost.

Significant opportunity costs are also incurred in forgone business and market opportunities that could have been pursued. Take, for example, the start-up firm noted above. When asked what level of sales the company would have achieved in the year had it spent the $100 000 of the founders' seed money on generating customers and business, the founder answered without hesitation, "We'd be at $1 million sales by now, and would probably be making a small profit."

UNDERESTIMATION OF OTHER COSTS

Entrepreneurs tend to underestimate the out-of-pocket costs associated with both raising the money and living with it. There are incremental costs after a firm becomes a public company. The Canadian regulatory bodies require periodic audited financial statements and various reports, there are outside directors' fees and liability insurance premiums, there are legal fees associated with more extensive reporting requirements, and so on. These can add up quickly, often to $100 000 or more annually.

Another "cost" that can be easily overlooked is of the disclosure that may be necessary to convince a financial backer to part with his or her money. An entrepreneur may have to reveal much more about the company and his other personal finances than he or she ever imagined. Thus, company weaknesses, ownership and compensation arrangements, personal and corporate financial statements, marketing plans and competitive strategies, and so forth may need to be revealed to people whom the entrepreneur does not really know and trust, and with whom he or she may eventually not do business. In addition, the ability to control access to the information is lost.

GREED

The entrepreneur—especially one who is out of cash, or nearly so—may find the money irresistible. One of the most exhilarating experiences for an entrepreneur is the prospect of raising that first major slug of outside capital, or obtaining that substantial bank line needed for expansion. If the fundamentals of the company are sound, however, then there is always some money somewhere out there. You owe it to yourself and your venture to take the best deal, not the first offer.

BEING TOO ANXIOUS

Usually, after months of hard work finding the right source and negotiating the deal, another trap awaits the hungry but unwary entrepreneur, and all too often the temptation is overwhelming. It is the trap of believing that the deal is done and terminating discussions with others too soon. Entrepreneurs fall into this trap because they want to believe the deal is done with a handshake (or perhaps with an accompanying letter of intent or an executed term sheet).

A masterful handling of such a situation occurred when an entrepreneur and a key vice president of a company with $30 million in sales had been negotiating with several venture capitalists, three major strategic partners, and a mezzanine source for nearly six months. The company was down to 60 days' worth of cash, and the mezzanine investors knew it. They offered the entrepreneur $10 million as a take-it-or-leave-it proposition. The vice president, in summarizing the company's relative bargaining position, said, "It was the only alternative we had left; everything else had come to rest by late last month and the negotiations with the three major companies had not reached serious stages. We felt like they were asking too much, but we needed the money." Yet the two had managed to keep the stalled negotiations with other investors from being apparent to the mezzanine. Each time negotiations with the mezzanine had been scheduled, the entrepreneur had made sure he also had scheduled a meeting with one of the other larger companies for later that afternoon (a two-hour plane ride away). In effect, he was able to create the illusion that these discussions with other investors were far more serious than they actually were. The deal was closed with the mezzanine on terms agreeable to both. The company went public six months later and is still highly successful today.

IMPATIENCE

Another trap is being impatient when an investor does not understand quickly, and not realizing each deal has velocity and momentum.

The efforts of one group to acquire a firm in the cellular phone business being sold by their employers provides an example. As members of the executive team, they were the first to know in May that the company was going to be sold by its owners. By early July, the investment bankers representing the sellers were expected to have the offering memorandum ready for the open market. To attempt to buy the company privately would require the team to raise commitments for approximately $150 million in three to four weeks, hardly enough time to put together even a crude business plan, let alone raise such a substantial sum. The train was moving at 200 kilometres per hour and gaining speed each day. The founders identified five top-notch, interested venture capital and leveraged buyout firms and sat down with representatives of each to walk through the summary of the business plan and the proposed financing. One excellent firm sent an otherwise very experienced and capable partner, but his questioning indicated just how little he knew about this business. The team knew they had to look elsewhere.

From 2009 to 2014 the tables were turning on the VCs and they were begging hard for money. Upstream from VC money exists a variety of institutional and other investors. The venture funds were simply dry, all tapped out and upstream investors were nervous and sitting tight. At that point, two of Canada's biggest firms, VenturesWest and Celtic House, were stalled in their own fundraising and had to suspend venture-funding activity.

For Brightspark it meant a reversal for new life. Brightspark was founded in 1999 with two parts: a software start-up incubator and VC. The VC arm invested in what came out of the other half. The incubator half (Brightspark Labs) was disbanded in 2002, having placed its employees and ideas in the real world while the other half (Brightspark Ventures) was going strong. In 2009, under dire economic conditions Brightspark was forced to start building software and launching—rather than funding—new ventures. Mark Skapinker, co-founder of Brightspark, said "We decided to go back to basics." The firm launched three Web-based businesses, all of which share a common architecture. Why would a VC firm launch its own businesses? "While it might seem counterintuitive for a VC firm to dream up, develop, fund, and launch its own companies, for the entrepreneurial veterans at Brightspark it's merely a case of

MARK SKAPINKER, COFOUNDER OF BRIGHTSPARK VENTURES

doing what comes naturally." "We hope that we are showing the market that great tech companies can be created and grown in the face of a brutal VC and financial market."

Question: With low interest rates, why would venture capital firms have such trouble finding investment dollars? Is Brightspark stepping into the role of start-up going to be a more common occurrence?

Sources: Timothy Hay, "O Canada VC, We Stand On Guard for Thee," *Wall Street Journal*, April 3, 2009; Mark Skapinker, "Say It Like You See It," www.blog.brightspark.com (accessed April 4, 2009); Canadian Venture Capital Association, "Venture Capital Investment Continued to Fall in Q1 2009," Press Release, May 12, 2009.

Had the group been too impatient simply because the train was moving so quickly, they would have exposed themselves to additional risk. That potential investor had a serious lack of elementary knowledge of the industry and the business model, and had not done his homework in advance. If they had waited for this investor to become knowledgeable about the business, it would have been too late.

TAKE-THE-MONEY-AND-RUN MYOPIA

A final trap in raising money for a company is a take-the-money-and-run myopia that invariably prevents an entrepreneur from evaluating one of the most critical longer-term issues—to what extent can the investor add value to the company beyond the money? Into this trap falls the entrepreneur who does not possess a clear sense that his or her prospective financial partner has the relevant experience and know-how in the market and industry area, the contacts the entrepreneur needs but does not have, the savvy and the reputation that adds value in the relationship with the investor—and yet takes the money.

As has been said before, the successful development of a company can be critically affected by the interaction of the venture's executive team and the financial partners. If an effective relationship can be established, the value-added synergy can be a powerful stimulant for success. Many founders overlook the high value-added contributions that some investors are accustomed to making and erroneously opt for a "better deal."

LEARNING OBJECTIVES SUMMARY

LO1 There is rarely a "fair fight" between users (entrepreneurs) and suppliers (investors) of capital. Entrepreneurs need to be prepared to negotiate equity proportions by learning how the capital markets determine valuation risk.

LO2 Several valuation methods are used to arrive at value for a company, the venture capital method being the most common. Successful deals are characterized by careful thought and sensitive balance among a range of important issues.

LO3 Investors prefer to stage their capital commitments, thereby managing and containing the risk and preserving their options to invest fur-

ther or cease. Deal structure can make or break an otherwise sound venture, and the devil is always in the details.

LO4 Numerous potential conflicts exist between users and suppliers of capital, and these require appreciation and managing. The economic consequences can be worth millions to founders. Negotiating the deal is both art and science, and also can make or break the relationship.

LO5 The entrepreneur encounters numerous strategic, legal, and other traps during the fundraising cycle and needs awareness and skill in coping with them. Advisors (chapter 8) can help.

STUDY QUESTIONS

1. Why can there be such wide variations in the valuations investors and founders place on companies? What are the determinants of value? What is a company worth: explain the theory and the reality of valuation.
2. Define and explain why the following are important: long-term value creation, investor's required IRR, investor's required share of ownership, discounted cash flow, and deal structure in fundraising.
3. Explain five prevalent methods used in valuing a company and their strengths and weaknesses, given their underlying assumptions.

4. What is a staged capital commitment, and why is it important?
5. What is a "cram down" or "down round"?
6. What are some of the inherent conflicts between investors and entrepreneurs, and how and why can these affect the venture's odds for success?
7. What are the most important questions and issues to consider in structuring a deal? Why?
8. What issues can be negotiated in a venture investment, and why are these important?
9. What are the pitfalls and traps in fundraising, and why do entrepreneurs sometimes fail to avoid them?

MIND STRETCHERS *Have you considered?*

1. Who should and should not have outside investors in their companies?
2. It is said that a good deal structure cannot turn a bad business into a good one, but many a good business has been killed by a bad deal structure. Why is this so? Find an example of each.

3. What beliefs and assumptions are revealed by the "bets" made in different deals?
4. What is a good deal? Why?
5. Is venture capital always structured to the advantages of the money lenders? Why?

Preparation Questions

1. Is Terracycle 'VC-able'?

2. Is Carrot Capital the right fit for Terracycle?

3. Should they take the deal anyway? Do they have a choice?

There was a bright burst of flashbulbs as Tom Szaky signed the electronic screen and pushed the button to signal the start of the NASDAQ's trading day. With his tousled bedhead, wearing a blazer over a T-shirt, the 21-year-old was visibly different from the CEOs, celebrities, and statespeople that usually preside over the market opening.

Szaky was a student on a leave of absence from Princeton University. He had put his studies on hold to found Terracycle, a New Jersey-based start-up that manufactured organic plant fertilizer from worm excrement. A week earlier, he'd pitched the concept to a panel of venture capitalists as part of the Carrot Capital Education Foundation Business Plan Challenge. His top performance in that competition earned him the right to ring the opening bell.

But it didn't stop there. Taking top honours also put Terracycle in line for up to US$1 million in seed funding from Carrot Capital, a New York-based venture capital company. Szaky next met with Carrot's managing director, setting up sessions for both companies to start conducting due diligence. While the judges had been enthusiastic about Terracycle's business model, an offer of VC funding was contingent on a closer inspection of the company's plans.

Szaky knew the stakes were high. With just $500 in the bank and $5000 coming in from another business-plan competition, Terracycle had barely enough cash to stay alive for another month. With no other venture capital deals on the horizon, Szaky and his six fellow staffers had only a few short weeks to either proceed with financing from Carrot—or find another way ahead with only their scarce bootstrapped cash to rely on.

"WORM POOP"

Just over a week later, Szaky found himself in more familiar, but less glamorous, surroundings. His brow glistening with sweat, he grunted with exertion as he shovelled compost from a metal biocomposter into a platformed worm gin in Princeton, N.J. Beside him was Bill Gillum, a former Bell Labs scientist with a Ph.D. in inorganic chemistry, who alternated between shovelling and adjusting settings on the biocomposter's computer.

The biocomposter and gin were two parts of a prototype system for producing nutrient-rich vermicompost on a large scale. The prototype was the latest step in a grand vision that had begun years earlier when Szaky took a road trip to Montreal. There, he had been impressed by the wriggling fertilizer factory installed under his Montreal friend's kitchen counter—a miniature vermicompost operation, where a bucket of red worms converted the house's kitchen waste into nutrient-rich plant food for the garden.

Now Szaky and Gillum were tinkering with an industrial-scale version of that same concept. A far cry from the kitchen-cupboard bucket, Terracycle's system used tens of thousands of worms, capable of producing thousands of pounds of fertilizer. Raw organic waste—from coffee grounds to paper sludge—was first heated and oxygenated to eliminate any harmful bacteria; then it was fed into a biotransformer, where red worms would chew through it, excreting nutrient-rich vermicompost castings in the process.

The final step saw these castings—"worm poop," in the candid language of Terracycle's founders—separated to remove any worms or undigested waste. The product could be bagged directly as a solid, or brewed and packaged as a liquefied plant food. This innovative separation and brewing process allowed the fertilizer to retain its nutrients on the shelf for years—a considerable improvement over the kitchen-cupboard system, whose output would lose its nutrients after only weeks.

Their working prototype could produce and bottle up to 80 half-litre containers per week—if Terracycle's staff chipped in enough manual labour. Often, they would spend their mornings in meetings, and then spend afternoons shovelling organic waste into the gin. The end product was bottled in spartan containers—the company had yet to settle on packaging design or a product name. Based on Bill's own anecdotal experience, the company's plant food was at least as effective as its chemical counterparts, such as Miracle-Gro.

Terracycle badly needed capital to turn the prototype into a working production facility. To convert a warehouse space

This case was written by Lukas Neville, PhD student, Queen's School of Business, and Professor Elspeth J. Murray, CIBC Teaching Fellow in Entrepreneurship, Queen's School of Business, Queen's University. This case was developed with the support of the CIBC Curriculum Development Fund at the Queen's Centre for Business Venturing, for purposes of classroom discussion.

in Trenton, N.J., into a fully functional production facility capable of producing 100 000 750-millilitre bottles per week would require $300 000; to scale up to 215 000 bottles per week, they would need $850 000 in facility upgrades and bottling and brewing equipment. The company also needed to undertake rigorous product testing—a process that, for each product, would take six months and cost $60 000 at Rutgers, the state university of New Jersey.

Terracycle had been focused on producing a liquid indoor plant food, but a number of other products were possible. Once the earthworm castings had been produced, they could be packaged in their solid form to be used as pellet fertilizers or growth media (soil substitute). Alternately, the castings could be brewed in distilled water to produce a sprayable liquid. Products for specialty applications such as rose bushes could be developed with small changes to the composition of the worms' organic-waste diet. And the company had a range of bottling options, from a spray applicator on small bottles for indoor use to a hose applicator affixed to a large jug for lawns and outdoor plants.

FIRST PRODUCT

Responsibility for setting product lines fell to Robin Tator. Tator, the company's vice president of marketing and sales, had given Szaky one of his very first jobs as a teen. Tator had joined the firm early in its development and had been dividing his time between Ontario and New Jersey ever since, steering sales and distribution efforts on both sides of the border.

Terracycle had already tentatively selected its first product: a sprayable, all-purpose indoor plant food aimed at the consumer market. Pricing was designed to match larger competitors like Miracle-Gro. While Terracycle couldn't match the scale economies of its competitors, the production process for its vermicompost was far less expensive than the energy-intensive production of chemical fertilizer products.

The size of the fertilizer and media market was appealing—in the United States alone, it was a US$6-billion segment of the US$37-billion lawn and garden market. But the segment was beset by sluggish growth—no more than 5 percent annually—and dominated by a handful of industry Goliaths. Scotts' Miracle-Gro controlled at least 35 percent of the consumer lawn and garden market—and had an even tighter grip on the all-purpose fertilizer market.

Tator considered the organic market a green field of opportunity: The market was small—perhaps $400 million—for "designer" soils and premium plant food, but it was growing at a rate of 16 percent per year. Sales of organic products, which made up at best 10 percent of the overall lawn and consumables market, had grown well over 400 percent between 1997 and 2002. Though one competitor, Schultz, had made tentative steps into the market and Scotts was planning an organic line, the organic market was still dominated by small, regionally focused competitors.

Tator advocated a consumer focus, even though the agricultural and commercial markets offered higher margins. First, he expected indoor home users to respond positively to the product's safe, non-chemical formulation. Second, he anticipated that consumers would more readily try out the Terracycle product—while agricultural users, whose livelihood depended on the product's efficacy, would take longer to experiment with and adopt the product.

TERRACYCLE VS. CARROT

While Terracycle refined its production process and planned for its product rollout, however, the relationship with its potential financier began to sour. The discussions were conducted by Szaky, CFO Doug Feltman, and interim CEO Thomas Pyle. Feltman had joined the team after serving as CFO of marketing firm Grey Worldwide. Pyle's career in banking included senior roles at Deutsche Bank, Chase Manhattan, and Skandinaviska Enskilda Banken.

Despite their resumes, the financial projections they presented reflected both the company's embryonic stage of development and the fact that the leadership was balancing dozens of competing priorities. Their submissions included neither detailed cash-flow projections nor a proposed use of proceeds for the financing round.

Carrot wanted more. It needed a clear picture of what stage of development the young company would reach with its round of financing. Szaky and partners soon discerned that the financing would be tranched—delivered in stages—based on set metrics for sales, development, and hiring. Having attributed their survival thus far to their adaptability, the Terracycle team worried that set metrics would limit their flexibility in the face of unpredictable change.

Terracycle and its prospective investors also clashed on spending priorities. The company had budgeted relatively modest amounts for marketing, preferring to build sales through guerrilla marketing and a network of unpaid student interns. They also planned to place the management team—who had been sleeping at the office and drawing meagre, infrequent paycheques—on salary. Carrot expected, by contrast, investments into professional branding and marketing. They considered the intern program an unacceptable distraction.

The VC also wanted to rethink the management line-up. In a letter, Carrot allowed that the management members were smart and capable, but argued they were the wrong people for the company. Carrot wanted to hire start-up veterans with deeper experience in consumer products and retail marketing. Those who were left, Carrot made clear, would be expected to continue working at modest salaries or for equity alone.

Carrot, as an act of good faith, was willing to keep the company afloat with a $20 000 bridge loan and agreed to give it additional time to work out a deal. But Terracycle's managers were skeptical, sensing a gulf between their vision and Carrot's aims. On top of those substantive challenges, Szaky felt uneasy with Carrot on a gut level, as if he was being cloistered from his team during the high-intensity negotiations with the VC.

Butting heads with Carrot over both strategy and spending, Terracycle was in an unenviable position. It would be months before they had a saleable product ready. Their coffers were empty. The company had some embryonic relationships with individual investors—enough, perhaps, to cobble together enough funding to survive a few more months—but there was still a very good chance that it would not survive if they rejected the venture capital deal.

connect®

CHAPTER 11

OBTAINING DEBT CAPITAL[1]

Leveraging a company is like driving your car with a sharp stick pointed at your heart through the steering wheel. As long as the road is smooth it works fine. But hit one bump in the road and you may be dead.

WARREN BUFFET

LEARNING OBJECTIVES

LO1 Describe the lender's perspective in making loans.

LO2 Identify sources of debt and how to access them in today's capital markets.

LO3 Explain the lender's criteria in making loans, how to prepare a loan proposal, and how to negotiate a loan.

LO4 Distinguish the key aspects of orchestrating the acquisition of debt capital.

LO5 Discuss how lenders estimate the debt capacity of a company.

LO6 Identify tar pits entrepreneurs need to avoid in considering debt.

Market cycles impact credit availability—often creating a lack thereof—for emerging companies. After a market meltdown (such as in 2000 and again in 2009), many old rules disappear and a harsher banking climate appears. This chapter aims to prepare you to cope better with those realities in the debt capital markets. And as debt markets improve, and they always do, lessons learned here will provide important competitive advantages.

A CYCLICAL PATTERN: THE GOOD OLD DAYS RETURN BUT FADE AGAIN

For entrepreneurs and their investors, the punishing credit crunch and stagnant equity markets give way to robust capital markets and once again are beaten down. Interest rates fluctuate and the credit environment turns from friend to foe in a short timeframe. The availability of bank loans and competition among banks changes dramatically from pursuer of entrepreneurs to playing hard to get. And as Jean-Etienne de Bettignies and James Brander, both of the University of British Columbia, observe: "With bank finance, the entrepreneur keeps full control of the firm and has efficient incentives to exert effort." This may not be the case with venture capital finance—the subject of the previous chapter.[2]

Regardless of the credit environment lenders are becoming more savvy in seeking growth companies with the potential to assert themselves in the new economy. When times are good, bank presidents and loan officers aggressively seek entrepreneurial companies as prospective clients. They work with local universities and business development associations to sponsor seminars, workshops, and small business fairs, all to cultivate entrepreneurial customers. This is a very welcome credit climate for entrepreneurs. In a more severe credit crunch, regardless of interest rates, money slows, lenders turn reluctant and are less encouraging. The availability of credit is cyclical, the good times will return and fade, but remember that the fundamentals of credit do not change that much.

A WORD OF CAUTION

personal guarantee: An entrepreneur's promise, which obligates him or her to personally pay back any debt on which his enterprise may default.

History suggests a favourable credit environment can and will change, sometimes suddenly. When a credit climate reverses itself, **personal guarantees** come back. Even the most creditworthy companies with enviable records for timely repayment of interest and principal could be asked to provide personal guarantees by the owners. In addition, there could be a phenomenon viewed as a perversion of the debt capital markets. As a credit crunch becomes more severe, banks face their own illiquidity problems. To cope with their own balance sheet dissipation, banks can and might call the best loans first. Thousands of high quality smaller companies can be stunned and debilitated by such actions. Also, as competition among banks lessens, pricing and terms can become more onerous as the economy continues to tighten credit. Debt reduction could then become a dominant financial strategy of small and large companies alike.

THE LENDER'S PERSPECTIVE   LO1

Lenders have always been wary capital providers. Because banks may earn as little as a 1 percent net profit on total assets, they are especially sensitive to the possibility of a loss. If a bank writes off a $1-million loan to a small company, it must then be repaid an incremental $100 million in profitable loans to recover that loss.

Yet lending institutions are businesses and seek to grow and improve profitability as well. They can do this only if they find and bet on successful, young, growing companies. Historically, points and fees charged for making a loan have been a major contributor to bank profitability. During parts of the credit cycle, banks may seek various sweeteners to make loans. Take, for instance, a lending proposal for a company seeking a $15-million five-year loan. In addition to the upfront origination fees and points, the bank further proposed a YES, or yield enhancement security, as part of the loan. This additional requirement would entitle the bank to receive an additional $3-million payment from the company once its sales exceeded $10 million and it was profitable, or if it was sold, merged, or taken public. While this practice has not happened frequently in the current economic climate, it could be revived, depending on the cycle.

SOURCES OF DEBT CAPITAL[3]

LO2

The principal sources of borrowed capital for new and young businesses are trade credit, commercial banks, finance companies, factors, and leasing companies.[4] But friends and family may be turned to for private financing structured as debt with flexible and favourable terms that reflect the relationship between the entrepreneur and creditor. Start-ups have more difficulty borrowing money than existing businesses because they do not have assets or a track record of profitability and/or a positive cash flow. Nevertheless, start-ups led by an entrepreneur with a track record and with significant equity in the business who can present a sound business plan can borrow money from one or more sources. Still, if little equity or collateral exists, the start-up will not have much success with banks.

The availability of such debt for high-tech start-ups can sometimes depend on where a business is located. Debt and leases as well as equity capital can be more available to start-up companies in such hotbeds of entrepreneurial activity than, say, in the prairies. The hotbed areas also feature close contact between venture capital firms and the high-technology-focused lending officers of banks. This contact tends to make it easier for start-ups and early-stage companies to borrow money, although banks rarely lend to new ventures. But even in these hotbeds, very few banks are active in the start-up environment.

The advantages and disadvantages of these sources, summarized in Exhibit 11.1, are basically determined by such obvious dimensions as the interest rate or cost of capital, the key terms, the conditions and covenants, and the fit with the owner's situation and the company's needs at the time.[5] How good a deal you can strike is a function of your relative bargaining position and the competitiveness among the alternatives.

EXHIBIT 11.1   **DEBT FINANCING SOURCES FOR TYPES OF BUSINESS**

SOURCE	START-UP COMPANY	EXISTING COMPANY
Trade credit	Yes	Yes
Finance companies	Occasionally, with strong equity	Yes
Commercial banks	Rare (if assets are available)	Yes
Factors	Depends on nature of the customers	Yes
Leasing companies	Difficult, except for start-ups with venture capital	Yes
Credit unions	Depends on strength of personal guarantee	Real estate and asset-based companies
Insurance companies	Rare, except alongside venture capital	Yes, depending on size

Source: Jeffry A. Timmons, *Financing and Planning the New Venture* (Acton, MA: Brick House Publishing Company, 1990).

Another consideration is the person with whom you will be dealing, in addition to the amount, terms, and institution. The industry and market characteristics, and the stage and health of the firm in terms of cash flow, debt coverage, and collateral are central to the evaluation process. Exhibit 11.2 summarizes the term of financing available from these different sources. Note the difficulty in finding sources for more than one year of financing.

Finally, an enduring question entrepreneurs ask is: What is bankable? How much money can I expect to borrow based on my balance sheet? Exhibit 11.3 summarizes some general guidelines in answer to this question. Because most loans and lines of credit are asset-based loans, knowing the lender's guidelines is very important. The percentages of key balance sheet assets that are often allowable as collateral are only ranges and will vary for different types of businesses, and for stages in the business cycle. For instance, non-perishable consumer goods versus technical products that

---

EXHIBIT 11.2   DEBT FINANCING SOURCES BY TERM OF FINANCING

SOURCE	TERM OF FINANCING		
	SHORT	MEDIUM	LONG
Trade credit	Yes	Yes	Possible
Commercial banks	Most frequently	Yes (asset-based)	Rare (depends on cash flow predictability)
Factors	Most frequently	Rare	No
Leasing companies	No	Most frequently	Some
Credit unions	Yes	Yes	Real estate and other asset-based companies
Insurance companies	Rare	Rare	Most frequently

Source: Jeffry A. Timmons, *Financing and Planning the New Venture* (Acton, MA: Brick House Publishing Company, 1990), p. 34.

EXHIBIT 11.3   WHAT IS BANKABLE? SPECIFIC LENDING CRITERIA

SECURITY	CREDIT CAPACITY
Accounts receivable	70%–85% of those less than 90 days of acceptable receivables
Inventory	20%–70% depending on obsolescence risk and saleability
Equipment	60%–70% of market value (less if specialized)
Chattel mortgage*	80% or more of auction appraisal value
Conditional sales contract	60%–70% or more of purchase price
Plant improvement loan	50%–70% of appraised value or cost

Source: Jeffry A. Timmons, *Financing and Planning the New Venture* (Acton, MA: Brick House Publishing, 1990).

*A lien on assets other than real estate backing a loan.

may have considerable risk of obsolescence would be treated very differently in making a loan collateral computation. If the company already has significant debt and has pledged all its assets, there may not be much room for negotiations. A bank with full collateral in hand for a company having cash flow problems is unlikely to give up such a position to enable the company to attract another lender, even though the collateral is more than enough to meet these guidelines.

TRADE CREDIT[6]

Trade credit is a major source of short-term funds for small businesses. Trade credit represents 30- to 40 percent of the current liabilities of non-financial companies, with generally higher percentages in smaller companies. It is reflected on the balance sheet as accounts payable, or sales payable-trade.

If a small business is able to buy goods and services and be given, or take, 30, 60, or 90 days to pay for them, that business has essentially obtained a loan of 30 to 90 days. Many small and new businesses are able to obtain such trade credit when no other form of debt financing is available to them. Suppliers offer trade credit as a way to get new customers, and often build the bad debt risk into their prices. Additionally, channel partners who supply trade credit often do so with more industry-specific knowledge than can be obtained by commercial banks.[7] Such credit is often termed *spontaneous credit* and is "subject to gradual and automatic modification in direct relation to the volume of business and profitability."[8] It should also be noted that a new venture's customers and clients may also wish to secure such terms.

The ability of a new business to obtain trade credit depends on the quality and reputation of its executive team and the relationships it establishes with its suppliers. Continued late payment or non-payment may cause suppliers to cut off shipments or ship only on a COD basis. A key to keeping trade credit open is to continually pay some amount, even if not the full amount. Also, the real cost of using trade credit can be very high; for example, the loss of discounts for prompt payment. Because the cost of trade credit is seldom expressed as an annual amount, it should be analyzed carefully, and a new business should shop for the best terms.

> *A key to keeping trade credit open is to continually pay some amount, even if not the full amount.*

Trade credit may take some of the following forms: extended credit terms; special or seasonal datings, where a supplier ships goods in advance of the purchaser's peak selling season and accepts payment 90 to 120 days later during the season; inventory on consignment, not requiring payment until sold; and loan or lease of equipment.

COMMERCIAL BANK FINANCING

Canadian chartered banks prefer to lend to existing businesses that have a track record of sales, profits, and satisfied customers, as well as a current backlog of orders. Their concern about the high failure rates in new ventures can make banks less than enthusiastic about making loans to such firms. They like to be lower-risk lenders, which is consistent with their profit margins. For their protection, they look first to positive cash flow and then to collateral, and in new and young enterprises (depending on the credit environment) they are likely to require personal guarantees of the owners. Like equity investors, commercial banks place great weight on the quality of the new venture's executive team.

term debt: Money to be repaid over a period of time, rather than as one lump sum.

demand loan: A loan with no specific maturity date, but payable at any time. The lender may demand full payment at any time. The open-ended repayment schedule may benefit the borrower if some time is needed to reach profitability or growth targets. But if revenue is not generated and payments are infrequent, the debt may balloon.

Notwithstanding these factors, certain banks do, rarely, make loans to start-ups or young businesses that have strong equity financings from venture capital firms. This has been especially true in centres of entrepreneurial and venture capital activity. Most **term debt** offered will be **demand loans**.

Commercial banks are the primary source of debt capital for existing (not new) businesses. Small business loans may be handled by a bank's small business loan department or through credit scoring (where credit approval is done "by the numbers"). Your personal credit history will also impact the credit-scoring matrix. Larger loans may require the approval of a loan committee. If a loan exceeds the limits of the local branch, part or the entire loan amount will be offered to the bank's central office loan department.

Most of the loans made by Canadian chartered banks are for one year or less. Some of these loans are unsecured, while receivables, inventories, or other assets secure others. Commercial banks also make a large number of intermediate-term loans (or term loans) with a maturity of one to five years. On about 90 percent of these term loans, the banks require collateral, generally consisting of shares, machinery, equipment, and real estate. Most term loans are retired by systematic, but not necessarily equal payments over the life of the loan. Apart from real estate mortgages and loans guaranteed by the Business Development Bank of Canada or a similar organization, commercial banks make few loans with maturities greater than five years.

Banks also offer a number of services to the small business, such as computerized payroll preparation, letters of credit, international services, lease financing, and money market accounts.

According to a World Economic Forum report, Canada has the world's soundest banking system. The World Economic Forum has come to the same conclusion five years in a row.

LINE OF CREDIT LOANS

A line of credit is a formal or informal agreement between a bank and a borrower concerning the maximum (and sometimes minimum, e.g., $10 000) loan a bank will allow the borrower for a one-year period. Often the bank will charge a fee of a certain percent of the line of credit for a definite commitment to make the loan when requested.

line of credit: A formal or informal agreement between a bank and a borrower concerning a loan a bank will allow the borrower for a one-year period.

Line of credit funds are used for such seasonal financings as inventory build-up and receivable financing. These two items are often the largest and most financeable items on a venture's balance sheet. It is general practice to repay these loans from the sales and reduction of short-term assets that they financed. Lines of credit can be unsecured, or the bank may require a pledge of inventory, receivables, equipment, or other acceptable assets. Unsecured lines of credit have no lien on any asset of the borrower and no priority over any trade creditor, but the banks may require that all debt to the principals and shareholders of the company be subordinated to the line of credit debt.

The bank will expect the borrower to pay off his or her open loan within a year and to hold a zero loan balance for one to two months. This is known as "resting the line" or "cleaning up." Canadian chartered banks may also generally require that a borrower maintain a chequing account at the bank with a minimum ("compensating") balance of 5 to 10 percent of the outstanding loan.

For a large, financially sound company, the interest rates for a "prime risk" line of credit will be quoted at the prime rate. A small, more risky, firm may be required to pay a higher rate. The true interest calculations should also reflect the multiple fees that may be added to the loan. Any compensating-balance or resting-the-line requirements or other fees will also increase effective interest rates.

ENTREPRENEURS ACROSS CANADA
The Canadian Angle

Richard Kinlough and Bill Holy of CIT Corporate Finance, Canada state that in Canada, "the mid-market never got as frothy as in the U.S., likely the result of our conservative banking system. Total leverage never reached the 6s, peaking at around 5× total, with senior pricing in the BA+250 to 300 range...which was about as borrower-friendly as it got in Canada. Because the mid-market was not as aggressive as in the U.S., the correction was not as severe. By the end of Q4 2008, pricing increased 100bps to BA+400 while total leverage came down a turn to around 4.0×"

"BA" stands for Banker's Acceptance and is a short-term credit note generated for investment purposes and guaranteed by a bank. BAs are discounted from face value and traded in secondary markets. Banker's Acceptances are similar to government-backed debt (e.g., treasury bills) and are generally found in money market funds.

100, 200, 300, 400 refers to 1, 2, 3, 4 percent. 100bps similarly refers to 100 basis points or 1 full percent; a basis point is 1/100 of a percent.

Kinlough and Holy go on to state, "In Canada, liquidity is less constrained and lending terms are set at levels that send an 'open for business' signal. But just like in the U.S., the market has become a bit more conservative and pricey. Senior leverage is around 2.5× to 3.0×, priced at BA+450. Total leverage is in the 4.0× range and should remain there for the foreseeable future."

What this assessment means is that being a bit behind the more risk-tolerant U.S. banking practices became good news for the Canadian banking sector. Canadian firms were not allowed to play the leverage games that firms in the U.S. played—thus avoiding driving with the sharp stick on the steering wheel that Warren Buffet warned of in this chapter's opening quote. Or in reference to another Warren Buffet quote: "It is only when the tide goes out that you know who was swimming naked." Prime Minister Harper stated, "The global economic crisis has revealed quite a few skinny dippers, but Canada is not one of them." It was over 25 years ago that Ben Bernanke, now Chairman of the U.S. Federal Reserve, noted that during the Great Depression (1930–1933) Canada avoided the catastrophic bank failures that plagued the United States. This Canadian austerity means that the highs and lows are avoided in favour of a moderate approach, which is not without critics—particularly in times of economic growth and free-flowing capital.

The European financial crisis impacted debt financing outside the region. For example, Greece's debt crisis was blamed for helping to bring Canada's market for fixed-income financings to a halt. But the debt market was turning around in Canada and globally. Apple sold $17 billion of bonds in 2013. "Canadian debt markets continued to provide good liquidity, affording debt capital to most comers with sensible transactions."

Question: The city of Detroit, Michigan, declared bankruptcy, and Greece, Portugal, and other European countries struggled with insolvency. Mark Carney left his post as Governor of the Bank of Canada to assume the same position for England. Even before assuming the role of Governor of the Bank of England in mid-2013, he made it clear that he disagreed with current leverage ratios and banking regulations. Liquidity plays a role at the macro and micro levels. Some countries and companies will fare much better than others. What other factors play a determining role in a country or company's output? Will entrepreneurial spirit around the world be stifled or fuelled?

Sources: Richard Kinlough and Bill Holy, "The Debt Market," *Private Capital*, Spring 2009; "Canada Will Emerge from Slump Faster, Stronger: PM," *CBC News*, March 10, 2009; Ben S. Bernanke, "Nonmonetary Effects of the Financial Crisis in the Propagation of the Great Depression," *American Economic Review* 73, no. 3 (1983): 257–276; Tim Kildaze, "Greece Weighs on Canada's Debt Market," *The Globe and Mail*, September 10, 2012; Avison Young, *Debt Market Monitor*, December 2012.

TIME-SALES FINANCE

Many dealers or manufacturers who offer instalment payment terms to purchasers of their equipment cannot themselves finance instalment or conditional sales contracts. In such situations, they sell and assign the instalment contract to a bank or sales finance company. (Some very large manufacturers do their own financing through captive finance companies. Most small retailers merely refer their customer instalment contracts to sales finance companies, which provide much of this financing, and on more flexible terms.)

From the manufacturer or dealer's point of view, time-sales finance is a way of obtaining short-term financing from long-term instalment accounts receivable. From the purchaser's point of view, it is a way of financing the purchase of new equipment.

Under time-sales financing, the bank purchases instalment contracts at a discount from their full value and takes as security an assignment of the manufacturer/dealer's interest in the conditional sales contract. In addition, the bank's financing of instalment note receivables includes recourse to the seller in the event of loan default by the purchaser. Thus, the bank has the payment obligation of the equipment purchaser, the manufacturer/dealer's security interest in the equipment purchased, and recourse to the manufacturer/dealer in the event of default. The bank also withholds a portion of the payment (5 percent or more) as a dealer reserve until the note is paid. Since the reserve becomes an increasing percentage of the note as the contract is paid off, an arrangement is often made when multiple contracts are financed to ensure that the reserve against all contracts will not exceed 20 percent or so.

The purchase price of equipment under a sales financing arrangement includes a "time-sales price differential" (e.g., an increase to cover the discount, typically 6 to 10 percent) taken by the bank that does the financing. Collection of the instalments may be made directly by the bank or indirectly through the manufacturer/dealer.

TERM LOANS

Bank term loans are generally made for periods of one to five years, and may be unsecured or secured. Most of the basic features of bank term loans are the same for secured and unsecured loans.

Term loans provide needed growth capital to companies. They are also a substitute for a series of short-term loans made with the hope of renewal by the borrower. Banks make these generally on the basis of predictability of positive cash flow.

Term loans have three distinguishing features: Banks make them for periods of up to five years (and occasionally more); periodic repayment is required; and agreements are designed to fit the special needs and requirements of the borrower (e.g., payments can be smaller at the beginning of a loan term and larger at the end).

Because term loans do not mature for a number of years, during which time the borrower's situation and fortunes could change significantly, the bank must carefully evaluate the prospects of the borrowing company. Even the protection afforded by initially strong assets can be wiped out by several years of heavy losses. Term lenders stress the entrepreneurial and managerial abilities of the borrowing company. The bank will also carefully consider such things as the long-range prospects of the company and its industry, its present and projected profitability, and its ability to generate the cash required to meet the loan payments, as shown by past performance. Pricing for a term loan may be higher, reflecting a perceived higher risk from the longer term.

To lessen the risks involved in term loans, a bank will require some restrictive covenants in the loan agreement. These covenants might prohibit additional borrowing, merger of the company, payment of dividends, sales of assets, increased salaries to the owners, and the like. Also, the bank will probably require financial covenants to provide early warning of deterioration of the business, like debt to equity and cash flow to interest coverage rates.

PERSONAL PROPERTY SECURITY ACT

"The Personal Property Security Act allows lenders and sellers to secure payment of a debt and to establish priority over other creditors by registering their security interest in the personal property of a debtor."[9] When a bank loans someone money to purchase a vehicle, the bank registers its security interest in the vehicle with the Personal Property Registry (PPR). Personal property is any machinery, equipment, or business property that is made the collateral of a loan in the same way as a mortgage on real estate. The personal property remains with the borrower unless there is

ENTREPRENEURS ACROSS CANADA
Insights from an Entrepreneurial Financing Specialist

- Commercial finance companies, factoring, and lines of credit from credit cards are some very high costs of financing.

- Find out exactly what the account manager at the bank has to fill in on the application forms he or she uses. Make sure to provide that person all of that exact information in a form that can readily be transcribed to the bank's forms and provide the appropriate summary write-ups about the company and the need for funds the account manager can use directly or copy for the application with some minor changes. Provide that information in hardcopy and electronically to facilitate an easy, error-free transfer of the information. Do the work for the account manager! He or she will have a lighter workload, ensure the application is accurate, speed up the process, and you appear co-operative.

- When the business cannot meet its covenants or otherwise "goes off the rails," the banker will no longer

seem to be a partner. That account manager is typically not an entrepreneur, he or she is an employee of a large institution that does not like errors of any kind. A lending recommendation from an account manager for a small business that gets into trouble is potentially a career limiting move and he or she will avoid that at all costs.

- If the borrower gets into trouble, the objective of most account managers will be to minimize his or her personal risk and decisions to help the borrower will become much more difficult to obtain.

Questions: A common pitfall is to think there is a "right" way to raise money to get the business started and growing, e.g., debt or equity financing. How can you best be prepared to appreciate that it is a fluid and dynamic process, one that changes on the go? Timing is also crucial; how will you know when the moment is right and can you plan in advance when you will need money?

default, in which case the personal property reverts to the bank. A lien charge against the title is registered with the province and priority is determined by the date of registration in the PPR.[10] Generally, credit against machinery and equipment is restricted primarily to new or highly serviceable and saleable used items.

PURCHASE MONEY SECURITY INTERESTS AND GENERAL SECURITY AGREEMENTS

A purchase money security interest is a specific form of security interest used as collateral. A loan to purchase goods is an example where the goods in inventory are the collateral. Another category is leases with a term greater than one year, where the leased asset becomes the collateral. A general security agreement is an additional assurance, typically collateral, provided to the lender; it is often necessary for the loan to be granted. The security agreement establishes the right of the lender with regard to the collateral.

A contract may be used to finance a substantial portion of the new equipment purchased by businesses. Under a sales contract, the buyer agrees to purchase a piece of equipment, makes a nominal down payment, and pays the balance in instalments over a period of from one to five years. Until the payment is complete, the seller holds title to the equipment.

A sales contract is financed by a bank that has recourse to the seller should the purchaser default on the loan. This makes it difficult to finance a purchase of a piece of used equipment at an auction. No recourse to the seller is available if the equipment is purchased at an auction; the bank would have to sell the equipment if the loan goes bad. Occasionally, a firm seeking financing on existing and new equipment will sell some of its equipment to a dealer and repurchase it, together with new equipment, in order to get a suitable contract financed by a bank.

instalment features:
A sum of money due as part of the agreed payback schedule over time for a debt.

The effective rate of interest on such a contract tends to be high, particularly if the effect of **instalment features** is considered. The purchaser/borrower should make sure the interest payment is covered by increased productivity and profitability resulting from the new equipment.

PLANT IMPROVEMENT LOANS

Loans made to finance improvements to business properties and plants are called plant improvement loans. They can be intermediate and long term and are generally secured by a first or second mortgage on that part of the property or plant that is being improved.

COMMERCIAL FINANCE COMPANIES

The commercial bank is generally the lender of choice for a business. But when the bank says no, commercial finance companies, which aggressively seek borrowers, are a good option. They frequently lend money to companies that do not have positive cash flow, although commercial finance companies will not make loans to companies unless they consider them viable risks. In tighter credit economies, finance companies are generally more accepting of risk than are banks.

The primary factors in a bank's loan decision are the continuing successful operation of a business and its generation of more than enough cash to repay a loan. By contrast, commercial finance companies lend against the liquidation value of assets (receivables, inventory, equipment) that it understands, knows how and where to sell, and whose liquidation value is sufficient to repay the loan. Today banks own many of the leading finance companies. As a borrower gains financial strength and a track record, transfer to more attractive bank financing can be easier.

In the case of inventories or equipment, liquidation value is the amount that could be realized from an auction or quick sale. Finance companies will generally not lend against receivables more than 90 days old, federal or provincial government agency receivables (against which it is very difficult to perfect a lien and payment is slow), or any receivables whose collection is contingent on the performance of a delivered product.

Because of the liquidation criteria, finance companies prefer readily saleable inventory items such as electronic components or metal in such commodity forms as billets or standard shapes. Generally, a finance company will not accept inventory as collateral unless it also has receivables. Equipment loans are made only by certain finance companies and against such standard equipment as lathes, milling machines, and the like. Finance companies, like people, have items in which they are more comfortable and therefore would extend more credit against certain kinds of collateral.

How much of the collateral value will a finance company lend? Generally, 70 to 85 percent of acceptable receivables under 90 days old, 20 to 70 percent of the liquidation value of raw materials and/or finished goods inventory that are not obsolete or damaged, and 60 to 70 percent of the liquidation value of equipment, as determined by an appraiser, is acceptable. Receivables and inventory loans are for one year, while equipment loans are for three to seven years.

All these loans have tough prepayment penalties: Finance companies do not want to be immediately replaced by banks when a borrower has improved its credit image. Generally, finance companies require a three-year commitment to do business with them, with prepayment fees if this provision is not met.

The data required for a loan from a finance company includes all that would be provided to a bank, plus additional details for the assets being used as collateral. For receivables financing, this includes detailed aging of receivables (and payables) and historical data on sales, returns, or deductions (all known as dilution), and collections.

For inventory financing, it includes details on the items in inventory, how long they have been there, and their rate of turnover. Requests for equipment loans should be accompanied by details on the date of purchase, cost of each equipment item, and appraisals, which are generally always required. These appraisals must be made by acceptable (to the lender) outside appraisers.

The advantage of dealing with a commercial finance company is that it will make loans that banks will not, and it can be flexible in lending arrangements. The price a finance company exacts for this is an interest rate anywhere from 0 to 6 percent over that charged by a bank, prepayment penalties, and, in the case of receivables loans, recourse to the borrower for unpaid collateralized receivables.

Because of their greater risk taking and asset-based lending, finance companies usually place a larger reporting and monitoring burden on the borrowing firm to stay on top of the receivables and inventory serving as loan collateral. Personal guarantees will generally be required from the principals of the business. A finance company or bank will generally reserve the right to reduce the percentage of the value lent against receivables or inventory if it gets nervous about the borrower's survivability.

FACTORING

Factoring is a form of accounts receivable financing. However, instead of borrowing and using receivables as collateral, the receivables are sold, at a discounted value, to a factor. Factoring is accomplished on a discounted value of the receivables pledged. Invoices that do not meet the factor's credit standard will not be accepted as collateral. (Receivables more than 90 days old are not normally accepted.) A bank may inform the purchaser of goods that the account has been assigned to the bank, and payments are made directly to the bank, which credits them to the borrower's account. This is called a notification plan. Alternatively, the borrower may collect the accounts as usual and pay off the bank loan; this is a non-notification plan.

Factoring can make it possible for a company to secure a loan that it might not otherwise get. The loan can be increased as sales and receivables grow. However, factoring can have drawbacks. It can be expensive, and trade creditors sometimes regard factoring as evidence of a company in financial difficulty, except in certain industries.

In a standard factoring arrangement, the factor buys the client's receivables outright, without recourse, as soon as the client creates them, by shipment of goods to customers. Although the factor has recourse to the borrowers for returns, errors in pricing, and so on, the factor assumes the risk of bad debt losses that develop from receivables it approves and purchases. Many factors, however, provide factoring only on a recourse basis.

Cash is made available to the client as soon as proof is provided (old-line factoring) or on the average due date of the invoices (maturity factoring). With maturity factoring, the company can often obtain a loan of about 90 percent of the money a factor has agreed to pay on a maturity date. Most factoring arrangements are for one year.

Factoring can also be on a recourse basis. In this circumstance, the borrower must replace unpaid receivables after 90 days with new current receivables to allow the borrowings to remain at the same level.

Factoring fits some businesses better than others. For a business that has annual sales volume in excess of $300 000 and a net worth over $50 000 that sells on normal credit terms to a customer base that is 75-percent credit rated, factoring is a real option. Factoring has become almost traditional in such industries as textiles, furniture manufacturing, clothing manufacturing, toys, shoes, and plastics.

The same data required from a business for a receivable loan from a bank are required by a factor. Because a factor is buying receivables with no recourse, it will analyze the quality and value of a prospective client's receivables. It will want a detailed aging of receivables plus historical data on bad debts, returns, and allowances. It will also investigate the credit history of customers to whom its client sells and establish credit limits for each customer. The business client can receive factoring of customer receivables only up to the limits so set.

The cost of financing receivables through factoring is higher than that of borrowing from a bank or a finance company. The factor is assuming the credit risk, doing credit investigations and collections, and advancing funds. A factor generally charges up to 2 percent of the total sales factored as a service charge.

There is also an interest charge for money advanced to a business, usually 2 to 6 percent above prime. A larger, established business borrowing large sums would command a better interest rate than the small borrower with a one-time, short-term need. Finally, factors withhold a reserve of 5 to 10 percent of the receivables purchased.

Factoring is not the cheapest way to obtain capital, but it does quickly turn receivables into cash. Moreover, although more expensive than accounts receivable financing, factoring saves its users credit agency fees, salaries of credit and collection personnel, and maybe bad debt write-offs. Factoring also provides credit information on collection services that may be better than the borrower's.

LEASING COMPANIES

The leasing industry has grown substantially in recent years, and lease financing has become an important source of medium-term financing for businesses. There are hundreds of leasing companies in Canada. In addition, many commercial banks and finance companies have leasing departments. Some leasing companies handle a wide variety of equipment, while others specialize in certain types of equipment—machine tools, electronic test equipment, and the like.

Common and readily resalable items such as automobiles, trucks, computers, and office furniture can be leased by both new and existing businesses. However, the start-up will find it difficult to lease other kinds of industrial, computer, or business equipment without providing a letter of credit or a certificate of deposit to secure the lease, or personal guarantees from the founders or from a wealthy third party.

An exception to this condition is high-technology start-ups that have received substantial venture capital. Some of these ventures have received large amounts of lease financing for special equipment from equity-oriented lessors, who receive some form of share purchase rights in return for providing the start-up's lease line. Like many financing options, availability of venture leasing may be reduced significantly in tight money markets.

Generally, industrial equipment leases have a term of three to five years, but in some cases may run longer. There can also be lease renewal options for 3 to 5 percent per year of the original equipment value. Leases are usually structured to return the entire cost of the leased equipment plus finance charges to the lessor, although some so-called operating leases do not, over their term, produce revenues equal to or greater than the price of the leased equipment.

Typically, an upfront payment is required of about 10 percent of the value of the item being leased. The interest rate on equipment leasing may be more or less than other forms of financing, depending on the equipment leased, the credit of the lessee, and the time of year.

Leasing credit criteria are very similar to the criteria used by commercial banks for equipment loans. Primary considerations are the value of the equipment leased, the justification of the lease, and the lessee's projected cash flow over the lease term.

Should a business lease equipment? Leasing has certain advantages. It enables a young or growing company to conserve cash and can reduce its requirements for equity capital. Leasing can also be a tax advantage, because payments can be deducted over a shorter period than can depreciation.

Finally, leasing provides the flexibility of returning equipment after the lease period if it is no longer needed or if it has become technologically obsolete. This can be a particular advantage to high-technology companies.

Leasing may or may not improve a company's balance sheet, because accounting practice currently requires that the value of the equipment acquired in a capital lease be reflected on the balance sheet. Operating leases, however, do not appear on the balance sheet. Generally, this is an issue of economic ownership rather than legal ownership. If the economic risk is primarily with the lessee, it must be capitalized and it therefore goes on the balance sheet along with the corresponding debt. Depreciation also follows the risk, along with the corresponding tax benefits. Start-ups that do not need such tax relief should be able to acquire more favourable terms with an operating lease.

BEFORE THE LOAN DECISION[11]   LO3

Choosing a bank and, more specifically, a banker is one of the more important decisions a new or young business will make. Entrepreneurs seeking to develop a constructive banking relationship should note:

✔ *Industry experience is critical.* Choose a banker who understands your particular industry. They will have other clients in the same industry and may serve as a valuable resource for networking and service professionals with relevant experience. In the case of funding requests, bankers with industry knowledge are more apt to make a quick and reasoned determination.

✔ *Understand their business model.* Every bank has different criteria with regard to working with new ventures and their lending decisions are largely based on quantitative credit-scoring metrics. The entrepreneur needs to have an understanding of how a particular bank works and determine whether that model is a fit with his or her venture.

✔ *Understand who you're dealing with.* Bankers are relationship managers whose job is to support their clients—including expediting the approval of loans and credit lines that fit with their bank's lending criteria. Like a lot of good vendors, the best of them have specialized knowledge, excellent contacts, and will take a genuine interest in your business.

Much of the following discussion of lending practices and decisions applies to commercial finance company lenders as well as to banks. A good lender relationship can sometimes mean the difference between the life and death of a business during difficult times. There have been cases where one bank has called its loans to a struggling business, causing it to go under, and another bank has stayed with its loans and helped a business to survive and prosper.

One bank's website specifically courts female entrepreneurs: "RBC Royal Bank has a long-standing involvement with women entrepreneurs and is committed to helping them start and grow their businesses. From market champions, to banking, to information and tips, we're dedicated to supporting the success of women business owners." RBC even sponsors the Canadian Women Entrepreneurs Awards. BDC has offered Aboriginal banking since 1996, offering "customized, long-term and flexible solutions specially designed for Aboriginal entrepreneurs." BMO offers "SmartSteps" for business—an online interactive tool to assess your enterprise.

Those banks that will not make loans to start-ups and early-stage ventures generally cite the lack of operating track record as the primary reason for turning down a loan. Lenders that make such loans usually do so for previously successful entrepreneurs of means or for firms backed by investors with whom they have had prior relationships and whose judgment they trust (e.g., established venture capital firms when they believe that the venture capital company will invest in the next round).

In centres of high technology and venture capital, the main officers of the major banks will have one or more high-technology lending officers who specialize in making loans to early-stage, high-technology ventures. Through much experience, these bankers have come to understand the market and operating idiosyncrasies, problems, and opportunities of such ventures. They generally have close ties to venture capital firms and will refer entrepreneurs to such firms for possible equity financing. The venture capital firms, in turn, will refer their portfolio ventures to the bankers for debt financing.

What should an entrepreneur consider in choosing a lender? What is important in a lending decision? How should entrepreneurs relate to their lenders on an ongoing basis? In many ways, the lender's decision is similar to that of the venture capitalist. The goal is to make money for his or her company, through interest earned on good loans. The lender fears losing money by making bad loans to companies that default on their loans. To this end, he or she avoids risk by building in every conceivable safeguard. The lender is concerned with the client company's loan coverage, its ability to repay, and the collateral it can offer. Finally, but most important, he or she must judge the character and quality of the leadership team of the company to which the loan is being made.

Exhibit 11.4 outlines the key steps in obtaining a loan. Because of the importance of a banking relationship, an entrepreneur should shop around before making a choice. The criteria for selecting a bank should be based on more than just loan interest rates. We have all become accustomed to looking at the price of what we purchase. But the cost of borrowing is just one element; details of payback matter greatly too: how much and how often. Equally important, entrepreneurs should not wait until they have a dire need for funds to try to establish a banking relationship. The choice of a bank and the development of a banking relationship should begin when you do not urgently need the money. When an entrepreneur faces a near-term financial crisis, the venture's financial statements are at their worst and the banker has good cause to wonder about the venture team's financial and planning skills—all to the detriment of the entrepreneur's chance of getting a loan.

Has the bank had lending experience in your industry? If it has, your chances of getting a loan are better, and the bank will be more tolerant of problems and better able to help you exploit your opportunities. Is there good personal chemistry between you and your prospective lending officer? Remember, the person you talk to and deal with is the bank. Does this person know your industry and competition? Can this officer competently explain your business, technology, and uniqueness to other loan officers? Is he or she experienced in administering loans to smaller firms? Can you count on this person consistently? Does he or she have a good track record? Does his or her lending authority meet or exceed your needs? Does he or she have a reputation for being reasonable, creative, and willing to take a sound risk?

How does an entrepreneur go about evaluating a bank? First, the entrepreneur should consult accountants, lawyers, and other entrepreneurs who have had dealings with the bank in question. The advice of entrepreneurs who have dealt with a bank through good and bad times can be especially useful. Second, the entrepreneur should meet with loan officers at several banks and systematically explore their attitudes and approaches to their business borrowers. Who meets with you, for how long, and with how many interruptions can be useful measures of a bank's interest in your account. Finally, ask for small business references from their list of borrowers and talk to the entrepreneurs of those firms. Throughout all of these contacts and discussions, check out particular loan officers; they are a major determinant of how the bank will deal with you and your venture.

EXHIBIT 11.4 **KEY STEPS IN OBTAINING A LOAN**

Before choosing and approaching a banker or other lender, the entrepreneur and his or her venture team should prepare by taking the following steps:

- Decide how much growth they want, and how fast they want to grow, observing the dictum that financing follows strategy.

- Determine how much money they require, when they need to have it, and when they can pay it back. To this end, they must:

  — develop a schedule of operating and asset needs

  — prepare a real-time cash flow projection

  — decide how much capital they need

  — specify how they will use the funds they borrow

- Revise and update the "corporate profile" in their business plan. This should consist of:

  — the core ingredients of the plan in the form of an executive summary

  — a history of the firm (as appropriate)

  — summaries of the financial results of the past three years

  — succinct descriptions of their markets and products

  — a description of their operations

  — statements of cash flow and financial requirements

  — descriptions of the leadership team, owners, and directors

  — a rundown of the key strategies, facts, and logic that guide them in growing the corporation

- Identify potential sources for the type of debt they seek, and the amount, rate, terms, and conditions they seek.

- Select a bank or other lending institution, solicit interest, and prepare a presentation.

- Prepare a written loan request.

- Present their case, negotiate, and then close the deal.

- After the loan is granted, borrowers should maintain an effective relationship with the lending officer.

Source: Jeffry A. Timmons, *Financing and Planning the New Venture* (Acton, MA: Brick Housing Publishing, 1990).

APPROACHING AND MEETING THE BANKER

Obtaining a loan is, among other things, a sales job. Many borrowers tend to forget this. An entrepreneur with an early-stage venture must sell himself or herself as well as the viability and potential of the business to the banker. This is much the same situation that the early-stage entrepreneur faces with a venture capitalist.

The initial contact with a lender will likely be by telephone. The entrepreneur should be prepared to describe quickly the nature, age, and prospects of the venture; the amount of equity financing and who provided it; the prior financial performance of the business; the entrepreneur's experience and background; and the sort of bank financing desired. A referral from a venture capital firm, a lawyer or accountant, or other business associate who knows the banker can be very helpful.

If the loan officer agrees to a meeting, he or she may ask that a summary loan proposal, description of the business, and financial statements be sent ahead of time. A well-prepared proposal and a request for a reasonable amount of equity financing should pique a banker's interest.

The first meeting with a loan officer will likely be at the venture's place of business. The banker will be interested in meeting the venture's executive, seeing how team members relate to the lead entrepreneur, and getting a sense of the financial controls and reporting used and how well things seem to be run. The banker may also want to meet one or more of the venture's equity investors. Most of all, the banker is using this meeting to evaluate the integrity and business acumen of those who will ultimately be responsible for the repayment of the loan.

Throughout meetings with potential bankers, the entrepreneur must convey an air of self-confidence and knowledge. If the banker is favourably impressed by what has been seen and read, he or she will ask for further documents and references and begin to discuss the amount and timing of funds that the bank might lend to the business. Exhibit 11.5 provides a snapshot of the relationship between Canadian banks and entrepreneurs. Additional resources are found on the Canadian Business Network website, www.canadabusiness.ca when you search for the term "banker."

WHAT THE BANKER WANTS TO KNOW[12]

You first need to describe the business and its industry. Exhibit 11.6 suggests how a banker "sees a company" may differ from what the entrepreneur might say. What are you going to do with the money? Does the use of the loan make business sense? Should some or all of the money required be equity capital rather than debt? For new and young businesses, lenders do not like to see total debt-to-equity ratios greater than one. The answers to these questions will also determine the type of loan (e.g., line of credit or term).

1. *How much do you need?* You must be prepared to justify the amount requested and describe how the debt fits into an overall plan for financing and developing the business. Further, the amount of the loan should have enough cushion to allow for unexpected developments (see Exhibit 11.7).

EXHIBIT 11.5	**FAST FACTS ABOUT SMALL AND MEDIUM-SIZED ENTERPRISES (SMES) AND CANADA'S BANKS**

▶ Banks authorized $87.7 billion in financing to 1.6 million SMEs in 2012

▶ 79% of SMEs use a teller mostly frequently for banking; 66% use the Internet most frequently; 79% of SME owners say banking online has made their business more efficient

▶ 91% of SMEs think provision of low cost products and services is important; 92% think face-to-face relationships are important

▶ 77% of SMEs maintain a credit relationship with a financial institution; 90% describe the relationship as "good"; 58% describe it as "very good"

▶ 43% of SMEs have held a credit relationship with their financial institution for more than 10 years; 21% report a relationship for over 20 years

▶ 20% have only one credit relationship; 17% have two credit relationships; 33% have more than five credit relationships

Source: Canadian Bankers Association, www.cba.ca.

Sales	What do you sell?
Cost of goods	Whom do you sell to?
	How do you buy?
	What do you buy?
	Whom do you buy from?
Gross margin	Are you a supermarket or a boutique?
Selling	How do you sell and distribute the product?
G&A: General and Administration	How much overhead and support is needed to operate?
R&D	How much is reinvested in the product?
Operating margins	Dollars available before financing costs?
Interest expense	How big is this fixed nut?
Profit before taxes	Do you make money?
Taxes	Corporation or not?
Profit after taxes	How much and to whom?
Dividends/withdrawals	How much money is left in the company?

Source: This exhibit was created by Kathie S. Stevens and Leslie Charm as part of a class discussion and is part of a presentation titled "Cash Is King, Assets Are Queen, and Everybody Is Looking for an Ace in the Hole." Ms. Stevens is former chief lending officer and member of the credit committee for a Boston bank.

2. *When and how will you pay it back?* This is an important question. Short-term loans for seasonal inventory build-ups or for financing receivables are easier to obtain than long-term loans, especially for early-stage businesses. How the loan will be repaid is the bottom-line question. Presumably you are borrowing money to finance activity that will generate enough cash to repay the loan. What is your contingency plan if things go wrong? Can you describe such risks and indicate how you will deal with them?

3. *What is the secondary source of repayment?* Are there assets or a guarantor of means?

4. *When do you need the money?* If you need the money tomorrow, forget it. You are a poor planner. On the other hand, if you need the money next month or the month after, you have demonstrated an ability to plan ahead, and you have given the banker time to investigate and process a loan application. Typically, it is difficult to get a lending decision in less than three weeks.

One of the best ways for all entrepreneurs to answer these questions is from a well-prepared business plan. This plan should contain projections of cash flow, profit and loss, and balance sheets that will demonstrate the need for a loan and how it can be repaid. Particular attention will be given by the lender to the value of the assets and the cash flow of the business, and to such financial ratios as current assets to current liabilities, gross margins, net worth to debt, accounts receivable and payable periods, inventory turns, and net profit to sales. The ratios for the borrower's venture will be compared to averages for competing firms to see how the potential borrower measures up to them.

For an existing business, the lender will want to review financial statements from prior years prepared or audited by a CA, a list of aged receivables and payables, the turnover of inventory, and lists of key customers and creditors. The lender will also want to know that all tax payments are

EXHIBIT 11.7	SAMPLE OF A SUMMARY LOAN PROPOSAL

Date of request:	May 30, 2014
Borrower:	Cole Graham & Sons, Inc.
Amount:	$4 200 000
Use of proceeds:	A/R, up to $1 600 000
	Inventory, up to 824 000
	WIP, up to 525 000
	Marketing, up to 255 000
	Ski show specials 105 000
	Contingencies 50 000
	Officer loans due 841 000
	$4 200 000
Type of loan:	Seasonal revolving line of credit
Closing date:	June 15, 2014
Term:	One year
Rate:	Prime plus 1/2 percent, no compensating balances, no points or origination fees.
Takedown:	$500 000 at closing
	$1 500 000 on August 1, 2014
	$1 500 000 on October 1, 2014
	$700 000 on November 1, 2016
Collateral:	70 percent of acceptable A/R under 90 days
	50 percent of current inventory
Guarantees:	None
Repayment schedule:	$4 200 000 or balance on anniversary of note
Source of funds for repayment:	a. Excess cash from operations (see cash flow).
	b. Renewable and increase of line if growth is profitable.
	c. Conversion to three-year note.
Contingency source:	a. Sale and leaseback of equipment.
	b. Officer's loans (with a request for a personal guarantee).

Source: Updated and adapted from Jeffry A. Timmons, *Financing and Planning the New Venture* (Acton, MA: Brick House Publishing, 1990).

current. Finally, he or she will need to know details of fixed assets and any liens on receivables, inventory, or fixed assets.

The entrepreneur-borrower should regard his or her contacts with the bank as a sales mission and provide data that are required promptly and in a form that can be readily understood. The better the material entrepreneurs can supply to demonstrate their business credibility, the easier and faster it will be to obtain a positive lending decision. The entrepreneur should also ask, early on, to meet with the banker's boss. This can go a long way to help obtain financing. Remember you need to build a relationship with a bank, and not just a banker.

THE LENDING DECISION   LO4

One of the significant changes in today's lending environment is the centralized lending decision. Traditionally, loan officers might have had up to several million dollars of lending authority and could make loans to small companies. Besides the company's creditworthiness as determined by analysis of its past results via the balance sheet, income statement, cash flow, and collateral, the lender's assessment of the character and reputation of the entrepreneur was central to the decision. As loan decisions are made increasingly by loan committees or credit scoring, this face-to-face part of the decision process has given way to deeper analysis of the company's business plan, cash flow drivers and dissipaters, competitive environment, and the cushion for loan recovery given the firm's game plan and financial structure.

The implication for entrepreneurs is a demanding one: You can no longer rely on your salesmanship and good relationship with your loan officer alone to continue to get favourable lending decisions. You, or the key team member, need to be able to prepare the necessary analysis and documentation to convince people (who you may never meet) that the loan will be repaid. You also need to know the financial ratios and criteria used to compare your loan request with industry norms and to defend the analysis. Such a presentation can make it easier and faster to obtain approval of a loan because it gives your relationship manager the ammunition to defend your loan request.

LENDING CRITERIA   LO5

First and foremost, as with equity investors, the quality and track record of the leadership team will be a major factor. Historical financial statements, which show three to five years of profitability, are also essential. Well-developed business projections that articulate the company's sales

Prescott Ensign's brother-in-law has an earth/snow moving equipment business. He has stated "My account manager has to know me and my business—it's feast or famine. I work in the winter, but don't get paid till the spring. That's just because our contracts are for 90 days plus—and they are always late in settling, often because they are late in getting paid. In the summer business is brisk and payments are half before the job even starts and the remainder due on completion. Basically, I have expenses year-round but only get paid in the summer! Right now, I am breaking in a new account manager. The last one understood all this and she was comfortable; the new guy is terrible. I've actually put in a call to the bank for someone new who gets it."

Question: When is the right time to request a loan officer or account manager be replaced? Are there any dangers in asking for a switch or voicing complaints/concerns?

estimates, market niche, cash flow, profit projections, working capital, capital expenditure, uses of proceeds, and evidence of competent accounting and control systems are essential.

In its simplest form, what is needed is analysis of the available collateral, based on guidelines such as those shown in Exhibit 11.3, and of debt capacity determined by analysis of the coverage ratio once the new loan is in place. Interest coverage is calculated as earnings before interest and taxes divided by interest (EBIT/interest). A business with steady, predictable cash flow and earnings would require a lower coverage ratio (say, in the range of two) than would a company with a volatile, unpredictable cash flow streams, for example, a company with risk of competition and obsolescence (which might require a coverage ratio of five or more). The bottom line, of course, is the ability of the company to repay both interest and principal on time.

LOAN RESTRICTIONS[13]

A loan agreement defines the terms and conditions under which a lender provides capital. With it, lenders do two things: try to assure repayment of the loan as agreed and try to protect their position as creditor. Within the loan agreement (as in investment agreements) there are negative and positive covenants. Negative covenants are restrictions on the borrower; for example, no further additions to the borrower's total debt, no pledge to others of assets of the borrower, no payment of dividends, or limitation on owners' salaries.

Positive covenants define what the borrower must do. Some examples are maintenance of some minimum net worth or working capital, prompt payment of all federal and provincial taxes, adequate insurance on key people and property, repayment of the loan and interest according to the terms of the agreement, and provision to the lender of periodic financial statements and reports.

Some of these restrictions can hinder a company's growth, such as a flat restriction on further borrowing. Such a borrowing limit is often based on the borrower's assets at the time of the loan. However, rather than stipulating an initially fixed limit, the loan agreement should recognize that

CANWEST GLOBAL COMMUNICATIONS IN CRISIS

The Winnipeg-based media conglomerate was "scrambling to cut costs and reduce debt" in hopes of appeasing banks and other nervous lenders. The lenders conditions were not being met: "The covenants require Canwest to stick below numbers that measure the company's financial leverage." With quarterly figures revealing bad news, credit was permanently reduced to $112 million from $300 million and certain borrowing requirements had to be waived. But with $92 million already drawn, Canwest has little breathing room. "And if the company's cash runs out, it could face an extreme makeover in CCAA." The Companies' Creditors Arrangement Act permits financially troubled enterprises to restructure and hopefully avoid bankruptcy.

"President and CEO Leonard Asper, whose family controls Canwest, blames the tanking economy." But Chris Diceman, a senior VP of DBRS, indicates "management should have focused on paying down debt...Instead, Canwest embarked on international expansion." Too much leverage at an inopportune time was catching up with them. "The company's shares have lost 95 percent of their value in a year." Falling from $4 to 20¢ per share; it should be noted that $4 itself was a fair distance from share prices of over $20 in 2000, $15 in 2005, and about $11 in 2007. And if Canwest heads toward bankruptcy and the courts takeover, "that would likely mean an end to the Asper family's control."

After missing a $30-million interest payment earlier in 2009, Canwest failed to make $10 million in debt payments at the end of May 2009. Acknowledging it was in default it moved to negotiate "broader restructuring of its finances." Grappling with $3.9 billion in debt during an economic recession was not easy.

It was years prior that Canwest developed an appetite for debt. Numerous expensive acquisitions seemed like a good idea at the time. Driving along on a smooth road on a sunny day with a sharp stick on the steering wheel may not have seemed threatening at the time, but Warren Buffet's wisdom about leverage comes through now that the driving conditions are looking treacherous and economic uncertainty looms. Canwest filed for bankruptcy in late 2009. It was subsequently delisted from the TSX and the final closing of the settlement agreement occurred in October 2011. This was the first successful equity committee campaign in Canada under CCAA.

Sources: Calvin Leung, "The Good, The Bad & The Ugly," *Canadian Business*, March 30, 2009; "Most Actively Traded Companies on Canadian Stock Markets," *Canadian Free Press*, May 30, 2009; "Canwest Media Gets Bondholder Reprieve," *United Press International*, May 21, 2009.

as a business grows and increases its total assets and net worth, it will need and be able to carry the additional debt required to sustain its growth; however, banks (especially in tighter credit periods) will still put maximums after allowed credit as it gives them another opportunity to recheck the loan. Similarly, covenants that require certain minimums on working capital or current ratios may be very difficult, for example, for a highly seasonal business to maintain at all times of the year. Only analysis of past financial monthly statements can indicate whether such a covenant can be met.

COVENANTS TO LOOK FOR

Before borrowing money, an entrepreneur should decide what sorts of restrictions or covenants are acceptable. Lawyers and accountants of the company should be consulted before any loan papers are signed. Some covenants are negotiable (this changes with the overall credit economy), and an entrepreneur should negotiate to get terms that the venture can live with next year as well as today. Once loan terms are agreed upon and the loan is made, the entrepreneur and the venture will be bound by them, so think through what to do if the bank says, "Yes, but..."

- wants to put constraints on your permissible financial ratios
- stops any new borrowing
- wants a veto on any new management
- disallows new products or new directions

- prevents acquiring or selling any assets
- forbids any new investment or new equipment

What follows are some practical guidelines about personal guarantees: when to expect them, how to avoid them, and how to eliminate them.

PERSONAL GUARANTEES AND THE LOAN

Personal guarantees may be required of the "lead" entrepreneur or, more likely, shareholders of significance (more than 10 percent) who are also members of the executive team. Also, personal guarantees are often "joint and severable"—meaning that each guarantor is liable for the total amount of the guarantee.

When to Expect Them

- If you are under collateralized.
- If there are shareholder loans or lots of "due to" and "due from" officer accounts.
- If you have had poor or erratic performance.
- If you have management problems.
- If your relationship with your banker is strained.
- If you have a new loan officer.
- If there is turbulence in the credit markets.
- If there has been a wave of bad loans made by the lending institution, and a crackdown is in force.
- If there is less understanding of your market.

How to Avoid Them

- Good to spectacular performance.
- Conservative financial management.
- Positive cash flow over a sustained period.
- Adequate collateral.
- Careful management of the balance sheet.

How to Eliminate Them (if you already have them)

- See "How to Avoid Them."
- Develop a financial plan with performance targets and a timetable.
- Negotiate elimination *upfront* when you have some bargaining chips, based on certain performance criteria.
- Stay active in the search for backup sources of funds.

BUILDING A RELATIONSHIP

After obtaining a loan, entrepreneurs should cultivate a close working relationship with their bankers. Too many businesspeople do not see their lending officers until they need a loan. The astute entrepreneur will take a much more active role in keeping a banker informed about the business, thereby improving the chances of obtaining larger loans for expansion and cooperation from the bank in troubled times.

Some of the things that should be done to build such a relationship are fairly simple.[14] In addition to monthly and annual financial statements, bankers should be sent product news releases and any trade articles about the business or its products. The entrepreneur should invite the banker to the venture's facility, review product development plans and the prospects for the business, and establish a personal relationship with him or her. If this is done, when a new loan is requested, the lending officer will feel better about recommending its approval.

What about bad news? Never surprise a banker with bad news; make sure he or she sees it coming as soon as you do. Unpleasant surprises are a sign that an entrepreneur is not being candid with the banker or that the venture team does not have the business under the proper control. Either conclusion by a banker is damaging to the relationship.

If a future loan payment cannot be met, entrepreneurs should not panic and avoid their bankers. On the contrary, they should visit their banks and explain why the loan payment cannot be made and say when it will be made. If this is done before the payment due date and the entrepreneur–banker relationship is good, the banker may go along. What else can he or she do? If an entrepreneur has convinced a banker of the viability and future growth of a business, the banker really does not want to call a loan and lose a customer to a competitor or cause bankruptcy. The real key to communicating with a banker is candidly to inform but not to scare. In other words, entrepreneurs must indicate that they are aware of adverse events and have a plan for dealing with them.

To build credibility with bankers further, entrepreneurs should borrow before they need to and then repay the loan. This will establish a track record of borrowing and reliable repayment. Entrepreneurs should also make every effort to meet the financial targets they set for themselves and have discussed with their banker. If this cannot be done, the credibility of the entrepreneur will erode, even if the business is growing.

Bankers have a right to expect an entrepreneur to continue to use them as the business grows and prospers, and not to go shopping for a better interest rate. In return, entrepreneurs have the right to expect that their bank will continue to provide them with needed loans, particularly during difficult times when a vacillating loan policy could be dangerous for a business's survival. But what should occur and what does happen are different things!

HANDLING A BANKER OR OTHER LENDER

1. Your banker is your partner, not a difficult minority shareholder.
2. Be honest and straightforward in sharing information.
3. Invite the banker to see your business in operation.
4. Always avoid overdrafts, late payments, and late financial statements.
5. Answer questions frankly and honestly. *Tell the truth.* Lying is illegal and undoubtedly violates loan covenants.
6. Understand the business of banking.
7. Have an "**ace in the hole**."

ace in the hole: Something that can be revealed to provide victory, such as a resource or advantage held secret until an opportunity arises. The phrase originates from poker, where a card dealt face down and kept hidden is the "hole card." With an ace being the best card.

WHAT TO DO WHEN THE BANK SAYS "NO"

What do you do if the bank turns you down for a loan? Regroup, and review the following questions.

1. Does the company really need to borrow now? Can cash be generated elsewhere? Tighten the belt. Are some expenditures unnecessary? Sharpen the financial pencil: be lean and mean.

2. What does the balance sheet say? Are you growing too fast? Compare yourself to published industry ratios to see if you are on target.

3. Does the bank have a clear and comprehensive understanding of your needs? Did you really get to know your loan officer? Did you do enough homework on the bank's criteria and their likes and dislikes? Was your loan officer too busy to give your borrowing package proper consideration? A loan officer may have 50 to as many as 200 accounts. Is your relationship with the bank on a proper track?

4. Was your written loan proposal realistic? Was it a normal request, or something that differed from the types of proposals the bank usually sees? Did you make a verbal request for a loan, without presenting any written backup?

5. Do you need a new loan officer, or a new bank? If your answers to the above questions put you in the clear, and your written proposal was realistic, call the head of the commercial loan department and arrange a meeting. Sit down and discuss the history of your loan effort, the facts, and the bank's reasons for turning you down.

6. Who else might provide this financing (ask the banker who turned you down)?

You should be seeing multiple lenders at the same time so you don't run out of time or money.

TAR PITS: ENTREPRENEURS BEWARE   LO6

Modern corporate financial theory has preached the virtues of zero cash balances and the use of leverage to enhance return on equity. When applied to closely held companies whose dream is to last forever, such thinking can be extremely destructive. The excessive leverage used by so many larger companies engaging in leveraged buyouts (LBOs) was apparently just not worth the risk: Two-thirds of the LBOs done in the 1980s have ended up in serious trouble. The serious erosion of IBM began about the same time as the company acquired debt on its balance sheet for the very first time, in the early 1980s. This problem was manifested in the acquisition binges of the early 1990s and in the high-technology feeding frenzy of the late 1990s. Following the 2000–2003 downturn, LBOs once again emerged as a popular growth vehicle. The same can be expected after the economic turmoil that began in late 2008 and pushed on into 2010 and beyond subsides. Those on the inside embrace risk, thinking they know better and can do better. Those are the skinny dippers left exposed as the tide goes out!

BEWARE OF LEVERAGE: THE ROE MIRAGE

According to the theory, one can significantly improve return on equity (ROE) by utilizing debt. Thus, the present value of a company would also increase significantly as the company went from a zero debt-to-equity ratio to 100 percent, as shown in Exhibit 11.8. On closer examination, however, such an increase in debt only improves the present value by 17 to 26 percent, given the 2 to 6 percent growth rates shown. If the company gets into any trouble—and the odds of that happening sooner or later are high—its options and flexibility become seriously constrained by the covenants of the senior lenders. Leverage creates an unforgiving capital structure, and the potential additional ROI often is not worth the risk. If the upside is worth risking the loss of the entire company should adversity strike, then go ahead. This is easier said than survived, however.

EXHIBIT 11.8 TOTAL PRESENT VALUE

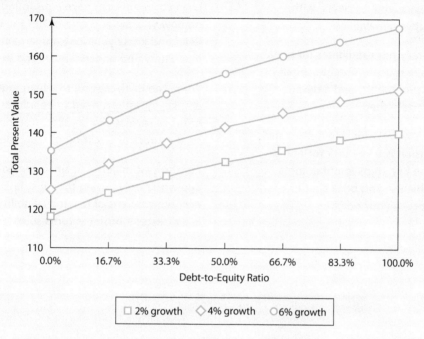

Source: William A. Sahlman, "Note on Free Cash Flow Valuation Models," Harvard Business School, 2003.

Ask any entrepreneur who has had to deal with the workout specialists in a bank and you will get a sobering, if not frightening, message: It is hell and you will not want to do it again.

NEITHER A LENDER NOR A BORROWER BE, BUT IF YOU MUST...

Canadian billionaire investor and philanthropist Stephen Jarislowsky repeats the words of Shakespeare "neither a borrower nor a lender be,"[15] which is good advice for early-stage entrepreneurs in this time of "economic war."[16] The following may serve as useful tips if you must borrow:

1. Borrow when you do not need it (which is the surest way to accomplish No. 2).

2. Avoid personal guarantees. Put caps and time limits on the amounts based on performance milestones, such as achieving certain cash flow, working capital, and equity levels. Also, don't be afraid in many markets to offer your guarantee and then negotiate ways to get it back in whole or in part!

3. The devil is in the details. Read each loan covenant and requirement carefully—only the owner can truly appreciate their consequences.

4. Try to avoid or modify so-called hair-trigger covenants, such as: "If there is any change or event of any kind that can have any materially adverse effect on the future of the company, the loan shall become due and payable."

5. Be conservative and prudent.

LEARNING OBJECTIVES SUMMARY

LO1 Business cycles impact lending cycles, with more or less restrictive behaviour.

LO2 Start-ups are generally not candidates for bank credit, but numerous sources of debt capital are available once profitability and a decent balance sheet are established.

LO3 Managing the banking relationship before and after the loan decision is a key task for entrepreneurs. Know the key steps in obtaining a loan and select a banker and bank that can add value and improve your odds.

LO4 Loan covenants can have a profound impact on how you can and cannot run the business. Read and know your loan agreement line by line. Study and understand all the details.

LO5 When the bank says no to a loan request, several key questions need to be addressed in an effort to reverse the decision. You may need to seek sources of credit other than banks.

LO6 For the vast majority of small companies, leverage works only during the most favourable economic booms of credit availability. Leverage is a disaster if business turns sour.

STUDY QUESTIONS

1. Define and explain the following terms and tell why they are important: sources of debt financing, trade credit, line of credit, accounts receivable financing, time-sales factoring, commercial finance company.
2. What security can be used for a loan, and what percentage of its value do banks typically lend?
3. What are the things to look for in evaluating a lender, and why are these important?
4. What does "value-added banker" mean, and how and why is this crucial?
5. What criteria do lenders use to evaluate a loan application, and what can be done before and after the loan decision to facilitate a loan request?
6. What restrictions and covenants might a lender require, and how and why should these be avoided whenever possible?
7. What issues need to be addressed to deal with a loan request rejection?
8. Why do entrepreneurs in smaller enterprises need to be especially wary of leverage?
9. At what stages should a venture borrow money?

MIND STRETCHERS *Have you considered?*

1. With the recent "credit crunch," capital is scarce. You have knocked on the doors of quite a few banks and had your loan applications denied. What next? Do you keep trying traditional lending options? What about an Internet or off-shore bank? Someone gives you the name of a guy in Las Vegas who can front you some cash off the books; do you follow up?

2. Why is Warren Buffet so wary about leverage?
3. Can you calculate the debt capacity of your proposed venture three to four years hence if it achieves positive cash flow and profitability?

Preparation Questions

1. Based on the information given and your own understanding of the issues, estimate the range of value for MLR in 2012.

2. How much financing do you think MLR will need during the next year? Where do you think it can or should obtain this financing?

3. Do you think there is an under-valuation problem with MLR, as Ronald Stanfield suggests? Explain why or why not.

4. How do factors other than those used in your valuation affect the share price for MLR? What could Ronald Stanfield do to increase the share price of MLR?

Ronald Stanfield wondered what it would take for investors to recognize the value of his company. For several years he had shepherded Minto Lake Resources Ltd. (MLR), a junior gold exploration company,[2] through exploration and early development of mining operations. Now, in the summer of 2012, the company had several promising gold properties. Still, the share price of Minto Lake Resources Ltd. on the Toronto Stock Exchange Venture Exchange (MLL-V) did not seem to reflect the potential of the resources in the ground. Although Ronald had long experience as a geologist and developer of resource deposits, it was frustrating that others could not see the value of his own company. He wondered what he could do to change this situation. Ronald was sure that the Wolf Lake gold project would create great value for MLR.

In 2007 Ronald had negotiated with Northway Inc. executives about joint development projects. He had angrily expressed his dismay at the poor prospects Northway had offered him. "Surely with all the high-powered brains around this table, you guys can give me a better offer." Ronald eyed each of the six committee members individually, then sat back and waited. Finally, Northway's head geologist spoke up. "Perhaps there is something. We have a gold property at Wolf Lake in Labrador you might be interested in."

By the end of that 2007 meeting Ronald had negotiated a seven-year deal to explore the property for gold and any other minerals present. By expending $750 000 in exploration over the next seven years Minto Lake would receive 50% ownership of the property. If MLR proved one million ounces of gold on the property, it would have the right to take over the entire project from Northway by spending a further $3 500 000 on a new mine start-up. MLR would then pay Northway royalties on the mine production. However, Northway also retained the right to back into the project again for 70% by developing a mine on the site itself. If Northway exercised this option, MLR would be left with 30% net ownership in the new mine without having to expend any extra cash.

Ronald had been very satisfied with the Wolf Lake agreement. The contract would keep the costs to his junior exploration company at a manageable level, while giving reasonable assurance that Northway would develop any significant find without further MLR expenditures.

Ronald believed strongly in the value of his company, and had expected it to increase steadily. However, even by 2012 it seemed that investors on the Venture Exchange did not. He knew his current financial challenge was to estimate the evolving value of MLR's gold mining prospects to determine MLR's total share value, and to ensure that new investors recognized that value.

Ronald was not sure why investors did not seem to recognize the value he did from MLR's financial statements, management forecasts, and exploration results. The company's financial reporting and management discussion showed responsible investment and efficient use of financing, in Ronald's opinion.[3]

THE CANADIAN MINING INDUSTRY

The Canadian mining industry was extensive. The large land mass provided several different areas of mineralization. The very old Canadian Shield rock, which crossed from northern Saskatchewan and Manitoba all the way to Quebec and Labrador, provided much of the base and precious metal finds. A second major area of exploration was in the Rocky Mountains and associated ranges. Further exploration was underway in the north, especially due to recent diamond finds.

The Canadian mining industry had existed from before confederation, but most large finds were made during the early to mid-1900s. The companies associated with these finds had evolved into international giants, such as Noranda,

---

This case was written by Charles Mossman, University of Manitoba, and Carter Berezay, Greaten Consulting Group.

[1] This case is for instructional use. It has been updated, simplified, and disguised from earlier information.

[2] A junior mining company is an exploration company that looks for new deposits of gold, silver, uranium, or other precious minerals. These companies target properties that are believed to have significant potential for finding large mineral deposits. (Investopedia.com—http://www.investopedia.com/articles/stocks/07/junior_mining.asp#axzz2Kc4Knged)

[3] Financial statements and management forecasts for MLR are found in Exhibits 1 and 2. Press release information is provided in Exhibit 3.

Falkenbridge, and Inco, now subsidiaries of foreign companies. Many other large and mid-size firms were also fully integrated, including exploration, development, mining, smelting, refining, and marketing operations. Some small and mid-size firms limited themselves to exploration, development, and mining. Other small firms, especially junior ones, focused on exploration with limited mining and development. Both international and junior Canadian firms participated in the worldwide mining industry due to the expertise gained in exploring for minerals within Canada.

The industry had created a vibrant equity market, with the majors listed mainly on the Toronto Stock Exchange[4] and smaller, especially junior firms listed on a speculative exchange, such as the Vancouver Stock Exchange (VSE). Unfortunately, during the 1980s and early 1990s, the VSE became "infamous" for being home to many share manipulators. They created "pump and dump" scams with thinly traded shell companies promoted by the controlling shareholders. These shareholder–promoters would find a new obscure mining or oil and gas exploration or development project for their shell company. Then they would promote the project and their company to unsuspecting new investors and selectively bid up the shell company's shares to higher and higher levels (the pump). Next, they would begin selling their own shares to incoming new shareholders (the dump) at a huge profit. As it became known that the mining project was a "bust," the share price of the shell company would drop to only a few cents. The share manipulators would buy back their controlling interest in the shell company very cheaply, then "discover" a new project and start the same scam over again.

It was recognized worldwide that Canada's VSE was home to many shady dealers and rip-off artists. These boiler room shenanigans had to be stopped, since their existence threatened the ability of legitimate companies to receive shareholder investments, and the Canadian government supported a change. The rules were improved, but the VSE's shady reputation was hard to shake. Finally, in 1999 the Vancouver and Alberta Stock Exchanges merged into a brand new Canadian Venture Exchange. Once again, the investment rules were changed to preclude share manipulations.

In 2001, the Toronto Stock Exchange bought the Canadian Venture Exchange, and renamed it the Toronto Stock Exchange Venture Exchange. Further rules to enhance transparency and disclosure were included in the new Exchange listing requirements. These changes greatly improved the environment for Canadian junior firms to raise funds for their operations.

RONALD STANFIELD

Ronald Stanfield was born in November 1947 and grew up in Thetford Mines, Quebec. During the summers of his college years, Ronald worked as a mine labourer and as a geological assistant doing surveys, diamond drilling supervision, prospecting, and geological and drift mapping. Upon graduation he joined a subsidiary of Nortanda Inc. During the first few years of his career, he quickly moved from one geology position to another. In December 1961 Ronald joined a subsidiary of De Beers, the biggest diamond miner in the world. During the next several years he supervised diamond mining in southern Africa. In July 1964 Ronald was promoted to Chief Geologist in charge of the Ivory Coast Operations, supervising 7 geologists, 2 prospectors and about 175 labourers. In 1970 he moved back to Canada and joined Inco Limited, where his career lasted the next 30 years, often in overseas locations.

Ronald retired from Inco in December 2002 at age 55, moving to Nova Scotia. He planned to spend his retirement years completing geological consulting projects for mining companies using the many personal contacts he had made during his career as a geologist. He had already established a separate personal geological consulting firm during the last 15 years of his employment.

MINTO LAKE RESOURCES INC.

In 1995 Ronald completed an independent geological assessment for Minto Lake Resources Inc. (MLR), a small exploration firm listed on the VSE.[5] Ronald was paid by an issue of 400 000 MLR common shares. During his geology work, Ronald decided that MLR was a shell company going nowhere, with no ongoing projects. He thought he could provide the expertise to give it a better future. He asked the previous president to step aside, and with his acquiescence took over the reins in November 1996. At that time, the company had about 7 million shares outstanding, trading for about $0.65 a share. MLR was debt free and had three employees.

From the outset, Ronald Stanfield's objective was to create shareholder value for his varied shareholders. Minto Lake would start as a gold and base metal exploration company.

---

[4] In 2002 the Toronto Stock Exchange abbreviation was changed from TSE to TSX, and the Canadian Venture Exchange, which became the TSX Venture Exchange in 2002, replaced the abbreviation CDNX with TSXV.

[5] On July 28, 2001, Minto Lake Resources became part of the new Canadian Venture Exchange.

The ultimate goal was to develop MLR into a dividend-paying junior company that found resources, kept a small percentage for itself, and sold the rest of each new discovery to a major producer for further development into a functioning mine. MLR would generate continuing income by retaining 2%–3% of the net smelter proceeds from each project.

From 1996 through 2005 Ronald's objective of developing MLR into a dividend-paying company did not change. Ronald continued to pursue gold and base metal discoveries. MLR signed land leases, prospected the land, and then sold off or abandoned the leases as dictated by the outcome. Ronald made a deal at a small brokerage to find the net funding needed by selling shares in the company. However, this deal eventually fell through. The 1997 Bre-X mining scandal[6] had all but killed the market for small exploration company funding. Investor money was not available anywhere. Then gold prices plummeted for several years, so there was little investment interest in exploration. Gold prices recovered sharply and grew rapidly after the World Trade Centre terrorism of 2001. Yet there was still limited general interest in gold exploration companies.

PURSUING SHAREHOLDER VALUE

By mid-2005, Ronald had become very frustrated. Nothing was happening to make his dream of a dividend-paying company a reality. In October 2005, Ronald decided to sell the entire company including all the gold and base metal leases carried on pieces of land throughout Canada to Ether Resources Inc., a Nova Scotia-based junior exploration company in a share exchange. Ether would provide one of its shares for every two of MLR received. MLR was valued at approximately $7 000 000 in total. For approval of the share exchange, Ronald needed 75% of MLR's current shareholders to accept the offer. However, MLR shareholders tendered only 71% of the outstanding shares. The deal fell through in February 2006.

Ether was still interested in buying control of several gold concessions that MLR had not yet developed. It made another offer in early 2006 to buy 75% of MLR's Northern British Columbia assets by purchasing 75% of the BC location rights in return for a US$2 million investment commitment to begin development of a mine within five years of signing.

MLR would not have to contribute any further cash to assure the mine was developed. For this opportunity, Ronald Stanfield did not need shareholder approval. He signed the deal as President of MLR. Many of Ether's management personnel saw the potential in the MLR deal. They were the biggest subscribers for the MLR private placement. The subsidiary established by Ether Resources Ltd. to develop the BC mine was known as Ether BC Ltd. and MLR owned 25% of this company.

Ronald Stanfield could now turn his efforts to concentrating on other gold and base metal exploration leases it already had in its inventory. At last his plan to develop shareholder value for MLR shareholders was coming to fruition. He continued to acquire land rights judiciously, and focused on Wolf Lake.

As progress continued on the various MLR gold exploration and development projects, Ronald developed a World Wide Web site for the company. This site became operational on April 10, 2009, and was used to update current shareholders and interested investors with company news. During the spring and summer of 2012, Ronald also reported frequently to business publications through press releases (Exhibit 3). Significant events during this period were as follows:

- The Candaga Property was optioned out to Hallbridge Mining Company for future income considerations.
- Wolf Lake (a favourite project of Ronald's from the start) was financed by the issue of a $160 000 private placement to existing shareholders.[7]
- The J.K. Gold Project in Montana, USA, was eliminated by abandoning the mining rights. It was a very good prospect but about 10 residential homes had been built in the mine site area in 2004. Environmental testing considerations now made the project too costly and time consuming.
- Results from the BC location (Ether BC Ltd.) being developed by Ether Resource Inc. were favourable, and Ether Resources announced that it planned to develop a mine in 2012, with production to begin during 2013. Ronald expected that high quality gold production would result.

MLR's Board of Directors had recognized Ronald Stanfield's leadership contribution to the company's growth over the years and had rewarded him with common shares as remuneration for his management and operational expertise. By the end of October, 2011 he owned about two million of MLR's 14 587 000 outstanding shares.

---

[6] From 1995 to 1997 Bre-X share price soared first on the Vancouver Stock Exchange and then on the Toronto Stock Exchange due to reports of extraordinary quantities of gold reserves at its property in Busang, Indonesia. Share prices rose to over $200 in pre-split value, making the company worth over $6 billion. In March 1997, after Bre-X's senior geologist fell from an aircraft and went missing, its mining partner, Freeport McMoran, announced that it had found very little gold at Busang. The Bre-X share price collapsed, creating large losses for pension funds and individuals. Fraud cases were pursued against senior management of Bre-X, but eventually nobody was found guilty.

[7] If the Wolf Lake drilling program were successful in proving one million ounces of mineable gold in the property, MLR would have the right to take over the entire project from Northway Inc. in return for a net profit royalty. To obtain the final 50% of the Wolf Lake MLR would have to spend a further $2 500 000 on a new mine start-up. Even in the improving market for small business financings, it might prove too much for MLR to obtain enough financing. Thus, Ronald expected to sell the project back to Northway or to another major gold miner for a lump sum payment, retaining a 30% ownership percentage for MLR.

PLANS FOR MINE DEVELOPMENT

Although he was gratified during the spring of 2012 that Ether Resources Inc. was now developing its mine, Ronald was very excited when MLR began to see very promising results at its Wolf Lake project. The Wolf Lake property was expected to show assets leading to up to one million ounces of mineable gold when the drilling and assays were completed in late June. Ronald expected that a mine developed at Wolf Lake by 2014 would produce 200 000 tonnes of ore per year by the time it reached full capacity in 2018, and that it would produce at 20 percent, 30 percent, and 50 percent of capacity in 2015, 2016, and 2017 respectively.

Wolf Lake

Depending on the share of the mine retained by MLR, different amounts of financing would be needed. For valuation of this mine, Ronald first assumed that MLR would keep a 50 percent share of mine income and cash flows, and then would consider the change in costs or revenues of alternatives to either own 100 percent or to revert to 30 percent ownership, should Northway exercise its option. Under the 50 percent ownership alternative, no royalties were payable by the Wolf Mine project. Ronald made all his revenue and cost estimates in 2013 Canadian dollars. From 2015 onward, he expected the mine to incur variable production costs of $20.00 per tonne and fixed production costs of $4 000 000 per year (in 2013 dollars). Administration and salary costs would be about $800 000 and non-cash mine depreciation and depletion (capital amortization) expenses would be about $600 000 per year. Due to favourable tax treatment, the effective Canadian tax rate for the mine (and MLR) would be about 22 percent after depreciation and depletion, once the mine was profitable. Once it showed a profit after tax, an additional small investment of $50 000 per year in inventory would be deducted.[8] Then the mine would distribute 75 percent of the remaining net cash flows after tax to its partners.

Ronald started with conservative estimates of ore recovery rates and current (2012) prices for gold, silver, copper, and zinc from the ore. In order to earn 50 percent of the Wolf Lake property mine income, MLR itself had to make further capital investments estimated at $250 000 (Canadian) in 2013 and $500 000 in each of the following three years. Although Ronald would try to raise equity funds, for planning purposes, he assumed he would borrow the funds at a 10 percent interest rate and repay $175 000 of principal plus annual interest starting at the end of 2014 and continuing for 10 years. (All borrowing, interest, and

principal repayment was assumed to occur at fiscal year end. Exhibit 4 shows more detailed information.)

Two other alternatives could occur for Wolf Lake. If MLR wished to earn 100 percent ownership of the mine, it could make capital expenditures estimated at $250 000 in 2013 and 2014, and $600 000 for each of the next five years instead of those specified under the 50 percent ownership alternative. For planning purposes, Ronald assumed MLR would borrow these amounts each year, and repay $150 000 plus 10 percent accrued interest in 2014 and 2015, then $400 000 plus accrued interest each year until 2023. MLR would receive 100 percent of net mine profits, except that it would pay Northway royalties of about 2.6 percent of gross mining revenues from mineral production plus 5 percent of net mining profits.

The third alternative was that if the mine looked profitable based on further exploration, it was possible that Northway could exercise its option to take over 70 percent of the ownership in 2013. If that occurred, MLR would receive only 30 percent of the net after-tax cash flows from Wolf Lake over its economic life, but would only be required to make a further capital expenditure of $160 000 already committed in the 2013 fiscal year. MLR would not have to borrow for this expenditure. Although this alternative would not please Ronald, since he wanted to own more of the potentially profitable mine, it would eliminate the need to take on more debt in order to finance mine development. This could also make more funding available for exploration of other MLR prospects.

Ether BC Ltd. Mine

The British Columbia mine being developed by Ether was expected to begin production in 2013. MLR's share of net cash flows was 25 percent. Based on Ether's estimates, Ronald projected that it would generate about $US1 500 000 in before tax cash flows in 2013, and that these cash flows would grow at 25 percent per year for five years until 2018, and continue production at the 2018 level until 2023, followed by a final year of $US1 000 000 in 2024. After that time the mine might be fully depleted, so cash flows would end. However, under the mine agreement, MLR was not responsible for any further costs, including returning the mine site to its original condition.

Corporate Expenditures

Besides the cash flows from British Columbia and Wolf Lake minerals, regardless of the situation, MLR would also have some corporate expenses that affected the value of its shares. Ronald estimated that in 2002 dollars, each year

---

[8] This inventory investment would be constant in $US each year, and the cumulative amount would be returned to the partners when the mine ceased operations in 2024.

it would invest and charge to expense $80 000 per year on exploration for its other small properties which were not expected to produce any revenue for the next few years, $25 000 on office expenses and administration, and $88 000 in salary to Ronald. These expenses would offset profit, so the 22 percent Canadian tax rate would decrease the net annual corporate expense.

Once the value of the mining projects and corporate expenses was found, after interest and debt changes, the value per share was simply the total value of the common equity divided by the number of shares outstanding.

WHAT IS THE CORRECT SHARE PRICE?

Ronald Stanfield's plan for creating value was coming together. He was the sole employee of Minto Lake Resources Inc., and had drawn limited salary income from the company. He had charged small company expenses to his own Visa card and was reimbursed on a sporadic basis. The company was now "debt free" and Ronald felt that he had created a high potential and stable gold exploration and development company. However, he believed that the market still had not recognized his efforts, talent at finding minerals, and honesty in his dealings. On July 1, 2012, the common shares of Minto Lake Resources Inc. closed at $1.10 on the Toronto Stock Exchange Venture Exchange, down from a recent $1.35 high.[9] The recent share price decline for the company was attributed to the recent decrease in gold prices from about $1620 per ounce to about $1330 per ounce.

Ronald was still concerned about the low level of MLR's share price that made it difficult to raise share capital at a reasonable cost. He consulted with a financial analyst who followed mining shares to see if he could get more insight into what drove value. The analyst told Ronald that in general, value was obtained from current profitability and future prospects. The primary quantitative method of valuing small mining companies with little production to give current value was to estimate their future potential cash flows and discount them at a rate reflecting their risk. Often, to estimate value of mining ventures, the cash flows to equity after all debt payments had been made were discounted at the cost of equity. Simple price multiples were not of much use for companies that did not have profits. But the estimation process using discounted cash flows was as much an art as a science, since both the cash flows and the discount rate were estimates that might vary widely.

The analyst provided some guidance on the factors needed for quantitative valuation of MLR's investments, and Ronald worked to obtain estimates (see Exhibit 4). However, as the analyst warned, "Value is often in the eyes of the beholder for small precious metal mining shares. Share prices for resource exploration shares are often driven by speculation on gold, silver, base metals, or oil and natural gas prices rather than fundamentals." He said that current and expected future supply and demand as well as market sentiment for the target commodity could drive commodity and related share prices up or down independent of the fundamental value.

Ronald decided to put together some financial assumptions for determining the value of each of MLR's investments. He could then hire an analyst to determine MLR's share price based on fundamentals. Ronald knew that it would be difficult to deal with the market sentiment issues out of MLR's control, but at least he would know whether the share price was trading above or below its fundamental value.

Ronald believed that MLR suffered from a lack of exposure to prospective new investors. The company needed major exposure to many market participants if their shares were to attain maximum value for their existing shareholders. Gaining investor exposure for all the value-enhancing activities of MLR was his next challenge. At 65 years of age, Ronald wanted to ensure Minto Lake Resources Inc. was on a strong financial footing. He said, "When Minto Lake is successful, I'll retire again!"

[9] The historic high price for MLR shares was $1.40 set on April 25, 2004. MLR's all-time low price was $0.28 on December 17, 2000.

MINTO LAKE RESOURCES INC.
BALANCE SHEET (AUDITED)

	JUNE 30	
	2012	2011
	$	$
ASSETS		
Current		
Cash	231 493	40 301
Accounts receivable	5 451	60 976
Due from a Director	12 794	15 407
	249 738	116 684
Investments In Ether Resources Inc. Project	850 205	–
Resource Property Interests	355 771	1 473 186
Office Equipment	3 857	2 495
	1 459 571	1 592 365
LIABILITIES		
Current		
Accounts payable and accrued liabilities	26 625	91 851
Current portion of long-term debt	–	74 378
	26 625	166 229
Long-Term Debt (Note 5)	176 750	202 346
SHAREHOLDERS' EQUITY		
Share Capital (Note 6)	4 605 173	4 438 473
Deficit	(3 348 977)	(3 214 683)
	1 256 196	1 223 790
	1 459 571	1 592 365

MINTO LAKE RESOURCES INC.
STATEMENT OF OPERATIONS AND DEFICIT (AUDITED)

	YEARS ENDED JUNE 30	
	2012	**2011**
	$	$
Administrative Expeditures		
Audit fees	11 500	9 700
Legal fees	12 928	14 968
Compensation expense	78 000	37 750
Share transfer, listing, and filing fees	10 589	13 791
Travel	11 909	9 444
Office supplies and services	6 195	16 914
Telephone	3 557	7 193
Shareholder information and communications	6 718	15 366
Amortization of equipment	531	500
	(141 927)	(125 626)
(Other Expenses) Recoveries		
Equity share of loss of investee	(1 409)	–
Interest and sundry income	91	–
Interest expense on long-term debt	(19 659)	(15 700)
Foreign exchange gain (loss)	25 005	(4 253)
Resource property acquisition and exploration expenditures (written off) recovered:		
B.N. claims, Ontario	8 560	–
J.K. gold project, Montana	(1 900)	(411 207)
G.W project, New Brunswick	(3 055)	(349 766)
M.C. project, Ontario	–	(24 375)
Merger agreement cancellation payment	–	50 000
	7 633	(755 301)
Loss For The Year	(134 294)	(880 927)
Deficit, Beginning of Year	(3 214 683)	(2 333 756)
Deficit, End of Year	(3 348 977)	(3 214 683)
Loss Per Share	($0.01)	($0.06)

MINTO LAKE RESOURCES INC.
STATEMENT OF CASH FLOW

	YEARS ENDED JUNE 30	
	2012 ($)	**2011 ($)**
Operating Activities		
Loss for the year	(134 294)	(880 927)
Expenses (recoveries) not involving current cash outlay		
Deferred property and exploration expenditures		
charged (credited) to operations	(6 999)	785 348
Amortization of equipment	531	500
Compensation expense deferred	78 000	37 750
Equity share of loss of investee	1 409	–
Cash provided by (used by) changes in non-cash working capital		
Accounts receivable	39 113	(43 845)
Due from a Director	2 613	(15 407)
Accounts payable	(33 586)	18 515
	(53 213)	(98 066)
Financing Activities		
Repayable advances from Ether Resources Ltd.	61 000	–
Long-term debt	77 650	43 474
Shares issued	166 700	20 000
Payments of long-term debt	(104 343)	(47 280)
	201 007	16 194
Investing Activities		
Cash held by subsidiary on de-commission (Note 3)	(31 704)	–
Resource property option payments received	60 000	50 000
Exploration expenditures	16 995	(16 150)
Purchase of office equipment	(1 893)	(2 995)
	43 398	30 855
Increase (Decrease) In Cash in the year	191 192	(51 017)
Cash, beginning of year	40 301	91 318
Cash, end of year	231 493	40 301

RONALD LAKE RESOURCES INC.
       SUPPLEMENTARY INFORMATION: SELECTED FINANCIAL RATIOS

	2012	2011
Liquidity		
Current Ratio	9.38	0.70
Leverage		
Current Liabilities / T Assets	1.8%	10.4%
Long-Term Debt / T Assets	12.1%	12.7%
Total Liabilities / T Assets	13.9%	23.1%
Long-Term Debt / Equity	14.1%	16.5%
Total Assets / Equity	1.16	1.30
Profitability Ratios		
Admin. Exp. / Total Loss	105.7%	14.3%
Return on Assets *	(8.8%)	(55.3%)
Return on Equity *	(10.8%)	(72.0%)

* For 2012 these ratios are based on the average total asset or equity balances outstanding. For 2011 they are based on the closing balances.

MINTO LAKE RESOURCES LTD.
EXCERPTS FROM OF NOTES TO THE FINANCIAL STATEMENTS
FROM THE ANNUAL REPORT, JUNE 30, 2012

1. The Company is a development stage enterprise in the business of mineral exploration. It is in the process of exploring resource properties and has not yet determined whether these properties contain ore reserves that are economically recoverable....The Company holds an option interest in an exploration property in Labrador, Canada. It also holds a 25 percent interest in Ether BC Limited, a company currently developing another gold property.

2. The Company accounts for its 25 percent interest in Ether BC Limited by the equity method. Under the equity method of accounting, the investment is recorded at cost adjusted for the Company's share of net income or loss reported by the investee. Dividends are recorded as a reduction in the carrying value of the investment.

   The Company follows the practice of capitalizing all costs relative to the acquisition, exploration, and development of resource properties. These costs are to be amortized over the estimated productive life of the property if it is placed into commercial production. If a property is abandoned as an exploration prospect or allowed to lapse, the related costs are charged to operations in the year. All proceeds from the sale of resources prior to the commencement of commercial production by the Company are recorded as recovery of exploration costs incurred.

3. BC Gold Project

   The Company's interest in Ether BC Limited was reduced from 100 percent to 25 percent effective January 11, 2012, upon receiving notice from Ether Resources Ltd. that it had earned a 75 percent interest under the terms of an agreement dated June 21, 2005, with respect to the BC gold project. The 2011 financial statements include the accounts of Ether BC Limited on a fully consolidated basis.

4. Wolf Lake

   The option agreement of August 2, 2007, entitled the Company to earn up to a 100 percent interest in 3 impost mineral holdings in Labrador, subject to a 2.6 percent blended average net smelter returns royalty on precious metals and base metal production, and a 5 percent net profits royalty.

   In order to earn its 100 percent interest the Company is required to incur a total of $3 250 000 in exploration expenditures; at least $750 000 by April 13, 2012 (subsequently completed), a further $500 000 by July 13, 2014, and a further $600 000 annually to July 13, 2019. The Company must also issue 1 000 000 common shares to Northway Inc. The Company may elect to enter into a 50 percent joint venture interest in the property based on expenditures incurred to April 13, 2012. In that event, it will be required to fund its share of further expenditures to avoid dilution of its interest. Deferred exploration expenditures related to this project are currently valued at $355 771.

5. Minto Lake Resources has no bank indebtedness. On the 2012 Balance Sheet, long-term debt of $176 750 includes deferred compensation to senior Company officers of $115 750 and Ether Resources Inc. advances and accrued interest of $61 000. The advances are repayable commencing the earlier of the date Ether BC Ltd. begins to pay dividends of not less than $96 000 annually, or the date it transfers the gold properties back to the Company for nominal consideration. The advances bear interest at prime plus 2 percent.

6. Authorized share capital is 50 000 000 common shares without par value. At June 30, 2011, there were 14 567 314 shares outstanding with a share capital value of $4 438 473. During 2012 a private placement of shares (plus 500 000 warrants to buy shares at $1.00 for one year), worth $155 200 after issue costs, and two exercises of share options occurred. At June 30, 2012, there were 15 117 314 shares outstanding with a share capital value of $4 605 173.

   At year-end there were 1 480 000 management options and 25 000 non-management options outstanding. In addition, 524 457 shares are reserved for issue (the remainder of 1 000 000 shares under agreement) related to acquisition of gold concessions.

7. The potential benefit of net operating loss carry forwards has not been recognized in the financial statements since the Company cannot be assured that it is more likely than not. Potential operating loss carry forwards, expiring from 2013 to 2019 total $393 000 and undeducted resource properties acquisition and exploration expenditures total $1 165 000. These losses and expenditures could be available to offset future tax liabilities.

EXHIBIT 2

MINTO LAKE RESOURCES LTD.
EXCERPTS OF MANAGEMENT DISCUSSION
FROM THE ANNUAL REPORT AND OTHER FILINGS, JUNE 30, 2012

DESCRIPTION OF BUSINESS

The Company's principal business activities are the exploration and development of mineral properties. It has not yet determined whether the properties contain mineral reserves that are economically recoverable….In some cases the Company, through its own efforts, stakes mineral claims or acquires exploration permits. In other cases the Company acquires interest in mineral properties from third parties. An acquisition from a third party is typically made by way of an option agreement which requires the Company to make specified option payments and to incur a specified amount of exploration expenditures on the property within a given time in order to earn an interest in the property. Most option agreements provide that once the Company has made any required option payments and incurred the specified exploration expenditures, the parties will enter into a joint venture requiring each party to contribute toward future exploration and development costs based on its percentage interest in the property, or suffer dilution of its interest.

The company advances its projects to varying degrees by prospecting, mapping, geophysical analysis, and drilling. Once a property is determined to have limited exploration potential the property is abandoned or sold. In cases where exploration work on the property reaches a stage where the expense and risk of further exploration and development are too high the Company may seek a third party to earn an interest by furthering the exploration process….The mineral exploration business is high risk and most exploration projects will not become mines.

CURRENT OPERATIONS

BC Mine

Minto Lake has a 25 percent share of Ether BC Limited, which is developing a mine in British Columbia. The major shareholder and operator is Ether Resources Inc. with 75 percent ownership. Based on the work it has already completed, Minto Lake is not required to make further capital or expenditure contributions. It is expected that the mine will begin producing gold and minor quantities of other metals in 2013, and will continue operating until 2024. The majority, 75 percent, of net cash flows will be paid to the owners in proportion to their holdings annually. The remainder will be used to cover expenses, and any further capital investments required after Ether Resources Inc. completes its capital expenditure commitment. Any funds remaining at the end of the mine's economic life will be returned proportionately to the owners. However, Minto Lake is not responsible for any shortfalls.

Wolf Lake Project, Labrador

The Company completed a private placement of 200 000 shares, of which 120 000 consisted of flow-through shares, at $0.88 per share to raise net proceeds after issuing costs and expenses of $160 000 for the continued exploration of this project. The Wolf Lake Project consists of 158 square kilometres, including a 25 kilometre strike length of mineralized contact, of which contact only 20 percent has been drill tested to date. Drilling results completed to date have been favourable, and indicates further work is merited.

The Company was required to spend a total of $750 000 in order to obtain a 50 percent undivided interest in the property from Northway Inc. With the exploration work to be completed in July 2012, the company will be able to achieve this goal, and will earn the 50 percent interest. The Company has the further option to earn an undivided 100 percent interest in the project by spending an additional $3.5 million over the next seven years in exploration or development costs, and issue to Northway 1 000 000 shares of the Company. Northway would retain net smelter royalties on base metals and precious metals, less payment of any royalties to third parties.

(continued)

EXHIBIT 2   (CONTINUED)

Candaga Property, Ontario

On April 8, 2012, the Company sold its interests in this property to Hallbridge Mining Limited, a TSX listed mining company, for a nominal amount and warrants to purchase 100 000 shares of Hallbridge at an exercise price of $0.75 per share until March 31, 2017. The Company also reserved a 3 percent net smelter royalty on precious metals and a 2 percent net smelter returns royalty on base metals, less payment of any royalties to third parties.

J.K. Gold Project, Montana

On April 3, 2012 the Company's Option Agreement with the owners of the J.K. Gold Property mineral rights was terminated. About ten new homes have been built during the past year around the project site, which has become a recreational destination area. The Company abandoned the property, since environmental permits for any mine development would have been virtually impossible to obtain.

RISKS

The Company's ability to generate future revenue from its BC gold project will be dependent upon a number of factors including Ether's ability to bring the mine into commercial production. The Company is dependent upon Ether's experience, expertise, and capital resources to develop and successfully operate the planned mine. The price of gold will also factor greatly into the profitability of this venture.

Mineral exploration and development involve a higher degree of risk and few properties are ultimately developed into producing mines. There is no assurance that the Company's future exploration and development activities will result in any discoveries of commercial bodies of ore. Whether an ore body will be commercially viable depends on a number of factors including the particular attributes of the deposit such as size, grade, and proximity to infrastructure, as well as mineral prices and government regulations, including regulations relating to prices, taxes, royalties, land tenure, land use, importing and exporting of minerals, and environmental protection. The exact effect of these factors cannot be accurately predicted, but the combination of these factors may result in a mineral deposit being unprofitable.

COMPETITION

The mining industry in which the Company is engaged is in general highly competitive. Competitors include well-capitalized mining companies, independent mining companies, and other companies having financial and other resources far greater than those of the Company. The Company competes with other mining companies in connection with the acquisition of mineral properties. In general, properties with a higher grade of recoverable mineral and/or which are more readily mineable afford the owners a competitive advantage in that the cost of production of the final mineral product is lower. Thus, a degree of competition exists between those engaged in the mining industry to acquire the most valuable properties. As a result, the Company may eventually be unable to acquire attractive mining properties.

1. March 7, 2012: Gold Quality of Ether BC Ltd. Mine

Ether Resources Inc. and Minto Lake Resources Inc. jointly announced continued positive results from the Ether BC Ltd. gold mine property. Construction has commenced on the initial phase on the property, which is 100 percent owned by Ether and Minto Lake. Ether, the operator of the project, will begin to mine and recover gold from the East Lake deposit in September 2012. It is hoped that this initial deposit will be the beginning of a gold mine development.

2. April 2, 2012 - Minto Lake Arranges Financing

Mr. Ronald Stanfield reports that Minto Lake Resources has arranged a private placement of 200 000 units at a price of 95 cents per unit, to raise net proceeds of $160 000. Each unit will consist of one common share and one non-transferable share purchase warrant. Two warrants plus $1.05 are required to purchase one additional common share for a period of one year from the closing date of the offering. The net proceeds from the offering will be used for the general working capital requirements of the company. The private placement is subject to the acceptance of the Canadian Venture Exchange.

3. April 17, 2012 - Hallbridge Mining Company Limited Purchases Candaga Property

Hallbridge Mining Company Limited and Minto Lake Resources Inc. are pleased to announce the purchase by Hallbridge of 100 percent interest in Minto Lake's 143 unpatented mining claims and 13 patented mining claims, totaling approximately 2500 hectares. The Candaga property contains a polymetallic prospect hosting broad dispersion halos of silver, zinc, gold, and copper. Under the terms of the agreement, Minto Lake will receive a nominal payment and an option to purchase 100 000 shares of Hallbridge at $1.75 per share for a period of five years from the date of signing. In addition, Minto Lake will retain a Net Smelter Return (NSR) of 2 percent on base metals and NSR of 3 percent on precious metals. Hallbridge can choose to purchase 50 percent of these NSRs for $1 million, before the start of commercial production.

4. June 26, 2012 - Minto Lake to Start Exploring Wolf Lake

Mr. Ronald Stanfield reports Minto Lake Resources will immediately commence a diamond-drilling program on its Wolf Lake gold property located in Labrador. Once the program is completed in late July 2012, Minto Lake will have earned a 50-percent interest in the property. The program will focus on two areas, the Silver Wolf Pond and Wolf East prospects.

The Silver Wolf Pond deposit has been drill tested with 49 drill holes over a strike length of three kilometres. Higher-grade intersections of 9.1 grams per tonne of gold over 9.6 metres and 14.9 grams per tonne over 2.1 metres are found in wider zones of lower grade mineralization of 4.6 grams per tonne gold over 23.1 metres and 2.1 grams per tonne gold over 29.5 metres. The zone remains open along strike and at depth. Gold mineralization at the Wolf East prospect, located along the same geological contact approximately 12.5 kilometres to the northeast, is the same as at Silver Wolf Pond. Previous trenching carried out by CR Canada uncovered gold mineralization assaying up to four grams per tonne gold over four metres in channel sampling and up to 25.4 grams per tonne gold in grab samples. Minto Lake drilled 12 holes and detected two parallel zones of gold mineralization in the area.

The Wolf Lake property consists of 178 square kilometres covering a 25-kilometre strike length of the mineralized contact. Minto Lake signed an option in 2006 to earn a 50-percent interest in the property by spending $750 000 in exploration expenditures. In order to acquire the remaining 50-percent, Minto Lake will have to spend an additional $3.5-million by July 2019, and pay Northway net smelter royalties on gold and base metals.

Ronald Stanfield, president and chief executive officer of Minto Lake, stated: "I am very excited about the enormous potential of this property. The overall strike length of Wolf Lake exceeds 25 kilometres and only 20 percent of the mineralized contact has been drill tested to date. The objective of this drilling program is to test other geophysical-geochemical targets on the property and I am confident that we will be successful."

EXHIBIT 4

MINTO LAKE RESOURCES
SUMMARY OF PLANNING INFORMATION
IN FY2013 DOLLARS

Ether BC Ltd. (25 percent owned by MLR)

Operator Ether Resources Inc. (75% owner)

Estimated mine life	12 years at original ore reserves and capacity estimates (FY2013–2024).
Minto Lake's original investment	$Cdn 850 205 (carrying value at FY2012), previously paid; no further investment needed
Estimated net cash flows from mine	US$1 500 000 per year for both partners in 2013; increase of 25% per year from 2014 to 2018; continued at the level of 2018 from 2019 to 2023; US$3 000 000 in 2024; all cash flows and their growth were assumed to include inflation, so no further adjustment for it was necessary
Cash flow sensitivity to the price of gold	$1000 per $1.00 change in the price of gold above or below $1600 in 2013. The 25% growth rate applies to this change until 2018. Then there is no further growth in cash flow.
Salvage value at end of project (2024)	zero, reclamation costs to be paid by Ether Resources in 2024; no other terminal costs or continuing value assumed

Wolf Lake Project (Currency in Canadian Dollars, except where indicated)

As shown below, through various scenarios, the resulting ownership of MLR in the Wolf Lake could be 50%, 30%, or 100%, with varying capital investment responsibilities and royalties.

Assumed ore available (from assays)	Estimated total: 2 500 000 tonnes
Capacity of mine production	200 000 tonnes of ore/year from 2018 to 2023
Capacity in pre-full production years	Before 2015: 0% capacity; 2015: 20%, 2016: 30%, 2017: 60%
Average gold recovery (net)	0.08 ounces/tonne of ore
Price of gold	US$1600/ounce
Average silver recovery	(net) 1.5 ounces/tonne of ore
Price of silver	US$28.00/ounce
Average copper recovery (net)	0.25%
Price of copper	US$3.20/lb.
Average zinc recovery (net)	1.5%
Price of copper	US$0.80/lb.
Shipping, refining and smelting costs (variable)	$50.00/tonne
Operating costs (fixed)—excl. depreciation	$3 000 000/year
Depreciation and Depletion (Capital Amortization)	$600 000/year

EXHIBIT 4 CONTINUED

Administrative costs (fixed)	$800 000/year
Effective Canadian tax rate on profits	22%
Salvage value at end of project (2024)	Zero, with ($2 000 000 site clean-up costs); no other terminal or continuing value; recovery of cumulative working capital investment
Assumed annual distribution rate (share of cash flow after capital expenditures)	75% paid to investment partners
Payout of accumulated cash not distributed (2014)	Remaining 25% of cash profit, assuming not invested, distributed to partners
Prices and costs increase at inflation rate	2.5%/year after 2013
Current ownership interest (50%)	Must pay 50% of mine development
Receives 50% of Wolf Lake distributions	Costs, less $355 771 (net) already spent; expected to spend another $250 000 in FY 2003, and $500 000 for each of the following 3 years—assume MLR will borrow these funds (at year-end), repaying $175 000 principal for 10 years beginning in 2014 plus annual interest of 10% on the outstanding loan balance (previous year-end)—part of corporate expenses.
Royalties	No royalty payments or receipts.
Investment to obtain 100%, less royalties by July 13, 2014 and the following years	Must make additional capital investments as follows: – The incremental total investments for MLR would now be $250 000 in 2013 and 2014, and $600 000 for each of the following five years – debt principal would be repaid at $150 000 in 2014 and 2015, and $400 000 per year from 2016 to 2023 plus annual interest of 10% on the outstanding loan balance (previous year-end) – part of corporate expenses – MLR must also issue 1 000 000 shares to Northway, increasing MLR's total shares outstanding from its current 15 157 314 shares
MLR must pay royalties to Northway and others	About 2.6% of total gross WL mineral revenues; and 5% of pre-tax profits from Wolf Lake; no royalty receipts for MLR
Northway exercises option to develop the mine, and MLR reverts to 30% ownership	Capital expenditures stop after August, 2013; MLR investment of only $160 000 in 2013;
No Royalty Payments Royalty Receipts (in addition to net profit share)	5% of net mine profits

Other Information/Assumptions

Assumed exchange rate (subject to change)	$1.00 Cdn. = US$0.98,
Discount rate (cost of equity)	20%, based on high equity risk
Corporate expenses and other projects	Executive compensation of $88 000 / year; other exploration expenditures of $80 000/yr. ; other admin. expenses (net) of $25 000/year; all before income tax.

(continued)

EXHIBIT 4   **CONTINUED**

Interest costs	Project interest costs are charged as an after-tax corporate expense in the following year; principal cash flows are also shown under corporate.
Effective income tax rate on profits	22% on all Canadian income; assume income tax offsets in same year for any negative project income or corporate expenses.

No other projects are assumed to be developed except for the minor exploration expenditures indicated. The major projects are subject to fluctuations in prices of commodities, production rates, recovery rates, and costs. Inflation is included in the cash flows from Ether BC Ltd., but needs to be added to the cash flows from the Wolf Lake project.

Various organizational structures are possible. However, to compare the alternatives, it is assumed that the Ether BC Ltd. operations are self-contained, providing MLR with net cash flows as a partner (25% of net earnings paid out in dividends plus a 25% share of residual value).

For Wolf Lake a flow-through partnership or wholly-owned entity is assumed, with the owner or owners each receiving their portion of operating cash flows, tax deductions, etc., and paying their portion of expenses. The Wolf Lake mine valuation assumes that the mine operates independently using its own cash flows, but needs planned capital injections. It is assumed that MLR uses its own debt to finance the investment, and is interested in its net return to shareholders and their equity, so a free cash flow to equity approach is suggested.

connect

For more information on the resources available from McGraw-Hill Ryerson, go to www.mcgrawhill.ca/he/solutions.

PART

V

START-UP AND BEYOND

Under conditions of rapid growth, entrepreneurs face unusual paradoxes and challenges as their companies grow and the leadership modes required by these companies change.

Whether they have the adaptability and resiliency in the face of swift developments to grow fast enough as leaders and whether they have enough courage, wisdom, and discipline to balance controlled growth with growing fast enough to keep pace with the competition and industry turbulence will become crystal clear.

Entrepreneurs face enormous pressures and physical and emotional wear and tear during the rapid growth of their companies. It goes with the territory. Entrepreneurs after start-up find that "it" has to be done now, that there is no room to falter, and that there are no "runners-up." Those who have a personal entrepreneurial strategy, who are healthy, who have their lives in order, and who know what they are signing up for fare better than those who do not.

Among all the stimulating and exceedingly difficult challenges entrepreneurs face—and can meet successfully—none is more liberating and exhilarating than a successful harvest. Perhaps the point is made best in one of the final lines of the musical *Oliver*: "In this life, one thing counts. In the bank, large amounts!"

Obviously, money is not the only thing, or everything. But money can ensure both independence and autonomy to do what you want to do, mostly on your terms, and can significantly increase the options and opportunities at your discretion. While value creation was the goal, the measure of success is wealth creation, and how one chooses to distribute and use that wealth. In effect, for entrepreneurs, net worth is the final scorecard of the value creation process.

CHAPTER 12

LEADING RAPID GROWTH: ENTREPRENEURSHIP BEYOND START-UP[1]

"You can fight without ever winning, but never ever win without a fight.
NEIL PEART
Musician, Author

LEARNING OBJECTIVES

LO1   Discuss how higher potential, rapidly growing ventures have invented new organizational paradigms to replace brontosaurus capitalism.

LO2   Describe how higher potential ventures "grow up big" and the special problems, organization, and leadership requirements of rapid growth.

LO3   Explore concepts of organizational culture and climate, and how entrepreneurial leaders foster favourable cultures.

LO4   Examine the leadership practices that distinguish high-growth companies.

INVENTING NEW ORGANIZATIONAL PARADIGMS   LO1

At the beginning of this text we examined how nimble and fleet-footed entrepreneurial firms have supplanted aging corporate giants with new leadership approaches, a passion for value creation, and an obsession with opportunity that have been unbeatable in the marketplace for talent and ideas. These entrepreneurial ventures have experienced rapid to explosive growth and have become the investments of choice of the venture capital community.

Because of their innovative nature and competitive breakthroughs, entrepreneurial ventures have demonstrated a remarkable capacity to invent new paradigms of organization. They have abandoned the organizational practices and structures typical of the industrial giants from the post-World War II era to the 1990s. One could characterize those approaches thus: What they lacked in creativity and flexibility to deal with ambiguity and rapid change, they made up for with rules, structure, hierarchy, and quantitative analysis.

The epitome of this pattern is the Hay System, which by the 1980s became the leading method of defining and grading management jobs in large companies. Scoring high with "Hay points" was the key to more pay, a higher position in the hierarchy, and greater power. The criteria for Hay points include number of people who are direct reports, value of assets under management, sales volume, number of products, square feet of facilities, total size of one's operating and capital budget, and the like. One can easily see who gets ahead in such a system: Be bureaucratic, have the most people and largest budget, increase head count and levels under your control, and think up the largest capital projects. Missing in the criteria are all the basic components of entrepreneurship we have seen in this book: value creating, opportunity creating and seizing, frugality with resources, bootstrapping strategies, staged capital commitments, team building, achieving better fits, and juggling paradoxes.

Contrast the multilayered, hierarchical, military-like levels of control and command that characterize traditional capitalism with the common patterns among entrepreneurial firms: they are flat—often only one or two layers deep—adaptive, and flexible; they look like interlocking circles rather than ladders; they are integrative around customers and critical missions; they are learning- and influence-based rather than rank- and power-based. People lead more through influence and persuasion, which are derived from knowledge and performance rather than through formal position or seniority. They create a perpetual learning culture. They value people and share the wealth with people who help create it.

ENTREPRENEURIAL LEADERS ARE NOT ADMINISTRATORS OR MANAGERS

In the growing business, owner-entrepreneurs focus on recognizing and choosing opportunities, allocating resources, motivating employees, and maintaining control—while encouraging the innovative actions that cause a business to grow. In a new venture the entrepreneur's immediate challenge is to learn how to dance with elephants without being trampled to death! Once beyond the start-up phase, the ultimate challenge of the entrepreneur is to develop the firm to the point where it is able to lead the elephants on the dance floor.

Henry Mintzberg of McGill University believes that most MBA programs encourage the wrong behaviour and develop the wrong skills.[2] The standard business education compartmentalizes business functions into discrete silos, when they should be integrative. Mintzberg finds few signs that this is appreciated or understood. Like medicine and like engineering, it is a "practice, which is fed by intuition. In a practice, one achieves mastery in the doing and has to pull together disparate knowledge to apply to situations at hand."[3] Steven Dunphy and David Meyer find evidence of differences in the roles of entrepreneurs and managers.[4] Such differences may help to explain the stagnancy and eventual demise of brontosaurus capitalism. Until the 1980s, virtually all the cases, problems, and lectures in MBA programs were about large, established companies.

LEADING PRACTICES OF HIGH-GROWTH COMPANIES[5]

In chapter 2 we examined a summary of research conducted on fast-growth companies to determine the leading practices of these firms. Now this research will likely take on new meaning for the reader. As one examines each of these four practice areas—marketing, finance, management, and planning—one can see the practical side of how fast-growth entrepreneurs pursue opportunities; devise and orchestrate their financial strategies; build a team with collaborative decision making; and plan with vision, clarity, and flexibility. Clearly, rapid growth is a different game, requiring an entrepreneurial mindset and skills.

GROWING UP BIG   LO2

STAGES OF GROWTH REVISITED

Higher potential ventures do not stay small for long. While an entrepreneur may have done a good job of assessing an opportunity, forming a new venture team, marshalling resources, planning, and so forth, leading and growing such a venture is a different game.

Ventures in the high growth stage face the problems discussed in chapter 5. These include forces that limit the creativities of the founders and team; that cause confusion and resentment over roles, responsibilities, and goals; that call for specialization and therefore erode collaboration; that require operating mechanisms and controls; and more.

Recall also that founders of rapidly growing ventures are usually relatively inexperienced in launching a new venture and yet face situations where time and change are compounded and where events are nonlinear and nonparametric. Usually structures, procedures, and patterns are fluid, and decision making needs to follow counterintuitive and unconventional patterns.[6]

Chapter 5 discussed the stages or phases companies experience during their growth. Recall that the first three years before start-up are called the research-and-development (R&D) stage; the first three years, the start-up stage; years 4 through 10, the early-growth stage; the 10th year through the 15th or so, maturity; and after the 15th year, stability stage. These time estimates are approximate and may vary somewhat.

Various models, and our previous discussion, depicted the life cycle of a growing firm as a smooth curve with rapidly ascending sales and profits and a levelling off toward the peak and then dipping toward decline. But it is probably more like Queen's business school professors Elspeth Murray and Peter Richardson have depicted the ride:

> You've mapped out what you believe is a great game plan to move your organization forward. You think everyone is on board. You believe you've allocated the right resources and enough of them, but nothing's happening. There's no sense of urgency, no pressure to move more quickly on initiatives that are critical to the organization's future viability and profitability.[7]

In truth, however, few new and growing firms experience smooth and linear phases of growth. If the actual growth curves of new companies are plotted over their first 10 years, the curves will look far more like the ups and downs of a roller-coaster ride than the smooth progressions usually depicted. Over the life of a typical growing firm, there are periods of jerks, bumps, hiccups, indigestion, and renewal interspersed with periods of smooth sailing. Sometimes there is continual upward progress through all this, but with others, there are periods where the firms seem near collapse or at least in considerable peril. Ed Marram, an entrepreneur and educator for 35 years, characterizes the five stages of a firm as Wonder, Blunder, Thunder, Plunder, Asunder (see Exhibit 12.1). Wonder is the period that is filled with uncertainty about survival. Blunder is a

EXHIBIT 12.1   GROWTH STAGES

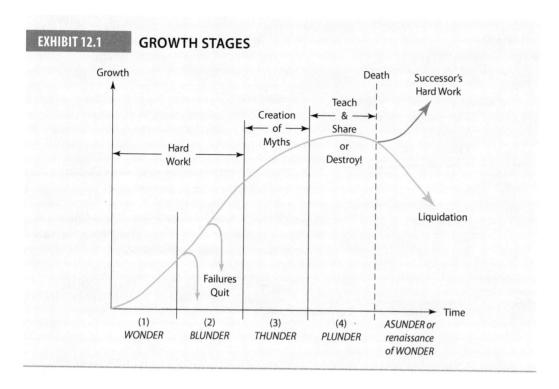

growth stage when many firms stumble and fail. The Thunder stage occurs when growth is robust and the entrepreneur has built a solid new venture team. Cash flow is robust during Plunder, but in Asunder the firm needs to renew or will decline.

CORE LEADERSHIP MODE

As was noted earlier, changes in several critical variables determine just how frantic or easy transitions from one stage to the next will be. As a result, it is possible to make some generalizations about the main leadership challenges and transitions that will be encountered as the company grows. The core leadership mode is influenced by the number of employees a firm has, which is in turn related to its dollar sales.[8]

Recall, as shown in Exhibit 5.3, that until sales reach approximately $5 million and employees number about 25, the core leadership mode is one of *doing*. Between $5 and $15 million in sales and 25 to 75 employees, the core leadership mode is *leading*. When sales exceed $10 million and employees number over 75, the core leadership mode is *leading team leaders*. Obviously, these revenue and employment figures are broad generalities. The number of people is an indicator of the complexity of the leadership task, and suggests a new wall to be scaled, rather than a precise point.

Sales per employee (SPE) can vary widely among firms; by virtue of an online model and a tremendously effective supply chain management system, Apple Canada can generate a higher SPE than a real estate–based service business. SPE numbers are boundaries, constantly moving as a result of inflation and competitive dynamics. SPE figures can illustrate how a company stacks up in its industry, but remember that the number is a relative measurement. Business Development Bank of Canada also reminds that the costs attributed to making those sales must be considered.[9] Explosive sales per employee was one of the failed promises of the Internet, and to some extent the irrational dot-com valuations of the late 1990s were an anticipation of technology massively leveraging variable employee expense.

The central issue facing entrepreneurs in all sorts of businesses is this: As the size of the firm increases, the core leadership mode likewise *changes from doing to leading to leading leaders.*

During each growth stage of a firm, there are entrepreneurial crises, or hurdles, that most firms will confront. Exhibit 12.2 and the following discussion consider some indications of crisis by using the stages of growth as a framework.[10] As the exhibit shows, for each fundamental driving force of entrepreneurship, a number of "signals" indicate crises are imminent. While the list is long, these are not the only indicators of crises—only the most common. Each of these signals does not necessarily indicate that particular crises will happen to every company at each stage, but when the signals are there, serious difficulties cannot be too far behind.

THE PROBLEM IN RATE OF GROWTH

Difficulties in recognizing crisis signals and developing appropriate mitigating measures are compounded by rate of growth itself. The faster the rate of growth, the greater the potential for difficulty, because of the various pressures, chaos, confusion, and loss of control. It is not an exaggeration to say that these pressures and demands increase geometrically, rather than in a linear way (see discussion in chapter 5).

Growth rates affect all aspects of a business. Thus, as sales increase, as more people are hired, and as inventory increases, sales outpace manufacturing capacity. Facilities are then increased, people are moved between buildings, accounting systems and controls cannot keep up, and so on. The cash burn rate accelerates. As such acceleration continues, learning curves do the same. Worst of all, cash collections can lag behind, as shown in Exhibit 12.3.

Distinctive issues caused by rapid growth were raised with the founders and presidents of rapidly growing companies—companies with sales of at least $1 million and growing in excess of 30 percent per year. These founders and presidents pointed to the following:

- *Opportunity overload.* Rather than lacking enough sales or new market opportunities (a classic concern in mature companies) these firms faced an abundance. Choosing from among these was a problem.
- *Abundance of capital.* While most stable or established small or medium-sized firms often have difficulties obtaining equity and debt financing, most of the rapidly growing firms were not so constrained. The problem was, rather, how to evaluate investors as "partners" and the terms of the deals with which they were presented.

| EXHIBIT 12.2 | CRISES AND SYMPTOMS |

PRE-START-UP (YEARS −3 TO 0)

Entrepreneurs:

Focus. Is the founder really an entrepreneur, bent on building a company, or an inventor, technical dilettante, or the like?

Selling. Does the team have the necessary selling and closing skills to bring in the business and make the plan—on time?

Leadership. Does the team have the necessary skills and relevant experience, or is it overloaded in one or two areas (e.g., the financial or technical areas)?

Ownership. Have the critical decisions about ownership and equity splits been resolved, and are the members committed to these?

Opportunity:

Focus. Is the business really user-, customer-, and market-driven (by a need), or is it driven by an invention or a desire to create?

Customers. Have customers been identified with specific names, addresses, and phone numbers, and have purchase levels been estimated, or is the business still only at the concept stage?

Supply. Are costs, margins, and lead times to acquire supplies, components, and key people known?

Strategy. Is the entry plan a **shotgun** and **cherry-picking** strategy, or is it a rifle shot at a well-focused niche?

Resources:

Resources. Have the required capital resources been identified?

Cash. Are the founders already out of cash (OOC) and their own resources?

Business plan. Is there a business plan, or is the team "**hoofing it**"?

START-UP AND SURVIVAL (YEARS 0 TO 3)

Entrepreneurs:

Leadership. Has a top leader been accepted, or are founders vying for the decision role or insisting on equality in all decisions?

Goals. Do the founders share and have compatible goals and work styles, or are these starting to conflict and diverge once the enterprise is under way and pressures mount?

Leadership. Are the founders anticipating and preparing for a shift from doing to leading and letting go—of decisions and control—that will be required to make the plan on time?

Opportunity:

Economics. Are the economic benefits and payback to the customer actually being achieved, and on time?

Strategy. Is the company a one-product company with no encore in sight?

Competition. Have previously unknown competitors or substitutes appeared in the marketplace?

Distribution. Are there surprises and difficulties in actually achieving planned channels of distribution on time?

Resources:

Cash. Is the company facing a cash crunch early as a result of not having a business plan (and a financial plan)? That is, is it facing a crunch because no one is asking: When will we run out of cash? Are the owners' pocketbooks exhausted?

Schedule. Is the company experiencing serious deviations from projections and time estimates in the business plan? Is the company able to marshal resources according to plan and on time?

shotgun: An approach to target as wide a swath as possible; in contrast to a rifle approach for which a specific target is aimed.

cherry-pick: To selectively choose the best element or opportunity from what is available; in a game, like basketball, hover near the net and wait for a pass for an easy shot. In politics, to register voters who are predisposed to the candidate. In music, to select songs, not the entire album.

hoofing it: To go on foot, often as a tough slog over the countryside compared to an easy ride on horse or vehicle.

(continued)

EXHIBIT 12.2   **CONTINUED**

EARLY GROWTH (YEARS 4 TO 10)

Entrepreneurs:

Doing or leading. Are the founders still just doing, or are they leading the team for results by a plan? Have the founders begun to delegate and let go of critical decisions, or do they maintain veto power over all significant decisions?

Focus. Is the mindset of the founders operational only, or is there some serious strategic thinking going on as well?

Opportunity:

Market. Are repeat sales and sales to new customers being achieved on time, according to plan, and because of interaction with customers, or are these coming from the engineering, R&D, or planning group? Is the company shifting to a marketing orientation without losing its killer instinct for closing sales?

Competition. Are price and quality being blamed for loss of customers or for an inability to achieve targets in the sales plan, while customer service is rarely mentioned?

Economics. Are gross margins beginning to erode?

Resources:

Financial control. Are accounting and information systems and control (purchasing orders, inventory, billing, collections, cost and profit analysis, cash management, etc.) keeping pace with growth and there when they are needed?

Cash. Is the company always out of cash—or nearly OOC, and is no one asking when it will run out, or is sure why or what to do about it?

Contacts. Has the company developed the outside networks (directors, contacts, etc.) it needs to continue growth?

MATURITY (YEARS 10 TO 15 PLUS)

Entrepreneurs:

Goals. Are the partners in conflict over control, goals, or underlying ethics or values?

Health. Are there signs that the founders' marriages, health, or emotional stability are coming apart (i.e., are there extramarital affairs, drug and/or alcohol abuse, or fights and temper tantrums with partners or spouses)?

Teamwork. Is there a sense of team building for a "greater purpose," with the founders now leading leaders, or is there conflict over control of the company and disintegration?

Opportunity:

Economics/competition. Are the products and/or services that have gotten the company this far experiencing unforgiving economics as a result of perishability, competitor blind sides, new technology, or off-shore competition, and is there a plan to respond?

Product encore. Has a major new product introduction been a failure?

Strategy. Has the company continued to cherry-pick in fast-growth markets, with a resulting lack of strategic definition (deciding on those opportunities on which to say no)?

Resources:

Cash. Is the firm OOC again?

Development/information. Has growth gotten out of control, with systems, training, and development of new leaders failing to keep pace?

Financial control. Have systems continued to lag behind sales?

EXHIBIT 12.2   **CONTINUED**

HARVEST/STABILITY (YEARS 15 TO 20 PLUS)

Entrepreneurs:

Succession/ownership. Are there mechanisms in place to provide for succession and the handling of tricky ownership issues (especially family)?

Goals. Have the partners' personal and financial goals and priorities begun to conflict and diverge? Are any of the founders simply bored or burned out, and are they seeking a change of view and activities?

Entrepreneurial passion. Has there been an erosion of the passion for creating value through the recognition and pursuit of opportunity, or are turf-building, acquiring status and power symbols, and gaining control favoured?

Opportunity:

Strategy. Is there a spirit of innovation and renewal in the firm (e.g., a goal that half the company's sales come from products or services less than five years old), or has lethargy set in?

Economics. Have the core economics and durability of the opportunity eroded so far that profitability and return on investment are nearly as low as that for the Fortune 500?

Resources:

Cash. Has OOC been solved by increasing bank debt and leverage because the founders do not want—or cannot agree—to give up equity?

Accounting. Have accounting and legal issues, especially their relevance for wealth building and estate and tax planning, been anticipated and addressed? Has a harvest concept been part of the long-range planning process?

- *Misalignment of cash burn and collection rates.* These firms all pointed to problems of cash burn rates racing ahead of collections. They found that unless effective integrated accounting, inventory, purchasing, shipping, and invoicing systems and controls are in place, this misalignment can lead to chaos and collapse.

- *Decision making.* Many of the firms succeeded because they executed functional day-to-day and week-to-week decisions, rather than strategizing. Strategy had to take a back seat. Many of the representatives of these firms argued that in conditions of rapid growth, strategy was only about 10 percent of the story.

- *Expanding facilities and space...and surprises.* Expansion of space or facilities is a problem and one of the most disrupting events during the early explosive growth of a company. Leaders of many of these firms were not prepared for the surprises, delays, organizational difficulties, and system interruptions that are spawned by such expansion.

INDUSTRY TURBULENCE

The problems just discussed are compounded by the amount of industry turbulence surrounding the venture. Firms with higher growth rates are usually found in industries that are also developing rapidly. In addition, there are often many new entrants, both with competing products or services and with substitutes.

The effects are many. Often, prices fluctuate. The turbulence in the semiconductor industry is a good example. From June 1984 to June 1985, the price to original equipment manufacturers

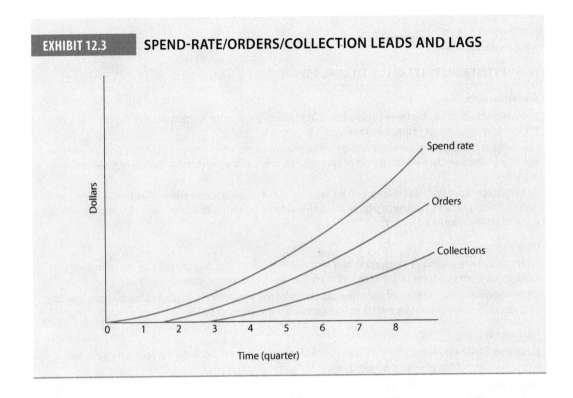

(OEMs) of 64K memory chips fell from $2.50 each to 50 cents. The price to OEMs of 256K chips fell from $15 to $3. The same devastating industry effect manifested in the years 2000–2002 when cellular airtime pricing plunged by more than 50 percent. And more recently the price for flat screen displays (LCD, plasma, LED, etc.) has plummeted. Imagine the disruption this caused in marketing and sales projections, in financial planning and cash forecasting and the like for firms in these industries. Often there are also rapid shifts in cost and experience curves. The consequences of missed steps in growing a business are profound.

THE IMPORTANCE OF ORGANIZATIONAL CULTURE AND CLIMATE   LO3

SIX DIMENSIONS

The organizational culture and climate, either of a new venture or of an existing firm, are critical in how well the organization will deal with growth. Studies of performance in large businesses that used the concept of organizational climate (i.e., the perceptions of people about the kind of place it is to work) have led to two general conclusions.[11] First, the climate of an organization can have a significant impact on performance. Further, climate is created both by the expectations people bring to the organization and by the practices and attitudes of the key leaders.

The climate notion has relevance for new ventures, as well as for entrepreneurial efforts in large organizations. An entrepreneur's style and priorities—particularly how he or she handles tasks and people—are well known by the people being led and affect performance. Roger Enrico of Pepsi describes the entrepreneurial climate, where the critical factors included setting high performance standards by developing short-run objectives that would not sacrifice long-run results,

A SHINY GREEN TRUCK, READY FOR ACTION

©Rene Johnston/GetStock.com

Dovigi quickly forged impressive connections in the North American waste management industry. According to his father, Patrick is "moving faster in street shoes than he did in skates." In 2007 Dovigi left Waste Excellence Corp. and formed Green For Life by merging several local haulers. He was supported by Bay Street financiers with cash and connections. Soon after his departure, Waste Excellence Corp. was mired in scandal.

Another lesson in business propriety came when the City of Toronto excluded a competitor of Green For Life's from the bidding process after the competitor lured a city waste management official to join the company. Green For Life won city contracts and grew.

Green For Life was more directly involved in scandal when in late 2103, Elections Ontario was called in to investigate a photo op of Liberal candidate Doug Holyday having a media moment in front of Green For Life garbage trucks. The west end of Toronto had privatized collection in 2012.

In 2013, Green For Life began a 10-year contract with Sault Ste. Marie. As a result, Green For Life invested in special recycling trucks and wheeled collection barrels. Some wondered if this would lock the city into Green For Life or vice versa!

Question: Sometimes governmental customers will mix efficiency with other motives—particularly when taxpayers and voters chime in—such as after a mid-summer garbage collection strike. Green For Life must balance political and legal threats and opportunities. How can Patrick Dovigi best make use of connections but avoid improprieties or the appearance of them?

Earlier, we introduced Green For Life, the company that acquired Turtle Island Recycling. Green For Life was founded by Patrick Dovigi, a graduate of Ryerson University, who "got his first exposure to waste management in 2002" while working for a holding company that had a stake in Keele North Recycling.

Growing up in Sault Ste. Marie, Ontario, Dovigi was a second-round draft pick of the Edmonton Oilers. However, his prospects on the ice ended and he was soon "involved in ventures ranging from the gritty world of car-leasing to a stint on the board of an entertainment startup led by KISS founder Gene Simmons." Dovigi was no stranger to celebrity and the media.

Sources: "Roark Capital Commits C$105 million to GFL Waste & Recycling Solutions Corp." Canada NewWire, November 30, 2010; John Lorinc, "Toronto's new garbage magnate stickhandles his way to the front," *The Globe and Mail,* September 6, 2012; Darren Tayler, "Expect to receive one of these soon," www.sootoday.com, August 2, 2013.

providing responsive personal leadership, encouraging individual initiative, helping others to succeed, and developing individual networks for success.

Evidence suggests that superior teams function differently than inferior teams when setting priorities, resolving leadership issues, deciding what and how roles are performed by team members, displaying attitudes toward listening and participation, and dealing with disagreements. Further, evidence suggests that specific approaches to leadership can affect the climate of a growing organization. For example, gains from the motivation, commitment, and teamwork that are anchored in a consensus approach to leadership, while not immediately apparent, are striking later. At that time, there is swiftness and decisiveness in actions and in follow-through, since the negotiating, compromising, and accepting of priorities are history. Also, new disagreements that emerge generally do not bring progress to a halt because there is both high clarity and broad acceptance of overall goals and underlying priorities. Without the prior consensus building, each new problem or disagreement often necessitates time-consuming and painful confrontation and renegotiation simply because it was not done initially.

Bella Dance Academy

"Lina Ball has taken her passion for dance and built it into a thriving business that is growing by leaps and bounds." With an opening like that on the Canadian Newswire, Lina Ball received much attention when she won BDC's Young Entrepreneur of the Year Award for the Northwest Territories. Born and raised in Nanaimo, British Columbia, where she began dancing at the age of three, two decades later, in 2003, Lina Ball moved with her husband and opened Bella Dance Academy in Yellowknife in a warehouse with high ceilings. To promote her dance school she did it all. That first season she offered ballet, tap, jazz, modern, and hip hop classes. Students ranged from 16 months to 65 years old. In addition to teaching 120 students in 25 different classes single-handedly, "I did everything and anything I could to promote the classes that first year. I worked at festivals, handed out flyers, did a mail-out, ran radio and newspaper advertising, talked to daycares and schools—just anything." In the second year Lina added four instructors as the number of students and classes grew. In late 2008 they moved to a new location with two studios.

Adding more instructors to her staff resulted in additional challenges. Clearly Lina was not simply doing, she had to lead her team and create a culture of those who shared her passion. The Canadian Newswire reported that "Lina's business plan has been carefully thought out" and quotes her as saying: "We set goals every year and we've always met our enrollment numbers. It's really important to me to increase at a steady pace, but also to keep the quality of the programs and to create a positive environment for the students." Lina notes staffing in a remote location is a problem: "It takes at least a year to train a student to teach, and most of the kids leave Yellowknife after they graduate. So I train them for a year to teach for one or two years and then they're gone. That's been hard." But her Bella Dance Academy has recently benefited from an instructor that in 2009 tried out for CTV's "So You Think You Can Dance" and returned to teaching. Lina and her dancers of all ages and abilities have become part of the community performing throughout the year for public events and at a seniors' residence. Bella Dance Academy also puts on its own recitals and shows, e.g., *Nutcracker*. Now, over ten years since inception, the studio is thriving. It boasts 70 classes per week and 15 instructors.

Questions: Where should Lina Ball go from here if she wants to expand her business? Yellowknife, the capital of the Northwest Territories, has a population under 20 000. The next largest cities in the Northwest Territories have 3600, 3460, and 2100 inhabitants! Bella Dance could expand to Whitehorse, in the Yukon—population 22 000. Or would it make more sense to go after regions in southern Canada? Can growth be fueled by additional services offered to existing customers or can new customers be reached?

Sources: "Lina Ball Has Yellowknife Dancing! Owner of Bella Dance Academy Wins BDC's Young Entrepreneur Award for the Northwest Territories," Canadian Newswire, October 21, 2008; Daron Letts, "Hip Hop is On Top," Northern News Service, September 10, 2008; Daron Letts, "Dancer Mum on Results of Her Star Audition," Northern News Service, April 24, 2009.

Organizational climate can be described along six basic dimensions:

- *Clarity*. The degree of organizational clarity in terms of being well organized, concise, and efficient in the way that tasks, procedures, and assignments are made and accomplished.
- *Standards*. The degree to which the venture's leaders expect and put pressure on employees for high standards and excellent performance.
- *Commitment*. The extent to which employees feel committed to the goals and objectives of the organization.
- *Responsibility*. The extent to which members of the organization feel responsibility for accomplishing their goals without being constantly monitored and second-guessed.
- *Recognition*. The extent to which employees feel they are recognized and rewarded (non-monetarily) for a job well done, instead of only being punished for mistakes or errors.
- *Esprit de corps*. The extent to which employees feel a sense of cohesion and team spirit, of working well together.

In achieving the entrepreneurial culture and climate described above, certain approaches to leadership (also discussed in chapter 5) are common across core leadership modes. David Halabisky, Erwin Dreessen, and Chris Parsley, all of the Small Business Policy Branch of Industry Canada, concede that entrepreneurial behaviour may be the "most crucial component in determining the growth path of a firm."[12]

Entrepreneurial Leadership

No single leadership pattern seems to characterize successful ventures. Leadership may be shared, or informal, or a natural leader may guide a task. What is common, however, is an individual who defines and gains agreements on who has what responsibility and authority and who does what with and to whom. Roles, tasks, responsibilities, accountabilities, and appropriate approvals are defined.

There is no competition for leadership in these organizations, and leadership is based on expertise, not authority. Emphasis is placed on performing task-oriented roles, but someone invariably provides for "maintenance" and group cohesion by good humour and wit. Further, the leader does not force his or her own solution on the team or exclude the involvement of potential resources. Instead, the leader understands the relationships among tasks and between the leader and his or her followers and is able to lead in those situations where it is appropriate, including managing actively the activities of others through directions, suggestions, and so forth.

This approach is in direct contrast to the communal approach, where two to four entrepreneurs, usually friends or work acquaintances, leave unanswered such questions as who is in charge, who makes the final decisions, and how real differences of opinion are resolved. While some overlapping of roles and a sharing in and negotiating of decisions are desirable in a new venture, too much looseness is debilitating. This approach also contrasts with situations where a self-appointed leader takes over, where there is competition for leadership, or where one task takes precedence over other tasks.

Consensus Building

Leaders of most successful new ventures define authority and responsibility in a way that builds motivation and commitment to cross-departmental and corporate goals. Using a consensus approach to management requires working with peers and with the subordinates of others (or with superiors) outside formal chains of command and balancing multiple viewpoints and demands.

In the consensus approach, the founder is seen as willing to relinquish his or her priorities and power in the interests of an overall goal, and the appropriate people are included in setting cross-functional or cross-departmental goals and in making decisions. Participation and listening are emphasized.

In addition, the most effective individuals are committed to dealing with problems and working problems through to agreement by seeking a reconciliation of viewpoints, rather than emphasizing differences, and by blending ideas, rather than playing the role of hard-nose negotiator or devil's advocate to force their own solution. There is open confrontation of differences of opinion and a willingness to talk out differences, assumptions, reasons, and inferences. Logic and reason tend to prevail, and there is a willingness to change opinions based on consensus.

Communication

The most effective leaders share information and are willing to alter individual views. Listening and participation are facilitated by such methods as circular seating arrangements, few interruptions or side conversations, and calm discussion versus many interruptions, loud or separate conversations, and similar behaviours in meetings.

Encouragement

Successful leaders build confidence by encouraging innovation and calculated risk-taking, rather than by punishing or criticizing what is less than perfect, and by expecting and encouraging others to find and correct their own errors and to solve their own problems. Their peers and others perceive them as accessible and willing to help when needed, and they provide the necessary resources to enable others to do the job. When it is appropriate, they go to bat for their peers and subordinates, even when they know they cannot always win. Further, differences are recognized and performance is rewarded.

Trust

The most effective leaders are perceived as trustworthy and straightforward. They do what they say they are going to do; they are not the corporate rumour carriers; they are more open and spontaneous, rather than guarded and cautious with each word; and they are perceived as being honest and direct. They have a reputation of getting results and become known as the creative problem solvers who have a knack for blending and balancing multiple views and demands.

Development

Effective leaders have a reputation for developing human capital (i.e., they groom and grow other effective leaders by their example and their mentoring). As noted in chapter 5, Bradford and Cohen distinguish between the heroic leader, whose need to be in control in many instances may actually stifle cooperation, and the post-heroic leader, a developer who actually brings about excellence in organizations by developing entrepreneurial mid-level leaders. If a company puts off developing mid-level leaders until price competition appears and its margins erode, the organization may come unravelled. Linking a plan to grow human capital at the mid-level leader and the supervisory levels with the business strategy is an essential first step.

ENTREPRENEURSHIP FOR THE 21ST CENTURY: BIG BREAKTHROUGHS

Extraordinary individuals and enterprises have been built in recent years and contributed to the entrepreneurial revolution: Austin Hill has had a slew of ventures; Gabrielle Chevalier has brought her company Solutions 2 GO to $500 million in annual revenue in just four years; Nina Gupta envisions taking Greenlite public and to $100 million in annual sales; Doug and Danny Elder aim to take their already successful promotional events "on tour" to other Western Canadian cities. These entrepreneurs created "high standard, perpetual learning cultures," which create and foster a "chain of greatness." The lessons from such great entrepreneurial leaders and enterprises provide a blueprint for entrepreneurship in the twenty-first century. They set the standard and provide a tangible vision of what is possible. Not surprisingly, the more exciting, faster growing, and more profitable companies in Canada today share striking similarities.

AUSTIN HILL

Serial entrepreneur and angel investor Austin Hill was born in Ottawa in 1973 and grew up in Calgary, where he developed a passion for computer technology. He created his first venture, Cyberspace Data Security, when he was 17 years old. In 1994, Hill started an Internet provider in Montreal called Infobahn Online Services with his brother. They merged with another ISP to create TotalNet, which they sold in 1997.

In 1997, with his brother and father, Austin Hill launched Zero-Knowledge Systems and raised $65 million in venture capital. After much turmoil, including "reducing head count by the hundreds because of undisciplined growth," in early 2003, Zero-Knowledge started to generate positive cash flow. Hill played a vital role for a decade including running a spinout "Synomos" that ultimately failed in 2005, the same year that Zero-Knowledge Systems changed its name to Radialpoint. "We wanted the world to know what we stood for—power to the people—privacy for all—we were passionate about changing the way the future would look. We were social entrepreneurs believing that we could both make a profitable company and a contribution to the betterment of society at the same time."[13] Their recruiting included a mobile billboard driven past Montreal software companies with the enticing phrase "wanna make Internet history?"

In his blog, Austin Hill points out:

The process of building innovative enterprises requires experimentation and failure.[14] How much experimentation is a function of risk appetite and cost of money. The cost of money was incredibly low and the risk appetite for technology stocks were so much in abundance that we were fielding random calls from retail investors looking to buy stock or get on a waiting list for the IPO for almost 2 years before we even had revenue.

We proved ourselves able to play by the rules of that time and raised money and built real products and teams in a way that the market was rewarding (getting big fast, become the market leader by the size of your brain trust and the broad range of your opportunities).

When the rules of the market changed, we changed with them and made sure we could continue to work with customers finding a business model and customer profile that would grow with us. We made a lot of mistakes that in hindsight now seem obvious. But we rushed into our mistakes recognizing them as valuable lessons and we were eager students.

When we started Zero-Knowledge my internal email signature carried the phrase "Make new mistakes more often." Our team culture helped us to react and evolve as we saw new opportunities, identified failing products and responded to the dramatic shifts that occurred in the capital markets.

Austin Hill became the CEO and Executive Investigator of Akoha in March of 2008 and the company raised $1.9 million in angel funding in April 2008. Despite its "cool factor," expenses outstripped revenues and Akoha was shuttered in August of 2011.

Austin Hill co-founded Standout Jobs and launched its first product in January 2008. It received $1.57 million in series A funding in late January 2008 and by May 2010 Standout Jobs announced that it had been acquired.

GABRIELLE CHEVALIER

The owner of Mississauga, Ontario-based Solutions 2 GO Inc., Gabrielle Chevalier was ranked number two on a list of the top 100 women entrepreneurs in Canada in 2007, 2008, and again in 2009, and finally number one in 2010! With revenue growth from $37 million in 2004 to $453 million in 2008 and $750 million in 2010, Solutions 2 GO is a video game distributor carrying hundreds of titles by Nintendo, Sony, and Microsoft. A typical day calls for processing up to 10 000 orders from clients that include major Canadian retailers such as Walmart, HMV, Blockbuster, Future Shop, and Best Buy.

According to Chevalier, "In our business, we exist solely to connect manufacturers and retailers. Neither will accept any excuses from us. As a start-up with very aggressive growth plans, Solutions 2 GO wanted an IT partner who was knowledgeable, experienced, and responsive."[15] Gabrielle Chevalier chose Lynn Cooke's 360 Visibility Inc.—also listed on Canada's Top Women Entrepreneurs. Cooke co-founded 360 Visibility in 2003 "around a vision of providing all enterprise participants in a client organization with the information

GABRIELLE CHAVALIER OF SOLUTIONS 2 GO

they need to make swift, well-informed, coordinated, and above all profitable business decisions." Lynn Cooke must be on the right track because 360 Visibility experienced three-year revenue growth of 883 percent.

NINA GUPTA OF GREENLITE

NINA GUPTA

Another one of Canada's Top Women Entrepreneurs, Nina Gupta, is at the helm of Greenlite—a leading manufacturer of energy efficient lighting products created in 1996 when her instincts told her that "North America's lighting business was going green." Based on years of experience in the family's automotive lighting business, she ventured into the residential and industrial lighting sector.[16] Those instincts have paid off as Greenlite revenues broke $30 million in 2008, a fair jump from $6 million just four years prior.

Beyond promoting her product she is a social activist; her goal is to encourage us to switch to CFLs (compact fluorescent light bulbs) to save the natural environment. She also boasts of Greenlite's workforce being 80 percent female. Nina Gupta describes herself as "tenacious, hardworking, focused, and honest." She also admits to being "a compulsive neurotic list maker writing down plans for everything." In the future she hopes that "a public offering will raise enough money to purchase factories and assembly facilities to become a $100-million company in the next five years." Nina Gupta was selected as a finalist for the 2012 RBC Canadian Women Entrepreneur Awards. Today the company's products serve four markets: residential, commercial, agricultural, and automotive. Greenlite also has a presence in the United States.

DOUG AND DANNY ELDER

Two brothers, Doug and Danny Elder, established Off Axis in 2001 in Regina, Saskatchewan, to cater to the "lifestyles of both males and females in the boarding culture." While they have a sizeable physical inventory with snowboards, skateboards, wakeboards, footwear, clothing, and accessories as well as a solid website, their real breakthrough was the events they put on to promote their business and the lifestyle of the sports. In 2008, BDC gave the Elders a Young Entrepreneur Award noting that the two had their finger on the pulse of Regina's youth culture and much of their success was due to stellar "guerilla" marketing tactics. The events Doug and Danny organized got bigger and bigger, attracting big-name corporate sponsors "eager to capitalize on the Elders' expertise in youth marketing."[17] Off Axis' multi-day Jibfest and Summer Invasion events "attract well over 10 000 attendees and include vendor villages featuring a wide variety of youth-related items."[18] The SaskTel 2013 Jibfest was no exception and neither was SaskTel Summer Invasion 2013.

Off Axis was associated with a wakeboarding school near Regina, which hosted the National Wakeboard Championships in 2008 and Doug and Danny were contemplating an event tour with stops in various Western Canadian cities appealing to their demographic—15 to 24-year-olds. Off Axis boasted two shops in Regina (OffAxis East and OffAxis North) and a new foray, "SuperGrom,"

Doug Elder, OffAxis

DOUG ELDER OF OFF AXIS

offering "surf, snow, and skateboard culture clothing and footwear for boys and girls from infant to pre-teen" which created a dedicated Facebook page in 2010. In 2011, Doug bought his brother out and Doug's wife became his new business partner.

THE CHAIN OF GREATNESS

As we reflect on these great individuals and enterprises, we can see that there is clearly a pattern, with some common denominators in both the ingredients and the process. This chain of greatness becomes reinforcing and perpetuating (see Exhibit 12.4). Leadership that instills a vision of greatness and the owner's mentality across the company is a common beginning. A philosophy of perpetual learning throughout the organization accompanied by high standards of performance is key to the value-creating entrepreneurial cultures at the three firms. A culture that teaches and rewards teamwork, improvement, and respect for each other provides the oil and glue to make things work. Finally, a fair and generous short- and long-term reward system, as well as the necessary education to make sure that everyone knows and can use the numbers, creates a mechanism for sharing the wealth with those who contributed to it. The results speak for themselves: extraordinary levels of personal, professional, and financial achievement.

EXHIBIT 12.4   **THE CHAIN OF GREATNESS**

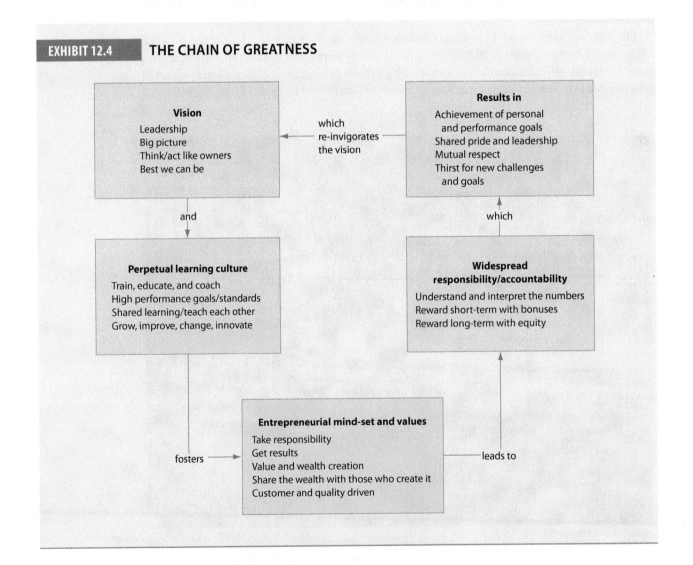

LO1 The demands of rapid growth have led to the development of new organizational and leadership paradigms. The entrepreneurial organization today is flatter, faster, more flexible and responsive, and copes readily with ambiguity and change. It is the opposite of the hierarchy, layers of management, and the more-is-better syndrome prevalent in brontosaurus capitalism.

LO2 As high-potential firms "grow up big" they experience stages (Wonder, Blunder, Thunder, Plunder, and Asunder or Wonder redux), each

with its own special challenges and crises, which are compounded the faster the growth.

LO3 Establishing a culture and climate conducive to entrepreneurship is a core task for the venture team.

LO4 A chain of greatness characterizes some breakthrough approaches to entrepreneurial leadership. Entrepreneurs in high-growth firms distinguish themselves with leading entrepreneurial practices in marketing, finance, management, and planning.

STUDY QUESTIONS

1. Why have old hierarchical management paradigms given way to new organizational paradigms?
2. What special problems and crises can new ventures expect as they grow? Why do these occur?
3. Explain the stages many ventures experience and why these are unique.
4. What role does the organizational culture and climate play in a rapidly growing venture? Why are many large companies unable to create an entrepreneurial culture?
5. What is the chain of greatness and why can entrepreneurs benefit from the concept? Can it be used to diagnose and correct a bad situation?
6. Why is the rate of growth the central driver of the organization challenges a growing venture faces?

MIND STRETCHERS *Have you considered?*

1. Many large organizations are now attempting to reinvent themselves. What will be the biggest challenge in this process, and why?
2. How fast should a company grow? How fast is too fast, organizationally and financially?
3. In your ideal world, how would you describe what it is like to live and work within the perfect entrepreneurial organization?
4. Do you have what it takes to lead a rapid-growth enterprise? Will you know when to do less, trust others, and lead more?

Preparation Questions

1. Tensions exist at Parlance Communications. Identify these tensions and propose solutions to remedy them.

2. Should ParCom enter the Mexican market? What resources are necessary to do so successfully? Compare what resources ParCom has versus what ParCom needs.

3. Parlance Communications is at a crossroads—torn in several directions. ParCom needs to prioritize and focus. What should ParCom tackle immediately? What changes if any need to be made at ParCom?

GROWING TENSIONS

Wednesday 12:51 p.m., November 23, 2010

While eating lunch at her desk, Beth Reuben reviewed her new emails. Dwight Andrews, the VP of Sales sent a high priority email notifying Beth that she would be required to attend a trade show in Ft. Lauderdale, Florida from January 24 to 28, 2011. Beth slumped in her chair and thought "How can he expect me to recruit new product resellers in Mexico and manage my accounts if he is constantly diluting my priorities?"

Beth, an experienced international business developer, was hired 13 months earlier by Parlance Communications to open Mexico and the CALA markets (Central America and Latin America). Her sales experience and her understanding of the business culture in these markets was excellent. As well, her language profile was exceptional, she was fluent in Spanish, English, French, and Portuguese. Beth had a proven track record of business development successes in the telecommunications and software industries. It seemed a wonderful fit for a company seeking international expansion and new revenue streams beyond Canada and the United States.

In her first year with Parlance Communications (ParCom), her orientation had been orchestrated by Dwight Andrews. Beth was assigned to manage one of the company's largest reseller accounts. In parallel, she was responsible for recruiting resellers in the United States and wherever possible stimulating sales in the Spanish-speaking segment of the US market. For the past two months, she had been working 12–14 hours a day and was beginning to find the workload incredibly taxing and the VP Sales to be without empathy.

It the first week of October 2010 the company's CEO, Emmanuel Cole, came to Beth's desk and directly assigned her the task of assessing the Mexican market for expansion. She was to conduct comprehensive market research and then develop the company's tactical plan for market penetration—no small task. Adding to the pressure was the deadline: the CEO wanted the full report and a tactical plan by November 25, 2010. In addition, as a part of the market research efforts, he wanted the recruitment of resellers in Mexico to begin immediately. He believed that a sales-driven effort would best measure response and could be used to feed into the sales forecasts for first quarter of 2011.

With a smile, the CEO then congratulated her recent work in the Spanish-speaking segment of the United States. He was impressed with the revenue her efforts had generated in the short time she had been with the company. And then he dropped the bomb, "I would like marketing and sales activities to begin in time for Mexico City's ExpoComm—with our complete product line. I would like you to host a booth at the trade show in four months: on February 14–17, 2011."

Fast forward to present. After Beth Reuben completed the market research, she was convinced that expansion into Mexico was a good move, but she was not confident that ParCom management was aware of the challenges that needed to be overcome to penetrate this market. A fiercely competitive pricing strategy was necessary to compete in Mexico, especially considering that Panasonic already delivered a similar product in Mexico.

Adding further doubt was Dwight Andrews' recent "request" to participate in a trade show in Florida—just two weeks before ExpoComm in Mexico. In quiet frustration she wondered, "How can I prepare for ExpoComm when I'll be in Florida? I'm only one person. Doesn't VP Sales understand the importance of the ExpoComm to the CEO and all the work I have been doing on this project?"

With a few minutes remaining before her 1 p.m. meeting with the company's product manager, Dan Asher, Beth quickly fired off an email to the VP Sales, Dwight Andrews, explaining to him that her involvement at the Ft. Lauderdale trade show would have to be limited. Given that she is scheduled to prepare for the Mexican ExpoComm, it would be difficult to walk the floor and conduct product demonstrations and follow-ups for the Florida tradeshow. After all, she needed this time to meet the CEO's expectations. Beth looked at the clock in the upper right hand corner of her monitor; it was 12:56 p.m. and time was ticking away.

This case was written by Andrew R. Lunney, Canadian International Development Agency, Gatineau, Quebec, and Prescott C. Ensign.

BACKGROUND ON PARLANCE COMMUNICATIONS

Parlance Communications, a privately-owned corporation with 140 employees based in Kanata, Ontario, was the product of an accomplished electrical engineer, Emmanuel Cole, PhD (Figure 1). In 1996, Cole launched his communications technology into the rapidly growing telecommunications industry and met immediate success in the small office/home office (SOHO) market segment.

Traditionally, advanced telephone technology could not be deployed by countless small enterprises because of its high cost and complexity. Designed for larger enterprises that could afford complicated systems and the technical staff to maintain them, sophisticated phone systems were beyond the reach of small organizations. ParCom devoted itself to engineering a product that would increase productivity, reduce communication costs, and improve the professional image of those small businesses adopting ParCom systems.

In 2003 the company launched its award-winning small business and home office telephone system: Synergy. Hailed as a breakthrough product by customers and analysts, Synergy delivered advanced communications capabilities such as automated attendant, fax detection, music on hold, and remote extensions for environments with one to three phone users.

The ParCom line of all-in-one PBXs[1] was launched in 2005, building on the features developed for Concerto (the next generation of technology following Synergy). With advanced call features like voicemail, auto attendants, and remote extension capabilities, ParCom systems were powerful, flexible solutions for environments with 1 to 32 phone users. ParCom systems were hybrid PBXs that affordably combined the best of both worlds; that is, traditional landline telephone and the Internet. IP/PSTN acts as a gateway between telephones and applications, including things like instant messaging and even voice over the Internet.

Parlance Communications continued to develop innovative telecommunications solutions. The company cemented customer loyalty with a program of free software and firmware upgrades that extended the capabilities of ParCom systems. The company's active in-house research-and-development lab continually leveraged its expertise in small business telephony to develop future telecommunications products.

Sales History

In Canada and the United States the SOHO market represented approximately 7 million consumers and a market value of over US$8 billion. In 2009 ParCom's domestic sales (United States and Canada) reached US$16 million, represented a steady increase at an average rate of 12 percent per year since 2004.

International revenue also increased in 2010 to reach US$780 000 in the first three quarters of the year. England, Ireland, and Australia represented 62 percent of the sales with the remaining revenues—as a result of unsolicited orders—coming from Mexico, Brazil, the Caribbean, and various other sources.

FIGURE 1   **ORGANIZATIONAL CHART**

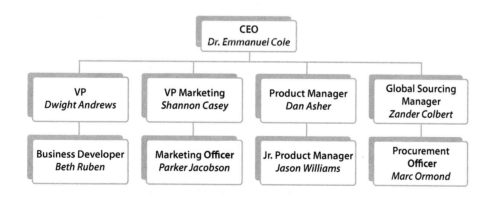

---

[1] Private branch exchange is an exchange or switch owned by a private enterprise, rather than a switch owned by a carrier (telephone company). Having a PBX eliminates the need for a business to have all of its telephones individually connected to the public telephone system. This saves monthly fees as well as avoids intra-office calls having to be routed to the external phone lines and then back again.

Revenue generated from Mexico alone represented 24 percent of total international sales. Most impressive was that sales to date had been achieved in an un-nurtured business environment. Despite the absence of product market adaptation, prohibitive import duties, and zero marketing efforts, ParCom somehow had amassed gross sales in Mexico of US$120 700 in 2009 and US$187 200 in the first three quarters of 2010.

Beth Reuben's investigation into sales performance in Mexico revealed that each product reseller experienced a surge in sales initially, but consistently gave up selling ParCom products after one year. Beth's recent conversations with former resellers in Mexico exposed lack of support and excessive import duties as the reason for abandoning the ParCom line of products.

In 2007, Dwight Andrews spearheaded a penetration strategy for Parlance Communications to establish sales activities in Brazil, Argentina, Chile, and Venezuela. After 13 months of sales and marketing investment the company had not achieved the CEO's desired results. Various reasons were cited for the poor performance, but rumours among staff speculated that "Dwight's ambition got the best of him." Dwight Andrews and the CEO stated that company resources were not positioned to respond to market expansion. In the end, all funding was pulled from the expansion effort and resellers in these countries eventually faded away.

Three years after the "botched attempt" to enter the four South American markets, increased volume of unsolicited orders have again caught senior management attention. This time the CEO believed that a more conservative approach to market penetration was needed. Seeking to satisfy investors created pressure to grow beyond the Canadian and US markets. This, combined with a desire for stronger international presence, motivated senior management to again review the potential Mexico held. Given the task of developing a tactical strategy to enter Mexico's market, Beth was now expected to achieve where her boss, Dwight Andrews, had failed.

MEXICO—A BRIEF PRIMER

In most of the areas of the United Mexican States (i.e., Mexico) that ParCom considered good target markets, Beth expected to encounter mid-level managers and higher who would be fluent in spoken and written English, while support staff might be much less so. The target for telecommunications services in Mexico was dominated by demand from the government sector, followed by demand from the financial services and IT sectors. The Mexican Ministry of the

Economy estimated the total local market to be approximately US$2 billion annually.

Beth thought that things were looking up for ParCom's foray into Mexico this time around, but why had Dwight Andrews failed in South America? And could she pull this off if she did not get additional resources including, perhaps, release from the Florida assignment?

PREPARING THE REPORT

The file on Beth Reuben's desk was a work-in-progress and still growing. Thus far she had identified the following:

1. In terms of telephone infrastructure, Telmex claimed to have 18 million telephone lines in service, 3.6 million data lines, and 1.9 million Internet access accounts.
2. General assessment: low telephone density with about 17.2 main lines per 100 persons; the state-owned telephone carrier had been privatized in December 1990; opened to competition in 1997 to improve prospects for development, but Telmex today controlled 95 percent of the domestic fixed-line market, 80 percent of the long-distance market, and 74 percent of international traffic (all according to Cofetel, Mexico's Federal Telecommunications Commission).

Beth noted that there was a chink in Telmex's armour. Smaller competitors were making inroads with:

1. Voice over Internet Protocol (VoIP). The press had even noted that Telmex used VoIP for internal operations even though it had not yet offered such a service to its customers.
2. Telephone service was adequate for business and government, but the population was poorly served. This was at least partially responsible for mobile subscribers outnumbering fixed-line subscribers (35 million mobile phone lines were expected by the close of 2010). In place was a domestic satellite system with 120 earth stations. Mexico had an extensive microwave radio relay network and made considerable use of fibre-optic and coaxial cable.

Telecommunications Industry

Mexico's demand for telecommunications equipment had shown a strong rebound following the recent economic downturn in the Americas and Europe. Overall, Mexico's economy had demonstrated resilience in the face of flat or very moderate growth in other western economies. Mexico experienced a 16 percent growth in the consumption of telecommunications goods and services in 2010. Industry analysts expected this level of growth to continue into the foreseeable future.

SWOT Analysis

Beth was planning on including Table 1 in her report, but she determined that it still needed work. For one, it did not provide clear evidence on the course of market entry and steps to be taken. It was pretty clear, given Emmanuel Cole's predilection to enter Mexico, that ParCom would go ahead. But resolving how to do so and implementation were her responsibility.

Trade Environment—NAFTA

North American companies benefited from NAFTA. The trade agreement maintained a stable, tariff-free status for Canadian and US exporters of telecom equipment destined to Mexico. This trade environment would allow Parlance Communications and its Mexican resellers to effectively compete on price. NAFTA's 10-year anniversary in 2004 meant that nearly all telecom equipment moved cross-border tariff free. This included new and refurbished equipment. Beth dismissed the notion of taking old ParCom technology from the United States or Canada and delivering it in Mexico. Though she made a note to run it by Dan Asher just to be certain; a lot of old equipment was reclaimed in upgrades. Could this "uninstalled" equipment be re-deployed? She believed that there was no market for such used equipment locally.

To gain tariff exemption under NAFTA, ParCom products (hardware and software) must be at least 51 percent North American content. A certificate of origin was also required and must be presented during the import process.

Certification and Standards

Safety standards for electronics in Mexico were established and regulated by Normalización y Certificación Electrónica (NYCE). The role of NYCE was to review and grant product certification based on a specific set of standards—the Norma Oficial Mexicana (NOM). Passing the NOM standard was a necessary hurdle for ParCom to overcome. NOM provided a guarantee to the buyer and was necessary to legally sell telecom equipment in Mexico.

Upon successful completion of the application process NYCE would issue a certificate under NOM. This application/certification process typically required two weeks and for new equipment it expired after one year and renewal was required.

The Mexican embassy in Ottawa informed Beth that the turnaround for NOM certification is rarely delayed and should ParCom submit multiple products at one time, the two weeks required would not be cumulative.

Dan Asher, the senior Product Manager, would be required to conduct compliance testing with ParCom products and the Mexican telecommunications infrastructure. Once this assessment was complete products may need to be further modified to ensure quality connections (sound fidelity, system stability, etc.).

| TABLE 1 | SWOT ANALYSIS |

STRENGTHS	WEAKNESSES
• Political stability (overall) • Geographic proximity—easy travel • Similar time zones • NAFTA member • General English proficiency • Good telecom and energy infrastructure	• Very limited number of vendors • Lack of financing for IT companies • Monopolized telecommunications industry: Telmex—acts as a national regulator

OPPORTUNITIES	THREATS
• Limited number of competitors in the same telecommunications segment (Panasonic, Avaya, Nortel, etc.) • Product adaptation for Mexico enhances ParCom service to Spanish segment in the United States • Products adaptation for Mexico provides a foundation for future expansion to service other Spanish-speaking markets (CALA)	• Economy has been slow to recover from recent recession • New elections: July 2, 2006 (potential political instability) • Recent efforts by government to boost the IT industry have had limited success • Government efforts to battle corruption have had limited success • Security concerns for Parlance personnel while travelling in Mexico

Sourcing/Product Assembly

Parlance Communications had recently completed major shifts in its sourcing strategy, adopting a global model for product assembly of the entire product line. This initiative was championed by Zander Colbert, who had been recruited by ParCom in March 2006 to manage sourcing. After graduating from Simon Fraser University's MBA program he had successfully implemented a global sourcing strategy for Verizon, a major telecommunications player. His proactive approach to seek quality sources of labour in foreign markets combined with a strategic sense of his company's expansion plans endeared him to ParCom's senior management

Since the inception of Zander Colbert's global sourcing/assembly strategy in 2007, per product profitability had increased to an average of 42 percent. Zander's efforts also stabilized the company's supply chain with a diversified supplier procurement system. Prior to 2007, all company products were sourced from one supplier in Burnaby, British Columbia—now product assembly contracts were also in place in Israel and Taiwan (Table 2).

Product Line

Overall, Parlance Communication's product line was considered high quality, reliable, and had been positioned to reach high-end users. The P100 was the original product with all-in-one features, simple industrial design, and a user-friendly window interface that allowed users to enhance their professional appearance with quality calling features. The most popular features included voicemail and music while on hold.

Complete with all-in-one features, ergonomic profile, and an award-winning industrial design, the P150 and P150X were the best-selling products regardless of the market. The P150X had a larger internal memory card included as a standard installation. Both the P150 and P150X had the same set of features as the P100.

Building upon the success of the P150 series of phones, the P180 was the company's newest telephone and showcased a sleek design, increased memory capacity, and improved feature design. The P180 garnered industry accolades for its functionality, reliability, and was expected to surpass the P150 system's sales due to an innovative new voicemail feature. When a voice message was received the phone automatically converted it to an audio file and sent it to the user via email as an attachment. This consolidation of messages into the user's email inbox meant that the user no longer needed to check voicemail separately. This convenient and time-saving feature was particularly beneficial for mobile business professionals (e.g., BlackBerry users).

The P200 was a switchboard system, not a phone. The P200 was designed to accommodate companies "on-the-grow" by permitting the development of an internal phone network. All ParCom phone systems connected via a LAN connection and standard ports allowed seamless integration and improved internal telecommunications.

Product Adaptation

Although English was a functional business language in Mexico, Spanish translation (system and voice prompts, product manual, etc.) was necessary to compete in the SOHO market. Beth knew that any product adaptations must be coordinated through Dan Asher and Jason William, the product management team. In an earlier discussion with Dan Asher, Beth was informed that "firmware" (the phones internal operating system) was a low-priority for re-work as the end user would never see this aspect of the product. But even Dan pointed out "our direct competitors—Panasonic and Alcatel—currently sell products with Spanish language capabilities built in as standard system options." Dan Asher had given Beth a chart identifying the current state of the adaptation process for ParCom products (Table 3).

TABLE 2	SOURCING/ASSEMBLY BY PRODUCT				
PHONES	**P100**	**P150**	**P150X**	**P180**	**P200**
Origin	Burnaby, BC	Israel	Israel	Burnaby, BC	Taiwan
Manufacturer	Premtel	Canaan IT	Canaan IT	StoneCom Inc.	TH Techs
Import Duties					
Brazil	27%	100%	100%	27%	100%
Ireland	10%	20%	20%	10%	80%
Mexico	0%	120%	120%	0%	120%

Competition

Within the telecom industry the strongest presence in the market were the major US telecom firms (Verizon, AT&T, etc.) with European firms battling aggressively for market share and Chinese firms leveraging their ability to compete on price. Although low prices had been a decisive factor for many clients, most were also demanding high quality, long-term warranties and training.

There were five main voice equipment manufacturers in the Mexican SOHO market with Panasonic leading the group with 19.2 percent market share as of the end of 2008—the most recent year for which Beth could find data that seemed believable (Table 4). Avaya was next with 7.4 percent market share. Other important players were Alcatel and Siemens. These competitors typically used exclusive local distributors to sell their equipment and also offered site tests, network design, and system installation.

Smaller players combined held 58 percent of the market for voice equipment with sales totalling over US$411 million in 2008. Beth noted both the plurality of customer preferences and knew the trend—telecom demand in Mexico was still booming; these factors signalled that Parlance Communication technology was well positioned to compete for market share.

Product Features

Depending upon the company and its product positioning strategy, products could contain any number of standard or extra features. Nearly all telecom companies in this segment offered the same set of features (call waiting, forwarding, cascading, call answer, call display, voicemail, etc.). From a purchaser's standpoint, research indicated that calling features were secondary to price as a determinant of selection.

Panasonic, Alcatel, and Siemens all offered their products as a base model with standard features and an upgrade option with an array of premium features and a larger memory card installed. The cost for the add-ons varied by company (see Table 4) and were only available as bundles. Avaya offered fewer features, but similar to Parlance sold their products with all features already installed.

In recent discussions with past and present Mexican resellers Beth found out that very few people used voicemail for

---

TABLE 3	MODIFICATIONS BY PRODUCT				
PHONES	**P100**	**P150**	**P150X**	**P180**	**P200**
System Prompts	English French Spanish	English French Spanish	English French Spanish	English	English French Spanish
Voice Prompts	English	English	English	English	English
Firmware	English	English	English	English	English
Product Manual	English	English	English	English	English

TABLE 4	COMPETITION IN MEXICO'S SOHO MARKET				
PHONES	**MARKET SHARE**	**PRODUCTS (MARKET READY)**	**STANDARD FEATURES/PRODUCT**	**ADD-ON FEATURES**	**COST OF ADD-ON FEATURES***
ParCom	0%	0	17	0	US$0
Panasonic	19.2%	6	10	6	US$120
Avaya	7.4%	2	12	0	US$0
Alcatel	2.5%	2	8	8	US$105
Siemens	2.4%	3	10	6	US$127

* Costs incorporate Mexican import tariffs

business in Mexico. The cultural preference was direct person-to-person communication or even indirectly whereby messages would be relayed via an office secretary. Failing these options, people would simply call back at a later time. Email correspondence was increasingly popular in Mexico, but the "human" element was accepted to be an integral component to successful business relations.

Product Pricing

In the domestic market (Canada and the United States) ParCom positioned its products as high-end and pricing reflected this strategy—permitting significant profit margins. Gleaned from ParCom's past foray into the CALA markets was the criticism from resellers and product distributors that ParCom's set profit margins were unrealistic (too high) and therefore limited sales. In addition, Beth understood that a new international market would have much greater price sensitivity due to lower disposable income levels—this was especially true in Mexico and competitors' pricing in Mexico reflected this.

Beth was aware of the numbers—ParCom's average product cost was calculated to be 28 percent of the suggested retail sales price. In September 2010, the marketing department compiled a comparative list of retail pricing for competitors' products in Mexico (Table 5). The list matched ParCom's products' with that of the competitor's closest counterpart in terms of design. All ParCom prices excluded the cost of Mexican import tariffs, which varied by product origin.

Distribution/Sales Channels

Strategic Alliances Establishing Parlance Communications in Mexico would depend on partnerships through reseller and distributor recruitment activities conducted by the sales department.

Resellers Typical resellers were consulting firms and system integrators who would bundle ParCom's products with other products and services for direct sales to end-users.

Distributors Distributors were limited to reselling ParCom merchandise through existing Mexican resellers and typically had exclusivity over a geographic area. Distributors would be responsible for added services: product/technical support, training centres for their channel sales, marketing/promotion, trade shows, etc. Distributors with stable and superior sales performance would be rewarded (e.g., incentives and higher discounts) for additional revenue coming from managed resellers.

End-users ParCom would refrain from selling directly to Mexican end-users and would pass sales leads to the existing channel (reseller) in Mexico. Based on ParCom's level of success in Mexico, Beth surmised ParCom should consider a local sales presence to generate end-user revenues. This could be accomplished through an extension of ParCom's existing online e-commerce site translated into Spanish as well as some adaptation for Mexico.

Marketing/Promotions

In many ways the Mexican business culture was similar to that of the United States and Canada, but there were a number of stark differences—even compared to the Spanish-speaking segment of the United States (including Mexican-Americans). For example, the use of voicemail was inconsistent, even in the IT sector. For business in Mexico, great value was placed upon personal interaction, face-to-face was universally the preferred mechanism for getting things done. Personal interaction with resellers and distributors would play a fundamental role in developing, nurturing, and maintaining successful sales channels in Mexico. In Mexico, the person who sold a product, might also install it and then provide technical and product support.

TABLE 5	PRICING COMPARISON—PARCOM VS. COMPETITORS				
	P100	**P150**	**P150X**	**P180**	**P200**
Parlance	US$280	US$450	US$540	US$1200	US$2300
Panasonic	US$189	US$350	US$320	N/A	US$1108
Avaya	US$220	N/A	N/A	N/A	US$1400
Alcatel	N/A	N/A	US$390	N/A	US$1420
Siemens	US$210	N/A	US$385	N/A	US$1730

For Mexico's business environment, throughout the nation, "word of mouth" promotion was the most effective way to reach decision makers and those with the power to make purchases. Beth believed that success in Mexico would depend on ParCom's ability to "meet and greet" resellers and distributors in Mexico—the sources of Mexican demand for ParCom products.

A recent meeting with the company's VP of marketing, Shannon Casey, revealed her preliminary plan to reach Mexican resellers and distributors—largely through the use of Internet-based marketing techniques. Shannon Casey was confident that resellers and distributors could be reached through annual Yellow Page advertisements. There would be an initial round to blitz larger cities with print advertisements combined with cold calling sales activities; another blitz campaign would follow with advertising on popular websites; and finally ParCom would work to obtain high Google search results in Mexico or perhaps be a sponsored link.

While some of these ideas would certainly work in Canada or the United States, Beth was unconvinced about their applicability and reach in Mexico. Beth's experience in Mexico and other Latin American countries caused her to conclude that the best use of resources would be print media and face-to-face contact. In the past, the Canadian and Mexican embassies had been useful in setting up meetings with industry leaders. Given that Google was a relatively US- and Canadian-centric search engine, it was unlikely to achieve the desired results. Beth muttered, "maybe they don't use Google in Mexico—Shannon doesn't really seem to know their preferences," and Beth already knew that Mexicans did not use the Internet for the same reasons as Americans and Canadians.

Overall, Beth thought the VP's plan was weak, "Besides, where is the human contact in all of this? And what about trade shows?"

Trade Shows

Beth viewed trade shows as the epitome of Mexican business culture—direct contact with resellers and distributors under an IT/telecommunications theme.

To effectively use trade shows to reach resellers and distributors a significant quantity of work was required before, during, and after the event. Preparation for a trade-show typically began three weeks in advance of the actual show. Cold calling potential resellers and distributors to set up meetings to do group presentations and product demonstrations in parallel with the trade show were essential (these meetings were commonly referred to as "road

shows"). Follow-up calls usually consumed the two weeks after the trade show and were necessary to qualify the resellers and distributors that expressed interest in carrying ParCom's product line. Once qualified and the partnership formed the sales cycle began.

ExpoComm

ExpoComm would be the key national sales point for ParCom. ExpoComm was Mexico's premiere IT and telecommunications event of the year—all market players would have their own promotional booth and attendance was essential to create brand awareness.

Held annually in Mexico City, this trade show was the single most important opportunity for Parlance Communication to showcase its wares with all key market players present. In recent years, ExpoComm had grown at an average rate of 15 percent per year and for 2011 attendance was projected to reach 4300 companies.

As the only person in the sales department who spoke Spanish, the pre-trade show preparation for this event would be handled exclusively by Beth. All "road show" presentations, all product demos, and all follow-ups to qualify clients for the sales cycle would also be entirely on Beth's shoulders. This would require much more time than the standard timeframe for trade show preparation.

RESOLVING THOSE TENSIONS

The 1 p.m. meeting with the product manager was enlightening. With a tone of contention, Dan Asher informed Beth, "Cole's timeline is completely unreasonable. There is no way I can deliver for that timeline; besides each product requires at least two weeks for testing and modification—and another week for adaptation to the Spanish language."

Again at her desk, Beth reviewed the meeting notes; she now realized that the current level of resources might not be sufficient to meet Emmanuel Cole's stipulations in time for ExpoComm. She also knew that outsourcing the product testing was not an option as Emmanuel Cole was unwilling to allow a third party to access the company's proprietary software platform (of which he was the author).

In addition to the time required by product management, each product intended for export to Mexico required two weeks for the NOM certification. With only nine weeks remaining before ExpoComm, Beth now realized that she was in a battle against time to bring Dr. Cole up to speed on her findings and to action tactical recommendations if time permitted.

Time was the critical resource now and Beth wondered how much time she could personally contribute. She also wondered which people should be expected to play a key role in the tactical plan. Adding injury to an earlier insult an email from the VP Sales' office had arrived. The email was not even from Dwight Andrews, but from his assistant and did not acknowledge the contents of her earlier message.

From: Susan R. Redmond
Sent: Wednesday, November 23, 2010 - 2:44 PM
To: Beth Reuben
Subject: Ticket for Beth Reuben - Jan 24, 2011

ELECTRONIC TICKET - ITINERARY/RECEIPT

NAME: Reuben / Beth Ms
ISSUING AIRLINE: AIR CANADA   DATE OF ISSUE: 22NOV10
DATE AIRLINE   FLT CLASS STATUS

24JAN US AIRWAYS   356 COACH CL CONFIRMED
LV: OTTAWA ON   AT: 120
AR: MIAMI   AT: 819

27JAN AIR CANADA 910 ECONOMY CONFIRMED
LV: MIAMI   AT: 935 DEPART: TERMINAL 2
AR: OTTAWA ON   AT: 1455

Have a pleasant trip. Bon voyage.

- Susie Redmond

---

connect®

For more information on the resources available from McGraw-Hill Ryerson, go to www.mcgrawhill.ca/he/solutions.

CHAPTER 13

FRANCHISING

Franchisees are chosen based on a number of criteria, including entrepreneurial drive.

DON SCHROEDER
President and CEO, Tim Hortons

LEARNING OBJECTIVES

LO1 Explain what franchising is and discuss the nature of the role of the franchisor and the franchisee.

LO2 Articulate the process of becoming a franchisor.

LO3 Describe a basic screening method for evaluating franchises with a higher success probability.

LO4 Compare the profile of a successful franchisee to the profile of a successful entrepreneur.

LO5 Analyze the franchise relationship model and its use as a guide for developing a high-potential franchise.

INTRODUCTION

In this chapter we will explore what franchising is and how it fits the Timmons Model definition of entrepreneurship. We consider the scope of franchising and examine the criteria for determining a franchise's stature, from the perspective of an existing or prospective franchisor. We present several templates and models that can be helpful in conducting due diligence on a franchise opportunity.

Let us consider how well franchising fits our definition of entrepreneurship from chapter 1. Just as the focus of our definition of entrepreneurship is opportunity recognition for the purpose of wealth creation, so too is the focus of franchising. Franchising offers a thoughtful system for reshaping and executing a delivery system designed to extract maximum value from the opportunity. Just as opportunity, thought, and action are essential elements of an entrepreneurial venture, so too are they important components of a franchise opportunity. Franchising also fulfills our definition of entrepreneurship because each partner understands the expectation for wealth of the other and they work together toward that goal; their "bond" is sealed as partners in the franchise alliance.

Franchising is, at its core, a partnership between two organizations, the franchisor and the franchisee. The successful franchise relationship defines and exploits an opportunity as a team. The franchisor is the concept innovator who grows by seeking partners or franchisees to operate the concept in local markets. A franchisor can be born when at least one company store exists and the opportunity has been beta tested. Once the concept is proven, the franchisor and the franchisee enter into an agreement to grow the concept based on a belief that there are mutual advantages to the alliance. The nature of these advantages is defined by the ability of the partners to execute a particular aspect of the opportunity for which each is respectively better suited than the other. The heart of franchising is entrepreneurship, the pursuit of and intent to gain wealth by exploiting the given opportunity. The unique aspect of franchising is that it brings together two parties that both have individual intentions of wealth creation through opportunity exploitation, but who choose to achieve their goals by working together. Because franchising aligns the different skill sets and capabilities of the franchisor and franchisee as a partnership, the whole of a franchise opportunity is greater than the sum of its parts.

At its most fundamental level, franchising is a large-scale growth opportunity based on a partnership rather than on individual effort. Once a business is operating successfully, then according to the Timmons Model, it is appropriate to think about franchising as a growth tool. The sum of the activities between the partners is manifest in a trademark or brand. The mission of the entrepreneurial alliance is to maintain and build the brand. The brand signals a price–value relationship in the minds of customers. Revenue is driven higher because the marketplace responds to the brand with more purchases or purchases at a higher price than the competition.

JOB CREATION VERSUS WEALTH CREATION

As a franchise entrepreneur, we can control the growth of our franchise opportunity. For those whose life goal is to own a pizza restaurant and earn a comfortable income, the opportunity is there. Franchising allows us to do this, but it also allows us to build 30 pizza restaurants and to participate fully in the wealth-creation process. One strength of franchising is that it provides a wide breadth of options for individuals to customize opportunities to meet their financial goals and business visions, however conservative or grandiose.

The ability to create wealth in any venture starts with the initial opportunity assessment. For example, a franchise company may decide to limit its geographic territories in terms of the number of stores. Therefore, the expansion market is limited from the start for potential franchisees. Even if franchisees work hard and follow all the proven systems, they may be buying a job versus creating wealth.

But some companies are designed to reward successful franchisees with the opportunity to buy more stores in a particular market or region. Franchisees who achieve prosperity with single units are rewarded with additional stores. The entrepreneurial process is encouraged, and wealth is created.

Much of the goal of New Venture Creation is to increase the odds for success in a new venture and increase its scope. Franchising can be an excellent vehicle for growth for the franchisor.

FRANCHISING: A STORY OF ENTREPRENEURSHIP

The franchise entrepreneurial spirit in Canada has never been more alive than today. More than 900 different brand names with 78 000 outlets populate the marketplace; estimates vary, but these businesses make up somewhere between 20 and 40 percent of all retail sales nationwide, or approximately $100 to $200 billion, the latter figure would represent 10 percent of Canada's GDP. In Canada, a franchise opens every two hours every day of the year.[1] The belief that franchising can be an exciting entrepreneurial venture is supported by the continued success of established franchise systems, the proliferation of new franchises, and the profitability reported by franchisors and franchisees.[2] These statistics hint at the scope and richness that franchising has achieved in a relatively short period. The process of wealth creation through franchising continues to evolve as we witness an increase not only in the number of multiple outlet franchisees,[3] but also in the number of franchisees that operate multiple outlets in different franchise systems. Exhibit 13.1 reveals several aspects of contemporary Canadian franchises.

Shoppers Drug Mart boasts having over 1250 stores and annual revenue of well over $10 billion. The franchising concept was to have pharmacists own and operate their own stores. Pharmacist Murray Koffler inherited two stores at the age of 20. In 1962 he had grown to 17 pharmacies and adopted the name Shoppers Drug Mart. Through acquisitions and aggressive expansion the brand grew to the presence it has today.

EXHIBIT 13.1	CANADIAN FRANCHISE FACTS
Average franchise fee*	$27 500
Average renewal fee	$3000 to $5000
Average franchisee investment	$175 000
Typical length of franchise agreement	5 to 10 years**
97% of franchises opened in the last five years are still in business, 86% are under the original ownership†	
Typical royalty rate***	5% to 8%
Typical advertising rate	3%

Source: Canadian Franchise Association.

* fees range from $5000 to $75 000.

** 15- and 20-year agreements are also common.

*** ongoing royalty fees vary from 0% to 20%.

† www.canada.franchiseek.com/franchise-statistics.htm/

Home Hardware is another chain whose footprint has grown to a formidable level—over 1100 stores strong and annual collective retail sales of over $5 billion. In 1964, 122 independent Ontario hardware retailers banded together to form a "dealer-owned co-operative—an answer to the challenge posed by 'big box' retailers who enjoyed the advantage of direct-from-manufacturer buying power."[4] Like Shoppers Drug Mart it offers a number of store brands in addition to those of popular manufacturers.

Cara Operations Ltd. provides catering services to airlines and operates Harvey's, Swiss Chalet, Kelsey's, Milestone's, Montana's, and formerly Outback and Second Cup. The corporate vision is to become "Canada's leading branded restaurant and airline services company."[5] Cara was founded by the Phelan family in 1883. The name "Cara" is derived from the first two letters of the words "Canadian Railway"—the enterprise's initial focus. The company went public in 1968 and later was taken private in 2004.

Anyone considering and exploring entrepreneurial opportunities should give serious consideration to the franchising option. As franchisor, this route can be a viable way to share risk and reward, create and grow an opportunity, and raise human and financial capital.

FRANCHISING: ASSEMBLING THE OPPORTUNITY   LO2

As we saw in earlier chapters, the Timmons Model identifies the three subsets of opportunity as market demand, market size and structure, and margin analysis. The franchise organization must understand the nature of demand both as it resides in the individual consumer and in society. At the most fundamental level, the primary target audience is the defining quality of the opportunity recognition process. Without a customer, there is no opportunity; without an opportunity, there is no venture; and without a sustainable opportunity, there can be no franchise.

As we discussed earlier in the chapter, our goal is to look at franchising as it presents opportunities for both franchisees and franchisors. We will now investigate several aspects of franchise opportunity recognition: primary target audience identification; service concept; service delivery system design; training and operational support; field support, marketing, advertising, and promotion; and product purchase provision. Prospective franchisors should understand the nature and quality of each of these franchise components. Those considering growth through franchising must pay attention to the detail of their system offering.

PRIMARY TARGET AUDIENCE

Defining the target customer is essential because it dictates many diverse functions of the business. Most important, it measures the first level of demand. Once the primary target audience is defined, secondary targets may be identified. The degree of market penetration in the secondary target is less than that of the primary target. Although measuring market demand is not an exact science, a franchisor must continually collect data about its customers. Even after a franchise is established, the franchisor and franchisee compare local market demographics with national profiles to decide the potential of the local market in terms of the number of outlets that can be developed. Revenue projections are made from the definition of the target audiences and the degree of market penetration that can be expected based on historical information. Three major areas of data collection can be integral to refining the primary target audience.

Demographic Profiles

A demographic profile is a compilation of personal characteristics that enables the company to define the "average" customer. Most franchisors perform market research as a central function, developing customer profiles and disseminating the information to franchisees. That research

may include current user and non-user profiles. Typically, a demographic analysis includes age, gender, income, home address (driving or walking kilometres from the store), working address (driving or walking kilometres from the store), marital status, family status (number and ages of children), occupation, race and ethnicity, religion, and nationality. Demographics must be put into context by looking at concept-specific data such as mean number of automobiles for a Jiffy Lube franchise or percentage of disposable income spent on clothes for a Mexx franchise.

Psychographic Profiles

Psychographic profiles segment potential customers based on social class, lifestyle, and personality traits. Economic class and lifestyle address such issues as health consciousness, fashion orientation, or being a "car freak." Personality variables such as self-confidence, conservativism, and independence are used to segment markets.

Behavioural variables segment potential customers by their knowledge, attitude, and use of products to project usage of the product or service. By articulating a detailed understanding of the target market and why consumers will buy our or our competitors' product or service, great knowledge of the competitive landscape is gained. Why will a consumer change their habits to spend their money with us instead of where they currently find value?

Geographic Profiles

The scope of a franchise concept can be local, regional, national, or international.[6] Regions are divided by population density and described as urban, suburban, or rural, can also be grouped as having from under 5000 residents to having 4 million or more.

THEORY INTO PRACTICE: MARKET DEMAND, A MOVING TARGET FOR RADIO SHACK

Target markets are dynamic, often metamorphosing very quickly. Radio Shack (later known in Canada as "The Source by Circuit City" and after Circuit City declared bankruptcy in early 2009, became just "The Source" under Bell Canada ownership) had to change its business to reflect the shift in its target market. In the 1970s and 1980s, Radio Shack grew by addressing the needs of technophiles—young men with penchants for shortwave radios, stereo systems, walkie-talkies, and the like. The national retail chain supplied this audience with the latest gadgets and did very well.

Then, starting in the early 1990s, technology became more sophisticated. Personal electronic equipment began to include cellphones, handheld computers, and electronic organizers. The market for these products was expanding from a smaller group of technophiles to a larger group of middle-aged males who loved gadgets and who had more disposable income. Yet Radio Shack remained Radio Shack. Its audience dwindled while the personal electronics market boomed.

In the early 1990s, Radio Shack refocused its business to target this new demographic. Its advertising addressed the needs of the 44-year-old upper-middle-class male versus the 29-year-old technophile. That 29-year-old who used to shop at Radio Shack was now 44! He was not going to make a radio, but he would buy a cellphone or GPS for his vehicle. Radio Shack made dramatic changes in its marketing and inventory. As a result, it made dramatic changes in its profitability. Under Bell Canada, The Source dropped its exclusivity agreement with Rogers Communications at the end of 2009 when contracts expired and in 2010 begin promoting the Bell line of products and services. The Source had over 700 stores as of 2013 and planned to open another 20 annually as well as renovate 50 per year.

The "smart" franchise uses the ever-growing system of franchisees and company outlets to continually gather data about customers. This helps dynamically shape the vision and therefore the opportunity. The analysis of system data must include a link to the vision of the concept and to what seems possible for the vision. For example, if we launched an earring company a generation ago, we could have defined the target market as women ages 21 to 40, and the size of the market as the number of women in this age group in Canada. But perhaps looking beyond the existing data and anticipating the larger market that now exists can shape our vision. The target market for earrings could be defined as women and men ages 12 to 32, with an average of three earrings (or more properly piercings) per individual, not two. The identification of the target market requires that we combine demographic data with our own unique vision for the venture.

The focus on primary target audience development as the core to franchise opportunity recognition is essential to determine the consumer appeal of a franchise and to establish validity of the opportunity. We will consider a set of criteria that will help define due diligence in assessing how a franchise has exploited the opportunity. This discussion holds value for an overall understanding of franchising for existing franchisors and potential franchisors alike.

EVALUATING A FRANCHISE   LO3

Before looking at the detail of a franchise offering, the prospective franchisee must mine an offering from the 900 franchises in Canada. Although the next section is appropriate for prospective franchisees, the savvy franchisor will use this information to better craft his/her franchise offering for potential franchisees.

Exhibit 13.2 provides a franchise screening template designed to make a preliminary assessment of the key variables that constitute a franchise. The exercise is crafted to help map the risk profile of the franchise and highlight areas that will most likely need further due diligence. If the following criteria are important to the potential franchisee, then they also provide a map of the growth and market positioning objectives a stable franchisor should be pursuing.

EXHIBIT 13.2 FRANCHISE RISK PROFILE TEMPLATE

CRITERIA	Low Risk Average Return 15%–20%	Acceptable Risk Incremental Return 30%	High Risk Marginal Return 40%–50%	Extreme Risk Large Return 60%–100%
Multiple Market Presence	National	Regional	Provincial	Local
Outlet Pro Forma Disclosed or Discerned	Yes, 90%+ apparently profitable	Yes, 80% apparently profitable	Yes, 70%+ apparently profitable	No, less than 70% profitable
Market Share	No. 1 and dominant	No. 1 or 2 with a strong competitor	Lower than No. 2	Lower than No. 3 with a dominant player
National Marketing Program	Historically successful creative process, national media buys in place	Creative plus regional media buys	Creative plus local media buys	Local media buys only
National Purchasing Program	More than 3%+ gross margin advantage in national purchasing contract	1%–3% gross margin advantage versus independent operators	Regional gross margin advantages only	No discernible gross margin advantages
Margin Characteristics	50% gross + margin 18%+ net outlet margin	40%–50% gross margin 12%–17% net outlet margin	30%–40% gross margin less than 12% net outlet margin	Declining gross margin detected, erratic net outlet margin
Business Format	Sophisticated training, documented operations manual, identifiable feedback mechanism with franchisees	Initial training and dynamically documented operations manual, some field support	Training and operations but weak field support	Questionable training and field support and static operations
Term of the Licence Agreement	20 years with automatic renewal	15 years with renewal	Less than 15 years or no renewal	Less than 10 years
Site Development	Quantifiable criteria clearly documented and tied to market specifics	Markets prioritized with general site development criteria	General market development criteria outlined	Business format not tied to identifiable market segment(s)
Capital Required per Unit	$15 000–$25 000 working capital	Working capital plus $50 000–$100 000 machinery and equipment	Working capital plus machinery and equipment plus $500 000–$1 000 000 real estate	Erratic, highly variable, or ill-defined
Franchise Fee and Royalties	PDV* of the fees are less than the demonstrated economic advantages (reduced costs or increased revenue) of the franchise versus stand-alone		PDV of the fees are only projected to be less than the expected economic advantages (reduced costs or increased revenue) of the franchise versus stand-alone	PDV of the fees are not discernibly less than the expected value of the franchise

*PDV is an abbreviation for present discounted value. If franchising is a risk-reduction strategy, then the discount of future revenue should be less. Concurrently, the economies of scale in marketing should increase the amount of revenue a franchise can generate versus a "stand-alone" operation.

This exercise is not designed to culminate in a "go or no go" decision. Rather, prospective franchisees should use it to help evaluate if the franchise meets their personal risk/return profile. Franchisors should also review the exercise to examine the risk signals they may be sending to prospective franchisees. It is especially important to understand this risk profile in the context of the alternative investments a prospective franchisee can make.

FRANCHISOR AS THE HIGH-POTENTIAL VENTURE   LO4

As Ron Joyce, Tim Horton's partner in their business demonstrates, becoming a franchisor can be a high-potential endeavour. Growth and scale are the essence of the franchise mentality. Throughout this chapter we have taken the approach of franchising as entrepreneurial behaviour by the franchisor. In this section, we focus principally on franchisors and their rewards. In a study of *publicly traded franchisors*, the size and scope of the firms that achieved public capital is impressive. The capital marketplace has rewarded many franchisors, which have measured well against the criteria for a high-potential venture franchise. They, in turn, have performed well vis-à-vis return to shareholders. The performance of public franchisors generally exceeds that of the TSX index. The relative buoyancy of franchisor performance can be attributed to being heavily weighted in the food category. During a recession, when household budgets are tight, consumers seek out dining establishments that offer the best value, the primary driver of many food-based franchise organizations.

Even more interesting are those exceptional performers among the high achieving franchisors. Take, for example, the quintessential Canadian franchise, Tim Hortons. Surpassing McDonald's, Tim Hortons is the largest Canadian food service organization with more than 4000 restaurants. Its infrastructure includes a network of suppliers and resources that allows it to achieve economies of scale and offer great value to customers. In 2008, system-wide sales reached nearly $2 billion, operating income approached $500 million, and earnings per share were strong. That year also marked the 500th store in the United States.[7] In late 2009 Tim Hortons Inc. announced a reorganization to become a Canadian public company. In 2011 a Master License Agreement was signed with a group in Dubai for up to 120 restaurants in the Gulf Cooperation Council. Total revenues in 2012 surpassed $3.1 billion.

KEY COMPONENTS OF A FRANCHISE OFFERING

In this section, we describe the major aspects of delivering a franchise system. It is excellence in both concept and delivery that has created wealth for the franchisors in publicly traded companies. We have analyzed the features that propel the high performance franchisor to exceptional return. The excellent franchisor supports the franchisee, and the symbiotic nature of the relationship leverages return for both partners. After prospective franchisees narrow their search for a franchise (by using the screening guide among other activities), they should begin a detailed analysis of the exact nature of a franchise. Franchisors should note the following in terms of how they might construct their offerings, knowing that prospective franchisees will conduct a detailed due diligence around these franchise components.

SERVICE DELIVERY SYSTEM

The road map for marshalling resources for the franchise comes from establishing the service delivery system. The opportunity dictates that certain tasks are performed to meet consumer demand. The assets put into place to meet these demands are largely the resources needed to launch the concept. In the franchise alliance, the franchisor develops a method for delivering the product or service that fills customer demand. In its most basic essence, the service delivery system is the way in which resources are arrayed so that demand can be extracted from the marketplace. This service delivery system has to be well defined, documented, and tested by the company or prototype operation. The end result of the organization, execution, and transfer of the service delivery system is the firm's competitive advantage.

The Timmons Model first looks at opportunity assessment, which demands a clear understanding of the target market and customer. Next it looks at resource marshalling or, in franchising, the establishment of the service delivery system. The service delivery system is the fundamental means by which customers will be served, and the fashion, often proprietary in design, in which the service delivery resources are arrayed can create competitive advantage in the marketplace. In franchising, this aspect is sometimes called the *business format*. A successful service delivery system's form and function will reflect the specific needs of the target customer. Highly successful and visible examples of business format innovations are the drive-through in fast-food restaurants and the bi-level facilities in quick-oil-change facilities. Every franchise has a well-defined service delivery system, however overt or transparent it may seem to an outside observer.

Because the service delivery system is truly the essence of the successful franchise, the detail given to it should not be underestimated. For the concept innovator, the common phrase, "The devil is in the details," never takes on more meaning than when designing the service delivery system for the franchise. Stephen Spinelli can corroborate this fact from experiences while expanding the Jiffy Lube franchise. One particular component of Jiffy Lube's expansion plans paints a vivid picture as to the intricacy of the development of the service delivery system and reveals what a great benefit this design paid over time.

Jiffy Lube franchises must meet specific location criteria: high volume of car traffic, side of the street located for inbound or outbound traffic, high profile retail area, and the far corner of any given street or block, among other requirements. Through trial and error, Jiffy Lube has determined the optimal location of the structure on any given property. Once these aspects are met, the building specifications follow. Structural specifications regarding the angle of the building and the width, depth, and angle of the entrance allow the optimal number of cars to stack in line waiting for the car in front to complete the service. On several occasions, facilities that met location criteria were failing to perform as expected. Analysis of the situation determined the bend in the driveway was too sharp, preventing customers from driving their cars completely into the line and giving the inaccurate impression that the lot was full. Driveways were adjusted to accommodate an increased number of cars waiting for service.

This same level of refinement and detail orientation is encouraged for concept innovators while looking at their conceptual and actual service delivery system. Unless examined under a microscope, essential components of the service delivery system will be missed, deteriorating the value of the franchise. Jiffy Lube's experience also reinforces the benefits of a beta site, providing a real-world laboratory that can be adjusted and modified until the outlet reaches optimal performance.

Another part of the complete Jiffy Lube service delivery system was the design of the maintenance bay. Considering the limitations inherent in the use of hydraulic lifts, Jiffy Lube faced the dilemma of providing 30 minutes of labour in only 10 minutes. To deliver this 10-minute service, three technicians would need to work on a car at once without the use of a lift. This quandary led to the design of having cars drive into the bay and stop above an opening in the floor. This allowed one technician to service the car from below, another to service the car underneath the hood, and a third to service the car's interior. Without developing such a disruptive system, Jiffy Lube would not have been able to succeed as it did.

The soundness of the decision to use the drive-through/bi-level system was confirmed when competitors, gas stations and car dealers, failed to deliver on offering a "quick lube" using hydraulic lifts and traditional bays. The sum of Jiffy Lube's intricately designed parts created the value of the service delivery system. Such is the level of detail needed for a service delivery system to deliver both value to the customer and cost efficiencies to the operator. In much the same way, the example highlighting Wendy's in the box above examines how the specific design components of the service delivery system can create value.

TRAINING AND OPERATIONAL SUPPORT

Formal franchisor training programs transfer knowledge of the service delivery system to the franchisees, to both managers and line workers. Continuous knowledge gathering and transfer is important both before launch and on an ongoing basis. The licence agreement must define the specific form in which this franchisor responsibility will be performed. It should extend significantly beyond a manual and the classroom. Training will vary with the specifics of the franchise, but it should include organized and monitored on-the-job experience in the existing system for the new franchisee and as many of the new staff members as the franchisor will allow. Established and stable franchise systems such as Jiffy Lube and Tim Hortons require such operational experience in the existing system for as long as a year before the purchase of the franchise; however, this level of dedication to the franchisee's success is not the norm. Once the franchise is operational, the franchisee may be expected to do much or all of the on-site training of new hires. But as we will discuss in the next section, field support from the franchisor is often a signal of franchise stability and a reflection of the strength of the franchise partnership. Manuals, testing, training aids such as videos, and certification processes are often provided by the franchisor as part of this ongoing field support.

As discussed previously, the trade name and trademark are the most valuable assets in a franchise system. A franchisee's success rests soundly on the sales of products that are based on the brand equity and strength of the franchisor. As important as a sound service delivery system is to the concept's foundation for success, the prospective training regimen is equally important.

Without appropriately instructed individuals an exceptional product will never reach the consumer's hands. As such, a poor training program will inevitably dilute the standardized, consistent delivery of the product and eventually erode the brand's value.

FIELD SUPPORT

Akin to the training program mentioned above is ongoing field support. This will take at least two forms, one in which a franchisor's representative will visit the franchisee's location in person, and the other in which the franchisor will retain resident experts in each of the essential managerial disciplines for consultation at the corporate headquarters. Ideally the licence agreement will provide for scheduled visits by the franchisor's agents to the franchisee's outlet with prescribed objectives, such as performance review, field training, facilities inspection, local marketing review, and operations audit. Unfortunately, some franchisors use their field role as a diplomatic or pejorative exercise rather than for training and support. The greater the substance of the field function, the easier it is for the franchisee to justify the royalty cost. Additionally, in the litigious environment in which we presently live, a well-documented field support program will mute franchisee claims of a lack of franchisor support.

One means of understanding the franchisor's field support motive is to investigate the manner in which the field support personnel are compensated. If field staff are paid commensurate with franchisee performance and ultimate profitability, then politics will play a diminished role. Key warning signs in this regard are when bonuses are paid for growth in the number of stores versus individual store growth, or for product usage (supplied by franchisor) by franchisee. Clearly, as with the training program prescribed by the franchisor and agreed to by the franchisee, a quality field support program is another integral factor to success, and a poor support program will eventually become evident.

MARKETING, ADVERTISING, AND PROMOTION

Marketing activities are certainly one of the most sensitive areas in the ongoing franchise relationship because they imprint the trade name and trademark in the mind of the consumer to gain awareness—the most important commodity of the franchise. If the delivery of the product validates the marketing message, then the value of the franchise is enhanced, but if it is not congruent, then there can be a detrimental effect at both the local and national level. As outlet growth continues, marketing budgets increase and spread across the growing organization, thereby optimizing the marketing program.

Generally, marketing programs are funded and implemented at three different levels: national, regional, and local. A national advertising budget is typically controlled by the franchisor and each franchisee contributes a percentage of top-line sales to the fund. The franchisor then produces materials (television, radio, and newspaper advertisements; direct-mail pieces; and point-of-sale materials) for use by the franchisees and, depending on the size of the fund, also buys media time or space on behalf of the franchisees. Because it is impossible to allocate these services equally between franchisees of different sizes across different markets, the licence agreement will specify the use of "best efforts" to approximate equal treatment between franchisees. Although "best efforts" will invariably leave some franchisees with more advertising exposure and some with less, over time this situation should balance itself. This is one area of marketing that requires careful monitoring by both parties.

Regional marketing, advertising, and promotion is structured on the basis of an area of dominant influence (ADI). All the stores in a given ADI (e.g., Winnipeg) would contribute a percentage of their top-lines sales to the ADI advertising co-operative.[8] The co-operative's primary function is usually to buy media using franchisor-supplied or approved advertising and to coordinate regional site promotions. If the franchise has a regional advertising co-operative requirement in the licence agreement, it should also have standardized ADI co-operative bylaws. These bylaws will outline such areas as voting rights and expenditure parameters. Often a single-store franchisee can be disadvantaged in a poorly organized co-operative, but even a major contributor to the co-operative may find his voting rights disproportionately low, so it is important to read and understand the bylaws.

The third and final scenario for marketing is typically dubbed local advertising or local store marketing. At this level, the franchisee is contractually required to make direct expenditures on advertising. There is often a wide spectrum of permissible advertising expenditures, depending on the franchisor guidelines in the licence agreement; unfortunately, the licence agreement will probably not be specific. Franchisors will try to maintain discretion on this issue for maximum flexibility in the marketplace, while franchisees will vie for control of this area. Company-owned stores should have advertising requirements equal to those for the franchised units to avoid a franchisor having a free ride; in this regard, historical behaviour is the best gauge of reasonableness.

The franchisor should monitor and enforce marketing expenditures. For example, the customer of a franchisee leaving one ADI and entering another will have been affected by the advertising of adjacent regions. Additionally, advertising expenditures not made are marketing impressions lost to the system. When this happens, the marketing leverage inherent in franchising is not optimized.

Mad Science was started in 1985 by Ariel and Ron Schlien, two brothers in Montreal, Quebec. As teenagers they put on science demonstrations and two moms asked if the Schliens would do a child's birthday party. The brothers were a hit and demand grew. In 1990, they had registered the name and the brothers had all the business that they could manage. Marketing was primarily word of mouth and attention snowballed. By 1995, offices were open in Toronto and Miami, Florida, and requests from parents, teachers, and organizations across North America flooded them. With over 200 franchises in 28 countries, the brothers have certainly been successful, despite little spent on advertising. But this is atypical, most franchises spend considerable time and money on building awareness.

SUPPLY

In most franchise systems one major benefit is bulk purchasing and inventory control. In the licence agreement there are several ways to account for this economy-of-scale advantage. Because of changing markets, competitors and antitrust laws make it impossible for the franchisor to be bound to best-price requirements. The franchise should employ a standard of best efforts and good faith to acquire both national and regional supply contracts. According to John Pozios of the University of Manitoba, franchise-specific laws vary significantly from province to province, "Alberta, Ontario, Prince Edward Island and most recently New Brunswick have passed laws targeting franchising. Québec offers limited protection in its Civil Code."[9] He states that with franchise-specific laws that differ from province to province, and no legislation in many provinces, "the need for uniformity in franchise legislation in Canada is greater than ever." Regulations protect the franchisee with disclosure requirements for the franchisor, obligations for fair dealing, and other duties of good faith. Inconsistency in law and expectations create a burden on the home-grown, developing franchise systems in Canada. The international franchisors have perfected their business models, are accustomed to variety in legal requirements, and have the experience and resources to take advantage of Canada's obstacles.

Depending on the nature of the product or service, regional deals might make more sense than national ones. Regional contracts may provide greater advantages to the franchisee because of shipping weight and cost or service requirements. The savvy franchisor will recognize this and implement a flexible purchase plan. When local advantages exist and the franchisor does not act appropriately, the franchisees will fill the void. The monthly ADI meeting then becomes an expanded forum for franchisees to voice their appreciations and concerns. The results of such ad hoc organizations can be reduced control of quality and expansion of franchisee association matters outside the confines of the licence agreement. Advanced activity of this nature can often fractionalize a franchise system and even render the franchisor obsolete. In some cases, the franchisor and franchisee-operated buying co-operatives peaceably coexist, acting as competitors and lowering the costs to the operator. However, the dual buying co-ops usually reduce economies of scale and dilute system resources, not to mention provide fertile ground for conflict within the franchise alliance.

For purposes of quality control, the franchisor will reserve the right to publish a product specifications list. The list will clearly establish the quality standards of raw materials or goods used in the operation. From those specifications, a subsequent list of approved suppliers is generated. This list can evolve into a franchise "tying agreement," which occurs when the business format franchise licence agreement binds the franchisee to the purchase of a specifically branded product. This varies from the product specification list because brand, not product content, is the qualifying specification. The important question here is: does the tying arrangement of franchise and product create an enhancement for the franchisee in the marketplace? If so, then are arm's-length controls in place to ensure that pricing, netted from the enhanced value, will yield positive results? Unfortunately, this is impossible to precisely quantify. However, if the tying agreement is specified in the licence agreement, then the prospective franchise owner is advised to make a judgment before purchasing the franchise. With this sort of decision at hand, the franchisor should prove the value of the tying agreement or abandon it.

Another subtle form of tying agreements occurs when the licence agreement calls for an approved suppliers list that ultimately includes only one supplier. If adding suppliers to the list is nearly impossible, there is a de facto tying arrangement. Additionally, another tying arrangement can occur when the product specification is written so that only one brand can qualify. A franchisor should disclose any remuneration gained by the franchisor or its officers, directly or indirectly, from product purchase in the franchise system. In this case, the franchisor's market value enhancement test is again proof of a credible arrangement.

FRANCHISING FRICTIONS AND LEGAL CONSIDERATIONS

In addition to considerable variation in legislated treatment of franchises from province to province, additional legal and other matters must be considered. Profitguide.com reports that "the franchising model contains an inherent tension that can lead to open conflict." According to Don Sniegowski, editor of franchise-news website, "Franchisees make their money on profits. Franchisors make their money on a percentage of gross sales. What's good for gross isn't necessarily good for profit—you've got a built-in conflict of interest." For example, the franchisor may try to boost sales through promotions. One of the authors of this textbook recently

FOOD FRANCHISES WITH AN APPETITE FOR SUCCESS

ST-HUBERT

1951 was the year that Hélène and René Léger opened their first St-Hubert restaurant in Montréal. Today the yellow and red rooster is found in approximately 100 locations throughout Québec, with a few more stores in New Brunswick and Ontario, and signals rotisserie chicken served with that delectable sauce. Adding home delivery and takeout increased consumption of their BBQ chicken and the young married couple realized they were really on to something. Their recipe for chicken, sauce, and service delivery system was easy for franchisees to follow. The sauce was then offered to grocery retailers. The Légers served thousands of visitors at the '67 Expo each day and their reputation grew. By 1979 about 50 St-Hubert restaurants were in existence.

Groupe St-Hubert Inc.

HARVEY'S

1959 was the year that Richard "Rick" Mauran and George B. Sukornyk—equal partners—opened the first Harvey's location in Richmond Hill, Ontario. They arrived at the name in a search for "something simple"—"Harvey's" was the name of the sign of a car dealer at 2300 Danforth Avenue (which today is the location of "Toronto Honda"). Franchising began in 1962 and in 1964 Harvey's Foods Ltd. went public and that year expanded from 7 to 17 locations. By 1965 there were 27 locations including Buffalo, New York. A handful of years later Rick's company merged with Industrial Growth Management to become Foodcorp and Rick and Bernie Syron lead expansive growth. In 1979 Foodcorp and the 80 Harvey's locations were acquired by Cara Operations Ltd. In the mid-1990s Harvey's partnered with Home Depot Canada and opened their first in-store kiosk in Whitby, Ontario. Today, there are 700+ restaurants across Canada with sales of almost $1.5 billion.

Robyn Craig

PIZZA NOVA

1963 marked the start of Pizza Nova. The Italian-born Primucci brothers opened one Pizza Nova restaurant in Scarborough, Ontario, and demand grew. In 1969 the Primucci family began franchising and today boasts over 130 franchises in Southern Ontario. Today, after 50 years of Pizza Nova, the company continues to thrive, grow, and evolve in an ever-changing food service industry. For more information on their franchising opportunities visit www.pizzanova.com.

Pizza Nova

MR. SUB

In 1968, during the hippie era, the first Mr. Sub opened at 130 Yorkville Avenue in downtown Toronto to customers in tie-dyed shirts and bell-bottom jeans. Two friends raised $1500 and started making fresh submarine sandwiches. After an "overwhelming response" the co-founders opened a second location five months later. In 1972 their first franchise opened. It expanded the menu and operations and remained privately held with the original owners/directors. In November of 2011, MTY Food Group Inc. acquired Mr. Submarine and its 338 Mr. Sub outlets for $23 million in cash. MTY was founded by Stanley Ma in 1979 with one restaurant, and today he remains Chairman, President, and CEO. Stanley Ma's empire includes 22 fully-owned franchise brands and 4 others that are under exclusive license agreements.

MTY Group-Mr. Sub Division

Sources: www.st-hubert.com; www.harveys.com; www.pizzanova.com; www.mrsub.ca.

encountered a Marble Slab Creamery franchisee complaining of these practices. It cannot be good for business relations when a customer hears a franchisee bad-mouthing her franchisor! In a similar situation Quiznos franchisees refused to honour franchisor-issued coupons that cut into store profits.[10]

Cautionary tales of frictions between franchisees and franchisors abound. As mentioned earlier, you must know and thoroughly understand any contract you enter into. For example, a **master franchise** differs significantly from a single or individual franchise. It will be more difficult for the franchisor to find someone suitable for a master franchise but is generally rewarded with rapid growth and the franchisee can obtain a sizable empire quickly too. Geographic rights define the territory that the master franchisee has exclusive purview over. An **area developer** is akin to a multi-unit franchisee. An area developer is tasked with building brand awareness quickly. In the rush, quantity may be valued above quality. There may also be incentives that do not promote doing things well.

What, if anything, is negotiable? The answer will vary from absolutely nothing to many reasonable requests. Covenants should also be examined carefully. It is common for relationships and business models to evolve, but check whether this is permitted or even encouraged—most likely not. When a franchise relationship is terminated or simply expires, what transpires next can be an amicable parting or hostility. Typically a non-compete element of the contract is enforceable. The franchisee will be sidelined for a period of time unable to compete in the business realm. But the courts have on occasion had different interpretations, and much depends on the particular circumstances.

FRANCHISE RELATIONSHIP MODEL   LO5

Now that we have established the nature and components of the franchise relationship, we can connect these principles to the franchise relationship model, which we have developed over the years (see Exhibit 13.3). The franchise relationship model takes the entrepreneurial framework provided by the Timmons Model and connects the specific processes that are unique to franchising. We have argued that franchising is a powerful entrepreneurial alliance because it fits the Timmons Model and because it creates wealth. The franchise relationship model illustrates both how a concept innovator (i.e., potential franchisor) can most efficiently construct a franchising company and how a concept implementer (i.e., potential franchisee) can determine which company to join. The franchise relationship model further helps to distinguish between those tasks best executed under a corporate umbrella and those best done by the individual franchisee. Just as franchising is itself a risk-ameliorating tool for the entrepreneur; the franchise relationship model is also a tool that both franchisors and franchisees can use to judge the efficiency or success potential of a franchise opportunity. By overlaying the franchise relationship model template onto any given franchise, we can forecast to a great extent where the bottlenecks will impede success or where improvements can be made that will offer a competitive advantage.

The franchise relationship model is a puzzle, a series of franchise principles, each of which fit into the others to form a powerful interlocking business concept that solidifies itself as the linkages are implemented more efficiently. While the process starts in the centre with the customer, moves to the service delivery system and follows from there, the outer perimeter of means and mechanisms drives the competitive advantage of a franchise system. The major areas of concern

master franchise: A franchise agreement that allows a person or corporation to purchase the rights to sub-franchise in a particular territory. Often the franchise fee and royalty fees for the sub-franchises are divided equally between the franchisor and the master franchisee. The master franchisor is in the middle of this hierarchy with sub-franchisees below and the franchisor above.

area developer: Someone who invests in a local territory or region, grows that area through franchisee recruitment and existing store growth, acts as mentor/coach in assisting with business development including site selection, opening, and ramp-up of business, provides ongoing support, and makes marketing and promotion decisions for the area.

EXHIBIT 13.3	FRANCHISE RELATIONSHIP MODEL

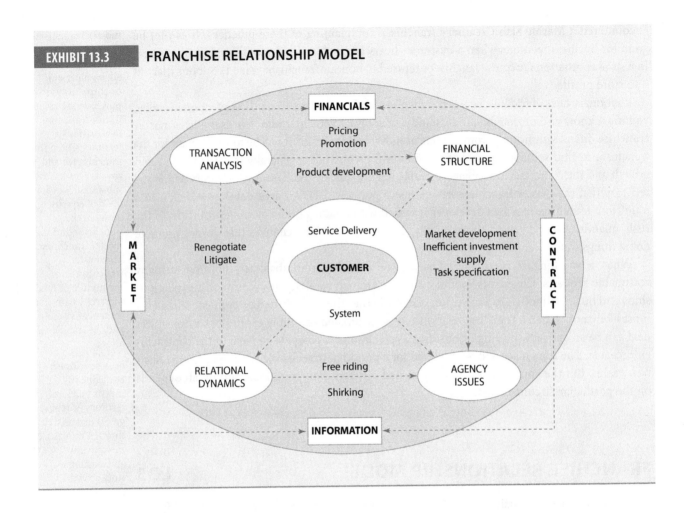

other than the customer and the service delivery system are transaction analysis, financial structure, agency issues, and relational dynamics.

Transaction analysis considers which transactions are better served at a national level by the franchisor and which at the local level by the franchisee.[11] Typically the franchisor functions are centred on economies of scale. Franchisee functions include those that require local knowledge for hiring and local promotion. The financial structure flows from pro forma analysis of customer demand and the cost associated with development and execution of the service delivery system. Agency issues concern delegating responsibility to a partner.[12] No franchisor can know absolutely that the franchisee is "doing the right thing" at the store level. There is always the possibility of shirking, but if incentives are aligned both parties will pursue the same interests for value creation. Franchisees cannot possibly know that the franchisor is always acting in their best interest. Relational dynamics is the area that allows the partnership between franchisor and franchisee to continually change and develop as the business continues to expand.[13] Any partnership that strictly adheres to a contract will end in litigation.

The franchise relationship model (Exhibit 13.3) is dynamic—as events affect one aspect of the model, all other aspects must be reviewed in an iterative process. For example, if renegotiation of the licence agreement were to result in a reduced royalty, the financial model would be altered. A change in royalty could dictate a change in the services that the franchisor provides. Any change creates a cascading effect throughout the system—a reconstruction of the puzzle.

The franchise relationship model begins with opportunity recognition and shaping (customer) and then articulates the competitive advantages and costs of the service delivery system that will extract the demand and create a return on investment. The competitive sustainability of the franchise is embedded in the delineation of responsibilities between franchisor and franchisee and in the conscious design of the service delivery system. The franchisor's tasks are centrally executed and focus on economies of scale; the franchisee concentrates on those responsibilities that require local on-site managerial intensity (transaction analysis). The emergent financial structure is the manifestation of the interaction between the primary target customer and the service delivery system. By sharing both the burden of the service delivery system and the potential for return on investment, the franchise entrepreneurial alliance is formed.

Central to the long-term stability of the franchise system is the proper selection of partners and monitoring of key partner responsibilities (agency issues). However, even in the most stable relationship, a dynamic business environment dictates adjustments in the relationship to ensure continued competitive advantage. Understanding the partner's tolerance zone in performance and reacting to market changes can be standardized by formal review programs and kept unstructured by informal negotiations (relational dynamics). Failure to recognize the need for dynamic management of the relationship can often result in litigation, as noted.

The franchise relationship model illustrates how a concept innovator can construct a franchising company and the pathway for implementing it in the most entrepreneurial way. The model also eliminates those ideas that are best developed using another growth strategy, such as distributorships, licensing, or corporate-owned outlets. We now understand that franchising is entrepreneurial and we understand the unique components of franchising that enable the building of a high-growth enterprise.

LEARNING OBJECTIVES SUMMARY

LO1 Franchising is an inherently entrepreneurial endeavour. Franchising shares profits, risk, and strategy between the franchisor and the franchisee.

LO2 In this chapter we argue that opportunity, scale, and growth are at the heart of the franchise experience.

LO3 A unique aspect of franchising is the wide spectrum of opportunity that exists and the matching of scale to appetite for a broad spectrum of entrepreneurs. Using the franchise screening template provided will help determine if the match is a suitable one.

LO4 The success of franchising is demonstrated by the fact that it accounts for more than one-fifth of all Canadian retailing. Equally important is the demonstrated performance of the top publicly traded franchise companies that outperforming the S&P TSX Composite Index.

LO5 Two tools have been provided in this chapter to help the entrepreneur. For those interested in creating a franchise, the franchise relationship model articulates the dynamic construction of the franchisor–franchisee alliance. The franchise risk profile helps assess the risk–return scenario for any given franchise opportunity.

STUDY QUESTIONS

1. Can you describe the difference between the franchisor and the franchisee? How are these differences strategically aligned to create a competitive advantage?
2. We describe franchising as a "pathway to entrepreneurship" providing a spectrum of entrepreneurial opportunities. What does this mean to you?
3. What are the most important determinants of whether franchising is an appropriate method of rapidly growing a concept?
4. What are the five components of the franchise relationship model? Can you describe the interactive nature of these components?
5. What are the key components of a franchise offering from the franchisor's viewpoint?

MIND STRETCHERS   *Have you considered?*

1. Why do you think that publicly held franchisors consistently outperform the TSX?
2. What would be the most attractive aspects of franchising to you? What is the least attractive part of franchising?
3. Can you list the top 10 franchises in the world? What criteria would you use to make your judgment?
4. Do you know anyone who owns a franchise? Do you think they work more or less hard than a "stand-alone" entrepreneur?
5. Who is franchising for and not for? What sectors are naturals for franchises?

IVEY | Publishing

Preparation Questions

1. What growth options are available and which one(s) should Eveline Charles pursue?

2. Assess market characteristics and market potential?

3. Will any resources need to be re-deployed? Any change in focus?

Eveline Charles looked pleased as she walked through her beauty salon and spa in Edmonton's Southgate Mall. It was late in the day, most of her staff had gone home, and the shop—one of nine outlets in her eponymous chain—was spic and span, just as she liked it.

Looking out through her storefront window, Charles watched as the last of the day's shoppers wandered towards the exits, bags in hand. Charles, however, wouldn't be heading out like the rest of them. On this mid-December evening, she was staying behind with her chief operating officer, Lina Heath, for a meeting. The subject: where to take the company next.

Turning her attention to that task, Charles sank down into one of the large black chairs in the reception lounge and looked up at Heath. "We've come a long way since we first added spa services to our salon business in 1995," she said. "Most of our stores are doing well. We've improved our decor, introduced new items and special services. And we've stayed true to our formula of offering a luxurious and fashion-forward salon where our clients can be pampered for a few hours."

Heath nodded. Both of the women knew that EvelineCharles was in good shape. Revenue and profit had grown steadily with the business. The company had launched a successful line of beauty products, it had created a training school in partnership with the Northern Alberta Institute of Technology and it had established EvelineCharles as a premium brand in western Canada, with annual sales of $17 million.

Still, Charles was puzzled over where her next phase of growth would come from. At least she had options. For starters, she had a large line of branded products—upwards of 1800 share-keeping units (SKUs), including beauty products and salon equipment—which meant she had the potential to become a supplier to other high-end salons. Heath liked

this idea. The company had $2 million worth of shares in its inventory, and she reminded Charles that becoming a supplier would increase turnover and generate cash. Charles agreed. But she had bigger ideas on her mind. "What about our thoughts on franchising our concept?" she asked Heath. "How should we assess that option? This is a unique industry where every operator wants to be an owner. We can give them the tools to build a business. With our school, we can even provide them with business training."

Both Charles and Heath were intrigued by the potential that franchising offered. But neither had experience as franchisors. Was it a good business model for EvelineCharles? They just didn't know and they were wary of pitfalls. Still, the idea was tempting. Growing by opening corporate stores would be time-consuming and expensive. Both women knew that well. But they also had a track record for getting it right. What was their best way forward—franchising or organic growth? Charles and Heath hoped this evening's meeting would shed some light on that question.

If Charles and Heath knew one thing as they pondered their options, it was that they were in a strong business category. The professional beauty-service market in North America was worth more than $60 billion in 2007, encompassing services that ranged from hair cuts and facials to massage and body scrubs. It was also extremely fragmented, with single, owner-operated stores accounting for most of the business.

Charles was such an owner when she opened her first business, a beauty salon in Edmonton, in 1984—but she wasn't content to stay that way. By the early 1990s, she had opened two more salons and, more importantly, had a plan for future growth. Charles had detected an early-stage trend in the industry of adding spa services to the menu of haircuts and manicures offered at traditional salons. She saw promise and, in 1995, launched her first combined salon-spa. She opened a second location in 1998, and set her sights on developing even more.

Part of Charles's strategy centred on developing signature services, such as hot-stone massages and mango body washes. To further differentiate her company, she also began developing branded lines of beauty products, like shampoos, lotions and cosmetics, a job she and Heath (who had joined the company by this time) attacked with relish. "Lina and I have spent months in all corners of the world sourcing our products," Charles says. "We have our skin-care products and

This case was written by Ken Mark, Eric Morse, and Mary Weil, Pierre L. Morrissette Institute for Entrepreneurship, Richard Ivey School of Business, University of Western Ontario, for purposes of classroom discussion.

aromatherapy products sourced in France. Our nail colours come from Italy. We source from the best manufacturers and those with the strongest traditions in beauty care. And every single component is 100 percent customized for us. Everything we offer is unique and very difficult to replicate."

That focus on customization didn't stop at the EvelineCharles product lines. As the chain grew, Charles and Heath paid careful attention the to the details of opening each new store. They oversaw construction at each location, designed the layouts, and picked the colours and the lights to create a feel consistent with the company's high-end positioning. Customers certainly noticed. Many asked if the new stores were part of a U.S. chain making its way into Canada. Industry peers were paying attention, too, and Charles started to win industry awards, including Entrepreneur of the Year for Canada in the Global Salon Business Awards, in both 2004 and 2006. By the middle of this decade, it had become a major player in the salon and spa business, with stores in Edmonton, Calgary, Vancouver and Kelowna, B.C.

Back in the salon, Charles and Heath continued to discuss their options. Their existing growth strategy had taken them a long way. But opening stores themselves was a slow process. Real estate had to be found, leases negotiated and construc-tion managed. Bringing stores to maturity in terms of sales also tied up working capital. And even though EvelineCharles had a source of recruits thanks to its beauty academy, hiring was still a major task.

For these reasons, among others, Charles and Heath were intrigued by the prospect of franchising the EvelineCharles brand. For starters, franchising would help the brand grow quickly, as EvelineCharles would be able to leverage the financial resources of its franchise partners. On the revenue side, the company would earn a percentage from each franchise and create a whole new market for its inventory of branded products.

Of course, franchisees would have to be selected carefully to maintain the quality of the EvelineCharles brand. And they'd have to be committed to growing their locations, keeping a close watch on local trends and ensuring that costs were controlled. Still, the prospects looked very tempting. "One day, EvelineCharles could become a nationwide brand," Heath mused.

But their inexperience as franchisors left Charles and Heath with nagging doubts, no matter how much they liked the idea. Turning to Heath, Charles had only one question: "What do you think we should do?"

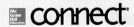

CHAPTER 14

THE FAMILY AS ENTREPRENEUR[1]

The very elements that foster success, as well as the attitudes bred by success itself, can precipitate failure. The systems that built great companies often work to destroy them.[2]

DANNY MILLER & ISABELLE LEBRETON-MILLER
HEC Montréal and University of Alberta

LEARNING OBJECTIVES

LO1 Describe the significant economic and entrepreneurial contribution families make to communities and countries worldwide.

LO2 Evaluate the different roles families play as part of the entrepreneurial process.

LO3 Assess a family on the mindset and methods continua for family enterprising and identify key issues for family dialogue.

LO4 Examine key questions on the six dimensions for family enterprising.

LO5 Plot a family's resource and capabilities on the "familiness f+ and f– assessment continuum" and understand their advantages and constraints.

LO6 Analyze succession in a transgenerational enterprise.

FAMILIES, ENTREPRENEURSHIP, AND THE TIMMONS MODEL

The tension among generations in families can often revolve around the aggressive younger executives seeking to explore new and exciting deals and the older executive who seeks to march forward on the pathway that created the family's fortune. The purpose of this chapter is to help families (and those working with families!) understand that opportunity recognition and balance in the Timmons Model help guide the family's decision-making process. By encouraging the discussion toward the model, we ask, "What is the richest opportunity?" and "Are the opportunity, team, and resources well balanced?" Families have special knowledge, experience, and often resources that bring competitive advantages.[3] We aspire to leverage these special factors to create a "familiness" advantage that creates value. But there also exist pitfalls with which enterprising families need to be aware. As Lloyd Steier of the University of Alberta, James Chrisman of Mississippi State University, and Jess Chua of the University of Calgary indicate, "family based approaches to organizing enterprise might yield advantages or disadvantages."[4]

> *Family based approaches to organizing enterprise might yield advantages or disadvantages."*

BUILDING ENTREPRENEURIAL FAMILY LEGACIES[5] LO1

When we hear the phrase *family business*, images of high-flying, harvesting entrepreneurs are not usually the first thoughts that come to our mind. We more often think of the small mom-and-pop businesses, or the large business family fights that hold the potential for reality TV. It is fair to say that family businesses do not always look and act entrepreneurially. They can focus on serving local markets, sustaining the family's lifestyle, or providing jobs to family members. They are often conflicted due to family dynamics, constrained by nepotism, or limited by their conservative risk profile.

But these realities should be held in tension with the corresponding truth that families comprise the dominant form of business organization worldwide and provide more resources for the entrepreneurial economy than any other source.[6] We must be careful that we do not form mental caricatures about either family businesses or entrepreneurs that might keep us from exploring the link between entrepreneurship and family or, more importantly, keep us from understanding the significance the linkage holds for social and economic wealth creation in our communities and countries worldwide.

The purpose of this chapter is to deepen our understanding of entrepreneurship in the family context. We will explore the entrepreneurial commitments, capabilities, and contributions of families and their businesses. To describe families who leverage the entrepreneurial process in the family context we use the phrase *family enterprising*. As enterprise refers to economic activity, enterprising is the action of generating economic activity. Consistent with earlier definitions of entrepreneurship, families who are enterprising generate new economic activity and build long-term value across generations. We refer to this outcome as *transgenerational entrepreneurship and wealth creation* and it is how to build entrepreneurial family legacies. This chapter will provide families with three sets of assessment and strategy tools to assist them in knowing how to become enterprising and build their family legacy.

LARGE COMPANY FAMILY LEGACIES

We must first begin by understanding the economic and entrepreneurial significance of families. It is difficult to walk into a Marriott Hotel, see the father and son picture of J. Willard Marriott Jr.

ENTREPRENEURS ACROSS CANADA
BC Bearing Engineers Ltd.

Robert MacPherson founded Northern Metals and Engineering in 1936. The company became BC Bearing Engineers Ltd. in 1944. Robert joined the RCAF in 1943 and gave his wife Wendy power of attorney over his business. When Robert returned home in 1946, Wendy returned to being a housewife. But she had tasted the life of an entrepreneur. "Well, I wasn't happy at all," she recollected.

Robert died in an airplane crash in 1950 and Wendy took over as president; "she needed the company's cash flow to raise four children." Business flourished in the 1960s and 1970s, fueled by growth in the resources economy. In 1988, Robby MacPherson was appointed president/COO and Wendy became chairman/CEO. Scott MacPherson also continued to play a role in the company. Wendy guided the BC Bearing Group for over 50 years to global stature and more than $200 million in annual sales. In March of 2010, Genuine Parts Co. of Atlanta, Georgia, completed the purchase of the North American assets of BC Bearing. The family retained the Latin American business, their real estate holdings, and a provider of hydraulic and pneumatic components. Wendy celebrated her 90th birthday with a big bash and died seven months later on December 30, 2012, leaving behind 8 children, 27 grandchildren, and 36 great-grandchildren.

©Dave Roels

WENDY MCDONALD OF BC BEARING ENGINEERS LTD.

Question: Would you work until you're 90 years old like this matriarch?

Sources: www.bearings.com; Gordon Pitts, "Wendy McDonald was an Indomitable Force in Canadian Business," *Globe and Mail*, February 8, 2013.

and Sr., and not think about entrepreneurial family legacies. From a small root beer concession stand, who would have expected the emergence of a $12-billion and 127 000-employee company? The Marriotts are now operating in their third generation of family leadership and are just one example of the many companies and branded products that are synonymous with family names and legacies. Of course, the Hilton family's namesake is not far behind.

John Molson founded his brewery in Montreal in 1786. In speaking with employees in 1825, he asserted "We are all members of a larger community which depends on everyone playing a part." In 2004 the Molson family united with the Coors family of Colorado to form the Molson Coors Brewing Company, of which a sixth generation family member, Eric Molson, is chairman. Molson is presently North America's oldest beer brand, in Canada it employs 3000 and has $7 billion in sales. Seventh generation members of the Coors family are engaged in the business including Eric's sons Geoff, a VP, and Andrew, who sits on the board of Molson Coors Brewing Company.[7]

While it is often assumed that family companies cannot play in the technology and telecommunications arena, the Rogers family has shown otherwise and grown one of Canada's largest communications companies with revenues over $12 billion and nearly 30 000 employees.

Many of the popular branded-product companies are controlled by families including Tyson Foods, an Arkansas-based $32-billion company in which the family controls 80 percent and the grandson of the founder is the current chairman. Walmart, of course, is probably the best-known family firm from Arkansas. Mars, the makers of M&M's, is still 100-percent family owned and the

$55-billion company has multiple generations of family members at all levels of top leadership. Cosmetic, fragrance, and skin care products company Estee Lauder generates approximately $7.5 billion in revenues with the founding family controlling approximately 88 percent of its voting shares with six members in top management bearing the Lauder name. Wrigley's gum, a $6-billion company currently run by the founder's great-grandson, William Wrigley Jr. II, far outperforms its rivals with a 20-percent return on assets. Smucker's Jam—"With a name like Smucker's, it has to be good"—has sales of over $2.2 billion with brothers Tim and Richard continuing to grow the 117-year-old company.

Another interesting category of entrepreneurial family involvement is the investment-holding company. Warren Buffet may be one of the most famous examples. Buffet's company, Berkshire Hathaway, owns many recognizable companies such as GEICO Insurance, Fruit of the Loom, and Dairy Queen. For nearly 50 years, Buffet's investments in companies have provided an average annual return of 20 percent and have increased the value of Berkshire by over 195 000 percent since 1965. His 38-percent stake in Berkshire Hathaway makes him one of the richest people in the world. Warren's son, Howard G. Buffet, is a director at several Berkshire subsidiaries and currently sits on the board at Berkshire. While succession planning at Berkshire is highly secretive, it is anticipated that Howard Buffet will take over as chairman of the board.

In keeping with this picture of family legacy contributions, a recent survey showed that 35 percent of Fortune 500 companies are controlled and or managed by families. These family-influenced companies consistently outperform non-family businesses on annual shareholder return, return on assets, and both annual revenue and income growth.[8] A study of firms listed on the TSX and included in the S&P/TSX composite index reveals that Canadian family firms "carry more long-term debt than non-family firms."[9] Anthony Markin of Simon Fraser University finds that "stock return volatility is substantially lower for family firms....It appears that the family firm's long-term perspective translates into a more efficient utilization of the firm's assets." But these large family companies only begin to tell the story of the entrepreneurial and economic contribution made by business families. (See Exhibit 14.1.)

SMALLER AND MID-SIZE FAMILY LEGACIES

In many regards, the real heart and often-overlooked segment of the Canadian economy and entrepreneurial activity is the smaller and mid-size companies. This segment is substantively controlled by families, and they are not all your typical "mom-and-pop" operations.

Vector Construction Group began in 1965 in the earthworks business, building roads. "After several years of highway grading, dam building, site development, and other heavy construction projects, the opportunity came to take on a significant concrete repair project on a hydro-electric facility for Manitoba Hydro. This start in concrete rehabilitation soon led to new opportunities to

---

| EXHIBIT 14.1 | CANADA'S FAMILY FIRMS |

▶ Employ 4.7 million people on a full-time basis and 1.3 million part-time
▶ Total annual sales of $828 billion
▶ 27% of family business leaders will retire within 5 years, another 29% will retire in 6 to 10 years
▶ 44% of family firms have an exit strategy, 29% have a succession plan
▶ 3 out of 10 family firms make it to the second generation
▶ 1 out of 10 family firms make it to the third generation

provide the latest concrete restoration and protection technologies to a broad range of clients." Donald Whitmore's two partners retired in 1980 but he kept going. From their home base in Winnipeg, Vector Construction expanded to Saskatchewan and Sarnia, Ontario. Later they opened branches in Alberta and Fargo, North Dakota. They expanded further to Thunder Bay and Stoney Creek, Ontario, and in the United States to Nebraska, Iowa, Florida, Illinois, and Colorado. Vector Construction Group has been known for its advanced technologies and for itself pushing the technology frontier in its field. In early 2009 it acquired an electrochemical products business from a global leader in the field so that it could prevent and treat concrete corrosion. Donald P. Whitmore remains at the helm. As the company moves past the 50-year milestone in 2015, the future looks promising.

Richard Stewart Sr. arrived in the Okanagan Valley in 1908 from Ireland. Having worked in the greenhouses of Lord Guinness in Ireland, with his brother Bill he started Stewart Brothers' Nurseries. "Inspired by Richard, his son Dick ventured out on his own in 1956 and purchased the site on the slopes of Mt. Boucherie, Kelowna, which is now the home of Quails' Gate Winery. As Dick neared retirement, he called on his eldest son Ben to come home to the family farm."[10] They then transformed the family farm from its diverse crops to high-density premium vinifera and became wine producers. Ben, with his siblings Tony, Cynthia, and Andrea, have pursued the creation of wonderful wines. This pursuit has meant looking outside the family to recruit those with expertise in winemaking.

Many family companies may not have brand names consumers recognize, but they are dominant in their industries because of the important part they play in the supply chains of large multinationals. They may make ingredients or inputs for other known wares or may produce goods in their entirety under another's moniker—take Magna for example. The list of these "everyday" family entrepreneurs is endless. They may be a regional or a national distributor behind the scenes, or an unnamed printer.

In this montage of families we have not even mentioned the nascent entrepreneurs and smaller companies that will become the next-generation Marriot, Reitman, Smucker, or Bronfman family company. Nor have we considered the children in existing family firms who will

© Quails' Gate Winery

IN 1956, DICK STEWART PURCHASED A SITE ON THE SLOPES OF MT. BOUCHERIE, KELOWNA, WHICH IS NOW THE HOME OF QUAILS' GATE WINERY.

ENTREPRENEURS ACROSS CANADA

Samuel, Son & Co.: A Growth-Oriented Family Enterprise

LARGE-SCALE INDUSTRIAL ACTIVITY AT SAMUEL, SON & CO.

Samuel, Son & Co., Limited

Samuel, Son & Co., Limited began in 1855 as "M & L Samuel" by Lewis and Mark Samuel in the metal and hardware business with operations in Toronto, Ontario, and Liverpool, England. In the late 1880s Lewis Samuel's son Sigmund became president and did away with "shelf" hardware and focused on metals and heavy hardware. In 1931, when a non-family partner retired, Sigmund took over that individual's sizeable stake in the company and became a sole proprietor. In 1962 a grandson of Sigmund, Ernest Samuel, became president. Ernest died in 2000, having opened and acquired facilities throughout Canada and the United States. Having been at the helm for 38 years, Ernest left a strong legacy. Samuel, Son & Co., Limited has become one of the top 10 processors and distributors of metals in North America and saw $3.1 billion in revenues in 2011. "We have a history we can be proud of and a strong future to look forward to." His wife, Elizabeth, already a board member, was elected chair. In 2006, their son Mark Samuel succeeded her as Chairman of the Samuel Group of Companies, having previously served as both President and CEO of Samuel Manu-Tech Inc. Nearly 160 years later, and still under the same family's control, the enterprise is still growing. Over the years it has acquired a number of businesses, chiefly in North America, to add capacity or reach particular markets.

Question: What do you think the future holds for Samuel, Son & Co., Limited?

Sources: http://www.metalcenternews.com/Editorial/CurrentIssue/September2012/tabid/5833/articleType/ArticleView/articleId/8408/Top-50.aspx; www.samuel.com.

become nascent entrepreneurs. In a recent undergraduate class on family entrepreneurship, more than 80 percent of the students said that they wanted to start *their own company* as an extension of their family business. They were not just looking to run their family company. Students like Toby Donath created a business plan to move his mother's business, Bäckerhaus Veit, from manufacturing and wholesaling to retailing and branded products. Brothers Colby and Drew West started auctionPAL with their parents as "support investors" based on ideas developed by Drew. Student Jonathan Gelpey had a plan to commercialize a product for which his grandfather holds the patent. All of these young entrepreneurs fulfill our vision for next-generation entrepreneurship and family enterprising.

THE FAMILY CONTRIBUTION AND ROLES   LO2

It is clear from our descriptions of family companies that families still dominate the Canadian economy and even more fully the economies of other countries worldwide. The most recent economic impact study in Canada reported that family businesses contribute more than 45 percent of Canada's GDP and paycheques for about half of working Canadians.[11] Family-controlled businesses in Canada create nearly 70 percent of new jobs. One-quarter of the top 50 Canadian companies (by market capitalization) are controlled by family, and the top six families generate $100 billion in annual revenues.[12] Family businesses in Canada provide 55 percent of all charitable donations. Worldwide, the economic numbers are similar to those in countries like Italy, reporting 93 percent of their businesses are family controlled, and Brazil, 90 percent.[13] (See Exhibit 14.2.)

EXHIBIT 14.2 WORLDWIDE HIGHLIGHTS OF FAMILY BUSINESSES

COUNTRY	% OF FAMILY BUSINESSES	CONTRIBUTION TO GNP
Brazil	90%	63%
Chile	75%	50%–70%
USA	96%	40%
Belgium	70%	55%
Finland	80%	40%–45%
France	>60%	>60%
Germany	60%	55%
Italy	93%	
Netherlands	74%	54%
Poland	Up to 80%	35%
Portugal	70%	60%
Spain	79%	
UK	70%	
Australia	75%	50%
India		65%

Once we acknowledge the economic relevance of families we can better understand the significant pool of resources and potential they represent for entrepreneurial activity. There was a day when "business" meant "family" because the family was understood to be foundational to all socioeconomic progress.[14] Today, however, we must more intentionally categorize the roles families play economically and entrepreneurially. Exhibit 14.3 presents five different roles families can play in the entrepreneurial process and distinguishes between a formal and informal application of these roles.

In this regard the categories are both descriptive and prescriptive. They describe what role families play and how they play them, but also hint at a prescription for a more formal approach to entrepreneurship in the family context. By "formal" we mean establishing individual and organizational disciplines and structure of the entrepreneurial process. We do not mean "bureaucratic." Many family entrepreneurs, particularly senior-generation entrepreneurs, embrace the myth that any formalization will constrain their entrepreneurial behaviour. Nothing could be further from the truth. With informed intuition, disciplined processes, clear financial benchmarks, and organizational accountability, family teams can generate higher potential ventures and get the odds in their favour for transgenerational entrepreneurship and wealth creation.

The first and dominant role families play is what we call *family-influenced start-ups*. Data from the Global Entrepreneurship Monitor indicate that worldwide there are about 25 million "new family firms" started every year.[15] Because families are driven by social forces of survival, wealth creation, and progeny, it is natural that start-up businesses think family first. Family-influenced start-ups are new businesses where the family ownership vision and/or leadership influence impacts the strategic intent, decision-making, and financial goals of the company. They may have family involvement in the beginning, intend to have family involvement, or end up having family involvement during the formative stages of the company. Some families begin their collective

EXHIBIT 14.3 ROLES FAMILIES PLAY IN THE ENTREPRENEURIAL PROCESS

	FAMILY-INFLUENCED START-UPS	FAMILY CORPORATE VENTURING	FAMILY CORPORATE RENEWAL	FAMILY PRIVATE CASH	FAMILY INVESTMENT FUNDS
Formal	An entrepreneur with no legacy assets/existing business, but who formally launches a new business with family and/or intending to involve family	Family holding companies or businesses that have formal new venture creation and/or acquisition strategies, plans, departments, or capabilities	Family-controlled companies with a formal strategic growth plan for creating new streams of value through change in business strategy, model, or structure	Start-up money from family member or business with a formal written agreement for market-base ROI and or repayment	Stand-alone professional private equity or venture capital fund controlled by family and/or using family generated capital
Informal	An entrepreneur with no legacy assets/existing business who happens to start a new business out of necessity and begins to involve family members	Family holding companies or businesses that grow through more informal, intuitive, and opportunistic business start-up and acquisitions	Intuitive growth initiatives that result in a change in business strategy, model, or structure and new streams of value for the family company	Start-up money or gift from family member or business with no agreement or conversation about ROI or repayment	Internal capital and/or funds used by family owners to invest in real estate, passive partnerships, or seed new businesses

entrepreneurship experience with a more formal vision and planning process that delineates how the family will capture a new opportunity. This approach often clarifies the role family members will play in the start-up and puts them on a faster path for successfully meeting their family and financial goals.

The *family corporate venturing category* is when an existing family company or group starts new businesses. Families are often, and quite naturally, portfolio entrepreneurs who build numerous businesses under a family umbrella. While they may not always grow each of the businesses to its fullest potential, the new businesses are often synergistic, create jobs for a community, and grow the net worth of the family. Often they are started so that family members have their own business to run. The more formal approach to family corporate venturing makes the new business process part of an overall strategic plan for growing family wealth while leveraging the resources and capabilities of family members.[16]

Family corporate renewal is where the family's entrepreneurial activity is focused on creating new streams of value within the business or group through innovation and transformational change activities. Companies that launch new products or services, enter new markets, or establish new business models are renewing their strategies for the future. This type of strategic or structural renewal is particularly prevalent during family generational transitions or when a family realizes their legacy business can no longer compete. A more formal approach to corporate renewal is proactive, continuous, and institutionalized versus waiting for transitions or competitive triggers to start the renewal processes.

One of the primary roles families play is to provide *family private cash* to family members who want to start a business. More than 63 percent of businesses in the planning stage and up to 85 percent of existing new ventures used family funding. Between 30 and 80 percent of all informal (non-venture capital) funding comes from family. In Canada this amounts to nearly

0.25 percent of GDP and as high as 3 percent of GDP in South Korea.[17] Most often the family cash is given based upon altruistic family sentiments rather than having more formal investment criteria. While providing seed capital, whether it is formal or informal, is clearly a significant role in the entrepreneurial process, having some formal investment criteria can avoid future confusion or conflict among family members. It also creates more discipline and accountability for family entrepreneurs, which is a good thing. (See Exhibit 14.4.)

Family investment funds are pools of family capital that families use for entrepreneurial activities. These family funds, both formal and informal, are becoming increasingly more common as families find themselves flush with cash. Most often, the formal family investment funds are created after a family has liquidated all or part of their family group. These funds are generally formed in conjunction with a family office. Informal family investment funds are pools of money, generally from cash flows, that family leaders invest in entrepreneurial activities as a way to diversify their family portfolios and/or have fun. They often invest within their network of peers and the investments are usually non-operating investments in businesses or real estate deals. These investments are often significant portions of their total wealth.

When we catalogue the wide range of informal and formal roles families can play in the entrepreneurial process, we see the contribution they are capable of making to the entrepreneurial economy. We believe business families who are interested in transgenerational entrepreneurship and wealth creation must cultivate the more formal approach to entrepreneurship. The remainder of this chapter assists families in formalizing their entrepreneurship roles. We present three strategy frames that are based on the Timmons Model introduced in chapter 2. The frames focus on the controllable components of the entrepreneurial processes that can be assessed, influenced, and altered.

FRAME ONE: THE MINDSET AND METHOD FOR FAMILY ENTERPRISING
LO3

Families who are enterprising are a particular type of family and *not* just a family who is in business. Enterprising families understand that today's dynamic and hypercompetitive marketplace requires families to act entrepreneurially. That is, they must generate new economic activity if they intend to survive and prosper over long periods of time. The Timmons Model shows us that at the heart of the entrepreneurial process is the opportunity. Those families who intend to act entrepreneurially must be opportunity focused. Consistent with this focus, enterprising is seen as the decision that leaders and organizations make to investigate opportunity and seek growth "when expansion is neither pressing nor particularly obvious."[18] The enterprising decision to search for opportunity precedes the economic decision to capture the opportunity. The "spirit of

---

EXHIBIT 14.4   **DISTRIBUTION OF BUSINESSES WITH FAMILY VENTURE BACKING**

	PLANNING STAGE START-UPS	NEW FIRMS	ESTABLISHED FIRMS
Number of Cases	1425	1594	3743
Family-Sponsored Ventures	63%	76%	85%

Source: Joseph H. Astrachan, Shaker A. Zahra, and Pramodita Sharma, "Family-Sponsored Ventures" First Annual Global Entrepreneurship Symposium, United Nations, April 29, 2003.

12 CHALLENGES TO FAMILY ENTERPRISING

Like the gravitational pull that keeps us bound to the earth, families face a number of inherent challenges that may keep them bound to past strategies rather than pursuing new opportunities.

1. Families assume that their past success will guarantee their future success.

2. Family members attribute "legacy value" to their businesses or assets, but that value does not translate into a market value or advantage.

3. Families want a "legacy pass" in the market—"We are 50 years old and we deserve another 50 years since we have been such good citizens."

4. Leaders try to balance the risk profile (risk and reward expectations) of their shareholders with the risk and investment demands of the marketplace.

5. Senior and successor generations have different risk profiles and goals for how the business should grow in the future.

6. Families find it hard to pass the entrepreneurial commitments and capabilities from the senior generation to a less "hungry" successor generation.

7. Families build their first-generation businesses on the founder's intuition, but the business never establishes more intentional entrepreneurial processes to keep the entrepreneurial contributions alive.

8. Families will not use many of the financial strategies that entrepreneurs use to grow businesses—i.e., debt, equity capital, strategic alliances, and partnerships.

9. Families do not "shed" unproductive assets and underperforming businesses to reallocate resources to more productive places.

10. Successor-generation family members feel entitled to get a business rather than seek next-generation entrepreneurial opportunity.

11. Senior leaders communicate to the next generation that business planning and entrepreneurial analysis is a waste of time.

12. Family members are given a business to run as part of their legacy and that is viewed as entrepreneurship in the family.

enterprising" is evidenced when families are faced with a decision (knowingly or unknowingly) to continue along their existing path or to expend effort and commit resources to investigate whether there are higher potential opportunities that are not yet obvious. We thus define family enterprising as the proactive and continuous search for opportunistic growth.

Enterprising families institutionalize the opportunity seeking processes in the mindset and methods of both their family ownership group and their business organizations. Those families who simply try to maintain their local advantage, safeguard their brands, assets, and customers, or hone their operational efficiencies put themselves at a competitive risk in the shorter run. In the longer run, if their strategic planning is mainly focused on how to pass their business from one generation to the next, rather than developing people and strategies for creating new streams of value, their future may be limited. We would certainly not describe these types of families as enterprising or assume that they are transgenerational.

ENTERPRISING MINDSET AND METHODS

The first assessment and strategy frame for family enterprising is the Mindset and Methods Model (Exhibit 14.5). The model shows that family enterprising is the combination of a financial ownership mindset and entrepreneurial strategic methods. The purpose of the model is to ensure that families talk about both the ownership *and* leadership requirements for carrying out the entrepreneurial process in their family and business. The mindset and methods assessment instruments[19] for this chapter (see end of chapter exercises) will enable families to determine their level of congruence on the two dimensions. It will also allow them to have a strategic conversation about where they currently are and how they might need to change to become more enterprising.

| EXHIBIT 14.5 | **MINDSET AND METHODS ENTERPRISING MODEL** |

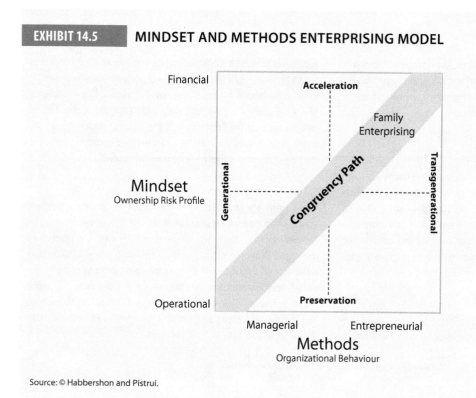

Source: © Habbershon and Pistrui.

The mindset continuum is primarily a measure of the financial risk profile of the family owners–shareholders. In general, it reflects the financial premise that entrepreneurial leaders gain strategic advantage and find above-normal rents by deploying their resources to points of highest return and by developing strategies that exploit new opportunity. Family leaders who have an operational mindset predominately focus on management strategies, operational efficiencies, and the perpetuity of a particular business. A financial mindset moves beyond the operational focus to an investor focus with a view toward the overall capital strategy of the family, creating new streams of value and finding a return on the totality of their assets. While the operational mindset is a requirement for running an efficient business, the financial focus is a requirement for transgenerational entrepreneurship and wealth creation.

The financial mindset for enterprising includes the following characteristics:[20]

- a proclivity for higher risk and above-normal returns
- a willingness to sell and redeploy assets to seek higher returns
- a desire to grow by creating new revenue streams with higher returns
- a commitment to generating next-generation entrepreneurship
- a willingness to continuously revisit the existing business model
- an assumption that a percentage of the business will become obsolete
- a willingness to leverage the business to grow and find higher returns
- a desire to reinvest versus distribute capital
- a willingness to enter into partnerships and alliances to grow

- a strategy to manage the family's wealth for a total return
- a commitment to innovation in business strategies and structures
- a belief that bold, wide-ranging acts are necessary to achieve investment objectives in today's environment

The *methods continuum* is a measure of the entrepreneurial orientation and the actions in the business organization. It assumes that enterprising organizations are taking bold, innovative, market leading actions to seek a competitive advantage and generate new streams of value. It also reflects the premise that to be enterprising (proactively and continuously seeking new opportunities for growth) organizations must have a collection of individuals who act like an entrepreneur and not just a single leader or small group of family leaders. A single leader acting entrepreneurially might generate entrepreneurial actions in the business during their generation, but it will not create a transgenerational family business or group. Enterprising organizations move beyond managerial methods that focus on maintaining the existing and implementing incremental change. They are seeking and creating "the new" and establishing entrepreneurial renewal processes. Dave Valliere of Ryerson University calls this entrepreneurial alertness.[21] While entrepreneurial methods do not replace the need for managerial actions, managerial actions are not sufficient conditions for enterprising and transgenerational wealth creation.

The entrepreneurial methods for enterprising include the following characteristics:[22]

- allocating disproportionate resources to new business opportunities
- systematically searching for and capturing new investment opportunities
- seeking new opportunities beyond the core (legacy) business
- creating a core competency in innovation at the business unit level
- making significant change in products, services, markets, and customers
- initiating competitive change to lead the market

- investing early to develop or adopt new technology and processes

- typically adopting an "undo the competitor" posture in the markets

- having institutionalized the entrepreneurial process in the organization

- having formal routines for gathering and disseminating market intelligence

- having people at every level in the organization "think like competitors"

- typically adopting a bold, aggressive posture to maximize the probability of exploiting potential investment opportunities

CREATING THE DIALOGUE FOR CONGRUENCE

The Mindset and Methods Model helps families fulfill key process conditions for family enterprising and transgenerational wealth creation:

> Creating a healthy *dialogue* in the family ownership group and organization around the mindset and methods issues.
>
> Establishing *congruence* between the mindset of the owner-shareholder group and the methods of the business organization(s).

One of the major differences between family enterprising and entrepreneurship as it is normally envisioned is that by definition the team includes the family. Family entrepreneurs are either currently working with family members or planning to work with family members; they are either multigenerational teams or hope to be a multigenerational team; they either have multiple family member shareholders and stakeholders or will have them as they go through time. This inherent familial condition requires families to cultivate effective communication skills to build relationship capital for family enterprising. Families know that it takes financial capital for entrepreneurial activity, but they do not always know that it also requires relationship capital. Relationship capital allows families to have healthy dialogue and find congruence around the mindset and methods for enterprising.[23]

Sabine Veit, founder of Bäckerhaus Veit in Toronto, realized the importance of dialogue and congruence when her son came home from university toting a business plan for aggressive growth. She had built her artisan bread manufacturing company into a $24-million force in the industry. When her son Toby won a business planning competition she was definitely proud, but she also knew she was in trouble. The plan was to grow *her* business. Sabine loved the thought of working with Toby and he definitely shared her passion for artisan breads. In fact, during university Toby took every class with the artisan bread industry in mind. How could a parent hope for anything more?

But Toby did not want to just run her company someday. He wanted to move the business beyond manufacturing and wholesaling into branded products and retailing, and he wanted to do it now. On the Mindset and Methods Model (Exhibit 14.6), Bäckerhaus Veit was on the congruency path as an operationally focused, managerially sound business. Sabine had a self-defined lifestyle firm that was competitive in her niche with a clear harvest strategy. But Toby was committed to family enterprising and wanted to be a growth firm. This meant moving beyond their current niche and lifestyle expectations. Clearly Toby had a mindset for much higher risk than Sabine.

On the methods continuum, Bäckerhaus Veit did not have the entrepreneurial methods to exploit Toby's plan. Sabine individually had the capabilities and Toby believed he did, but the entrepreneurial team and organization would have to be built. There was clearly significant incongruence as a family and business. The challenge for Sabine and Toby was to establish a plan and process for aligning their mindset and methods if they want to capture the new opportunity and become an enterprising family.

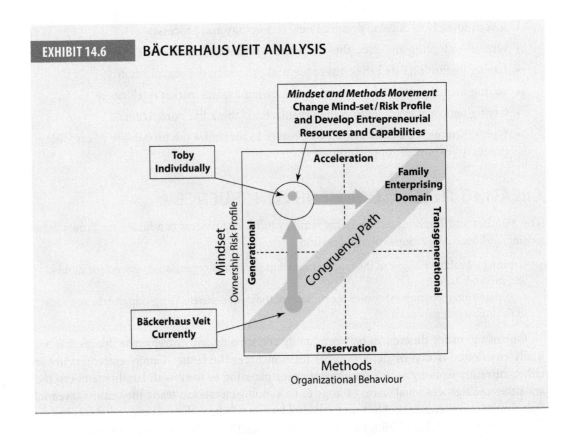

EXHIBIT 14.6   BÄCKERHAUS VEIT ANALYSIS

- Mindset and Methods Movement — Change Mind-set / Risk Profile and Develop Entrepreneurial Resources and Capabilities
- Toby Individually
- Acceleration
- Family Enterprising Domain
- Mindset — Ownership Risk Profile
- Generational
- Congruency Path
- Transgenerational
- Bäckerhaus Veit Currently
- Preservation
- Methods — Organizational Behaviour

SUCCESSFUL NEXT GENERATION ENTREPRENEURSHIP

The challenge for multigenerational family teams like Toby and Sabine is to "keep it in dialogue" rather than letting it turn into a debate or disconnect. Debates become personal and disconnects cut off opportunity. When family members turn the situation into right and wrong, good and bad, winning or losing, there is very little listening, give-and-take, or changing one's position. In contrast, the word dialogue actually means "talking through" an issue. It assumes the ability to challenge each other's assumptions, to keep an open mind, and to test different options. It looks at the big picture, considers the long-term perspective, and discusses the process for getting there. Most important, dialogue does not follow hierarchical roles like parent-child, boss-employee, or the one who owns the business versus the one who does not. The goal of dialogue is to find solutions that are not constrained by the boundaries of either of the original positions.

There are a number of things Toby and Sabine need to do to ensure they are an enterprising family. First, they need to develop communication skills to have an effective dialogue. Most families assume they are able to carry on a dialogue simply because they are a family. In actuality the familiarity of a family can make it very difficult to challenge assumptions and talk about differing views. Often families need a facilitator to help them develop communication skill and have a dialogue.

Second, they need to make sure their views of the future are the same. Families often have a vague notion of "working together" and they assume that they will figure the details out over time. This is a clear formula for future discontent and conflict. In reality, Toby and Sabine had very different visions for their futures. Sabine's vision was to enjoy her passion for breads while balancing growth with her lifestyle interests. Toby's vision was to exploit his passion for breads by building new businesses on the family's reputation and skills.

Third, Toby and Sabine had very different risk profiles. What Sabine was willing to risk for future returns was different from what Toby was willing to risk and the returns he desired. It is not surprising that the successor generation is willing to risk more than the senior generation. The key is to keep talking until you understand each other's perspective. Once you understand each other you can create a business model and structure that accommodates the risk profiles of both generations. Locking into one generational perspective or the other undermines the collective strengths of a multigenerational team.

Fourth, timing is everything. Usually for the successors the time is now and for the seniors the time is *someday*. Chances are that both generations will end up out of their comfort zones a little. Toby and Sabine realized that timing was really a strategy question of how they would proceed, not just if or when they would proceed.

Fifth, get creative. You can be sure that the final outcome will not look exactly like either of you envisioned. Through dialogue it became clear to Toby and Sabine that the range of options was fairly extensive. We often tell family members to "remember their algebra" when it comes to dialogue. Just because "a equals b" it does not mean that "a" might not equal "c, d, or even e, f, and g." The point is that once you start a true dialogue, you may find many more options than you originally envisioned.

Even among entrepreneurs with no family directly involved with their venture, family concerns persist—just as they do for any individual in the workforce. Such work-family conflicts may hit entrepreneurs harder than those who are simply employees.[24] Jennifer Jennings and Megan McDougald, both of the University of Alberta, suggest "greater work-family conflict is likely to be experienced by female entrepreneurs" and that "growth facilitating" strategies will be more likely with lower levels of work–family conflict.[25] The Canadian Association of Family Enterprise, cafecanada.ca, regularly features discussions on work/life, multigenerational issues for Canadian family-owned firms.[26]

FRAME TWO: THE SIX DIMENSIONS FOR FAMILY ENTERPRISING   LO4

The second assessment and strategy frame for family enterprising addresses the team component of the Timmons Model. In family enterprising "team" is a much broader and complex concept. It encompasses the family ownership group and the family and non-family entrepreneurial capabilities. The entrepreneurial process cannot occur unless there is alignment in the team's ownership mindset and entrepreneurial methods as described above. When the entrepreneurial leader is a family member there is potentially another layer of team complexity around issues such as parent-child relationships, altruistic versus entrepreneurial decision-making, nepotism and competency, family versus personal equity and compensation, and success measures. In essence, the family as team can create more perfect balance in the Timmons Model or can cause imbalance. One key is to stay focused on the opportunity and stress that the team is in support of exploiting that opportunity.

The six dimensions for family enterprising provide family teams with six areas that they can address to assist them in aligning their mindset and methods and moving up the congruency path toward the enterprising domain. The six dimensions and the corresponding strategic questions apply key entrepreneurial considerations to the family context. As family owners and leaders answer the questions they are creating unity within the team for entrepreneurial action. The six dimensions are as follows:

- ✔ Leadership
- ✔ Relationship

- ✔ Vision
- ✔ Strategy
- ✔ Governance
- ✔ Performance

There is an internal logic and order to the six dimensions. We begin with the *leadership dimension* because leaders are the catalyst for organizational behaviour and have the responsibility for creating the team. Leaders also set the tone for the relationship commitments and culture in the family and organization. The *relationship dimension* is often overlooked, but it is the foundation for organizational effectiveness and health, especially in family teams and enterprising. For an entrepreneur, the vision dimension involves knowing or seeing where you want to go, even if the in-between details have yet to be resolved. The *strategy dimension* flows out of the leadership and relationship dimensions. At the end of the day, strategy and planning are simply extended organizational conversations. Organizational strategy is only as effective as the leadership and relationships in the family and organization. Governance structures and policies simply enable organizations to carry out their strategies. The *governance dimension* must, therefore, follow both ownership and business strategy formulation. In an interesting way, the *performance dimension* is the last dimension because it is an organizational outcome, but it is also feedback that leaders use to frame their leadership actions.

LEADERSHIP DIMENSION—DOES YOUR LEADERSHIP CREATE A SENSE OF SHARED URGENCY FOR ENTERPRISING AND TRANSGENERATIONAL WEALTH CREATION?

Entrepreneurial leaders create a sense of shared urgency in the organization. The goal is to have everyone, from the owners to those carrying out routine tasks, thinking and acting to find an advantage over the competition.[27] Families traditionally and systemically follow hierarchical and stereotypical patterns—parent-child, older-younger siblings, male-female—and their family organizations often embody these stereotypes in their leadership models. A transgenerational commitment requires families to move beyond the "great leader" model to the "great group."[28] Family leaders who strive to turn their families into a team based upon the great group philosophy overcome many of the negative caricatures often associated with family business leadership and empower the family and organization to be enterprising.

Leadership Dimension Diagnostic Questions

- Do family leaders understand the requirements to be transgenerational?
- Do they develop next-generation leadership?
- Do they move the family beyond the "great leader" model?
- Do they promote a sense of openness and mutuality?
- Do they encourage participation by family members at all levels in the family and organization?
- Do they lead others to think and act like entrepreneurs?
- Do they help the family grow beyond a hierarchical model of leadership to become the "great group"?

RELATIONSHIP DIMENSION—DOES YOUR FAMILY HAVE THE RELATIONSHIP CAPITAL TO SUSTAIN THEIR TRANSGENERATIONAL COMMITMENTS?

Effective teams are built upon healthy relationships. We describe healthy relationships as those that build relationship capital and allow efficient interpersonal interactions in the team. Relationship capital is the reserve of attributes such as trust, loyalty, positive feelings, benefit of the doubt, goodwill, forgiveness, commitment, and altruistic motives. Relationship capital is a necessary condition for long-lasting teams and transgenerational families. Now here are two opposite but simultaneously true statements: Families have the natural potential to build relationship capital better than other social groups *and* families have the natural potential to destroy relationship capital more ruthlessly than any other social group. Is this good news or bad news for family enterprising? It depends. Those families who intentionally gain the skills and strive to build relationship capital leverage the natural advantage of family teams. But those families who assume they will always have relationship capital or take their relationships for granted open themselves up to potentially destructive tendencies of families. Families who have relationship capital reserves are more likely to create the dialogue that moves them up the congruence path to the family enterprising domain.

Relationship Dimension Diagnostic Questions

- Is your family intentionally building relationship capital?
- Are you investing in the communication and relationship building skills you need to build relationship capital?
- Are there healthy relationships between family siblings, branches, and across generations?
- Does your family have formal family meetings to discuss family ownership and relationship issues?
- Do you experience synergy in your family relationships?
- Do you have a positive vision for working together as a family?
- Do family members see relationship health as part of their competitive advantage?

VISION DIMENSION—DOES YOUR FAMILY HAVE A COMPELLING MULTIGENERATIONAL VISION THAT ENERGIZES PEOPLE AT EVERY LEVEL?

A compelling vision is what creates the shared urgency for family enterprising and mobilizes people to carry out the vision. By compelling we mean that it "makes sense" to people in light of tomorrow's marketplace realities. Often a vision might make sense for the moment, but it does not make sense for the future. For enterprising families, the vision must describe how the family will collectively create new streams of wealth that allow them to be transgenerational. It also has to be multigenerational. It is easy for the different generations to craft their personal visions for the future. Transgenerational families must craft a vision that is compelling to all generations and in a sense transcends generational perspectives. This multigenerational necessity also underscores the importance of establishing participatory leadership and building relationship capital.

Vision Dimension Diagnostic Questions

- Does your family have a vision that makes sense of tomorrow's marketplace?
- Would all generations describe the vision as compelling?
- Was the vision developed by everyone in the family?

- Does the vision have relevance for your decision making and lives?
- Does your family regularly review and test the vision as an ownership group?
- Is the vision transgenerational?
- Is the vision larger than the personal interests of the family?
- Does the vision mobilize others to create new streams of value?
- Do all family members share in the rewards from the vision?

STRATEGY DIMENSION—DOES YOUR FAMILY HAVE AN INTENTIONAL STRATEGY FOR FINDING THEIR COMPETITIVE ADVANTAGE AS A FAMILY?

We have already said that there is a more intentional and formal application of the entrepreneurial process within the family context. Part of that formal approach is developing strategies for both cultivating and capturing new business opportunities. But for families it means much more. The family's strategic thinking and planning should be based on determining how to exploit their unique family-based resources and capabilities to find advantages in enterprising. While we will address this more specifically in the next section, it includes things like finding synergies with current assets, leveraging their networks of personal relationships, cultivating next-generation entrepreneurs, and extending the power of their family reputation. Because families tend to take their family-influenced resources and capabilities for granted they often fail to see the opportunities they represent for providing them with a long-term advantage for enterprising.

Strategy Dimension Diagnostic Questions

- How does your family provide you with an advantage in entrepreneurial wealth creation?
- What resources and capabilities are unique to your family?
- Does your family have a formal planning process to direct their enterprising?
- Does your organization have formal systems for cultivating and capturing new opportunities?
- Does your family mentor next-generation family members to become entrepreneurs?
- Does your strategic thinking and planning empower your family to fulfill their transgenerational vision?
- What role does your family play in the strategy process?

GOVERNANCE DIMENSION—DOES YOUR FAMILY HAVE STRUCTURES AND POLICIES THAT STIMULATE CHANGE AND GROWTH IN THE FAMILY AND ORGANIZATION?

Few family leaders would consider that governance structures and policies could actually stimulate growth and change. Most would equate the word *governance* with bureaucracies and, at best, acknowledge that structures and policies are a necessary evil to be tolerated and minimized. But we offer two different perspectives. First, the lack of effective governance structures and policies creates significant ambiguity in families and constrains enterprising. Second, when entrepreneurial processes are institutionalized through the governance structures and policies it promotes growth and change activities. For example, when ownership, equity, or value realization is unclear or un-discussable it dis-incentivizes family entrepreneurs. But when financial conversations are part of the professional culture and there are transparent ownership structures, family entrepreneurs are clear on the rules of the game. Governance structures are thus critical to transgenerational entrepreneurship and wealth creation. Danny Miller of HEC Montreal and the University of Alberta, Isabelle Le Breton-Miller of the University of Alberta, and Richard Lester of Texas A&M University find that family owners' ties to one another lead to entrenchment, resource extraction, and conservative strategies, whereas entrepreneur owners without family ties pursue growth priorities and invest more in the firm.[29]

Governance Dimension Diagnostic Questions

- Does your family view governance as a positive part of their family and business lives?
- Are your governance structures static or fluid?
- Do your structures and policies promote family unity?
- Do your governance structures and policies give an appropriate voice to family members?
- Do your governance structures and policies assist you in finding your family advantage?
- Do you have formal processes that institutionalize the entrepreneurial process in your family and businesses?
- Do your governance structures and policies promote next-generation involvement and entrepreneurship?

PERFORMANCE DIMENSION—DOES YOUR PERFORMANCE MEET THE REQUIREMENTS FOR TRANSGENERATIONAL ENTREPRENEURSHIP AND WEALTH CREATION?

The performance dimension is where families clarify whether or not they are really committed to family enterprising. Families who are enterprising are market driven and seek to accelerate their wealth creation through their opportunistic entrepreneurial actions. They have clear financial benchmarks and information for assessing their performance against the market. Lifestyle firms often assume that they are performing well because they are sustaining their lifestyles. Enterprising also implies a process of matching the organization's core competencies with external opportunities to create new streams of value. Enterprising families do not rely on past performance as an indicator that they will perform well in the future, nor do they define success simply by the preservation of an asset. Their success measures are their ability to fulfill their transgenerational vision for social and economic wealth creation.

Performance Dimension Diagnostic Questions

- Does your family talk openly about financial performance issues or are finances secretive?
- Are you in lifestyle or enterprising mode?
- Are your performance and strategies driven by a clear market orientation?
- Do family owners agree on their risk and return expectations?
- Are performance expectations clear to next-generation entrepreneurs?
- Are there clear transparency and accountability structures in relation to meeting performance expectations?
- Is there family dialogue about performance expectations—growth, dividends, reinvestment, ROE?

FRAME THREE: THE FAMILINESS ADVANTAGE FOR FAMILY ENTERPRISING

All entrepreneurial success and the opportunity to capture above-average returns is premised upon finding an advantage over your competitors. Correspondingly, the potential for finding an advantage is rooted in the distinctive resources and capabilities that an organization possesses. The "resources" aspect of the Timmons Model is where enterprising can get exciting for families. Because every family is unique, they can generate idiosyncratic bundles of resources and capabilities that can give them an advantage in the entrepreneurial process if they know how to identify and leverage them. We refer to this idiosyncratic bundle of resources and capabilities as their *familiness*.

The Family Systems Model in Exhibit 14.7 shows how the familiness bundle of resources and capabilities is generated. As the vision, history, and capabilities of the collective family interact with the goals, skills, and commitments of the individual family members, and they both in turn interact with the organizational history, culture, and resources of the business entities, it creates this familiness effect or the "f factor" of resources$_f$ and capabilities$_f$. If we think of the four resource categories in chapter 8—people, financial, assets, and plan—we can explore how the systemic family influence impacts, changes, or somehow reconfigures the properties of the resource. We identify familiness resources and capabilities with a subscript "f" such as capital$_f$, leadership$_f$, networking$_f$, knowledge$_f$, reputation$_f$.

The familiness assessment frame helps families become realists. What we mean is the assessment process leads families to realistically evaluate where their family influence might be positive and where it might be negative. One of the key insights from this model is the understanding that family cannot be characterized as either good or bad. Rather, family influence must be viewed as one of the inputs that entrepreneurs need to intentionally manage. As family leaders manage the

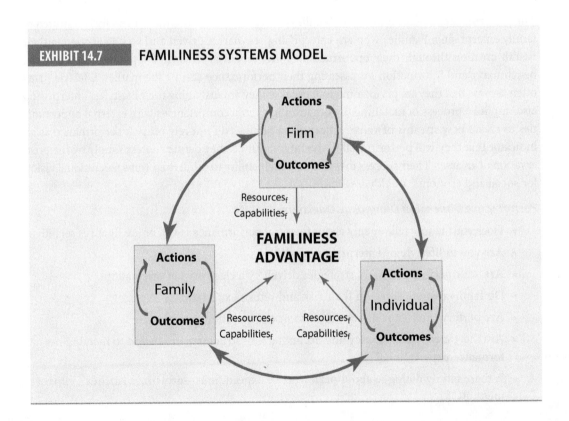

EXHIBIT 14.7 **FAMILINESS SYSTEMS MODEL**

actions and outcomes within the subsystems—family unit, individuals, and business entities—and between the subsystems, they are managing their bundle of resources$_f$ and capabilities$_f$.

When these familiness resources$_f$ and capabilities$_f$ lead to a competitive advantage for the family we refer to them as "distinctive familiness" or an "f+." When they constrain the competitive enterprising ability of the family we refer to them as "constrictive familiness" or "f–." Exhibit 14.8 allows families to place their resources and capabilities on an assessment continuum. The job of families who desire to be enterprising is to determine how to generate and exploit their distinctive familiness and to minimize or shed their constrictive familiness. When families begin assessing and planning based upon their distinctive and constrictive familiness, they move from an intuitive and informal to the intentional and formal mode of family enterprising.

To better understand familiness let's return to the family enterprising decision that Toby and Sabine have to make in regard to Bäckerhaus Veit (BV). If we analyze the distinctive (f+) and constrictive (f–) familiness in their situation we can bring significant focus to the dialogue and move them along the mindset and methods congruence path.

Exhibit 14.9 is their familiness resources and capabilities continuum as it relates to the new venture opportunity. When you see the f+ f– assessment it is a comprehensive and revealing picture of their individual and organizational contribution to the new venture. But it is not only the

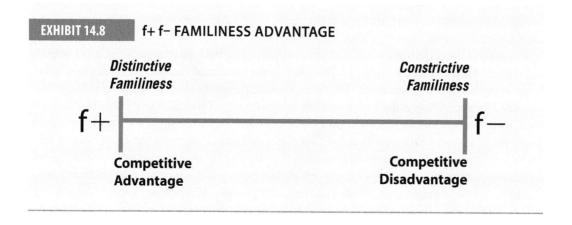

EXHIBIT 14.8   f+ f– FAMILINESS ADVANTAGE

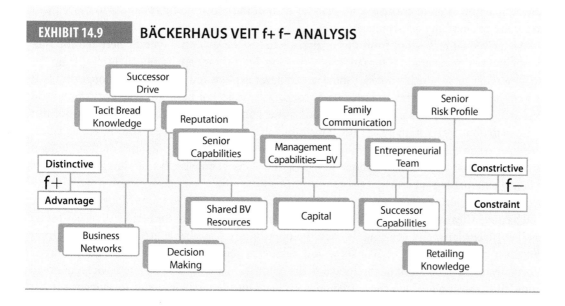

EXHIBIT 14.9   BÄCKERHAUS VEIT f+ f– ANALYSIS

final picture that is useful to families. The conversation to identify the resources and capabilities and to determine where they should be placed is the real learning outcome.

First, there are clear resources and capabilities specifically associated with the senior and successor generations and others that are mixed. While Toby's successor drive is an f+ his business capabilities and lack of experience are an f–. Sabine readily admits that without Toby's drive she would never consider this opportunity. But Sabine's advisors are concerned that Toby may overestimate his capabilities and contribution. This discussion is very natural in next-generation entrepreneurship and families should "normalize" it and not allow it to become personal. Conversely, Sabine's senior capabilities, business networks, and reputation are an f+ for Toby's new venture. Toby readily admits that Sabine's role makes his business plan a much higher potential venture. On the other hand, Sabine's risk profile and lifestyle goals are a significant f– and constraint to enterprising. But we need to remember that they fit very well for her current strategy.

Second, there are resources and capabilities associated with BV; in many ways BV *is* Sabine. Toby's business plan calls for BV to provide valuable shared resources such as wholesale bread supply, bookkeeping, used equipment, repair services, and the like. This opportunity creates a very significant resource advantage that we would call "plan$_{f+}$" because only family members with existing businesses could incorporate these into their plan. The existing venture team capabilities are also an f+, but because the existing team is not entrepreneurial (in fact, they see the new venture as a drain on the existing business), we have to give an f– to entrepreneurial team.

Third, there are certain resources that are associated with both Sabine and Toby. Most important is the f+ for tacit bread knowledge. They both know bread making, but the particularly interesting point is to see how advanced Toby is as a young person because he grew up in the bread industry. Correspondingly, the f– for retailing is significant. While Sabine grew up in the retail bread industry (her family has 70 retail bakeries in Germany), she does not know the casual dining bread industry (like Panera Bread Company) and this is the target for Toby's plan. While decision making is an f+, family communication is an f–. The family has great relationships, but in the business setting, they sometimes communicate like mother and son rather than business peers.

The f+ to f– continuum makes Toby's and Sabine's "pre-launch" work very clear. Managing the f+ to f– continuum is how families build their resources and capabilities bundle as part of formalizing the entrepreneurial process. It is a critical step in getting the odds more in their favour. Toby and Sabine now need to create a work plan for each of the constraining resources to move them to a point of neutrality or advantage.

An additional realization from this analysis is to see the potential synergy between the successor and senior generations for family enterprising. Four things are immediately clear from the analysis. First, as we already noted, Sabine would never explore and/or capture this opportunity if it were not for Toby driving the process. Second, Toby does not have the synergistic familiness resources and capabilities if he tries to do the business on his own. Third, while there are positive reasons to do it together, there are also constraints that must be addressed. Fourth, family enterprising is when they decide to do it together as a family, rather than not doing it, or Toby doing it on his own. That is not to say that one way is right or wrong, but simply that doing it together is a family enterprising approach.

We will provide a final assessment of Sabine and Toby using the Timmons Model to discuss fit and balance. Clearly the opportunity for Bäckerhaus Veit to move into the retail fast-casual-eating market is very large and growing. In fact, the opportunity is probably greater than the current resources and capabilities of BV, Toby, and Sabine to meet them without outside resources. Currently, the weakest link in the model is the team. While Toby and Sabine have great bread knowledge, they do not have the entrepreneurial team for the retailing initiative. Further, the BV leaders and advisors are strongly committed to managing their current assets, rather than launching an entrepreneurial business. Exhibit 14.10 shows that the model is "out of balance" and reaffirms the conclusions from our previous assessment that there is significant pre-launch work to be done to ensure a "fit." If they do this pre-launch work and can get the Timmons Model into balance, however, they have a great high potential venture for the family.

Ultimately, Sabine moved BV to a fresh-frozen product. BV was relocating into a new facility in 2014, double the size of the current location. According to Sabine "Aside from moving, we're investing money in getting more efficient."[30] Toby worked for BV in a sales and marketing capacity. He and his mom received a consultation with his class and created a board of advisors, and together determined what his job and salary would be when he graduated. Eventually Toby left BV to pursue studies at IMD in Switzerland and then became a management consultant at Fidelity Investments in Boston, Massachusetts.

SUCCESSION

LO6

Familiness can be an advantage when it comes to succession as well. According to Grant Walsh, Director of KPMG Canada's Centre for Family Business, "History has proven that the influence of the family (active and non-active family members) on the business is too important not to make it one of, if not the major component of the succession process."[31]

Four generations have managed to keep Butler Byers Insurance Ltd. going for 100 years. The Byers family is at the helm of one of the largest family-owned insurance brokers in Western Canada. Drew Byers, president, indicates that succession was "a very natural process that came about during a restructuring of the companies...buying out his father was a natural process with no real drama attached to it." It was Drew's desire to take over, not a sense of obligation or duty that led him on a long path to president of the firm. The next handover is "way off," but they are already making certain that the groundwork is "laid early for that process." The Byers family has recently started a "family council to open the lines of communication that they know are vital to healthy business families."[32]

EXHIBIT 14.10   **TIMMONS MODEL FOR BÄCKERHAUS VEIT**

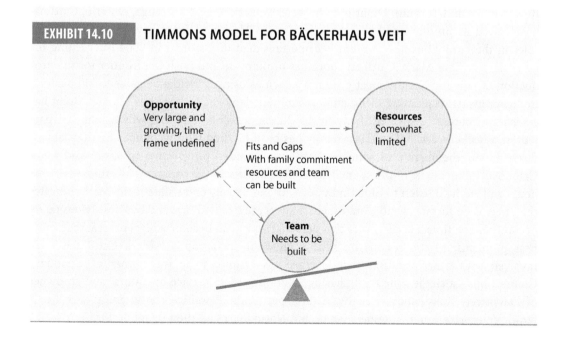

The third generation of Teppermans, Andrew and Noah, transitioned to take charge of the family's four furniture stores in Southwestern Ontario in 2006, becoming president and treasurer respectively. Noah even maintained the company's twitter account. The brothers' parents, Rochelle and Bill Tepperman, still maintained important roles in the family business, as chair and vice-chair of the board respectively. The brothers knew the family story well and had an appreciation for their grandfather's hard work. In 1925, Nate Tepperman, a Russian immigrant, began working as a door-to-door peddler; four years later he opened his first store in Windsor, Ontario.[33] With his wife, Bill took over the business in 1970 when his father drowned while swimming in the ocean. In 1992, their one-year-old store in Chatham, Ontario, burned to the ground, but this did not halt growth and the Teppermans continued to expand. In 1997, Andrew became general manager of the London, Ontario, store and in 2000 Noah became Director of Human Resources, overseeing a staff of nearly 300 employees.[34]

The Wilson family has been in business in Nova Scotia for eight generations! Wilson Fuel's original incarnation was as a distributor of wood and coal for home heating. They moved to heating oil and then became a full service home heating company offering equipment sales and leasing, delivery of furnace oil, propane, and biofuel. Today they have nearly 300 retail gas stations throughout Atlantic Canada. Ian Wilson recounts how he got to where he is now:

> I did not see myself working in the family business when I was growing up. I did not grow up sweeping the floors at the business or with any regular involvement. I would occasionally visit the office with my father but never felt any pressure to become involved. I did not work at Wilson Fuel until after achieving a university degree and even then, it was a summer job to earn money for further education. Once I became involved with the business I did not really think about taking a leadership role. After seven years of work and at the age of thirty, I was thrust into the role when my father, the president of the company, died unexpectedly. I was the only family member who was active in a day to day role at the business and I volunteered to become the president of the company.[35]

Family lore has it that Jack Cator started in the meat business with a sledgehammer and knife. He would buy a steer, butcher it in a barn, and sell the meat. His son Ralph Cator founded Cardinal Meat Specialists Ltd. in 1966. From the farm to butcher shops in Bowmanville and Toronto, Ontario, to burger production in Mississauga, Ontario, Cardinal has evolved its products and processes. Jack's sons Mark and Brent have played important roles in the family business.[36] Brent became President of Cardinal in 2004, succeeding his father and brother Mark. Cardinal continues to innovate and push the frontier for the production of safe and healthy meat products—such as using a "oxidative gases to kill bacteria in the air inside its plants, a tactic more commonly deployed in hospitals." In fact, Brent has a separate venture "dedicated solely to developing a technology that will at long last pasteurize a beef carcass."[37] The Cator family has been holding family councils for 20 years—a dozen family members plus spouses; "We even included prospective spouses," said Mark Cator. Not all members of the council are active partners in the company. Meetings last three hours and are held seven to nine times per year and usually end with a meal. Mark indicates that there is no formal agenda, but urgent matters are handled first and business issues rarely occupy half the time. He also notes that personal issues can become a bigger threat than business problems, so discussions on raising children are apropos.[38] Mark Cator has been involved with other ventures that leverage his resources: he was owner of Coolinary Connection—"a single source purchasing solution for foodservice operators" and co-owner of Pawsitively Raw Foods—healthy, natural pet foods. Pawsitively Raw Foods was also a family enterprise run by founders Janice and Norm Starr and their daughter Lisa.

SUCCESSION? MAYBE.

With its start as a "humble farm harvesting blueberries," the Bragg Group of Companies today holds the biggest slice of the global blueberry market, is a large producer of carrots, includes a building-supply chain, a company that reclaims airplane de-icing fluid, and Canada's largest privately owned cable-TV company. John Bragg, with a net worth estimated at $811 million in 2012, is the fifth generation and at age 74 has no succession plan and does not know when he will retire. In fact he has not decided if control will pass to one of his four children (Lee, Matthew, Carolyn, and Patricia), all of whom are involved in the Bragg Group, or an outsider such as David Hoffman, co-CEO of the Bragg Group of Companies. John Bragg knows he cannot control the fate of the company, but would prefer to see the Bragg Group stay together under family control. Finally he says, "I want them to think of themselves as trustees, rather than inheritors. If it's an inheritance, you think it's for you. If you're a trustee, you know it's for the next generation."[39]

SUCCESSION? NO.

For Kenneth Levene, the third generation owner of his family's Crescent Furniture, the solution to succession was to exit the business and sell the chain. And he has no regrets, confident that he made the right decision, particularly given the rise of the big box stores and national chains. According to Levene, "Succession planning can be difficult, especially when two adult children who are close in age are involved in the process...always expect the unexpected and have some provisions for unanticipated events. In many cases with a family business, those who started the business have a driven personality and are successful at the beginning; however, often the qualities and skills needed to start a business may not be adequate once the business grows and becomes established."[40] Kenneth Levene went on to focus on other matters of interest and 21 years after selling his family's furniture business he donated $4 million to the University of Regina's Graduate School of Business.

SUCCESSION WOES

The Avedis Zildjian Company is a cymbal manufacturer founded nearly 400 years ago in Turkey by an Armenian named Avedis Zildjian. For centuries, the family tradition was to keep metallurgical secrets and pass the business to one heir. In 1908 Avedis Zildjian III and his uncle Aram Zildjian began manufacturing cymbals in Quincy, Massachusetts, and began competing with K. Zildjian company back in Turkey around 1928! In 1968 Avedis Zildjian Co. bought K. Zildjian Co. and all European trademarks and opened production in Meductic, New Brunswick, to complement production in Massachusetts and Istanbul, Turkey. In early 1977 Armand Zildjian, Avedis Zildjian III's eldest son, was appointed president. Avedis Zildjian III died in 1979 at age 90. Avedis had broken tradition by passing the secrets to both his sons Armand and Robert. Armand passed the secrets and family namesake to his daughters Craigie and Debbie, and now their daughters Cady, Emily, and Samantha are involved in the family enterprise.

In 1981 Robert Zildjian, son of Avedis Zildjian III, continued the family tradition and started making Sabian cymbals in the Meductic facility. After a family feud and legal proceedings Robert became a rival of his older brother. The name Sabian is derived from the first two letters of the names of his three children Sally, Billy, and Andy. Today Andy is the president of Sabian. There appears to be another Zildjian family feud brewing, this time between Bill Zildjian and Sabian.

The Phelan family took Cara Operations, which was founded in 1883, public in 1968. But in 2004 sisters Gail and Rosemary, along with a deceased sister's daughter Holiday took the company private against the wishes of the sisters' estranged brother Paul. It was the death in 2002 of 84-year-old father of Gail, Rosemary, and Paul that caused the ill feelings. He failed to provide a clear succession plan before his health deteriorated. A full-on family feud ensued. But this is not an isolated case, within Canada, or even within this industry. The McCain family split over control over their empire resulting in one brother breaking off to head Maple Leaf Foods. The Bata family too has squabbled over the family shoe business. Eaton's and Canwest Global's economic woes are tied to family turmoil. Meanwhile the Sobey family and Westons have stuck to business as they battle in the competitive supermarket space. The Comrie and Leon families behind the Brick Warehouse and Leon's Furniture respectively have also managed to keep an eye on economic competition rather than family battles.

CONCLUSION

For those business families who would like to act more entrepreneurially and become an intentional enterprising family that has multiple generations seeking higher potential opportunities we suggest that there are four strategic shifts that may need to occur:

- From a lifestyle firm that has the goal of personal comfort to an enterprising family committed to transgenerational entrepreneurship and wealth creation.

- From an intuitive family business that "kicks around" to see what new opportunities turn up (as one family entrepreneur described it) to an intentional entrepreneurial process that seeks to generate and capture new opportunities.

- From a senior-generation entrepreneur who does it to a successor-generation entrepreneurial process and team that create opportunities for others to do it.

- From a "low potential" entrepreneurial family that creates one-off businesses as they can to a "higher potential" entrepreneurial family that mobilizes resources to create transgenerational wealth.

LEARNING OBJECTIVE SUMMARY

LO1 We began by demonstrating the significant contributions families make to the economy and entrepreneurial process. It is often overlooked that the majority of the businesses worldwide are controlled and led by families, including many of the largest businesses that we normally do not associate with family.

LO2 Families play a diverse number of formal and informal roles in the entrepreneurial process. We described them as (a) the family-influenced start-up, (b) family corporate venturing, (c) family corporate renewal, (d) family private cash, and (e) family investment funds.

LO3 The mindset continuum assesses the family's risk profile and those interested in a move from an operational to a financial investor strategy. The methods continuum assesses the organizational behaviour of leaders and organizations and requires a move from managerial to entrepreneurial strategies for enterprising.

LO4 There are six dimensions for family enterprising that were described as antecedents from the entrepreneurship literature: leadership, relationship, vision, strategy, governance, and performance. The chapter presented key questions on each dimension to assist families in becoming more enterprising.

LO5 We defined the familiness of an organization as the unique bundle of resources and capabilities that result from the interaction of the family and individual family members with the business entities. Families can have positive and negative family influence, which we described as an f+ or f–.

LO6 Family enterprising was defined as the proactive and continuous search for opportunistic growth when expansion is neither pressing nor particularly obvious. The outcome of family enterprising is transgenerational entrepreneurship and wealth creation through balance in the Timmons Model. Succession planning is an important part of family enterprising.

STUDY QUESTIONS

1. What are the entrepreneurial implications of not appreciating or understanding the role and contribution of families to the economies of our communities and countries?
2. Describe the advantages of a more formal approach on each of the roles families play in the entrepreneurial process. Give a few contrasting examples from a family firm with which you are familiar.
3. Define family enterprising, familiness, and relationship capital and relate each of them to the Timmons Model of the entrepreneurial process.
4. How do the six dimensions for family enterprising relate to one another? How do they enhance family enterprising? Describe how the six dimensions can be used to stimulate positive family dialogue.
5. If a family is trying to find their competitive advantage, how can the familiness assessment approach help them? How is the familiness approach a more formal application of the entrepreneurial process? How can the familiness approach change the family dialogue?
6. Given the familiness assessment of Bäckerhaus Veit in this chapter, describe why Sabine should or should not partner with Toby to implement his business plan. Describe the familiness action steps that they should take if you say they should launch the business. Describe the familiness reasons for why they possibly should not launch the business.

MIND STRETCHERS   *Have you considered?*

1. Like a bumblebee that should not be able to fly, it is said that family businesses should not be able to compete. Why might this be a true statement? Why are families so economically dominant worldwide if they are like the bumblebee?
2. How can a lifestyle firm be both a fine choice for a family and a dangerous choice for a family at the same time?
3. Give 10 reasons why dialogue can be harder for families than non-families even though families are supposed to have closer relationships.
4. If you were a Bronfman successor-generation family member, what expectations would you have about your future?
5. Research the children of entrepreneurs, such as Jamie Johnson, Howard Buffet, Paris Hilton, and Jennifer Gates, perhaps by watching the documentary *Born Rich* by Jamie Johnson (heir to the Johnson & Johnson fortune). What did you learn about wealth and entrepreneurship? Are wealthy families the same as entrepreneurial families? Is Jamie Johnson entrepreneurial? Is Paris Hilton entrepreneurial? Is this the same as family enterprising? What are their family legacies?

Determine where your family is on the mindset and methods continuum and what familiness advantage you might have for enterprising. Fill out the assessment surveys, plot your family group on the Family Enterprising Model, and fill out the resources and capabilities continuum.

Mindset Continuum

The mindset continuum establishes the family's financial risk and return expectations and their competitive posture in relation to the marketplace. There are no right and wrong answers. The point of the assessment is to surface family members' beliefs and fuel the family dialogue.

Using the assessment continuums, have the family member shareholders and future shareholders answer the questions on the mindset continuum listed below. Circle the number between the two statements that best reflects the strength of your belief about the family as a shareholder group. Total scores are between 12 and 84 reflecting views from the most traditional to the most enterprising.

In general, family member shareholders…

Have a strong proclivity for low-risk businesses and investment opportunities (with normal and certain returns).	1 2 3 4 5 6 7	Have a strong proclivity for high-risk business and investment opportunities (with chances for high returns).
Would sacrifice a higher return to preserve the family's legacy business.	1 2 3 4 5 6 7	Are willing to sell and redeploy their assets to find a higher return in the market.
Tend to think about cultivating our current businesses for current returns.	1 2 3 4 5 6 7	Desire to grow by creating new revenue streams with higher possibilities for returns.
Have a commitment to operating the business and providing job opportunities for family.	1 2 3 4 5 6 7	Have a commitment to mentoring next-generation entrepreneurs to create new streams of value.
Feel we have a good business model that will take us into the future.	1 2 3 4 5 6 7	Feel we should continuously revisit the assumptions of our business model.
Feel that our current businesses and products will serve us well in the future.	1 2 3 4 5 6 7	Assume that a significant percentage of our businesses will become obsolete.
Desire to avoid debt and grow with internally generated cash as we can.	1 2 3 4 5 6 7	Are willing to leverage the businesses to grow and find higher returns in the market.
Desire to increase our financial ability to provide distributions and/or liquidity.	1 2 3 4 5 6 7	Desire to reinvest more aggressively for faster growth and higher returns.
Desire to grow within our current financial and equity structures in order to ensure control over our destiny.	1 2 3 4 5 6 7	Are willing to use alliances, partnerships, share equity, or dilute share positions in order to grow.
Would describe ourselves more as a conservative company meeting our family's financial and personal goals.	1 2 3 4 5 6 7	Would describe ourselves as a risk taking group seeking higher total returns for our family as an investment group.
Would describe our business models and strategy as making us steady rather than opportunistic.	1 2 3 4 5 6 7	Are willing to be innovative in our business models and structures to be opportunistic.
Believe that a steady and consistent approach will allow us to fulfill our family's vision and goals for the future.	1 2 3 4 5 6 7	Believe that bold, wide-ranging acts are necessary to achieve our family investment objectives in today's environment.

TOTAL:

Methods Continuum

The methods continuum establishes the organization's entrepreneurial orientation and actions. It reflects the beliefs of the shareholders and stakeholders on how the leaders incite entrepreneurship in the organization.

Using the assessment continuums, have the family member shareholders and future shareholders answer the questions on the methods continuum listed below. Circle the number between the two statements that best reflects the strength of your belief about the family as a shareholder group. Total scores are between 12 and 84 reflecting views from the most traditional to the most enterprising.

In general, senior leaders in our family organization(s)...

Spend their time nurturing the existing businesses.	1 2 3 4 5 6 7	Pay a disproportionate amount of attention to new business opportunities.
Place a strong emphasis on pursing returns by reinvesting in tried and true businesses.	1 2 3 4 5 6 7	Place a strong emphasis on searching for and capturing new business investment opportunities.
Have pursued no new investment opportunities outside of our core operating arena (in last five years).	1 2 3 4 5 6 7	Have pursued many new investment opportunities beyond our core operating arena (in last five years).
Believe our core competency is in managing efficient businesses.	1 2 3 4 5 6 7	Believe our core competency is in innovating for opportunistic growth.
Have made minor changes in our businesses, products, services, markets, or business units during the current generation of leaders.	1 2 3 4 5 6 7	Have made significant changes in our products, services, markets, or business units as the market required it.
Typically respond to actions that competitors or the market initiates.	1 2 3 4 5 6 7	Typically initiate actions and competitive change to lead the market and competitors.
Are generally moderate to slow in adopting new technologies and technological processes in our industry.	1 2 3 4 5 6 7	Are often early in investing to develop or adopt new technologies and technological processes in our industries.
Tend to avoid competitive clashes, preferring friendly "live and let live" competition.	1 2 3 4 5 6 7	Typically adopt a competitive "undo-the-competitor" posture when making investment decisions.
Are more intuitive and informal in how the organization seeks or captures new opportunities.	1 2 3 4 5 6 7	Have established formal structures and policies to institutionalize the entrepreneurial process in the organization.
Rely on family leaders to know the markets and customers and get the information to the organization.	1 2 3 4 5 6 7	Have more formal plans and approaches to how they gather and disseminate market intelligence.
Rely on family leaders to set the tone and ensure that the organization is competitive through time.	1 2 3 4 5 6 7	Encourage and empower people at every level of the organization to think and act like competitors.
Typically adopt a cautious "wait and see" posture to minimize the probability of making costly investment decisions.	1 2 3 4 5 6 7	Typically adopt a bold, aggressive posture to maximize the probability of exploiting potential investment opportunities.

TOTAL:

Family Enterprising Model

Plot your score totals from the mindset and methods assessment surveys above. The lowest possible score is a 12 and the highest possible score is an 84. Plotting the scores provides you with a visual basis for your family dialogue. Does the plotted score rightly describe your family? Is your family on the "congruence path"? Does everyone agree on where your family is on the model? Develop strategies to move your family on the model if necessary.

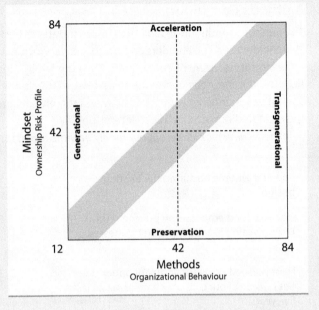

Familiness f + and f– Continuum

Identify where the family influences on your resources and capabilities are part of a competitive advantage (f+) and a competitive constraint (f–). You can conduct this analysis on many levels. The "meta" analysis would be of the larger family group as a whole, while the "micro" analysis would be of a particular business unit, or in relation to a specific innovation or new venture (such as the Bäckerhaus Veit example in the chapter). Identify the unit of analysis you are assessing and list the f+ and f– resources and capabilities.

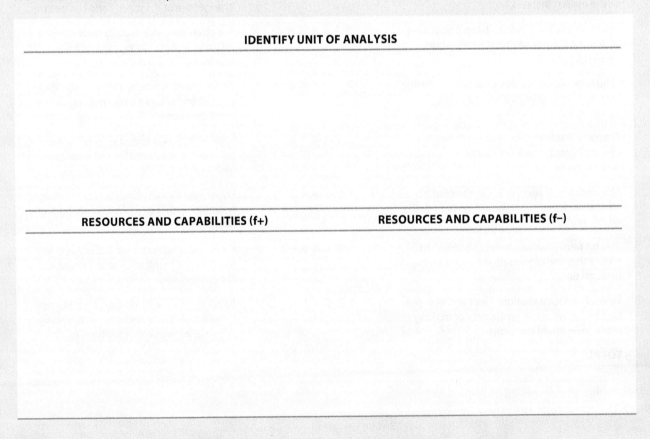

IDENTIFY UNIT OF ANALYSIS

RESOURCES AND CAPABILITIES (f+)

RESOURCES AND CAPABILITIES (f–)

Plot the f+ and f– resources and capabilities from the chart on the continuum below. Place them in position relative to one another so that you see a picture of how the resources and capabilities are related, similar to Exhibit 14.9.

A list of potential resources and capabilities to choose from:

SUCCESSOR LEADERSHIP	EXPERIENCED LEADERSHIP	ENTREPRENEURIAL PROCESSES	TEAM
Land	Treatment of employees	Firm specific knowledge	Patient capital
Location	Conflict resolution	Firm specific skills	Debt structure
Cash	Effective communication	Leadership development	Strategic alliances
Access to capital	Decision making	Leadership talent	Compensation
Distribution systems	Learning environment	Employee productivity	Strategy making and planning
Intellectual property	Openness to ideas	Network of relationships	Information flow
Raw materials	Cross functional communication	Employee commitment	Organizational culture
Contracts/alliances	Reputation of company	Personal values	Unified beliefs and goals
Manufacturing processes	Market intelligence gathering	Flexible work practices	Time horizons
Innovation processes	Reporting structures	Trustworthiness	Brand name
Reputation of company	Coordination and control	Training	Governance structure

Preparation Questions

1. What leadership behaviour pattern would you say Sayed uses most? Is this the best type for him or is there one leadership behaviour pattern that would be more effective with his employees?

2. The majority of Sayed's employees are young, middle to upper class, and of European descent. Do you think this is a cause of the problem? Why or Why not?

3. Given the language and cultural barriers that exist between Sayed and his employees as well as his current leadership style, what recommendations for change would you give him?

Dairy Queen® is a fast-food restaurant franchise that was founded in 1940. With 5900 restaurants in 22 countries as of 2008, it is one of the largest chains in the world. Much of its early growth occurred in rural areas of the United States, and references to "DQ®" occur repeatedly in both the popular and literary culture. For many years the franchise's slogan was "We treat you right!" in recent years it has been changed to "DQ® something different." The company is a wholly owned subsidiary of Berkshire Hathaway.

The Dairy Queen® franchisee-franchisor relationship is simple yet effective. Prospective franchisees are required to have a certified operator working in the store. To qualify as a certified operator, one must attend training at Dairy Queen®'s head office. The program offers training in employee and financial management, hiring and recruitment, product training, community involvement, customer service, and Dairy Queen® procedures and policies. To successfully complete the training program operator candidates must complete a set of examinations covering all of these different areas. After completing the program and commencing the operation of a franchise location, operators are required to adhere to DQ® Procedures and Policies, follow national marketing campaigns, pay monthly royalties, and pass quarterly on-site evaluations. DQ® District Managers conduct these evaluations by spending a full day on site examining operations, product consistency, cleanliness, and customer service. Franchise locations that fail these evaluations are given a warning and opportunity to rectify shortcomings. If shortcomings are not remedied by a specified date, the franchisor (Dairy Queen® Inc.) has the right to terminate the contract. As consistency and customer service are of the utmost importance, Quarterly Evaluations are often supplemented by the use of mystery shoppers.

The franchisor-franchisee relationship is facilitated through the use of a DQ® Field Consultant from and to whom the franchisee is encouraged to seek guidance and communicate questions or concerns.

ST. THOMAS

St. Thomas (population 36 110) ranks 51st in size among 912 Ontario cities. Residents of St. Thomas are mostly upper-middle class to wealthy individuals and families, mostly of French roots and Catholic. The small size of the city allows better acquaintance between its residents and for word of mouth to travel quickly. It is a prosperous city with ample opportunity for business growth and success.

ST. THOMAS DAIRY QUEEN

The St. Thomas Dairy Queen® was first opened in 1995 by Ted Smith and his wife Ronnie. They opened it as a "full Brazier store," which is the Dairy Queen® terminology for a fast food restaurant that serves "hot eats" and "cold treats." Prior to opening the St. Thomas location Ted and Ronnie had gained experience as owners of the Dairy Queen® location in White Oaks mall in neighbouring London, Ontario. With their lease expiring at the mall, the Smiths decided to open up a new DQ® location in the emerging city of St. Thomas. With the assistance of two full-time managers, Ted and Ronnie created a successful business realizing nearly $550 000 in revenue in their second year of operation.

St. Thomas's DQ® was perceived as the "cool" place to work by the local high school students. Each year tens of applicants would apply in hopes of a part-time position. During summer weekends DQ® would open until midnight making it a popular hangout for teens, families, and couples alike. The St. Thomas DQ® also became involved in the community though sponsorship of local baseball and hockey little league teams.

Although Ted was both proud and loyal to the brand, he was very cynical of the Franchisor. He often wanted to do things his way and found it difficult to follow DQ® Policies. He often challenged head office and had developed a very antagonistic relationship. He was also known to be strict and firm in managing his business and employees often viewed him as a tyrant, avoiding him at all costs.

After six successful years of running the St. Thomas DQ®, Ted and Ronnie decided they were ready for retirement and put the store up for sale in 2000.

This case was written by Zeina Haidar and Francine K. Schlosser, Odette School of Business, University of Windsor, Canada, for purposes of classroom discussion.

THE HASHEM FAMILY

In 1990 Sayed Hashem and his family immigrated to Canada from civil war–torn Lebanon. The Hashem family consisted of Sayed, the patriarch, his wife Nora, and their six children, the youngest of which was born in Canada shortly after arrival. In January 2001 the Hashem family purchased the St. Thomas Dairy Queen® from the Smiths.

At the time of the Dairy Queen® purchase, Sayed's two eldest children, Yasmine and Khalil, were enjoying living away from home to complete their professional educations. Yasmine, a dentist, and Khalil, a doctor, had always described living at home as "boot camp" living with the discipline of a strict father. Sayed's parenting skills were much like those of parents from any war-torn and dangerous region; where strict discipline was a necessity more than an option.

The four youngest children; Aliya, Mira, Hanna, and Bassil were to become integral parts of the Hashem family Dairy Queen. Nora, on the other hand, had no intention of becoming involved with the newly acquired Dairy Queen®. Past experience had taught the Hashems that Nora and Sayed working together put a tremendous strain on their relationship and created problems and unhappiness.

Sayed—Father, Manager, Boss

In June 2001, five months after purchasing the St. Thomas Dairy Queen®, Sayed Hashem completed his three-week training course and officially became a Dairy Queen® operator. While Sayed had immigrated to Canada in 1990 at the age of 37, he still struggled to perfect the English language and assimilate into the Canadian culture. Although Sayed had previous business experience in Canada, the fast food industry was a completely new venture. Prior to being interested in purchasing a Dairy Queen® franchise, Sayed's only experience with Dairy Queen® had involved a single visit during which he enjoyed a banana split and a sunny day with his children.

In Lebanon, Sayed had simultaneously worked three jobs to support his relatively large family. He was a math teacher, the first sales manager for Lebanon's first and largest super store, and an exporter on the side. Clearly not a stranger to hard work, Sayed would soon learn that the restaurant industry would require much more.

Aliya—Daughter, Employee, Manager

Aliya, the eldest of the Hashem children remaining at home, had completed the Dairy Queen® training program with her father and was also qualified to operate the franchise. Her father had been concerned about failing the training program due to the language barrier and as such had asked her to at-tend as a backup. At the time the Hashem family took over the St. Thomas Dairy Queen®, Aliya was a 19-year-old first year university student. Aliya also played a key role in the acquisition of the business as both translator and negotiator for her English-challenged father. Sayed often referred to Aliya as his "right hand man" or his "tongue" because of his less than perfect English.

Having been brought up in Canada, Aliya had several advantages over her father. She was fluent in English and completely understood and fit in with the Canadian culture. At the same time, she had been born in Lebanon and spent the first eight years of her life there. This gave her the ability to appreciate the differences in culture and society and communicate from both perspectives. Aliya was a quick learner who, as a teenager raised in Canada, had far more exposure to the fast food industry. Through school, sports, and extra-curricular activities Aliya had gained experience in group work and leadership.

In contrast to Aliya's perspective, her father considered much of the Dairy Queen® requirements, managerial tasks, roles, and tactics to be "just another way to steal money from the Franchisee." He often expressed his opinion that $10 000 for a transfer of ownership, $8000 for new menu boards, and $10 000 for a required training course were just a few of the many techniques DQ® was using to gouge the Franchisee. Aliya on the other hand was able to understand, appreciate, and explain the necessity and benefits of these and other costs.

With Aliya by his side, Sayed would grow to value the DQ® trademark and operating procedures. More importantly, he would learn to train, manage, and retain approximately 25 employees, 90 percent of which are Caucasian teenagers who in the past would have certainly clashed with Sayed's way of doing things.

Mira

Mira was 16 years old when her father acquired the St. Thomas DQ®. She began working for her father immediately after the end of the 2001 school year. She was a quick study and within a short period of time became a key employee in the store. She disliked working at the family business and avoided taking on any additional responsibility. On a given shift, Mira would come in and get straight to task. She would have little communication with other staff except the occasional reminder to get something done or stop "fooling around." She felt that it was easier to get things done on her own and delegated little to the staff. She constantly complained about the staff being slow and inefficient.

Mira and Sayed were very similar and as such would often bump heads resulting in a low tolerance for one another. Unlike Aliya, Mira had little compassion for issues troubling her father. If he told her that a staff member was underperforming and needed retraining her immediate recommendation was to fire them. When asked to do anything outside her normal shift duties she would conveniently "forget."

Today, Mira is 21 years old. She is an efficient and fast employee that makes excellent products and offers great customer service. She still dislikes her job, mainly because she does not enjoy working with her father, and continues to avoid responsibility. Mira works very flexible hours and covers shifts whenever needed. She feels this is a significant contribution to the family business and to expect anything more of her is unreasonable.

Hanna

Hanna was 14 years old at the time her father acquired the St. Thomas DQ®. Working at the family business was her first job. Like her sisters, she was quick to absorb and had perfected her role as a cashier. She displayed great customer service and was often complimented by customers on her attitude.

Today, Hanna is 19 years old. She has a pleasant personality but can also be very stubborn. She insists on doing tasks her own way and on her own schedule. Sayed depends on his children and as such has given them authority over the other employees. Hanna often abuses her authority and uses it to avoid work by ordering the staff around.

Hanna has difficulty taking orders and refuses the authority of her older sisters, Aliya and Mira. Mira and Hanna often get into "sisterly fights" at work. Hanna and Aliya have also butted heads. Hanna has been known to refuse Aliya's orders and display rude behaviour to the point of having to be sent home. Hanna often takes out her frustration by ordering around her younger brother Bassil, which results in countless arguments at work.

After five years of working at DQ®, Hanna refuses to learn supervisory responsibilities, and her capabilities are limited.

Bassil

Bassil is the youngest member to the Hashem family. He started working at DQ® only a year ago, at the age of 13. When he started working his primary responsibilities were to keep the dining room tables clean and the floors spotless. A year later, he is a top kitchen worker.

WHY DQ®?

Prior to 2001, the Hashem family resided in London, Ontario. Sayed had purchased a failed variety store that he remodelled, restocked, and reopened. The business was a success! The store location had failed under the previous management of Becker's and Mac's Milk, but Sayed was able to get it back on its feet.

Sayed and the family operated the store for nearly six years before Sayed decided he had enough. He was unhappy with the nature of the job. He did not enjoy standing on his feet all day in what seemed a mindless job. He detested dealing with his three employees who he felt were unreliable or not worthy of trust. In addition, neither he nor his wife Nora enjoyed living in London. They wanted to relocate to St. Thomas as they had many family and friends in the area. They felt that being near family would benefit the children and their own social life and happiness. With this in mind, Sayed sold the variety store in September of 2000, and with a mere $150 000 travelled to St. Thomas in search of the perfect opportunity.

After nearly nine months of networking and searching for an appropriate business, Sayed began to run out of time. A family of eight with two children in medical school could not sustain itself without a substantial income. Sayed had to move quickly to avoid having to tap into the $150 000 business investment account.

The St. Thomas market made Sayed's business searching task a difficult one. Businesses in the appropriate price range were far too risky and less risky businesses were not for sale. Finally, a realtor approached Sayed about a business for sale in St. Thomas where the owner was willing to finance a mortgage. Immediately, Sayed's interest was piqued.

Sayed met with Ted Smith the owner of the St. Thomas Dairy Queen® that was for sale. Sayed noticed it was a very well run and clean facility that had a constant inflow of customers. He also loved the location and the manageable size of the business. Ted had prepared all of the appropriate financial statements, which he revealed to Sayed as soon as he had communicated his interest and signed a confidentiality agreement. Sayed was impressed by the numbers. Over $550 000 in sales, profits were still healthy even though Ted was paying four managerial salaries each year!

Sayed considered the facts. The St. Thomas Dairy Queen® was already established and in a growing area at a busy intersection. Also the staff was already trained and experienced. In addition, the business had a competitive advantage; it was a fast food restaurant that also served soft serve treats that the competition could not compete with. The financials of the business looked great and with Ted willing to finance a five-year mortgage, Sayed could get the most for his money. He knew he had no experience in the industry, but he was determined to learn quickly.

DQ®'S SENIOR STAFF

Sayed and Aliya's Relationship

Sayed became heavily reliant on Aliya. Sayed took care of the ordering, cost control, scheduling, maintenance, and training. He expected Aliya to communicate with head office and to train and manage front counter staff. The DQ® staff generally consists of five kitchen workers and 20 cashiers. Kitchen workers would prepare food while cashiers were responsible for taking orders, preparing soft serve treats, making frozen cakes, stocking, and cleaning. Aliya is also responsible for keeping up to date with policies, rules, and regulations and making sure that staff understands and follows them. Further, she has to ensure that the employees are performing to their fullest potential, providing superior customer service, and keeping their morale up. She was also responsible for disciplining those employees that were not performing to standard.

Often Sayed would express a concern, frustration, or problem to Aliya and expect her to resolve it. If a shift task was not completed (e.g., staff not making enough frozen cakes) then Sayed would confront Aliya. He would often say something along the lines of: "Didn't you tell so-and-so to make 20 cakes last night? Why didn't they? What kind of manager are you if your staff won't listen to you? So-and-so is just good at talking and fooling around! Before her next shift you talk to her!"

Although Sayed was often critical of, and hard on, Aliya, she usually did not let it get to her. She remained task oriented and got the job done. She knew that her father's concerns were valid, but she also knew that he had difficulty expressing them fairly and/or calmly. She adapted to his hostile style and was able to calm him down, make him feel better about a situation and eventually solve it. She also realized that it was not easy for her siblings and other staff to cope with his behaviour. Aliya cared about the well-being of both her father and the business and for that reason could put up with the stress and demand. But she knew that it was unrealistic to expect regular staff to deal with her father's style. Aliya vocalized this concern to her father and he apologized for his behaviour and noted that he should be more careful. In time Sayed learned to better control himself in front of employees, but remained hard on Aliya. She accepted this and assumed the role of "counsellor" to her father. She allowed him to vent to her and after he was done his spiel she would dilute the problem making him feel that "it's not a big deal, we'll take care of it."

In 2006, after five years of working hand in hand with her father, Aliya got married and abruptly distanced herself from the family business. She became a full-time graduate student juggling two other part-time jobs while working on building a career in banking. Career combined with married life left her no time to help with the family business. Sayed was left to pick up all of Aliya's responsibilities. He found himself hiring as many as six cashiers in order to be able to retain two of them. He quickly realized that he needed a more gentle management style, especially with the younger and newer employees. He left the training up to Mira and senior staff members Rose and Meredith but constantly interfered with his own input. For example, Meredith would teach a new employee how to make a certain product one way, and then he would tell that employee that he wants it done another. Sayed attempted to have Mira pick up Aliya's responsibilities, but she was not interested. She made it clear to her father that she was working because he was making her and that she did not want to be there or get involved any further. Soon thereafter, Hanna and Bassil carried the same attitude towards the family business. Sayed felt that dealing with the employees was not his job. In an attempt to solve his problem, he promoted Meredith to chief of staff and made her responsible for communicating his needs and expectations to the staff while at the same time training and resolving employee problems.

Other Senior Staff

Rose and Meredith were two senior employees that had worked at the St. Thomas location for six years even before Sayed had purchased it. They were the most experienced and only full-time employees. They often resisted any change but eventually adapted to the new management and did as asked. They were hard working, dedicated employees that cared about the business as if it were their own. But they often did not see eye to eye with Sayed. They quickly came to respect and follow Aliya, for she proved she was competent and caring as well as a hard worker who always set a good example. Aliya often met with them to discuss new changes or ideas and ask for their opinion. Sayed on the other hand, often met with them to complain about an issue and try to get consensus from them.

Rose

Sayed and Rose did not always get along. In one incident, Sayed was speaking to Rose about incomplete tasks on a previous shift that she had supervised and he said, "You know Rose, that kitchen staff Adam is terrible. I've told him a million times not to leave the lettuce uncovered. He doesn't listen, he doesn't care. You know there's some stupidity in his head, he doesn't understand."

Rose, clearly upset by Sayed's constant attacks and language replied in a seemingly mocking and patronizing voice, "Sayed, I think he's a great worker and very intelligent, he wants to be a doctor one day. I think he's doing fine."

At this response, Sayed became upset with her lack of support and her inability to accept Adam's underperformance. He responded in an aggressive tone "A doctor? He'll never be a doctor; he can't even make an order correctly. None of the kitchen staff is doing well, even you don't perform the kitchen duties perfectly! You need to see that and make things better, not say 'ohhhh, it's okay!'"

Another issue that often created friction between Rose and Sayed was how Sayed would say "my kids are not to be treated as employees here and they are free to do whatever they want. When I'm not here, they are here in charge in my place." On any given summer afternoon, if business was more than expected, Sayed would simply call one of his children to pop in to work for just an hour or so during the peak period. Often, Mira, Hanna, Bassil, and even Aliya would have to leave whatever they were doing just to come in for an hour to help out. In these situations they were likely to come in wearing jeans and a t-shirt and provide the necessary support until things were under control and then head out again.

Rose almost always complained about what they were wearing. Sayed would remind her that his kids were also owners and that they came in unscheduled to help so they could do as they pleased. As owners who were just there as unscheduled help, he felt they could wear and do as they pleased. Rose considered this to be unfair treatment and often voiced her opinion in front of the staff.

In another point of conflict, Rose would often say or imply that the Hashem children were spoiled. It was common for Sayed to instruct Rose to have her staff accomplish certain tasks during her shift. Rose often replied, "Well, what if we're busy? You should have Aliya come in to do the extra work!" Sayed replied, "I always told you customer comes first so if it is busy I'll understand. But it's not busy now, so why are you arguing? Also, Aliya works very hard, she was in earlier today making blanks!" Rose replied, "Well she should work hard, you gave her a car and everything!" Sayed was outraged by her comment and told her to mind her own business, he said "she's my daughter, and it's my responsibility to give her everything she wants. She works harder than everyone here and without her I would have lost the business long ago."

Meredith

Meredith and Sayed on the other hand had an easier time communicating because Sayed found it easier to explain things to her. He perceived her as being less cynical, where he felt that Rose just always wanted to disagree first regardless of the issue.

Meredith was a diligent employee. She displayed great customer service and always completed her required tasks. Meredith was very task oriented and had great difficulty planning ahead, forecasting product needs, and disciplining employees. For example, if an employee called in sick multiple times and was frequently late she would accept whatever excuse she was given.

It was not long before Sayed realized that Meredith was not management material, so he began interacting directly with the employees. When business was going well and tasks were being completed as needed Sayed would often compliment the staff and give them free desserts and meals. He attempted to be flexible with the employee needs and scheduled them as conveniently as possible. He encouraged them to talk to him about any concerns or problems they may have at work and reminded them that if they did not understand him because of his English or his accent to please ask him to explain again. He also gave raises as soon as he saw an employee show slight improvement. Things seemed to be going great until an employee would call in sick or a customer would complain. After these mistakes Sayed would often say something like "When you want you can be excellent and other times you are terrible." He would call employees into his office and interrogate them on their mistake. Employees would often respond with an apology. But the mistakes were often repeated.

When Sayed called an employee into the office Meredith would attempt to interfere and try to find out what was going on. Sayed's direct management of the employees and Meredith's disagreement with his approach soon created friction between them as well. Meredith became easily irritable and often voiced her disagreements.

EMPLOYEE CRISIS

With Aliya gone Rose and Meredith were integral despite their relationships with Sayed. Soon, the difficult relationships would create an employee crisis for the St. Thomas Dairy Queen®. Meredith began to come in late, ask for more days off, and stopped returning calls on days she was called to cover a shift. Rose submitted a note saying that she would be retiring in May, which was only six months away. Further, nearly all of the remaining employees were newly hired and not very reliable. Their willingness to work depended on how much money they needed at the time. They often exhibited no sense of responsibility or dedication.

CURRENTLY

Aliya discusses the business with her father on a daily basis and visits the DQ® periodically. Lately, she has been consumed with worry. She feels that her father is overworked and has become quite unhappy. For the past five years her father has worked seven days a week every week. He appears to be physically and mentally exhausted. He told Aliya that he was worried about the behaviour of Meredith and Rose, but he felt helpless because without them he cannot develop and retain employees. He also mentioned to her that although a high employee turnover rate is expected in the fast food restaurant industry, he has noticed his turnover rate is excessively high.

There is also a concern about the increasing number of customer complaints being delivered to him through head office. Yearly revenues have remained steady and are not growing at the same rate as in previous years. He confessed that "I feel like I am losing the business and I don't know what more to do. Your sisters and brother don't care about the business. If they don't care how are the employees going to care?"

Aliya knows that by correcting some of the main problems at work she would also be able to ensure her father's health and well being. She realizes that she does not have the time to go back to work at DQ® because her schedule was still being consumed by school, career, and marriage. She feels she has to find a way to pinpoint the root of the problems and help her father resolve them. She suspected that part of the problem was her father's expectation that she would solve his problems for him. She knew that the first step was to make him realize that he had to change his ways and take responsibility for his business and actions.

But how does she tell her father he needs to change his ways? How does she tell him that he needs to work on his managerial skills or that he may need outside help? She worries that figuring out the problems and solutions would be the easy part, but implementing them would be near impossible. Regardless, she feels that she must intervene for the sake of the family business and her father's well being.

For more information on the resources available from McGraw-Hill Ryerson, go to www.mcgrawhill.ca/he/solutions.

CHAPTER 15

LEADING THROUGH TROUBLE, THE HARVEST, AND BEYOND[1]

> " *It's better to burn out than it is to rust.* "
>
> NEIL YOUNG, MUSICIAN

LEARNING OBJECTIVES

LO1 Identify specific signals and clues that can alert entrepreneurial leaders to impending crises, and describe both quantitative (ratio analysis) and qualitative symptoms of trouble.

LO2 Describe the principal diagnostic methods used to devise intervention and turnaround plans, and identify remedial actions used for dealing with lenders, creditors, and employees.

LO3 Articulate why it is important to first build a great company in order to create harvest options.

LO4 Explain why harvesting is an essential element of the entrepreneurial process and does not necessarily mean abandoning the company.

LO5 Identify the principal harvest options, including trade sale, going public, and cash flow ("capital cow").

LO6 Discuss the importance of creating a longer-term legacy from personal and family wealth by pursuing philanthropic activities and contributing to community renewal.

This chapter tackles issues that generally arise in the latter stages of a venture's existence. The first part of this chapter deals with problems after time has elapsed and the venture has made it through growing pains. With experience comes both comfort and an array of problems associated with apathy. Alternatively the entrepreneur may come to the realization that what served the enterprise so well in the past may now be a source of sub-par performance. The second part of this chapter deals with the harvest—the end of one venture—an action that may lead to a foray into another endeavour.

Perhaps the analogy of the automobile serves to demonstrate how the service period and final kilometres of a vehicle are similar to events for an enterprise. A new car may require a period of breaking in—any number of things might go wrong early on—but once those bugs are ironed out, it should run fine for quite a while. Tuning-up your vehicle or your venture ensures the highest price when you part ways. Later on—depending on how well it is maintained and how hard it is driven—the car comes to the end of its useful life with its owner. The owner may upgrade to a bigger and better car; however, unlike a venture, vehicles seldom increase in value.

WHEN THE BLOOM IS OFF THE ROSE LO1

We now turn our attention to the entrepreneur and the troubled company. We'll trace a firm's route into and out of crisis and provide insight into how a troubled enterprise can be rescued by a turnaround specialist.

Many times in history, companies have experienced times of financial troubles, such as the recent economic downturn. Both corporate and personal bankruptcies increased during this period, and entrepreneurs needed a new and special set of skills to lead through the shoals.

There is a saying among horseback riders that the person who has never been thrown from a horse probably has never ridden one! Jim Hindman, founder of Jiffy Lube, is fond of saying, "Ultimately it is not how many touchdowns you score but how fast and often you get up after being tackled." Professional golfer Mike Weir said "Playing hockey, there were a lot of guys bigger than me, so I knew I was going to get hit and have to deal with it. Gotta hit back." These insights capture the essence of the ups and downs that can occur during the growth and development of a new venture.

GETTING INTO TROUBLE—THE CAUSES

Trouble can be caused by external forces not under one's control. Among the most frequently mentioned are recession, interest rate changes, changes in government policy, inflation, the entry of new competition, and industry/product obsolescence.

However, those who lead turnarounds find that while such circumstances define the environment to which a troubled company needs to adjust, they are rarely the sole reason for a company's failure. External shocks impact all companies in an industry, and only some of them fail. Others survive and prosper.

Most causes of failure can be found within company leadership. Although there are many causes of trouble, the most frequently cited fall into three broad areas: inattention to strategic issues, general management problems, and poor financial/accounting systems and practices. There is striking similarity between these causes of trouble and the causes of failure for start-ups given in chapter 2. Exercise 10, "Flaws, Assumptions, and Downside Consequences—Risk Reconsidered," in the Venture Opportunity Screening Exercise that accompanies chapter 3 and is found online with Connect is a tool worth visiting.

STRATEGIC ISSUES

- *Misunderstood market niche.* The first of these issues is a failure to understand the company's market niche and to focus on growth without considering profitability. Instead of developing a strategy, these firms take on low-margin business and add capacity in an effort to grow. They then run out of cash.

- *Mismanaged relationships with suppliers and customers.* Related to the issue of not understanding market niche is the failure to understand the economics of relationships with suppliers and customers. For example, some firms allow practices in the industry to dictate payment terms, when they may be in a position to dictate their own terms.

- *Diversification into an unrelated business area.* A common failing of cash-rich firms that suffer from the growth syndrome is diversification into unrelated business areas. These firms use the cash flow generated in one business to start another without good reason. As one turnaround consultant said, "I couldn't believe it. There was no synergy at all. They added to their overhead but not to their contribution. No common sense!"

- *Mousetrap myopia.* Related to the problem of starting a firm around an idea, rather than an opportunity, is the problem of firms that have "great products" and are looking for other markets where they can be sold. This is done without analyzing the firm's opportunities.

- *The big project.* The company gears up for a "big project" without looking at the cash flow implications. Cash is expended by adding capacity and hiring personnel. When sales do not materialize, or take longer than expected to materialize, there is trouble. Sometimes the "big project" is required by the nature of the business opportunity. An example of this would be the high-technology start-up that needs to capitalize on a first-mover advantage. The company needs to prove the product's "right to life" and grow quickly to the point where it can achieve a public market or become an attractive acquisition candidate for a larger company. This ensures that a larger company cannot use its advantages in scale and existing distribution channels, after copying the technology, to achieve dominance over the start-up.

- *Lack of contingency planning.* As has been stated over and over, the path to growth is not a smooth curve upward. Firms need to be geared to think about what happens if things go sour, sales fall, or collections slow. There need to be plans in place for layoffs and capacity reduction.

LEADERSHIP ISSUES

- *Lack of leadership skills, experience, and know-how.* As was mentioned in chapter 5, when companies grow entrepreneurs need to change their leadership mode from doing to leading to leading leaders.

- *Weak finance function.* Often, in a new and emerging company, the finance function is nothing more than a bookkeeper. One company was five years old, with $20 million in sales, before the founders hired a financial professional.

- *Turnover in key personnel.* Although turnover of key personnel can be difficult in any firm, it is a critical concern in businesses that deal in specialized or proprietary knowledge. For example, one firm lost a bookkeeper—the only person who really understood what was happening in the business.

- *Big-company influence in accounting.* A mistake that some companies often make is to focus on accruals, rather than cash.

POOR PLANNING, FINANCIAL/ACCOUNTING SYSTEMS, PRACTICES, AND CONTROLS

- *Poor pricing, overextension of credit, and excessive leverage.* These causes of trouble are not surprising and need not be elaborated. Some of the reasons for excess use of leverage are interesting. Use of excess leverage can result from growth outstripping the company's internal financing capabilities. The company then relies increasingly on short-term notes until a cash flow problem develops. Another reason a company becomes overleveraged is by using guaranteed loans in place of equity for either start-up or expansion financing. One entrepreneur remarked, "[The guaranteed loan] looked just like equity when we started, but when trouble came it looked more and more like debt."

- *Lack of cash budgets/projections.* This is a most frequently cited cause of trouble. In small companies, cash budgets/projections are often not done.

- *Poor management reporting.* While some firms have good financial reporting, they suffer from poor management reporting. As one turnaround consultant stated, "[The financial statement] just tells where the company has been. It does not help manage the business. If you look at the important management reports—inventory analysis, receivables aging, sales analysis—they're usually late or not produced at all. The same goes for billing procedures. Lots of emerging companies don't get their bills out on time."

- *Lack of standard costing.* Poor management reporting extends to issues of costing, too. Many emerging businesses have no standard costs against which they can compare the actual costs of manufacturing products. The result is they have no variance reporting. The company cannot identify problems in process and take corrective action. The company will know only after the fact how profitable a product is.

  Even when standard costs are used, it is not uncommon to find that engineering, manufacturing, and accounting each has its own version of the bill of material. The product is designed one way, manufactured a second way, and costed a third.

- *Poorly understood cost behaviour.* Companies often do not understand the relationship between fixed and variable costs. For example, one manufacturing company thought it was saving money by closing on Saturday. The thinking was that this would save paying overtime. It had to be pointed out to the lead entrepreneur by a turnaround consultant that, "He had a lot of high-margin product in his manufacturing backlog that more than justified the overtime."

  It is also important for entrepreneurs to understand the difference between theory and practice in this area. The turnaround consultant mentioned above said, "Accounting theory says that all costs are variable in the long run. In practice, almost all costs are fixed. The only truly variable cost is a sales commission."

GETTING OUT OF TROUBLE

The major protection against and the biggest help in getting out of these troubled waters is to have a set of advisors and directors who have been through this in the past. They possess skills that are not taught in school or in most corporate training programs. An outside "vision" is critical. The speed of action for an entrepreneurial firm has to be different, control systems have to be different, and the organization generally needs to be different.

Although uncontrollable external factors such as new government regulations do arise, an opportunity-driven firm's crisis is usually the result of management error. Yet in these management errors are found part of the solution to the troubled company's problems. It is pleasing to see

ENTREPRENEURS ACROSS CANADA
Choices in Accounting Rules

LEE BRAGG AND HIS FATHER, JOHN

The Bragg Group of Companies, introduced in the previous chapter, had to make a decision. As a privately held company they could follow a simpler version of GAAP (generally accepted accounting rules) or they could adopt what is required of publicly traded companies—IFRS (International Financial Reporting Standards). The CFO stated, "When we looked at what IFRS would mean to us, we didn't see the benefit." Centra Industries, a maker of airframe and landing gear components for aircraft, was in a different situation; shares were not all held by a single family as with the Bragg Group. Nevertheless, Centra chose the same course and its shareholders (that include employees and non-employees) as well as a U.S. private-equity firm were satisfied. "The company's customers include major manufacturers such as Boeing and Lockheed Martin with stringent vendor require-

ments for financial reporting. Centra provides detailed operational information to owners and lenders. Some customers even received financial statements. "So why not just go ahead with IFRS? Cost." According to Centra's CFO, "Adopting a robust system like IFRS and setting up the controls to capture and track the information becomes expensive, as do the annual audit fees." The Bragg Group's CFO stated, "it doesn't preclude us from making a change later—it's not an irreversible move for us."

The National Post published a news story in 2013 with the headline: "Most Small Business Owners Can't Pass a Basic Financial Test." The article went on to report the results of a recent survey:

83 percent of business would have trouble passing a test on basic finance, which may be why 'financial literacy' for entrepreneurs has suddenly become a big thing. Entrepreneurs haven't suddenly become stupid. Running a business requires a wide range of talents and skills, from production savvy to employee empathy and marketing mojo. Throw in P&Ls, cash flow and taxes, and that's more breadth of knowledge than is expected of line managers. According to former tech entrepreneur Lance Laking, "I think any entrepreneur who is going to put their stick on the ice must realize that financial literacy is a core requirement for their success."

Question: How will you determine what financial knowledge is necessary? Over the life of your venture, how will you determine what financial reporting is beneficial and when?

that many enterprises—even enterprises that are insolvent or have negative net worth or both—can be rescued and restored to profitability.

PREDICTING TROUBLE

Since crises develop over time and typically result from an accumulation of fundamental errors, can a crisis be predicted? The obvious benefit of being able to predict crisis is that the entrepreneur, employees, and significant outsiders, such as investors, lenders, trade creditors—and even customers—could see trouble brewing in time to take corrective actions.

There have been several attempts to develop predictive models. Two are presented below and have been selected because each is easy to calculate and uses information available in common financial reports. Because management reporting in emerging companies is often inadequate, the predictive model needs to use information available in common financial reports.

Each of the two approaches below uses easily obtained financial data to predict the onset of crisis as much as two years in advance. For the smaller public company, these models can be used by all interested observers. With private companies, they are useful only to those privy to the information and are probably only of benefit to such non-management outsiders as lenders and boards of directors.

The most frequently used denominator in all these ratios is the figure for total assets. This figure often is distorted by "creative accounting," with expenses occasionally improperly capitalized and carried on the balance sheet or by substantial differences between tangible book value and book value (i.e., overvalued or undervalued assets).

NET-LIQUID-BALANCE-TO-TOTAL-ASSETS RATIO

The model shown in Exhibit 15.1 was developed to predict loan defaults. This ratio has been shown to predict loan defaults with significant reliability as much as two years in advance. But the science of prediction is ever improving. Marissa Mayer, at the time a Google vice president, pointed out that credit card companies are generating detailed psychometric profiles and accurately assessing behaviour; the credit card company knows that you will be getting divorced two years before you do.[2]

This approach is noteworthy because it explicitly recognizes the importance of cash. Among current accounts, it distinguishes between operating assets (such as inventory and accounts receivable) and financial assets (such as cash and marketable securities). The same distinction is made among liabilities, where notes payable and contractual obligations are financial liabilities and accounts payable are operating liabilities.

The model then subtracts financial liabilities from financial assets to obtain a figure known as the net liquid balance. Net liquid balance can be thought of as "uncommitted cash," cash the firm has available to meet contingencies. Because it is the short-term margin for error should sales change, collections slow, or interest rates change, it is a true measure of liquidity. The net liquid balance is then divided by total assets to form the predictive ratio.

NON-QUANTITATIVE SIGNALS

In chapter 12 we discussed patterns and actions that could lead to trouble, indications of common trouble by growth stage, and critical variables that can be monitored.

Turnaround specialists also use some non-quantitative signals as indicators of the possibility of trouble. As with the signals discussed in chapter 12, the presence of a single one of these does not necessarily imply an immediate crisis. However, once any of the following signals surfaces and if the others follow, then trouble is likely to mount:

- inability to produce financial statements on time
- changes in behaviour of the lead entrepreneur (such as avoiding phone calls or coming in later than usual)

EXHIBIT 15.1   **NET-LIQUID-BALANCE-TO-TOTAL-ASSETS RATIO**

Net-Liquid-Balance-to-Total-Assets Ratio = NLB/Total Assets
Where
NLB = (Cash + Marketable securities) − (Notes Payable + Contractual obligations)

Source: Ismael G. Dambolena and Joel M. Shulman, "Primary Rule for Detecting Bankruptcy: Watch the Cash," *Financial Analysts Journal* 44, no. 5 (1988): 74–78.

- change in executive team or advisors, such as directors, accountants, or other professional advisors
- accountant's opinion that is qualified and not certified
- new competition
- launching of a "big project"
- lower research and development expenditures
- special write-offs of assets and/or addition of "new" liabilities
- reduction of credit line

THE GESTATION PERIOD OF CRISIS   LO2

Crises rarely develop overnight. The time between the initial cause of trouble and the point of intervention can run from 18 months to five years. Zellers was on the ropes for years and Sears Canada's present prospects are dim[3] but are they dire? What happens to a company during the crisis gestation period has implications for the later turnaround of the company. Thus, how the lead entrepreneur reacts to crisis and what happens to morale determine what will need to happen in the intervention. Usually, a demoralized and unproductive organization develops when its members think only of survival, not turnaround, and its entrepreneur has lost credibility. Further, the company has lost valuable time.

In looking backward, the plot of a company's key statistics shows trouble. One can see the sales growth rate (and the gross margin) have slowed considerably. This is followed by an increasing rise in expenses as the company assumes that growth will continue. When the growth does not continue, the company still allows the growth rate of expenses to remain high so it can "get back on track."

THE PARADOX OF OPTIMISM

In a typical scenario for a troubled company, the first signs of trouble (such as declining margins, customer returns, or falling liquidity) go unnoticed or are written off as teething problems of the new project or as the ordinary vicissitudes of business. For example, one entrepreneur saw increases in inventory and receivables as a good sign, since sales were up and the current ratio had improved. However, although sales were up, margins were down, and he did not realize he had a liquidity problem until cash shortages developed.

Although the lead entrepreneur may miss the first signs, outsiders usually do not. Banks, board members, suppliers, and customers see trouble brewing. They wonder why the venture team does not respond. Credibility begins to erode.

Soon the venture team has to admit that trouble exists, but valuable time has been lost. Furthermore, requisite actions to meet the situation are anathema. The lead entrepreneur is emotionally committed to people, to projects, or to business areas. Further, to cut back in any of these areas goes against instinct, because the company will need these resources when the good times return.

The company continues its downward fall, and the situation becomes stressful. Turnaround specialists mention that stress can cause avoidance on the part of an entrepreneur. Others have likened the entrepreneur in a troubled company to a deer caught in a car's headlights. The entrepreneur is frozen and can take no action. Avoidance has a basis in human psychology. One organizational behaviour consultant who has worked on turnarounds said, "When a person under stress does not understand the problem and does not have the sense to deal with it, the

Michele Romanow, Anatoliy Melnichuk, and Ryan Marien, all of whom were students at Queen's University, launched Evandale Caviar after winning five competitions and over $100 000 in cash. Michele and other classmates had earlier founded The Tea Room on campus, a place for exotic teas, espresso, and sandwiches. A very different model was developed for The Tea Room—it was purportedly North America's first zero consumer waste coffee shop—pushing the bounds of environmentally friendly technologies and practices. For Evandale Caviar, Michele stated, "We chose New Brunswick, where we lived for three months to establish the fishery, then went on the road, visiting high-end restaurants to sell our product." A profitable business was grown "before two disasters struck, the 2008 recession that drastically affected luxury purchasing and new federal legislation that effectively put an end to their ability to export their product."

Michele went on to a business improvement position at Sears Canada. "I had a wonderful time there developing growth strategies for the company, looking at how to take a department store, one of the oldest models in retail, and update it." Trying to refresh that dinosaur in peril, Romanow was introduced to the group-buying concept. She and two others started Buytopia.ca, an online group-buying site for consumers to get good deals where they live and offer charities a percentage of proceeds for traffic directed to Buytopia.

Question: Having been through a fatal crisis at Evandale Caviar and having worked for Sears Canada, is Michele Romanow better prepared to diagnose and tackle threatening situations?

Sources: Lisa Jemison, "Tea Room Manager Receives Tricolour Award," *The Journal*, April 5, 2007. Shelley Pleiter, "Group-Buying Power" *Queen's School of Business Magazine*, Winter 2012. Travis Myers, "Women of the Week: Michele Romanow," *Women's Post*, May 29, 2013.

person will tend to replace the unpleasant reality with fantasy." The consultant went on to say, "The outward manifestation of this fantasy is avoidance." This consultant noted it is common for an entrepreneur to deal with pleasant and well-understood tasks, such as selling to customers, rather than dealing with the trouble. The result is that credibility is lost with bankers, creditors, and others. (These are the very people whose co-operation needs to be secured if the company is to be turned around.)

Often, the decisions the entrepreneur does make during this time are poor and accelerate the company on its downward course. The accountant or the controller may be fired, resulting in a company that is then flying blind. One entrepreneur, for example, running a company that manufactured a high-margin product, announced across-the-board cuts in expenditures, including advertising, without stopping to think that cutting advertising on such a product only added to the cash flow problem.

Finally, the entrepreneur may make statements that are untrue or may make promises that cannot be kept. This is the death knell of his or her credibility.

THE BLOOM IS OFF THE ROSE—NOW WHAT?

Generally, when an organization is in trouble some telltale trends appear:

- principals ignore outside advice
- the situation goes from bad to worse
- people (including and usually, most especially, the entrepreneur) stop making decisions and also stop answering the phone
- nobody in authority talks to the employees
- rumours fly

- inventory gets out of balance and does not reflect historical trends
- accounts receivable aging increases
- customers become afraid of new commitments by the organization
- a general malaise settles in while a high-stress environment continues to exist

DECLINE IN ORGANIZATIONAL MORALE

Among those who notice trouble developing are the employees. They deal with customer returns, calls from creditors, and the like, and they wonder why the executive team does not respond. They begin to lose confidence in their leader(s).

Despite troubled times, the lead entrepreneur talks and behaves optimistically or hides in the office declining to communicate with employees, customers, or vendors. Employees hear of trouble from each other and from other outsiders. They lose confidence in the formal communications of the company. The grapevine, which is always exaggerated, takes on increased credibility. Company turnover starts to increase. Morale erodes.

It is obvious there is a problem and that it is not being dealt with. Employees wonder what will happen, whether they will be laid off, and whether the firm will go into bankruptcy. With their security threatened, employees lapse into survival mode. As an organizational behaviour consultant explains:

> The human organism can tolerate anything except *uncertainty*. It causes so much stress that people are no longer capable of thinking in a cognitive, creative manner. They focus on survival. That's why in turnarounds you see so much uncooperative, finger-pointing behaviour. The only issue people understand is directing the blame elsewhere [or in doing nothing].

Crisis can force intervention. The occasion is usually forced by the board of directors, lender, or a lawsuit. For example, the bank may call a loan, or the firm may be put on cash terms by its suppliers. Perhaps creditors try to put the firm into involuntary bankruptcy. Or something from the outside world fundamentally changes the business environment.

THE THREAT OF BANKRUPTCY

Unfortunately the heads of most troubled companies usually do not understand the benefits of bankruptcy law. To them, bankruptcy carries the stigma of failure; however, the law merely defines the priority of creditors' claims when the firm is liquidated.

Although bankruptcy can provide for the liquidation of the business, it also can provide for its reorganization. Bankruptcy is not an attractive prospect for creditors because they stand to lose at least some of their money, so they are often willing to negotiate. The prospect of bankruptcy can also be a foundation for bargaining in a turnaround. Of the late Ted Rogers, the *Globe and Mail* noted: "his greatest expectation-smashing act was escaping bankruptcy, as his flagship Rogers Communications Inc. survived a parade of near-death experiences, buried under the debt amassed by its risk-embracing owner."[4]

VOLUNTARY BANKRUPTCY

When legal bankruptcy is granted to a business, the firm is given immediate protection from creditors. Payment of interest or principal is suspended, and creditors must wait for their money. Generally the current executive team (a debtor in possession) is allowed to run the company, but sometimes an outsider, a trustee, is named to operate the company, and creditor committees are formed to watch over the operations and to negotiate with the company.

The greatest benefit of bankruptcy is that it buys time for the firm. The firm has 30 to 90 days to come up with a reorganization plan and time to obtain acceptance of that plan by creditors. Under a reorganization plan, debt can be extended. Debt also can be restructured (composed). Interest rates can be increased, and convertible provisions can be introduced to compensate debt holders for any increase in their risk as a result of the restructuring. Occasionally, debt holders need to take part of their claim in the form of equity. Trade creditors can be asked to take equity as payment, and they occasionally need to accept partial payment. If liquidation is the result of the reorganization plan, partial payment is the rule, with the typical payment ranging from zero to 30 cents on the dollar, depending on the priority of the claim.

BARGAINING POWER

For creditors, having a firm go into bankruptcy is not particularly attractive. *Bankruptcy, therefore, is a tremendous source of bargaining power for the troubled company.* Bankruptcy is not attractive to creditors because once protection is granted to a firm, creditors must wait for their money. Further, they are no longer dealing with the troubled company but with the judicial system, as well as with other creditors. Even if creditors are willing to wait for their money, they may not get full payment and may have to accept payment in some unattractive form. Last, the legal and administrative costs of bankruptcy, which can be substantial, are paid before any payments are made to creditors.

Faced with these prospects, many creditors conclude that their interests are better served by negotiating with the firm. Because the law defines the priority of creditors' claims, an entrepreneur can use it to determine who might be willing to negotiate. One anonymous reviewer of the present edition of this textbook noted:

> It is important when dealing with lenders—especially banks—to take action well before the bank may consider appointing a receiver. Once that step is taken, or even someone from outside comes into the business and monitors daily activities, the options for the owners have mostly evaporated.

INTERVENTION

A company in trouble will usually want to use the services of an outside advisor who specializes in turnarounds. In their book, *Fast Forward: Organizational Change in 100 Days*, Professors Elspeth Murray and Peter Richardson open with this scenario:

> You've mapped out what you believe is a great game plan to move your organization forward. You think everyone is on board. You believe you've allocated the right resources and enough of them, but nothing's happening. There's no sense of urgency, no pressure to move more quickly on initiatives that are critical to the organization's future viability and profitability. In the face of a seemingly endless stream of disruptive technologies, increasing customer expectations, new competitors coming out of nowhere, unrelenting globalization, and increasing shareholder expectations, you are trying to changed your organization to meet new demands, and you're not making any progress. In fact, no one seems to understand what they have to do.[5]

The situation the outside advisor usually finds at intervention is not encouraging. The company is often technically insolvent or has negative net worth. It already may have been put on a cash basis by its suppliers. It may be in default on loans, or if not, it is probably in violation of loan covenants. Call provisions may be exercised. At this point, as the situation deteriorates more, creditors may be trying to force the company into bankruptcy, and the organization is demoralized.

The critical task is to quickly diagnose the situation, develop an understanding of the company's bargaining position with its many creditors, and produce a detailed cash flow business plan for the turnaround of the organization. To this end, a turnaround advisor usually quickly signals that change is coming. He or she will elevate the finance function, putting the "cash person" (often the consultant himself) in charge of the business. Some payments may be put on hold until problems can be diagnosed and remedial actions decided upon.

DIAGNOSIS

Diagnosis can be complicated by the mixture of strategic and financial errors. For example, for a company with large receivables, questions need to be answered about whether receivables are bloated because of poor credit policy or because the company is in a business where liberal credit terms are required to compete.

Diagnosis occurs in three areas: the appropriate strategic posture of the business, the analysis of the venture team, and "the numbers."

Strategic Analysis

This analysis in a turnaround tries to identify the markets in which the company is capable of competing and decide on a competitive strategy. With small companies, turnaround experts state that most strategic errors relate to the involvement of firms in unprofitable product lines, customers, and geographic areas. It is outside the scope of this book to cover strategic analysis in detail.

Analysis of Leadership

Analysis of leadership consists of interviewing members of the executive team and coming to a subjective judgment of who belongs and who does not. Turnaround consultants can give no formula for how this is done except that it is the result of judgment that comes from experience.

The Numbers

Involved in "the numbers" is a detailed cash flow analysis, which will reveal areas for remedial action. The task is to identify and quantify the profitable core of the business.

- *Determine available cash.* The first task is to determine how much cash the firm has available in the near term. This is accomplished by looking at bank balances, receivables (those not being used as security), and the confirmed order backlog.

- *Determine where money is going.* This is a more complex task than it appears to be. A common technique is called subaccount analysis, where every account that posts to cash is found and accounts are arranged in descending order of cash outlays. Accounts then are scrutinized for patterns. These patterns can indicate the functional areas where problems exist. For example, one company had its corporate address on its bills, rather than the lockbox address at which cheques were processed, adding two days to its dollar days outstanding.

- *Calculate percent-of-sales ratios for different areas of a business and then analyze trends in costs.* Typically, several of the trends will show flex points, where relative costs have changed. For example, for one company that had undertaken a big project, an increase in cost of sales, which coincided with an increase in capacity and in the advertising budget, was noticed. Further analysis revealed this project was not producing enough in dollar contribution to justify its existence. Once the project was eliminated, excess capacity could be reduced to lower the firm's break-even point.

- *Reconstruct the business.* After determining where the cash is coming from and where it is going, the next step is to compare the business as it should be to the business as it is. This involves reconstructing the business from the ground up. For example, a cash budgeting exercise can be undertaken and collections, payments, and so forth determined for a given sales volume. Or the problem can be approached by determining labour, materials, and other direct costs and the overhead required to drive a given sales volume. What is essentially a cash flow business plan is created.

- *Determine differences.* Finally, the cash flow business plan is tied into pro forma balance sheets and income statements. The ideal cash flow plan and financial statements are compared to the business's current financial statements. For example, the pro forma income statements can be compared to existing statements to see where expenses can be reduced. The differences between the projected and actual financial statements form the basis of the turnaround plan and remedial actions.

The most commonly found areas for potential cuts/improvements are these: (1) working capital management, from order processing and billing to receivables, inventory control, and, of course, cash management; (2) payroll; and (3) overcapacity and underutilized assets. More than 80 percent of potential reduction in expenses can usually be found in workforce reduction.

THE TURNAROUND PLAN

The turnaround plan not only defines remedial actions but, because it is a detailed set of projections, also provides a means to monitor and control turnaround activity. Further, if the assumptions about unit sales volume, prices, collections, and negotiating success are varied, it can provide a means by which worst-case scenarios—complete with contingency plans— can be constructed.

Because short-term measures may not solve the cash crunch, a turnaround plan gives a firm enough credibility to buy time to put other remedial actions in place. For example, one firm's consultant could approach its bank to buy time with the following: by reducing payroll and discounting receivables, it can improve cash flow to the point where the firm can be current in five months. If it is successful in negotiating extended terms with trade creditors, then the firm can be current in three months. If the firm can sell some underutilized assets at 50 percent off, it can become current immediately.

The turnaround plan helps address organizational issues. The plan replaces uncertainty with a clearly defined set of actions and responsibilities. Since it signals to the organization that action is being taken, it helps get employees out of their survival mode. An effective plan breaks tasks into the smallest achievable unit, so successful completion of these simple tasks soon follows and the organization begins to experience success. Soon the downward spiral of organizational morale is broken.

Finally, the turnaround plan is an important source of bargaining power. By identifying problems and providing for remedial actions, the turnaround plan enables the firm's advisors to approach creditors and tell them in very detailed fashion how and when they will be paid. If the turnaround plan proves that creditors are better off working with the company as a going concern, rather than liquidating it, they will most likely be willing to negotiate their claims and terms of payment. Payment schedules can then be worked out that can keep the company afloat until the crisis is over.

Quick Cash

Ideally, the turnaround plan establishes enough creditor confidence to buy the turnaround consultant time to raise additional capital and turn underutilized assets into cash. It is imperative, however, to raise cash quickly. The result of the actions described below should be an improvement in cash flow. The solution is far from complete, however, because suppliers need to be satisfied.

For the purpose of quick cash, the working capital accounts hold the most promise. Accounts receivable is the most liquid non-cash asset. Receivables can be factored, but negotiating such arrangements takes time. The best route to cash is discounting receivables. How much receivables can be discounted depends on whether they are securing a loan. For example, a typical bank will lend up to 80 percent of the value of receivables that are under 90 days. As receivables age past the 90 days, the bank needs to be paid. New funds are advanced as new receivables are established as long as the 80 percent and under-90-day criteria are met. Receivables under 90 days can be discounted no more than 20 percent, if the bank obligation is to be met. Receivables over 90 days can be discounted as much as is needed to collect them, since they are not securing bank financing. One needs to use judgment in deciding exactly how large a discount to offer. A common method is to offer a generous discount with a time limit on it, after which the discount is no longer valid. This provides an incentive for the customer to pay immediately.

Consultants agree it is better to offer too large a discount than too small a one. If the discount is too small and needs to be followed by further discounts, customers may hold off paying in the hope that another round of discounts will follow. Generally it is the slow payers that cause the problems and discounting may not help. By getting on the squeaky-wheel list of the particular slow-pay customer, you might get attention. A possible solution is to put on a note with the objective of having the customer start paying you on a regular basis; also, adding a small additional amount to every new order helps to work down the balance.

Inventory is not as liquid as receivables but still can be liquidated to generate quick cash. An inventory "fire sale" gets mixed reviews from turnaround experts. The most common objection is that excess inventory is often obsolete. The second objection is that because much inventory is work in process, it is not in saleable form and requires money to put in saleable form. The third is that discounting finished-goods inventory may generate cash but is liable to create customer resistance to restored margins after the company is turned around. The sale of raw materials inventory to competitors is generally considered the best route. Another option is to try to sell inventory at discounted prices to new channels of distribution. In these channels, the discounted prices might not affect the next sale.

One interesting option for the company with a lot of work-in-process inventory is to ease credit terms. It often is possible to borrow more against receivables than against inventory. By easing credit terms, the company can increase its borrowing capacity to perhaps enough to get cash to finish work in process. This option may be difficult to implement because, by the time of intervention, the firm's lenders are likely following the company very closely and may veto the arrangements.

Also relevant to generating quick cash is the policy regarding current sales activity. Guiding criteria for this needs to include increasing the total dollar value of margin, generating cash quickly, and keeping working capital in its most liquid form. Prices and cash discounts need to be increased and credit terms eased. Easing credit terms, however, can conflict with the receivables policy described above. Obviously, care needs to be taken to maintain consistency of policy. Easing credit is really an "excess inventory" policy. The overall idea is to leverage policy in favour of cash first, receivables second, and inventory third.

Putting all accounts payable on hold is the next option. Clearly, this eases the cash flow burden in the near term. Although some arrangement to pay suppliers needs to be made, the most important uses of cash at this stage are meeting payroll and paying lenders. Lenders are important, but if you do not get suppliers to ship goods you are out of business. Getting suppliers to ship is critical. A company with negative cash flow simply needs to "prioritize" its use of cash. Suppliers are the least likely to force the company into bankruptcy because, under the law, they have a low priority claim.

Dealing with Lenders

The next step in the turnaround is to negotiate with lenders. To continue to do business with the company, lenders need to be satisfied that there is a workable long-term solution.

However, at the point of intervention, the company is most likely in default on its payments. Or, if payments are current, the financial situation has probably deteriorated to the point where the company is in violation of loan covenants. It also is likely that many of the firm's assets have been pledged as collateral. To make matters worse, it is likely that the troubled entrepreneur has been avoiding his or her lenders during the gestation period and has demonstrated that he or she is not in control of the situation. Credibility has been lost.

It is important for a firm to know that it is not the first ever to default on a loan, that the lender is usually willing to work things out, and that it is still in a position to bargain. Strategically, there are two sources of bargaining power. The first is that bankruptcy is an unattractive result to a lender, despite its senior claims. A low-margin business cannot absorb large losses easily. (Recall that banks typically earn 0.5 percent to 1.0 percent total return on assets.)

The second is credibility. The firm that, through its turnaround specialist, has diagnosed the problem and produced a detailed turnaround plan with best-case/worst-case scenarios, the aim of which is to prove to the lender that the company is capable of paying, is in a better bargaining position. The plan details specific actions (e.g., layoffs, assets plays, changes in credit policy, etc.) that will be undertaken, and this plan must be met to regain credibility.

There are also two tactical sources of bargaining power. First, there is the strength of the lender's collateral. The second is the bank's inferior knowledge of aftermarkets and the entrepreneur's superior ability to sell.

The following example illustrates that, when the lender's collateral is poor, it has little choice but to look to the entrepreneur for a way out without incurring a loss. It also shows that the entrepreneur's superior knowledge of his business and ability to sell can get himself and the lender out of trouble. One company in turnaround in the leather business overbought inventory one year, and, at the same time, a competitor announced a new product that made his inventory almost obsolete. Since the entrepreneur went to the lender with the problem, the lender was willing to work with him. The entrepreneur had plans to sell the inventory at reduced prices and also to enter a new market that looked attractive. The only trouble was he needed more money to do it, and he was already over his credit limit. The lender was faced with the certainty of losing 80 percent of its money and putting its customer out of business or the possibility of losing money by throwing good money after bad. The lender decided to work with the entrepreneur. It got a higher interest rate and put the entrepreneur on a "full following mechanism," which meant that all payments were sent to a lockbox. The lender processed the cheques and reduced its exposure before it put money in his account.

Another example illustrates the existence of bargaining power with a lender who is under-collateralized and stands to take a large loss. A company was importing knockoffs of a particular fad doll from Europe. This was financed with a letter of credit. However, when the dolls arrived in this country, the company could not sell the dolls because the particular craze was over. The dolls, and the bank's collateral, were worthless. The company found that the doll heads could be replaced, and with the new heads, the dolls did not look like copycat dolls. It found also that one toy buyer would purchase the entire inventory. The company needed $30 000 to buy the new heads and have them put on, so it went back to the bank. The bank said that if the company wanted the money key members of the venture team had to give liens on their houses. When this was refused, the banker was astounded.

Lenders are often willing to advance money for a company to meet its payroll. This is largely a public relations consideration. Also, if a company does not meet its payroll, a crisis may be precipitated before the lender can consider its options.

When the situation starts to improve, a lender may call the loan. Such a move will solve the lender's problem but may put the company under. While many bankers will deny this ever happens, some will concede that such an occurrence depends on the loan officer.

Dealing with Trade Creditors

In dealing with trade creditors, the first step is to understand the strength of the company's bargaining position. Trade creditors have the lowest priority claims should a company file for bankruptcy and, therefore, are often the most willing to deal. In bankruptcy, trade creditors often receive just a few cents on the dollar.

Another bargaining power boost with trade creditors is the existence of a turnaround plan. As long as a company demonstrates that it can offer a trade creditor a better result as a going concern than it can in bankruptcy proceedings, the trade creditor should be willing to negotiate. It is generally good to make sure that trade creditors are getting a little money on a frequent basis. Remember trade creditors have a higher gross margin than a bank, so their getting paid pays down their "risk" money faster. This is especially true if the creditor can ship new goods and get paid for that, and also get some money toward the old receivables.

Also, trade creditors have to deal with the customer-relations issue. Trade creditors will work with a troubled company if they see it as a way to preserve a market.

The relative weakness in the position of trade creditors has allowed some turnaround consultants to negotiate impressive deals. For example, one company got trade creditors to agree to a 24-month payment schedule for all outstanding accounts. In return, the firm pledged to keep all new payables current. The entrepreneur was able to keep the company from dealing on a cash basis with many of its creditors and to convert short-term payables into what amounted to long-term debt. The effect on current cash flow was very favourable.

The second step is to prioritize trade creditors according to their importance to the turnaround. The company then needs to take care of those creditors that are most important. For example, one entrepreneur told his controller never to make a commitment he could not keep. The controller was told that, if the company was going to miss a commitment, he was to get on the phone and call. The most important suppliers were told that if something happened and they needed payment sooner than had been agreed, they were to let the company know and it would do its best to come up with the cash.

The third step in dealing with trade creditors is to switch vendors if necessary. The lower priority suppliers will put the company on cash terms or refuse to do business. The troubled company needs to be able to switch suppliers, and its relationship with its priority suppliers will help it to do this, because they can give credit references. One firm said, "We asked our best suppliers to be as liberal with credit references as possible. I don't know if we could have established new relationships without them."

The fourth step in dealing with trade creditors is to communicate effectively. "Dealing with the trade is as simple as telling the truth," one consultant said. If a company is honest, at least a creditor can plan.

Workforce Reductions

With workforce reduction representing 80 percent of the potential expense reduction, layoffs are inevitable in a turnaround situation.

A number of turnaround specialists recommend that layoffs be announced to an organization as a onetime reduction in the workforce and be done all at once. They recommend further that layoffs be accomplished as soon as possible, since employees will never regain their productivity until they feel some measure of security. Finally, they suggest that a firm cut deeper than seems necessary to compensate for other remedial actions that may be difficult to implement. For example, it is one thing to set out to reduce capacity by half and quite another thing to sell or sublet half a plant.

LONGER-TERM REMEDIAL ACTIONS

If the turnaround plan has created enough credibility and has bought the firm time, longer-term remedial actions can be implemented.

These actions will usually fall into three categories:

- *Systems and procedures.* Systems and procedures that contributed to the problem can be improved, or others can be implemented.

- *Asset plays.* Assets that could not be liquidated in a shorter time frame can be liquidated. For example, real estate could be sold. Many smaller companies, particularly older ones, carry real estate on their balance sheet at far below market value. This could be sold and leased back or could be borrowed against to generate cash.

- *Creative solutions.* Creative solutions need to be found. For example, one firm had a large amount of inventory that was useless in its current business. However, it found that if the inventory could be assembled into parts, there would be a market for it. The company shipped the inventory to Jamaica, where labour rates were low, for assembly, and it was able to sell the entire inventory very profitably.

As was stated at the beginning of the chapter, many companies—even companies that are insolvent or have negative net worth or both—can be rescued and restored to profitability.

Although we opened this chapter with the assertion that purchasing an automobile seldom provides a positive financial return—we do know that those who restore cars find great joy in the activity. Rescuing a wreck from the scrapyard or taking a jalopy from a barn and returning it to working condition is rewarding for those who have a passion for it. While diagnosing and overcoming troubles for a venture need not result in harvest, and harvest can be undertaken regardless of the venture's condition, often the two are related. While driving a car into the ground may be prudent with a fully depreciated vehicle, this certainly is not the ideal modus operandi for a viable business. We now turn our attention to exit strategy and execution.

A JOURNEY, NOT A DESTINATION

A common sentiment among successful entrepreneurs is that it is the challenge and exhilaration of the journey that gives them the greatest kick. Actor Jim Carrey captures the spirit: "Desperation is a necessary ingredient to learning anything, or creating anything. Period. If you ain't desperate at some point, you ain't interesting." It is the thrill of the chase that counts. And of course, many entrepreneurial individuals cannot sit still—they are always restless. In Jim Carrey's case: "My report card always said, 'Jim finishes first and then disrupts the other students.'"[6]

Entrepreneurs also talk of the venture's incredibly insatiable appetite for not only cash but also time, attention, and energy. Some say it is an addiction. Most say it is far more demanding and difficult than they ever imagined. Most, however, plan not to retire and would do it again, usually sooner rather than later. They also say it is more fun and satisfying than any other career they have had.

For the vast majority of entrepreneurs, it takes 10, 15, even 20 years or more to build a significant net worth. According to the popular press and government statistics, there are more millionaires than ever in Canada. One report estimated 315 000 Canadian millionaires in 2001 and 900 000 in 2010.[7] According to Statistics Canada "surging real estate values and a strong economy helped drive up the number of millionaire families in Canada."[8] Another report proclaimed that the number of millionaires in Canada grew 7.7% in 2012, placing Canada in 7th place for number of millionaires worldwide.[9] Nearly half of Canada's high net-worth individuals are immigrants or first-generation Canadians. According to Yannick Archambault, VP and COO of BMO Harris Private Banking, it is because they "bring a strong work ethic, a lot of determination and entrepreneurship."[10] Although the Bare Naked Ladies affirmed in 1992, "If I had a million dollars I'd be rich," sadly, a million dollars is not really all that much money today as a result of inflation, and while lottery winners become instant millionaires, entrepreneurs do not. The number of years it usually takes to accumulate such a net worth is a far cry from the instant millionaire associated with lottery winners or depicted in TV shows.

THE JOURNEY CAN BE ADDICTIVE

The total immersion required, the huge workload, the many sacrifices for a family, and the burnout often experienced by an entrepreneur are real. Maintaining the energy, enthusiasm, and drive to get across the finish line, to achieve a harvest, may be exceptionally difficult. For instance, one entrepreneur in the computer software business, after working alone for several years, developed highly sophisticated software. Yet, he insisted he could not stand the computer business for another day. Imagine trying to position a company for sale effectively and to negotiate a deal for a premium price after such a long battle.

Some entrepreneurs wonder if the price of victory is too high. One very successful entrepreneur put it this way:

> What difference does it make if you win, have $20 million in the bank—I know several who do—and you are a basket case, your family has been washed out, and your kids are a wreck?

Entrepreneur Brett Wilson recalls:

> It was hard not to enjoy the success we were having, doing a deal a day. It was enthralling to be at the office. I got as caught up in my career as any investment banker could be. I had always told myself that I worked so hard because of my family. Suddenly, I was facing the possibility of no family at all.[11]

The message is clear: Unless an entrepreneur enjoys the journey and thinks it is worthy, he or she may end up on the wrong train to the wrong destination.

FIRST BUILD A GREAT COMPANY   LO3

One of the simplest but most difficult principles for non-entrepreneurs to grasp is that wealth and liquidity are results—not causes—of building a great company. They fail to recognize the difference between making money and spending money. Most successful entrepreneurs

HARD WORK AND BAD LUCK

Sam Tilden bought a Hertz Rent-a-Car franchise for Montréal in 1925. When Hertz took the franchise back in 1929 thinking it could make more money, Sam went into the miniature golf business for a few years, and in 1932 Sam reclaimed his old franchise! He expanded to Ottawa and Hamilton, Ontario. In 1953, Sam Tilden and several Hertz franchises walked—and founded Tilden Rent-a-Car. (Hertz had a cancellation policy that allowed them to revoke a franchise without cause on 60-days' notice.) By 1954, they had 100 Tilden locations across Canada. Sam formed partnerships (50–50 joint ventures) with U.S.-based National Car Rental for Europe and Japanese Nippon Rent-a-Car for Asia. In 1973, at the age of 76, Sam died of a heart attack. His sons Walter and Ted took over and moved headquarters from Montréal to Toronto. In 1991, Ted died of a heart attack.

Two months later a Tilden car was involved in a gruesome accident in New York City involving a gasoline tanker truck. Nearly a dozen stores were burned as 200 firefighters fought the blaze. The trucking company did not have insurance and over 20 lawsuits were aimed at Tilden's deeper pockets. For estate planning reasons, Walter looked to sell the company. His niece, Patricia Tilden, took over as president and CEO of the family company. Tilden sought protection from potential liability and sought protection under the Companies' Creditor Arrangement (bankruptcy protection) a month before the lawsuits were expected to go to trial. Walter's son, Bruce, witnessed the claims being tossed out of court and within a week National Car Rental paid $115 million for Tilden's fleet with Tilden retaining about $4 million in real estate assets. Walter died in 2008 at age 80.

Source: Anthony J. Patterson, "Canada's Tildens: Waving the Flag That Works for Them," *Financial Times*, March 24, 1975; "Car Rental Industry's Ted Tilden Dies at 60," *Calgary Herald*, March 7, 1991; "Court Clears Way for Tilden Sale," *Financial Post*, June 8, 1996; Sandra Martin, "He Helped Build Tilden Rent-a-Car Into a Thriving, All-Canadian Concern," *The Globe and Mail*, July 30, 2008.

possess a clear understanding of this distinction; they get their kicks from growing the company. They know the payoff will take care of itself if they concentrate on proving and building a sustainable venture.

CREATE HARVEST OPTIONS

Here is yet another great paradox in the entrepreneurial process: Build a great company but do not forget to harvest. This apparent contradiction is difficult to reconcile, especially among entrepreneurs with several generations in a family-owned enterprise. Perhaps a better way to frame this apparent contradiction is to keep harvest options open and to think of harvesting as a vehicle for reducing risk and for creating future entrepreneurial choices and options, not simply selling the business and heading for the golf course or the beach, although these options may appeal to a few entrepreneurs.

It is not difficult to think of a number of alternative outcomes for those wanting to exit the venture. By stubbornly and steadfastly refusing to explore harvest options and exiting as a natural part of the entrepreneurial process, owners may actually increase their overall risk and deprive themselves of future options. Innumerable examples exist whereby entrepreneurs sold or merged their companies and then went on to acquire or to start another company and pursued new dreams:

- At the age of six Ted Rogers' father died. At the urging of family, his mother sold off industrial assets, including radio station CFRB, which Ted promised his mother he would one day buy back.

- Edgar Bronfman expanded the family fortune as Seagram expanded and then divested ownership in favour of other financial and personal pursuits. The decision to divest the family stake in DuPont Chemical was controversial and received much criticism.

The Canadian Press/Frank Arcuri

Born in Saskatoon, Saskatchewan, Jim Pattison has amassed an amazing empire. Born in 1928, he is still going strong and making acquisitions one after the other. Forbes lists him as the 6th wealthiest Canadian and like many other high net-worth individuals he devotes much time, effort, and money to causes he finds worthy. When CBC television announced that during the NHL playoffs they could not afford to rent high-definition broadcast trucks during away games, Pattison announced that Save-On Foods, his western Canadian grocery chain, would cover the costs—$100 000.

Despite his age, Jim Pattison shows no signs of cashing out. As the sole owner of the third-largest privately held Canadian company, he is not required to reveal any "harvest" plans.

Question: When would you cash out? Will you keep working when you are in your eighties?

JIM PATTISON, SOLE OWNER OF THE THIRD-LARGEST PRIVATELY HELD COMPANY IN CANADA

Source: www.jimpattison.com

- E.D. Smith & Sons of Winona, Ontario, had been a family business making jams, spreads, marmalades, etc. since 1882. In 2002, Llewellyn S. Smith, chairman of E.D. Smith & Sons Ltd., sold the company to Imperial Capital Corporation. E.D. Smith went on to acquire other food processors. In late 2007, E.D. Smith & Sons was sold to Treehouse Foods Inc. for $220 million in cash.

- While in his early 20s, Stephen Spinelli was recruited by his former college football coach, Jim Hindman, to help start and build Jiffy Lube International. As a captain of the team, Spinelli had exhibited the qualities of leadership, tenacity, and competitive will to win that Hindman knew were needed to create a new company. Spinelli later built the largest franchise in America, and after selling his 49 stores to Pennzoil in 1993, he returned to his MBA alma mater to teach. So invigorated was he by this new challenge he even went back to earn his doctorate and eventually become a university president.

- Dominion Loose Leaf Company was started in 1918; the Nicholds family purchased the company in 1956 creating an exit for the previous owners. The printing services company was renamed Dollco Printing and in 2001 ownership passed to the third generation. Cousins Krista Nicholds, VP of Marketing, and Kevin Nicholds, President, became co-owners of an enterprise with 300 employees and operations in Ottawa, Toronto, Québec, Halifax, and the northeastern United States. In 2012, Dollco was acquired by the Lowe-Martin Group.

These are a tiny representation of the tens of thousands of entrepreneurs that build on their platforms of entrepreneurial success to pursue highly meaningful lives in philanthropy, public service, and community leadership. By realizing a harvest, such options become possible, yet the vast majority of entrepreneurs make these contributions to society while continuing to build their companies (see Jim Pattison). This is one of the best-kept secrets in our culture: The public has very little awareness and appreciation of just how common this pattern of generosity is of their time, their leadership, and their money. One could fill a book with numerous other examples. The entrepreneurial process is endless.

A HARVEST GOAL LO4

Having a harvest goal and crafting a strategy to achieve it are what separate successful entrepreneurs from the rest of the pack. Many entrepreneurs seek only to create a job and a living for themselves. It is quite different to grow a business that creates a living for many others, including employees and investors, by creating value—value that can result in a capital gain.

Setting a harvest goal achieves many purposes, not the least of which is helping an entrepreneur get after-tax cash out of an enterprise and substantially enhancing his or her net worth. Such a goal also can create high standards and a serious commitment to excellence over the course of developing the business. It can provide, in addition, a motivating force and a strategic focus that does not sacrifice customers, employees, and value-added products and services just to maximize quarterly earnings.

There are other good reasons to set a harvest goal as well. The workload demanded by a harvest-oriented venture versus one in a venture that cannot achieve a harvest may actually be less and is probably no greater. Such a business may be less stressful than running a business that is not oriented to harvest.

There is a significant societal reason as well for seeking and building a venture worthy of a harvest. These are the ventures that provide enormous impact and value added in a variety of ways. These companies contribute disproportionately to technological and other innovations, to new jobs, to returns for investors, and to economic vibrancy.

Also, the seeds of renewal and reinvestment are sown within the harvest process. Such a recycling of entrepreneurial talent and capital is at the very heart of our system of private responsibility for economic renewal and individual initiative. Entrepreneurial companies organize and execute for the long haul in ways that perpetuate the opportunity creation and recognition process and thereby ensure economic regeneration, innovation, and renewal.

Thus, a harvest goal is not just a goal of selling and leaving the company. Rather, it is a long-term goal to create real value added in a business. (It is true, however, that if real value added is not created, the business simply will not be worth much in the marketplace.)

CRAFTING A HARVEST STRATEGY: TIMING IS VITAL

Consistently, entrepreneurs avoid thinking about harvest issues. In a survey of the computer software industry, 80 of the 100 companies had only an informal plan for harvesting. The rest of the sample confirmed the avoidance of harvest plans by entrepreneurs—only 15 of the companies had a formal written strategy for harvest in their business plans and the remaining five had a formal harvest plan written after the business plan.[12] When a company is launched, then struggles for survival, and finally begins its ascent, usually the farthest thing from its founder's mind is selling out. Selling is often viewed by the entrepreneur as the equivalent to complete abandonment of his or her very own "baby." But a harvest "makes perfect sense" when the entrepreneur "finds it is the appropriate timing for capturing the value that has been created through the venture."[13]

Thus, time and again, a founder does not consider selling until terror, in the form of the possibility of losing the whole company, is experienced. Usually, this possibility comes unexpectedly: New technology threatens to leapfrog over the current product line, a large competitor suddenly appears in a small market, or a major account is lost. A sense of panic then grips the founders and shareholders of the closely held firm, and the company is suddenly for sale—for sale at the wrong time, for the wrong reasons, and thus for the wrong price. Selling at the right time, willingly, involves hitting a strategic window, one of the many strategic windows that entrepreneurs face.

Entrepreneurs find that harvesting is a non-issue until something begins to sprout, and again there is a vast distance between creating an existing revenue stream of an ongoing business and ground zero. Most entrepreneurs agree that securing customers and generating continuing sales revenue are much harder and take much longer than they could have imagined. Further, the ease with which those revenue estimates can be cast and manipulated on a spreadsheet belies the time and effort necessary to turn those projections into cash.

At some point, with a higher potential venture, it becomes possible to realize the harvest. It is wiser to be selling as the strategic window is opening than as it is closing. Business financier and stock market speculator Bernard Baruch's wisdom is as good as it gets on this matter. He has said, "I made all my money by selling too early." For example, a private candy company with $150 million in sales was not considering selling. After contemplating advice to sell early, the founders recognized a unique opportunity to harvest and sold the firm for 19 times earnings, an extremely high valuation. Another example is that of a cellular phone company that was launched and built from scratch. Only 18 months after purchasing the original rights to build and operate the system, the founders decided to sell the company, even though the future looked extremely bright. They sold because the sellers' market they faced at the time had resulted in a premium valuation—30 percent higher on a per capita basis (the industry valuation norm) than that for any previous cellular transaction to date. The harvest returned over 25 times the original capital in a year and a half. (The founders had not invested a dime of their own money.)

If the window is missed, disaster can strike. Shaping a harvest strategy is an enormously complicated and difficult task. Thus, crafting such a strategy cannot begin too early. Companies declare bankruptcy after bubbles burst and stock markets crash. The toll includes large corporations and dozens of lesser-known small and mid-size companies. This is one history lesson that seems to repeat itself. While building a company is the ultimate goal, failure to preserve the harvest option and utilize it when it is available can be most disheartening.

In shaping a harvest strategy, some guidelines and cautions can help:

- *Patience.* As has been shown, several years are required to launch and build most successful companies; therefore, patience can be invaluable. A harvest strategy is more sensible if it allows for a time frame of at least three to five years and as long as 7 to 10 years. The other side of the patience coin is not to panic as a result of precipitate events. Selling under duress is usually the worst of all worlds.

- *Realistic valuation.* If impatience is the enemy of an attractive harvest, then greed is its executioner. For example, an excellent, small firm, which was nearly 80 years old and run by the third generation of a line of successful family leaders, had attracted a number of prospective buyers and had obtained a bona fide offer for more than $25 million. The owners, however, had become convinced that this "great little company" was worth considerably more, and they held out. Before long, there were no buyers and market circumstances changed unfavourably. In addition, interest rates skyrocketed. Soon thereafter, the company collapsed financially, ending up in bankruptcy.

- *Outside advice.* It is difficult but worthwhile to find an advisor who can help craft a harvest strategy while the business is growing and, at the same time, maintain objectivity about its value and have the patience and skill to maximize it. A major problem seems to be that people who sell businesses, such as investment bankers or business brokers, are performing the same economic role and function as real estate brokers; in essence, their incentive is their commissions during a quite short time frame, usually a matter of months. However, an advisor who works with a lead entrepreneur for as much as five years or more can help shape and implement a strategy for the whole business so that it is positioned to spot and respond to harvest opportunities when they appear.

HARVEST OPTIONS   LO5

There are seven principal avenues by which a company can realize a harvest from the value it has created. Described on the next pages, these most commonly seem to occur in the order in which they are listed. No attempt is made here to do more than briefly describe each avenue, since there are entire books written on each of these, including their legal, tax, and accounting intricacies. As you read through these harvest options consider Roots. Established in 1973, Roots is "Canada's leading lifestyle" brand known worldwide, particularly after outfitting Olympic athletes.[14] But Roots has had ups and downs. Roots is owned by its co-founders Michael Budmand and Don Green who met one summer at camp in Algonquin Park, Ontario. When would you "harvest" Roots and how? What signals would tell you? It is worth visiting exercise 7, "Capital and Harvest—How Will You Realize Dollars from the Venture?" in the Venture Opportunity Screening Exercise that accompanies chapter 3 and is found online with Connect.

CAPITAL COW

A "capital cow" is to the entrepreneur what a "cash cow" is to a large corporation. In essence, the high-margin profitable venture (the cow) throws off more cash for personal use (the milk) than most entrepreneurs have the time and uses or inclinations for spending. The result is a capital-rich and cash-rich company with enormous capacity for debt and reinvestment. Take, for instance, a health care–related venture that realized early success and went public. Several years later, the founders decided to buy the company back from the public shareholders and to return it to its closely held status. Today the company has sales in excess of $100 million and generates extra capital of several million dollars each year. This capital cow has enabled its entrepreneurs to form entities to invest in several other higher potential ventures, which included participation in the leveraged buyout of a $150-million sales division of a larger firm and in some venture capital deals. Sometimes the creation of a capital cow results in substantial real estate holdings by the entrepreneur, off the books of the original firm. This allows for greater flexibility in the distribution of cash flow and the later allocation of the wealth.

EMPLOYEE SHARE OWNERSHIP PLAN

Employee share ownership plans have become popular among closely held companies as a valuation mechanism for shares for which there is no formal market. They are also vehicles through which founders can realize some liquidity from their shares by sales to the plan and other employees. And since an ESOP usually creates widespread ownership of shares among employees, it is viewed as a positive motivational device as well. Part of WestJet's public persona is that employees are committed, caring, and have a stake in the venture's success: "Because we're also WestJet owners." In General Motors' 2009 restructuring, Magna sought to acquire GM's European product group Opel. Although the deal never went through, it called for 10 percent of the shares to be turned over to Opel employees.

The Bauer family was running the Western Shoe Company when in 1927 it established Bauer as a brand of hockey skates. The family was the first to produce skates where the blade was permanently attached to the boot—the Bauer Supreme it was called. (CCM marketed "Tacks," which were worn by all NHL scoring champions from 1939 to 1969. The patent for the skate had been sold (harvested) to CCM by Helen Tackaberry in 1937 on her husband's death.) The Bauer family realized a harvest when their namesake became a division of family-controlled shoe company Greb Industries. The Bronfman family's Warrington Products purchased Greb in 1974. Bauer took the bold step of paying superstar Bobby Hull to endorse their skates and later introduced the Tuuk skate chassis. From 1971 to 1982 Warrington Products had five years of annual losses and shares tanked from an IPO of $8.75 to less than $1. After a tour of Warrington's skate factory in 1975, ski boot entrepreneur and inventor Icaro Olivieri became a competitor and by 1981 merged with Warrington. Olivieri reinvested 2–3 percent of revenues into R&D. By 1987, 70 percent of the NHL pros were wearing his Micron Mega skate.

A wild spree of acquisitions proved disastrous. The diversification strategy resulted in losses and massive debt. Bronfman family disputes also made matters worse. A leveraged buyout of the family's 30 percent stake resulted in a company re-focused on just hockey. The turnaround specialist placed at the helm was ousted a few years later and Olivieri sold his 46 percent stake to Nike. Nike paid $430 million for the entity in 1994, the year it sponsored the NHL. Roustan Inc., led by W. Graeme Roustan, and private-equity firm Kohlberg & Co. purchased Nike's Bauer assets for $200 million

BOBBY HULL STEALS THE PUCK FROM A CZECHOSLOVAKIAN PLAYER AT THE CANADA CUP, SEPTEMBER 13, 1976

in 2008. Bauer purchased Mission-Itech that same year. In 2011, Bauer complete an IPO on the TSX. In 2012, Bauer acquired Cascade. In 2013, Kohlberg & Co. announced that it would begin cashing out its position through a secondary offering.

Question: Was Bobby Hull realizing a harvest when he took the deal with Bauer to play in their skates? For every divestiture, someone else is jumping in. Many entrepreneurs invest in new activities (another start-up, a charity, a hobby, etc.) after they realize a harvest. What might you do with your newfound time and money if you realized a harvest?

MANAGEMENT BUYOUT

Another avenue, called a management buyout (MBO), is one in which a founder can realize a gain from a business by selling it to existing partners or to others in the business. If the business has both assets and a healthy cash flow, the financing can be arranged via banks, insurance companies, and financial institutions that do leveraged buyouts (LBOs) and MBOs. Even if assets are thin, a healthy cash flow that can service the debt to fund the purchase price can convince lenders to do the MBO.

Usually, the problem is that those who want to buy out the owners and remain to run the company do not have the capital. Unless the buyer has the cash up front—and this is rarely the case—such a sale can be very fragile, and full realization of a gain is questionable. MBOs typically require the seller to take a limited amount of cash up front and a note for the balance of the purchase price over several years. If the purchase price is linked to the future profitability of the business, the seller is totally dependent on the ability and integrity of the buyer. Further, under such an arrangement, the price can be lowered by growing the business as fast as possible, spending on new products and people, and showing very little profit along the way. In these cases, it is often seen that after the marginally profitable business is sold at a bargain price it is well positioned with excellent earnings in the next two or three years. As can be seen, the seller will end up on the short end of this type of deal.

MERGER, ACQUISITION, AND STRATEGIC ALLIANCE

Merging with a firm is still another way for a founder to realize a gain. For example, two founders who had developed high-quality training programs consummated a merger with another company. These entrepreneurs had backgrounds in computers, rather than in marketing or general management, and the results of the company's first five years reflected this gap. Sales were under $500 000 based on custom programs and no marketing, and they had been unable to attract venture capital. The firm with which they merged was a $15-million company that had an excellent reputation for its leadership training programs, had a large customer base, had repeat sales of 70 percent, and had requests from the field sales force for programs to train leaders in the use of personal computers. The buyer obtained 80 percent of the shares of the smaller firm, to consolidate the revenues and earnings from the merged company into its own financial statements, and the two founders of the smaller firm retained a 20-percent ownership in their firm. The two founders also obtained employment contracts, and the buyer provided nearly $1.5 million of capital advances during the first year of the new business. Under a put arrangement, the founders will be able to realize a gain on their 20 percent of the company, depending upon performance of the venture over the next few years.[15] The two founders now are reporting to the president of the parent firm, and one founder of the parent firm has taken a key executive position with the smaller company, an approach common for mergers between closely held firms.

In a strategic alliance, founders can attract badly needed capital, in substantial amounts, from a large company interested in their technologies. Such arrangements often can lead to complete buyouts of the founders downstream.

OUTRIGHT SALE

Most advisors view outright sale as the ideal route to go because upfront cash is preferred over most shares, even though the latter can result in a tax-free exchange.[16] In a shares-for-shares exchange, the problem is the volatility and unpredictability of the share price of the purchasing company. Many entrepreneurs have been left with a fraction of the original purchase price when the share price of the buyer's company declined steadily. Often the acquiring company wants to lock key executives into employment contracts for up to several years. Whether this makes sense depends on the goals and circumstances of the individual entrepreneur. Recall from chapter 2 that John W. Sleeman sold his namesake in 2004 and agreed to stay on to serve as CEO under the new owner Sapporo Breweries of Japan.

PUBLIC OFFERING

Probably the most sacred business school cow of them all—other than the capital cow—is the notion of taking a company public.[17] The vision or fantasy of having one's venture listed on one of the stock exchanges arouses passions of greed, glory, and greatness. For many would-be entrepreneurs, this aspiration is unquestioned and enormously appealing. Yet, for all but a chosen few, taking a company public, and then living with it, may be far more time and trouble—and expense—than it is worth. Richard L'Abbé of Med-Eng Systems Inc. was strongly opposed to becoming a publicly traded company. His board of directors pushed him out and sold the company to Allen Vanguard in 2007 for $650 million. Allen Vanguard plummeted on the TSX and its shares were subsequently delisted in 2009. Despite having "regrets" over the deal, "shareholders get nothing." In 2013, Allen-Vanguard was seeking damages alleging fraudulent misrepresentations on the part of Med-Eng shareholders.

After the market crash of October 1987, the market for new issues of shares shrank to a fraction of the robust IPO market of 1986 and earlier years. The number of new issues and the volume of IPOs did not rebound; instead, they declined between 1988 and 1992. Beginning in 1993 the IPO window opened again. During this IPO frenzy, small companies with total assets under $500 000 issued most of the IPOs. Previously, small companies had not been as active in the IPO market. Now most of the firms that go public in Canada have small capitalizations.

This cyclical pattern repeats itself regularly. As the dot.com, telecommunications, and networking explosion accelerated from 1995 to 2000, the IPO markets exploded as well. In 1996, for instance, despite twice the number of IPOs as in 2005, the total dollar value in 2006 was

EXHIBIT 15.2(A)   NUMBER OF CANADIAN IPOs

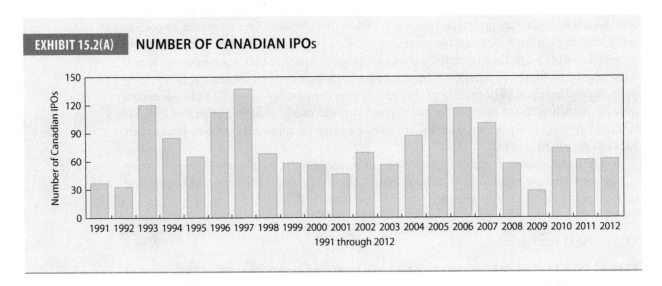

EXHIBIT 15.2(B)   VALUE OF CANADIAN IPOs ($MILLIONS)

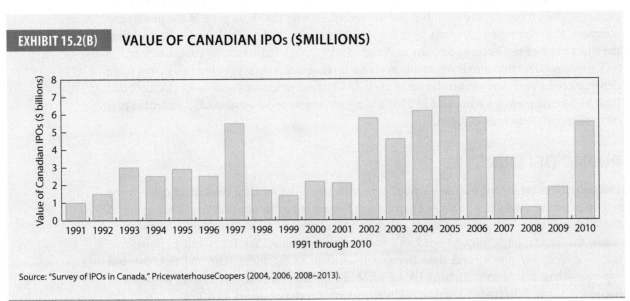

Source: "Survey of IPOs in Canada," PricewaterhouseCoopers (2004, 2006, 2008–2013).

lower than in 2005. In 2008, there were months when not a single IPO occurred on the Toronto Stock Exchange! Few signs of recovery were evident in 2009. The lesson is clear: Depending upon the IPO market for a harvest is a highly cyclical strategy, which can cause both great joy and disappointment. Such is the reality of the stock markets. Exhibits 15.2(A) and 15.2(B) show this pattern vividly.

There are several advantages to going public, many of which relate to the ability of the company to fund its rapid growth. Public equity markets provide access to long-term capital, while also meeting subsequent capital needs. Companies may use the proceeds of an IPO to expand the business in the existing market or to move into a related market. The founders and initial investors might be seeking liquidity, but restrictions limiting the timing and the number of shares that the officers, directors, and insiders can dispose of in the public market are increasingly severe. As a result, it can take several years after an IPO before a liquid gain is possible. A public offering not only increases public awareness of the company but also contributes to the marketability of the products, including franchises. Tim Hortons went public in 2006 on the New York Stock Exchange and the Toronto Stock Exchange.

However, there are also some disadvantages to being a public company. For example, 50 percent of the computer software companies surveyed in one study agreed that the focus on short-term profits and performance results was a negative attribute of being a public company.[18] Also, because of the disclosure requirements, public companies lose some of their operating confidentiality, not to mention having to support the ongoing costs of public disclosure, audits, and tax filings. With public shareholders, the executives of the company have to be careful about the flow of information because of the risk of insider trading. Thus, it is easy to see why companies need to think about the positive and negative attributes of being a public company. When considering this decision, you may find it useful to identify the key components of the IPO process and to assess which investment bankers, accountants, lawyers, and advisors might be useful in making this decision.

BEYOND THE HARVEST   LO6

A majority of highly successful entrepreneurs seem to accept a responsibility to renew and perpetuate the system that has treated them so well. They are keenly aware that our system of opportunity and mobility depends in large part upon a self-renewal process.

There are many ways in which this happens. Some of the following data often surprise people:

- *University endowments.* Entrepreneurs are the most generous regarding larger gifts and the most frequent contributors to school endowments, scholarship funds, and the like. One study showed that eight times as many entrepreneurs, compared to *all other graduates*, made large gifts to the schools that they attended.[19] On college and university campuses across Canada, a huge number of dorms, classroom buildings, arts centres, and athletic facilities are named for the contributor. In virtually every instance, these contributors are entrepreneurs whose highly successful companies enabled them to make major gifts of shares to their alma mater.

- *Community activities.* Entrepreneurs who have harvested their ventures very often reinvest their leadership skills and money in such community activities as symphony orchestras, museums, and local colleges and universities. These entrepreneurs lead fundraising campaigns, serve on boards of directors, and devote many hours to other volunteer work. Martin Prosserman, the founder and CEO of men's business attire retailer

"Moores Clothing for Men," sold the venture and went after charitable activities where he could make a difference in the community.

- *Investing in new companies.* Post-harvest entrepreneurs also reinvest their efforts and resources in the next generation of entrepreneurs and their opportunities. Successful entrepreneurs behave this way since they seem to know that perpetuating the system is far too important and too fragile to be left to anyone else. They have learned the hard lessons. As angel investors, experienced entrepreneurs are the key source of capital for start-up firms.

Innovation, job creation, and economic renewal and vibrancy are all results of the entrepreneurial process. Government does not cause this complicated and little understood process, though it facilitates and/or impedes it. It is not caused by the stroke of a legislative pen, though it can be ended by such a stroke. Rather, entrepreneurs, investors, and hardworking people in pursuit of opportunities create it.

Fortunately, entrepreneurs seem to accept a disproportionate share of the responsibility to make sure the process is renewed. And, judging by the new wave of entrepreneurship in Canada, both the marketplace and society once again are prepared to allocate the rewards to entrepreneurs that are commensurate with their acceptance of responsibility and delivery of results.

THE ROAD AHEAD: DEVISE A PERSONAL ENTREPRENEURIAL STRATEGY

GOALS MATTER—A LOT!

Of all the anchors one can think of in the entrepreneurial process, two loom above all the rest:

1. A passion for achieving goals.
2. A relentless competitive spirit and desire to win, and the will to never give up!

These two habits drive the quest for learning, personal growth, continuous improvement, and all other development. Without these good habits, most quests will fall short. In chapter 1 and online with Connect you will find the "Crafting a Personal Entrepreneurial Strategy" exercise. Completing this lengthy exercise will help you develop these good habits.

VALUES AND PRINCIPLES MATTER—A LOT!

We have demonstrated in numerous places throughout the book that values and principles matter a great deal. We encourage you to consider those of others as you develop your own anchors. This is a vital part of your leadership approach, and who and what you are:

- treat others as you would want to be treated
- share the wealth with those high performers who help you create it
- give back to the community and society

We would add a fourth principle in the Aboriginal spirit of considering every action with the seventh generational impact foremost in mind:

- be a guardian and a steward of the air, land, water, and environment

One major legacy of the coming generations of entrepreneurial leaders can be the sustainability of our economic activities. It is possible to combine a passion for entrepreneurship with love of the land and the environment. The work of such organizations as the Nature Conservancy, the World Wildlife Fund, Direct Relief International, and dozens of others is made possible by the contributions of money, time, and leadership from highly successful entrepreneurs. It is also one of the most durable ways to give back. Practising what he preached, Professor Jeffry Timmons, who built the foundation for this textbook, and his wife made a permanent gift of nearly 500 acres of their New Hampshire farm to a conservation easement. Other neighbours joined in for a combined total of over 1000 acres of land preserved forever, never to be developed. This has led to a regional movement as well, which involves landowners from a dozen surrounding towns.

Another purposeful environmental action to preserve space for future generations to enjoy is the Trans Canada Trail, which aims to be the longest recreational path in the world when finished. Depending on section, the trail allows a variety of uses: walk, cycle, ski, canoe, horse, ATV, or snowmobile. Much of the trail is former railroad lines donated by provincial, federal, and commercial entities. Kilometres of the trail are sponsored by individuals, families, and corporations. It began on Canada's 125th anniversary in 1992 and upon completion will be 21 500 kilometres long, connecting 1000 communities and 33 million Canadians.

SEVEN SECRETS OF SUCCESS

The following seven secrets of success are included for your contemplation and amusement:

1. There are no secrets. Understanding and practising the fundamentals discussed here, along with hard work, will get results.

2. As soon as there is a secret, everyone else knows about it, too. Searching for secrets is a mindless exercise.

3. Happiness is a positive cash flow.

4. If you teach a person to work for others, you feed him or her for a year, but if you teach a person to be an entrepreneur, you feed him or her, and others, for a lifetime.

5. Do not run out of cash.

6. Entrepreneurship is fundamentally a human process, rather than a financial or technological process. You—and the people you choose to work with—can make an enormous difference.

7. Happiness is a positive cash flow.

LO1 Numerous signals of impending trouble—strategic issues, poor planning and financial controls, and running out of cash—invariably point to a core cause: leadership at the top. Crises do not develop overnight. Often it takes 18 months to 5 years before the company is sick enough to trigger a turnaround intervention. Both quantitative and qualitative signals can predict patterns and actions that could lead to trouble.

LO2 Turnaround specialists begin with a diagnosis of the numbers—cash, strategic market issues, and management—and develop a turnaround plan. Bankruptcy, usually an entrepreneur's nightmare, can actually be a valuable tool and source of bargaining power to help a company survive and recover. The turnaround plan defines remedial action to generate cash, deal with lenders and trade creditors, begin long-term renewal, and monitor progress.

LO3 First and foremost, successful entrepreneurs strive to build a great company; wealth follows that process.

LO4 Entrepreneurs thrive on the challenges and satisfactions of the game: It's a journey, not a destination.

LO5 Harvest options mean more than simply selling the company, and these options such as trade sale, going public, and cash flow ("capital cow") are an important part of the entrepreneur's know-how.

LO6 Entrepreneurs know that to perpetuate the system for future generations, they must give back to their communities and invest time and capital in the next entrepreneurial generation.

STUDY QUESTIONS

1. What do entrepreneurs need to know about how companies get into and out of trouble? Why?
2. Why do most turnaround specialists invariably discover that it is the venture's leadership that is the root cause of trouble?
3. Why is it difficult for existing leaders to detect and to act early on signals of trouble?
4. Why can bankruptcy be the entrepreneur's ally?
5. What are the main components of a turnaround plan and why are these so important?
6. Why is it essential to focus first on building a great company, rather than on just getting rich?
7. Why is a harvest goal so crucial for entrepreneurs and the economy?
8. Define the principal harvest options, the pros and cons of each, and why each is valuable.
9. Beyond the harvest, what do entrepreneurs do to give back, and why is this so important to their communities and the nation?

MIND STRETCHERS   *Have you considered?*

1. General Motors was forced to "harvest" a few of its divisions. Oldsmobile was eliminated in 2004. Saab, founded in 1937 in Sweden, came under GM's full control in 2000. GM placed Saab on the auction block during the economic turmoil of 2009, but was that the best time to sell? With GM under bankruptcy protection, plans were to shrink Pontiac. Saturn, a fresh new venture within GM created in 1985, was to be folded or sold off—Penske eventually bid on it. After only a decade under GM's control Hummer was sold to a machinery company in China. Meanwhile Magna International was poised to purchase GM's European lines: Opel and Vauxhall. The deal included a Russian bank and Opel employees taking a 10-percent stake. How important is harvest timing?

2. CanWest Global Communications was in dire financial distress. Was it just another brontosaurus heading for a fall? What are the signals and what is the remedy?

3. With so much positive spin on restructuring, has the stigma of bankruptcy (personal and corporate) completely been eliminated?

4. Would you go to work for a troubled company? Why and under what conditions?

Preparation Questions:

1. What are the strengths and weaknesses of Cavendish Cove Cottages (CCC's) current strategy?

2. Should Sherry Noonan make an offer? What is the value of the business?

3. What is the business's financial position now and for the future?

4. What valuation methods can be used to construct an estimate?

"I just don't know if the asking price is fair," Sherry Noonan explained to Martin Heaney, one of her business professors at the University of Prince Edward Island (UPEI). It was December 10, 2008, and Sherry had just finished writing her final exam for the semester. She was now finished with the first half of her fourth and final year of the business program at UPEI. Sherry was considering making an offer on a cottage rental business located in the heart of Cavendish, the very popular tourist destination on Prince Edward Island (PEI). While Sherry would have some financial support from her family if she bought the cottage business, she knew that a key to ensure the future success of the business was to pay a fair price for it, and to be able to exploit marketing opportunities.

As Sherry left Martin Heaney's office, she reflected on the conversation with her professor. At this point in her university career, Sherry had completed courses in all of the functional areas of business (marketing, operations management, corporate finance, organizational behaviour, and accounting) and she felt that she should be able to analyze the information she had available regarding the cottage property. The work required to make an offer on the business would have to be completed over the next few days. That would allow Heaney and her parents the time to review her work. It would also give Sherry the time to negotiate with the business's owners, Fran and Ted Baker. It was important to get all of this work done before the activities of Christmas began, and before she would begin her final semester of classes. It would also ensure that she would have plenty of time to prepare for the opening of the cottages in May 2009, if her bid was successful.

The price for the cottages was $800 000, and Martin Heaney had asked Sherry whether she thought that was a fair price for the business. Heaney had focused on some of the key questions that had to be answered: How should the value of the cottage business be estimated? Could a new market-

ing strategy increase the value of the business to Sherry? If so, how would the new marketing strategy differ from the one employed by the current owners? What is the business worth? If a deal was negotiated, how should the purchase be financed? Now all Sherry had to do was answer these questions using the concepts she had learned over the last three-and-a-half years of her business education.

PEI AND THE CAVENDISH AREA

Prince Edward Island is Canada's smallest province, with a population of just 140 000 and 5684 square kilometres of land. The Island, as it was known to locals, was often called "the million acre farm," though PEI actually consisted of 1.4 million acres. About 55 percent of the population lived in rural areas. PEI, in the Gulf of St. Lawrence, was separated from its sister provinces of Nova Scotia and New Brunswick by the Northumberland Strait. In 1997, the Confederation Bridge was opened, providing PEI with a permanent link to New Brunswick. A ferry service also ran between PEI and Nova Scotia for about eight months of the year. At the turn of the 21st century, PEI continued to rely heavily on three industries that had seen it through the last century: agriculture, tourism, and fishing.

From May 1 to October 31, 2008, 1 105 264 visitors in 393 681 tourist parties spent a total of $345.6 million while vacationing on PEI. Compared to 2007, this was a decrease of 3.8 percent in numbers and 2.1 percent in expenditures. In 2008, 93.9 percent of the visitors and 90.6 percent of the tourist parties visited PEI for pleasure (rather than business), and accounted for 90.6 percent of the expenditures. The average party size was 2.91 people, and they spent an average of 4.5 nights on PEI.

Tourism on PEI was seasonal with mid-July to late-August being the peak of the tourism season. The early season (pre-July) is quite slow in many areas of PEI, and winter tourism is almost non-existent, except when special events are held. These are normally on weekends. The fall season was starting to become popular after many years of marketing by the Provincial Government Tourism Department and individual operators. The primary visitors during the fall were older and retired couples who liked the cooler temperatures and smaller crowds. While some came on bus tours, many were independent travellers who valued quality products and services.

The largest share of visitors (27.8 percent) came from Ontario, followed by the United States with 19.4 percent and

This case was written by Dr. Sean M. Hennessey, University of Prince Edward Island, for purposes of classroom discussion.

Nova Scotia was a close third. New Brunswick and Québec accounted for 18 percent of visitors. About 56 percent of the pleasure visitors were repeat customers, and 47 percent were in the 40–59 age bracket. Over 74 percent reported household incomes greater than $50 000. The primary activities of pleasure visitors in 2008 were: sightseeing (84 percent), soft outdoor adventure (77 percent), beach visits (71 percent), and craft shopping (69 percent). Golf was enjoyed by 15 percent of visitors.

Cavendish was located on the north shore of PEI, on the Gulf of St. Lawrence, in the centre of the province. It was about a 30-minute, very scenic, drive from Charlottetown, the capital city. Cavendish was a favourite destination for many visitors since the area has much to offer in terms of tourist attractions. In the area there were national parks, beaches, amusement parks, and many other types of tourist attractions, eight golf courses within a 15-minute drive and eight more within 30 minutes, numerous restaurants, shopping, a nightclub for night life, miniature golf, as well as beautiful scenery.

In addition, there were all types of accommodations from campgrounds to self-catering cottages, to hotels and resorts, to four-star B&Bs and country inns. A major draw was the famous Cavendish Beach, within the PEI National Park, with its rolling dunes and beautiful sandstone rock facings. The beach attracted many visitors to PEI either to swim in its warm waters, or walk the long stretches of red sandy shoreline. Young and old could always find something to do in the area.

Market research statistics for the 2008 tourism season, as collected by the government agency Tourism PEI, indicated that Cavendish was the main overnight destination for 263 600 pleasure visitors, or 25.4 percent of all pleasure visitors to PEI. Cavendish was the second most popular destination for visitors with Charlottetown being the first (32.9 percent of visitors). Other statistics for the pleasure visitors whose main overnight destination was Cavendish indicated that:

- 95 percent stayed in paid accommodations. Of these, 34 percent rented cottages or cabins.
- 55 percent were repeat customers.
- 46 percent made their decision to come to PEI more than 12 weeks prior to their departure.
- 49 percent of visitors were adult couples, while families with children less than 18 years old accounted for 38 percent.
- They spent an average of 4.1 nights on PEI.
- Expenditures averaged $919 per tourist party, similar to the level in 2007.
- Accommodations, restaurant meals, and souvenirs accounted for 66 percent of total expenditures.

- Total expenditures were $65.5 million in 2008.
- The top activities enjoyed by visitors to Cavendish in 2008 were: sightseeing (85 percent), beach visits (81 percent), souvenir shopping (73 percent), visiting the National Park (63 percent), visiting "Anne attractions" (51 percent), driving tours (50 percent), and lobster suppers (48 percent).[1]

"Anne attractions" referred to the book *Anne of Green Gables* written by the well-known Island author Lucy Maud Montgomery. Montgomery was born and raised in the Cavendish area where she lived until she was 36. *Anne of Green Gables*, published in 1908, was based in Cavendish. It has been translated into 15 different languages, put on film, and was the title of a musical stage production that had been staged at the Confederation Centre of the Arts in Charlottetown since 1965. The production also toured around the world. The story imparted an image of PEI that each year drew thousands of visitors to Cavendish from around the world. As a result, *Anne* was a major focus of the tourism industry in Cavendish with many attractions and names of businesses based on characters and locations in the book.

CAVENDISH COVE COTTAGES

Cavendish Cove Cottages (CCC) was located in the heart of the community of Cavendish on Route 6, Cavendish Road, a few hundred metres inland from the shoreline. Route 6 was the main road running along the north coastline of central PEI and was easily reached from all parts of PEI. All of the main tourist attractions in Cavendish and the neighbouring communities were on this main road. Cavendish beach, a significant attraction in its own right, was a four-minute drive away from the main entrance to CCC. Those with more time could easily walk to the beach in less than 15 minutes.

Also within 200 metres of the business were grocery stores, restaurants, a laundromat, shopping, and numerous family-oriented attractions. These included amusement parks such as Rainbow Valley (water and ride park), Sandspit (roller coasters, racing cars, and other park rides), and Avonlea Village (a re-creation of a village from 1908 that allows visitors to interact with characters from the *Anne of Green Gables* novel). Also close by was the Green Gables heritage site that includes the famous Green Gables House. The house and farm site were once owned by relatives of Lucy Maud Montgomery and were the inspiration for her book. Also on the site were numerous other family-oriented attractions.

Finally, within 10 minutes of the cottages were four championship golf courses, with two of these within walking dis-

[1] Data were taken from "Economic impact: Tourism 2008" published by the Province of PEI.

tance. One was the brand new, five-star, 27-hole, championship Eagles Glenn Golf Course that bordered the cottage complex. The other was the scenic, ocean-side Green Gables golf course, designed and built in 1939 by world-renowned architect Stanley Thompson. The cottage business had been in operation in the same location, under the same name, for over 50 years. The complex was zoned as "resort commercial" and, for property tax purposes, was assessed a value of $417 250 with property taxes of $5340. On the income statement, this expense was included within licences.

The business was owned and operated by an older couple, Fran and Ted Baker. They started the business in the 1950s when land and building costs were quite low. Fran and Ted each owned half of the common shares of the business. The property consisted of 19 rental units and one owner's unit on 2.4 acres of land. Of the rental units, seven were 1-bedroom, four were 2-bedroom, and eight were 3-bedroom. The units were further divided into standard, deluxe, and executive categories. The rental units ranged in size from 226 to 784 square feet. There were five smaller (226 to 270 square feet) units with the remainder generally between 435 and 784 square feet. Exhibit 1 provides a listing of the cottage complex with rental rates for the 2008 tourism season. Given the low rate of inflation and the need to set rental rates up to a year in advance, the Bakers were quoting and taking bookings for the 2009 season based on the 2008 rental rates.

Seventeen of the units were built many years earlier but, within the past three years, 11 had been upgraded with new interiors, windows, and flooring. Dishwashers and whirlpool tubs were installed in some units. These upgrades were in addition to the yearly outlays for repairs and maintenance. Six of the units still required work. The real estate agent listing the property indicated that these units, while structurally sound, were "looking tired." The two executive 2-bedroom cottages were new additions to the property and were very popular. These units were usually the first to rent. Construction of these 784-square foot units had started in the fall of 2006, and were first rented in the spring of 2007. The owner's unit was 1170 square feet with 3 bedrooms, an office, and laundry. There was also a 480-square foot garage on the property.

CCC was rated as a three-star rental accommodation by Canada Select. Canada Select was the only national accommodations rating program for all types of properties. Their ratings range from one star to five stars. There were at least 75 other accommodation providers within a five-minute drive of CCC. These included over 50 cottage operations ranging in size from two to three rental units to as many as 40 units. In addition, there were 10 motel properties, 11 B&Bs, and four campgrounds. The ratings of these properties range from 2

to 4 stars. Most properties in the Cavendish area were rated 2.5 to 4 stars. There were no properties that were rated less than two stars or more than four. About half of the properties were rated 3.5 or four stars. Exhibit 2 provides a brief discussion of some of the local competitors.

Many of the local competitors had 3.5 or higher star ratings (see Exhibit 2). As a consequence, CCC's average nightly rates were lower than many of their competitors. In addition to the cottages, the complex had an in-ground heated swimming pool, old-fashioned wooden swing benches, and a playground for children. All cottages had cable television, fridge, stove, microwave, barbeque, picnic table, as well as the other standard amenities normally expected with a rental unit.

Rental rates for cottages were often set six months to one year in advance since many repeat guests booked for the following year when checking out in the current year. Many cottage operators were fully booked for the peak season six to 12 months ahead of time. CCC's long history meant that many of their visitors were repeat. Recently, however, a few long-time clients had been lost to competitors who had newer and additional amenities such as ocean-view rooms, hot tubs, fireplaces, and fitness centres. Many competitors also had very well-designed websites featuring attractive pictures and detailed information concerning the property, the area, and PEI, in general.

In the high season CCC employed four workers, three full-time and one part-time. In the low season, this was reduced to one full-time and one part-time employee. They worked as housekeepers and on the front desk. Two of the employees had been on the staff for over 20 years. This provided a consistent vision and level of service for repeat guests. In the Cavendish area, it was relatively easy to hire low-skilled workers. Pay rates were usually $6.50 to $7.50 per hour, including benefits. Long-term employees often received $2 to $3 more per hour. The Bakers actively worked and managed the business and drew a salary.

Exhibit 3 provided income statements for CCC for the 2006–2008 fiscal years. Exhibit 4 provides balance sheets for the same period, while Exhibit 5 is the notes to the statements. The cottages were open from May 17 to September 30. Fran and Ted indicated that CCC's occupancy rate in 2007 and 2008 was 93 percent in the high season and 30 percent in the low. The asking price for CCC was $800 000. In discussions with Sherry, the real estate agent listing the property indicated that this was a reasonable price given that it was essentially a turn-key operation, the location of the property, the goodwill created by the Bakers, and given the high value of the assets.

Martin Heaney had told Sherry that there might be tax consequences for the Bakers from the sale. On the sale of a small business in Canada, each of the owners of the common shares would be exempt from tax on the first $500 000 of capital gains. But, 50 percent of any remaining gain would be taxed at about 45 percent. Sherry wondered if this should be considered in her analysis of the business.

MARKETING ISSUES

Fran and Ted believed that there were two primary target markets for their cottages. The principal market was middle-income families with children residing in the Maritime provinces who came to PEI for sightseeing and rest and relaxation. These customers stayed at CCC because they were close to all the major attractions of Cavendish, there was entertainment for their children, the price was affordable, and the accommodations were clean, friendly, and adequate. These were customers who might return year after year because they were satisfied with the services provided for the price paid, and they did not require luxuries.

The second and newer target market was more upscale consumers who came to PEI with friends for a golfing vacation. These customers were also from the Maritime provinces but tended to have more money to spend and visit primarily with other adults. CCC's location made it a good choice for these visitors since there were two exceptional golf courses within walking distance. CCC also offered their customers golf packages with reduced rates on green fees.

Fran and Ted listed CCC in the *PEI Visitors Guide*, and had brochures and a website. These were the only forms of advertising used, but that was the case with many of the smaller accommodation providers on PEI. The current website could be best described as "lean." The home page and all linked pages only used about 40 percent of the screen space due to a coding problem in the page design. The site itself provided basic information on the property including a brief description of the units, a list of amenities, rates, contact details, golf package details, four short reviews by guests totalling 24 words, and some pictures of the grounds, pool, and cottages. There was also a virtual tour of the grounds and of two cottages, but this was very slow and one of the cottages used looked very average with poor lighting. Most of the pictures were very small and lacked clarity and excitement. While it was not possible to make reservations online, there was a toll-free number and an email address available.

The competition in the accommodations sector in the Cavendish area was fierce. In the area there were four campgrounds, five hotels, and dozens of cottage rental properties. Exhibit 2 provides a listing of the major accommodation properties in the area, and some facts concerning each. With a short season, all operators aggressively competed for the tourist business.

CONCLUSION

Sherry Noonan considered all of the information she had collected and knew she had better get to work on trying to determine the amount she should offer for Cavendish Cove Cottages. If she bought the business, Sherry planned to be the manager. Her family had run a very successful hotel operation in Charlottetown for many years and she had worked in the business since she was 12. But still, there were many questions she had to consider: Was this a business worth buying? What marketing strategy would she use if she purchased the cottage? Was the $800 000 asking price fair? How should she determine a fair price? With a fair price calculated, how would she finance the purchase?

Her parents indicated that they would provide a portion of the purchase price as equity. Sherry wondered how large an investment she should request from her parents and what rate of return her parents would require on this investment. From her corporate finance course, Sherry knew that the market risk premium on Canadian common shares over the 69 years to 2006 was 6.7 percent. Sherry also questioned where she would access the remainder of the money required. Borrowing from a bank was a possibility. But, after the courses she took, Sherry knew that a bank would not lend her the full purchase price. All lenders required someone to sign that the owners were committed to the business.

After phoning the bank, Sherry knew that prime rate was currently 4.5 percent, while commercial mortgage rates were 4.75 percent for a one-year term, 5.9 percent for a three-year term, and 6.45 percent for a five-year term. Sherry felt she should develop a monthly amortization schedule for the loan for at least the first five years of the planned loan amortization period so she would know the cash flow required to service the loan. But first she had to decide on the loan amortization period, the number of years she would take to repay the loan in full.

Sherry only had a few days to come up with the answers to these questions and to finalize an offer to Fran and Ted Baker. Martin Heaney had volunteered to review her analysis and Sherry wanted to be sure to take advantage of the free expert advice. Also, before making an offer, her parents had indicated that they wanted to review the work behind the proposed offer price. Sherry knew she had better get to work and develop answers to the ever-expanding list of questions that were popping into her head.

EXHIBIT 1   CAVENDISH COVE COTTAGES: CATEGORIES AND PRICING OF COTTAGES

COTTAGE TYPE	NUMBER OF COTTAGES	DAILY RATE FOR 2008[1]	
		HIGH SEASON	LOW SEASON
1-bedroom Deluxe	7	$131	$76
2-bedroom Standard	1	$131	$76
2-bedroom Deluxe	1	$151	$81
2-bedroom Executive	2	$176	$96
3-bedroom Standard	5	$131	$76
3-bedroom Deluxe	3	$146	$81
Total	19		

Notes:

1. The stated rate for each cottage is for 1 to 4 people. Extra people cost $8.00 per day. The business is open from about May 17 (the date changes every year since the actual opening date is the Friday of the Victoria Day holiday that falls on the Monday preceding May 25 in Canada) to September 30. High season is from June 25 to Labour Day (the first Monday in September). Low season is before June 25 and after Labour Day. The Bakers were taking bookings and quoting the 2008 rates for the 2009 season. This was due to the need to set rental rates up to a year in advance, and the current low rate of inflation.

EXHIBIT 2   COMPETITION IN THE CAVENDISH AREA

GREEN GABLES BUNGALOW COURT 2.5*

40 cottages on beautiful treed grounds. Bed sitting, one and two bedroom housekeeping bungalows. Kitchenettes and gas barbecues. Located beside Green Gables House and golf course. Excellent playground and heated pool. Ideal for families, golfers. Popular destination for families of all ages for 50 years. Walking distance to golf, restaurants, and shops. Walk, bike or jog to the beach and trails—less than 1 km by path through the National Park. Daily rate: $65 to $145; weekly rate: $655 to $980; based on cottage type and season.

CAVENDISH BOSOM BUDDIES COTTAGES & SUITES 3.5*

On Route 6, 1 km east of main Route 6 and 13 intersection. Ten modern, heated, spacious, well equipped deluxe two, three, and four bedroom cottages. Jacuzzi, dishwasher, microwave, skylight, gas barbecues, sun decks, laundromat. Deluxe efficiency suites with double Jacuzzis. Large, well equipped, safe play area. Panoramic view of ocean and sunsets. Golf course, beach, and other major attractions nearby. Daily rate: $85 to $295; weekly rate: $560 to $2,065; based on cottage type and season.

Get a 2008/09 visitor guide at www.cavendishbeachresort.com/search_maps_accommodations.php.

EXHIBIT 3 **CAVENDISH COVE COTTAGES**

INCOME STATEMENTS FOR THE YEAR ENDED DECEMBER 31

	2006	2007	2008*
Rental Income	$158 375	$196 881	$210 499
less: Operating Expenses			
Advertising	4 483	4 221	6 528
Amortization	20 258	25 965	27 573
Cable	1 284	1 095	2 088
Electric	8 753	9 281	10 270
Heat	1 146	1 436	1 183
Insurance	6 729	7 988	10 471
Interest and bank charges	2 216	4 131	3 149
Interest on long-term debt	10 321	14 966	11 700
Licences	6 963	7 159	6 706
Office	879	1 919	1 489
Professional fees	3 583	4 649	3 460
Repairs and maintenance	15 935	20 541	18 955
Supplies	11 586	6 844	8 479
Telephone	3 995	2 914	3 801
Vehicle and travel	4 965	2 911	3 035
Wages and benefits	63 425	49 460	47 388
Total Fixed Expenses	166 519	165 480	166 273
Earnings Before Taxes and Other	–8 144	31 401	44 226
Net Other Income	$0	$6 305	$568
Earnings Before Taxes	–8 144	37 706	44 794
Taxes	1 340	8 174	9 436
Net Income after Tax	**–$6 804**	**$29 533**	**$35 358**

* Note: The results for the 2008 fiscal year have not yet been certified.

EXHIBIT 4   CAVENDISH COVE COTTAGES

BALANCE SHEETS AS AT DECEMBER 31

	2006	2007	2008*
ASSETS			
Cash	$0	$8 113	$4 084
Marketable securities	0	18 750	6 250
Accounts receivable	2 944	189	1 605
Income taxes receivable	1 340	0	0
Total Current Assets	4 284	27 051	11 939
Land	16 655	16 495	16 495
Gross fixed assets (Note 1)	518 700	580 604	612 986
less: Accum amortization	242 210	268 175	295 748
Net value	276 490	312 429	317 238
Total Fixed Assets	293 145	328 924	333 733
Other assets (Note 2)	1	1 919	1 493
Total Assets	**$297 430**	**$357 894**	**$347 164**
LIABILITIES AND EQUITY			
Line of credit (Note 3)	$2 784	$0	$0
Accounts payable	7 223	4 300	4 818
Income taxes payable	0	8 209	8 405
Bonus payable	7 500	10 000	10 000
Demand loan (Note 4)	31 250	31 250	37 500
Current portion of long-term debt	21 796	22 271	22 271
Total current liabilities	70 553	76 030	82 994
Long-term debt (Note 5)	116 040	149 544	127 273
Payable to shareholder (Note 6)	38 440	30 390	24 610
Total liabilities	225 033	255 964	24 876
EQUITY			
Common shares (Note 7)	3 125	3 125	3 125
Retained earnings	69 273	98 805	109 163
Net equity	72 398	101 930	112 288
Total liabilities & equity	**$297 430**	**$357 894**	**$347 164**

* Note: The results for the 2008 fiscal year have not yet been certified.

| EXHIBIT 5 | CAVENDISH COVE COTTAGES INC. |

CAVENDISH COVE COTTAGES INC.
NOTES TO THE FINANCIAL STATEMENTS (UNAUDITED)

The company is incorporated under the Companies' Act of Prince Edward Island, and is primarily engaged in the cottage rental industry. The financial statements have been prepared in accordance with Canadian generally accepted accounting principles and include the following significant accounting policies:

1. **Capital Assets**

   Capital assets are recorded at cost, net of government assistance. Amortization is computed using the declining-balance method at the following annual rates, which were the same as the Capital Cost Allowance (CCA) rates for the applicable asset classes.

Building	5%
Equipment	20%
Vehicle	30%
Pool	8%
Pavement	8%

	2008			2007
	COST	ACCUMULATED AMORTIZATION	NET BOOK VALUE	NET BOOK VALUE
Buildings	$350 804	$104 636	$246 168	$237 478
Equipment	189 985	128 202	61 783	63 648
Vehicle	43 181	40 281	2 900	4 350
Pool	22 323	19 709	2 614	3 261
Pavement	6 693	2 920	3 773	3 693
Totals	**$612 986**	**$295 748**	**$317 238**	**$312 429**

   Government assistance of $27 953 has been deducted from the cost of the buildings while $10 655 has been deducted from the cost of the equipment.

2. **Other Assets**

	2008			2007
Website development	$2 131	$639	$1 492	$1 918
Goodwill	1	0	1	1
Totals	**$2 132**	**$639**	**$1 493**	**$1 919**

   Website development costs are being amortized on a straight-line basis over a five-year period.

3. **Line of Credit**

   The line of credit is authorized to a maximum of $20 000 and is payable on demand. The interest rate is based on prime plus 1.5 percent. The line is secured by land and cottages, and the personal guarantee and postponement of claims by shareholders.

4. **Demand Loan**

   The demand loan is payable on demand and bears interest at prime plus 2 percent. The average prime rate during 2008 was 5 percent (2007—5 percent, 2006—6.5 percent). The demand loan is secured by a collateral first mortgage on the cottages, and personal guarantees of the shareholders.

(continued)

5. Long-Term Debt

The long-term debt is secured by a mortgage on the land and cottages, personal guarantees of the shareholders, and life insurance on the shareholders.

	2008	2007	2006
Loan at 8.5%, payable to 2010 in annual amounts of $5000 plus interest	$30 000	$35 000	$40 000
Loan at prime +1.5%, payable to 2012 in annual amounts of $10 000 plus interest	$80 000	$90 000	$43 750
Loan at prime +1.5%, payable to 2011 in annual amounts of $2,271 plus interest	$4 544	$6 815	$9 086
Loan at prime +1.5%, payable to 2011 in annual amounts of $5000 plus interest	$35 000	$40 000	$45 000
Totals	$149 544	$171 815	$137 836
less: Current portion	22 271	22 271	21 796
	$127 273	$149 544	$116 040

Principal repayments required in each of the next four years are:

2009	2010	2011	2012
$22 271	$22 272	$20 000	$20 000

6. Due to Shareholders

This amount is due on demand without interest. However, the shareholders have indicated they will not request material repayment within the next fiscal year and consequently, the amount has not been classified as current.

7. Common Shares

There are 20 000 common shares at no par value authorized to be issued, 5000 common shares are issued for a total value of $3125. No dividends were paid during the 2006 fiscal year.

connect

For more information on the resources available from McGraw-Hill Ryerson, go to www.mcgrawhill.ca/he/solutions.

CASES

CASE 1   MEAL IN A JAR

Driving down the road, Irene and Carson were surrounded with a symphony of clinking jars that filled their car to the brim. It was Monday, and they were busy delivering 300 prepared meals across the Waterloo region in southern Ontario, Canada. Laughing out loud, Irene looked at Carson, "What the hell are we doing? All I wanted was solve my family's meal problems at home!" With deliveries to local businesses, individual homes, an upscale grocery store, a health food store, a skating rink, and a coffee shop, Irene and Carson were six months into their healthy food adventure.

They had some big questions on their mind: Could they grow their business idea into a profitable, repeatable and scalable business model? Would their current kitchen be able to produce the same quality of meals in the thousands? Were they delivering their product through the right distribution channels? And finally, were they growing fast enough to capture the market before their competitors could? They had many challenges ahead.

SOLUTION IN A JAR

In January 2013, Irene, with two working professional daughters and a working professional husband all living at home, started hearing the complaints. "There is nothing fresh and healthy in the fridge to take for lunch!" Irene always made enough dinner for lunches the next day, but her husband and youngest daughter were the first two out the door and had made a habit of taking all the leftovers. After a few weeks of hearing the complaints, Irene decided to do something about "her" problem.

Early one morning, Irene woke up before the rest of the family and grabbed a handful of ingredients from the fridge. She reached for the closest container, a glass Mason jar, and started layering. Irene had recently seen a page for mason jars meals on Pinterest, a popular social media site, and was now creating her own Mason jar meal. Her first meal in a jar was so beautiful that she snapped a photo and uploaded it to Facebook.

A friend suggested that she open her own Facebook page to feature her creation, which she titled *Meal in a Jar*. Later that day, Irene returned from the grocery store to make more Meal in a Jar. When she logged back into her Facebook page, she discovered 52 likes and a new thread:

"Do you sell Meal in a Jar?"

Without hesitation, Irene replied "Yes!"

"How much?"

"$10 each."

"Do you have a menu?"

"Yes, give me 5 minutes…"

Irene saw an opportunity to solve the healthy, tasty, and convenient lunch problem, and maybe even make some money in the process. After posting the menu, featuring her family's favourite recipes, Irene suggested that her customers buy five jars every week and pick them up on Sunday night from her house. She would take back the empty jars, wash them, and reuse them. By the end of week 1, Irene had 52 jars ordered through Facebook. Word began to spread quickly, by the end of week two, 75 jars were ordered!

Irene's background in the health and fitness industry, including ownership in two local gyms, granted her the credibility to capture the early attention of busy families with kids and young working professionals. Similar to her own family, her customers struggled to eat fresh, healthy, and convenient meal options as part of their daily routine. This was a great idea with early success, but how could she move forward?

COFOUNDING

In a parallel world, a graduating student from Wilfrid Laurier University had just entered an entrepreneurship incubator called the Laurier LaunchPad Program. Failing to find $10 meal options that were socially, environmentally, and health conscious, Carson was driven to build a food company to fill the gap.

Having described the problem to dozens of potential customers, he learned that there were, indeed, a limited number of fresh, wholesome and convenient meal options available on the market. The food landscape was rammed full of subs, pitas, wraps, and other takeout foods, none of which fully solved the problem. He learned that workplaces struggled most with healthier options, and that $11 was the most customers were willing to pay for a good solution.

After two weeks of customer discovery, Carson's closest solution was a mobile salad bar and healthy BBQ venture. He would require at least $150 000 in start-up capital for a kitchen or food truck. Though an interesting concept, his idea was far from unique. It seemed these trendy food places were opening everywhere. Frustrated and anxious about the financial risk involved, Carson decided it was time for a good haircut.

Upon taking his seat at the salon, his eye caught a glass Mason jar filled with visibly fresh and healthy ingredients. "What is that?" he exclaimed, reaching for the jar. His barber described it as a great new meal idea that his friend Irene had been creating for a couple of weeks now. Inspecting the jar from top to bottom, Carson knew this was exactly the product fit for his food vision and immediately asked for Irene's contact information.

Case written by Carson Kolberg, Wilfrid Laurier University

With a fresh new look from his barber, Carson called Irene and booked a meeting for that afternoon.

In their first introduction, the pair saw the immediate connection. Irene had a background in health and fitness, a keen sense of food trends, and deep roots within the local community. Carson had an entrepreneurial background, a strong local network, and sales charisma. Most importantly, they shared a common vision for the company to be. As Irene put it, "I wish everyone could eat at least one healthier meal made from clean ingredients every day." Carson envisioned the channels and outlets necessary to realize the concept into reality. They were ready to get started!

WHY THE JAR?

The Mason jar has been a trusted food container for over a hundred years. Made from high-quality glass, the 500 ml and 1 L sizes offer a clear and portable showcase for fresh wholesome ingredients. Just like any other glass container, Mason jars are susceptible to breaking and must be handled with care. This presented a challenge for distribution, which Carson and Irene solved initially with snug carrying containers, flexible ice packs, and non-slip sheets.

Mason jars retail for approximately $1 and can be washed to re-used many times in production. In the beer industry, a typical glass bottle will undergo 12 uses before being broken and recycled. In the first six months of production, Carson and Irene broke about a dozen jars and have re-used some jars over 25 times. Because of the cost, Carson and Irene charge a $1 deposit on every jar sold in retail. They initially purchased 1000 jars and after about six months had 300 jars remaining in their inventory. Many customers were keeping the jars as drinking containers or recycling them to save the hassle of the return.

After finishing up their first couple deliveries of the day, Irene turned to Carson and asked, "Is the glass Mason jar the best option? It seems to be integral to our brand, but will the deposit system even work at higher volumes?" Carson replied, "Do you think the deposit is causing customer friction and slowing our growth? What other industries manage a successful deposit system?" They both pondered the questions as they drove to their next stop.

THE MEAL

Irene's culinary experience was developed through raising a family, working in the health and fitness industry, and travelling extensively internationally. As such, she is a creative, wholesome, and health-oriented cook. She closely follows health trends including eat-clean principles (whole ingredients, no preservatives) and the gluten-free methodology (no wheat). She is also crafty at developing vegetarian meals.

The original menu for Meal in a Jar was completely gluten-free, using fresh, whole ingredients, without preservatives or processing and was nutritiously balanced, portion controlled, and diabetic friendly. A variety of serve-hot and serve-cold options, including Pulled Pork & Smashed Potatoes, No-Butter Chicken, Apple Chicken Salad, and Mediterranean Quinoa Salad were on the menu. After some early experiments, Carson and Irene learned that their jars had a one-week shelf life and must be kept continuously refrigerated. They were selling 1 L jars for $10 and the 500-ml mini versions for $7 each.

As they stopped for lunch, Irene and Carson continued their debate, "How can we make these meals safely and cost effectively in higher volumes? Which customers will be most have the greatest need for our solution? How will we overcome the "final mile" of commercial kitchen to home fridge as we grow? What are the fastest growing trends in the food industry? Is gluten-free fundamental to our unique value proposition? What is the biggest competitive threat? Who could provide the most credible endorsement to Meal in a Jar and its' growth?" The questions kept coming out!

"JARRED" INTO PRODUCTION

With orders reaching 100 jars per week, Irene and Carson knew that Meal in a Jar needed a commercial kitchen fast, so they went hunting. They found commercial kitchen spaces available for rent between $1000–$2000 per month. Though these kitchens were functional, there were minimum 1-year lease commitments and each kitchen would require variety of additional equipment. They knew that with an unpredictable growth path, committing to a lease was too risky.

Property of:
Meal in a Jar Inc.
fresh meals on-the-go
Mealinajar.ca
info@mealinajar.ca

Label Listing

Apple Chicken Salad (Gluten-Free, Dairy-Free)

Chicken, Black Beans, Cranberry Jar Dressing (Olive Oil, Red Wine Vinegar, Cranberry, Prepared Dijon Mustard, Honey, Salt), Green Apple, Carrots, Red Cabbage, Beets, Spring Mix Greens, Dried Cranberry

Allergens: Mustard
Prepared in a facility that uses Gluten, Nuts, Dairy

Greek Chicken Salad (Gluten-Free)

Chicken, Green Lentils, Sundried Tomato Dressing (Olive Oil, Red Wine Vinegar, Sundried Tomatoes, Prepared Dijon Mustard, Honey, Salt), Mixed Bell Peppers, Radish, Carrots, Spinach, Cherry Tomato, Green Onion, Feta Cheese, Kalamata Olive

Allergens: Mustard
Prepared in a facility that uses Gluten, Nuts, Dairy

As they continued their search, they found a local recreation cooking school that offered to rent them time and consulting support in exchange for $5 per jar produced. They took the deal. For two months, Meal in a Jar incubated in the cooking school while learning to scale up production while maintaining quality. Unfortunately, they soon learned that 150 jars filled the idle fridge space and idle time of the kitchen; any more than one production day a week became a challenge for the kitchen's normal operations. Carson and Irene decided to search again for a new, larger space.

They found a local restaurant that had idle time each Sunday and a production style layout. Carson and Irene offered a deal to pay the cost of food, labour, and $1 per jar fee for the kitchen's overhead and profit. The restaurant accepted. In this new facility, Meal in a Jar was able to capture a greater efficiency of scale. To provide some context, a typical meal involves 20% food cost, 15% labour cost, and 10% kitchen overhead, representing just under 50% revenue. Production costs at the restaurant dropped to just below $4.50 per large jar and below $3.50 per mini jar. More importantly, Irene and Carson had time to focus on growing their weekly orders. They quickly grew to 300 jars per week, but realized they once again had a major capacity issue of fridge space.

Rather than building the jars on-site and storing them elsewhere for sorting and delivery, Irene and Carson knew it was time to go hunting again for a larger scale production facility. They approached the largest catering company in the region. Conveniently, this business partnered with other similar businesses, like Meals on Wheels, which provides mobile food service for seniors. The catering kitchen was experienced in large-scale production and open to taking on operations for Meal in a Jar on a non-exclusive manufacturing agreement.

To control costs, Meal in a Jar continued to produce their entire line in one day per week. Irene and Carson anticipated a production maximum of 3000 jars per week at the new facility. They were confident that they had the sales capacity to get them there.

Nearing the end of their delivery day, the debate continued and some big questions remained on their minds regarding production. Meal in a Jar began production in the new facility during the summer time when event catering was seasonally low. How would their production be affected by the Christmas season? Would the same care and attention be available to ensure the highest quality of production? Even bigger questions emerged: Is this the ideal method of production? What is the greatest capacity of jars produced in this facility? Will this single production facility be able to sustain orders within the Waterloo region? What if they had to build 10 000 Meal in a Jars? There were some big challenges ahead that they would have to solve.

GROWING DISTRIBUTION CHANNELS

In the first six months, Meal in a Jar had discovered three methods for distribution. Retail sales, direct-to-customer delivery, and hybrid pickup hubs. Carson and Irene learned that an typical grocery store expects margins between 25% and 45% for products placed in store. Products with a short shelf life are a particularly high risk to stores due to lost profit in waste (shrink). Local retailers were not quite as aggressive; asking between 20%–30% of sales was reasonable. They also learned that stores would be willing to trial product on consignment for 15%–20% of sales. Here is the breakdown of their current distribution channels:

Retailers

Balzac's Coffee Roasters is a southern-Ontario based coffee chain specializing in gourmet coffee and baked treats. They have seven prime locations in Toronto, Kitchener, Niagara-on-the-Lake, and Stratford. Meal in a Jar approached the coffee chain knowing they had a gap in food sales and a local demand for prepared meals. A gourmet sandwich company had launched product in the franchise a year earlier, but had failed to gain enough popularity; low turnover and high spoilage lead to discontinuation of the product.

After treating the owners of the coffee shop to a Meal in a Jar, Carson and Irene were invited to launch their product on consignment as a turn-key food solution. In their first week, Meal in a Jar sold 50 units, with strong reception from surrounding businesses. This got Irene and Carson thinking: What similar coffee chains might have this food problem that Meal in a Jar can help solve? What other major competitors sell meal options in coffee chains? What coffee chains align well with Meal in a Jar's values?

Vincenzo's is a locally owned and operated grocery store, featuring upscale and gourmet groceries. Their store includes a butcher, seafood counter, sushi counter, sandwich and deli counter, cheese bar, olive bar, and a coffee shop. Meal in a Jar began selling on consignment at Vincenzo's and saw a steady growth in weekly sales. Customers valued the convenience and quality of their options and sales remained steady around 40 units per week. Irene and Carson wondered: What is Meal in a Jar's unique value proposition in an upscale grocery store, especially one full of home meal replacement and takeout options? Is this a sustainable distribution outlet? What other independent stores or grocery chains might they be able to approach? Is a local retailer the ideal partner?

Healthy Foods and More is one of the largest health food stores in the Waterloo region. They specialize in gluten-free, organic, and local foods with a strong customer following from young professionals, families, and seniors. Meal in a Jar launched in Healthy Foods and More on consignment and in the first couple weeks the jars exceeded the sales volume of Vincenzo's. Meal in a Jar's offering of gluten-free, dairy free, and vegetarian options attracted an early following from employees and customers. Irene and Carson wondered: What other health food stores might consider giving shelf room to Meal in a Jar in their stores? How do their target segments distinguish Meal in a Jar in a health food store as compared to a gourmet grocery store?

After launching in the first three retail outlets, Meal in a Jar began attracting new vendor opportunities. The City of Waterloo had recently taken over food operations for the athletic and community centres throughout the region. One of these athletic centres holds an indoor soccer field, multiple skating rinks, outdoor facilities and basketball courts, and a bar, a coffee shop, and a café. Meal in a Jar had an existing fundraising relationship with the Kitchener-Waterloo Skating Club, based out of this particular athletic centre and had earned some credibility from parents, coaches, and athletes.

Meal in a Jar was invited to trial their product over a weekend and received a welcome reception from coaches, players, parents, and employees of the facility. They launched consignment sales, and were told that if first month sales went well, Meal in a Jar had an opportunity launch in more of the city's recreation facilities. Irene and Carson began to see an opportunity that might exist other urban areas. They wondered: Would they be able to grab the attention of more municipalities with their fresh, healthy, and environmentally friendly meal solutions?

As they were finishing their deliveries to each of the retail locations, Irene and Carson were in a fierce discussion. "Which of our four retail operations has the largest potential for growth? " said Irene. "I don't know, we'll have to do more market research and survey our customers." Carson replied. "We can't ignore that our customers have unique goals and each outlet might serve them differently." They continued onwards with home and office deliveries to the rhythmic jingle of jars.

Web Sales

Months before any retailer was approached, Irene and Carson had established a basic online process to preorder jars. It all started with Facebook, and slowly transitioned to online Google form submissions. Customers would place an order the week in advance, pay using their credit card over the phone or on delivery, and choose for jars to be delivered directly to home or office, or picked up from the production kitchen.

This method of sales increased their profit margins, reduced their risk of waste, and allowed a direct connection with customers. Two months into the venture, Meal in a Jar launched their website, mealinajar.ca, which featured an e-commerce platform traditionally used for non-perishable goods. The website streamlined the order process, allowing customers to choose individual jars, build packages, or even initiate a weekly subscription. Online sales permitted a "just-in-time" ordering and production schedule for Meal in a Jar and facilitated prepayment through PayPal and Stripe.

To support the web sales, Meal in a Jar needed a delivery service. Irene's personal vehicle was the most cost-effective solution so far, but with orders increasing, the founders were becoming overwhelmed. They had to commit the entirety of Monday and Tuesday to delivering jars around the city. Irene and Carson discovered a local delivery company, which provided a same day service for $9 per delivery within the Waterloo region. Each delivery included pick up and return for empty jars back to the commercial kitchen. As an alternative, a private driver could be hired for $50/hour, with a minimum of three hours, plus the cost

of fuel. They both wondered how delivery might be managed beyond their region. They also wondered if there was a better solution for delivering web orders to customers.

Hybrid Pickup Hubs

A unique opportunity was uncovered when interviewing a local retailer. A local butcher named Brady's Meat & Deli was interested in carrying the product, but had limited capacity to display the jars. They did, however, have a large amount of idle refrigerator space below their counters. The butcher was a trusted name in the city and conveniently located in a large residential area. For a 10% handling fee, the butcher offered to be a once per week pick up hub for pre-sold orders. This was a lucrative opportunity for both Meal in a Jar and the retailer. It decreased risk, increased distribution channels, guaranteed customer foot traffic in the store, and maintained a reasonable profit margin for all parties involved. Irene and Carson wondered: What other local pickup hubs would be ideal for customers? Could this be the ideal delivery solution for the "final mile"?

WHAT NOW?

As they finished their last delivery for the day, both co-founders let out a sigh of relief as they pulled into the driveway. Just then, the phone rang. With the car in park, they reached to put their BlackBerry on speakerphone. "Good afternoon, my name is Mike and I've been watching you grow since day one. I would like to book a meeting with you about the possibility of raising capital to grow your business. If you are interested, please put together a brief presentation and prepare your sales history and business plan for me to review."

They knew they had a great idea with lots of potential and wondered what they would do with additional funding. Were they ready to give up equity in their business or bring on additional expertise? Was it too early to scale? They had many challenges ahead for production and distribution and it would not be long before competitors started to enter the market. Irene turned to Carson, and with a smile on her face and a sparkle in her eye said, "What the hell have we gotten ourselves into, this is incredible," to which Carson replied, "Jar Up, it's going to be a wild ride."

CASE 2 WILLY DOG

In 1989, having taken losses on a string of real estate plays, Kingston resident Will Hodgskiss found himself close to broke. Entrepreneurial to the end, he leveraged the last few dollars in his savings account and bought a hot dog cart. It wasn't much, but Hodgskiss was convinced that, with the right discipline and vision, he could start with his lowly hot dog cart and build a serious growth business.

He was right. In less than a decade, Hodgskiss's business, Willy Dog, had grown from a one-cart operation to a substantial franchise network with cart owners patrolling North American streets. And—thanks to Hodgskiss's decision in his first years as a vendor to trade in his standard metal cart for one in the shape of an eight-foot-long wiener—it had developed a distinct and instantly recognizable brand.

This case was written by Lukas Neville, PhD student, Queen's School of Business, and Professor Elspeth J. Murray, CIBC Teaching Fellow in Entrepreneurship, Queen's School of Business, Queen's University. This case was prepared with the assistance of Kimberley Mosher and Gillian Shiau. Developed with the support of the CIBC Curriculum Development Fund at Queen's School of Business, for purposes of classroom discussion.

By 2006, Hodgskiss's company was enjoying annual sales of about $1 million. It had diversified from its roots as a franchiser and had become one of the world's leading manufacturers of specialty carts for street-food vendors. Hodgskiss had travelled a great distance from his humble roots—but he was not yet ready to call it a day. He had set a goal of growing Willy Dog's annual sales to $5 million within three years. When he reached that goal, he planned to step back from the company to either retire or start another business. Meeting that target, however, wouldn't be easy. For all Hodgskiss's success, Willy Dog faced a number of issues. It wasn't growing as quickly as it had in the past, and it was facing heightened competition. On top of that, Hodgskiss was wrestling with staffing issues, customer relations, and breaking into new markets. In short, he needed to develop a fresh strategy to foster growth at his firm. But knowing that he needed a plan wasn't enough. Hodgskiss also needed time—something he didn't have, given the chaotic schedule that managing all the minutiae of his company forced him to keep. And without it, he was left wondering how he could plot a course to carry Willy Dog into the future.

Back in 1999, when Willy Dog was celebrating its 10th anniversary, Hodgskiss was sitting on top of a thriving franchise network. But his company was starting to have problems. The revenue from franchise fees that had fuelled growth during Willy Dog's first decade was starting to dry up, and Hodgskiss's margins were thinning rapidly.

Looking for ways to generate new income, he began to experiment with making and selling his firm's distinctive carts. His revenue growth picked up dramatically. "I was making $2000 to $5000 per sale, with none of the follow-up of franchising," Hodgskiss recalls with a grin.

And so, a manufacturer was born: Hodgskiss changed his franchising revenue model to encourage owners to buy the cart rather than the franchise, and he moved production of the carts in-house, hiring a staff of fabricators to operate the production line.

But even though his company was back on a growth footing, Hodgskiss remained a classic founder, involved in every dimension of the firm he started. Three separate hotlines—for support, orders, and other inquiries—were often routed to his cellphone. As a result, that phone was practically glued to his ear.

Hodgskiss felt it was important that Willy Dog customers be able to reach the "top dog" directly; that personal touch had been a hallmark of the company since its inception. But since he was involved in all aspects of Willy Dog's operations, he could be anywhere when a call came in. Customers liked dealing with Hodgskiss directly, but were occasionally frustrated when he didn't have all their information on hand. Hodgskiss, for his part, loved talking with his customers—but hated having to spend time reciting information easily found on the company's Web site. He valued the relationships, but wished that there was a more effective way of handling inquiries.

Part of the problem stemmed from Willy Dog's internal structure. Almost all of the company's 18 employees worked on the shop floor as machinists and fabricators. Under the leadership of the shop foreperson, this staff spent its days producing the company's signature carts. The rest of the operations, from finance to marketing, were handled by Hodgskiss, his general manager, and an office clerk.

For Hodgskiss, this meant he had to keep up a frenzied pace of activity to manage the company's operations. In a typical day, he rose at 5:00 a.m. to tackle his email inbox before breakfast and his morning run. At the office, he would handle everything from clerical work to minor errands, though two-thirds of his usual day would be consumed by supervising staff.

Though Hodgskiss described his ideal leadership approach as "hands-off," he could not resist getting involved in the day-to-day details of the business, from staffing to equipment. But his enthusiasm for running the business, he realized, left Willy Dog vulnerable. If he ever took ill, his general manager could handle only some of the company's operations for a limited time. Hodgskiss knew he was personally still indispensable to the firm.

By this year, cart sales had come to account for 80 percent of Willy Dog's annual revenue. But as the cart business grew, Hodgskiss began running into stiff competition from an entrenched U.S. manufacturer called All-American Hot Dogs Co. With fierce rhetoric on their graphic-saturated Web sites, the two titans clashed over features, quality and, eventually, price. It was war, and the battles bit deep into Hodgskiss's margins. His price woes didn't end with a single competitor. He also competed against a range of small local players, who Hodgskiss described as "backyard mechanics." Worse, his market for high-end carts was being eroded by online marketplaces for used carts. On any given day, dozens of carts could be found for sale on eBay.

Short-handed on sales and marketing staff, and faced with intensifying competition, Willy Dog turned to a distributorship model. Though it involved parcelling out a portion of the company's modest margins, Willy Dog's five American distributors contributed marketing and sales resources, and their high-volume purchases cut down dramatically on the cost of shipping the bulky carts. Finally, the local presence allowed for improved customer service and local regulatory knowledge for new vendors.

But while the distributor network had improved Willy Dog's outlook, Hodgskiss still wondered how to sustain his firm's competitive advantage. With individual vendors accounting for most of his cart sales, the majority of revenue came from one-off purchases. Hodgskiss's customer service and personal touch had built customer loyalty, but it didn't often translate to repeat sales. And while Willy Dog had invested considerable effort in product innovation, customers were highly price-sensitive and often indifferent about the firm's higher-gauge steel or other technical improvements.

Having to fight for every last sale to small-scale customers was an unappealing part of Willy Dog's business model. Over 70 percent of the company's sales came from small-time owner-operators and seasonal "hobby" entrepreneurs—often leaving the company saddled with bad debt from failed clients. The last 30 percent of Willy Dog's sales, by contrast, was to business managers: franchised restaurants and professionally managed local chains. Earlier this year, for instance, Willy Dog completed an order for 10 carts from an ice cream vendor. But how, Hodgskiss wondered, could he go about finding more customers in this appealing segment? His own market research offered clues about how strong the hot dog market was: At major-league baseball parks, hot dog sales had increased by over 13 percent between 2004 and 2005, Hodgskiss learned. And "curbside take-out," the market that included Willy Dog-built stands, was growing even more quickly. With street-side vendors propagating rapidly, Hodgskiss knew his market was relatively secure.

At the same time, with increasing health concerns and a globalizing palate, would the lowly hot dog be abandoned in favour of sushi or samosas? The demand for frankfurters was enough to sustain Willy Dog at its present level, but Hodgskiss wanted more than comfortable, flat growth. He wanted to quintuple his annual sales and then make a graceful exit.

To do that, he had to find a growth market, but he wondered how his modest manufacturing operation would scale up. Between resignations and seasonal layoffs, his staff suffered annual turnover of 30 percent. On top of that, it was hard to keep trained staff in a market starved for skilled workers. Earlier in the year, Hodgskiss had to establish employee health and dental plans as a retention measure.

Intermittently starved for production capacity, Hodgskiss had experimented with contracting out production. The strat-egy worked out exceptionally well—until the contracting firm decided to launch its own cart manufacturing business, directly competing with Willy Dog.

Willy Dog was also highly reliant on steel to build the carts. With slender margins, Hodgskiss wondered whether manufacturing was necessarily the most appealing part of his industry's value chain. With labour and input prices on the rise and mixed experiences with outsourcing, Hodgskiss would need to carefully consider how to grow his manufacturing operations to keep pace with the growth he hoped to foster.

Though growth was a priority for Willy Dog's founder, his schedule didn't afford him much time for strategic planning sessions. Busy revamping his cart models, dealing with his steel suppliers, and handling the constant barrage of customer calls, Hodgskiss's days were already a flurry of activity. He had built Willy Dog into a million-dollar enterprise. But with so little time, he had no idea how to begin dealing with eroding margins and stiff competition.

CASE 3   MATCHA MEN

Tea is in Brian Takeda's blood. His childhood memories are dotted with scenes of tea ceremonies with his grandmother, and his family lineage includes more than one Japanese tea master. So in 2001, when an entrepreneurship professor at an Ontario business school challenged Takeda and fellow student Mars Koo to develop a business plan for a new venture, Takeda's thoughts turned immediately to tea. Having seen Japan's fast-growing green tea market firsthand, he felt that North America was an untapped well of opportunity. The pair built a business plan that envisioned a chain of premium, fresh-brewed loose-leaf tea retailers across Canada and the United States.

EAST MEETS WEST

Their model was an elegant meeting of East and West: the high-end teas of the Japanese salon and the chado ceremony, transplanted into the accessible, high-volume retail model of the café. The concept followed the lead of chains like Starbucks and Second Cup, offering customers premium products, a space for social gathering, and a focus on customer education. As Starbucks reshaped consumer tastes a decade earlier by promoting superior arabica premium beans, so Infuze planned to cultivate a Canadian taste for premium tea, far beyond flat, forgettable supermarket varieties.

In 2002, shortly after graduation, the pair began planning for a Vancouver-area store to test their concept. Their parents thought enough of their plan that they put up the $200 000 they needed to get rolling. A short time later, Infuze Holdings had its first location—a spot in Vancouver's Gastown district, tucked amidst large hotels and shopping areas. Although cash was scarce, the company chose a high-end design group to create a sleek, Zen-inspired interior. It also hired a noted branding expert to develop a minimalist logo and packaging treatment. "It was expensive," Takeda admits. "But we always pledged to be the best at what we do, and to partner with those who are the best at what they do."

The obsession with quality extended to their products as well. When their first store opened in early 2003, Infuze offered a range of more than 50 freshly brewed loose-leaf teas. The selection included green, black, oolong and white teas, fruit and herb-infused teas, and iced tea. In each category, Infuze offered both premium and regular teas, distinguished by price (from $1.50 to $4 per cup) and by packaging. Introducing teas at super-premium price points was novel—at the time, even at chains such as Starbucks, tea was still served in bags at price levels ranging from $1.30 to $2.00. Yet Infuze's premium teas were exceptional, including rare Taiwanese oolongs and sencha green teas. Even its lower-priced regular beverages used high-grade loose-leaf teas.

While Infuze had little money for marketing and promotion, its designs and products succeeded in attracting a discriminating and well-connected clientele. The founders, sensing an opportunity, began to leverage the knowledge and networks of those early customers. Within a month, Infuze-branded teas were being offered at a local boutique hotel and in tea-flavoured martinis at another stylish eatery.

This case was written by Lukas Neville, PhD student, Queen's School of Business, and Professor Elspeth J. Murray, CIBC Teaching Fellow in Entrepreneurship, Queen's School of Business, Queen's University. This case was developed with the support of the CIBC Curriculum Development Fund at the Queen's Centre for Business Venturing, for purposes of classroom discussion.

MATCHA

To further increase Infuze's prestige, Takeda and Koo gambled on a product that had almost no North American exposure—matcha. Matcha is a jade-green powder made by grinding shade-grown, hand-picked tea leaves and stems with granite wheels. It can be whisked with hot water for a frothy tea drink or used in blended drinks and baked goods. Matcha contains an amino acid called theanine, which is reputed to offer its users an energy boost similar to caffeine—but without causing the jitters. This tea is perhaps the world's best, and Infuze hoped that offering it would differentiate its menu and help encourage a culture of tea connoisseurship. It's also pricey. Shortly after its first store opened, Infuze launched its matcha-based drinks at prices ranging from $3.50 for a whisked cup of matcha tea to $5 for a matcha smoothie.

It wasn't long before good luck gave Takeda and Koo a boost. It turned out that many of their first customers were from the nearby offices of *The Vancouver Sun*. The store's uniqueness, coupled with the founders' penchant for giving customers lessons on their teas' history, cultivation, health benefits, and flavour profiles, led to some immediate and favourable press coverage. The attention grew as the founders exploited their story. The media treated matcha as a made-in-Vancouver success, playing up Takeda's family history and the heresy of shilling tea in Starbucks country. Coverage continued to spread. "We've never sent out a press release," says Takeda. "We've never cold-called an editor."

Infuze had other advantages. Most significant was its exclusive distribution rights to matcha in Vancouver. In the company's planning stages, the founders secured a commitment from Aiya Corp. of Japan, the market leader in ceremonial green tea production. Side stepping usual distribution channels, Aiya pledged to offer just-in-time delivery of its high-end teas, which could otherwise be difficult to source and procure. Infuze was offered exclusivity in their area, giving its tea rooms a virtual monopoly on the green powder.

Before long, Infuze's business took a turn. Takeda and Koo knew that their pair of tea houses was too small to drive and sustain mainstream consumer demand for matcha alone. So even though their original business plan identified other retailers as a serious competitive threat, the duo found themselves supplying an increasing number of those same competitors with matcha powder. The biggest was a 40-store regional chain, which Takeda and Koo helped to develop its own matcha latte and "matcha chillo" drinks. This deal put matcha drinks into a competitor's store not five minutes away from one of their own.

Since Infuze was young, it was difficult for the founders to quantify the effects of this change in tactics—but they felt that wholesaling and retail beverage sales seemed to form a virtuous circle for the company. "Sure, we gave up being the only place in town for matcha," says Takeda. "But the more prevalent it was, the more popular it became. We were making money whether it was being sold wholesale or through our store, so it wasn't in our interests to clutch onto exclusivity on the retail side." With the chain's aggressive PR campaign, matcha grabbed national coverage. In less than six months, Infuze's bulk sales increased from 5 percent to 20 percent of gross revenue.

Even then, however, wholesale distribution was still a sideline. That changed after a meeting in late 2004. Takeda and Koo were invited to San Francisco to meet with senior decision-makers at a 500-location chain of smoothie stores. The smoothie giant was enthralled with matcha and was prepared to order it in bulk from Infuze in unprecedented volumes. It was also ready to move fast. "Product development in the beverage industry can be a year-long cycle," Takeda says. "They were ready to push it forward in three months."

But the new deal was fraught with peril. "There was nothing to stop our client from dealing with Aiya directly," said Takeda. "We were two guys in Vancouver working as middlemen between two massive corporations." And even if they could continue working with the client directly, Infuze stood to gain only a very modest markup on the cost of the bulk matcha—hardly commensurate with the resources Infuze was investing to close the deal.

By this time, Infuze had done a second round of financing. And Takeda and Koo's worries were echoed by their new investors, who insisted that Infuze's relationship with Aiya needed retooling. Infuze's management took their business case to Aiya: Infuze's bulk business was growing quickly, they had a 500-location chain waiting in the wings, but the present structure of the deal left Infuze no incentive for continuing to pursue bulk sales. Aiya responded with a "working understanding." Says Takeda: "Aiya basically promised me that we would find a fair way to share the risks and rewards of growing the matcha market. But they wouldn't commit to any details."

Aiya had a corporate culture that valued deliberation, and negotiations plodded on for months. Yet Infuze was still able to help its big, fast-moving client debut its matcha smoothie. The arrangement was held together by the good faith of Infuze's founders and two equity investments from Aiya as evidence of its commitment. Takeda, Koo, and their staff joined Aiya at trade fairs and conventions. Takeda and Koo were used to conveying matcha's value proposition clearly and concisely. "Behind the counter at Infuze, you've got 20 seconds of the customer's attention," Takeda says. They used their 20-second elevator pitch at the trade shows they attended to considerable effect. "We were getting 10 business cards for every one that Aiya's staff were getting."

NEW DEAL

In May 2005, Aiya finally returned with a new deal for Infuze. The offer involved a five-year term, entitling Infuze to 33.3 percent of its gross margin for all sales to new or expanded Canadian and American accounts. Infuze, as a non-exclusive supplier and marketer, would be required to make "reasonable commercial efforts" to expand its own chain of branded tea houses, sell Aiya tea in its tea houses, and maximize North American sales.

The night they received Aiya's memorandum of understanding, Takeda and Koo stayed up late digesting its contents. Under its terms, Aiya and Infuze would share the cost of direct marketing and employees. Aiya would cover two-thirds of the costs and Infuze the remaining third. Infuze's spending would be subsidized by an injection of $250 000 from Aiya, in exchange for a modest share of equity. "We were ecstatic. It was an unbelievable deal," says Takeda. "When we first talked with Aiya in January, they had been talking about performance milestones, contingent on growth levels. By the time we had a written deal, there were no performance requirements." The trust built during the two companies' long courtship allowed Aiya to feel comfortable with a flexible contract free of formal obligations beyond a commitment to revenue-sharing.

But for all their enthusiasm, Takeda and Koo were daunted by the road that lay ahead: Would Infuze miss its retail opportunity by moving into wholesale? What would it need to do to switch from retail to wholesaling? And how were two guys in Vancouver going to make Americans clamour for matcha and bring industry giants to their doorstep? "It was going to be a 180-degree turnaround in the direction of our business. And we needed strategy on the fly, in real time," says Takeda.

Infuze's founders were worn out and overwhelmed. They had been successful at retailing. Their first experiments in wholesaling had been extraordinarily promising. But were they ready to switch gears mid-race?

CASE 4   WATCH THAT NEXT STEP

Wally Haas had much to celebrate as 2007 slipped into 2008. As he welcomed the new year, he could proudly look back on a banner performance at his firm, St. John's, N.L.-based Avalon Microelectronics. Haas had founded the company—a maker of specialized software for microchips used in high-speed data transfer—just four years earlier as a tiny start-up in a remote location with little more than a good idea. Over the past 12 months, it had generated sales of $1.5 million, a ten-fold increase from the year before. Better yet, Haas was projecting sales to grow as much as 40 percent in 2008, a pace he expected to maintain for several years to come.

But even as the metaphorical champagne flowed, Haas knew that the outlook for Avalon wasn't all wine and roses. Serious issues were beginning to emerge, and Haas's company was struggling to keep up as demand for its products and services began to outstrip the company's capacity. Much to Haas's chagrin, Avalon was starting to turn down business. Fortunately, Haas's market position was protected for the time being as there were no direct competitors in Avalon's niche to snatch the clients the company couldn't take on right away. But Haas was certain that it was only a matter of time before someone would try. The only solution to his problem was to expand Avalon, fast. The question was, how—and where?

"I'm worried about the near future," Haas would say when asked about his business. "What happens when firms in our space start to encroach on our turf? We may be growing at 40 percent a year, but what happens five years down the road if our competitors are growing at 400 percent a year?"

Haas's capacity problems stemmed from the fact that he'd had a hard time convincing software engineers to leave major industry centres and move to Newfoundland to join his company. Few that had been trained in North America or Europe had been tempted by his overtures, mainly because they could earn higher salaries and work for larger, more prestigious companies in tech-savvy cities like Ottawa and San Francisco. Avalon had attracted international interest from engineers in developing countries, such as India and China. But Haas—a native Newfoundlander who'd spent 12 years in Ottawa with Nortel Networks and PMC Sierra before returning home to start Avalon—worried that most of these candidates were more interested in getting to Canada and acquiring citizenship than in working specifically for Avalon. They might be willing to start out in St. John's, but he feared they would leave for other cities as soon as they acquired legal status to remain in the country. Understandably, Haas was reluctant to invest in a hire only to see that person move on as soon as the opportunity presented itself.

One solution to his problem was to open a second Avalon design centre in an established tech hub, where it would be in the middle of existing talent pools. But where? Haas had been investigating the issue and had yet to come to any firm conclusions. He could, for instance, open a design centre in California's famed Silicon Valley, but that would be expensive due to the salary expectations of local engineers, whose skills were already in high demand and richly compensated. A cheaper option would be to open an office in an Asian hub. But whatever cost savings Haas would realize overseas would be offset by lower productivity. A third option, going to Ottawa, would strike a balance between cost and productivity, but even then Haas would have to find a manager to run the office while he managed headquarters in St. John's. No matter where he was located, he would need someone he could trust fully and completely.

Even if Haas resolved these issues, the very nature of Avalon's work would make it difficult to move some of its operations. Avalon develops what are known as "IP cores." Essentially, these cores are bits of software that enable inexpensive, generic microchips to perform customized functions. This allows firms in the data-transfer business, such as Nortel or Cisco, to buy off-the-shelf chips—at less cost than buying or developing their own custom chips—and then program them in ways to differentiate their hardware products from those of competitors. The work is highly collaborative, Haas says, meaning that it would be difficult for Avalon to function with geographically dispersed teams. And if this is true for branching out in Canada, it's doubly so for

This case was written by Ken Mark, Eric Morse, Stewart Thornhill, and Mary Weil, Pierre L. Morrissette Institute for Entrepreneurship, Richard Ivey School of Business, University of Western Ontario, for purposes of classroom discussion.

setting up in another country. "We need to consider factors like cultural proximity," he says. "We may speak the same language as engineers in other countries, but we rely on different expressions and have different expectations."

If Haas had one advantage as he confronted his expansion issues, it was his familiarity with the challenges of running a software company in a region better known for its troubled fishery and booming energy sector than its technological prowess. He had already overcome a number of them in getting Avalon this far. When it came to financing his new venture back in 2004, for example, Haas was certain he was onto a good thing and he saw the potential for decades of growth. But because his idea tapped a new area of expertise—and because he was proposing an unusual business for Newfoundland—he found it difficult to attract investors.

Tenacity paid off, though, and Haas was eventually able to secure government financing, using his personal investment in Avalon as leverage, as well as the company's acceptance into a local tech business incubator. Within a year, Avalon released its first product. Before long it was winning customers with large and deep pockets. Soon, however, Avalon found itself operating at maximum capacity—and then beyond, leaving Haas to greet the new year in a quandary: "We just can't find enough qualified engineers. Should we only expand in St. John's or should we open an office in Ottawa, or Silicon Valley or Asia? We're growing fast, but we could be growing much faster."

CASE 5   WYSE DESIGN & DEVELOPMENT INC.

Brian Lundrigan typed his company's name, Wyse Design & Development Inc., into Google. Then he clicked on the link leading to a promotional video for its main product—a portable winch system—that he had posted on YouTube. The clip told a simple story: A man driving an all-terrain vehicle through soggy muskeg suddenly becomes stuck in a deep mud hole. He hops off his vehicle and pulls out a small case holding the winch. He hooks one end of the winch's cable to his ATV, the other to a tree, with the winch's motor slung between the two points. He flips on the motor and, a few moments later, is out of the muck and back on his way.

"Putting the demo on YouTube was a good idea," Lundrigan thought to himself as he watched the clip one more time. It helped him deal with one of the key tasks facing his St. John's, N.L.-based firm—specifically, educating consumers and retailers accustomed to fix-mounted winches about his unique, portable product, dubbed the Wyse Mid-Span Winch System. Instead of listening to him explain it, potential customers could see it in action. Best of all, posting videos on YouTube was free—a major consideration for a young company like Wyse, which had little money to spend on a full-scale advertising campaign yet dearly needed to get word out about its product.

Until this point—approximately three years since he launched Wyse—Lundrigan had built up a small but enthusiastic roster of clients that included individual customers as well as local institutional users such as Fisheries and Oceans Canada, the Newfoundland and Labrador Search and Rescue Association, and the Newfoundland Department of Resources. But long-term success could only be achieved if he extended his reach. On the plus side, Lundrigan was convinced there was a much wider market for his winch, as well as a soon-to-be-launched kit option that would allow owners of fix-mounted winches to con-

vert their units into portable devices using Wyse's design. He saw his biggest opportunity in the mass retail market, even though it was (and remains) dominated by cheaper imports. He believed his product's quality and flexibility would convince consumers to accept his price.

The problem was, how could he get the word out when he had no resources to invest in a major marketing campaign? Posting videos on YouTube was a start. But Lundrigan knew he'd need to do much more than that. But what?

Lundrigan, who had worked for a major food distributor before founding Wyse, came up with the idea for his winch system in 2003. It happened one day while he was visiting a friend, sitting in the man's garage and talking about a new snowmobile he had bought.

"This man, who was about 50 years old at the time, was telling me about how he had been out in the backcountry by himself and had gotten his new snowmobile stuck," Lundrigan recalls. "He complained that it had taken him an hour to walk back to his cabin, an hour back to the sled, and a third hour to dig the machine out." While the man was talking, Lundrigan found himself staring at an ATV in the corner of the garage that had a fix-mounted winch system. "I'm an avid fan of snowmobiles myself and I'd been in a lot of similar predicaments. I kept looking at the winch on the ATV and thinking: This can be made much more useful."

Inspired, Lundrigan spent the next few months sketching out his idea for what would become the Wyse (an acronym for "When You've Struggled Enough") mid-span winch. In 2004, he pulled some funding together and applied to a local business incubator for technology startups called the Genesis Centre, which was affiliated with Newfoundland's Memorial University. The centre believed that Lundrigan's concept had potential to compete in the global market and accepted his fledgling company as a client.

Initially, Lundrigan simply planned to design his winch system and license it to a manufacturer. As it turned out, his timing couldn't have been worse. Since early in the decade, the domestic winch industry had been facing stiff competition in

This case was written by Eric Morse, Ken Mark, and Mary Weil, Pierre L. Morisette Institute for Entrepreneurship, Richard Ivey School of Business, University of Western Ontario, for purposes of classroom discussion.

the form of cheap imports from Asia. Mass merchandisers had been selling the imports for as low as $69, much cheaper than the $200 to $600 charged for winches made in North America. The Asian winches were of lesser quality, but they had gained market share rapidly. "The traditional winch manufacturers were going through a particularly hard time trying to recapture market share they had lost to the cheaper Asian products," he says. "It seemed that most were in survival mode and focused primarily on cutting costs, not so much on new product development."

Undaunted, Lundrigan continued to test designs and develop prototypes. In the end, he decided to build the business on his own. In 2006, after sourcing his own components and finding a manufacturer, he went to market with the final version that retailed in the range of $300 to $400. Lundrigan decided to call his product a mid-span winch—not a "portable winch"—because he wanted to avoid being confused with various imported winches, some of which gave the impression of being a portable product. "It can be confusing to the consumer because these 'portable winches' are only portable while you are carrying them from the place of purchase to your home," Lundrigan says. "Then they have to be permanently bolted down to something for it to be used."

The name of Lundrigan's winch system may have been a mouthful for casual consumers, but that didn't stop it from having a successful launch. It scored great reviews and generated decent business, much of it via word of mouth. While that interest alone was enough to convince Lundrigan that he needed to reach a wider market, the issue grew more acute when he came up with the idea of the conversion kit.

From his research and meetings with retailers, Lundrigan knew that many consumers had purchased imported fixed winches on a whim, either due to the low shelf price or for a spe-

cific but infrequent use. But industry contacts were also telling Lundrigan that many of these winches were not actually being put to use by the people who bought them, due to their impracticality and the added cost of having them mounted on vehicles.

This insight led him back to the design process to develop a product he would call the Wyse Winch Kit. The final version was essentially his mid-span winch system, minus the winch. The customers he was targeting already owned those. What they lacked was the true portability that came with his mid-span concept—and, thus, the motivation to pay to have their inexpensive Asian winches fix-mounted on a single vehicle. Lundrigan was hoping that his solution to the mounting issue would give winch owners a whole new reason to open their pocketbooks.

Lundrigan is now ready to launch the Wyse Winch Kit and is looking for an affordable marketing strategy for both his mounting kit and his mid-span system. "The question is, how do we effectively educate potential customers about our products?" he asks. "If consumers realized how useful their winches—either fix-mounted or sitting unused—could be with our kit, I'm confident that they would look for our products at their local retailers. And if they wanted a full winch system, we'd gladly be able to serve their needs as well."

Lundrigan also faces another, related hurdle—getting his products placed at retailers. "Every major retail chain is offering winches in their product line, but what they seem to forget is that every winch they sell will require a mounting solution," he says. "We think we have the solution with our kit, but I'm having a hard time convincing the retailers. How can I get them to see the potential profit that walks out their door every day?"

Indeed, although word about Wyse products is spreading, Lundrigan needs something more to take his business to the next level—specifically, a marketing strategy that's both high-impact and low-cost. What to do?

CASE 6   ROCKY MOUNTAIN SOAP

It was meant to be a coup. Cam Baty and Karina Birch, owners of Canmore-based Rocky Mountain Soap, were offered an opportunity at a national trade show to create a new packaged-goods brand and were given space to sell it on retail shelves in supermarkets nationwide. They jumped at the chance, buoyed by the success of their own thriving trio of retail shops. After all, they reasoned, in the decade since they first founded their company, Rocky Mountain's all-natural soaps and skin-care products had inspired near-fanatical devotion in their customers and created a vibrant, highly profitable regional brand.

The new packaged-goods line was called Glacier, in a nod to the glacier water used in all of Rocky Mountain's soaps, and it was distributed to large-scale retailers across the country. Based on their initial assumptions, Baty and Birch projected at least $800 000 in annual sales for their new line.

But what began as a victory march onto retail shelves ended in bloody trench warfare. The distribution and logistics involved in serving hundreds of retail locations were challenging. Glacier's packaging and branding, though far more sophisticated than Rocky Mountain's previous products, were nonetheless lost in the visual clutter of crowded retail shelves. And, most importantly, supermarket retailers weren't prepared to engage in the loyalty-building customer-education campaigns that were the daily norm at Rocky Mountain's own stores.

Consumers, unfamiliar with the Glacier brand and unmoved by its presentation, reacted tepidly. Annual sales for the Glacier line fizzled, finishing just shy of $100 000 for the year.

The failed project left Rocky Mountain's owners with a dilemma. In early 2006, after winding down the Glacier brand and returning their focus to their three stores, they had to rec-

This case was originally written by Peggy Cunningham, R.A. Jodfrey Chair at Dalhousie University, and was adapted by Lukas Neville, PhD student and Professor Elspeth J. Murray, CIBC Teaching Fellow in Entrepreneurship at the Queen's School of Business. The adaptation of this case was supported by the CIBC Curriculum Development Fund at Queen's School of Business, for purposes of classroom discussion.

oncile their ambitions for the brand with the dissatisfying results of their growth experiment. Baty still longed to build a national brand, and looked with a degree of envy at their competitors in the natural skin-care market. Burt's Bees of Durham, North Carolina, for instance, had grown from a small honey bottler to a $250-million hyper-growth consumer brand, while the U.K.'s Lush Handmade had expanded internationally, ratcheting its annual sales well beyond $100 million. While Baty's and Birch's aspirations for Rocky Mountain weren't quite on that scale, they nonetheless hoped to build their company into a national presence—and add to their sales by an order of magnitude.

They had reason for their enthusiasm. Since the start of 2000, Rocky Mountain's same-store sales had grown at a healthy clip, and per-square-foot sales in its stores (the touchstone metric for all retailers) ranged from an enviable $900 to a staggering $1700. But the brand's impact on its consumers was even more evident in their correspondence than in their cash-register receipts. Gushing, evangelical testimonials arrived at the company's headquarters almost daily. One eczema sufferer tried their soap once, and then described returning to the store for four more bars the same day. A chemotherapy patient weighed in on the relief afforded by Rocky Mountain's foot butter, and noted that they frequently gave the cream as a gift to others.

Rocky Mountain had also developed a successful brand imprint in Alberta. Their logo was a stylized depiction of the Three Sisters mountain range outside Canmore—Baty's mountain-bike stomping grounds and the company's birthplace. Their slogan, "Be Kind, Be Real, Be Natural," was as much a personal mantra as a corporate motto. Since the company's inception, it had eschewed the usual lineup of chemical cleansers, preservatives, and colouring agents. Instead, Rocky Mountain's soaps deployed a range of essential oils, grains, and berries. As natural products moved from a niche market in the 1990s to mainstream consciousness in this decade, enthusiasm picked up for the company's high-priced but all-natural offerings. Once converted, customers would frequently spread the word: "Customers are often our best salespeople," Baty noted with a laugh.

Wasting little time after mothballing Glacier, Rocky Mountain's owners started to ruminate about the potential for another type of expansion. Rather than turning their products over to another retailer, Baty and Birch began to consider the prospect of expanding their own retail chain. After all, they figured, the failing of their Glacier-brand, packaged-goods venture was primarily the result of their lack of control over the retail environment. What they recognized was that a customer visit to one of their stores wasn't mere shopping—it was a well-rounded body and mind experience.

It started with the smells of the company's 27 different soaps. Upon entering a store, you might first catch a whiff, say, of pumpkin patch soap, whose pumpkin pulp was designed to soothe rough, sore skin—or of Citrus Smoother, a soap whose sweet orange essential oils were a panacea for acne-prone faces.

But equally important was the embrace of its service. Rocky Mountain didn't owe its success just to its products; it owed it to the company's staff, its intimate, personal marketing efforts and its unique approach to product development. The small chain's employees were remarkably knowledgeable and conscientious.

They could readily match customers' skin conditions to the right product. Their capability wasn't an accident—nor was it easy to achieve. Throughout this decade, Rocky Mountain had worked hard to build employee talent. It recognized the contributions of individual staffers on their Web site, was in the midst of launching a daycare program, had instituted open-book management and a profit-sharing plan, and had worked out a sales incentive scheme that rewarded teams for sales achievement without encouraging overzealous commission-chasing.

Employees were also intimately involved with the products. For the dozens of items, staffers could recite ingredients and explain how specific oils, extracts, and grains each affected the skin. The staff were also a conduit for customer knowledge, relaying feedback, suggestions, and requests to the owners. Such customer requests were still at the heart of the company's product-development process. Where a competitor like The Body Shop had access to the R&D resources of French parent firm L'Oréal, Rocky Mountain's products sprang forth from small-scale experiments conducted by Birch in the company's Canmore factory. Product ideas came from (and were often tested by) customers and staff. Some, like a salt scrub, went through 17 iterations before the founders settled on the final formulation. Others came about more quickly. Their strong-selling Summer Lemonade Soap, for instance, was the result of a suggestion from a local eighth-grade student.

These tight-knit customer relationships had been reinforced in the decade since Rocky Mountain's inception through its marketing efforts. Customer newsletters read like personal notes from Birch, sharing internal goings-on (their Wednesday morning staff yoga sessions, for instance) and describing new products. As the company grew, it began experimenting with more sophisticated marketing techniques, including opt-in email marketing and custom tailored mailings offering premiums such as a free bar of soap on customers' birthdays. The company's marketing also served to help educate consumers, deepening their clients' commitment to natural products. Alongside product updates and contests, Rocky Mountain's newsletters often contained information about natural products and aromatherapy trends. This type of communication was critical, because consumer education took time, particularly when clients had to adjust to things like unorthodox packaging—the stores' body butters, for instance, were packaged in plastic containers more commonly used for men's deodorant.

The owners had also leveraged the tourist economies of Banff and Canmore to grow their brand. Many local hotels in these tourist hubs offered Rocky Mountain soaps in their guest suites, providing customers with an all-important first trial. And from experience, the owners knew that much of the company's sales came from tourists eager for mountain-themed Canadiana. Their retail locations and branding catered to these distinctly local dynamics.

Traditional marketing at Rocky Mountain wasn't quite an afterthought—but it came close. Print advertising was limited and exclusively local. The company took out small ads in low-circulation local newspapers and often left rack cards in hotel lobbies. In Banff and Canmore, whose small populations were served by a single newspaper each, such advertising was relatively inexpensive. In Edmonton, they had tried to scale up their efforts by purchasing billboards, mall posters, and space in the

Edmonton Journal—all with limited success. On reflection, Baty and Birch realized that they weren't as comfortable managing high-gloss campaigns as they were building deep relationships with customers, one at a time.

With wholesaling all but ruled out, Rocky Mountain needed a unique strategy if it truly wanted to grow nationally. As Baty and Birch discussed their experiences—both their successes with retailing and setbacks with wholesaling—their aims began to crystallize. They decided they should open 30, perhaps 40 stores, with a rollout schedule of four to seven new company-owned outlets per year.

Envisioning growth was easy—getting there, the owners knew, would be an entirely different story. After the failed Glacier launch, Baty and Birch felt a natural trepidation about entering new markets without answers to a range of questions. Among them: How could they translate their personal marketing techniques to a much larger chain? Would the Rockies-themed brand resonate outside the Canadian West? Could they keep their intuitive and organic approach to product development as they entered the turf of larger competitors like The Body Shop? Could they replicate the personal service provided by their long-serving staff members as the chain grew?

Burt's Bees and Lush had both transformed themselves from tiny startups to retailing juggernauts on the strength of their organic and natural product niches. Baty hoped to follow in their footsteps but, as a final question, wondered how much space was left in this already crowded market—particularly for a small company with a limited marketing arsenal. As he and Birch surveyed their factory floor and watched employees carve out blocks of soap, they wondered: Did they have what it takes to build a national retail brand?

CASE 7   MELVILLE CORPORATE FINANCE INC.

12 September 2008, 3:58 p.m., Melville Corporate Finance Inc., Vancouver Office

Just 72 hours after returning from a week's holiday, Chris Haselbach was about to join a 4:00 p.m. progress briefing on the new financing deal in China. Chris was CEO and founder of Melville Corporate Finance Inc. (Melville). The US$3.4 million deal had got off to a quick start two weeks earlier. A financing request had come in from an existing client, Kohen Manufacturing (KM), in Edmonton, Alberta. During the holiday with his family, Chris had used his BlackBerry to gather requirements from the KM sales lead, James Chui, and relay that information back to Nathaniel Shaw, Senior Vice President in Melville's office in Vancouver, British Columbia. Nathaniel's coordination with the Vancouver office and the existing rapport between KM and Melville fast-tracked the preparations. Yet, Chris wondered if it was reasonable to expect the deal to materialize. He knew that he could not pursue this further without a full agreement from Export Development Canada (EDC). The deal could not proceed unless an EDC Account Manager in Ottawa, Ontario, endorsed the deal. EDC would provide a loan guarantee for 85% of the loan value if they all came to the same conclusion. The EDC Account Manager had been great in the past and EDC's knowledge and expertise complemented that of Melville's team. Together they were good at rapidly and properly evaluating risks.

Melville had financed previous KM deals and was accustomed to the time pressures of multi-million dollar, multi-year, international financing deals. Chui revealed that another manufacturer—one of KM's competitors—would be sought if the financing could not be in place by 15 October 2008. Chui confided that a quarterly bonus hinged on this deal closing by 31 September 2008. Chris enjoyed a challenge.

ABOUT THE DEAL

On 1 September 2008, KM finalized the technical specifications for the sale of two large-scale preform production bottling systems. The machine created plastic soft drink bottles; essentially taking a PET (polyethylene terephthalate) preform starter through an injection molding system to produce a beverage container. The preform looked like a rigid deflated balloon, where the open end already had the threads for the bottle cap. The purchaser was Bottle King Zhongshan (BK), a bottler in Zhongshan, China (see Figure 1). BK had existing contracts with PepsiCo Inc. and The Coca-Cola Company for regional bottling operations. BK was facing an ongoing cash flow crunch as a result of rapid year-to-year growth (accounting reports estimated growth at 90% over the three previous years). As well, the contract renewal process with Pepsi was scheduled to begin in 18 months; renewal would be contingent on a satisfactory inspection of operations.

BK's continued operations and growth depended on purchasing modern plastic preform production bottling technology. Through improved automation, higher quality controls, and a greater operational capacity to meet demand, BK management was pleased the KM sales team was able to match their requirements with the right equipment. The new equipment from KM would increase production capacity by 25%. This was sufficient to meet growth projections for the next three years. Unfortunately, the company's on-hand cash supply could not cover this purchase cost. Until now the natural second option to finance the purchase of the equipment would be mainland Chinese banks. However, BK was a family-owned business with 100% equity owned by Chinese citizens. Regulations restricted Chinese bank participation in international financing deals for any company without partial foreign ownership. Even if financing were obtained it would not be US or Canadian dollars.

Case written by Andrew Lunnie, Canadian International Development Agency, Gatineau, Québec, Angeline Pacione, Export Development Canada, Santiago, Chile, and Prescott C. Ensign.

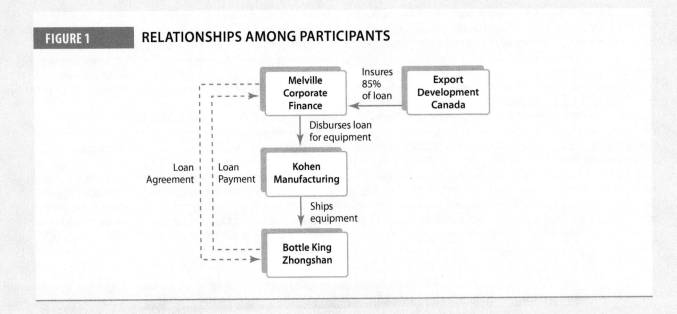

FIGURE 1   RELATIONSHIPS AMONG PARTICIPANTS

It was nearly impossible for a private Chinese enterprise to obtain foreign currency. Other financing options in China were explored, but without success. An alternative financing option needed to be found quickly.

On 6 September 2008, KM's sales team took the lead to identify financing in Canada and sought help from Melville, their proven partner for export financing. Using Melville provided several advantages. First and foremost was Melville's ability to quickly step in, assess merit, and close the deal. If EDC's and Melville's requirements were met, financing would be made available immediately and the equipment would be shipped to Zhongshan within two weeks of approval. This deal, however, was unlike previous deals and had a number of unusual characteristics that needed to be explored.

Melville provided another advantage for KM in that their approval would simplify the deal. If approved, KM would be paid in full and have no further transactions with BK on this sale. Melville would assume full responsibility to recover the loan from BK directly. In other words, Chui and the KM sales team would earn their quarterly bonus without any strings attached and could move their energies onto the next sale. KM did not know or appreciate EDC's role in the outcome. All KM knew was that Melville somehow made things happen. The truth was that EDC did a lot of the work to pull the deal together. As usual, the EDC Account Manager and EDC team would have to be convinced of the merits of this particular transaction before providing a guarantee. Critical analysis of risks and mitigants would be performed by EDC and Melville.

It was up to EDC and Melville to assess the viability and decide. On the surface the Zhongshan deal needed to be considered carefully due to the rapidly changing global economy. Apart from the financials—which required the usual scrutiny—this deal was directly with a Chinese private company. There would be no guarantee by the Government of China or reputable Chinese bank as the intermediary. The rewards from this deal would be significant for Melville and would include: a strengthened relationship with KM, an opportunity to gain expertise inside

a rapidly growing market, and financial yield. While Melville's reputation was built on its agility and speed to close deals, this had never equated with hasty decisions. EDC also knew that no reward was completely divorced from risk.

Melville had plenty of ongoing projects in Latin America and there were numerous financing arrangements to be explored. There were even those at EDC that thought prospecting in Latin America was easier. Spanish was the most common language to be overheard at Melville offices and despite Chris Haselbach's affinity for China, just one-fifth of their deals were linked to mainland China. Turning down a deal that might have been lucrative was not nearly as detrimental as approving a deal that should have been turned down. Knowing when to pass up a deal was an important part of the business. Something else would always come along if EDC and Melville chose to pass on this one. Neither Chris nor the EDC Account Manager wanted to be swayed by BK choosing not to go with KM if this deal could not be resolved in time.

BUILDING THE NECESSARY DECISION CRITERIA

Meeting with Nathaniel Shaw

12 September 2008, 4:00 p.m., Melville's Executive Boardroom, Vancouver

Chris walked into the boardroom to find Nathaniel ready and waiting. Nathaniel looked up to greet Chris, and indicated that this deal would be the first of its kind in China for Melville and apparently, it would be the first EDC deal in this part of China in this industry. Without Chinese government authorities or a trusted local bank working with them, they were on their own dealing directly with a private Chinese company.

Nathaniel informed Chris that Melville had shared with EDC what his team had compiled so far. It had only been a week, but the file was not nearly complete. At this point the proposal was missing some fundamental information. Nathaniel pointed out that with what they had right now Melville would likely not approve a domestic company for this amount. And given EDC's high standards for new situations, the Account Manager would need some convincing as well.

This deal represented a significant use of capital by Melville and it was crucial to ascertain that this capital was being applied very cautiously and that risks of losses would be minimized as much as possible. Melville had a 15% uncovered risk on this deal. Documentation and information had to be complete.

Company documents from BK were quite revealing. BK was not nearly as large as Chris and Nathaniel had expected, particularly considering the size of the loan for which Chui was lobbying. Based on this financial snapshot document that arrived from Zhongshan, China, through Chui, BK was requesting a loan that was close to one-third of their annual revenues. Nathaniel knew that if this did not stop the process it should at least merit serious consideration of the financing terms. Nathaniel paused and passed the annual revenues snapshot to Chris (see Table 1).

Chris scanned over the report, then reviewed the document again. He questioned Chui's judgment and wondered if he was misinterpreting what he was seeing. Melville would not normally follow through on such a disproportionate financial request. Nathaniel also recognized that something was missing. Chui called that morning and pointed out that this could be the first of many sales to BK. Chui highlighted BK's rate of growth and the stability of their multi-year bottling contracts with Pepsi and Coca-Cola.

KM's position was understood but neither Chris nor Nathaniel could envision approving a deal based on the facts at hand. On paper the numbers looked strange considering the size of the financing BK was requesting. Also, Bottle King Zhongshan's income statement indicated that they were running a high debt to equity ratio. Melville would need to be able to have influence over how BK managed future cash flow. At a minimum, if Melville were to proceed, it would need BK to maintain a specific

debt to equity ratio. Further, EDC had discovered that placing an enforceable lien on the equipment might be possible.

Nathaniel would have Melville's legal advisor include a reasonable debt to equity ratio into the letter of intent and explore the right to place a lien on the equipment as well. Chris would then send that draft letter over to BK to communicate Melville's expectations during the repayment period. BK's response to this control might allow Melville to gauge BK's intent to pay.

Nathaniel confirmed that he would push Chui for confirmation on the revenue levels and ensure Melville's legal advisor got updates and forwarded the revised letter of intent. BK would see it in a couple of days. BK seemed eager to get this resolved too.

Nathaniel knew that from a fundamental standpoint, BK's size was at the lower end of the spectrum of deals Melville would typically approve, but their growth over the past four years and their projections for the next four provided merit for approval. Nathaniel considered those "5 Cs of credit" he had studied in finance. Those '5 Cs' now played a prominent role in his daily work life. They were key in seeing creditworthiness and unlocking a borrower's willingness and ability to repay a debt. There were both qualitative and quantitative measures to determine the chance of default (see Table 2).

Bottle King Zhongshan's year-to-year growth was impressive but hard to fathom (see Table 3). Chris reminded Nathaniel that Melville's high growth domestic market clients were not even close to this. It was hard to gain proper perspective. Nathaniel wished they had performance data for this company or even others from a similar sector in China—EDC was unable to turn up anything concrete for comparison. The EDC Account Manager and his team had checked EDC databases and found almost nothing at all on BK and very little on this manufacturing segment in China. Typically both EDC and Melville relied on industry and

TABLE 2	FIVE Cs OF CREDIT
Character	Borrower's reputation. Are they responsible? Past behaviour, expected future actions.
Capacity	Borrower's ability to repay based on a comparison of income and debts. Are they financially overextended?
Capital	Capital the borrower puts toward the investment; the larger the contribution the less chance of default, *ceteris paribus*. How much cash is on hand?
Collateral	Property or large assets used to secure the loan. What do they own? Can we get our hands on it?
Conditions	Interest rate, amount of principal, and payment schedule. Are things (revenue stream, customers, market, etc.) stable?

TABLE 1	BOTTLE KING ZHONGSHAN ANNUAL REVENUES

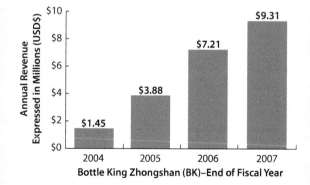

Source: Company financial statements as of September 2008.

TABLE 3 — BOTTLE KING ZHONGSHAN PROJECTED ANNUAL REVENUES

Projected Annual Revenue Expressed in Millions (USD$)

Bottle King Zhongshan (BK)–End of Fiscal Year	Value
2008	$12.56
2009	$17.10
2010	$22.98
2011	$29.78

Source: Company financial statements as of September 2008.

company historical information to feed into their interpretations. EDC and Melville were both tentative about proceeding without a good fundamental analysis.

EDC was able to determine that the accounting practices were unique compared to those in North America. The Chinese government required each company to complete a standard form and this form established the basis for annual corporate taxation. It was a very rough financial picture, full of gaps by Western standards. Both Nathaniel and the EDC Account Manager were skeptical about the form's veracity. They wondered if any penalty existed in China for non-compliance or submitting a misleading report.

Nathaniel and Chris had the suspicion that no respectable accounting firm in Canada or the United States would let this go—there were just too many gaps. And there was no way to validate it without actually going to China. While Melville had approved deals with unique risk variables in the past, this one would be challenging.

Chris received a call from the EDC Account Manager in Ottawa. The EDC Account Manager wondered if Chris could meet to review the BK dossier via conference call. Chris looked to Nathaniel. Nathaniel nodded indicating the documentation could be ready next week. Nathaniel and he agreed to join EDC via conference call from Vancouver.

Chris and Nathaniel resolved to maintain momentum until a decision could be resolved on BK. Working closely with the EDC Account Manager was expected to help identify and qualify the risks.

Nathaniel conveyed to Chris that if Melville continued to proceed with assessing ability to pay (viability), Melville would need to be certain that Melville's legal advisor was satisfied with the legal recourse to place a lien on the equipment. If BK could not pay, Melville would need the legal framework in place to quickly seize ownership of the equipment. Nathaniel concluded that they would be awaiting BK's response to the revised letter of intent.

Chris too felt it was essential to get a reaction to the letter of intent—Melville might thus learn how serious BK was about making the deal happen.

DOCUMENT REVIEW WITH EDC

19 September 2008, 8:45 a.m., Export Development Canada, Ottawa, Ontario

Meeting Attendees:

EDC Account Manager

Several EDC small and medium-sized enterprises relations Team Leads

Chris Haselbach, CEO, Melville (via teleconference)

Nathaniel Shaw, Senior Vice President, Melville (via teleconference)

The EDC Account Manager welcomed Chris and Nathaniel to the conference call and explained that several members of the EDC team were in the room. The EDC Account Manager indicated that Melville's documents were being projected onto a screen and asked them to walk through BK's company profile, financials, and then the credit application and assessment.

Nathaniel informed those assembled in Ottawa that he had received a surprising update. Nathaniel announced that Chui had sent Melville an email to correct a misinterpretation with BK's financial statements. According to James, the translators missed a key detail when they translated the Chinese government financial statements for each year. Melville now had in its possession confirmation that the financial statements were off by a factor of 10.

Nathaniel explained that the accounting practices in China, and that province in particular, removed a zero at the end of financial statements. It was a Chinese accounting method that the Canadian translators had missed. Bottle King Zhongshan was not a US$9.3 million company, but a US$93.1 million company. James had verified this accounting practice with the existing BK accountant who had sent over documents used in negotiating with Coca-Cola three years prior (see Tables 4, 5, and 6).

TABLE 4 — BOTTLE KING ZHONGSHAN REVENUES

Projected Annual Revenue Expressed in Millions (USD$)

Actual Revenues (from corrected financial statements)

Bottle King Zhongshan (BK)–End of Fiscal Year	Value
2004	$14.54
2005	$38.80
2006	$72.04
2007	$93.15

Incorrect Revenues (from incorrect financial statements)

Bottle King Zhongshan (BK)–End of Fiscal Year	Value
2004	$1.45
2005	$3.88
2006	$7.20
2007	$9.31

Source: Company financial statements as of September 2008.

| TABLE 5 | BOTTLE KING ZHONGSHAN ANNUAL REVENUES |

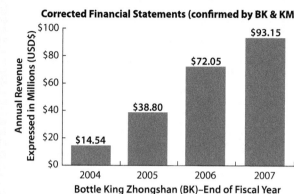

Corrected Financial Statements (confirmed by BK & KM)

Source: Company financial statements as of September 2008.

| TABLE 6 | BOTTLE KING ZHONGSHAN PROJECTED ANNUAL REVENUES |

Corrected Financial Statements (confirmed by BK & KM)

Source: Company financial statements as of September 2008.

Nathaniel then relayed that EDC's legal counsel made them aware that a new law in China would allow for liens to be taken. Melville's lawyer called to confirm the enforceability of a lien on the equipment under Chinese law in case of a default on the loan. It was not a certainty, but they were confident the Chinese government could step in. However, Melville's lawyer did confirm that there was no record of the successful application of a lien in Zhongshan. In summary, if BK did not pay, Melville would have little recourse but to seize the equipment and try to recoup some of its losses but through a very new and untried Chinese law.

Nathaniel navigated through the key points of the deal and the EDC Account Manager used this time to underscore EDC's reliance on formal financial analysis. Forty-five minutes into the documentation review, all of the essential documents were covered. Nathaniel remained tentative on the potential of this deal. Given that BK had no previous relationship with KM, Melville, or EDC, Chris would have preferred better quality information to guide their decisions. If only there was another way to gauge BK's intentions and capabilities to handle this debt load.

Chris divided the arguments into points for and against providing financing to BK. In his mind he weighed the impact of a defaulted loan. What would it mean for Melville? How would it affect his team and his relationship with EDC and KM?

Continuing now, the EDC Account Manager shared that EDC had held off on making comments so that Nathaniel could maintain his objectivity through this process. EDC would like to help support KM and Melville in making this happen, but it must be understood that although this was a strategic opportunity, the EDC Account Manager was not yet comfortable forwarding this for approval.

Chris revealed that he too saw this as a tough decision. He appreciated the EDC Account Manager and EDC team's frankness and noted that for Melville and him there too was no clear pathway on this deal and that time pressures only further complicated it.

Nathaniel shared that BK had approved the letter of intent without requesting further revisions. A signed copy was due to arrive tomorrow at the Vancouver office via air-courier.

Chris sat quietly for a few seconds assessing these new pieces of information carefully. Breaking the silence he asked their EDC Account Manager if he wanted to visit Zhongshan early next week with Nathaniel. Chris would need a recommended course of action on their return from China. He would need a justification of how they should continue and whether or not they should approve or deny BK's request for funding.

Both the EDC Account Manager and Nathaniel needed to prepare if they were going to get at Bottle King Zhongshan's ability and intent to repay a loan from Melville Corporate Finance: Who should they visit? What questions would need to be asked?

Appendix A: About the Players

MELVILLE CORPORATE FINANCE INC.

Principals

Chief Executive Officer: Chris Haselbach—founder and major shareholder. He was a former employee of the Department of Foreign Affairs and International Trade, Business Development Bank of Canada, and Export Development Canada. Under Haselbach's leadership Melville had maintained strong partnerships with Canadian exporters and EDC.

Senior Vice President: Nathaniel Shaw—in charge of overall management and operations for Melville's team of 16 employees, with offices in Vancouver, Toronto, Montreal, and Calgary. He worked on analyzing risk and creditworthiness. He had the ability to gain insight quickly to support decision making. He was trusted for new and high value proposals—his industry experience was an asset.

Background

Melville was a private firm created to support Canadian exporters by offering financing to creditworthy buyers of eligible Canadian goods and services. Melville's acted as a unifying partner between the private sector and Canadian public sector actors (federal and provincial bodies). Melville worked with the support of various provincial and federal export-related institutions such as EDC, Western Economic Diversification Canada, Business Development Bank of Canada (BDC), Canadian Commercial Corporation (CCC), and DFAIT (currently the Department of Foreign Affairs, Trade and Development Canada). Melville was profitable because they operated in the niche market of export financing for small and medium-sized transactions. They were able to dedicate more time and attention to smaller and more complicated foreign loans that the large Canadian banks did not have the expertise and risk appetite to support directly.

Melville's target market in Canada was small and medium-sized enterprises (SMEs). SMEs were a major economic engine of growth for the Canadian economy and an area of strategic importance to EDC. Melville relied on EDC to provide insurance against nonpayment by the foreign companies. In order to be eligible for financing, exported goods and services had to satisfy Canadian benefits requirements of EDC.

Through Melville's agile assessment, approval, and financing mechanisms Canadian exporters could expand into the global market with minimal risk. A Melville-financed transaction allowed the Canadian exporter to be paid immediately while the buyer paid Melville over time at the agreed upon terms. Most of the risk of nonpayment was absorbed by EDC through insurance coverage provided to Melville.

Every deal posed direct risk to Melville's financial health. Depending on the terms of the financing, Melville could be exposed significantly. This made EDC's role vital. If a deal failed, i.e., a borrower defaulted on their loan, this would hurt Melville's balance sheet considerably. Other forces included waiting periods, interest, collection costs, etc. Despite the reality of these constant concerns, Melville had a consistent record of accomplishment in qualifying good deals. Without EDC's insurance, Melville could not proceed with this or any financing. Melville, or for that matter any Canadian company venturing abroad, could expect to encounter all sorts of problems in collecting payment. Even if a party were willing to make payment, barriers might exist, such as restrictions on currency exchange and transfer.

Melville's Performance in Recent Years:

- Annual disbursements of US$160 million, stable and increasing revenue
- Solid track record of backing growth companies and good deals

Melville Offered:

- Export financing for SMEs
- Payment within 10 days of shipment to the foreign buyer (provided all obligations under the sales contract with the buyer had been met)

- Quick application processing that did not hold up the sales process
- Loan negotiations

Benefits for International Buyers when Using Melville:

- Quick turnaround of buyer applications for buyer financing (within 10 days)
- Loans available to the buyer in several approved currencies
- Loan documentation standardized for greater efficiency
- Competitive interest rates
- A fixed interest rate that would not fluctuate with the movements of interest rates on international money markets (alternatively, variable interest rates were available to suit client needs)

Benefits for Term Finance

Fixed-rate, medium-term loans, from two to five years were available from Melville to foreign buyers, providing them with a regular repayment schedule. These loans were for amounts up to US$5 million, and were secured by a registered lien[1] on the exported goods.

EDC's Export Guarantee Program

To compensate EDC for taking on their spread of the loan's risk (85%), EDC charged an annual fee of 2.25% of the total loan (paid each year for the life of the term and re-calculated annually based on the outstanding principle). For this loan, the terms were 3-year repayment term at a fixed rate of 6% payable to Melville. EDC charged an additional 2.25% on top of this rate.

EXPORT DEVELOPMENT CANADA

Personnel

EDC Account Manager—had worked directly with Chris Haselbach and Nathaniel Shaw on several deals over the past three years and served as an essential partner in identifying and assessing risk management issues.

Background

Supporting Canadian exports and foreign direct investment, EDC was Canada's export credit agency. EDC offered innovative financing, insurance, and risk management solutions to help Canadian exporters and investors expand their international business. Every year, EDC's knowledge and partnerships were used by over 6400 Canadian companies and their global customers in up to 200 markets worldwide. Approximately 80% of EDC's customers were SMEs. EDC was a crown corporation wholly owned by the Government of Canada. The corporation was financially self-sustaining and operated on commercial principles.

Export Development Canada's mandate was to grow and develop Canada's trade and the capacity of Canadian companies to participate in and respond to international business opportunities. EDC provided trade finance and risk mitigation services

---

[1] A lien allowed the holder of it to take possession or control of property belonging to another until a debt owed by that party is discharged.

to Canadian companies to help them compete internationally. Partnering with Melville Corporate Finance, EDC had participated in approximately C$1.6 billion in deals.

EDC provided a number of risk mitigation solutions to Canadian exporters. EDC offered Canadian companies the creditworthiness ratings of potential foreign customers. This gave them an idea of the likelihood of repayment by that buyer. For Melville, such a credit check would give them an idea as to whether or not a foreign corporation could fulfill its payment obligations. EDC also provided other financing mechanisms for foreign and Canadian companies to gain access to working capital.

BOTTLE KING ZHONGSHAN

Personnel

CEO and Chairman of the Board: Hong Zhen, company founder, who, despite his age, still maintained direct involvement in operations and decision making, thus leveraging his more than three decades of experience in the industry. His political clout in the local region was also known to be strong. Hong Zhen was admired and respected for his contribution to the community.

Background

Bottle King Zhongshan was founded in 1982; its head office and principal manufacturing facilities were across from Macau, in a special economic development zone in Zhongshan in the province of Guangdong. When BK was established, its original activity was boat repair. From those humble beginnings, the company quickly entered into two new areas: textiles and plastic packaging. In 1985, BK purchased from Japan its first injection molding equipment to manufacture the bottles locally to save cost, and it was able to secure contracts with The Coca-Cola Company and PepsiCo Inc. for their bottling needs.

Over this time period, BK's business expanded rapidly. BK grew from one small local factory to 10 large modern industrial enterprises in Zhongshan, and approximately 100 subsidiaries located throughout the whole of China. BK employed 4000 workers and administrators, including 600 engineers and technicians. Every employee was a shareholder of the company.

For the past decade, Bottle King Zhongshan had been dedicating itself to the development of food and beverage packaging and non-woven cloth products. Following a regional development strategy, whereby the company was no further than 600 kilometers from its most important clients, BK had become a China-wide enterprise.

Additionally, there was a current drive at BK to increase exports, which only comprised 2% of the company's revenues. BK was placing a significant focus on Southeast Asia with its relatively new operation in Thailand (the market that would be served with this equipment from KM).

Market & Competition

Based on performance statements from Coca-Cola and Pepsi the following summary had been compiled.

> With regard to the soft drink industry in China, the market has experienced rapid development in the food industry. The

key drivers were hot weather and increasing prosperity. The Chinese market however has proven to be very diverse with great variations in the market demand for different products. Carbonated drinks have shown strong demand throughout. Growth in almost all types of drinks is expected to continue to see strong growth in the near term.

BK had been a manufacturer of PET bottles and a major vendor for Coke and Pepsi in China for over two decades. BK supplied 40% of Coca-Cola's needs, 15% of PepsiCo's, and about the same for a leading Chinese beverage company. It was expected that the bottling industry would consolidate and BK was in a position to benefit as the total volume of soft drinks in China was expected to increase at 3 to 5 percent annually.

Regional Connections and Strategic Investments

Rapid growth rates in Guangdong Province as a whole was mirrored by many companies. This presented a synergistic opportunity for BK to expand via stronger and more integrated business relationships with these growing enterprises.

Hong Zhen sought to leverage his family's business network to establish shared ownership arrangements and strategic investments in Yingde City (population 1 050 000) and Dongguan (population 8 000 000). As it happened, two of his uncles were minority owners of a Chinese holding company, Guangdong Corporation, that was aggressively franchising convenience stores (franchising a well-known Japanese convenience store brand). As Guangdong Corporation worked to establish its supply chain locally, they also sought a local partner through whom they could "integrate" and balance supply risk variables. The president offered a minority ownership stake to Bottle King Zhongshan and additional shares to Hong Zhen and his two uncles in mid-2004. As a sign of good faith and desire for partnership, Hong Zhen arranged for Guangdong Corporation to own a small mix of preferred and minority equity in BK.

The growth of BK's joint venture/ownership portfolio surged in 2005 as Guangdong Corporation opened 40 convenience stores; another 12 were opened in 2006. The return on investment was modest; however, it was the assurance of demand for BK's products that pleased Hong Zhen. Furthermore, the relationship ensured alternative suppliers would not be sought in the foreseeable future and BK would be best positioned to adapt if supply requirements changed for the convenience store chain. Strategically, the timing of the move made sense for all those involved and aligned key persons to a common set of business objectives and gained leverage within the supply chain. As an additional, unexpected, reward for his business acumen, Guangdong Corporation subtly informed Coca-Cola and Pepsi's regional account managers of their deal with BK—in effect, this benefit of this relationship, was leverage over Coca-Cola and Pepsi for current and future contracts in the region.

BK's financial statements (balance sheet and income statement) are found in Exhibits 1 and 2.

EXHIBIT 1 **BOTTLE KING ZHONGSHAN BALANCE SHEET**

IN MILLIONS OF USD	YEAR ENDING 2007-12-31	YEAR ENDING 2006-12-31	YEAR ENDING 2005-12-31	YEAR ENDING 2004-12-31
Cash on Hand	0.90	0.60	1.90	0.08
Government Certificates of Deposit Held	7.80	1.95	0.80	0.01
Investments in Subsidiaries and Joint Ventures	12.00	19.50	15.00	4.00
Loans and Advances to Customers	24.52	22.30	19.81	12.30
Current Assets (including land value)	33.50	21.80	15.55	4.50
Inventory	2.03	7.80	2.92	2.80
Total Assets	**80.75**	**73.95**	**55.98**	**23.69**
Short Term Debt	17.35	13.50	11.60	3.98
Long Term Debt	38.60	37.45	24.66	9.88
Chinese Government Currency Notes in Circulation	7.90	5.65	4.69	0.73
Other Liabilities	3.50	1.51	5.73	3.44
Owner's Equity	11.30	12.94	9.30	5.66
Minority Interests Equity	0.50	0.40	0.00	0.00
Preferred Share Equity	1.60	2.50	0.00	0.00
Total Liabilities	**80.75**	**73.95**	**55.98**	**23.69**

EXHIBIT 2 **BOTTLE KING ZHONGSHAN INCOME STATEMENT**

IN MILLIONS OF USD	YEAR ENDING 2007-12-31	YEAR ENDING 2006-12-31	YEAR ENDING 2005-12-31	YEAR ENDING 2004-12-31
Revenue	**93.15**	**72.04**	**38.80**	**14.54**
Operating Income	91.35	67.88	36.00	14.50
Other Operating Income (joint ventures' operations)	0.90	2.06	1.80	1.14
Interest Income	4.25	4.25	2.25	1.25
Interest Expense	−3.35	−2.15	−1.25	−2.35
Total Operating Expenses (including depreciation)	**88.90**	**68.14**	**24.55**	**6.28**
Gross Profit (before taxation)	**4.25**	**3.90**	**14.25**	**8.26**
Taxation Rate (%)	13.86%	13.89%	15.41%	15.80%
Taxation	0.59	0.54	2.20	1.31
Profit/(loss) after taxation	**3.66**	**3.36**	**12.05**	**6.95**
Minority Interest Payments	0.05	0.04	0.00	0.00
Preferred Share Payments	0.08	1.20	0.00	0.00
Net Profit	**3.53**	**2.12**	**12.05**	**6.95**
Revenue Growth (%)	**29.30%**	**85.67%**	**166.85%**	**...**

KOHEN MANUFACTURING

Personnel

Asian Markets Sales Lead: James Chui was born in Hong Kong. He immigrated to Canada and graduated from the University of Ottawa. He was recruited in 2001 by KM's VP Sales to lead a major expansion into non-domestic markets of China, Thailand, Japan, South Korea, and Taiwan. Chui had worked in the industry since 1990.

Background

Founded in 1977 in Edmonton, Alberta, KM was a diversified manufacturer and exporter of products ranging from standard plastics preform production equipment to large-scale custom mold design. KM plastic preform and molds equipment used industry leading engineering and design for the production of plastics found in everyday life (bottles, containers, bottle caps, and more).

Beginning in mid-2006 Kohen Manufacturing had decided to actively pursue sales growth in Asia. Soft drink consumption—the key driver of demand for KM's technology—was rapidly increasing in this region of the world. KM's market share had continued to climb and in the past year, sales were sufficient in Asia to begin strategic planning to open a new production facility in South Korea. During the last three years KM had completed transactions in over 35 countries and now had a substantial base of users in Asia. Being located in the Asia-Pacific region offered a number of benefits in serving these customers. First, it showed commitment and a willingness to interact with Asian customers. This aided in understanding requirements and technical specifications. Finally, being located in Asia reduced costs associated with design, development, and transportation of bottling equipment.

According to their website:

> KM's goal is manufacturing the best quality products while maintaining competitive pricing and prompt delivery time for our customers. Quality control is a major competitive advantage within the industry and KM achieved ISO9001 (2000 version) in the fall of 2002 and are now a fully certified manufacturer.

KM had established a worldwide reputation for quality products with a relatively favourable benefit-cost realization for purchasers. In addition, a major advantage over their competitors was a continuous focus on innovation in design. Over the past three years several PET preform equipment designs received awards for being economical and having short production start-up times.

Previous and Ongoing Deals with Melville

Since Chui had arrived, KM had relied on Melville's flexible and responsive services to streamline its rapid expansion into Asia. KM had established itself as a high-quality exporter with good business values and trustworthy conduct during the exporting process. Total cumulative value of KM–EDC/Melville deals reached US$100 million in 2006. Currently, Melville was working on financing for additional KM sales; most of which were multi-year financing in Asia and Eastern Europe.

Relationship with Export Development Canada

Kohen Manufacturing had maintained an excellent record of performance and repayment when directly using EDC services. However, since the arrival of Chui at KM, the sales team had preferred the immediate financing advantage provided by Melville over managing a loan within KM's finance department.

Direct Competitors

Sidel, Inc. was located in Georgia—the home of The Coca-Cola Company. Sidel was part of the Tetra Laval Group, a global leader in food packaging and equipment. There was every likelihood that Sidel had been considered by BK. Sidel was pushing an alternative technology—stretch blow molding. KM believed that their own equipment could generate greater throughput (volume of PET bottles formed per minute) than any current Sidel models.

Hovert Impex was based in Ahmedabad, India. While Kohen could argue that Hovert Impex's technology was much less modern, it had been proven to be cost-effective in developing countries. Maintenance costs were low for Hovert Impex customers, even if the equipment was not nearly as state-of-the-art as KM's fully automated machines.

Nissei and Aoki were two prominent players in the PET bottle production equipment industry. These companies from Japan were well established in the region and it was likely that BK had a number of their bottle production lines currently in use. While Nissei and Aoki already had market penetration in China, they did not have unblemished reputations in day-to-day operations. Nissei and Aoki equipment had reliability issues and were known to be over-engineered, requiring knowledgeable operators to keep the finicky machines running.

Appendix B: Risks and Mitigating Factors

China was a massive country with the highest of expectations for growth and prosperity (see Exhibit 3). But with very little comparable data available broken down on regional and sectoral performance, both EDC and Melville were nervous. EDC's office in Beijing had existed for quite some time, but the office in Shanghai had just opened in late 2006. This office covered the booming Yangtze River Delta region and was getting to know that part of China. EDC's Shanghai office boasted being in the business capital of China and focused on the provinces of Jiangsu, Zhejian, and Anhui. Despite being an economically well-off province (its GDP was US$522 billion), Guangdong was politically distant from Beijing. Guangdong was relegated to a lower status when it came to most matters. Other regions with more political clout received greater attention from national authorities.

The stability of the central federal government authority was striking and local leaders had to stay in line. But still there were wide discrepancies from region to region. The EDC Account

EXHIBIT 3   **EDC's POSITION ON CHINA**

CHINA

China consistently ranks as one of Canada's top five export destinations. The country's strong economic growth continues to offer extensive opportunities for Canadian export businesses and investors. China is the base of manufacturing operations for many Canadian companies that have incorporated the advantages of China's low cost of production into their global supply chains. However, in a market experiencing rapid evolution, there are potential credit, regulatory, and Corporate Social Responsibility risks that must be mitigated wherever possible.

Country Risk : Medium

EDC's Position

• Actively seeking new business

• Open under all programs, subject to EDC's regular approval criteria

Canada's strengths in natural resources, agricultural, information and communication technologies, educational services, automotive and environmental technologies make China a natural business partner to explore. In addition to these sectors, EDC will look at transactions in any sector in which Canadian companies have found opportunities.

With representations in Beijing and Shanghai covering Greater China, EDC provides on-the-ground support to Canadian companies doing business in China. EDC's regional representatives have developed strong relationships with major local clients and have created an extensive network of local contacts. EDC is well positioned to help Canadian companies finance and manage credit risk associated with sales to Chinese buyers, and to support Canadian Direct Investment Abroad and Canadian affiliate operations in China.

WHAT IS CHINA BUYING FROM CANADA?

CANADIAN EXPORT TO CHINA, 2007

RANKING	SECTOR	C$
1	Industrial Chemicals	1,485,261,032
2	Paper & Products	1,454,335,988
3	Non-Ferrous Metals	997,763,065
4	Metals, Ores, Non-metallic Minerals	987,208,476
5	Agriculture, Hunting, Forestry, Fishing	651,777,518

CHINA'S FASTEST GROWING SECTORS

FORECAST OF DOMESTIC MARKET GROWTH, 2009

RANKING	SECTOR	%
1	Non-Ferrous Metals	32.4
2	Pottery & China	26.1
3	Motorcycles & Bicycles	23.3
4	Textiles	22.8
5	Agriculture, Hunting, Forestry, Fishing	22.5

Source: EDC website, September 2008.

Manager had firsthand observations and stories relayed by EDC colleagues confirming that a local mayor or business family could take his or her[2] town in a direction that could shake things up for outside interests. While political risk was not great, it was real. EDC's political risk insurance covered the scenarios in Exhibit 4.

Zhongshan, China

Zhongshan was a prefecture-level city situated in the centre of the Pearl River Delta of Guangdong Province (see Map of Region). It faced Hong Kong on the east across the Lingding Ocean, Xinhui and Taishan on the west, with Macau and Zhuhai to the south. It was 100 kilometers away from Guangzhou and a high-speed ferry serviced Hong Kong. Zhongshan held historic and political significance as it was renamed for Dr. Sun Zhonghsan (a.k.a. Sun Yat-sen), the "father" of modern China who overthrew the feudal Qing Dynasty. The city authorities had attempted to balance a pleasant living environment with industrial growth. Most visitors found it warm and charming and less frenetic than other high-growth areas of China. The city boasted having operations for 20 of the Fortune Global 500 and a thriving high-tech sector.

Unusual by Chinese standards it was missing an administrative layer—Zhongshan had no county-level division. Zhongshan held 22 townships under its control and itself fell under the guidance of Guangdong authorities. In additional to the 22 towns, Zhongshan city government directly oversaw four district offices and the Zhongshan Torch Park (high-tech industrial development zone). While holding on to its lineage as the "Fragrant Mountain" town, Zhongshan welcomed the move to diversify from its traditional agricultural base, including rice, lychee, banana, sugar cane, and its famous flowers—particularly chrysanthemum.

GUANGDONG, CHINA

MAP OF REGION ZHONGSHAN, GUANGDONG

| EXHIBIT 4 | POLITICAL RISK SCENARIOS |

Breach of contract risk: The breach of a contractual obligation by a foreign government or state-owned entity and the ensuing refusal by the government or entity to honour an arbitral award in your favour.

Nonpayment by a sovereign obligor: The refusal or inability of a foreign government to make scheduled loan payments or to make a payment under a guarantee.

Expropriation risk (including gradual or creeping expropriation): An act or a series of acts taken by a foreign government to seize, confiscate or otherwise expropriate your assets or investments, or foreign government acts that have had the effect of expropriation.

Political violence risk: Terrorism or other forms of political turmoil aimed at influencing the policies of the host country government that damage assets or force you to shut down foreign operations.

Conversion risk: The inability to convert the local currency of a foreign country into hard currency.

Transfer risk: The inability to transfer hard currency outside a foreign country.

Repossession risk: Measures that a foreign government may take that prevent you from repossessing or re-exporting physical assets brought into the country (e.g. machinery, equipment, rolling stock, an aircraft, etc.).

Source: EDC Website, September 2008.

[2] The People's Daily newspaper reported on 5 July 2002 that about 10 percent of China's 5000 major cities had a female mayor or vice-mayor. The Chinese government affirmed in its Program for the Development of Chinese Women (2001–2010) that "more efforts should be made to improve women's capacity in management and decision making in state and social affair, and increase the proportion of women leaders."

Zhongshan was one of the Four Little Tigers in Guangdong, the others being: Dongguan, Nanhai, and Shunde. These four economically virile centres served as exemplars for others to emulate. Zhongshan's thriving state-owned enterprises in the 1980s gave way to township and village enterprises and more recently to foreign multinationals. Zhongshan was known by the credo "One industry in one town." Pillar industries included: mahogany furniture from Dachong (500 local enterprises accounted for 60% of China's output), electric household appliances manufactured in Dongfeng, lighting fittings manufactured in Guzhen (over 3000 lighting enterprises; 95% of Guzhen's GDP came from lighting), food from Huanpu, casual wear (blue jeans and shirts) made in Shaxi, and locks, hardware, and electronic acoustics from Xiaolan.

CASE 8   KEENGA RESEARCH

Jeron sat back contemplating the next steps at his young enterprise. It had been four years since he graduated with his MBA and with the idea for Keenga Research, and for the first time he faced competitors and tough business decisions. Now, in the middle of 2011 and based in Utah, with a young family and still-large aspirations, he needed to determine the direction of his efforts and resources. He worked hard, full time at a venture capital firm and was a devout Mormon, spending a lot of time and energy involved with the church. He would need to make some critical choices about where he would allocate his time and effort going forward.

KEENGA RESEARCH—PHASE ONE

Keenga Research had begun as many companies do, an idea crafted on the back of a scrap of paper in a discussion with one of his professors at Ben's—a local establishment that served fresh bagels and sold used books. In 2007, Jeron's concept was to reverse the venture capitalist relationship with entrepreneurs—letting those that had been funded rate the VC that gave them the money. Reports would then be generated and sold to pension and wealth funds giving a numerically based way to evaluate VC firms. Jeron believed "This would provide a solution to the problem many small funds faced—a two- or three-person organization that was required to place several billions of investment but did not have the resources and could not afford the overhead to search through the thousands of VCs now present to find the best opportunities."

What made the business model more interesting was that there were really only two major players in the market (defined as assisting funds with investment decisions). Cambridge Associates and Thompson Financial Consultants were both helping funds find investments, but they were at the high end of the market. A report, for example, cost $50 000 and would require multiple rounds of diligence and include great overhead. Although powerful in evaluating a single fund, it did not help in identifying market opportunities. Jeron remarked, "Though lacking in some of the elements of the fancy, full-service outfits it seemed Keenga—as sketched out on a cream cheese smeared scrap of paper at Ben's—could work well at meeting a gap in the market."

Jeron contacted and initially worked with one of his capable colleagues, Jeff, to get the idea off the ground. The first step was to go after the entrepreneurs. Together they spent many months creating a process by which they could isolate individual entrepreneur's email addresses and tie that person back to a fund. So for example, they could identify a thousand entrepreneurs that had been funded by Benchmark Capital and get the email addresses of those individuals. The process was manual, and time consuming, but very effective. On average, each email address took about five minutes to produce.

They partnered with a contact centre based in the Philippines to do the manual work. They negotiated over a month with the centre and finally arrived at a price point of $0.40 per email address through their process. They utilized the developed methodology and began to build their database. Jeron and Jeff were funding the project out of their own pockets and wrote an initial check for $2000 to their new partner.

The team then went about the next vital step in the project; they developed the methodology necessary to gather and statistically analyze the data. The survey that would be presented to entrepreneurs was drafted and pilot tested against some individuals they knew for feedback and refinement.

They were confident in the methodology that they developed and the contact list was growing, but the team almost immediately ran into an issue of financing. Although their initial outlay of $2000 had yielded 5000 email addresses, the team was only receiving a response rate to their requests of two percent and to date had only received 100 completed surveys—"nothing nearly statistically significant given that there were well over 2000 VCs in the marketplace for entrepreneurs to potentially provide feedback on," remarked Jeron.

Jeff admitted, "The entire process was moving slowly." Jeron and Jeff spent nearly two years doing the work ad hoc as it was a secondary project for the pair. Jeff was employed full time as the VP of sales for a major telecom provider. The team also realized that they were in a catch-22 on their initial business model. To sell reports they needed to create them based on statistically significant results—but to generate these results they would need 5000 or so surveys completed, which would likely cost approximately $100 000. Jeff sputtered, "We just can't get this kind of money without selling reports—and the next steps aren't clear."

Keenga Research—Phase Two

In 2009, the pair wrestled for several months to create a plan and finally identified a solution. Together they called their partner in the Philippines and spilled their guts. Jeron and Jeff outlined the

Case written by Anthony A. Woods and Prescott C. Ensign.

problem they were facing. Their partner responded in a unique way. He saw promise and they received their request for some extended credit. This allowed them to get up to 30 000 email addresses immediately and continue their work toward scale—but now focusing on a subset of VCs initially to generate reports. Their partner also identified that their efforts were moving slowly and needed some horsepower. Their partner therefore added a request: he wanted to get personally involved in the business and help the team move forward faster.

At the time, their partner Anthony had been working as the CEO of a Philippine call centre for five years and although he enjoyed running the business, he also longed to return to the Internet space. His company had provided lots of interesting learning opportunities, but ultimately he felt the call centre industry was not intellectually stimulating. Prior to his current work, he had been employed at multiple Internet startups and had some experience to bring to the table. The only weakness the two saw of working with Anthony was that he was not physically located in Utah.

After another negotiation period, Jeron and Jeff decided to accept the offer. Running his own company, Anthony actually brought something else that Jeff and Jeron needed—an ability to work on their venture at any time of day while they were tied down to their regular day jobs. "He could reach out to the market and respond to customers during the normal course of business as necessary," remarked Jeff.

The relationship flourished over the next six months, with both sides gaining trust in each other, and Anthony began to take more and more of a leadership role. At the same time, Jeff made a change in his day job that greatly reduced his ability to devote time and energy toward Keenga Research. His spare time became scarce, and after several years of working on the start-up he decided to step back and take himself out of a full-time management role. As an initial investor and one of the founders, he did maintain a fair share of equity and moved instead to a role of active investor. With an increasing role at his VC firm, Jeron was also having a hard time maintaining the two jobs. The decision was soon made to promote Anthony to be president of Keenga Research.

At this point Keenga Research had completed 450 surveys by focusing on some specific VCs, had done several revisions of the survey improving the data they were collecting, had completed a summary of results from these surveys, and had launched their preliminary website providing an overview of the company to those who wished to review it.

The team had also made the decision to move quietly. They had two concerns, the first being that they would receive an extremely negative reaction from venture capital companies who would then block entrepreneurs from participating. The second was of course that they felt that they had "a better mouse trap"—and wanted to launch it properly before telling the world.

They had also determined the process that they needed to make the data relevant. For example, they had often used a 1 to 5 scale system to judge criteria for the VCs—but there was no way to tell how good a rating of 3 was in the overall market. The team therefore used the first round of data to create a benchmark, placing VCs instead into quartiles on the respective survey questions thereby creating unique data.

Jeron remarked, "Things had been going well against initial goals, but the next steps required a transition from a data gathering company to one that produced revenue. Something tangible needed to be created that could then be sold."

Keenga Research—Phase Three

In late 2010, relying on the initial business model, Anthony and Jeron began to work on the template for a report. Their initial report (see sample report generated for Canaan Partners) contained more than just the survey data. It included data about the company, outlining investment strategies as well as strengths and weaknesses. Jeron asserted that the team developed "a unique rating system that highlights the potential volatility of a VC's investment strategy combined with their overall performance."

Anthony and Jeron had confidence that the report was a good piece of work and the team began making calls to pension and wealth funds to try to sell them. Until this time, the team had only done some preliminary inquiries to see if the product would be considered valuable and had universally received approval. They found that they were hitting a different response when they came back asking companies to pay for these reports. Not a single customer stepped forward to place an order.

The team took the opportunity to finally do a critical review of their business and where they were. They questioned these same potential customers again to determine what they would need to do to be successful. They found a few things and Anthony summarized them:

1. Although a unique concept, Keenga Research did not have a reputation as a research company. Keenga Research needed to gain credibility in the market. In another "chicken and the egg" scenario, it was surmised that if everyone was using the reports they would become an industry standard—but until others were reading them most funds would not feel that they were a valuable resource.

2. The team had not built an effective sales organization. Jeron had the contacts within the industry but he didn't have the time. Anthony had more time (although not enough he admitted) but lacked some of the industry understanding and all of the contacts.

3. The process of generating their first report had been an exciting experience, but in hindsight an extremely manual one. They had relied on their generated data for only a part of the report and had been forced to actively find sources of information to complete the remainder. Each report would require 30 hours of work to effectively complete.

4. The customers further highlighted that the only really unique part of the report was the numerical data they had generated from entrepreneurs. Some customers had indicated some pieces were helpful, but those comments were few and far between as compared to the interest in the core data.

5. The process of data collection was leveraging the web, but it then required manual manipulation to include it into quartiles, and an analyst to then clean up and present the data.

Jeron and Anthony saw their next steps as:

- work on credibility and enhancing their brand
- outline a way to sell their reports
- change the reports to be less manual and focus on the unique Keenga Research data
- find a way to automate their data collection process

REINVENTION

The team got together in person and attacked their original business model. What they had created would not survive their resources. They started to ask critical questions. Would people ever be willing to pay for the data? Should they give the data away for free? Is the business model one that can generate revenue in the originally designed fashion? How do they get to scale? How do you create a brand that can gain credibility in the market? How do we eliminate the manual processes involved?

Anthony explained "We came to the conclusion that we needed to shift the original business model and move the entire database online. We would build a web portal that would allow customers to leave surveys directly into a database. This database would automate the processes involved in analyzing the data, and provide all the results for free online." They also made a hard decision—they would move some of their core data online for free. Jeron and Anthony hoped this loss leader would provide the credibility to sell more complete reports. They basically identified two products, a short report that would be available online at no cost and a long report only available to premium members. Once they had established the base of business they needed, they would shift both reports into the premium section.

During one of Anthony's trips to Utah, the two used the brainstorming process to identify other spin-off business models they could pursue while they waited for critical mass. Back at Ben's for a "serious think session" fuelled by caffeine and carbs, they sketched out what they called the "Entrepreneur's Toolkit." The theory was to provide entrepreneurs with a source for useful documents, for example a sample term sheet for fundraising. Such documents (see Appendix) would be provided at no cost but would improve the stickiness of the web property.

Another idea that had not been done to date was providing online tools to allow entrepreneurs to determine a value for their companies. Daily stock market benchmarks, combined with some financial analytics, could provide individuals with a current and accurate benchmark for their companies. Because the approach used daily benchmarks, the data would also be fresh and hopefully once again sticky. They hoped the combination would create a community of entrepreneurs using Keenga Research as an ongoing resource, which would hopefully lead to more data collection for their core business, and new revenue opportunities.

To make the new model work, they also recognized that they would need funding. Neither of them had any ability to code, so they raised $15 000 to find someone to help build and code the site.

TOO SLOW

After three years of working on Keenga Research, Jeron felt like they were finally closing in on a sustainable business model. Things were looking up and moving forward. Then the other shoe dropped.

Jeron received an email from a colleague with whom he had shared the concept of Keenga Research. The friend knew the business model and sent over the worst possible news: despite their attempt at some secrecy a competitor had launched, TheFunded.com.

Although it was impossible to prove, Anthony and Jeron felt that TheFunded had received one of their surveys, evaluated their business model, and had come to all the same strategic conclusions that they had reached. The site was completely automated and streamlined. The site didn't have the depth of questions present at Keenga, but they immediately reached out to every major news forum and became the originator of the business idea. They were covered by every major press outlet as the company that was turning the tables on the VCs.

After four years of work, Keenga was now a "Me Too" website rather than a brilliant cutting-edge company.

CRITICAL LESSONS

Although they had been scooped, the team also had the ability to learn a great deal from their new competitor. The first lesson was how the TheFunded monetized their research. They learned that at this juncture people would not pay for the services. They knew that although novel, the general review on the street regarding the service was that it was "interesting" and "entertaining" but not "educational." Serious players in the industry were discounting the value and quality of the data.

In the end the team came to a conclusion. They felt that the idea still had merit and that in the long term when reputations were established money could be generated from it, but to get there would require a lot of time and investment. They still felt that TheFunded had managed to quickly become the incumbent, but that with their experience and their database of entrepreneurs they were still executing better than the new site.

NEXT STEPS

Jeron and Anthony spent time reviewing and planning a course of action. They had a decision to make. If they were to continue, one of them would need to make a greater time commitment. They had to make some critical decisions.

Was the business plan still valid? Could they make it as the second player in the market that was unproven for revenue and would require substantial investment? Could they maintain Keenga Research as a "hobby business" or would it require one or both of them to go full time? Would it be better to rally around the new products? Could these generate revenue? If so, what resources, including financial and human would be needed to launch the products? Both of them agreed that Keenga Research really needed people power to build clout. Should they try to sell? Could they get anything for their small enterprise? Who would purchase it? TheFunded, Cambridge Associates, or Thompson Financial Consultants?

Appendix:
Sample Report, Canaan Partners

Keenga would again like to thank you for your time and for providing us with insight into the areas that are valued by entrepreneurs. We researched the contact information of over 20,000 individuals who have been involved with companies that have raised capital. Of this group, we had over 400 responses providing us a solid benchmark of opinions. We have provided this report to those who completed the survey to highlight some of the most relevant information.

In our research, we found that the majority of entrepreneurs are between the ages of 41 and 50 years old and have started 1.4 companies (on average) and are generally male (92%).

Entrepreneurs value, above all, the ethic and trustfulness of the VC that they are working with. This is the most prominent area that is used in determining VCs. Our research also showed that the majority of entrepreneurs feel good

| FIGURE 1 | POLITICAL RISK SCENARIOS |

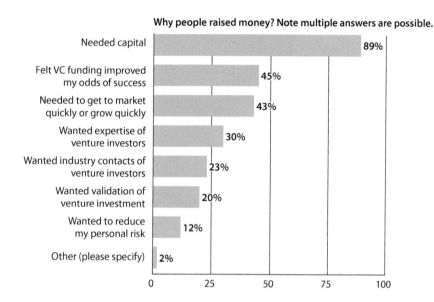

Why people raised money? Note multiple answers are possible.

Needed capital	89%
Felt VC funding improved my odds of success	45%
Needed to get to market quickly or grow quickly	43%
Wanted expertise of venture investors	30%
Wanted industry contacts of venture investors	23%
Wanted validation of venture investment	20%
Wanted to reduce my personal risk	12%
Other (please specify)	2%

| FIGURE 2 | |

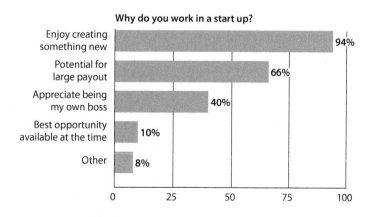

Why do you work in a start up?

Enjoy creating something new	94%
Potential for large payout	66%
Appreciate being my own boss	40%
Best opportunity available at the time	10%
Other	8%

FIGURE 3

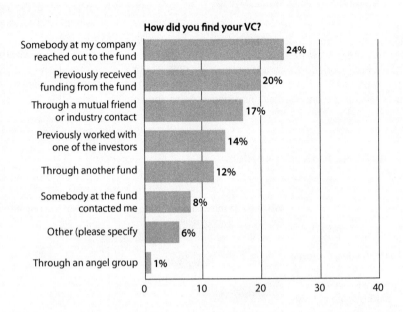

How did you find your VC?

Somebody at my company reached out to the fund	24%
Previously received funding from the fund	20%
Through a mutual friend or industry contact	17%
Previously worked with one of the investors	14%
Through another fund	12%
Somebody at the fund contacted me	8%
Other (please specify	6%
Through an angel group	1%

about their VCs on this front. After this area, entrepreneurs are primarily concerned with finding a long term partner and of course the economic terms of investment. This last item, economic terms, is where entrepreneurs feel that VCs have performed the weakest.

Likely to reinvest with same partner: 74%

The fund managed expectations appropriately during the process: 82%

Entrepreneurs feel they had a positive experience: 83%

Overall, entrepreneurs found that VCs are least helpful in two key areas for any young business. They found that they were not getting assistance for finding top talent and providing sales leads.

Keenga Research is your guide to the private economy. Our first product, Keenga Venture Reports, is a library of analyst reports on the world's most prominent venture capital firms. We provide these reports to a range of interested parties including:

- LPs, institutional investors and their advisors
- Venture capital funds
- Entrepreneurs

Keenga's founders have worked in management consulting, software and high-technology, venture capital, and as entrepreneurs. The founders have significant experience performing customer research, benchmarking, and consulting large and small companies in a variety of industries. They also have a great deal of experience being and working with entrepreneurs. Keenga founders benefit from strong personal networks of advisors in the private equity, fund of funds, and LP communities.

FIRM PROFILE: CANAAN PARTNERS A-2

Early through expansion-stage venture capital focusing on IT and life sciences in the US and Israel.

Rating

Return Rating	A—30 % + IRR
Volatility Rating	2—Normal
Entrepreneur Rating	High—2nd Quartile 4.44 / 5.00
Portfolio Benefits	Solid US mixed-stage venture with a solid risk-return profile

Summary

Fundraising
- Last fund heavily oversubscribed
- Not in market for 2-4 years
- Near complete shift to institutional investors in Fund VII

Performance
- Recent funds have generated very strong IRRs
- High percentage of investments have exited

Team
- Strong team with varied backgrounds
- At least two strong, young partners
- Some evidence older generation is less involved

Market
- US valuations creeping up
- US exits remain difficult
- Israel remains healthy with room for more investment

Investment Model
- Strong deal flow
- Rates high in ethics and relationships with entrepreneurs
- Rates low in industry expertise and treatment of entrepreneurs when startups fail

Red Flags
- Founder left firm in 2002
- Some partners seem less involved
- Not terribly good at building business for portfolio despite claims
- Canaan may lack deep industry expertise

Recommendation

Given Canaan's strong track record of returns, its solid base of institutional investors who all agree on its potential, its ability to source deals and generate exits, and its generally healthy rapport with entrepreneurs, we believe Canaan is a "buy." We believe that Canaan will continue to generate very strong IRRs so we rate Canaan an A for Returns. We do not have any evidence that indicates that Canaan's volatility will be lower than average or greater than average, so we gave it a Volatility Rating of 2—normal. Entrepreneurs think highly of Canaan and place it high in the 2nd quartile. In conclusion, we are convinced that Canaan has a good rapport with entrepreneurs, will typically generate solid returns, and has a viable and sustainable investment model with a strong next generation of younger partners.

Overview

Founded in 1987, Canaan Partners is an established, relatively large, US-based, early through expansion-stage venture capital firm with offices in Connecticut, the Bay Area, Israel and India (opened earlier this month). Canaan has established a great fundraising track record, most recently investing out of a $450M Fund VII and transitioning almost entirely to an institutional LP base. According to our analysis, Canaan has made 247 investments since inception and has had a significant number of exits. Over 51% of its investments have exited compared to our benchmark of 37%. While Keenga does not have access to Canaan's full historical returns data, we believe that its funds have performed quite strongly. According to Keenga's proprietary survey sent to over 21,000 entrepreneurs, entrepreneurs think very highly of Canaan. Comments are consistently positive, for example: "Canaan is wonderful. Straight shooters. Support the entrepreneur." When asked about the fund's weaknesses, entrepreneurs can only point to "limited time available to pay attention to the inner workings of our company during times of transition (financing, commercialization, etc.)." One entrepreneur also noted that occasionally Canaan gave "inconsistent advice" and gave advice "when they [were] not experts." Our research and survey identify that Canaan ranks at the high end of the 2nd quartile in the strength of their next generation of fund managers and our research confirms that young partners Brent Ahrens and Maha Ibrahim are widely viewed as capable successors. Overall entrepreneurs rated the fund 4.44/5.00 which places it at the top end of the 2nd quartile. Our investment rating is for Canaan is A-2 because we believe that it will continue to consistently generate stong returns.

Fundraising

Canaan has been very successful at fundraising over the past 18 years, raising over $2.82B. It began to fundraise for its most recent $450M fund in January 2005 and by May 2005 it was already $100M oversubscribed. New LPs in Fund VII have said that Canaan terms are pretty much standard. LPs have also mentioned that the firm's investment consistency and practice of promoting from within helped pique their interest. The firm believes that Canaan Equity III will be fully invested by the third quarter of 2006 and they will then begin investing out of Canaan Partners VII.

Performance

Canaan is best known for successful investments in DoubleClick (DCLK), Commerce One (CMRC), Copper Mountain Networks (CMTN), Immunicon (IMMC), ONI Systems (ONIS), and Combinatorx (CRXX). However, the fund has also performed well recently, in part due to due the success of a couple of new partners. One new partner, Brent Ahrens joined Canaan in May 1999 and was promoted to partner in May 2005. Since joining he has led investments in Revivant (sold to Zoll Medical), Peninsula Pharmaceuticals (sold to J&J for $245M) and Dexcom which concluded a $56M IPO in April of 2005. Although we do not have access to Canaan's complete performance record, we believe that Canaan's latest funds have generated strong IRRs.

Team

Canaan was founded by Harry Rein and Eric Young, though Mr. Rein considers himself the principal founder. The two started Canaan after spinning out from GE Venture Capital in 1987 and subsequently brought on other GE Capital investors like Stephen Green. Mr. Rein left Canaan in 2002 and subsequently became a general partner of Foundation Medical Partners. Canaan's partner have financial, operating, fund-of-funds, legal, and entrepreneurial experience. There are some indications, however, that the some of the "old guard" are much less actively involved in building the Canaan portfolio. The current partners are:

Brent Ahrens (joined 1999)—Led investments in Revivant, Penninsula, and Dexcom. Previously Kauffman Fellow; sales, business development and technical roles at J&J. MBA from Tuck.

John Balen (joined 1995)— Led investments in Commerce One and RightPoint. Previously, a managing director at Horsley, Bridge.

James Furnival (joined 1996)—Led investments in Indus River, Ganymede, and Network Engines. Previously, VP at 3i; VP at Atari; VP at PaineWebber. BSE, Princeton and MBA, Wharton.

Stephen Green (joined 1991)—Previously worked at GE and GE Venture Capital.

Maha Ibrahim (joined 2000)—Involved in Recourse Technologies investment. Previously, VP at Qwest; consultant at BCG and PWC. BA, MA from Stanford. PhD in Economics from MIT. One entrepreneur specifically mentioned as one of Canaan's firm strengths "the representation of Maha Ibrahim."

Deepak Kamra (joined 1991)—Led investments in DoubleClick and Match.com. Previously, Aspect Communications, ROLM,

Gregory Kopchinsky (joined 1990)—Unclear what investments he has led and whether or not he currently sits boards.

Seth Rudnick (joined 1998)—Previously, CEO of CytoTherapeutics; R&D at Ortho Biotech (J&J); Schering-Plough; Biogen. MD.

Eric Young (co-founder in 1987)—Led investments in CopperMountain Networks and Immunicon. Previously, held various positions at GE, GE Venture Capital.

COMPARABLE FUNDS
TL Ventures, Highland Capital Partners, ComVentures,

LPS
Pantheon Ventures (VII), Abbot Capital (VII), General Motors (earlier funds and VII), Winterthur (VII),

---

Our survey of Canaan entrepreneurs supports a conclusion that Canaan partners are capable and generally quite good at what they do. The following is a table summarizes entrepreneurs' ratings of the Canaan partners on a scale of one to five for various capabilities and attributes and their quartile ranking compared to the 87 other funds we profile.

ENTREPRENEUR PARTNER RATINGS

CAPABILITY	RATING	QUARTILE
Reputation	3.75	3rd Quartile
Analytical and quantitative ability	3.69	2nd Quartile
VC experience	3.81	3rd Quartile
Entrepreneurial experience	4.25	3rd Quartile
Personal honesty and trustworthiness	4.75	2nd Quartile
Industry experience and network	4.06	3rd Quartile
Friendship or previous relationship	3.50	Bottom
Interpersonal skills	3.06	Bottom
Ability to help find talented employees	4.00	2nd Quartile
Consistent involvement in the company	4.06	2nd Quartile
Ability to generate sales leads	2.81	3rd Quartile
Ability to provide good advice	4.44	2nd Quartile
Consistent rather than sporadic involvement	3.88	2nd Quartile
Patience in waiting for the company to succeed	4.38	3rd Quartile
Responsiveness	4.19	2nd Quartile

Market

Canaan invests most heavily in the US venture market, though it will begin to get more international exposure through its Israel office. To date, the company has only made 3 investments outside of the US. The US venture market is currently characterized by increased venture investing (highest levels since 2001), competition, and rising pre-money valuations. The US exit environment continues to be somewhat challenging. Sarbanes-Oxley has taken a significant toll on the number of venture-backed companies going public and foreign stock exchanges and the US M&A market has only picked up part of the slack. All of this is leading to more later-stage investing and longer median times to exit for venture-backed companies, decreasing IRRs ceteris paribus. US limited partners appear to be paring back investment in VC and encouraging US VCs to limit fund sizes to avoid destroying industry returns. US VCs are also being much more selective about the funds in which they invest, due to increasing information that only the best funds produce above-average returns. However, there is evidence that foreign institutional investors, especially in Europe and Japan remain eager to get into US venture capital and many are investing in even marginal funds. Firms like Canaan with strong track records are increasingly able to raise institutional money despite the difficult climate.

Israel continues to be a solid venture market, deploying just over $1B / year in venture capital (compared to $22B/year in the US). IT remains Israel's strong point and more money is flowing into the area leading to all-time highs in the size of the typical rounds. We continue to believe that Israel is a relative safe overseas bet and that it can absorb another venture fund.

Investment Model

Canaan appears to have a strong sourcing apparatus. They do not appear to be geographically constrained in their investments and are also willing to invest in both early and later-stage opportunities. They have invested in SAS, a very small Mid-Atlantic focused seed fund as another method of generating deal flow. Deal flow appears to be strong and growing in recent years, despite a slowdown after the market bust of 2000. The majority of Canaan's deals are IT focused but they have a very significant life sciences and services practices as well.

In general, entrepreneurs support our positive view of Canaan's investment model, value add and capabilities. The following table summarizes the results of our survey where we asked entrepreneurs to rate several of Canaan's firm capabilities on a scale of 1-5.

ENTREPRENEUR COMPANY RATINGS

CAPABILITY	RATING	QUARTILE
Pricing and terms	3.44	2nd Quartile
Prestige and reputation	4.19	2nd Quartile
Relationship with entrepreneurs	4.25	Top
Industry expertise	4.38	Bottom
Strength of fund's investment philosophy	3.75	3rd Quartile

Due diligence capabilities	3.75	3rd Quartile
Management assistance and advice	4.15	3rd Quartile
Ability to achieve exits	3.56	Bottom
Ability, willingness to invest in future rounds	4.56	Top
Treatment of entrepreneur when startups fail	2.69	Bottom
Consistent involvement in the company	4.25	3rd Quartile

Red Flags / Outstanding Questions

There are no significant red flags for Canaan, though we have a few outstanding questions. Entrepreneurs rated Canaan's ethics and trustworthiness a 4.56/5.00, placing it within the top quartile of the 87 venture capital funds we profiled. Our only questions are:

- Why did "principal founder" Harry Rein leave the firm in 2002?
- What is the current level of involvement of Gregory Kopchinsky and Stephen Green?
- Why do partners rate so poorly in helping their portfolio companies generate sales leads?
- Why do entrepreneurs rate Canaan so poorly on "industry expertise" and "treatment of entrepreneurs when startups fail?"

Investments

PACE

YEAR	DEALS	YEAR	DEALS
1999	49	2003	25
2000	56	2004	37
2001	31	2005	37
2002	40	2006 Q1	10

SECTORS

SECTOR	#	%
Software/internet	69	28
Services	42	17
Biopharmaceutical	26	11
Communications	24	10
Medical devices	22	09
Computers/electronics	22	09
Media/information	14	06
Semiconductors	10	04
Materials	03	01
Energy	00	00
Other	14	06

REGIONS

Roughly half of investments are in California, significant minority in Boston and Mid-Atlantic. Generally strong national presence.

PARTNERS

PARTNER	BOARDS	PARTNER	BOARDS
Brent Ahrens	8	Deepak Kamra	7
John Balen	8	Gregory Kopchinsk	NA
James Furnival	5	Seth Rudnick	5
Stephen Green	4	Eric Young	5
Maha Ibrahim	9		

FUNDS

FUND	YEAR	($ M)	IRR	X
Canaan Ventures	1987	141	NA	NA
Canaan Capital	1990	180	NA	NA
Canaan II	1993	54	NA	NA
Canaan SBIC	1994	14	NA	NA
Canaan Equity	1997	158	NA	NA
Canaan Equity II	2000	500	NA	NA
Canaan III	2001	700	NA	NA
Canaan VII	2005	450	NA	NA

PORTFOLIO STATUS

CATEGORY	#	%	BENCHMARK
Public	51	21	8
Acquired	73	30	29
Private	71	29	45
Out of Bus.	48	19	19
Other	4	2	0

FUNDRAISING

Last Fund	Canaan Equity III (2001)
Latest Fund	Canaan Partners VII (2006)
Fundraising	Probably in 2-4 years. Estimated size $400-500M

Fundamental Opinion Key:

Keenga's opinions include a Return Rating, a Volatility Rating and an Entrepreneur Rating. The Return Rating represents Keenga's belief about the expected IRR of the firm's existing and future funds. There are three possible Return ratings: A—representing an expected IRR of 30%+ or more, B—representing an expected IRR of 15%-30% and C—representing an IRR of less than 15%.

The Volatility Rating represents Keenga's belief about the volatility of returns from fund to fund. There are three possible Volatility ratings: 1—representing low volatility for the asset class and stage of the firm, 2—representing normal or moderate volatility for the asset class and stage of the firm, and 3—representing high volatility for the asset class and stage of the firm.

The Entrepreneur Rating represents Keenga's belief about the overall relationship and reputation that the firm has with its primary customers-entrepreneurs. We use a numeric number ranging from 0 to 5 based on a statistical polling of entrepreneurs. We also provide a benchmark comparison of the firm's performance in this area to all of the firms in our database based on quartiles. Hence there are 4 possible benchmark results: Top quartile, 2 nd quartile, 3rd quartile, and bottom quartile.

Example:

If Keenga believes that fund has very strong IRR prospects but has significant volatility, we would assign it an A-3 rating. If we believe that a fund has moderate IRR prospects but low volatility, we would assign it a B-1 rating. In either case, we will also provide information about what entrepreneurs think of the firm relative to others. A very strong entrepreneur perception would merit a Top Quartile rating whereas a weak perception would merit a Bottom Quartile rating.

Legal Disclaimer

Keenga Research, LP does not currently do business with the fund covered in this report and has no intention at this time to do so. However, it is possible that Keenga could sell this report to the fund in question or offer other services. As a result, investors should be aware that at some point Keenga could have a conflict of interest that could affect the objectivity of this report. Investors should consider this report as only a single factor in making an investment decision.

ENDNOTES

CHAPTER 1

1. The authors would like to thank Frederic M. Alper of Babson College for his insights and contributions to this chapter, in particular the graphic representation of entrepreneurial attributes and the development of the Quicklook Exercise to develop a personal entrepreneurial strategy.
2. Jeffry A. Timmons, *The Entrepreneurial Mind* (Acton, MA: Brick House Publishing, 1989).
3. Graeme Wearden, "The Big Interview: Sir Terry Matthews," ZDNet, November 21, 2006.
4. David Gow, "Terry Matthews: A Well-Connected Celt," *Guardian*, October 28, 2000.
5. Sally Watson, "Terry Matthews: Entrepreneur Extraordinaire," silicon.com, November 14, 2001.
6. Andrew Wahl "VoIP: When Sir Terry Talks…" *Canadian Business*, September 24, 2007.
7. Graeme Wearden, "The Big Interview."
8. L. H. Tiffany Hsieh, "Queen's Students Go Green with Bullfrog," *Kingston This Week*, September 3, 2008.
9. Boyd Cohen, "Sustainable Valley Entrepreneurial Ecosystems," *Business Strategy and the Environment* 15, no. 1 (2006): 1–14.
10. Richard Hudson and Roger Wehrell, "Socially Responsible Investors and the Microentrepreneur: A Canadian Case," *Journal of Business Ethics* 60, no. 3 (2005): 281–292.
11. See John W. Atkinson, *An Introduction To Motivation* (Princeton, NJ: Van Nostrand, 1964); John W. Atkinson, *Motives in Fantasy, Action and Society* (Princeton, NJ: Van Nostrand, 1958); David C. McClelland, *The Achieving Society* (Princeton, NJ: Van Nostrand, 1961).
12. John B. Miner, Norman R. Smith, and Jeffry S. Bracker, "Predicting Firm Survival from a Knowledge of Entrepreneur Task Motivation," *Entrepreneurship & Regional Development* 4, no. 2 (1992): 145–154.
13. John B. Miner, Norman R. Smith, and Jeffry S. Bracker, "Role of Entrepreneurial Task Motivation in the Growth of Technologically Innovative Firms: Interpretations from Follow-Up Data," *Journal of Applied Psychology* 79, no. 4 (1994): 627–630.
14. Jeffry A. Timmons and Howard H. Stevenson, "Entrepreneurship Education in the 80s: What Entrepreneurs Say," in *Entrepreneurship: What It Is and How to Teach It*, J. Kao and H. H. Stevenson, eds. (Boston, MA: Harvard Business School, 1985), 115–134.
15. Floyd Norris, "Low-Fat Problem at Ben & Jerry's," *New York Times*, September 9, 1992.
16. Ibid.
17. Donald K. Clifford, Jr., and Richard E. Cavanagh, *The Winning Performance* (New York, NY: Bantam Books, 1991).
18. Determining the attitudes and behaviours in entrepreneurs that are "acquirable and desirable" represents the synthesis of over 50 research studies compiled for the first and second editions of this book. See extensive references in J. A. Timmons, L. E. Smollen, and A. L. M. Dingee, Jr., *New Venture Creation*, 2nd ed. (Homewood, IL: Irwin, 1985), 139–169.
19. Monica Diochon, Teresa V. Menzies, and Yvon Gasse, "Attributions and Success in New Venture Creation Among Canadian Nascent Entrepreneurs," *Journal of Small Business & Entrepreneurship* 20, no. 4 (2007): 335–350; Karen D. Hughes, "Exploring Motivation and Success Among Canadian Women Entrepreneurs," *Journal of Small Business & Entrepreneurship* 19, no. 2 (2006): 107–120; Don A. Moore, John M. Oesch, and Charlene Zietsma, "What Competition? Myopic Self-Focus in Market Entry Decisions," *Organization Science* 18, no. 3 (2007): 440–454.
20. John A. Hornaday and Nancy B. Tieken, "Capturing Twenty-One Heffalumps," *Frontiers of Entrepreneurship Research* (Babson Park, MA: Babson College, 1983).
21. Alan J. Grant, "The Development of an Entrepreneurial Leadership Paradigm for Enhancing New Venture Success," *Frontiers of Entrepreneurship Research* (Babson Park, MA: Babson College, 1992).
22. David L. Bradford and Allan R. Cohen, *Managing for Excellence: The Guide to Developing High Performance in Contemporary Organizations* (New York, NY: John Wiley & Sons, 1997).
23. Thomas Hellmann, "Entrepreneurs and the Process of Obtaining Resources," *Journal of Economics and Management Strategy* 16, no. 1 (2007): 81–109; Yves Robichaud and Egbert McGraw, "Les motivations entrepreneuriales commes facteur explicatif de la taille des enterprises," *Journal of Small Business & Entrepreneurship* 21, no. 1 (2008): 59–73.
24. Dean A. Shepherd, Jeffrey S. McMullen, and P. Deveraux Jennings. "The Formation of Opportunity Beliefs: Overcoming Ignorance and Reducing Doubt," *Strategic Entrepreneurship Journal* 1, no. 1 (2007): 75–95.
25. Dave Valliere and Thomas Gegenhuber, "Deliberative Attention Management," *International Journal of Productivity and Performance Management* 62, no. 2 (2013): 130–155.
26. Paul Kedrosky, "Bless This Mess" *Canadian Business*, January 17, 2005.
27. Daryl G. Mitton, "The Compleat Entrepreneur," *Entrepreneurship Theory and Practice* 13, no. 3 (1989): 9–19.
28. John B. Miner, "Entrepreneurs, High Growth Entrepreneurs and Managers: Contrasting and Overlapping Motivational Patterns," *Journal of Business Venturing* 5, no. 4 (1990): 221–234.
29. David E. Gumpert and David P. Boyd, "The Loneliness of the Small-Business Owner," *Harvard Business Review* 62, no. 6 (1984): 18–24.
30. Maria Cook, "Investing in our Future," *Ottawa Citizen*, March 1, 2004.
31. Richard Martin, "Alumni Profile: Entrepreneur Angel," *Carleton University Magazine*, Fall 2006.
32. Timmons and Stevenson, "Entrepreneurship Education in the 80s: What Entrepreneurs Say," 115–134.
33. See Timmons, *The Entrepreneurial Mind* (1989).
34. Dean Tjosvold and David Weicker, "Cooperative and Competitive Networking by Entrepreneurs: A Critical Incident Study," *Journal of Small Business Management* 31, no. 1 (1993): 11–21.
35. Dev K. Dutta and Mary M. Crossan, "The Nature of Entrepreneurial

Opportunities: Understanding the Process Using the 4I Organizational Learning Framework," *Entrepreneurship Theory and Practice* 29, no. 4 (2005): 425–449.

36. Ronald K. Mitchell, J. Brock Smith, Eric A. Morse, Kristie W. Seawright, Ana Maria Peredo, and Brian McKenzie, "Are Entrepreneurial Cognitions Universal? Assessing Entrepreneurial Cognitions Across Cultures," *Entrepreneurship Theory and Practice* 26, no. 4 (2002): 9–32.

37. William Lee, "What Successful Entrepreneurs Really Do," Lee Communications, 2001.

38. John A. Hornaday and Nancy B. Tieken, "Capturing Twenty-One Heffalumps."

39. Jeffry A. Timmons, Daniel F. Muzyka, Howard H. Stevenson, and William D. Bygrave, "Opportunity Recognition: The Core of Entrepreneurship," *Frontiers of Entrepreneurship Research* (Babson Park, MA: Babson College, 1987).

40. G. Page West III and Terry W. Noel, "The Impact of Knowledge Resources on New Venture Performance," *Journal of Small Business Management* 47, no. 1 (2009): 1–22.

41. James J. Chrisman, Ed Mcmullan, and Jeremy Hall, "The Influence of Guided Preparation on the Long-Term Performance of New Ventures," *Journal of Business Venturing* 20, no. 6 (2005): 769–791.

42. "Rodney C. Shrader and Gerald E. Hills, "Opportunity Recognition: Perceptions of Highly Successful Entrepreneurs," *Journal of Small Business Strategy* 14, no. 2 (2003): 92–108.

43. Harvey "Chet" Krentzman, entrepreneur, lecturer, author, and nurturer of at least three dozen growth-minded ventures.

44. Brian O'Reilly, and Natasha A. Tarpley, "What It Takes to Start a Startup," *Fortune*, June 7, 1999.

45. Howard H. Stevenson, "Who Are the Harvard Self-Employed?" *Frontiers of Entrepreneurship Research* (Babson Park, MA: Babson College, 1983).

46. Henry Mintzberg, *Managers Not MBAs: A Hard Look at the Soft Practice of Managing and Management Development* (San Francisco, CA: Berrett-Koehler, 1992).

47. W. Ed McMullan and Vance Gough, "Developing Entrepreneurs in a Hybrid Management and Entrepreneurship MBA: A Case Study in Calgary," in *Innovation & Entrepreneurship in Western Canada: From Family Business to Multinationals*, J. J. Chrisman, J. A. D. Holbrook, and J. H. Chua, eds. (Calgary, AB: University of Calgary Press, 2002), 225–242.

48. B. Joseph White with Yaron Prywes, *The Nature of Leadership: Reptiles, Mammals, and the Challenge of Becoming a Great Leader* (New York, NY: Amacom Books, 2006).

49. William D. Estbeb, "Your Associate Knows," *Chiropractic Journal*, July 2000.

50. Sarah Scott, "Do Grades Really Matter?" *Maclean's*, September 10, 2007.

51. Atul Gupta, "Relationship between Entrepreneurial Personality, Performance, Job Satisfaction and Operations Strategy: An Empirical Examination." *International Journal of Business and Management* 8, no. 2 (2013): 86–95.

52. Simon C. Parker, "A Predator-Prey Model of Knowledge Spillovers and Entrepreneurship," *Strategic Entrepreneurship Journal* 4, no. 4 (2010): 307–322. Simon C. Parker, David J. Storey, and Arjen van Witteloostuijn, "What Happens to Gazelles? The Importance of Dynamic Management Strategy," *Small Business Economics* 35, no. 2 (2010): 203–226.

53. Stevenson, "Who Are the Harvard Self-Employed?"

54. Robert C. Ronstadt, "The Decision Not to Become an Entrepreneur," *Frontiers of Entrepreneurship Research* (Babson Park, MA: Babson College, 1983).

CHAPTER 2

1. Jeffry A. Timmons, Daniel F. Muzyka, Howard H. Stevenson, and William D. Bygrave, "Opportunity Recognition: The Core of Entrepreneurship," in *Frontiers of Entrepreneurship Research* (Babson Park, MA: Babson College, 1987), 409.

2. Ewing M. Kauffman, founder of Marion Laboratories.

3. William J. Dennis, Jr., "Business Starts and Stops," Wells Fargo/NFIB November 1999.

4. Joseph L. Bower and Clayton M. Christensen, "Disruptive Technologies: Catching the Wave," *Harvard Business Review* 73, no. 1 (1995): 43–53.

5. Ibid.

6. Ibid.

7. U. Srinivasa Rangan, "Alliances Power Corporate Renewal," Babson College, 2001; Elicia Maine, "Radical Innovation Through Internal Corporate Venturing: Degussa's Commercialization of Nanomaterials," *R&D Management* 38, no. 4 (2008): 359–371.

8. Mike Chiasson and Chad Saunders, "Reconciling Diverse Approaches to Opportunity Research Using the Structuration Theory," *Journal of Business Venturing* 20, no. 6 (2005): 747–767.

9. Dirk De Clercq and Maxim Voronov, "The Role of Cultural and Symbolic Capital in Entrepreneurs' Ability to Meet Expectations about Conformity and Innovation," *Journal of Small Business Management* 47, no. 3 (2009): 398–420.

10. Vincent Chandler, "The Economic Impact of the Canada Small Business Financing Program," *Small Business Economics* 39, no. 1 (2012): 253–264. Amarjit Gill and Nahum Biger, "Barriers to Small Business Growth in Canada," *Journal of Small Business and Enterprise Development* 19, no. 4 (2012): 656–668.

11. Library and Archives of Canada, "Joseph (Joey) Smallwood," www.collections canada.gc.ca

12. Paul Gompers, Anna Kovner, Josh Lerner, and David Sharfstein, "Performance Persistence in Entrepreneurship," *Journal of Financial Economics* 96, no. 1 (2010): 18–32.

13. Henry Mintzberg takes this metaphor quite far in "Crafting Strategy," *Harvard Business Review* 66, no. 4 (1987): 66–75.

14. See Howard H. Stevenson, *Do Lunch or Be Lunch* (Cambridge, MA: Harvard Business School Press, 1998) for a provocative argument for predictability as one of the most powerful of management tools.

15. Statistics Canada.

16. Harry P. Bowen and Dirk De Clercq, "Institutional Context and the Allocation of Entrepreneurial Effort," *Journal of International Business Studies* 39, no. 4 (2008): 747–767.

17. In response to a student question at Founder's Day, Babson College, April 1983. Pizza Time Theatre (a.k.a. "Chuck E. Cheese's") filed for bankruptcy in 1984.

18. Global Entrepreneurship Monitor 2008 Report, www.gemconsortium.org

19. Summaries of these are reported by Albert N. Shapero and Joseph Giglierano, "Exits and Entries: A Study in Yellow Pages Journalism," *Frontiers of Entrepreneurship Research* (Babson Park, MA: Babson College, 1982) and Arnold C. Cooper, William C.

Dunkelberg, and Carolyn Y. Woo, "Survival and Failure: A Longitudinal Study," *Frontiers of Entrepreneurship Research* (Babson Park, MA: Babson College, 1988).

20. Bizminer 2002 Startup Business Risk Index.

21. Monica Diochon, Teresa V. Menzies, and Yvon Gasse, "Exploring the Nature and Impact of Gestation-Specific Human Capital among Nascent Entrepreneurs," *Journal of Developmental Entrepreneurship* 13, no. 2 (2008): 151–165.

22. S. Venkataraman and Murray B. Low, "The Effects of Liabilities of Age and Size on Autonomous Sub-Units of Established Firms in the Steel Distribution Industry," *Journal of Business Venturing* 9, no. 3 (1994): 189–204.

23. Ibid.

24. Dev K. Dutta and Stewart Thornhill, "The Evolution of Growth Intentions: Toward a Cognition-Based Model," *Journal of Business Venturing* 23, no. 3 (2008): 307–332.

25. This reaffirms the exception to the failure rule noted above and in the original edition of this book in 1977.

26. "The Inc. 500 Almanac," *Inc.*, September 13, 2012.

27. Jim McElgunn, "Meet the New Stars of Growth," *Profit Magazine*, October 2012

28. Ibid.

29. Ibid.

30. VentureXpert Thompson Financial Data Services, 2001.

31. Jean-Etienne de Bettignies, "Financing the Entrepreneurial Venture," *Management Science* 54, no. 1 (2008): 151–166.

32. Michael S. Malone, "John Doerr's Startup Manual," *Fast Company*, December 18, 2007.

33. Ernie Parizeau, Norwest Venture Partners, June 2001.

34. Eleanor Beaton, "Launch and Learn: Management Lessons from the Profit Hot 50," *Canadian Business*, September 2008.

35. Howard H. Stevenson and Susan S. Harmeling, "Howard Head and Prince Manufacturing, Inc.," Harvard Business School Case, 1992.

36. William D. Bygrave and Jeffry A. Timmons, *Venture Capital at the Crossroads* (Boston, MA: Harvard Business School Press, 1992).

37. Michael Malone, "John Doerr's Startup Manual."

38. Toby E. Stuart and Olav Sorenson, "Strategic Networks and Entrepreneurial Ventures," *Strategic Entrepreneurship Journal* 1, no. 3-4 (2007): 211–227.

39. Simon C. Parker, "Can Cognitive Biases Explain Venture Team Homophily?," *Strategic Entrepreneurship Journal* 3, no. 1 (2009): 67–83.

40. Arthur Rock, "Strategy vs. Tactics from a Venture Capitalist," *Harvard Business Review* 65, no. 6 (1987): 63–67.

41. Mark Anderson, "Simplify. Electrify. Magnify. Shopify." *Profit Magazine*, January, 2013.

42. Donald L. Sexton and Forrest I. Seale, *Leading Practices of Fast Growth Entrepreneurs: Pathways to High Performance* (Kansas City, MO: Kauffman Center for Entrepreneurial Leadership, 1997).

CHAPTER 3

1. Wan Lin, Rajaram Veliyath, and Justin Tan, "Network Characteristics and Firm Performance: An Examination of the Relationships in the Context of a Cluster." *Journal of Small Business Management* 51, no. 1 (2013): 1–22. Moriah Meyskens and Alan L. Carsrud, "Nascent Green-Technology Ventures: A Study Assessing the Role of Partnership Diversity in Firm Success," *Small Business Economics* 40, no. 3 (2013): 739–759. Ronald K. Mitchell, J. Robert Mitchell, and J. Brock Smith, "Inside Opportunity Formation: Enterprise Failure, Cognition, and the Creation of Opportunities," *Strategic Entrepreneurship Journal* 2, no. 3 (2008): 225–242. Walter W. Powell, Kelley A. Packalen, and Kjersten Bunker Whittington, "Organizational and Institutional Genesis: The Emergence of High-Tech Clusters in the Life Sciences," Queen's School of Business Research Paper, no. 3 (2010). Kingston, Ontario.

2. See www.onset.com/resources/index.html for additional information.

3. See Jeffry A. Timmons, *New Business Opportunities* (Acton, MA: Brick House Publishing, 1989).

4. Derin Kent and M. Tina Dacin, "Bankers at the Gage: Microfinance and the High Cost of Borrowed Logics," *Journal of Business Venturing* 28 no. 6 (2013):759-773.

5. A. Wren Montgomery, Peter A. Dacin, and M. Tina Dacin. "Collective Social Entrepreneurship: Collaboratively Shaping Social Good," *Journal of Business Ethics* 111, no. 3 (2012): 375–388.

6. Prescott C. Ensign, "Small Business Strategy as a Dynamic Process: Concepts, Controversies, and Implications," *Journal of Business & Entrepreneurship* 20, no. 2 (2008): 25–43.

7. Tom Brzustowski, *The Way Ahead: Meeting Canada's Productivity Challenge* (Ottawa, Ontario: University of Ottawa Press, 2008).

8. Barrie McKenna, "More than the Sum of Its Parts," *The Globe and Mail*, February 23, 1993.

9. Tracy Corrigan, "Far More than the Viagra Company: Essential Guide to William Steere," *Financial Times*, August 31, 1998.

10. Joline Godfrey, *Our Wildest Dreams: Women Entrepreneurs, Making Money, Having Fun, Doing Good* (New York, NY: Harper Business, 1993).

11. A. Rebecca Reuber and Eileen Fischer, "Signaling Reputation in International Online Markets," *Strategic Entrepreneurship Journal* 3, no. 4 (2009): 369–386.

12. Hyoung-Goo Kang, Richard M. Burton, and Will Mitchell, "How Potential Knowledge Spillovers Between Venture Capitalists' Entrepreneurial Projects Affect the Specialization and Diversification of VC Funds when VC Effort has Value," *Strategic Entrepreneurship Journal* 5, no. 3 (2011): 227–246.

13. Herbert A. Simon, "What We Know About the Creative Process," in R. L. Kuhn (ed.) *Frontiers in Creative and Innovative Management* (Cambridge, MA: Ballinger Publishing, 1986), 3–20.

14. Alison Stein Wellner, "Creative Control: Even Bosses Need Time to Think," *Inc.*, July 2007.

15. Jessica Stillman "Go Ahead, Daydream" *Inc.* June 12, 2012.

16. Violina P. Rindova, Adrian Yeow, Luis L. Martins, and Samer Faraj, "Partnering Portfolios, Value-Creation Logics, and Growth Trajectories: A Comparison of Yahoo and Google (1995 to 2007)," *Strategic Entrepreneurship Journal* 6, no. 2 (2012): 133–151.

17. Amar Bhide, "Bootstrap Finance: The Art of Start-Ups" *Harvard Business Review* 70, no. 6 (1992): 109–117.

18. Small Business Policy Branch, Key Small Business Financing Statistics–December 2006 (Industry Canada).

19. Teri Lammers and Annie Longsworth, "Guess Who? Ten Big-Timers Launched from Scratch," *Inc.*, September 1991.

20. Prescott C. Ensign and Nicholas P. Robinson, "Entrepreneur Because They Are Immigrants or Immigrants Because They Are Entrepreneurs? A Critical Examination of the Relationship between the Newcomers and the Establishment," *Journal of Entrepreneurship*, 20 no. 1 (2011): 33–53.

21. Robert A. Mamis, "The Secrets of Bootstrapping," *Inc.*, September 1991.

22. Peter Nowak, "Canadian Cell Phone Bills Double U.S. Counterparts," *Financial Post*, January 30, 2007.

23. Edgar H. Schein, Peter S. Delisi, Paul J. Kampas, and Michael M. Sonduck, *DEC is Dead, Long Live DEC: The Lasting Legacy of Digital Equipment Corporation* (San Francisco, CA: Barrett-Koehler, 2003).

24. Ernie Parizeau, Norwest Venture Partners.

25. Mollie Neal, "Cataloger Gets Pleasant Results," *Direct Marketing*, May 1, 1992.

26. Brian Dumaine, "How to Compete with a Champ," *Fortune*, January 10, 1994.

27. Lionel Perron, "Canadian Fiddler Looks for Quick Payday Via eBay," *Reuters*, July 2, 2008.

28. Scott W. Kunkel and Charles W. Hofer, "The Impact of Industry Structure on New Venture Performance," *Frontiers of Entrepreneurship Research* (Babson Park, MA: Babson College, 1993).

29. Canada's Venture Capital & Private Equity Association, www.cvca.ca

30. For a more detailed description of free cash flow, see William Sahlman, "Note on Free Cash Flow Valuation Models," Harvard Business School Case, 2003.

31. William A. Sahlman, "Sustainable Growth Analysis," Harvard Business School Background Note, 1984.

32. R. Douglas Kahn, president, Interactive Images, Inc., speaking at Babson College about his experiences as international marketing director at McCormack & Dodge.

33. Dan McLean, "EDS Acquisition Better Late Than Never for HP," *Computerworld Canada*, May 16, 2008.

34. "Bulls, Bears, and Other Animals," *CBC News Online*, June 13, 2006.

35. Kara Aaserud, "Canada's Top Women Entrepreneurs—When Turncoats Attack," *Profit*, November 2006.

36. This point made by J. Willard Marriott, Jr., at Founder's Day at Babson College, 1988.

37. "Recognizing, Research Results in New Brunswick," hosted by the New Brunswick Innovation Foundation in October 2008.

38. Prescott C. Ensign, Audrey Giles, and Maureen G. Reed, "Labour Migration: 'What Goes around Comes Around'," in D. Carson, R.O. Rasmussen, P. Ensign, L. Huskey, and A. Taylor (eds.) *Demography at the Edge: Remote Human Populations in Developing Nations* (Farnham, UK: Ashgate, 2011), 189–212.

39. Janet White Bardwell, "Born to Launch," *Profit*, June 2007.

40. Allen C. Bluedorn and Gwen Martin, "The Time Frames of Entrepreneurs," *Journal of Business Venturing* 23, no. 1 (2008): 1–20.

41. Prescott C. Ensign, "International Channels of Distribution," *Multinational Business Review* 14, no. 3 (2006): 1–26.

42. Alexandra Dean, "Ben Gulak's DTV Shredder All-Terrain Vehicle," *Bloomberg Businessweek*, August 23, 2012.

43. See Steven Flax, "How to Snoop on Your Competitors," *Fortune*, May 14, 1984; and information such as *Sources of Industry Data* published by Ernst & Young.

44. Leonard M. Fuld, *Secret Language of Competitive Intelligence* (New York, NY: Crown Business, 2006).

45. Ibid.

46. Jonathan Calof, director of the Canadian Institute of Competitive Intelligence.

47. Fuld, *Secret Language of Competitive Intelligence*.

CHAPTER 4

1. Martin L. Martens, Jennifer E. Jennings, and P. Devereaux Jennings, "Do the Stories they Tell Get Them the Money They Need? The Role of Entrepreneurial Narratives in Resource Acquisition," *Academy of Management Journal* 50, no. 5 (2007): 1107–1132.

2. Yuval Deutsch and Thomas W. Ross, "You Are Known by the Directors You Keep: Reputable Directors as a Signalling Mechanism for Young Firms," *Management Science* 49, no. 8 (2003): 1003–1017.

3. Kevin Hindle and Brent Mainprize, "A Systematic Approach to Writing and Rating Entrepreneurial Business Plans," *Journal of Private Equity* 9, no. 3 (2006): 7–21.

4. Tomas Karlsson and Benson Honig, "Judging a Business by Its Cover: An Institutional Perspective on New Ventures and the Business Plan," *Journal of Business Venturing* 24, no. 1 (2009): 27–45.

5. Benson Honig and Mikael Samuelsson, "Planning and the Entrepreneur: A Longitudinal Examination of Nascent Entrepreneurs in Sweden," *Journal of Small Business Management* 50, no. 3 (2012): 365–388.

6. See also William A. Sahlman, "How to Write a Great Business Plan," *Harvard Business Review* 75, no. 4 (1997): 98–108.

7. Shelley L. MacDougall and Deborah Hurst, "Surviving the Transience of Knowledge: Small High-Technology Businesses Parting Ways with Their Knowledge Workers," *Journal of Small Business & Entrepreneurship* 20, no. 2 (2007): 183–199.

8. Gary G. Gorman, Peter J. Rosa, and Alex Faseruk, "Institutional Lending to Knowledge-Based Businesses," *Journal of Business Venturing* 20, no. 6 (2005): 793–819.

9. Young Rok Choi, Moren Lévesque, and Dean A. Shepherd, "When Should Entrepreneurs Expedite or Delay Opportunity Exploitation?" *Journal of Business Venturing* 23, no. 3 (2008): 333–355.

10. Moriah Meyskens, Colleen Robb-Post, Jeffrey A. Stamp, Alan L. Carsrud, and Paul D. Reynolds, "Social Ventures from a Resource-Based Perspective: An Exploratory Study Assessing Global Ashoka Fellows," *Entrepreneurship Theory and Practice* 34, no. 4 (2010): 661–680.

CHAPTER 5

1. George C. Rubenson and Anil K. Gupta, "Replacing the Founder: Exploding the Myth of the Entrepreneur's Disease," *Business Horizons* 35, no. 6 (1992): 53–57.

2. John Kenneth Galbraith, *The New Industrial State* (Princeton, NJ: Princeton University Press, 2007).

3. George C. Rubenson and Anil K. Gupta, "The Initial Succession: A Contingency Model of Founder Tenure," *Entrepreneurship Theory and Practice* 21, no. 2 (1996): 21–36.

4. Gary E. Willard, David A. Krueger, and Henry R. Feeser, "In Order to Grow, Must the Founder Go: A Comparison of Performance between Founder and Non-Founder Managed High-Growth Manufacturing Firms," *Journal of Business Venturing* 7, no. 3 (1996): 181–194.

5. For another useful view of the stages of development of a firm and required management capabilities, see Carroll V. Kroeger, "Management Development and the Small Firm," *California Management Review* 17, no. 1 (1974): 41–47.
6. Larry E. Greiner, "Evolution and Revolution as Organizations Grow," *Harvard Business Review* 50, no. 4 (1972): 37–46; and Herbert N. Woodward, "Management Strategies for Small Companies," *Harvard Business Review* 54, no. 1 (1976): 113–121.
7. David L. Bradford and Allan R. Cohen, *Power Up: Transforming Organizations Through Shared Leadership* (New York, NY: John Wiley & Sons, 1998).
8. Prescott C. Ensign, *Knowledge Sharing Among Scientists: Why Reputation Matters for R&D in Multinational Firms* (New York, NY: Palgrave Macmillan, 2009).
9. Bradford and Cohen, *Power Up.*
10. Neil C. Churchill, "Entrepreneurs and Their Enterprises: A Stage Model," *Frontiers of Entrepreneurship Research* (Babson Park, MA: Babson College, 1983).
11. Royston Greenwood and Roy Suddaby, "Institutional Entrepreneurship in Mature Fields: The Big Five Accounting Firms," *Academy of Management Journal* 49, no. 1 (2006): 27–48.
12. Joel West, "Cross-Cultural Differences in Entrepreneurship in the Asia-Pacific PC Industry," Working Paper, University of California, Irvine, 1997.
13. Rosabeth Moss Kanter, *When Giants Learn to Dance* (New York, NY: Simon & Schuster, 1989).
14. Ibid.
15. Ibid.
16. Rosabeth Moss Kanter, *The Change Masters* (New York, NY: Simon & Schuster, 1983).
17. The study was done by McKinsey & Company. See "How Growth Companies Succeed," reported in *Small Business Report*, July 1984, 9.
18. David L. Bradford and Allan R. Cohen, *Managing for Excellence* (New York, NY: John Wiley & Sons, 1984).
19. John Sculley with John A. Byrne, *Odyssey: Pepsi to Apple... A Journey of Adventures, Idea, and the Future* (New York, NY: HarperCollins, 1987).
20. Clayton M. Christensen, *The Innovator's Dilemma* (Boston, MA: Harvard Business School Press, 1997).
21. Geoffrey Moore, *Crossing the Chasm* (New York, NY: HarperCollins, 2002).

22. Geoffrey Moore, *Inside the Tornado: Marketing Strategies from Silicon Valley's Cutting Edge* (New York, NY: HarperCollins, 1999).
23. Stephen R. Covey, *The 7 Habits of Highly Effective People* (New York, NY: Simon and Schuster, 1989).
24. Donald F. Kuratko, "Entrepreneurial Leadership in the 21st Century," *Journal of Leadership & Organizational Studies* 13, no. 4 (2007): 1–11.
25. Ibid.
26. Donald F. Kuratko and Michael G. Goldsby, "Corporate Entrepreneurs or Rogue Middle Managers: A Framework for Ethical Corporate Entrepreneurship," *Journal of Business Ethics* 55, no. 1 (2004): 13–30.
27. Donald F. Kuratko, "Entrepreneurial Leadership in the 21st Century," *Journal of Leadership and Organizational Studies* 13, no. 4 (2007): 1–11.
28. Don A. Moore, John M. Oesch, and Charlene Zietsma, "What Competition? Myopic Self-Focus in Market-Entry Decisions," *Organization Science* 18, no. 3 (2007): 440–454.
29. Hao Ma and Justin Tan, "Key Components and Implications of Entrepreneurship: A 4-P Framework," *Journal of Business Venturing* 21, no. 5 (2006): 704–725.
30. Bruno Dyck and Frederik A. Starke, "The Formation of Breakaway Organizations: Observations and a Process Model," *Administrative Science Quarterly* 44, no. 4 (1999): 792–822.
31. W. Glenn Rowe, "Creating Wealth in Organizations: The Role of Strategic Leadership," *Academy of Management Executive* 15, no. 1 (2001): 81–94.
32. Jeffry A. Timmons and Howard H. Stevenson, "Entrepreneurship Education in the 80s. What Entrepreneurs Say," in *Entrepreneurship: What It Is and How to Teach It*, John J. Kao and Howard H. Stevenson, eds. (Cambridge, MA: Harvard Business School, 1985), 115–134.
33. Isabelle Giroux, "Problem Solving in Small Firms: An Interpretive Study," *Journal of Small Business and Enterprise Development*, 16, no. 1 (2009): 167–184; J. Brock Smith, J. Robert Mitchell, and Ronald K. Mitchell, "Entrepreneurial Scripts and the New Transaction Commitment Mindset: Extending the Expert Information Processing Theory Approach to Entrepreneurial Cognition Research," *Entrepreneurship Theory and Practice*, 33, no. 4 (2009): 815–844.

CHAPTER 6

1. Stephen Daze, "Planning Key to Success, Says Tech Vet," *Ottawa Business Journal*, July 14, 2008, 11.
2. Lowell W. Busenitz, Douglas D. Moesel, James O. Fiet, and Jay B. Barney, "The Framing of Perceptions of Fairness in the Relationship between Venture Capitalists and New Venture Teams," *Entrepreneurship Theory and Practice* 21, no. 3 (1997): 5–21.
3. Elicia Maine and Elizabeth Garnsey, "The Commercialization Environment of Advanced Materials Ventures," *International Journal of Technology Management* 39, no. 1/2 (2007): 49–71.
4. Elicia M. Maine, Daniel M. Shapiro, and Aidan R. Vining, "The Role of Clustering in the Growth of New Technology-Based Firms," *Small Business Economics*, 34, no. 2 (2010): 127–146.
5. David Boyd and David Gumpert, "The Loneliness of the Start-Up Entrepreneur," *Frontiers of Entrepreneurship Research* (Babson Park, MA: Babson College, 1982).
6. Henry Mintzberg, *Tracking Strategies: Towards a General Theory of Strategy Formulation* (London, UK: Oxford University Press, 2008).
7. Michael D. Ensley, James W. Carland, and Joann C. Carland, "Investigating the Existence of the Lead Entrepreneur," *Journal of Small Business Management* 38, no. 4 (2007): 59–77.
8. Stephen Daze, "Planning Key to Success."
9. Brett Bundale, "Layoffs at Spheric Technologies seen as 'Right-Sizing,'" *Telegraph Journal*, April 21, 2009.
10. Jean-René Halde, "BDC's Young Entrepreneur Awards," *Canadian Business*, November 24, 2008.
11. See Jeffry A. Timmons, "The Entrepreneurial Team: An American Dream or Nightmare?" *Journal of Small Business Management* 13, no. 4 (1975): 33–38.
12. Maria Minniti and Moren Lévesque, "Recent Developments in the Economics of Entrepreneurship," *Journal of Business Venturing* 23, no. 6 (2008): 603–612.
13. Jay W. Lorsch and Robert C. Clark, "Leading from the Boardroom," *Harvard Business Review* 86, no. 4 (2008): 104–111.
14. Tod D. Rutherford and John Holmes, "Entrepreneurship, Knowledge and Learning in Cluster Formation and

Evolution: The Windsor Ontario Tool, Die and Mould Cluster," *International Journal of Entrepreneurship & Innovation Management* 7, no. 3/4 (2007): 320–344.

15. Richard Grigonis, "Talking with Mahshad Koohgoli, CEO, Protecode," TMCcnet.com, March 11, 2009.

16. Research has even revealed that men and women see value in networks differently; Debra S. Malewicki and Cathleen A. (Folker) Leitch, "Female and Male Entrepreneurs' Perceived Value of Formal Networks: Are there Differences," *Journal of Small Business Strategy*, 22, no. 1 (2011): 1–20.

17. Jay W. Lorsch and Edward J. Waitzer, "Corporate Governance in Canada and the United States: A Comparative View," Woodrow Wilson International Center Breakfast, April 28, 2008, New York, NY.

18. See Howard H. Stevenson and William A. Sahlman, "How Small Companies Should Handle Advisers," *Harvard Business Review* 66, no. 3 (1988): 28–34.

19. Reference groups—groups consisting of individuals with whom there is frequent interaction (such as family, friends, and co-workers), with whom values and interests are shared, and from whom support and approval for activities are derived—have long been known for their influence on behaviour. See John W. Thibault and Harold H. Kelley, *The Social Psychology of Groups* (New York, NY: Transaction Publishers, 1986).

20. Jeffry A. Timmons presented a discussion of these entrepreneurial characteristics. See "Entrepreneurial Behavior" Proceedings, First International Conference on Entrepreneurship, Centre for Entrepreneurial Studies, Toronto, November 1973.

21. "Raising Venture Capital" seminar held at Babson College, co-sponsored by Venture Capital Journal and Coopers & Lybrand, 1985.

22. Steve Alper, Dean Tjosvold, and Kenneth S. Law, "Conflict Management, Efficacy, and Performance in Organizational Teams," *Personnel Psychology* 53, no. 3 (2000): 625–642.

23. John L. Hayes and Brian Haslett of Venture Founders Corporation have made a major contribution in the area of reward systems, and the following section is based on their work.

24. Ritch L. Sorenson, Cathleen A. Folker, and Keith H. Brigham, "The Collaborative Network Orientation: Achieving Business Success through Collaborative Relationships," *Entrepreneurship Theory and Practice* 32, no. 4 (2008): 615–634

25. Stephen Daze, "Planning Key to Success, Says Tech Vet," *Ottawa Business Journal*, July 14, 2008, 11.

26. See Prescott C. Ensign, "The Concept of Fit in Organizational Research," *International Journal of Organization Theory and Behavior* 4, no. 3 (2001): 287–306.

CHAPTER 7

1. Elizabeth Crawford, "MBA Students Want Programs to Put More Emphasis on Ethics, Survey Finds," *Chronicle of Higher Education*, May 21, 2003.

2. Donald L. McCabe, Kenneth D. Butterfield, and Linda Klebe Treviño, "Academic Dishonesty in Graduate Business Programs: Prevalence, Causes, and Proposed Action," *Academy of Management Learning and Education* 5, no. 3 (2006): 294–305.

3. J.D. Gravenor, "Is Cheating on the Rise?" *Gazette*, March 20, 2007.

4. Cathy Gulli, Nicholas Kohler, and Martin Patriquin, "The Great University Cheating Scandal," *Macleans*, February 9, 2007.

5. Sarath Nonis and Cathy Owens Swift, "An Examination of the Relationship between Academic Dishonesty and Workplace Dishonesty: A Multicampus Investigation," *Journal of Education for Business* 77, no. 2 (2001): 69–77.

6. Associated Press, "Canadian University Rules Against Expelling Student over Facebook Study Group," March 19, 2008.

7. Susan S. Harmeling, Saras D. Sarasvathy, and R. Edward Freeman, "Related Debates in Ethics and Entrepreneurship: Values, Opportunities, and Contingency," *Journal of Business Ethics* 84, no. 3 (2009): 341–365.

8. Olaf Fisscher, David Frenkel, Yotam Lurie, and Andre Nijhof, "Stretching the Frontiers: Exploring the Relationships between Entrepreneurship and Ethics," *Journal of Business Ethics* 60, no. 3 (2005): 207–209.

9. David A. Robinson, Per Davidson, Hennie Van Der Mescht, and Philip Court, "How Entrepreneurs Deal with Ethical Challenges—An Application of the Business Ethics Synergy Start Technique," *Journal of Business Ethics* 71, no. 4 (2007): 411–423.

10. Yves Fassin, "The Reasons Behind Non-Ethical Behaviour in Business and Entrepreneurship," *Journal of Business Ethics* 60, no. 3 (2005): 265–279.

11. Richard Hudson and Roger Wehrell, "Socially Responsible Investors and the Microentrepreneur: A Canadian Case," *Journal of Business Ethics* 60, no. 3 (2005): 281–292.

12. Albert Z. Carr, "Is Business Bluffing Ethical?" *Harvard Business Review* 46, no. 1 (1968): 143–153.

13. Jeannie Macfarlane, "Trio of Alumni Lead Three Canadian Universities," *The University of Western Ontario Alumni Gazette*, Spring 2009.

14. Alistair R. Anderson and Robert Smith, "The Moral Space in Entrepreneurship: An Exploration of Ethical Imperatives and the Moral Legitimacy of Being Enterprising," *Entrepreneurship & Regional Development* 19, no. 6 (2007): 479–497.

15. Kirk Frith and Gerald McElwee "Value-Adding and Value-Extracting Entrepreneurship at the Margins," *Journal of Small Business & Entrepreneurship* 22, no. 1 (2009): 39–54.

16. "New Places to Look for Presidents," *Time*, December 15, 1975.

17. Ibid.

18. Jeremy Hall and Philip Rosson, "The Impact of Technological Turbulence on Entrepreneurial Behavior, Social Norms, and Ethics: Three Internet-Based Cases," *Journal of Business Ethics* 64, no. 3 (2006): 231–248.

19. Andrew Stark, "What's the Matter with Business Ethics?" *Harvard Business Review* 71, no. 3 (1993): 38–48.

20. Ibid.

21. Ibid.

22. Derek Bok, *Universities and the Future of America* (Durham, NC: Duke University Press, 1990), 99–100.

23. Colin Campbell, "M.B.A.s Who Want to Save the World," Macleans.ca, September 11, 2008.

24. www.mbaswithoutborders.org

25. www.rotman.utoronto.ca/nexus

26. Colin Cambell, "M.B.A.s Who Want to Save the World."

27. Chitra Nayak, "Ethics Under the Microscope," *The Harbus*, 1989.

28. Eva-Maria Hammann, André Habisch, and Harald Pechlaner, "Values that Create Value: Socially Responsible Business Practices in SMEs—Empirical Evidence from German Companies," *Business Ethics: A European Review* 18, no. 1 (2009): 37–51.

29. Lynn Sharp Paine, "Managing for Organizational Integrity," *Harvard Business Review* 72, no. 2 (1994): 105–117.

30. Lynn S. Paine, "Putting codes in perspective," *Zeitschrift für Wirtschafts- un Unternehmensethik* 8, no. 1 (2007): 29–32.

31. David E. Allwright, "Detecting Social Landmines: Strategic Issues Management as an Integrative Theory of the Firm," PhD thesis, University of Calgary, 2002.

32. David Allwright and Harrie Vredenburg, "A New Species of Global Corporate Risk: Social Issues International Firm Expansion Theory an Crisis Avoidance in the Emerging Industry," *International Journal of Sustainable Strategic Management* 2, no. 2 (2010): 74–89.

33. BC Business, "Doing the Right Thing," September 1, 2006.

34. David McClelland, *Achieving Society* (New York, NY: Van Nostrand, 1961), 331.

35. Letter to the Editor, *Wall Street Journal*, October 17, 1975.

36. BC Business, "Doing the Right Thing," September 1, 2006.

CHAPTER 8

1. This definition was developed by Howard H. Stevenson and colleagues at the Harvard Business School.

2. Olivier Torrès, "Le divers types d'entrepreneuriat et de PME dans le monde," *International Management* 6, no. 1 (2001): 1–15.

3. Michael J. Roberts, Howard H. Stevenson, William A. Sahlman, Paul W. Marshall, and Richard G. Hamermesh, *New Business Ventures and the Entrepreneur* (Homewood, IL: McGraw-Hill/Irwin, 2007).

4. Ibid.

5. Emily Barker, "Start With Nothing," *Inc.*, February 2002, 66–72.

6. www.6nsilicon.com

7. Howard H. Stevenson and William H. Sahlman, "How Small Companies Should Handle Advisors," in *The Entrepreneurial Venture*, William H. Sahlman, Howard H. Stevenson, Michael J. Roberts, and Amar Bhide (eds.) (Boston, MA: Harvard Business School, 1999).

8. Per Davidsson and Benson L. Honig, "The Role of Social and Human Capital Among Nascent Entrepreneurs," *Journal of Business Venturing* 18, no. 3 (2003): 301–331.

9. Robert A. Baron and Gideon D. Markman, "Beyond Social Capital: The Roles of Entrepreneur's Social Competence in Their Financial Success," *Journal of Business Venturing* 18, no. 1 (2003): 41–60.

10. Olukemi O. Sawyerr, Jeffrey McGee, and Mark Peterson, "Perceived Uncertainty and Firm Performance in SMEs: The Role of Personal Networking Activities," *International Small Business Journal* 21, no. 3 (2003): 269–290.

11. Andrew Wahl, "Michael Doesn't Live Here Anymore," *Canadian Business*, October 8, 2007.

12. Ibid.

13. Olivier Torrès, "Le divers types d'entrepreneuriat et de PME dans le monde."

14. Douglas J. Cumming and Jeffrey G. MacIntosh, "Crowding Out Private Equity: Canadian Evidence," *Journal of Business Venturing* 21, no. 5 (2006): 569–609.

15. James J. Chrisman, Ed McMullan, and Jeremy Hall, "The Influence of Guided Preparation on the Long-Term Performance of New Ventures," *Journal of Business Venturing* 20, no. 6 (2005): 769–791.

16. Jean Lorrain and Sylvie Laferté, "The Support Needs of the Young Entrepreneur," *Journal of Small Business & Entrepreneurship* 19, no. 1 (2006): 37–48.

17. The authors are indebted to Leslie Charm and Carl Youngman, formerly of Doktor Pet Centers and Command Performance hair salons, respectively, for insights into and knowledge of boards of directors.

18. Jay W. Lorsch, Andargachew S. Zelleke, and Katharina Pick, "Unbalanced Boards," *Harvard Business Review* 79, no. 2 (2001): 28–30.

19. Ellyn E. Spragins, "Confessions of a Director: Hambro International's Art Spinner Says Most CEOs Don't Know How to Make Good Use of Boards," *Inc.*, April 1991, 119–121.

20. David E. Gumpert, "Tough Love: What You Really Want from Your Advisory Board," www.entrepreneurship.org

21. Joseph Rosenstein, Albert V. Bruno, William D. Bygrave, and Natalie T. Taylor, "The CEO, Venture Capitalists, and the Board," *Journal of Business Venturing* 8, no. 2 (1993): 99–113.

22. Ellyn E. Spragins, "Confessions of a Director."

23. Tara Gray, "Canadian Response to the US Sarbanes-Oxley Act of 2002: New Directions for Corporate Governance," October 4, 2005, Library of Parliament.

24. Monica Diochon, Teresa V. Menzies, and Yvon Gasse, "Exploring the Relationship between Start-Up Activities and New Venture Emergence: A Longitudinal Study of Canadian Nascent Entrepreneurs," *International Journal of Management & Enterprise Development* 2, no. 3/4 (2005): 408–426.

25. James J. Chrisman and W. Ed McMullan, "A Preliminary Assessment of Outsider Assistance as a Knowledge Resource: The Longer-Term Impact of New Venture Counseling," *Entrepreneurship Theory and Practice* 24, no. 3 (2000): 37–53.

26. Craig O. White with Gerda Gallop-Goodman, "Tap Into Expert Input—Learn How a Board of Advisors Can Benefit Your Firm," *Black Enterprise* 30, no. 12 (2000): 47.

27. Justene Adamec, "A Business Owner's Guide to Preventive Law," www.inc.com, January 1997.

28. Bradford W. Ketchum, Jr., "You and Your Attorney," *Inc.*, June 1982, 52.

29. Stevenson and Sahlman, "How Small Companies Should Handle Advisors," 297.

30. Jill Andresky Fraser, "How Many Accountants Does It Take to Change an Industry?" *Inc.*, April 1997, 63, 64, 66–69.

31. Susan Greco and Christopher Caggiano, "How Do You Use Your CPA?" *Inc.*, September 1991, 126.

32. Neil C. Churchill and Louis A. Werbaneth, Jr., "Choosing and Evaluating Your Accountant," in *Growing Concerns*, David E. Gumpert (ed.) (New York, NY: John Wiley & Sons, 1984).

33. Jill Andresky Fraser, "Do I Need a Top-Tier Accounting Firm?" *Inc.*, June 1998, 113.

34. Ibid.

35. Jill Andresky Fraser, "How Many Accountants Does It Take to Change an Industry?"

36. The following is excerpted in part from David E. Gumpert and Jeffry A. Timmons, *The Encyclopedia of Small Business Resources* (New York, NY: Harper & Row, 1984).

37. Karl Bayer, "The Impact of Using Consultants during Venture Formation on Venture Performance," *Frontiers of Entrepreneurship Research*. (Babson Park, MA: Babson College, 1991).

38. Ibid.

39. J. Finnegan, "Plug and Pay: The Fine Art of Finding a Consultant" *Inc.*, July 1997, 70–72, 75, 79, 80.

40. Alistair Croll, "6N Silicon Ramps Up Pure Silicon," www.earth2tech.com, February 29, 2008.

41. James McNeill Stancill, "When Is There Cash in Cash Flow?" *Harvard Business Review* 65, no. 2 (1987): 38–49.

42. Ibid.

43. www.springwise.com

44. www.trendwatching.com

CHAPTER 9

1. Mark Freel, Sara Carter, Stephen Tagg, and Colin Mason, "The Latent Demand for Bank Debt: Characterizing 'Discouraged Borrowers'," *Small Business Economics* 38, no. 4 (2012): 399–418.

2. Dave Valliere, "Venture Capitalist Signaling of Screening Skill," *Journal of Private Equity* 14, no. 2 (2011): 86–99. Dave Valliere, "Quality Signals in Early-Stage Venture Capital Markets," *International Journal of Entrepreneurial Venturing* 4, no. 3 (2012): 199–213.

3. Special appreciation is due to Bert Twaalfhoven, founder and chairman of Indivers, the Dutch firm that compiled this summary and that owns the firm on which the chart is based.

4. See Paul A. Gompers and William A. Sahlman, *Entrepreneurial Finance* (New York, NY: John Wiley & Sons, 2002).

5. Nancy A. Nichols, "Efficient? Chaotic? What's the New Finance?" *Harvard Business Review* 71, no. 2 (1993): 50–60.

6. Ibid., 52.

7. Ibid., 60.

8. Hugh Mackenzie "Timing is Everything: Comparing the Earnings of Canada's Highest Paid CEOs and the Rest of Us," www.growinggap.ca, January 2007.

9. Andrew James, "Ted Livingston: The Shape of Canadian Tech to Come," Pandodaily.com, July 11, 2012.

10. Darrell Etherington, "Kik Raises $19.5M Series B, Bets on Its Cards Platform Play to Take on WhatsApp and Others," techcrunch.com, April 22, 2013.

11. This section is drawn directly from William A. Sahlman, "Note on Free Cash Flow Valuation Models," Harvard Business School Case, 2003.

12. In addition to the purchase of common shares, equity financing is meant to include the purchase of both shares and subordinated debt, or subordinated debt with shares conversion features or warrants to purchase shares.

13. For lending purposes, commercial banks regard such subordinated debt as equity. Venture capital investors normally subordinate their business loans to the loans provided by the bank or other financial institutions.

14. William H. Wetzel, Jr., of the University of New Hampshire originally showed the different types of equity capital that are available to three types of companies. The exhibit is based on a chart by Wetzel, which the authors have updated and modified. See William H. Wetzel, Jr., "The Cost and Availability of Credit and Risk Capital in New England," in *A Region's Struggling Savior: Small Business in New England*, J. A. Timmons and D. E. Gumpert, eds. (Waltham, MA: Small Business Foundation of America, 1979).

15. Andrew Wahl, "VC Financing: Cold Realities," *Canadian Business*, March 16, 2009.

16. Taken from a lecture on March 4, 1993, at the Harvard Business School, given by Paul A. Maeder and Robert F. Higgins of Highland Capital Partners.

17. Robert A. Mamis, "The Secrets of Bootstrapping," *Inc.*, September 1992, 76.

18. Ibid.

19. Matthew McClearn, "The Good, the Bad & the Ugly," *Canadian Business*, March 30, 2009.

20. Robert Harrison and Colin Mason, eds., *Informal Venture Capital: Evaluating the Impact of Business Introduction Services* (Upper Saddle River, NJ: Prentice Hall, 1996).

21. Michael J. Robinson and Thomas J. Cottrell, "Investment Patterns of Informal Investors in the Alberta Private Equity Market," *Journal of Small Business Management* 45, no. 1 (2007): 47–67.

22. William H. Wetzel, Jr., "Informal Investors—When and Where to Look," in *Pratt's Guide to Venture Capital Sources*, 6th ed., S. E. Pratt, ed. (Wellesley Hills, MA: Capital Publishing, 1982).

23. New Brunswick Securities Commission, "Venturing Into a New Economy: Developing New Brunswick's Capital Markets," FullSail 2008.

24. Unless otherwise noted, this section is drawn from William D. Bygrave and Jeffry A. Timmons, *Venture Capital at the Crossroads* (Boston, MA: Harvard Business School Press, 1992).

25. "Note on the Venture Capital Industry," Harvard Business School Case, 1982.

26. Bygrave and Timmons, *Venture Capital at the Crossroads*.

27. Michael Vachon, "Venture Capital Reborn," *Venture Capital Journal*, (1993) 32–36.

28. For more specifics, see Harry A. Sapienza and Jeffry A. Timmons, "Launching and Building Entrepreneurial Companies: Do the Venture Capitalists Build Value?" *Frontiers of Entrepreneurship Research* (Babson Park, MA: Babson College, 1989). See also Jeffry A. Timmons, "Venture Capital: More Than Money," in *Pratt's Guide to Venture Capital Sources*, 13th ed., J. Morris, ed. (Needham, MA: Venture Economics, 1989).

29. The authors express appreciation to Thomas Huseby of Seapoint Ventures for his valuable insights in the following two sections.

30. Geoffrey H. Smart, "Management Assessment Methods in Venture Capital," PhD Thesis (Claremont, CA: Claremont Graduate University, 1998).

31. Business Development Bank, 2013 Annual Report, www.bdc.ca/EN/about/publications/annual_report/Pages/annual_report.aspx

32. This section was drawn from Donald P. Remey, "Mezzanine Financing: A Flexible Source of Growth Capital," in *Pratt's Guide to Venture Capital Sources*, D. Schutt, ed. (New York, NY: Venture Economics Publishing, 1993).

33. The following examples are drawn directly from Daniel R. Garner, Robert R. Owen, and Robert P. Conway, *The Ernst & Young Guide to Raising Capital* (New York, NY: Wiley, 1991), 51–52.

34. Ibid., 52–54.

35. Ibid., 281.

CHAPTER 10

1. Press Release, "Q1 2009 Private Equity Buyout Industry: Slowdown in Investments and Fundraising," www.cvca.ca, May 5, 2009.

2. www.vcaonline.com/news/news.asp?ID=2013021922#.UieNUhaIAqs

3. Press Release, "Venture Capital Investment Continued to Fall in Q1 2009," www.cvc.ca, May 12, 2009.

4. Ibid.

5. Ibid.

6. The venture capital method of valuation is adapted from William A. Sahlman and Daniel R. Scherlis, "Method

for Valuing High-Risk, Long-Term Investments: The 'Venture Capital Method'," Harvard Business School Background Note, 2009.

7. This paragraph is adapted from Sahlman and Scherlis, "Method for Valuing High-Risk, Long-Term Investments."

8. Ibid., 58–59.

9. Ibid., 24.

10. Jeffry A. Timmons, "Valuation Methods and Raising Capital," lecture at the Harvard Business School.

11. Note that it is WACC, not free cash flow, because of the tax factor.

12. Jeffry A. Timmons, "Deals and Deal Structuring," lecture at the Harvard Business School.

13. William A. Sahlman, "Structure of Venture Capital Organizations," *Journal of Financial Economics* 27, no. 2 (1990): 473–521.

14. William A. Sahlman, "Note on Financial Contracting Deals," Harvard Business School Background Note, 1989.

15. Ibid., 35–36.

16. Ergete Ferede, "Tax Progressivity and Self-Employment: Evidence from Canadian Provinces," *Small Business Economics* 40, no. 1 (2013): 141–153.

17. Ibid., 43.

18. Jeffry A. Timmons, Stephen Spinelli, and Andrew Zacharakis, *How to Raise Capital: Techniques and Strategies for Financing and Valuing Your Small Business* (New York, NY: McGraw-Hill, 2004).

19. Timmons, "Deals and Deal Structuring."

20. Herb Cohen, *You Can Negotiate Anything* (New York, NY: Bantam Books, 1982).

21. Ibid., 16.

22. Roger Fisher and William Ury, *Getting to Yes* (New York, NY: Penguin Books, 1991).

23. See, for example, Harold M. Hoffman and James Blakey, "You Can Negotiate with Venture Capitalists," *Harvard Business Review* 65, no. 2 (1987): 16–24.

24. Fisher and Ury, xviii.

25. Timmons, "Deals and Deal Structuring."

26. Ryan Roberts, "I Got a Term Sheet, Now What?" November 11, 2008, www.thestartuplawyer.com.

27. Mark Davis, "Term Sheets: Exploding Offers," November 10, 2008, www.markpeterdavis.com.

28. Douglass J. Cumming, "Capital Structure in Venture Finance," *Journal of Corporate Finance* 11, no. 3 (2005): 550–585.

29. This is a fictional name for an actual company.

30. David C. Roach, "The Impact of Product Management on SME Performance," *Journal of Small Business and Enterprise Development* 18, no. 4 (2011): 695–714.

CHAPTER 11

1. The authors wish to thank Leslie Charm of Babson College for his significant contributions to this chapter.

2. Jean-Etienne De Bettignies and James A. Brander, "Financing Entrepreneurship: Bank Finance Versus Venture Capital," *Journal of Business Venturing* 22, no. 6 (2007): 808–832.

3. Jeffry A. Timmons, *Financing and Planning the New Venture* (Acton, MA: Brick House Publishing, 1990).

4. Ibid., 68.

5. Ibid., 33.

6. Ibid., 68–80.

7. Neelam Jain, "Monitoring Costs and Trade Credit," *Quarterly Review of Economics and Finance* 41, no. 1 (2001): 89–110.

8. Gordon Donaldson, *Corporate Debt Capacity* (New York, NY: Beard Books, 2000)

9. Ministry of Justice, Government of Sakatchewan.

10. Canada Business, "Online Small Business Workshop," www.canadabusiness.ca

11. Jain, 81–82.

12. This section is drawn from Timmons, *Financing and Planning the New Venture* (Action, MA: Brick House Publishing, 1990).

13. Timmons, *Financing and Planning the New Venture*, 90–94.

14. Gordon Baty, *Entrepreneurship: Playing To Win.* (Reston, VA: Reston Publishing Company, 1974)

15. Interview with Anna Maria Tremonti, host of *The Current*, CBC Radio, May 18, 2009.

16. Christinne Muschi, "'This is Economic War!' Jarislowsky Warns," *Financial Post*, December 29, 2008.

CHAPTER 12

1. Special thanks to Ed Marram, entrepreneur, educator, and friend, for his lifelong commitment to studying and leading growing businesses and sharing his knowledge with the authors.

2. Henry Mintzberg, *Managers Not MBAs: A Hard Look at the Soft Practice of Managing and Management Development* (San Francisco, CA: Berrett-Koehler, 2004).

3. Ellyn Kerr, "Not Another MBA!" *McGill Reporter*, May 13, 2004.

4. Steven M. Dunphy and David Meyer, "Entrepreneur or Manager? A Discriminant Analysis Based on Mintzberg's Managerial Roles," *Journal of Business and Entrepreneurship* 14, no. 2 (2002): 17–36.

5. Special appreciation is given to Ernst & Young LLP and the Kauffman Center for Entrepreneurial Leadership for permission to include the Summary of their research here.

6. Dave Valliere, "Dynamic Capabilities in Entreprenerial Firms: A Case Study Approach," *Journal of International Entrepreneurship* 10, no. 2 (2012): 1–16.

7. Elspeth Murray and Peter Richardson, *Fast Forward: Organizational Change in 100 Days* (London, UK: Oxford University Press, 2002).

8. Harvey "Chet" Krentzman described this phenomenon to the authors many years ago. The principle still applies.

9. www.bdc.ca/en/business_tools/calculators/salesperemployee.htm

10. The crises discussed here are the ones the authors consider particularly critical. Usually, failure to overcome even a few can imperil a venture at a given stage. There are many more, but a complete treatment of all of them is outside the scope of this book.

11. Jeffry A. Timmons, "The Entrepreneurial Team: Formation and Development," paper presented at the Academy of Management Annual Meeting, Boston, MA, 1973.

12. David Halabisky, Erwin Dreessen, and Chris Parsley, "Growth in Firms in Canada, 1985–1999," *Journal of Small Business and Entrepreneurship* 19, no. 3 (2006): 255–268.

13. Austin Hill, "Inaugural Blog Post," www.billionswithzeroknowledge.com

14. Philip R. Walsh, "Innovation Nirvana or Innovation Wasteland? Identifying Commercialization Strategies for Small and Medium Renewable Energy Enterprises," *Technovation* 32, no. 1 (2012): 34–42.

15. www.360visibility.com

16. www.greenlite.ca

17. Jean-René Halde, "BDC's Young Entrepreneur Awards," *Canadian Business*, November 24, 2008.

18. Ibid.

CHAPTER 13

1. Canadian Franchise Association, www.cfa.ca
2. Stephen Spinelli, Jr., Benoit Leleux, and Sue Birley, "An Analysis of Shareholder Return in Public Franchisors," Society of Franchising Presentation, 2001.
3. Scott Shane, "Hybrid Organizational Arrangements and Their Implications for Firm Growth and Survival: A Study of New Franchisors," *Academy of Management Journal* 39, no. 1 (1996): 216–34.
4. www.homehardware.ca
5. www.cara.com
6. For a discussion of geographic diversification vs. market concentration, see Jerzy Cieślik, Eugene Kaciak, and Dianne H.B. Welsh, "The Impact of Geographic Diversification on Export Performance of Small and Medium-Sized Enterprise (SMEs)," *Journal of International Entrepreneurship* 10, no. 1 (2012): 70–93.
7. www.timhortons.com
8. Advertising co-operatives in franchising are common. A co-operative is a contractual agreement whereby franchisees in a geographic area are bound to contribute a percentage of their revenue to a fund that executes a marketing plan, usually including media purchases. The co-operative is typically governed by the participating franchisees and sometimes includes representation from the franchisor and advertising agency.
9. John Pozios, "Canada Needs Uniformity in Franchise Legislation," May 9, 2008, www.lawyersweekly.ca
10. Elaenor Beaton "Franchising: Can't We All Just Get Along?" Profitguide.com, February 18, 2010.
11. Oliver E. Williamson, "Comparative Economic Organizations: The Analysis of Discrete Structural Alternatives," *Administrative Science Quarterly* 36, no. 2 (1991): 269–296.
12. Francine Lafontaine, "Agency Theory and Franchising: Some Empirical Results," *Rand Journal of Economics* 23, no. 2 (1992): 263–283.
13. Ian R. Mcneil, "Economic Analysis of Contractual Relations: Its Shortfalls and the Need for a 'Rich Classificatory Apparatus,'" *Northwestern University Law Review* 75, no. 6 (1980): 1018–1063.

CHAPTER 14

1. The concepts and models presented in this chapter are based on the research and writing of Timothy Habbershon and colleagues, including Timothy G. Habbershon, Mary L. Williams, and Kenneth Kaye, "A Resource Based Framework for Assessing the Strategic Advantages of Family Firms," *Family Business Review* 12, no. 1 (1999): 1–25; Timothy G. Habbershon, Mary Williams, and Ian C. Macmillan, "A Unified Systems Perspective of Family Firm Performance," *Journal of Business Venturing* 18, no. 4 (2003): 451–465; Timothy G. Habbershon and Joseph Pistrui, "Enterprising Families Domain: Family-Influenced Ownership Groups in Pursuit of Transgenerational Wealth," *Family Business Review* 15, no. 1 (2002): 223–237.
2. Danny Miller and Isabelle Lebreton-Miller, *Managing for The Long Run: Lessons in Competitive Advantage from Great Family Businesses* (Boston, MA: Harvard Business School Press, 1995).
3. G. T. Lumpkin, Lloyd Steier, and Mike Wright, "Strategic Entrepreneurship in Family Business," *Strategic Entrepreneurship Journal* 5, no. 4 (2011): 285–306.
4. Lloyd P. Steier, James J. Chrisman, and Jess H. Chua, "Entrepreneurial Management and Governance in Family Firms: An Introduction," *Entrepreneurship Theory and Practice* 28, no. 4 (2004): 295–303.
5. Primary financial, performance, and ownership data from Hoovers Online.
6. Joseph H. Astrachan, Shaker A. Zahra, and Pramodita Sharma, "Family-Sponsored Ventures," United Nations. Entrepreneurial Advantage of Nations: Global Entrepreneurship Symposium, 2003.
7. www.molsoncoors.com
8. Joseph Weber, et al., "Family Inc.," *Businessweek*, November 10, 2003.
9. Anthony Markin, "Family Ownership and Firm Performance in Canada," Master's Thesis in Global Asset and Wealth Management, Simon Fraser University, 2004.
10. www.quailsgate.com
11. Peter Leach, Bruce Ball, and Garry Duncan, *Guide to the Family Business*, Canadian ed. (Scarborough, ON: Thomson Carswell, 2003).
12. Alberta Business Famiy Institute, www.business.ualberta.ca/Centres/ABFI.aspx
13. "IFERA, Family Businesses Dominate," *Family Business Review* 16, no. 4 (2003): 235.
14. Howard E. Aldrich and Jennifer E. Cliff, "The Pervasive Effects of Family on Entrepreneurship: Toward a Family Embeddedness Perspective," *Journal of Business Venturing* 18, no. 5 (2003): 573–596.
15. Global Entrepreneurship Monitor 2002, Special Report on Family Sponsored New Ventures.
16. G. T. Lumpkin, Lloyd Steier, and Mike Wright, "Strategic Entrepreneurship in Family Business," *Strategic Entrepreneurship Journal* 5, no. 4 (2011): 285–306.
17. Global Entrepreneurship Monitor 2002.
18. Edith T. Penrose, *The Theory of the Growth of the Firm*, 3rd ed. (New York, NY: Oxford University Press, 1995).
19. The content and questions from the mindset and methods inventories are based upon the following literature: Jeffrey G. Covin and Dennis P. Slevin, "Strategic Management in Small Firms in Hostile and Benign Environments," *Strategic Management Journal* 10, no. 1 (1989): 75–87; Rita Gunther McGrath, and Ian Macmillan, *The Entrepreneurial Mindset: Strategies for Continuously Creating Opportunity in an Age of Uncertainty* (Boston, MA: Harvard Business School Press, 2000); Daniel L. McConaughy, Charles H. Matthews, and Anne S. Fialko, "Founding Family Controlled Firms: Performance, Risk, and Value," *Journal of Small Business Management* 39, no. 1 (2001): 31–49; Danny Miller, "The Correlates of Entrepreneurship in Three Types of Firms," *Management Science* 29, no. 7 (1983): 770–791; Danny Miller and Peter H. Friesen, "Innovation in Conservative and Entrepreneurial Firms: Two Models of Strategic Momentum," *Strategic Management Journal* 3, no. 1 (1982): 1–25; Shaker Zahra "Entrepreneurial Risk Taking in Family Firms," *Family Business Review* 18, no. 1 (2002): 23–40.
20. Jeffrey G. Covin and Dennis P. Slevin, "Strategic Management in Small Firms in Hostile and Benign Environments," *Strategic Management Journal* 10, no. 1 (1989): 75–87.
21. Dave Valliere, "Towards a Schematic Theory of Entrepreneurial Alertness," *Journal of Business Venturing* 28, no. 3 (2011): 430–442.
22. Covin and Slevin, "Strategic Management in Small Firms."
23. Ramona K. Z. Heck, Frank Hoy, Panikkos Z. Poutziouris, and Lloyd P. Steier, "Emerging Paths of Family Entrepreneurship Research," *Journal of Small Business Management* 46, no. 3 (2008): 317–330.

24. Nicholas J. Beutell, "Self-Employment, Work-Family Conflict and Work-Family Synergy: Antecedents and Consequences," *Journal of Small Business & Entrepreneurship* 20, no. 4 (2007): 325–334.

25. Jennifer E. Jennings and Megan S. McDougald, "Work-Family Interface Experiences and Coping Strategies: Implications for Entrepreneurship Research and Practice," *Academy of Management Review* 32, no. 3 (2007): 747–760.

26. Bill Fields, "The Art of Delegating: A Critical Approach to Achieving Work/Life Balance," *Canadian Family Business*, November 2008.

27. Rita Gunther McGrath and Ian Macmillan, *The Entrepreneurial Mindset: Strategies for Continuously Creating Opportunity in an Age of Uncertainty* (Boston, MA: Harvard Business School Press, 2000).

28. Duane R. Ireland and Michael A. Hitt, "Achieving and Maintaining Strategic Competitiveness in the 21st Century: The Role of Strategic Leadership," *Academy of Management Executive* 13, no. 1 (1999): 43–57.

29. Danny Miller, Isabelle Le Breton-Miller, and Richard H. Lester, "Divided Loyalties: Governance, Conduct and Performance in Family and Entrepreneur Businesses," Academy of Management Proceedings, 2007.

30. Chuck McKenna and Jeanee Dudley, "Bäckerhaus," *CA Business Executive*, Winter 2013.

31. Grant Walsh, "Succession Strategy: Managing the All-Important Family Component," *Canadian Family Business*, April 2008.

32. "Sharing Success: Butler Byers Building on Community," *Canadian Family Business*, April 2008.

33. Hank Daniszewski, "Tepperman's Gets Bigger, Better," *London Free Press*, October 2, 2008.

34. www.teppermans.com

35. "Leadership Insights," *Canadian Family Business*, December 2007.

36. www.cardinalmeats.com

37. Tom Johnston, "Canadian Invasion – Brent Cator Eyes U.S. Expansion as Cardinal Meat Specialists Continues to Innovate." www.meatingplace.com February 25, 2013.

38. Margot Gibb-Clark, "Family Firms Learn to Share Power," *Globe and Mail Report on Business*, June 25, 1999.

39. Rick Spence, "'Stewards' of a Blueberry Empire: No Special Status for Heirs of Bragg Group Founder," *Financial Post*, June 8, 2009.

40. Jenna Lomas, "Kenneth Levene on Building a Family Legacy," *Small and Medium-Sized Enterprise & Entrepreneur Review*, August 2008.

CHAPTER 15

1. Special credit is due to Robert Bateman, Scott Douglas, and Ann Morgan for contributing material in this chapter. The material is the result of research and interviews with turnaround specialists. The authors are especially grateful to two specialists, Leslie B. Charm, who along with his partner has owned three national franchise companies, an entrepreneurial advisory and troubled business management company, and a venture capital company, AIGIS Ventures, LLC; and Leland Goldberg of Coopers & Lybrand, Boston, who contributed enormously to the efforts of Bateman, Douglas, and Morgan and to the material.

2. Charlie Rose, "A Conversation with Marissa Mayer, V.P. of Search Product and User Experience, Google," http://video.google.com/googleplayer.swf?showShareButtons=true&docId=2130473232539454111%3A88000%3A3273000&hl=en, March 5, 2009.

3. Michael Lewis, "Sears Canada: A Turnaround Story You Need to Watch," *The Motley Fool*, May 28, 2013.

4. Gordon Pitts, "He was Canada's Master Communicator," *The Globe and Mail*, December 3, 2008.

5. Elspeth Murray and Peter Richardson, *Fast Forward: Organizational Change in 100 Days*, (London, UK: Oxford University Press, 2002).

6. www.jimcarreyworld.com

7. CBC News, "Canada's Super Rich," www.cbc.ca, March 6, 2008.

8. CBC News, "Number of Millionaire Families Rises to 1.1 Million," www.cbc.ca, June 23, 2008.

9. Tom Keyser, "Rebel with a Cause," www.albertadventures.com, December 1, 2008.

10. Steven R. Holmberg, "Value Creation and Capture: Entrepreneurship Harvest and IPO Strategies," *Frontiers of Entrepreneurship Research* (Babson Park, MA: Babson College, 1991).

11. Joao C. Neves, "The Value of Financial Freedom and Ownership in Opportunities of Entrepreneurial Harvest," *International Journal of Entrepreneurship and Innovation Management* 5, no. 5/6 (2005): 469–482.

12. www.roots.com

13. This is an arrangement whereby the two founders can force (the put) the acquirer to purchase their 20 percent at a predetermined and negotiated price.

14. See several relevant articles on selling a company in *Growing Concerns*, David E. Gumpert, ed. (New York, NY: John Wiley & Sons, 1984).

15. The big accounting firms publish information on deciding to take a firm public, as does the TSX.

16. Holmberg, "Value Creation and Capture."

17. John A. Hornaday, "Patterns of Annual Giving," *Frontiers of Entrepreneurship Research* (Babson Park, MA: Babson College, 1984).

GLOSSARY

ace in the hole Something that can be revealed to provide victory, such as a resource or advantage held secret until an opportunity arises. The phrase originates from poker, where a card dealt face down and kept hidden is the "hole card," with an ace being the best card.

angel investor A high-net-worth individual who provides start-up or growth capital in exchange for equity or convertible debt. They often play an advisory role to the venture team.

area developer Someone who invests in a local territory or region, grows that area through franchisee recruitment and existing store growth, acts as mentor/coach in assisting with business development including site selection, opening, and ramp-up of business, provides ongoing support, and makes marketing and promotion decisions for the area.

boilerplate Originally referred to the steel label on a steam boiler. The boilerplate was cast iron and unalterable. Later the term referred to printing plates, which were also stamped iron. Today the term refers to a standard that can be changed little, if any. It may apply to legal contracts or even computer code.

bootstrapping A technique of starting with existing (minimal) resources and proceeding to accumulate resources and grow organically. "Pull oneself up by the bootstraps" is a metaphor of independence without external assistance.

business model A one-page flowchart or diagram describing the "engine of the enterprise" to demonstrate the value proposition of the venture, how it balances resources with the ecosystem in which it operates, and how it generates cash flow.

business plan A document that conveys the entrepreneur's vision for transforming an idea into a viable ongoing enterprise. It contains background on the venture team and how the goals will be realized.

buyback agreement Sale of a security with the provision that the seller can repurchase the security at a later date.

cherry-pick To selectively choose the best element or opportunity from what is available; in a game, like basketball, to hover near the net and wait for a pass for an easy shot. In politics, to register voters who are predisposed to the candidate. In music, to select songs, not the entire album.

creative destruction The idea that innovation displaces old ideas and ways. Capitalism and market forces call for annihilation and reconfiguring of the status quo. Something newer or better is always out there, ready to topple established market offerings.

demand loan A loan with no specific maturity date, but payable at any time. The lender may demand full payment at any time. The open-ended repayment schedule may benefit the borrower if some time is needed to reach profitability or growth targets, but if revenue is not generated and payments are infrequent, the debt may balloon.

escrow Money held in trust by a third party on behalf of the transacting parties until stipulated conditions are met.

founder An individual (founder) or individuals (co-founders) who were present and contributed at the inception of the venture.

hoofing it To go on foot, often as a tough slog over the countryside compared to an easy ride on horse or vehicle.

instalment features A sum of money due as part of the agreed payback schedule over time for a debt.

intrapreneurs Managers within an organization who develop innovative solutions.

kicker An exercisable warrant, right, or other feature added to a debt instrument to satisfy investors; the debt holder thus has the option to purchase shares. Often the kicker has a breakpoint that must be obtained (e.g., share price reaching a particular level) before having real value. Kickers are included to lure investors and seal the deal or reach the entire issue.

line of credit A formal or informal agreement between a bank and a borrower concerning a loan a bank will allow the borrower for a one-year period.

market failure The existence of another means by which a market participant can be better off.

master franchise A franchise agreement that allows a person or corporation to purchase the rights to sub-franchise in a particular territory. Often the franchise fee and royalty fees for the sub-franchises are divided equally between the franchisor and the master franchisee.

mezzanine financing Financing utilized to fund expansion of existing enterprises. It is a debt/equity hybrid: the lender has the right to convert debt capital to an equity position. It usually provides the borrower a quick hit of cash; with little due diligence or collateral the financing is priced aggressively and the lender expects a 20–30 percent return. In architecture, a mezzanine is a middle level between two other floors.

moonlighting Having a second job beyond one's regular "daytime" employment. Many entrepreneurs do not give up their steady job to focus on the start-up: employee by day, entrepreneur by night.

new venture A recently created enterprise involving risk with expectation of gain.

paradoxes Statements or relationships that are seemingly contradictory.

personal guarantee An entrepreneur's promise, which obligates him or her to personally pay back any debt on which his enterprise may default.

private equity Working capital provided to an enterprise that is not publicly traded; sources of private equity include a private equity firm, a venture capitalist, and an angel investor.

sea change A broad or substantial transformation.

senior debt Money borrowed that must be repaid first if the enterprise fails; debt that takes priority over other unsecured or "junior" or subordinate debt owed.

serial entrepreneur An individual who has repeatedly gone through the venture creation process.

share-vesting agreement A schedule indicating what an individual's shares are worth and when. The arrangement takes into consideration when the person joined and when they leave. The agreement is structured so that at early departure the equity can be purchased back at a discount, which diminishes over time—typically three to five years—at which point the employee is fully vested and the shares can no longer be purchased back at a pro-rated amount. The agreement does not take into account how hard the person worked and whether or not they deserve the shares; share vesting is to encourage loyalty and dedication and to provide a reward.

shotgun An approach to target as wide a swath as possible; in contrast to a rifle approach for which a specific target is aimed.

shotgun clause A buy–sell agreement delivered as an ultimatum. It generally occurs when a partnership is strained or an impasse is reached and a buy-out cannot amicably be reached. Cash on hand and accessible as well as ability to run the firm play a role in evaluation and offer.

start-up A newly established business.

team A group who put effort into a common purpose. In sports, a team forms one side in a competitive game. Horses can even be harnessed together as a team to pull collectively. Team can be used as a noun or a verb.

term debt Money to be repaid over a period of time, rather than as one lump sum.

term sheet A short, non-binding document outlining the conditions for financing a startup company that summarizes the acceptable terms of the agreement.

venture capital Cash invested in a new or expanding business or project in which there is significant risk.

venture capitalists Individuals who invest in a new or expanding business or project in which there is significant risk.

venture team The founder or co-founders and the core group responsible for the start-up's survival. websites

WEBSITES

CHAPTER 1:
THE ENTREPRENEURIAL MIND: CRAFTING A
PERSONAL ENTREPRENEURIAL STRATEGY

dhltd.com Davis and Henderson

CHAPTER 3:
THE OPPORTUNITY: SCREENING, CREATING,
SHAPING, RECOGNIZING, SEIZING

www.thefuntheory.com The Fun Theory
designthinking.ideo.com IDEO blog, Design Thinking
www.canadabusiness.ca/eng Canada Business Network
www.ipic.ca Intellectual Property Institute of Canada
Futurity.org Futurity
www.ic.gc.ca/Intro.html Industry Canada

CHAPTER 4:
THE BUSINESS PLAN

www.tedxtoronto.com/speakers/bruce-poon-tip Bruce Poon Tip
Ted Talk
www.eqjournal.org/?p=692 Bruce Firestone blog
www.junoawards.ca The Juno Awards
**www.cbc.ca/books/canadareads/2011/12/meet-canada-reads
-panelist-shad.html** Canada Reads
http://shadk.com/whenthisisover.html Shad

CHAPTER 10:
THE DEAL: VALUATION, STRUCTURE, AND
NEGOTIATION

**http://business.queensu.ca/centres/qcbv/tricolour_venture
_fund.php** TricClour Venture Fund

CHAPTER 11:
OBTAINING DEBT CAPITAL

www.canadabusiness.ca Canadian Business Network
www.cba.ca Canadian Bankers Association

CHAPTER 13:
FRANCHISING

www.pizzanova.com Pizza Nova

CHAPTER 14:
THE FAMILY AS ENTREPRENEUR

http://cafecanada.ca Canadian Association of Family Enterprise

CHAPTER 15:
LEADING THROUGH TROUBLE, THE HARVEST,
AND BEYOND

www.buytopia.ca Buytopia

INDEX

A

Abdelnour, Assaad, 92
accountants, 263–264
accounts receivable
    factoring, 359–360
    financial trouble, 482
    lending criteria, 352
    operating working capital, 287
    quick cash, 488
    time-sales financing, 355
ace in the hole, 371
ACE Security Laminates, 423
acquisition, 499
Adler, Fred, 277
Air Canada, 292–293
Air Canada Jazz, 83
Air Canada Rouge, 83
Aldrich, Howard, 253
Allen, Fred, 232
Allen Vanguard, 500
Allwright, David, 229
Almgren, Ake, 202
ambiguity
    entrepreneurial process, 61
    entrepreneurship, 9, 10, 13–14
    Timmons model, 55, 56
    transitions, 168
    venture team, 59
Amyris, 208
Anagnostakos, Louis, 396
angel investor. *See also* financing;
    venture capital
    contacting, 295
    debt capital, 10
    decision to have, 296
    defined, 51–52
    evaluation process, 295
    finding, 294–295
    who they are, 293–294
Angstrom Power Inc., 202
apprenticeship, 19–22
Archambault, Yannick, 492
area developer, 433
area of dominant influence (ADI), 430
Armstrong, Ann, 227
Asper, Leonard, 369
Avrio Ventures Ltd., 332
Awake, 230

B

Bäckerhaus Veit analysis, 451–452, 459,
    460–461
Ball, Lina, 402
bank financing. *See also* debt capital;
    financing

debt capital source, 351
defined, 353
demand loan, 354
financing term, 352
line of credit, 354
purchase money security interest,
    357–358
selection criteria, 263
term debt, 354
term loans, 356
time-sales financing, 355–356
bankers, 263
bankruptcy threat, 484–485
bargaining power, 485
Barnes, Wade, 342
Baruch, Bernard, 496
Bauer, 498
Baumol, William, 8
Bayer, Karl, 265
BC Bearing Engineers Ltd., 441
Beauchamp, Alyssa, 53
Bella Dance Academy, 402
Ben & Jerry's Ice Cream, 7
Benerji, Anamitra, 285
Bennis, Warren, 42
Berkowitz, David, 202
Billingsley, Jason, 199
bitHeads, 255
Black Box Technology Inc., 338
board of advisors, 260
board of directors, 256–260
    alternatives to, 260
    decision to have, 257
    harassment, 260
    liability, 259
    selection criteria, 258–259
    time and risk, 260
boilerplate, 336
Bok, Derek, 227
bOKnow, 330
Bond, Holly, 84
Bontis, Nick, 251, 268
bootstrapping
    defined, 27
    examples of, 91–92
    resources, 58, 252, 259
    Timmons model, 236
Boston Pizza, 89
Boudreau, Jocelyn, 332
Bowen, Harry, 46
Bowie, David, 98
Bradford, David, 167
Bragg Group of Companies, 480
brain trust, 256
Brander, James, 350
Bre-X, 232
Bricklin, Dan, 267

Brightspark, 344
Bronfman, Edgar, 493
brontosaurus capitalism, 62, 393
brontosaurus factor, 85
Brown, Michael, 227
Brusha, Patricia, 265
Brzustowski, Tom, 82
Budmand, Michael, 497
Buffet, Howard G., 442
Buffet, Warren, 349, 355, 442
Bulldog Interactive Fitness, 84
Bullfrog Power, 5
burn rate, 286–287
Bush, George, 226
Bush, George W., 226
Bushnell, Nolan, 46
Business Development Bank of Canada
    (BDC), 305–307
business ethics. *See* ethics
business model
    business plan vs., 136–137
    opportunity, 78
business plan
    audience, 133
    business model, 136–137
    checklist for, 138
    completeness of, 135–136, 137
    defined, 45, 127
    dehydrated business plan, 132
    do's and don'ts, 129
    goals and actions, 133–134
    investor input, 131–132
    organizing, 134
    paradox, 45
    SHAD case, 154–159
    steps of writing, 134–135, 142–153
    tips for, 130–131
    work in progress, 128
Butterfield, Stewart, 169
buyback agreement, 211

C

Calof, Jonathan, 113
Canada Business Network, 110–111
CanadaHelps.org, 268
Canada/Manitoba Business Service Centre,
    111
Canada's Venture Capital and Private
    Equity Association (CVCA), 302
Canadian banks, 354, 355. *See also* bank
    financing
Canadian inventions in the 20th century,
    108
Canica Design case study, 218–222
Canwest Global Communications, 369
capital cow, 497

capital market
    context, 103–104
    debt capital. *See* debt capital sources
    entrepreneurial process, 61–62
    equity source, 312–313
    food chain, 79–80, 290–292, 321
    private ventures, 282
    timing, 103–104
    Timmons model, 55
capital markets food chain, 79–80,
    290–292, 321
capital requirements, 102
Cara Operations Ltd., 422
Caron, Jean, 332
Carpentier, Cécile, 312
Carr, Emily, 3
Carrey, Jim, 491
case studies
    Canica Design, venture teams, 218–222
    Cavendish Cove Cottages, 505–513
    Dairy Queen, family enterprising,
        472–475
    ExerciseApp, resource requirements,
        271–276
    F&D Meats, entrepreneurial process, 69–75
    Minto Lake Resources Inc., debt capital,
        375–380
    Nanopix, opportunity, 118–125
    Parlance Communications, high-growth
        companies, 410–418
    Planet Bean, ethics, 242–248
    Scavenger Energy, venture financing,
        315–316
    SHAD, business plan, 154–159
    Torak Express, entrepreneurship, 34–37
    Which Way To Grow, franchising,
        437–438
cash flow
    discounted, 328
    financing, 282, 286–287
    positive, 101
    profit and loss, 103
Cavendish Cove Cottages case, 505–513
Celtic House Venture Partners, 5
Centra Industries, 480
chain of greatness, 408
Charade, Jim, 2
Charity auctions, 268
Charm, Leslie, 260, 261
Chemko, Harry, 199
cherry picking, 397
Chevalier, Gabrielle, 405–406
ChipCare, 206
Choi, Matthew, 268
Chrétien, Jean, 226
Chrisman, James, 256, 260, 440
Christensen, Clayton, 172, 229, 231
Christoff, Kalina, 91
Chua, Jess, 440
Churchill, Winston, 27
circle of ecstasy, 79
Clarity.fm, 198

CLIC Foods, 92
Cloherty, Patricia, 77
Coady, Theresa, 176
Cohen, Allan, 167
Cohen, Boyd, 5
cohesion, 198
commercial bank financing. *See* bank
    financing
commitment
    entrepreneurship theme, 8–11
    to the long haul, 198
    stages capital, 330–331
    to value creation, 199
competencies of entrepreneurial leaders.
    See also entrepreneurial leader
    entrepreneurial leadership, 178–179
    finance, 178
    informational technology, 180
    law and taxes, 180
    leadership paradigm, 12
    management skills, 17
    marketing, 177
    operations, 177–178
competitive advantage issues
    screening opportunities, 104
    venture opportunity evaluation criteria, 96
compliance strategy for ethics
    management, 228
consensus building, 403
consultants, 264–266
consulting and information, 112
Cook, Lynn, 405–406
corporate venture capital, 307
corporations and information, 111
co-sale provision, 337
cost structure, 101
Cottrell, Thomas, 294
covenants, 369–370
Covey, Stephen, 173
Cowpland, Michael, 4–5, 256
cram-down round, 323–325
Crate & Barrel, 89
creative destruction, 48
creativity
    enhancing, 89
    left-mode/right-mode brain
        characteristics, 90
    Timmons model, 55
credit unions, 351, 352
Crile, George, 86
critical mass
    opportunity, 106
    start-up stage of venture growth, 167
    threshold concept, 49
Crossing the Chasm, 172
Csikszentmihalyi, Mihaly, 90
Culligan, Tom, 319
Cumming, Douglas, 340

D

Dacin, Tina, 82

Dairy Queen, family enterprising case,
    470–475
D'Angelo, Dino, 69–75
D'Angelo, Franko, 69–75
Davis, Mark, 338
Daze, Stephen, 196
de Bettignies, Jean-Etienne, 53, 350
De Clercq, Dirk, 44, 46
deal structure, 331–336
    characteristics of successes, 332–333
    deal defined, 331
    deal elements, 333
    deal over time, 331–332
    minimizing surprises, 335–336
    risk management, 333
    understanding the bets, 334–335
debt, 350
debt capital. *See also* financing; venture
    capital
    ace in the hole, 371
    alternatives to, 371
    choosing a lender, 361–362
    covenants, 369–370
    credit capacity, 352–353
    economic cycles, 350–351
    factoring, 351, 352, 359–360
    instalment features, 358
    lending criteria, 367–368
    leverage, 372–373
    loan restrictions, 368–369
    location consideration, 351
    meeting the lender, 363–366
    personal guarantees, 370
    Personal Property Security Act, 356–357
    pitfalls, 372–373
    plant improvement loans, 358
    relationship building, 370–371
    return on equity (ROE), 372–373
    security agreements, 357–358
    sources of. *See* debt capital sources
    steps in obtaining a loan, 363
    term-of-financing consideration, 352
    type-of-business consideration, 351
debt capital sources. *See also* debt capital;
    lending decision
    bank financing, 351, 352, 353–354
    choosing a lender, 361–362
    considerations, 351–353
    credit unions, 351, 352
    demand loan, 354
    factoring, 351, 352, 359–360
    finance companies, 352, 358–359
    instalment features, 358
    insurance companies, 342, 351
    line of credit, 354
    meeting the lender, 363–366
    Personal Property Security Act, 356–357
    plant improvement loans, 358
    security agreements, 357–358
    term debt, 354
    term loans, 356
    time-sales financing, 355–356

trade credit, 351, 352, 353
Dees, J. Gregory, 227
degree of control, 104
degree of fit, 107
Dehtiar, Tal, 171, 227
dehydrated business plan, 132
Delorme, Lisa, 205
demand loan, 354
demand registration rights, 338
demographic profile, 422–424
Denomme, Robb, 253
Deremo, Adam, 230
Deshpande, Guraj, 226
Deshpande, Jaishree, 226
desirability criteria, 106–107
determination and entrepreneurship, 8–11
Deutsch, Yuval, 128
DHX Media, 84
Diceman, Chris, 369
Diochon, Monica, 48, 260
directors. *See* board of directors
discipline, 45
Discount Car & Truck Rentals, 98
discounted cash flow, 328
disruptive technologies, 42, 45, 62, 485
distribution channels, 109
Dominion Loose Leaf Company, 494
Donaldson, Lisa, 110
Donath, Toby, 444
Doriot, Georges, 58, 293
Dovigi, Patrick, 401
down round, 323–325
Drabinsky, Garth, 232
Dragons' Den, 44
Dreessen, Erwin, 403
Dubini, Paola, 253
due diligence
    business plan, 127
    entrepreneurial leader, 56
    evaluation process, 295
    franchising, 424
    mezzanine financing, 308
    research and development stage, 166
    two ways, 304–305
    venture capital history, 299
    venture capital process, 304–305
Duell, Charles, 94
Dunleavy, Michael, 251, 302
Dunn, Frank, 232
Dunphy, Stephen, 393
Dutta, Dev, 49
Dyck, Bruno, 174

E

early growth stage of venture growth, 398
Easthope, Steve, 34–37
Easthope Gerry, 34–37
eBay, 4
economics
    screening opportunities, 101–103
    venture opportunity evaluation criteria, 95

E.D. Smith & Sons, 494
Eddison, Thomas, 94
education for entrepreneurship, 26–29
Einstein, Albert, 94
Elastic Path, 199
Elder, Doug and Danny, 407–408
Emerson, Ralph Waldo, 87
employee share ownership plans (ESOPs),
    312, 479
Enrico, Roger, 400
Ensign, Prescott, 368
entrepreneurial culture, 170–171. *See also*
    entrepreneurial process;
    entrepreneurship
entrepreneurial domain, 164–165
entrepreneurial founder, 160–161. *See also*
    entrepreneurial leader
entrepreneurial leader, 163–180. *See also*
    entrepreneurs; entrepreneurship
    chain of greatness, 408
    coaching skill, 174, 175
    driving forces, 164–165
    entrepreneurial founder, 1, 4, 160–161
    entrepreneurial vs. managerial domains,
        164–165
    entrepreneurship theme, 9, 11
    entrepreneurship vs. leadership, 163–164
    ethical leadership, 173
    ethical stereotypes, 226
    ethics perspective, 229–231
    examples of, 404–408
    failure causes, 477–478
    finance competency, 178
    financial management myopia, 278–279
    high-growth companies, 395–396,
        403–404
    influence skills, 174, 175
    information technology competency, 180
    law/tax competency, 180
    leadership competency, 178–179
    management vs., 6
    marketing competency, 177
    necessary skills, 171–173
    operations/production competency,
        177–178
    paradigm, 11
    people skills, 174, 175–176
    personal strategy, 502–503
    rapid growth management, 167–171
    resource requirements approach,
        251–255. *See also* financing
    stages of venture growth and, 165–174
    team formation, 203–204
    Timmons model, 55, 56
entrepreneurial leadership paradigm, 11
entrepreneurial process. *See also*
    entrepreneurs
    ambiguity, 61
    criteria for success, 47–53
    entrepreneurship, 41–43. *See also*
        entrepreneurship
    requirements to launch, 45–46

Timmons model, 53–65
entrepreneurial reasoning, 17–19
entrepreneurial team. *See* venture team
entrepreneurial themes. *See also*
    entrepreneurs; entrepreneurship
    commitment and determination, 8–11
    leadership, 9, 11
    motivation to excel, 9, 16
    opportunity obsession, 9, 11–13
    self-reliance and resilience, 9, 14–16
    tolerance of risk, ambiguity, and
        uncertainty, 9, 13–14
entrepreneurs. *See also* entrepreneurial
    leader; entrepreneurial process;
    entrepreneurship
    apprenticeship, 19–22
    attitudes and behaviours, 7–8
    desirable attributes, 8, 10
    education for, 26–29
    entrepreneurial leadership paradigm, 11
    entrepreneurial reasoning, 17–19
    entrepreneur's creed, 22–23
    examples of, 4–5
    human resource management, 7
    leadership and, 6
    myths of, 23–25
    networking, 253–254
    nonentrepreneurial attributes, 10
    opportunity recognition, 17
    personal strategy, 502–503
    psychological motivation, 6–7
    themes of. *See* entrepreneurial themes
entrepreneur's creed, 22–23
entrepreneurship. *See also* entrepreneurial
    leader; entrepreneurial process;
    entrepreneurs
    Canada and, 254–255
    defined, 41
    established corporations vs, 41–43
    ethical stereotypes, 226
    ethics overview, 224–225
    failure, 477–491
    financial backing, 50–52
    financial management myopia,
        278–279
    financing perspective, 281–284
    franchising, 420
    harvest, 493–502
    journey vs. destination, 491–492
    lifestyle venture, 52–53
    paradoxes, 44–45
    personal strategy, 502–503
    post start-up, 41–42
    resource requirements approach,
        251–255. *See also* financing
    start-up, 41
    survival rates, 47–50
    thinking big, 45–46
    Timmons model, 53–65
entry barriers, 104–105
equal inequality, 199
equity financing, 288, 292–293

equity sources
  Business Development Bank of Canada
    (BDC), 305–307
  capital market context, 312–313
  corporate venture capital, 307
  employee share ownership plans
    (ESOPs), 312
  Industrial Research Assistance Program
    (IRAP), 307
  initial public offering (IPO) shares,
    309–312
  investor's required rate of return, 319,
    320
  investor's required share of ownership,
    319–321, 326
  mezzanine financing, 308
  private placements, 308–309, 310–311
  Scientific Research and Experimental
    Development Tax Credit Program,
    307
Ericsson, Anders, 88
escrow, 211
established vs. entrepreneurial firms, 41–43
Estee Lauder, 92, 442
ethics
  differing views, 232–233
  ends-and-means issues, 233–235
  entrepreneurial leader perspectives,
    229–231
  ethical dilemma examples, 231
  integrity, 228–229. See also integrity
  law, 225
  overview, 224–225
  Planet Bean case, 242–248
  pressure and, 231–232
  problems of law, 233
  social entrepreneurship, 235–237
  stereotypes, 226
  strategies for ethics management, 228
  teaching of, 227
  Timmons model and social
    entrepreneurship, 236–237
ethics management strategies, 228
Evandale Caviar, 483
executive summary, 130, 134, 138, 363
ExerciseApp, resource requirements case,
  271–276
existing businesses, 110
exit mechanism, 103
external environment influences, 11

F

F&D Meats, entrepreneurial process case,
  69–75
f+ f– analysis, 459–460
Fabian, Peter, 423
factoring, 351, 352, 359–360
failure
  bankruptcy threat, 484–485
  causes, 477
  crisis gestation period, 482–484

financial/accounting issues, 479
getting out of trouble, 479–480
intervention, 485–491
leadership issues, 478
net-liquid balance-to-total-assets ratio,
  481
non-quantitative signals, 481–482
paradox, 44–45
planning/practices issues, 479
predicting trouble, 480–481
strategic issues, 478
fairness, 200
Fake, Caterina, 169
familiness f+ f– analysis, 459–460
family business. See family enterprising
family corporate renewal, 446
family corporate venturing category, 446
family enterprising
  Bäckerhaus Veit, 451–452, 459, 460–461
  Dairy Queen case, 470–475
  defined, 440
  economic contribution, 444–445
  familiness advantage, 458–461
  family legacy companies, 440–444
  governance, 456–457
  leadership, 454
  mindset and method, 447–453
  performance, 457
  relationships, 455
  roles, 445–447
  strategy, 456
  succession, 458–461
  Timmons model, 440, 447, 453, 458,
    460–461
  transgenerational entrepreneurship and
    wealth creation, 440
  vision, 455–456
family investment funds, 446, 447
family private cash, 446–447
family-influenced start-ups, 445–446
Farmer's Edge, 342
Faseruk, Alex, 131
*Fast Forward: Organizational Change in
  100 Days,* 485
fatal-flaw issue
  screening opportunities, 106
  venture opportunity evaluation criteria, 96
finance companies, 351, 358–359
finance competency, 178
financial management myopia, 278–279
financial resources, 266–267
financial strategy framework, 284–286
financing. See also bank financing; debt
  capital; venture capital
  analyzing requirements, 266–267
  angel/informal investors, 293–297
  area developer, 433
  bootstrapping, 252. See also
    bootstrapping
  capital markets food chain, 290–292, 321
  cash flow, 282
  critical issues, 279–281

entrepreneurial approach to, 251–252
  equity, 292–293
  financial management myopia, 278–279
  financial strategy framework, 284–286
  free cash flow, 286–287
  leading financing practices, 65
  loans. See debt
  negotiating, 336–344
  other equity sources. See equity sources
  owner's perspective, 281–284
  resource requirements, 251–268
  spreadsheets, 267, 278–279
  strategy crafting, 287–290
  structuring the deal, 331–336
  survival rates and, 50–52
  term sheet, 285
  timing, 282, 293
  using other peoples', 252–254
  valuation, 318–329
  value creation, 52, 279–280
  venture capital, 298–313
  vigilance, need for, 297–298
financing life cycles, 288–290
financing strategy crafting, 287–290
  critical variables, 287–288
  financial life cycles, 288–290
  investor preferences, 290
First Chicago valuation method, 326, 327
Fischer, Eileen, 87
Fisher, Andrew, 132
fit and balance
  Bäckerhaus Veit analysis, 461
  Timmons model, 59, 236
  value creation, 54
  venture team, 55, 59
fixed costs, 104
flexibility
  capital cow, 497
  entrepreneurial leader, 21
  entrepreneurship, 45
  opportunity evaluation, 97
  paradox, 45
  resource ownership, 251
  strategic differentiation, 108
  venture team rewards, 210
Flickr, 169
Flowtown, 198, 201
food chain concept
  financing, 290–292
  opportunity, 79–80
  valuation, 321
forced buyout, 338
Forssman, Godfrey, 202
Foster, Bill, 199
founder, 1, 4. See also entrepreneurial
  leader
Fox, Terry, 230
franchises, 110
franchising
  Canada, 421
  conflicts, 431, 433
  defined, 420

entrepreneurship, 420
evaluation process, 424–426
field support, 429
franchise relationship model, 433–435
marketing, 429–430
master franchise, 433
rewards for franchiser, 426
service delivery system, 426–428
supply, 430–431
target audience, 422–424
Timmons model, 422, 427, 433
training and operational support,
    428–429
tying agreement, 431
Which Way To Grow, case, 437–438
Franks, Wilbur, 86
free cash flow
    characteristics, 102
    financing, 286–287
Friese, Lauren, 110
Fuld, Leonard, 113
fundamental valuation method, 326, 327
fundraising, 131, 287–290

G

G Adventures, 135
Galbraith, John Kenneth, 163
Gallagher, Sheila, 197
Gasse, Yvon, 48, 260
Gates, Bill, 94, 163
gathering information, 109–114
    ideas and, 109
    industry and trade contacts, 111–112
    Internet, 114
    published sources, 113
Gegenhuber, Thomas, 13
Geist, Joshua, 290
Gelpey, Jonathan, 444
Genuwine Cellars, 253
geographic profiles, 423–424
Gianforte, Greg, 252
Gilder's Law, 85
GiveMeaning.com, 268
Glavine, April, 110
Globe and Mail, 484
goals
    business plan, 133–134
    harvest, 495
    venture team formation, 206
goals and fit, 106
Google, 114
Gorman, Gary, 131
Gottlieb, Myron, 232
Graham, Nicholas, 92
Grant, Alan J., 11
Grant, Joyce, 234
Gray, Tara, 259
great mousetrap fallacy, 87–88
Green, Don, 497
Green For Life, 401
Greenlite, 406–407

Greenwood, Royston, 170
Grimm's Fine Foods Ltd., 72
Groh, Ortwin, 296
gross margins, 102–103
Grove, Andy, 163
growth rate, 100
growth stages of entrepreneurial ventures
    crises and, 397–399
    leadership, 172–173
    rapid growth management, 167–171
    stages, 165–167, 394–395
Guillon, Chris, 28
Gulak, Ben, 109
Gumpert, David, 257
Gupta, Nina, 406–407

H

Halabisky, David, 403
Hall, Jeremy, 226, 256
harassment, 260
Harvard Business Review, 224–225
harvest, 493–502
    acquisition, 499
    beyond harvest, 501–502
    capital cow, 497
    employee share ownership plans
        (ESOPs), 479
    examples, 493–494
    goals, 495
    management buyout, 498–499
    merger, 499
    options, 497–501
    public offering, 499–501
    sale, 499
    strategic alliance, 499
    strategy, 495–497
    timing, 495–496
harvest issues
    mindset, 198–199
    screening opportunities, 103
    sharing, 200
    venture opportunity evaluation criteria,
        96
harvest mindset, 198–199
harvest stage of venture growth, 399
Harvey's, 432
Hay system, 393
Head, Howard, 57–58, 86, 251
Heins, Thane, 296
Heintzman, Tom, 5
Hesjedal, Ryder, 234
high-growth companies, 394–400
    cherry-picking approach, 397
    growth rate problems, 396–399
    hoofing it, 397
    industry/market issues, 399–400
    leadership, 395–396, 403–404, 408
    leadership examples, 404–408
    organizational culture, 400–403
    Parlance Communications case, 410–418
    sales per employee (SPE), 395

shotgun approach, 397
stages of growth, 165–174, 394–395
high-growth stage of venture growth, 166,
    167. See also high-growth companies
Hill, Austin, 404–405
Hindle, Kevin, 129
Hindman, 201
Hindman, Jim, 477
Hofer, Charles, 101
Holmes, John, 203
Holy, Bill, 355
Home Hardware, 422
Honig, Benson, 129
hoofing it, 397
Horton, Tim, 2
How Will You Measure Your Life? (2012),
    229
Hudson, Richard, 5, 224
Hull, Bobby, 498
human resource management, 7
Hurst, Deborah, 131
Huseby, Thomas, 130, 304

I

idea
    information gathering, 109
    opportunity vs., 80–81, 83–85
    role of, 86–88
incentives for venture team, 208–212.
        See also venture team rewards
income statement, 365
Industrial Research Assistance Program
    (IRAP), 307
industry and market criteria, 95
industry and technical experience, 105
industry and trade contacts and
        information, 111–112
Industry Canada, 113
industry/market issues
    high-growth companies, 399–400
    screening opportunities, 99–101
influence
    area of dominant influence (ADI), 430
    entrepreneurial leader, 174–176
    family enterprising, 445–446
    rapid growth management, 167
informal investor
    contacting, 295
    decision to have, 296
    evaluation process, 295
    finding, 294–295
    who they are, 293–294
information gathering, 109–114
information technology competency, 180
initial public offering (IPO)
    equity source, 309–312
    harvesting, 499–501
    private placements, 310–311
    timing, 501
    venture team rewards, 208
INPEX, 111

instalment features, 358
insurance companies, 351, 352
integrity
    ethics and, 228–229
    team philosophy/attitude, 198
    venture team, 105
    venture team formation, 208
intellectual honesty, 105
Intellectual Property Institute of Canada, 111
internal rate of return potential, 102
Internet
    gathering information, 114
    resource requirements, 268
    as source of information, 114–115
intervention
    diagnosis, 486–487
    long-term remediation, 491
    turnaround plan, 487–491
intrapreneurs, 11
inventions of the 20th century, 108
inventureLab, 290
investor
    required rate of return, 319, 320
    required share of ownership, 319–321, 326
irrational exuberance, 85

J

Jarislowsky, Stephen, 373
Jennings, Dev, 11, 128
Jennings, Jennifer, 128
Jetsgo, 83
Jiffy Lube, 427–428
Jobs, Steven, 19, 44, 91, 163
Joe Boxer Corporation, 92
Johnsonville Sausage, 101
Jourdan Resources, 310–311
Journal of Business Ethics, 224
Julicher, Jack, 296

K

Kahn, Leo, 13
Kahneman, Daniel, 90
Kairos Society, 82
Kanter, Rosabeth Moss, 171, 172
Karlsson, Tomas, 129
Kedrosky, Paul, 13
Kent, Derin, 82
key-person insurance, 338
Kiessling, Greg, 5
Kik Interactive, 285
Kingma, Lance, 253
Kinlough, Richard, 355
Kleiner, Eugene, 211
Knexa, 268
Koffler, Murray, 421
Koohgoli, Mahshad, 196, 203, 211
Kumar, Pushkar, 28
Kunkel, Scott, 101
Kuratko, Donald, 173
Kutcher, Ashton, 20

L

La Senza, 89
L'Abbé, Richard, 99, 499
Laferté, Sylvie, 256
Lai, Albert, 44
Lake, Scott, 60–62
Lalonde, Coralie, 15
Large, David, 18
law competency, 180
lead entrepreneur, 11
leadership. See also entrepreneurial leader;
    entrepreneurship
leadership competency, 178–179
LeBreton-Miller, Isabelle, 439
Ledoux, Sean, 296
Lee, John, 202
left-mode/right-mode brain characteristics,
    90
legal circumference trap, 339–340
legal counsel
    decision to use, 260–262
    selection criteria, 262–263
Léger, René, 432
Lemieux, Mario, 337
lending decision, 367–371. See also
    debt capital
    covenants, 369–370
    lending criteria, 367–368
    loan restrictions, 368–369
    personal guarantees, 370
Letterman, David, 296
leveraged buyouts (LBOs), 372
Lewin, Laurence, 89
L'Her, Jean-François, 312
liability of board of directors, 259
Libretto Restaurant Group, 50
line of credit, 354
Little, Ryan, 28, 268
Livent Corporations, 232
Livingston, Ted, 285
loan restrictions, 368–369
loans. See debt
long-term borrowing, 288
Lorrain, Jean, 256
Loughati.com, 109
Lütke, Tobias, 60–62

M

Ma, Hao, 174
Ma, Stanley, 432
MacDougall, Shelley, 131
MacIsaac, Ashley, 98
MacPherson, Robert, 441
MacPherson, Wendy, 441
Madonna, 98
Maine, Elicia, 196, 203
Mainprize, Brent, 129
management, leading practices, 65
management buyout (MBO), 498–499
management team issues. See also venture
    team

screening opportunities, 105
    venture opportunity evaluation criteria,
        96
management versus leadership, 6
managerial domain, 164–165
Manitoba Harvest, 332
Manziaris, Ted, 396
Maple Leaf Angels, 204
Maple Leaf Foods, 71
Marien, Ryan, 483
market
    business plan, 137
    capacity, 100
    cost structure, 101
    failure, 57
    growth rate, 100
    high potential businesses, 99
    high-growth companies, 399–400
    industry criteria, 95
    low potential opportunities, 99
    readiness, 56
    research, 137, 177, 265
    sea change, 85
    share attainable, 101
    size, 99
    structure, 99–100
marketing
    competencies of entrepreneurial
        leaders, 177
    franchising, 429–430
    leading practices, 64–65
    plan, 177
Markin, Anthony, 442
Marram, Edward, 172, 394
Marriott Hotel, 440–441
Marriott Jr., J. Willard, 440–441
Mars, 441–442
Martell, Dan, 198, 201, 206
Martens, Martin, 128
master franchise, 433
Matten, Dirk, 227
Matthews, Terry, 4–5, 163
maturity stage of venture growth, 166,
    167, 398
Mauran, Richard "Rick," 432
Mayer, Marissa, 481
McBeth, Jim, 202
McClelland, David, 231
McLean, Ged, 202
McMullan, Ed, 256, 260
Mei, Monica, 110
Melnichuk, Anatoliy, 483
Melville, George, 89
Mentzer, Josephine Esther, 92
Menzies, Teresa, 48, 260
merger, 499
Merton, Robert, 282
Metcalfe's Law, 84, 85
Meyer, David, 393
mezzanine financing, 308
Middleton, Mike, 290
Miller, Danny, 439

Minto Lake Resources Inc. case, debt capital, 375–380
Mintzberg, Henry, 20, 197, 393
Mirzaee, Aydin, 77, 256, 330
Mitchell's Gourmet Foods Inc., 71
Mitel, 4–5
Moffatt, Brandon, 28
Molson, John, 441
Monster.com, 212
Monty, Jean, 232
moonlighting, 207
Moore, Don, 174
Moore, Geoffrey, 172
Moore's Law, 84, 85
Morgan, Tim, 19–20
motivation to excel
  entrepreneurship, 9
  entrepreneurship themes, 16
Motricity, 208
Mr. Sub, 432
Mulroney, Brian, 226
Mumford, Robyn, 296
Murray, Elspeth, 394, 485
Muzyka, Daniel, 202
myths of entrepreneurship, 23–25

N

Nanopix case, opportunities, 118–125
nascent stage of venture growth, 166–167
National Angel Capital Organization (NACO), 294
Naumman, Frank, 296
need for achievement, 7
need for affiliation, 7
need for power, 7
negative covenants, 368
negotiation traps
  anxiety, 343
  cost underestimation, 342–343
  greed, 343
  impatience, 343–344
  legal circumference, 339–340
  opportunity cost, 341–342
  status/size attraction, 340
  strategic circumference, 339
  take-the-money-and-run myopia, 344
  unknown territory, 340–341
negotiations, 336–344
  boilerplate, 335–336
  issues faced, 337–338
  principled, 336–337
  term sheet, 338
  traps, 339–344
net-liquid balance-to-total-assets ratio, 481
networking, 253–254
networking and information, 112
New Brunswick Small Business Investor Tax Credit, 294
new venture, 5
Nichol, Scott, 252
Nicholds, Kevin, 494

Nicholds, Krista, 494
Nichols, Nancy, 282
Nimcat Networks, 196
nonentrepreneurial attributes, 10
nonlinear/nonparametric events, 169
non-quantitative signals, failure, 481–482
Nortel, 232
not-for-profit research institutes and information, 111
notification plan, 359

O

O'Dea, Frank, 319
Oesch, John, 174
Off Axis, 407
Olivieri, Icaro, 498
Olsen, Ken, 94
OOC, 286–287
operations competency, 177–178
opportunity
  business model, 78
  circle of ecstasy, 79
  food chain concept, 79–80
  gathering information, 109–114
  great mousetrap fallacy, 87–88
  ideas, 86–88, 109
  ideas vs., 80–81
  market failure and, 57
  market readiness, 56
  Nanopix case, 118–125
  obsession, 11–13
  orientation, 108
  paradox, 44
  pattern recognition, 88–97
  reality, 78, 81
  recognition, 17, 77
  screening, 97–109, 115
  sea change, 83–85
  shaping it, 112–113
  Shopify example, 60–62
  spawners and drivers, 82, 85
  thinking big, 77
  Timmons model, 55, 56–57
  venture team formation, 204–205
opportunity cost
  negotiation traps, 341–342
  screening criteria, 106
opportunity obsession, 11–13
opportunity orientation, 108
Opti-Com, 341
optimism paradox, 482–483
optimistic realism, 16
organizational culture in high-growth companies, 400–403
organizational paradigms in high-growth companies, 393
Orr, Bobby, 230
Osborne Computer, 99
"Osborneing," 99
Out Of Cash, 286–287
Outliers (2008), 88

Owens, William, 232
ownership dilution, 326, 328
ownership paradox, 44
Oxtoby, David, 202

P

Paine, Lynn, 228
Paninguaki Kjærulff, Maria, 53
paradoxes, 44–45
Parlance Communications case, high-growth companies, 410–418
Parsley, Chris, 403
Partin, Paul, 226
patents, 110
patience paradox, 45
pattern recognition
  creativity, 89–91
  defined, 88
  evaluation criteria, 94–97
  examples of, 89
  limited capital resources, 91–92
  opportunity, 88–97
  window of opportunity, 93–94
Pattison, Jim, 494
Peart, Neil, 392
people resources, 256–266
  accountants, 263–264
  bankers/lenders, 263
  board of directors, 256–260
  brain trust, 256
  consultants, 264–266
  legal counsel, 260–263
  social capital, 254–255
  using, 255
Pereira, Aaron, 268
perseverance paradox, 45
personal criteria
  screening opportunities, 106
  venture opportunity evaluation criteria, 96
personal guarantees, 350, 370
Personal Property Registry (PPR), 356
Personal Property Security Act, 356–357
Peters, Tom, 172
piggyback registration rights, 338
Pilkington Brothers, 103
Pillars Sausages & Delicatessens Limited, 71
Pilon, Melanie, 19
Pintendre Auto Inc., 83
Pixar Canada, 20
Pizza Nova, 432
Planet Bean, ethics case, 242–248
planning practices, 65
plant improvement loans, 358
Polaroid Corporation, 86
Pond, Gerry, 226
Poon Tip, Bruce, 135
positive cash flow, 101
positive covenants, 368
Pozios, John, 430
Pratt, Steven, 202
pre-start-up stage of venture growth, 397

PricewaterhouseCoopers, 297
pricing, 109
private equity, 5
private investors, 51–52
private placements, 308–309, 310–311
product licensing, 110–111
production competency, 177–178
profits after tax, 101
Prosserman, Martin, 501–502
psychographic profiles, 423
published sources of information, 113–114
Purple Angel, 51

Q

Quails' Gate Winery, 443
QuickScreen, 115
Quinn, Pat, 198

R

Radio Shack, 424
rapid growth management
    counterintuitive/unconventional
        decision making, 169
    entrepreneurial culture, 170–171
    fluid structures/procedures, 170
    inexperience, 169
    influence, 167
    interpersonal relationships, 168
    necessary skills, 171–173
    nonlinear/nonparametric events, 169
    time and change, 168–169
    transitions, 168
ratchet anti-dilution protection, 337
Regan, David, 84
Rent frock Repeat, 205
research and development stage, 166–167
resilience, 9, 14–16
resource requirements
    analyzing financial requirements,
        266–267
    bootstrapping, 252
    control vs. ownership, 251–252
    entrepreneurial approach to, 251–255
    ExerciseApp case, 271–276
    financial resources, 267–268.
        See also financing
    Internet, 268
    people resources, 255–266
    social capital, 253–254
    Timmons model, 55, 57–58
    using other peoples', 252–254
return on equity (ROE), 372–373
return on investment potential, 101–102
Reuber, Becky, 87
rewards for venture team. *See* venture team
    rewards
Richardson, Peter, 394, 485
Riding, Allan, 133
Rifco National Auto Finance Corporation,
    312

right-mode/left-mode brain characteristics,
    90
Rimaldi, Max, 50
Rimaldi, Rocco, 50
risk
    board of directors, 260
    deal structure, 333
    entrepreneurship, 9, 13–14, 107
    financing, 279–280, 283
    franchising, 424–426
    management, 333
    tolerance, 9, 13–14, 107
risk/reward tolerance, 9, 13–14, 107
Roberts, Ryan, 338
Robinson, Michael, 294
Rock, Arthur, 46
Rocksteady Investments, 28
Rogers, Ted, 484
Rogers, Ted Jr., 163, 493
Rogers Communications, 441
Romanow, Michele, 483
room for error, 109
Roots, 497
Roots Air, 83
Rosa, Peter, 131
Ross, Thomas, 128
Rosson, Philip, 226
Roth, John, 232
Rowe, Glen, 175
Rowland, Pleasant, 98
rule-of-thumb valuation methods, 329
Rush, Cassandra, 110
Rutherford, Tod, 203

S

Sahlman, William, 253, 331
sales per employee (SPE), 395
Samuel, Son & Co., 444
Sarbanes-Oxley Act (SOX), 259
Saunders Farm, 18
Scavenger Energy, venture financing case,
    315–316
Schlien, Ariel and Ron, 430
Schnarr, Matt, 230
Schroeder, Don, 419
Schrooten, Jeremy, 202
Schumpeter, Joseph, 48
Schurman, Maynard Freeman, 13
Schwitzer, Eric, 202
Scientific Research and Experimental
    Development Tax Credit Program,
    307
screening opportunities, 97–109
    competitive advantage issues, 104
    criteria for success, 98
    economics, 101–103
    focus, 97
    harvest issues, 103
    industry/market issues, 99–101
    management team issues, 105
    personal criteria, 106

    QuickScreen, 115
    strategic differentiation, 107–109
    Venture Opportunity Screening
        Exercises, 115
Sculley, John, 172
sea change, 83–85
segmenting, 134
selection criteria
    accountants, 264
    bankers/lenders, 263
    board of directors, 258–259
    consultants, 265–266
    legal counsel, 262–263
self-reliance, 9, 14–16
serial entrepreneur, 4
service delivery system, 426–428
service management, 107
Shad, John, 227
SHAD case, business plans,
    154–159
Shapiro, Daniel, 203
share-vesting agreement, 198
Shopify, 60–62
Shoppers Drug Mart, 421
short-term debt, 288
shotgun approach, 397
shotgun clause, 319
Simon, Herbert, 88
Singer, Herb and Rhoda, 98
6N Silicon, 252, 266
Skapinker, Mark, 344
Skoll, Jeffrey, 4, 227
Skoll Foundation, 227
Sleeman, George, 63
Sleeman, John W., 63
Sloan, Sal, 163
Smallwood, Joseph, 44–45
SME Benchmarking Tool, 112
Smith, Gregory, 321–322
Snache, Julie, 129
Sniegowski, Don, 431
social capital, 253–254
social entrepreneurship, 235–237
societal sea change, 85
Solutions 2 GO, 405
Sorenson, Olav, 58
sources of information, 109–114
spawners and drivers, 83, 85
Spin Master, 92
Spinelli, Stephen, 201, 427, 494
Spinner, Art, 257, 259
spontaneous credit, 351. *See also* trade credit
spreadsheets, 267, 278–279
St. Hubert, 432
stability stage of venture growth, 166, 167,
    399
stages of venture growth. *See* growth stages
    of entrepreneurial ventures
Stancill, James, 267
Stanfield, Ronald, 375–380
Stark, Andrew, 227
Starke, Frederick, 174

start-up stage of venture growth
    critical mass, 166
    debt capital, 4
    described, 166–167, 394–395
    family-influenced, 445–446
    pre-start, 397
Steere, William, 85
Steier, Lloyd, 440
Steinley, Mark, 202
Stemberg, Tom, 12–13
Stevenson, Howard, 20, 253
Stewart Sr., Richard, 443
StormFisher Biogas, 28
"storytelling," 128
strategic alliance, 499
strategic circumference trap, 339
strategic differentiation, 97, 107–109
stress tolerance, 107
Stronach, Frank, 20
structuring the deal. *See* deal structure
Stuart, Toby, 58
succession, 458–461
Suddaby, Roy, 170
Sukornyk, George, 432
Sun Microsystems, 94
Sundback, Gideon, 86
Suret, Jean-Marc, 312
survival rates, 47–50
survival stage of venture growth, 397
sustainability, 55, 56
Sustronk, Phillip, 257
Suzy Shier, 89
Syron, Rick and Bernie, 432
Szaky, Tom, 346–348

T

Tackaberry, Helen, 498
take-the-money-and-run myopia, 344
Tan, Justin, 174
Tango, 83
tax competency, 180
Taylor, Jeff, 212
Teaching Kids News, 234
team. *See* venture team
teamwork, 198. *See also* venture team
technological sea change, 85
technology, 108
term debt, 354
term loans, 356
term sheet, 285, 338
Testa, Richard, 207
The 7 Habits of Highly Effective People, 173
The Innovator's Dilemma, 172
The Source, 424
The Way Ahead, 82
TheFunTheory.com, 87
theory of company pricing, 321–322
Thinking, Fast and Slow (2011), 90
thinking big enough
    entrepreneurs, 23
    higher-potential, 45–46

opportunity, 77, 79
Thompson Couplings Ltd., 257
Thornhill, Stuart, 49
360 Visibility Inc., 405–406
Tilden, Sam, 493
Tilden Rent-a-Car, 493
Tilly, Jonathan, 234
Tilly, Kathleen, 234
Tim Hortons, 426
time to breakeven, 101, 103
Time To Close, 286–287
time-sales financing, 355–356
timing
    capital market, 103–104
    deal structure, 331–332
    entrepreneurial process, 64
    financing, 267, 282, 293
    harvest, 495–496
    initial public offering (IPO), 501
    opportunity, 93–94
    strategic differentiation, 107
    succession, 453
    Timmons model, 64
    venture team rewards, 210–211
Timmons model
    brain trust, 256
    entrepreneurial team, 55, 58–59
    family enterprising, 440, 447, 453, 458,
        460–461
    fit and balance, 59
    franchising, 422, 427, 433
    leading practices, 64–65
    opportunity, 55, 56–57
    recent research, 64
    resources, 55, 57–58
    Shopify example, 60–62
    social entrepreneurship, 236–237
    theory plus practice, 53–54
    timing, 64
    value creation, 54–55
Todres, Elaine, 197
Torak Express, entrepreneurship case, 34–37
Tour Effel, 71
Townson, Bruce, 202
trade credit, 351, 352, 353
transgenerational entrepreneurship and
        wealth creation, 440
transitions
    ambiguity, 168
    entrepreneurial, 168
    family enterprising, 446
    rapid growth management, 168
    venture growth stages, 166
Treacy, Michael, 254–255
Treliving, Jim, 89
TriColour Venture Fund, 323
TTC, 286–287
turnaround plan, 487–491
    lenders, 489–490
    longer-term actions, 491
    quick cash, 488–489
    trade collectors, 490

uses of, 487
    workforce reductions, 491
Turtle Island Recycling, 396
tying agreement, 431
Tyson Foods, 441
Tzotsis, Dan, 230

U

uncertainty, 9, 13–14
Underwood, Dave, 296
universities and information, 111
upside/downside issues, 106

V

Valliere, Dave, 13, 278
valuation, 318–329
    capital markets food chain, 321
    cram-down/down round, 323–325
    determinants, 318
    investor's required rate of return, 319,
        320
    investor's required share of ownership,
        319–321, 326
    long-term value creation, 318
    methods. *See* valuation methods
    multiples and comparables, 103
    psychological factors, 318–319
    reality of, 322–323, 325
    shotgun clause, 319
    theory of, 319
    theory of company pricing, 321–322
valuation methods
    discounted cash flow, 328
    First Chicago method, 326, 327
    fundamental method, 326, 327
    ownership dilution, 326, 328
    rule-of-thumb methods, 329
    venture capital method, 325–326
value creation
    capital flows, 300
    commitment to, venture team, 199
    driving forces, 54–55
    entrepreneurial leader, 12
    financing, 52, 279–280, 284
    long-term, 318
    Timmons model, 54–55
value pie, 279, 280
value-added investor, 297–298, 302
value-added potential
    harvesting, 103, 495
    market, 99
    opportunity evaluation, 96
    take-the-money-and-run myopia, 344
van Berkel, Bas, 28
van der Velden, Peter, 322
van Lierop, Wal, 202
Vanderleeden, Olen, 202
variable costs, 104
Vector Construction Group, 442–443
Venetian Meat & Salami Co. Ltd., 72

venture capital. *See also* angel investor; debt capital; financing
    defined, 5, 298
    industry, 299
    negotiations. *See* negotiations
    other equity sources, 305–313. *See also* equity sources
    paradox, 44
    process, 298. *See also* venture capital process
    staged capital commitments, 330–331
    structuring the deal, 331–336
    survival rates, 50–51
    tar pits for entrepreneurs, 329–330
    valuation, 325–326. *See also* valuation
venture capital process
    core activities summary, 299–301
    dealing with investors, 303–304
    due diligence on investors, 304–305
    identifying investors, 301–303
    investment criteria, 301
    questions to ask investors, 304
    visual summary of, 298
venture capital valuation method, 325–326
venture capitalists, 5
venture growth stages. *See* growth stages of entrepreneurial ventures
venture modes, 164–165
Venture Opportunity Screening Exercises, 115
venture team
    ambiguity, 59
    board of directors, 256–260
    Canica Design case study, 218–222
    common pitfalls, 207–208
    defined, 59, 196
    formation, 197–208
    importance of, 196–197
    integrity, 105, 198
    moonlighting, 207
    rewards/incentives, 208–212
    screening criteria, 105
    screening opportunities, 105

share-vesting agreement, 198
Timmons model, 55, 58–59
venture opportunity evaluation criteria, 96
venture team formation, 197–208
    evolution, 200–201
    filling gaps, 201–205
    founder, 203–204
    goals, 206
    integrity, 208
    opportunity, 204–205
    outside resources, 205–206
    peer groups, 206
    pitfalls, 207–208
    role definitions, 206
    share-vesting agreement, 198
    vision and philosophy/attitudes, 197–200
venture team rewards, 208–212
    buyback agreement, 211
    differentiation, 209
    escrow, 211
    flexibility, 210
    initial public offering (IPO), 208
    performance, 210
    reward system, 209
    slicing the pie, 208
    timing considerations, 210–211
    value considerations, 211–212
veridical awareness, 16
Vining, Aidan, 203
VisiCalc, 267
Volkswagon, 87
voluntary bankruptcy, 484–485
von Sturmer, Lisa, 110
Voronov, Maxim, 44
Vredenburg, Harrie, 229

W

Walker, Marnie, 197, 204
Walt Disney Company, 92
Warrington Products, 498
washout financing, 338

Waterman, Bob, 172
Watsa, Prem, 225
Watson, Thomas, 94
Wehrell, Roger, 5, 224
Weir, Mike, 477
Wendy's, 428
Wesley Clover, 5
West, Colby and Drew, 444
Wester, Lyndon, 98
Wester's Garage, 98
WestJet Encore, 83
Wexler, Mark, 233
Whalen, Alicia, 265
Which Way To Grow, franchising case, 437–438
Whitmore, David, 443
Wieber, Kristy, 205
Williams, Mark, 199
Williams, Tom, 268
Wilson, Brett, 367
window of opportunity, 93–94
Winters, Owen B., 87
Woods, Anthony, 212
Wozniak, Steve, 19, 44
Wright, Wilbur, 94
Wrigley Jr. II, William, 442

Y

Young, Neil, 476
Yukon Small Business Investment Tax Credit, 294
Yzerman, Steve, 250

Z

Zafirovski, Mike, 232
Zero-Knowledge Systems, 405
Zietsma, Charlene, 174
Zimmerman, Brenda, 227
Zimmerman, Joerg, 202
Zimmerman, Paul, 202
Zip, 83